PHILIP'

G000136405

STRI

Devon

First published 2003 by

Philip's, a division of
Octopus Publishing Group Ltd
2–4 Heron Quays, London E14 4JP

First edition 2003
Second impression with revisions 2003

ISBN 0-540-08131-0 (pocket)

© Philip's 2003

oS Ordnance Survey®

This product includes mapping data licensed
from Ordnance Survey® with the permission
of the Controller of Her Majesty's Stationery
Office. © Crown copyright 2003. All rights
reserved. Licence number 100011710.

Printed and bound in Spain
by Cayfosa-Quebecor

Contents

II   **Administrative and Postcode boundaries**

III   **Key to map symbols**

IV   **Key to map pages**

VI   **Route planning**

1   **Street maps** at 1¼ inches to 1 mile

150   **Street maps** at 2½ inches to 1 mile

261   **Street maps of Exeter and Plymouth city centres** at 5 inches to 1 mile

264   **Index** of towns and villages

266   **Index** of streets, hospitals, industrial estates, railway stations, schools, shopping centres, universities and places of interest

Digital Data

The exceptionally high-quality mapping found in this atlas is available as digital data in
TIFF format, which is easily convertible to other bitmapped (raster) image formats.

The index is also available in digital form as a standard database table. It contains all the
details found in the printed index together with the National Grid reference for the map
square in which each entry is named.

For further information and to discuss your requirements, please contact
Philip's on 020 7644 6932 or james.mann@philips-maps.co.uk

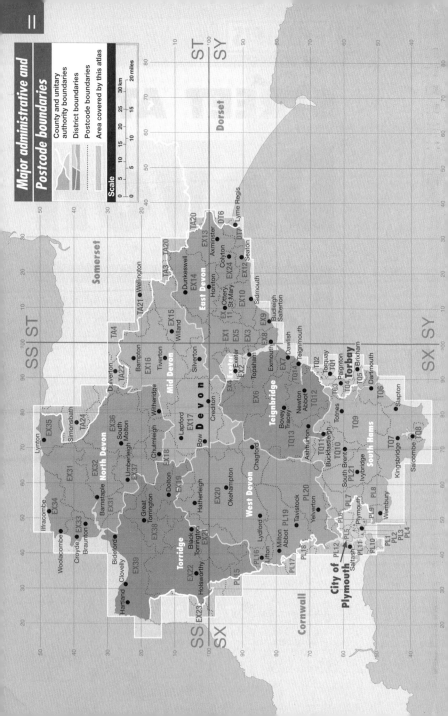

(22a)	**Motorway** with junction number
	Primary route – dual/single carriageway
	A road – dual/single carriageway
	B road – dual/single carriageway
	Minor road – dual/single carriageway
	Other minor road – dual/single carriageway
	Road under construction
	Tunnel, covered road
	Rural track, private road or narrow road in urban area
	Gate or obstruction to traffic (restrictions may not apply at all times or to all vehicles)
	Path, bridleway, byway open to all traffic, road used as a public path
	Pedestrianised area
DY7	**Postcode boundaries**
	County and unitary authority boundaries
	Railway, tunnel, railway under construction
	Tramway, tramway under construction
	Miniature railway
Walsall	**Railway station**
	Private railway station
South Shields	**Metro station**
	Tram stop, tram stop under construction
	Bus, coach station

◆	**Ambulance station**
◆	**Coastguard station**
◆	**Fire station**
◆	**Police station**
✚	**Accident and Emergency entrance to hospital**
H	**Hospital**
+	**Place of worship**
i	**Information Centre** (open all year)
P	**Parking**
P&R	**Park and Ride**
PO	**Post Office**
⚊	**Camping site**
⚊	**Caravan site**
▶	**Golf course**
⊠	**Picnic site**
Prim Sch	**Important buildings, schools, colleges, universities and hospitals**
River Medway	**Water name**
	River, weir, stream
	Canal, lock, tunnel
	Water
	Tidal water
	Woods
	Built up area
Church	**Non-Roman antiquity**
ROMAN FORT	**Roman antiquity**
87	**Adjoining page indicators and overlap bands** The colour of the arrow and the band indicates the scale of the adjoining or overlapping page (see scales below)
228	

Acad	**Academy**	Inst	**Institute**	Recn Gd	**Recreation**
Allot Gdns	**Allotments**	Ct	**Law Court**		**Ground**
Cemy	**Cemetery**	L Ctr	**Leisure Centre**	Resr	**Reservoir**
C Ctr	**Civic Centre**	LC	**Level Crossing**	Ret Pk	**Retail Park**
CH	**Club House**	Liby	**Library**	Sch	**School**
Coll	**College**	Mkt	**Market**	Sh Ctr	**Shopping Centre**
Crem	**Crematorium**	Meml	**Memorial**	TH	**Town Hall/House**
Ent	**Enterprise**	Mon	**Monument**	Trad Est	**Trading Estate**
Ex H	**Exhibition Hall**	Mus	**Museum**	Univ	**University**
Ind Est	**Industrial Estate**	Obsy	**Observatory**	Wks	**Works**
IRB Sta	**Inshore Rescue**	Pal	**Royal Palace**	YH	**Youth Hostel**
	Boat Station	PH	**Public House**		

■ The small numbers around the edges of the maps identify the 1 kilometre National Grid lines

■ The dark grey border on the inside edge of some pages indicates that the mapping does not continue onto the adjacent page

The scale of the maps on the pages numbered in blue is 3.92 cm to 1 km • 2½ inches to 1 mile • 1: 25344

0	¼	½	¾	1 mile
0	250m	500m	750m	1 kilometre

The scale of the maps on pages numbered in green is 1.96 cm to 1 km • 1¼ inches to 1 mile • 1: 50688

0	¼	½	¾	1 mile
0	250m	500m	750m	1kilometre

The scale of the maps on pages numbered in red is 7.84 cm to 1 km • 5 inches to 1 mile • 1: 12672

0	220 yards	440 yards	660 yards	½ mile
0	125m	250m	375m	½ kilometre

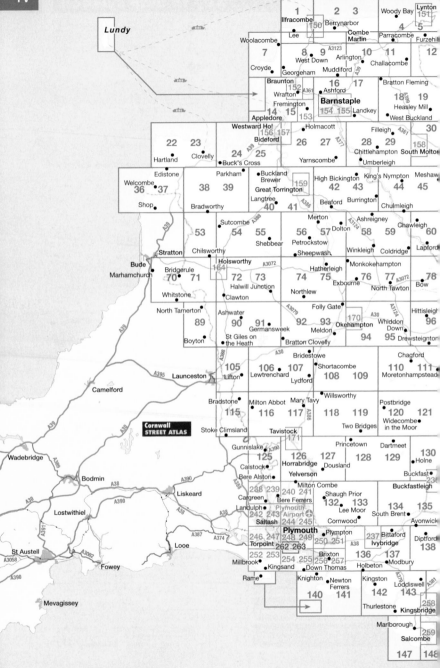

IV

Lundy

1 Ilfracombe
150
Lee
2 Berrynarbor
3
Woody Bay
Combe Martin
Parracombe
Lynton
151
4
5
Furzehill

Woolacombe
7
West Down
A3123
8
9 Arlington
10
Challacombe
11
12

Croyde
Georgeham
Muddiford

Braunton
152
Wrafton
A361
16 Ashford
17
Bratton Fleming
18
Heasley Mill
19

Fremington
Barnstaple
154 155 Landkey
West Buckland

Appledore
14 15 153
Westward Ho!
156 157
Bideford
Holmacott
Filleigh
A361
158
30

22 23
Hartland
Clovelly
24 25
Buck's Cross
26 27
Yarnscombe
28 29
Chittlehampton
South Molton

36 37
Welcombe
Edistone
38 39
Parkham
Bradworthy
Buckland Brewer
Great Torrington
159
Langtree
40 41
High Bickington
42 43
Beaford Burrington
King's Nympton
44 45
Meshaw

Shop

53 54 55
Sutcombe
Shebbear
56 57
Petrockstow
Dolton
58 59
Ashreigney
Chawleigh
60
Lapford

Stratton
Chilsworthy
Holsworthy
164
72 73
Halwill Junction
Sheepwash
74 75
Hatherleigh
Winkleigh Coldridge
Monkokehampton
76 77
Exbourne North Tawton
78
Bow

Bude
Marhamchurch
Bridgerule
70 71
Whitstone

North Tamerton
89 90 91
Ashwater
Germansweek
St Giles on the Heath
Clawton
Boyton
92 93
Meldon
Folly Gate
Northlew
Okehampton
170
94
Whiddon Down
95
Drewsteignton
Hittisleigh
96

Camelford
A395
Launceston
Lifton
105 106 107
Lewtrenchard
Bradstone
Lydford
Bridestowe
Shortacombe
108 109
Willsworthy
118 119
Two Bridges
Chagford
110 111
Moretonhampstead
Postbridge
120 121
Widecombe in the Moor

Stoke Climsland
115 116 117
Milton Abbot
Mary Tavy
Tavistock
171

Wadebridge
Bodmin
Liskeard
Gunnislake
125
Calstock
Bere Alston
126 127
Horrabridge
Yelverton
Dousland
128 129
Princetown
Dartmeet
130
Holne
Buckfast
238

Lostwithiel
St Austell
Looe
Cargreen
288 239
Landulph
242 243
Saltash
240 241
Milton Combe
Shaugh Prior
132 133
Lee Moor
Cornwood
134 135
South Brent
Buckfastleigh
Avonwick
Diptford
138
Bittaford
237
Ivybridge
A38

Fowey
Mevagissey
Torpoint
246 247
252 253
Millbrook
Kingsand
Rame
244 245
Plymouth
248 249
262 263
254 255
Down Thomas
Plympton
250 251
Brixton
256 257
Holbeton
136 137
Modbury

Knighton
140
Newton Ferrers
141
Kingston
142
Thurlestone
Loddiswell
143
Kingsbridge
258

Marlborough
259
Salcombe
147 148

Cornwall STREET ATLAS

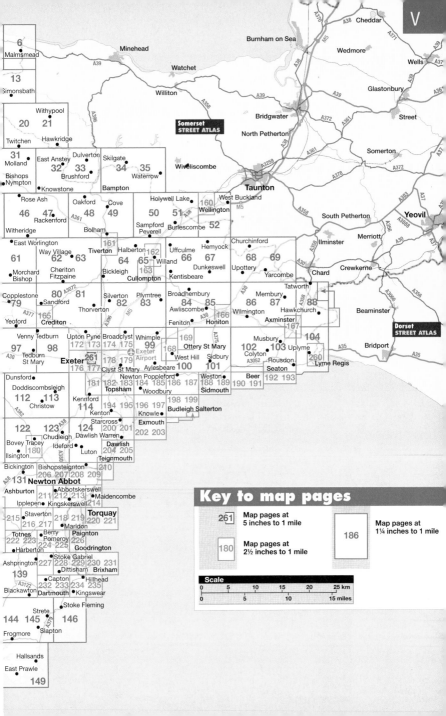

V

Cheddar
Burnham on Sea
Wedmore
Wells
Minehead
Watchet
Street
Glastonbury
6
Malmsmead
13
Simonsbath
Williton
Somerton
Withypool
20 21
Hawkridge
Bridgwater
Somerset
STREET ATLAS
North Petherton
Twitchen
31 East Anstey Dulverton Skilgate
Molland 32 33 34 35
Brushford Waterrow
Bishops
Nympton Knowstone Bampton
Rose Ash Oakford Cove
46 47 48 49 50 51 160 West Buckland Taunton
Rackenford Sampford Burlescombe Wellington M5
Witheridge Bolham Peverell 52
Wiveliscombe
South Petherton
Yeovil
Merriott
East Worlington Churchinford
61 Way Village Tiverton Halberton 162 Uffculme Hemyock 68 69 Ilminster
62 63 64 65 Willand 66 67 Crewkerne
Morchard Cheriton Bickleigh 163 Dunkeswell Upottery Chard
Bishop Fitzpaine Cullompton Kentisbeare Yarcombe Tatworth
Copplestone 80 81 Broadhembury Membury
79 Sandford Silverton Plymtree 84 85 86 87 88 Beaminster
Yeoford 165 82 83 Awliscombe 166 Wilmington Hawkchurch
A377 Crediton Thorverton Feniton Honiton Axminster Dorset
STREET ATLAS
Venny Tedburn Upton Pyne Broadclyst Whimple 169 Musbury 167 104
97 98 172 173 174 175 99 168 Ottery St Mary 102 103 Uplyme Bridport
Tedburn 261 178 179 100 West Hill Sidbury Colyton Rousdon 260
St Mary Exeter 176 177 Clyst St Mary 101 A3052 Seaton Lyme Regis
Exeter Newton Poppleford 184 185 186 187 Weston Beer
Dunsford Airport 181 182 183 Woodbury 188 189 190 191 192 193
Doddiscombsleigh Topsham 196 197 198 199 Sidmouth
112 113 Kennford 194 195 Knowle Budleigh Salterton
Christow 114 Kenton Exmouth
122 123 Starcross 202 203
Bovey Tracey 124 Dawlish Warren
Ilsington 180 Ideford Luton Dawlish
131 Bishopsteignton Teignmouth
206 207 208 209 210
Bickington Newton Abbot
Ashburton Abbotskerswell
211 212 213 Maidencombe
Ipplepen Kingskerswell 214
-215 Staverton 218 219 Torquay
216 217 Marldon 220 221
Totnes Berry Paignton
222 223 Pomeroy 226
Harberton 224 225 Goodrington
Ashprington 227 Stoke Gabriel 230 231
139 228 229 Brixham
Dittisham
Blackawton Capton Hillhead
Dartmouth Kingswear
144 145 Strete Stoke Fleming
146
Frogmore Slapton
Hallsands
East Prawle
149

Key to map pages

261	Map pages at 5 inches to 1 mile
180	Map pages at 2½ inches to 1 mile
186	Map pages at 1¼ inches to 1 mile

Scale
0   5   10   15   20   25 km
0   5   10   15 miles

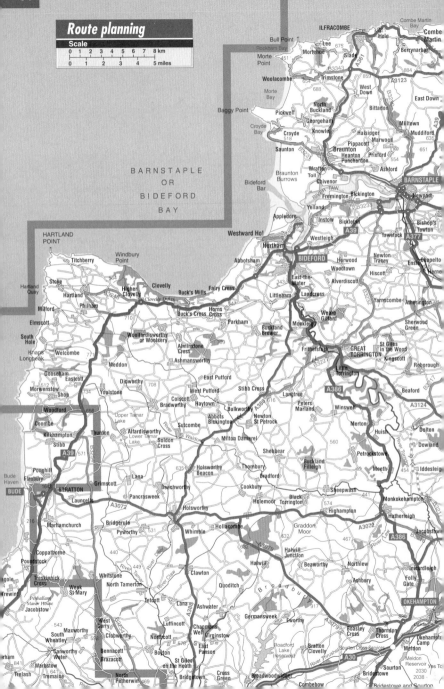

Foreland Point
723
LYNTON
Countisbury
Woody Bay
Heddon's Mouth
Trentishoe
Martinhoe
Toll
1036
Lynmouth
Porlock Bay
Bossington
Selworthy Beacon
1012
North Hill
Culbone Hill
Toll
284
Brendon
Malmsmead
Oare
A39
Porlock
Toll
Allerford
Selworthy
MINEHEAD
1145
Kemacott
A39
Barbrook
Cheriton
Heale
A399
Parracombe
Furzehill
Brendon Common
B3223
Shallowford
Kentisbury
1574
Patchole
1106
Blackmoor Gate
Pinkery Pond
1598
EXMOOR
FOREST
1527
1040
A39
Luccombe
968
Alcombe
Dunster
Wootton Courtenay
1403
Castle
Timberscombe
Carhampton
Withycombe
Dunkery Hill
1704
1426
River Exe
Arlington
Wistlandpound Reservoir
Arlington Court
A399
Challacombe
B3358
Croydon Hill
Knightacott
1079
Shoulsbarrow Common
Simonsbath
B3224
Luckwell Bridge
Wheddon Cross
1248
Luxborough
Loxhore
Bratton Fleming
Leworthy
Burcombe
EXMOOR
Exford
Lype Hill
1388
Kingsbridge
Shirwell
River Barle
1282
1265
A396
BRENDON HILLS
B3224
1350
1618
Lydcott
Long Holcombe
1454
Withypool Common
Withypool
Winsford
Goodleigh
Stoke Rivers
Brayford
1404
Winsford Hill
Exton
Withiel Florey
868
North Heasley
North Radworthy
1405
Gunn
Charles
Heasley Mill
South Radworthy
Loscombe
B3223
Bridgetown
Landkey
West Buckland
East Buckland
Brompton Regis
Wimbleball Lake
940
Twitchen
Molland Common
1238
Dane's Brook
Hawkridge
A361
732
River Barle
1039
Swimbridge
North Molton
Haddon Hill
Upton
Filleigh
Molland
West Anstey
Dulverton
1164
Bury
Cobbaton
River Mole
East Anstey
Skilgate
478
River Yeo
Battleton
B3227
Yeo Mill
Brushford
Chittlehampton
B3226
SOUTH MOLTON
Oldways End
Exebridge
Morebath
B3227
878
Clapworthy
George Nympton
Bishop's Nympton
Ash Mill
811
Umberleigh
567
Knowstone
786
Shillingford
B3137
518
Mariansleigh
Warkleigh
Satterleigh
Alswear
Roachill
Bampton
High Bickington
Chittlehamholt
Rose Ash
920
Remansleigh
Oakford
Huntsham
Portsmouth Arms Station
Meshaw
King's Nympton
Stoodleigh Beacon
Cove
753
782
Creacombe
Stoodleigh
937
Northcote Manor
987
Exe Valley
Rackenford
Dart River
King's Nympton Station
Week
A361
Loxbeare
Knightshayes Court
661
Cadbury Barton
Little
Washfield
Burrington
Elstone
A396
Uplowman
Lutworthy
Templeton Bridge
Bolham
Chevithorne
Ashreigney
Chulmleigh
Witheridge
Calverleigh
Chettiscombe
River Taw
Cheldon
Templeton
Sampford Peverell
Riddlecombe
B3096
Nomansland
Withleigh
TIVERTON
Chawleigh
Thelbridge Barton
Washford Pyne
Cruwys Morchard
B3137
788
Halberton
River Dalch
Eggesford Station
Pennymoor
Ash Thorverton
Hollocombe
Filleigh
B3042
820
Way Village
779
629
Puddington
River Exe
Eastington
Black Dog
Wembworthy
Upham
Woolfardisworthy
Poughill
Cadeleigh
Butterleigh
Winkleigh
Coldridge
Lapford
Brushford
Nymet Rowland
Kennerleigh
Bickleigh
River Taw
Morchard Bishop
591
Oldborough
Stockleigh English
Cullompton
B3220
Colebrook
River Yeo
Bickleigh Castle
East Leigh
East Village
Cheriton Fitzpaine
Morchard Road
828
857
Broadwoodkelly
Fursdon House
Bondleigh
Zeal
Monachorum
521
A3072
Cadbury
A3124
Newbuildings
Bradninch
Down St Mary
Stockleigh Pomeroy
Honeychurch
North Tawton
668
589
Sandford
Upton Hellions
Up Exe
Copplestone
A396
Exbourne
Hele
A3072
Bow
Silverton
Creedy Park
M5
A377
Thorverton
538
Sampford Courtenay
Nymet Tracey
Coleford
Knowle
CREDITON
Shobrooke
Efford
Nether Exe
Killerton
River Okement
Budlake
Itton
Colebrooke
Brampford Speke
Rewe
B3181
River Clyst
Sampford Courtenay Sta
Yeoford
Uton
Hookway
Newton St Cyres
A377
324
Stoke Canon
Broadclyst
B3215
Hillerton
Upton Pyne
Poltimore
A3124
Cowley
Taw Green
Spreyton
45
Dog Village
South Tawton
735
EXETER
Hittisleigh
Tedburn St Mary
Pinhoe
M5
Clyst Honiton
Sticklepath
Finch Foundry
Whitestone
Exeter Airport
Belstone
South Zeal
Cheriton Bishop
Pathfinder Village
A30
Whipton
29
A30
Sowton
Cosdon Hill
Whiddon Down
Exeter Services
Okehampton Common
Drewsteignton
Crockernwell
Longdown
30
Clyst St Mary
Throwleigh
B3212
Ide
A3052
637
Countess Wear
High Willhays
Wonson
Easton
River Teign
Alphington
Clyst St George
Gidleigh
Dunsford
Shillingford

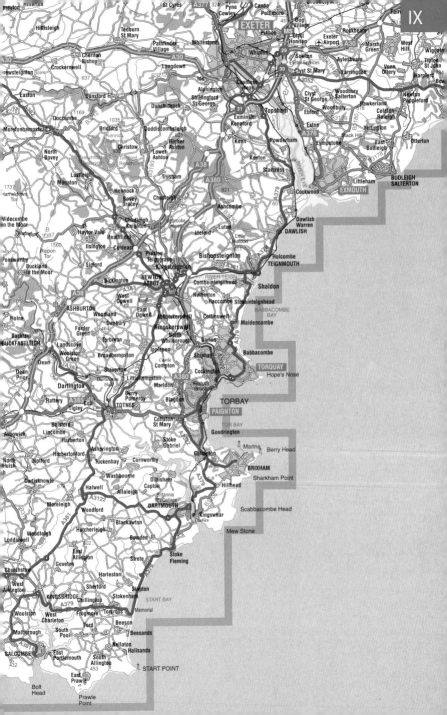

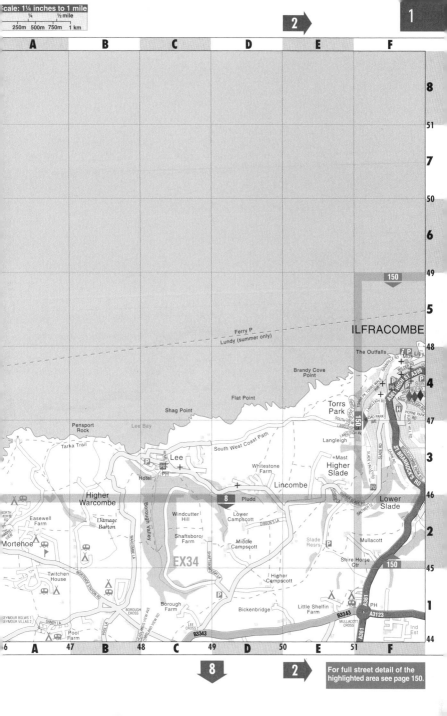

Scale: 1¼ inches to 1 mile
0   ¼   ½ mile
0   250m 500m 750m 1 km

BERRY LA 1
NEWBERRY LA 2
NEWBERRY RD 3
THE GABLES 4
WHITE GATES 5
SEASIDE 6
HANGMAN PATH 7
CROSS ST 8
MOORY MDW 9
REW'S CL 10
LIBRA GDNS 11
KING ST 12
UMBER CL 13
TRENODE AVE 14
BELMONT RD 15

Lundy (summer only)
Ferry P
Capstone Point
Chapel
ILFRACOMBE
Beacon Point
Hele Bay
Rillage Point
Samson's Bay
Widmouth Head
Burrow Nose
Water Mouth
Briery Cave
Combe Martin Bay
Lester Point
Wild Pea Beach

LB Sta
Hillsborough
CH
Widmouth
PORTLAND ST
A399
A3230
HIGHFIELD RD
WATERMOUTH RD
Hele Mill
Hele
Widmouth Hill
Lydford Farm
Watermouth Castle
Hotel
South West Coast Path
NEWBERRY
A399
Sch
Coll
Cemy
CHAMBERCOMBE LA
OLD BERRYNARBOR RD
Beara Farm
Hole Farm
Goosewell
BARTON HILL
Home Barton
Mast
The Castle
DOOM WAY
Chambercombe
Chambercombe Manor
West Haggington
Hagginton Hill
Lee Hills
Lee
Sch
Berrynarbor
NEWBERRY
NEW BARNSTAPLE RD
Shield Tor
Trayne Hills
Kitstone Hill
RECTORY HILL
PH
EASTER LA
WOOD HANGER'S LA
CROFTS LEA
Channe Farm
Trayne
EX34
Hill Barton
9
OLD BARNSTAPLE RD
Warmscombe Farm
Cockhill
Ruggaton Farm
Hodges
Oakridge Farm
Keypitts Farm
Bowden Farm
Bodstone Barton
Yetland Farm
Shelfin Farm
Francis Farm
Woolscott Barton
Smythen Farm
WHEEL CROSS
Two Pots
Mast
Mast
IRON LETTERS CROSS
Hempster Farm
Ettiford Farm
BERRYDOWN CROSS
LONG LA
WHEEL LA
A3123
A3230
A3123

A B C D E F

8

51

7

50

6

49

Hangman
Point

Little
Hangman

South West
Coast Path

Challacombe

Rawn's
Rocks

Blackstone Point

Great
Hangman

Girt Down

Girt
Farm

Knap
Down

KNAP DOWN LA

Combe Martin

Sherrycombe

Red
Cleave

Holdstone
Down

Holdstone
Farm

VILLACOTT LA

The Mare & Colt

Tarka
Trail

North
Cleave

5

Trentishoe
Down

Ladies Mile

48

Mill
Ham

4

47

Trentishoe
Manor

Tattiscombe

EX34

1 REW'S CL
2 ROSEA BRIDGE LA
3 ROCKY LA
4 FIVE TURNINGS
5 SPACKWAYS

NETHERTON
CROSS

SHUTE LA

CHAPEL LA

EAST CHALLACOMBE LA

1 LADDER LA
2 SPURWAY GDNS

CORNER LA

LOWER DEAN LA

HIGHER BUZZACOTT LA

Buzzacott
Manor

Coulscott

Verwill

VERWILL LA

STONY
CNR

COULSWORTHY
CROOK

EX31

3

46

PH
Libry

Mast
Clorridge
Hill

Ind
Units

HIGH ST

KING ST

VICTORIA ST

TOM SANDERCOCK LA

SEVERLEIGH LA

BUZZACOTT LA

BEARA LA

BUZZACOTT CL

NUTTS LA

NUTCOMBE HILL

THISTLEWAY

TRUCKHAM LA

10

Nutcombe

Truckham
Farm

Dean

LOWER
DEAN CROSS

Higher
Cowley

BRATTON LA

DEAN LA

2

45

Stonedith
Hill

Henstridge

RIDGE LA

River Umber

LEIGH RD

WESTLEIGH LA

Lower
Leigh

Combe Martin
Wildlife Park Rly

Combe Martin
Wildlife & Dinosaur
Park

Yellaton

Westleigh
Farm

Coulsworthy

COULSWORTHY LA

Waytown

DEAN CROSS

Silkenworthy
Knap

DOWN LA

A380

1

44

Indicknowle

Seven
Ash

SEVEN ASH
CROSS

A3123 **LONG LA**

South Ley

EASTER CLOSE
CROSS

SOUTH LEY
CROSS

SLADE LANE
CROSS

B3229

ELY LA

SLADE LA

A3123

58   **A**   59   **B**   60   **C**   61   **D**   62   **E**   63   **F**   44

A3
1 SUMMERLAND TERR
2 GENESIS LA
3 BARTON GATE LA
4 KINGSTON AVE
5 MANSION TERR
6 VALLEY LA
7 ORCHARD CL
8 KINGSLEY TERR
9 MILL MDW
10 WATER TERR
11 SPRINGFIELD TERR
12 HIGH CROSS
13 POUND LA
14 ROCK LA
15 WET LA
16 SUNNYSIDE COTTS
17 UMBERSIDE
18 PARK VIEW CL
19 ROWS LA
20 BROOKSIDE VILLAS

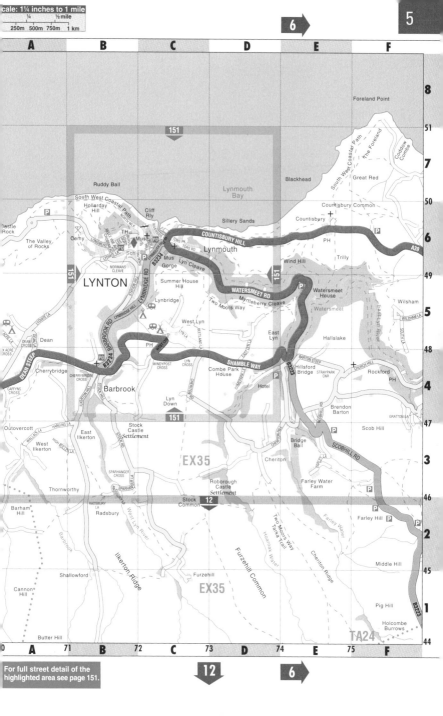

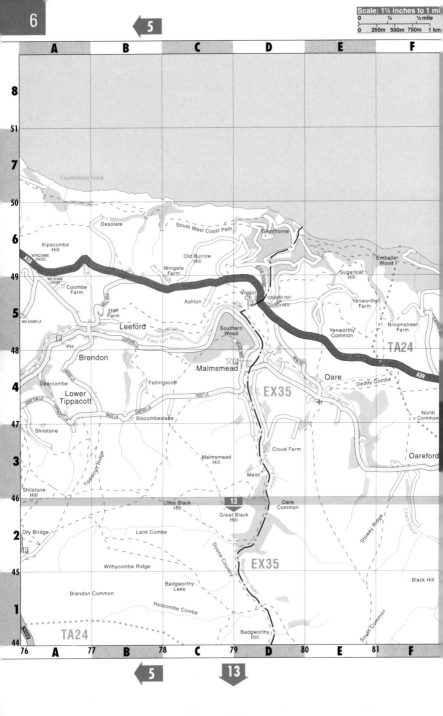

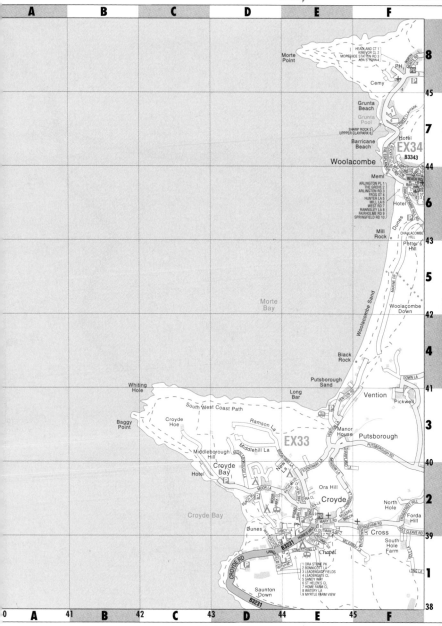

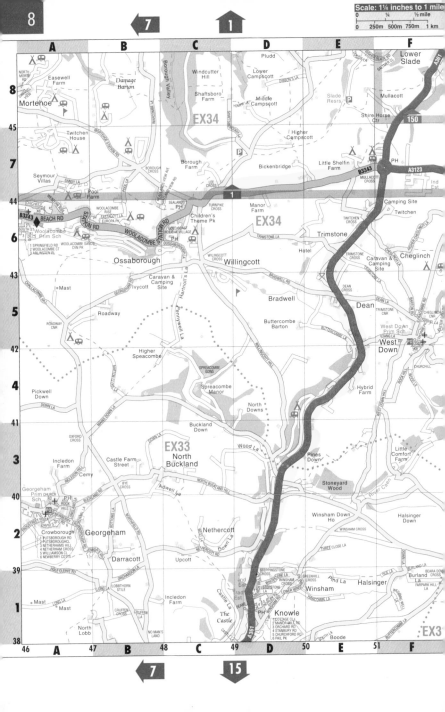

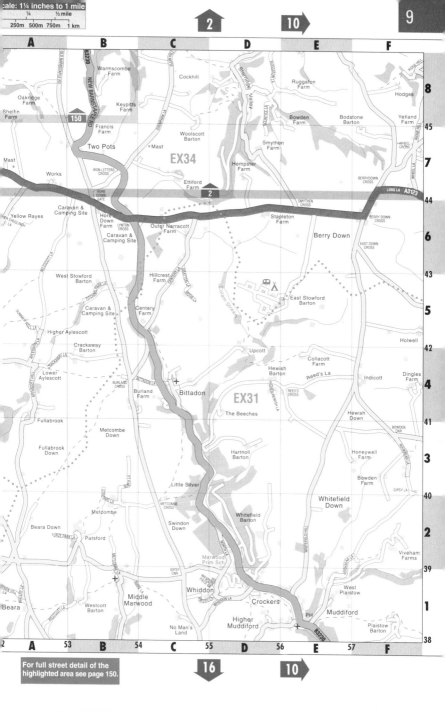

Scale: 1¼ inches to 1 mile

¼	½ mile	
250m	500m 750m	1 km

A **B** **C** **D** **E** **F**

8
45
7
44
6
43
5
42
4
41
3
40
2
39
1
38

B3230
NEW BARNSTAPLE RD
OLD BARNSTAPLE RD

Warmscombe Farm
Cockhill
Sterridge Valley
RUGGATON LA
Ruggaton Farm
Hodges

Oakridge Farm
150
Keypitts Farm
Bowden Farm
Bodstone Barton
Yetland Farm

Shelfin Farm
Francis Farm
Woolscott Barton
Smythen Farm
WHEEL CROSS
WHEEL LA
RIDGE LA

Two Pots
Mast
EX34
Hempster Farm
BERRYDOWN CROSS

Mast
Works
IRON LETTERS CROSS
Ettiford Farm
2
SMYTHEN CROSS
LONG LA A3123

HORE DOWN GATE
Caravan & Camping Site
Hore Down Farm
Yellow Rayes
NEW CHEGLINCH LA
Outer Narracott Farm
LYNTON CROSS
Stapleton Farm
Berry Down
BERRY DOWN CROSS

Caravan & Camping Site
West Stowford Barton
THORNE PARK LA
Hillcrest Farm
SILVER LA
GRATTON LA
ROBOROUGH LA
Colam Stream
East Stowford Barton
EAST DOWN CROSS

SUMMER WELL LA
WESTCOTT LA
Caravan & Camping Site
Centery Farm
Holwell

Higher Aylescott
Crackaway Barton
Upcott
Collacott Farm
Reed's La
Indicott
Dingles Farm

Lower Aylescott
CRACKAWAY HILL
BURLAND CROSS
BITTADON LA
Bittadon
Hewish Barton
HORE LA / MARTIN LA
REED'S CROSS
Hewish Down
BOWDEN CNR

Fullabrook
Burland Farm
EX31
The Beeches
ROOKERY LA

Fullabrook Down
Metcombe Down
Hartnoll Barton
Honeywell Farm

LEE LAND LA
Metcombe
Little Silver
Bowden Farm
GIPSY LA

METCOMBE CROSS
Whitefield Down

Beara Down
Patsford
FURZE PARK LA
Swindon Down
Whitefield Barton
WHITEFIELD THORN RD
Viveham Farms

CHURCH LA
Beara
Westcott Barton
Middle Marwood
METCOMBE LA
Marwood Prim Sch
GIPSY CNR
West Plaistow
ROOKERY LA

Whiddon
Crockers
PH
Muddiford
Plaistow Barton

No Man's Land
WHIDDON LA
Higher Muddiford
B3230

For full street detail of the highlighted area see page 150.

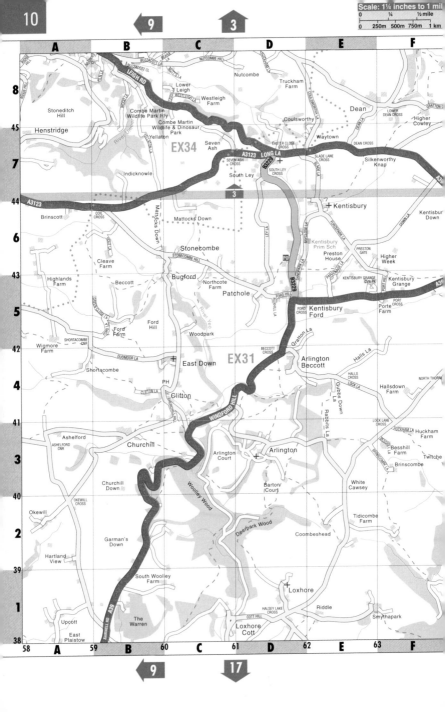

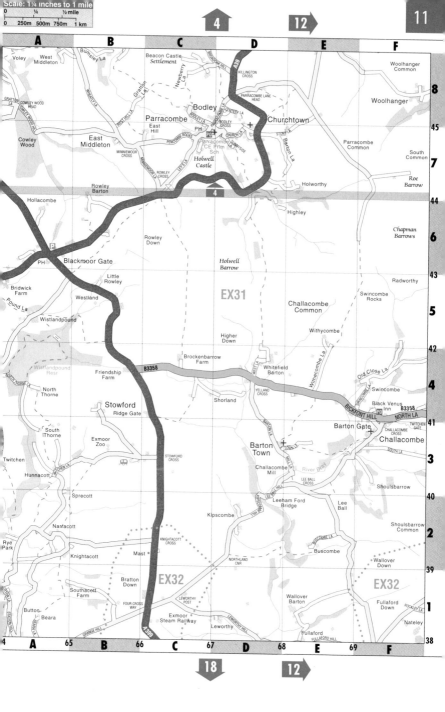

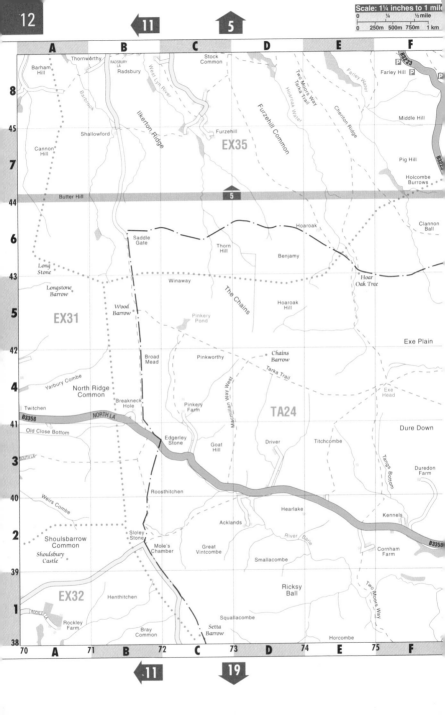

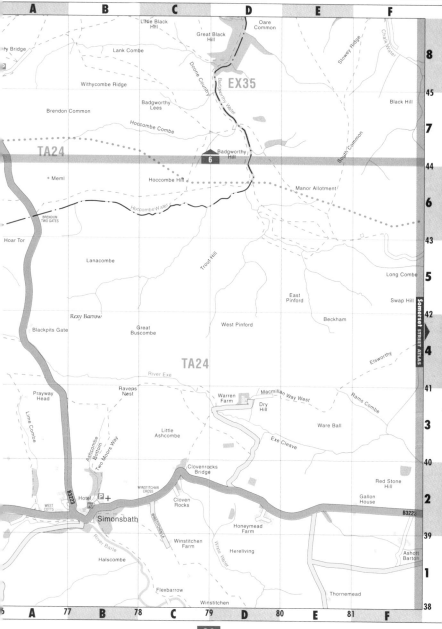

Scale: 1¼ inches to 1 mile

| 0 | ¼ | ½ mile |

| 0 | 250m | 500m | 750m | 1 km |

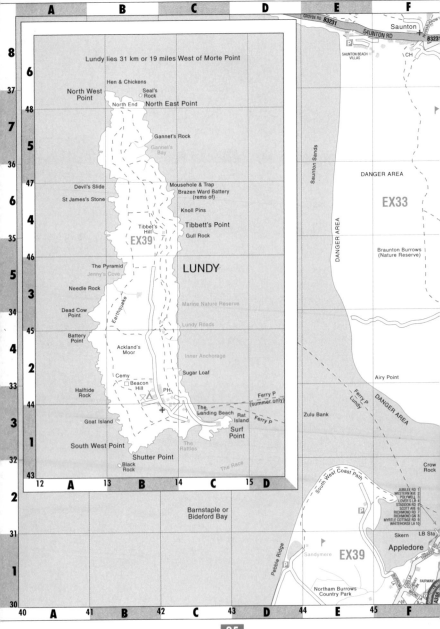

Lundy lies 31 km or 19 miles West of Morte Point

Hen & Chickens

North West Point

Seal's Rock

North End   North East Point

Gannet's Rock

Gannel's Bay

Devil's Slide

St James's Stone

Mousehole & Trap

Brazen Ward Battery
(rems of)

Knoll Pins

Tibbett's Point

Tibbett's Hill

EX39

Gull Rock

LUNDY

The Pyramid

Jenny's Cove

Needle Rock

Marine Nature Reserve

Dead Cow Point

Earthquake

Lundy Roads

Battery Point

Ackland's Moor

Inner Anchorage

Sugar Loaf

Cemy

Beacon Hill

PH

Halftide Rock

Ferry P
(summer only)

Zulu Bank

The Landing Beach

Rat Island

Ferry P

Goat Island

Surf Point

South West Point

The Rattles

Shutter Point

Black Rock

The Race

Saunton

SAUNTON RD

CROYDE RD B3231

B323

Saunton Sands

SAUNTON BEACH VILLAS

CH

DANGER AREA

EX33

DANGER AREA

Braunton Burrows
(Nature Reserve)

Airy Point

Ferry P Lundy

DANGER AREA

Crow Rock

South West Coast Path

JUBILEE RD 1
WESTERN AVE 2
POLYWALL 3
LOVER'S LA 4
STADDON RD 5
SCOTT AVE 6
RICHMOND RD 7
RICHMOND GR 8
MYRTLE COTTAGE RD 9
WHITEHORSE LA 10

Skern

LB Sta

Appledore

Barnstaple or
Bideford Bay

Pebble Ridge

Sandymere

EX39

FAIRWAY

Northam Burrows
Country Park

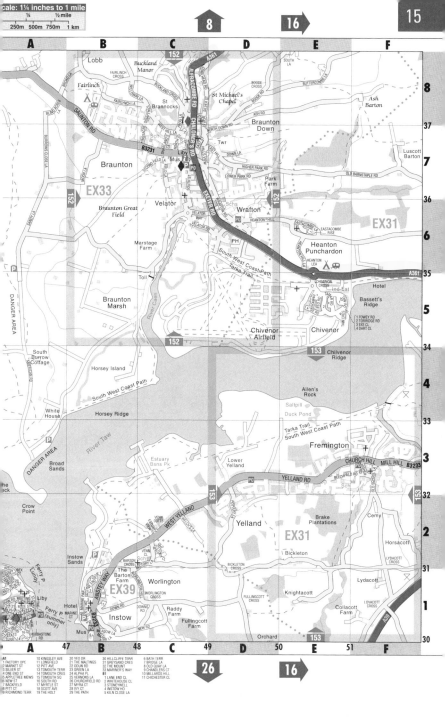

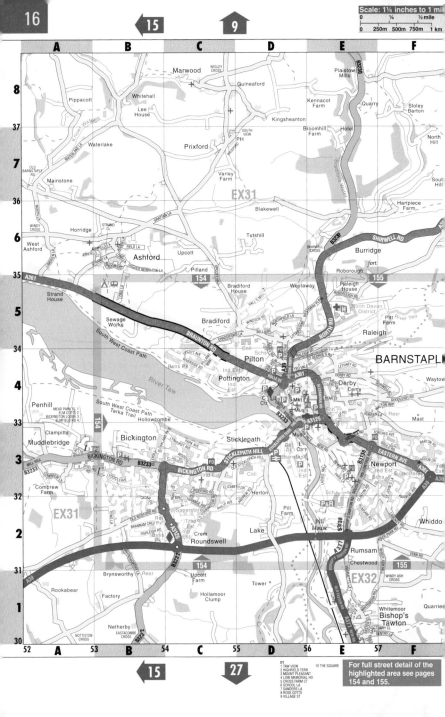

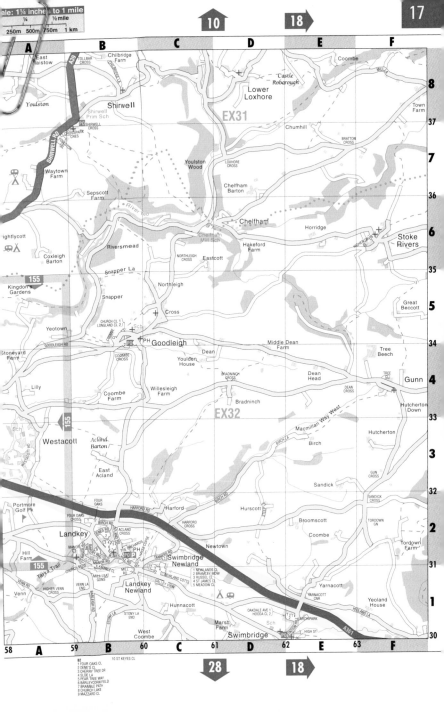

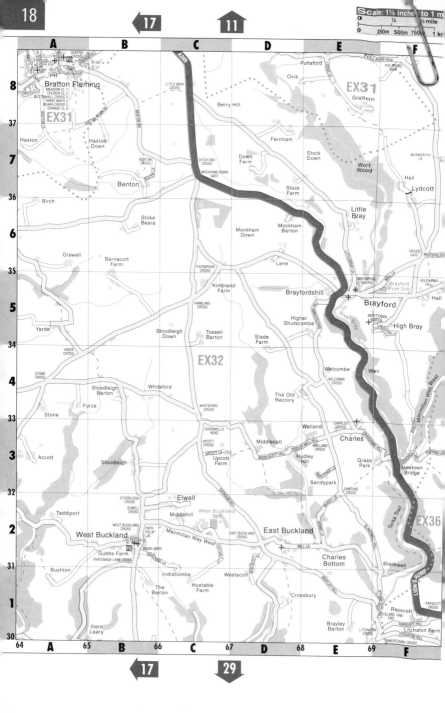

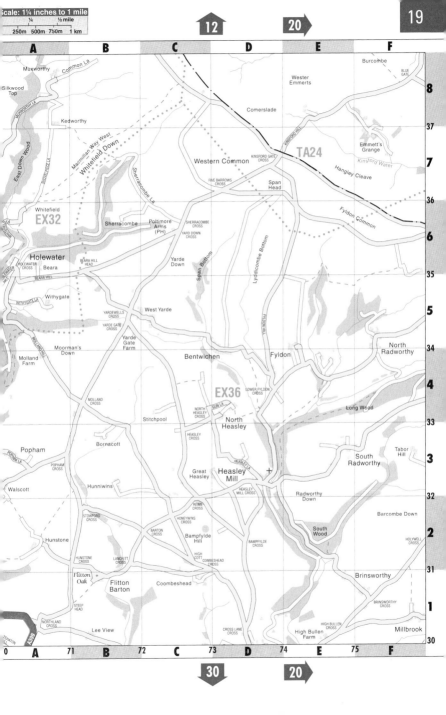

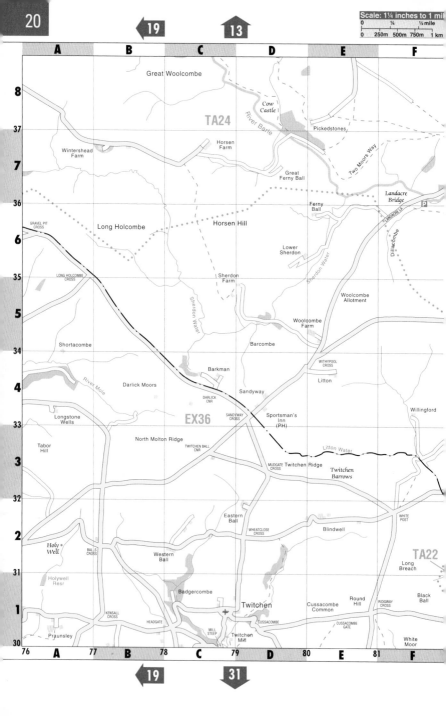

Scale: 1¼ inches to 1 mile

¼   ½ mile

250m 500m 750m 1 km

| A | B | C | D | E | F |

8

Pennycombe Water

Chibbet

B3223

Chibbet Hill

CHIBBET POST

Court Farm

Road Castle

Lyncombe

SLADES HILL RD

SELLBED CROSS

Buckworthy

37

Herne's Barrow

ROOM HILL RD

Road Hill

Halsgrove Farm

SPARROW LA

Blacklands

TA24

Room Hill

Nethercote

7

Hillway

KITRIDGE LA

Weatherslade

Foxwitchen

Lanacre

36

Brightworthy

Withypool

PH

COMER'S CROSS

ASH LA

Newland

Knighton

PH

King's Farm

Uppington

COMER'S GATE

Great Ash

Waterhouse Farm

MOORFIELD GDN

6

Withypool Common

South Hill

35

Knigthon Combe

Withypool Hill

5

Wambarrows

B3223

Stone Circle

Batsom Farm

Great Bradley

Somerset STREET ATLAS

34

Worth Hill

West Water

WORTH LA

River Barle

Two Moors Way

Two Moors Way

4

Porchester Post

Worth

Knaplock

EX36

Westwater Allotment

Westwater Farm

Liscombe

33

Humber's Ball

Parsonage Down

Tarr Farm

Little River

P

3

Hawkridge Plain

Old Barrow

Hill Farm

Parsonage Farm

Tarr Steps

Hotel

Ashway Side

32

Clogg's Down

WITHYPOOL CROSS

Hawkridge Common

TA22

Ashway

2

Moorhouse Ridge

Cloggs Farm

HAWKRIDGE CROSS

Hawkridge

PH

Slade

31

Lyshwell Farm

Shircombe Farm

BROAD LANE HEAD

BROAD LA

Hawkridge Ridge

1

Dane's Brook

Hollowcombe

Eve Valley Way

VENFORD HILL

30

| A | 83 | B | 84 | C | 85 | D | 86 | E | 87 | F |

Hartland
Point

Barley
Bay

Eldern
Point

Chapman
Rock

Radar
Tower

Shipload
Bay

Gawlish
Cliff

South West Coast Path

Titchberry

Cow & Calf

Upright
Cliff

Blagdon
Farm

Exmansworthy
Cliff

Fattacott

Damehole
Point

Gawlish
Farm

Exmansworthy

Long
Furlong

Moor

FATACOTT
CROSS

Beckland
Farm

Blegberry

Pitt

Dyer's
Lookout

PITT
CROSS

YOULTREE
CROSS

BECKLAND
CROSS

Downe

FATTARD
CROSS

Norton

Broad
Beach

The
Warren

Berry

Markadon

Abbey
(rems of)

Cheristow

Pattard

Hartland
Abbey

Hotel

COASTGUARD
COTTS

Abbey River

Ballhill

10 SCHOOL LA
11 JEFFREY CL
12 HEYWOOD CL
13 GOAMAN PK
14 HARTON WAY

Hartland
Quay
Mus

Stoke

EX39

Hartland

Rosedown

METTAFORD
CROSS

CUTLIFF LA

Waterfall

Chapel

St Leonards

NEWTON
CROSS

NORTHGATE 1
THE SQUARE 2
VICARAGE CL 3
WELL SPRING CL 4
PINES CL 5
TURNERS CRES 6
BROMACOMBE RD 7
MEADOW VW 8
THE GREENWOODS 9

FORE ST

FORD
HILL

PH

EASTDOWN

Kernstone
Farm

Little
Barton

Newton

Leigh
Farm

Wargery

Waterfall

LIBERTY
STILE

Hotel

SPUR
CROSS

NATCOTT LA

Farford

KERNSTONE
CROSS

Trellick

Ackworthy

Stowford

GREENLAKE
CROSS

PHILHAM
CROSS

GORRANS
DOWN

Mildford

Lymebridge

Galsham
Farm

Well

Philham

Docton
Mill

MILFORD
CROSS

PHILHAM
WATER

Staddon

Scale: 1¼ inches to 1 mile

0   ¼   ½ mile
0   250m 500m 750m 1 km

A B C D E F

8

29

7

28

6

27

5

26

4

Babbacombe Mouth
Babbacombe Cliff

Higher Rowden

25

3

Portledge

Chiddlecombe

The Gore

Gauter Point

Castle

24

South West Coast Path

Peppercombe

Gilscott

2

Sloo

Northway

PH

Horns Cross

Bideford Bay Holiday Village

Buck's Mills

Hoops PH

Holwell

PO

COTHERIDGE LA

23

Buck's Cross

Cemy

Watershute

EX39

Goldworthy

1

Bitworthy

Walland

Waytown

Hotel

Newhaven

BREWERS HILL

PARKHAM CROSS

22

Limebury

Broad Pakham

34   A   35   B   36   C   37   D   38   E   39   F

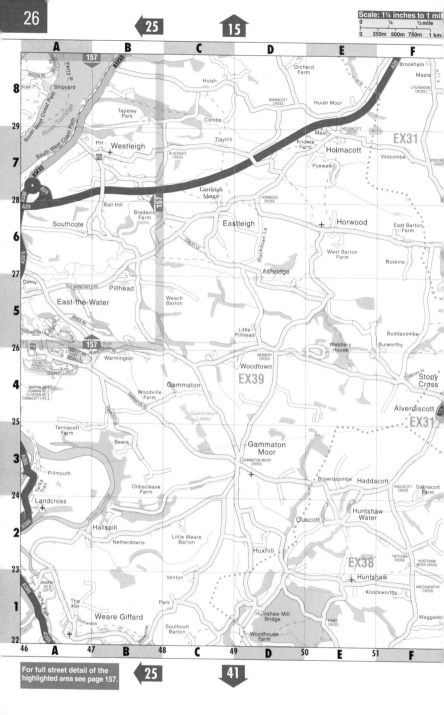

Scale: 1¼ inches to 1 mile

0   ¼   ½ mile
0   250m 500m 750m 1 km

A **B** **C** **D** **E** **F**

157
B233

8
WOODA RD
Shipyard
RONA LN
Huish
Orchard Farm
Brookham
Masts
LITCHARDON CROSS

29
River Torridge
Tapeley Park
Combe
BARNACOTT CROSS
Huish Moor
HOLMACOTT CROSS
EX31
Voscombe
VOSCON CROSS

7
South West Coast Path
PH
Westleigh
PO
BLACKGATE CROSS
Trayhill
Knowle Farm
Mast
Holmacott
Pyewell

28
A39
B233
A386
Ball Hill
Bradavin Farm
Eastleigh Manor
157
HORWOOD CROSS
Horwood
East Barton Farm

6
Southcote
CORLEY LA
Eastleigh
Blackdown La
West Barton Farm
Boskins

27
Cemy
Pillhead
Weach Barton
Ashridge

5
East-the-Water
MINES RD
Little Pillhead
Buddacombe

26
PO
TORRINGTON LA
BROAD-LANDS
157 Sch
Sch
ALVERDISCOTT RD
Warmington
WEBBERY CROSS
Webbery House
Bulworthy

4
BARTON HO 8
GOAMAN RD 2
CLIVEDEN RD 3
TENNACOTT HTS 4
CHUBB RD
CHURCHILL RD
CHOPES CLOSE
Woodville Farm
GAMMATON RD
Gammaton
Woodtown
EX39
BOUNDARY LN
Stony Cross

25
Tennacott Farm
Beara
Gammaton Lakes
Alverdiscott
EX31

3
A386
Tarka Trail
Pillmouth
Oldiscleave Farm
Gammaton Moor
GAMMATON MOOR CROSS
Brownscombe
Haddacott
HADDACOTT CROSS
Garnacott Farm

24
Landcross
River Torridge
Guscott
SCHOOL LA
CORLEY LA
Huntshaw Water

2
Hallspill
Netherdowns
Little Weare Barton
Huxhill
TWITCHEN CROSS
HUNTSHAW MOOR CROSS
EX38

23
A386
Tarka Trail
ANNERY KILN COTTS
Venton
Huntshaw
KNOCKWORTHY CROSS

1
The Hill
Weare Giffard
CHURCH MEW
Park
Southcott Barton
Huntshaw Mill Bridge
Woodhouse Farm
FOKES CROSS
Knockworthy
Waggado

22
46 **A** 47 **B** 48 **C** 49 **D** 50 **E** 51 **F**

For full street detail of the highlighted area see page 157.

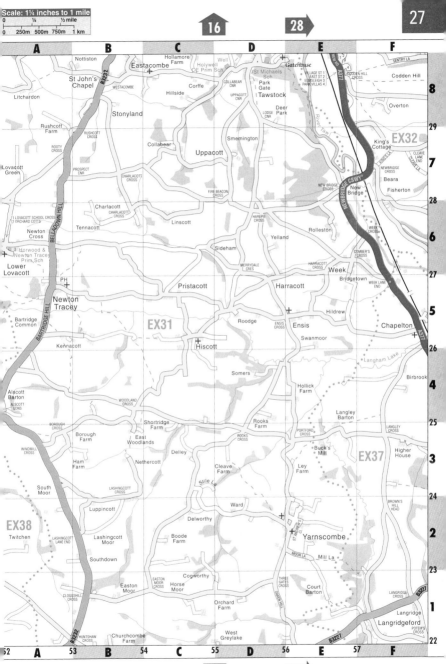

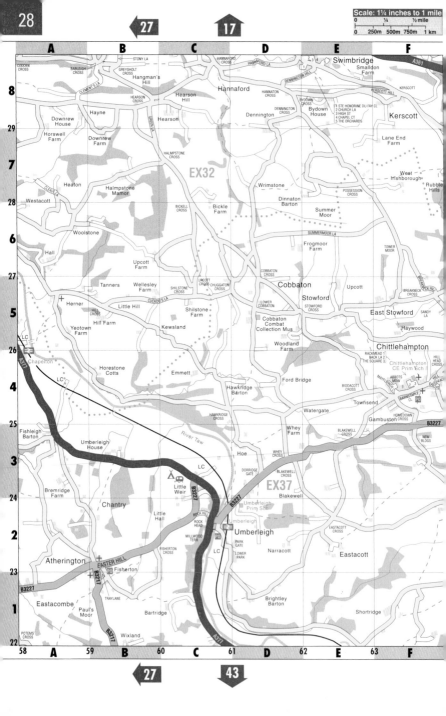

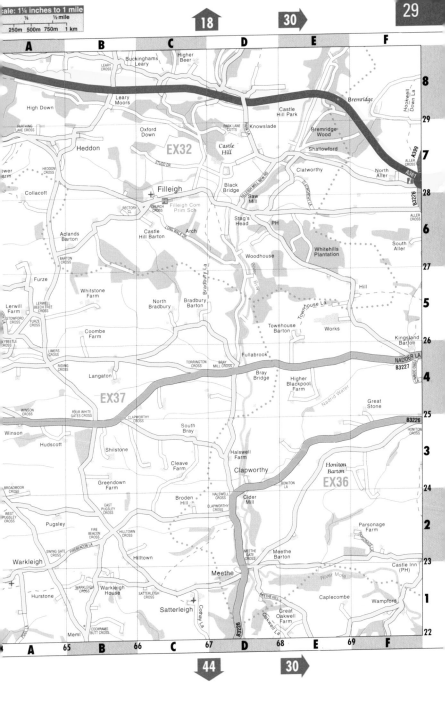

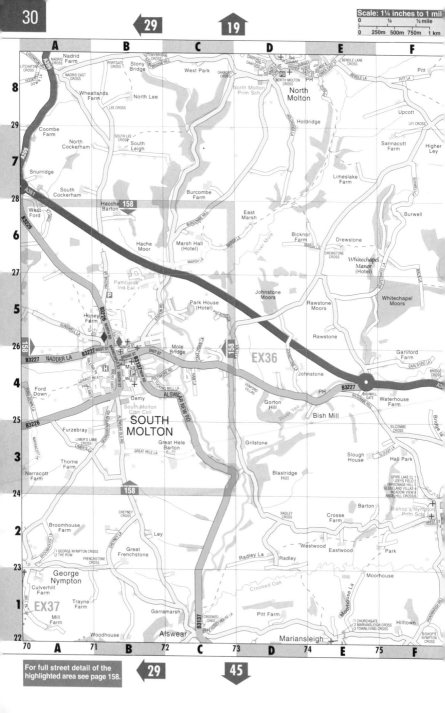

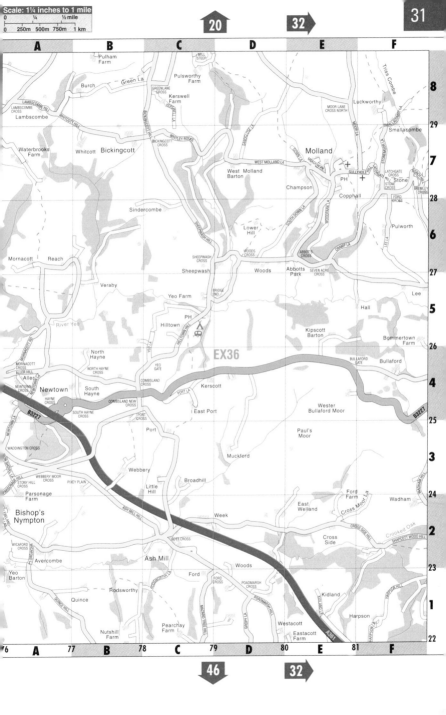

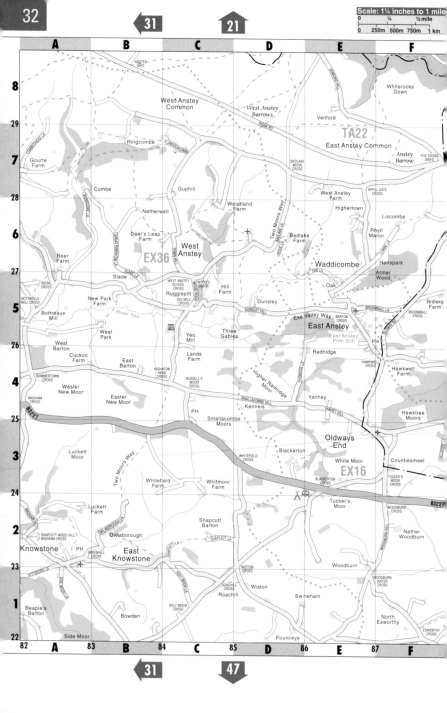

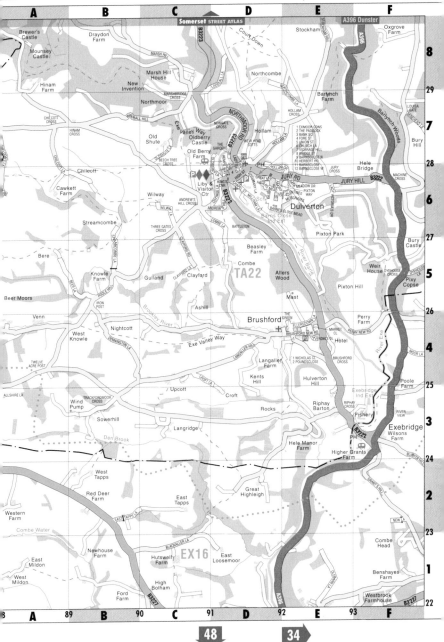

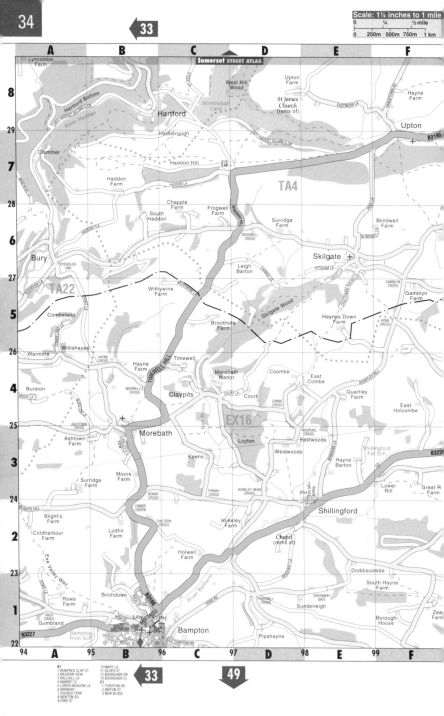

Scale: 1¼ inches to 1 mile

| 0 | ¼ | ½ mile |

| 0 | 250m 500m 750m | 1 km |

Somerset STREET ATLAS

Lyncombe Farm

Hartford Bottom

River Haddeo

Hartford

Clammer

Haddon Hill

Haddon Farm

Chapple Farm

South Haddon

Withywine Farm

Combeland

Warmore

Willishayes

Hayne Cross

Hayne Farm

Bury

DYEHOUSE CNR

Burston

West Hill Wood

Wimbleball Lake

Hadborough

Frogwell Farm

Frogwell Cross

Surridge Farm

Leigh Barton

Brockhole Farm

Timewell

Morebath Manor

Claypits

Court

Coombe

East Combe

Upton Farm

St James Church (rems of)

Upton

B3190

Hayne Farm

TA4

Blindwell Farm

Skilgate

Skilgate Wood

Haynes Down Farm

HONE CROSS

Gamblyn CROSS

Gamblyn Farm

TA22

Morrell's Cross

Ashtown CROSS

Ashtown Farm

Morebath

Keens

Moore Farm

Surridge Farm

Blight's Farm

Coldharbour Farm

Exe Valley Way

Rows Farm

Gumbland

Birchdown

Loyton

Westwoods

Eastwoods

HOOPERS CROSS

EX16

Hayne Barton

Shillingford Fst Sch

B3190

Lower Rill

Great R Farm

Quartley Farm

East Holcombe

COMBE CROSS

Bonny Cross

Lower Lodfin

CHILTERN CROSS

Lodfin Farm

Firway Cross

Hukeley Head CROSS

Hukeley Farm

Holwell Farm

Chapel (rems of)

Shillingford

PH

Doddiscombe

South Hayne Farm

Zea Far

Borough House

Sunderleigh

GREENWAY GATE

FORDMILL CROSS

Pipshayne

Bampton

River Batherm

Bampton Prim Sch

High CROSS

Gumbland

B3227

River Haddeo

B1
1 WINIFRED CLIFF CT
2 MEADOW VIEW
3 BALLHILL LA
4 MARKET CL
5 LORDS MEADOW LA
6 BARNHAY
7 CHURCH TERR
8 NEWTON SQ
9 FORE ST
10 MARY LA
11 SILVER ST
12 BOURCHER DR
13 BOURCHER CL
C1
1 TIVERTON RD
2 BRITON ST
3 NEW BLDGS

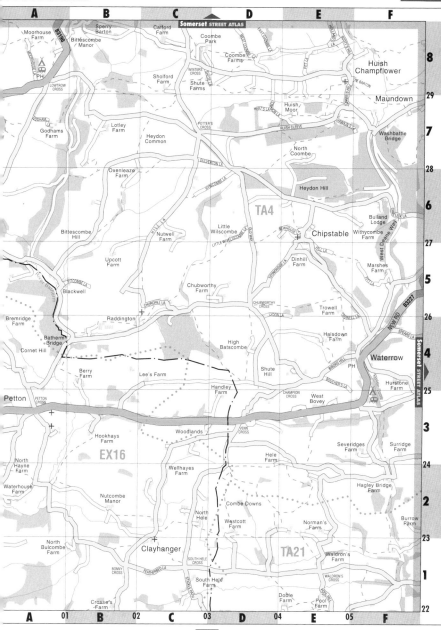

Me...

Nabor
Point

Emb
Bea...

Embury
Beach

EX39

Knaps
Head

The
Hermitage

Welcombe Mouth

Marsland Mouth

Gull
Rock

Marsland
Cliff

Cornakey Cliff

Marsland
Manor

Yeol Mouth

Cornakey
Farm

South West Coast Path

EX23

Henna
Cliff

Westcott
Farm

Hawker's
Hut

Well

Vicarage
Cliff

Morwenstow

Lucky Hole

Crosstown PH

Higher
Sharpnose Point

The Tidna

CROSSWATER

Tonacombe

WOODVILLE
CROSS

STANBURY
CROSS

WOODVILLE
RD.

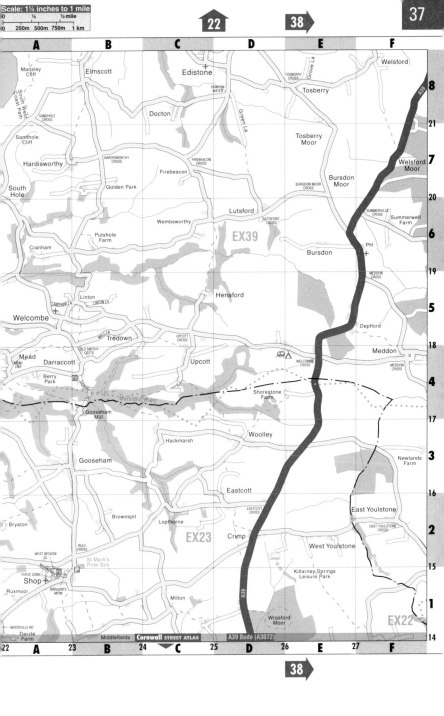

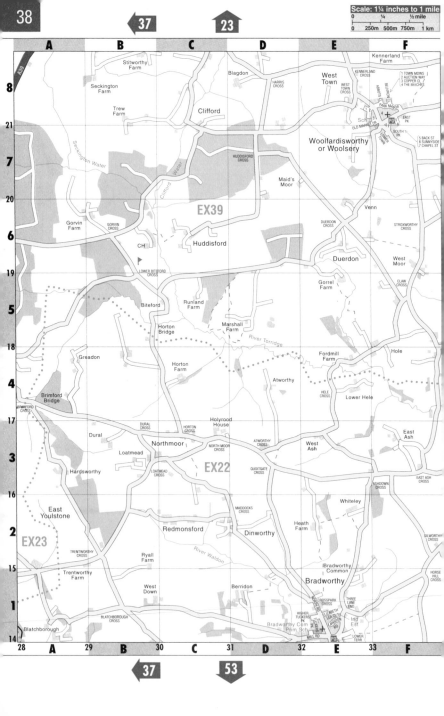

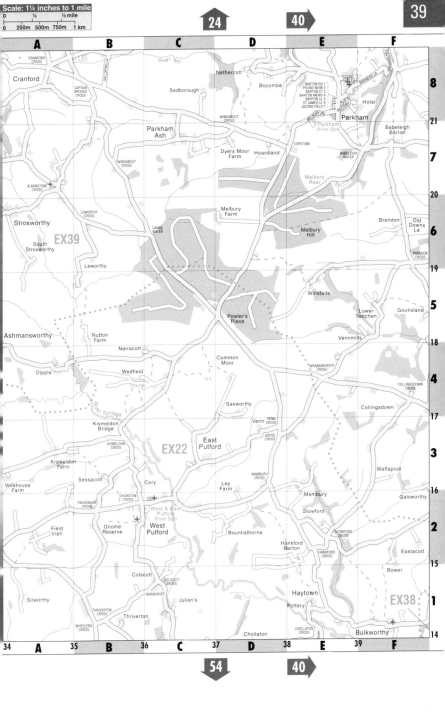

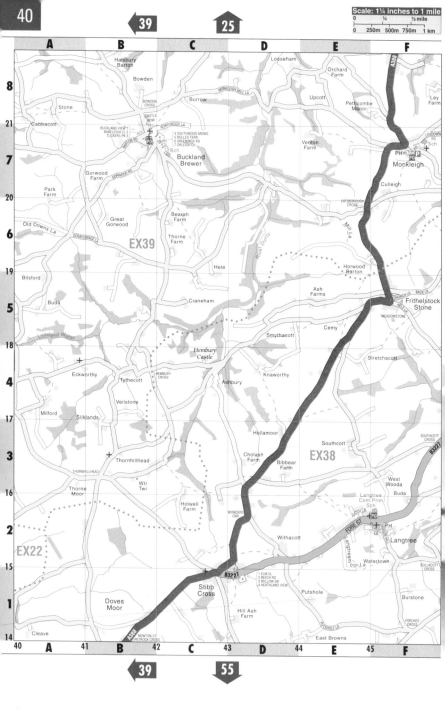

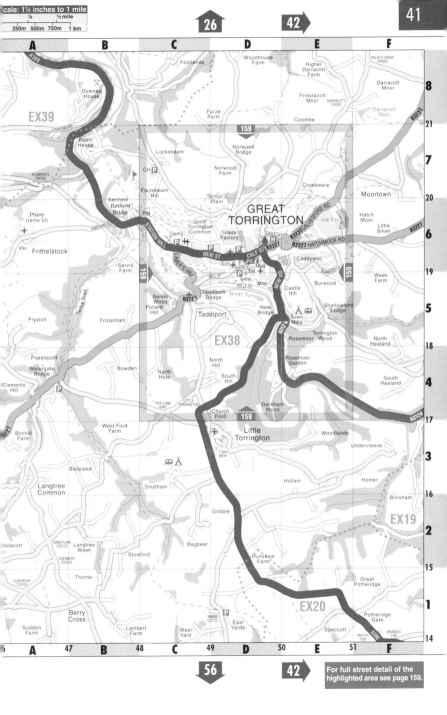

Scale: 1¼ inches to 1 mile

¼ ½ mile
250m 500m 750m 1 km

A B C D E F

A386

EX39

DELVE'S GRAVE CROSS

Footlands

Woodhouse Farm

Higher Darracott Farm

Darracott Moor

8

Downes House

Furze Farm

Priestacott Moor

DARRACOTT CROSS

Darracott Resr

21

B3232

Beam House

LOXDOWN RD

Locksbeam

Coombe

159

Norwood Bridge

7

PLUMPER'S CROSS

CH P

Norwood Farm

Crowbeare

Moortown

20

Kennels Rothern Bridge

Furzebeam Hill

Tanton's Plain

GREAT TORRINGTON

CALVSFORD RD

Ind Est

Hatch Moor

Little Silver

Priory (rems of)

PH

RAKEHAM HILL

PH

Great Torrington Common

Glass Factory

B3232

B3227

Sch

B3227

6

Frithelstock

STATION HILL

Cemy

P

NEW ST

CALF ST

B3227

B3227 HATCHMOOR RD

Caddywell

19

PH

Servis Farm

159

P

Sch

PO

Mus

Sch

Burwood

Week Farm

LIMER'S HILL

ROLLE RD

MILL ST

TH

Lby

Mon

NEW RD

Castle Hill

Shallowford Lodge

Pryston

Tarka Trail

Frizenham

Servis Wood Pollard Hill

B322

Taddiport Bridge

River Torridge

New Bridge

Town Mills

Torrington Wood

North Healand

5

Priestacott

Taddiport

EX38

A3124

Rosemoor

Rosemoor Wood

18

Watergate Bridge

Clements Hill

P

Bowden

North Hole

North Hill

South Hill

Rosemoor Garden

South Healand

4

B3227

Birchill Farm

FIVE LANE END

LITTLE TORRINGTON

West Ford Farm

Church Ford

159

Darkham Wood

A3124

17

Langtree Common

Badslake

Smytham

TOWN MDW

Little Torrington

Woodlands

Undercleave

3

Hollam

Homer

Blinsham

16

EX19

Sollacott

SANDYLANE CROSS

Langtree Week

SHEBBEAR CROSS

Stowford

Bagbear

Gribble

2

CUDEMOOR CROSS

Thorne

Hunshaw Farm

Great Potheridge

15

Berry Cross

YARDE COTTS

P

West Yard

East Yarde

EX20

Potheridge Gate

1

Suddon Farm

Lambert Farm

Speccott

PRETTY TOP

A386

BRANDIS CNR

14

A B C D E F

47 48 49 50 51

For full street detail of the highlighted area see page 159.

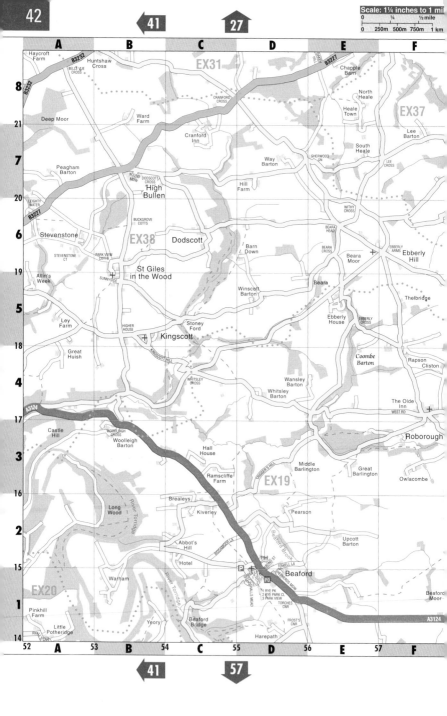

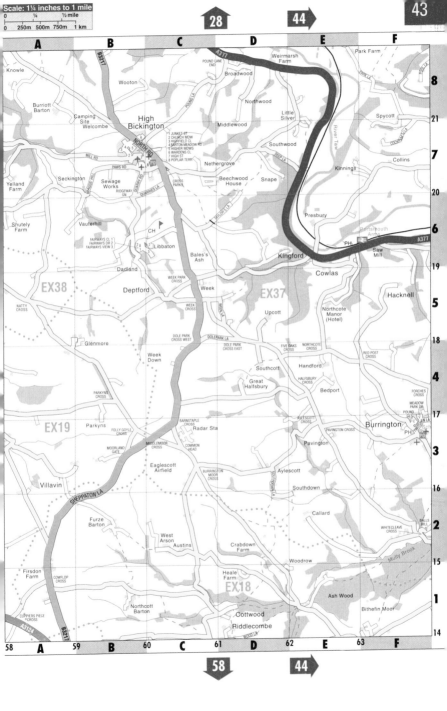

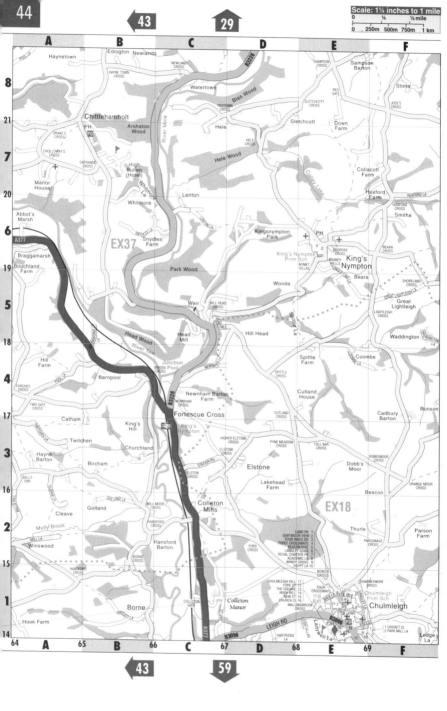

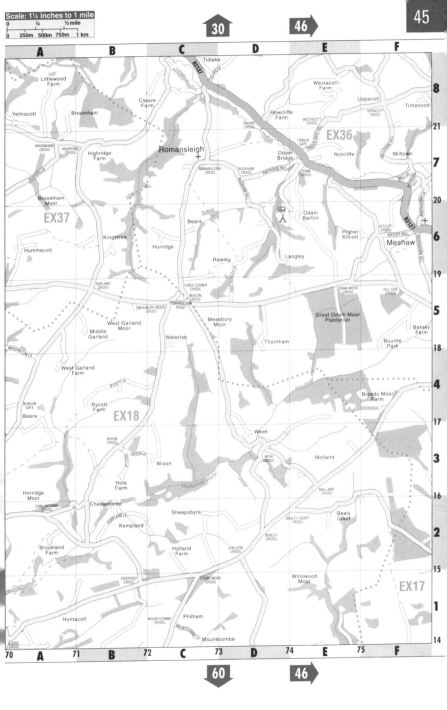

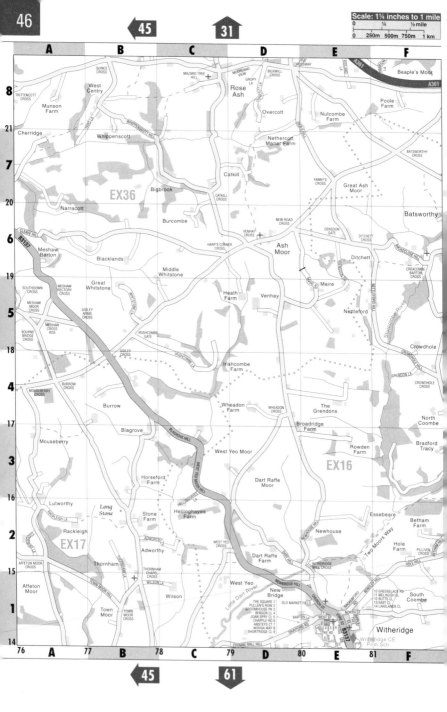

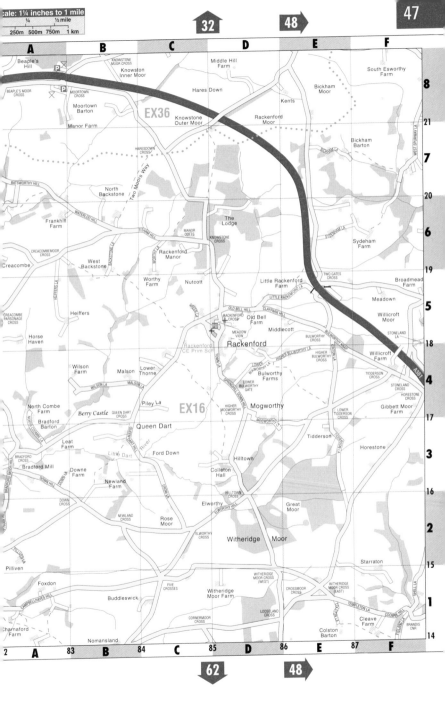

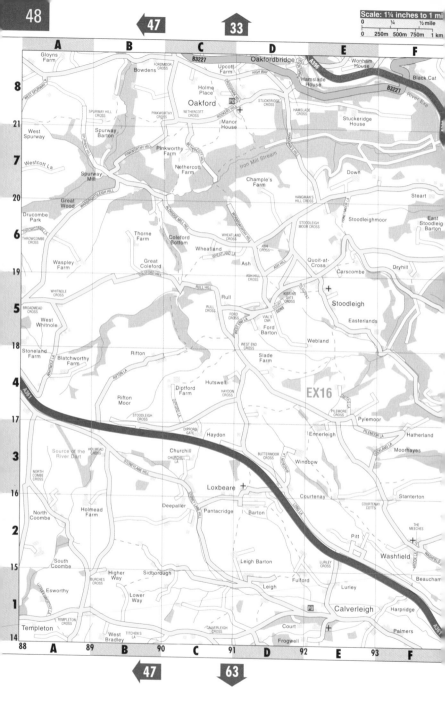

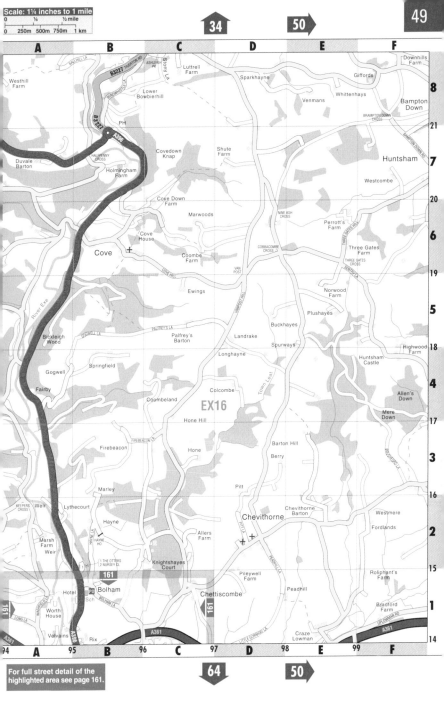

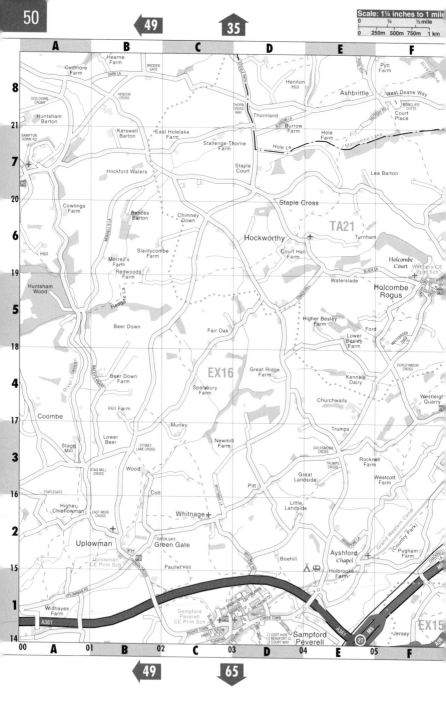

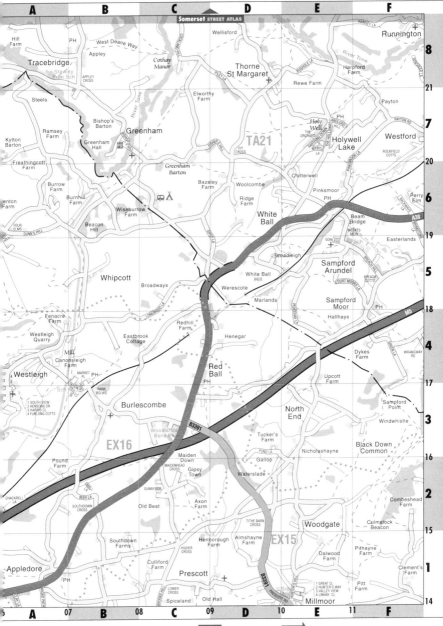

Runnington

Hill Farm

PH

West Deane Way

Wellisford

River Tone

8

Tracebridge

Appley

Cothay Manor

Thorne St Margaret

Rewe Farm

Harpford Farm

21

Stawley Prim Sch

APPLEY CROSS

Elworthy Farm

Payton

Steels

Bishop's Barton

Greenham

PH

Holy Well

Holywell Lake

PAYTON RD

7

Kytton Barton

Ramsey Farm

Greenham Hall

River Lane

THE ORCHARD

MYRTLE

Westford

ROCKFIELD COTTS

Freethingcott Farm

Greenham Barton

TA21

IVY CROSS

Chitterwell

20

Burrow Farm

Bazeley Farm

Woolcombe

Pinksmoor

Perry Elm

6

enton Farm

Burnhill Farm

Ridge Farm

White Ball

PH

Beam Bridge

A38

Easterlands

Wiseburrow Farm

WEEKES MEAD

19

FOUR ELMS

DUNN'S HILL

Beacon Hill

GORES LA

Sch

Broadleigh

Sampford Arundel

BREACH COTTS

Whipcott

Broadways

White Ball Hill

Werescote

COURT MOOR LA

M5

5

Marlands

Sampford Moor

PH

18

Fenacre Farm

Eastbrook Cottage

Redhill Farm

Henegar

Hallhays

Westleigh Quarry

Dykes Farm

WRANGWAY RD

4

Mill

Canonsleigh Farm

Red Ball

Upcott Farm

17

Westleigh

MARKET

PH

PH

Sampford Point

1 SOUTH VIEW
2 HENSONS DR
3 HARHS CL
4 FURLONG COTTS

PARK BGLWS

Burlescombe

North End

Windwhistle

3

EX16

B3391

Woodlands Bsns Pk

Tucker's Farm

Nicholashayne

Black Down Common

16

Maiden Down

POND LA

Gallop

Pound Farm

MAIDENHEAD CROSS

Gipsy Town

Waterslade

Combeshead Farm

2

CHACKRELL LA

BEER LA

SUNNYSIDE

Axon Farm

Culmstock Beacon

SOUTHDOWN CROSS

Old Beat

TITHE BARN CROSS

Woodgate

15

Appledore

Southdown Farms

HIGHER CROSS

Henborough Farm

Aimshayne Farm

EX15

Dalwood Farm

Pithayne Farm

Clement's Farm

1

PH

Culliford Farm

Prescott

PRESCOTT RD

1 GREAT CL
2 HUNTER'S WAY
3 VALLEY VIEW
4 LINHAY CL

Pitt Farm

LOWER CROSS

Spiceland

Old Hall

Sch

Millmoor

14

Scale: 1¼ inches to 1 mile

0   ¼   ½ mile

0   250m 500m 750m   1 km

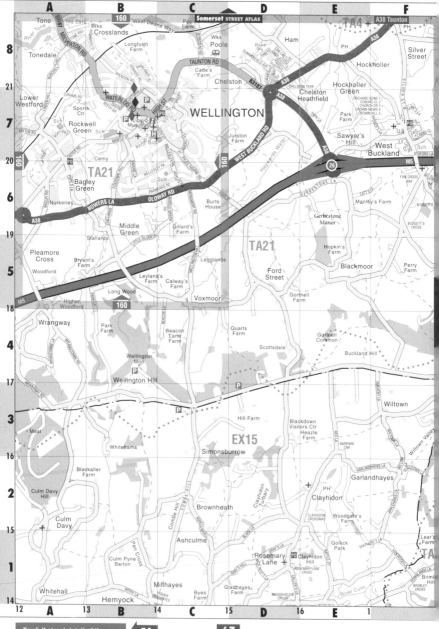

A   **B**   **C**   **D**   **E**   **F**

TA4   A38 Taunton

Somerset STREET ATLAS

160   West Deane Way

Crosslands

Tone

River Tone

Ind Ests

MILVERTON RD

Longforth Farm

Pool Farm

Ham

Silver Street

8

Tonedale

Lower Westford

Wks Poole

TAUNTON RD

Cade's Farm

Chelston

B3187

PH

Hockholler

Hockholler Green

21

Waterloo Rd

HIGH ST

Sch

A38

WELLINGTON

Chelston Heathfield

Park Farm

7

Sports Ctr

Rockwell Green

Lib & Mus

Jurston Farm

WEST BUCKLAND RD

Sawyer's Hill

West Buckland

20

Cemy

TA21

Haywards Water

A38

26

Five Cross Way

M5

6

Bagley Green

Nurseries

NOWERS LA

OLDWAY RD

Burts House

FORBESTONE LA

Manley's Farm

Gerbestone Manor

BUDGETT'S CROSS

A38

Middle Green

Gillard's Farm

Hopkin's Farm

19

Stallards

LITTLE SILVER LA

Legglands

TA21

Blackmoor

Perry Farm

5

Pleamore Cross

Woodford

Bryant's Farm

Leyland's Farm

Calway's Farm

Ford Street

Gortnell Farm

M5

Higher Woodford

Long Wood

160

Voxmoor

18

Wrangway

Park Farm

Beacon Lane Farm

Quarts Farm

Scottsdale

Gortnell Common

Buckland Hill

4

Wellington Mon

P

17

Wellington Hill

P

Hill Farm

Wiltown

3

Mast

Whitehams

EX15

Simonsburrow

Blackdown Visitors Ctr Heazle Farm

BARPARK CNR

Wiltown Valley

16

Blackaller Farm

Garlandhayes

2

Culm Davy Hill

Brownheath

Clayhidon Turbary

PH

Clayhidon

Woodgate's Farm

Culm Davy

Combe Hill

CLAYHIDON CROSSWAY

Golluck Park

15

Ashculme

Culm Pyne Barton

Rosemary Lane

Clayhidon Hill

Lear's Farm

1

Whitehall

Milhayes

Byes Farm

Gladhayes Farm

BRIDGEHOUSE CROSS

River Culm

Brimli

14

Hemyock

12   **A**   **13**   **B**   **14**   **C**   **15**   **D**   **16**   **E**   **1**

For full street detail of the highlighted area see page 160

51

67

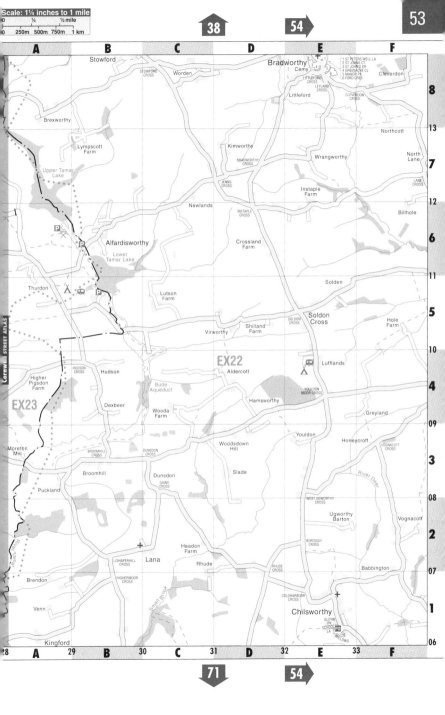

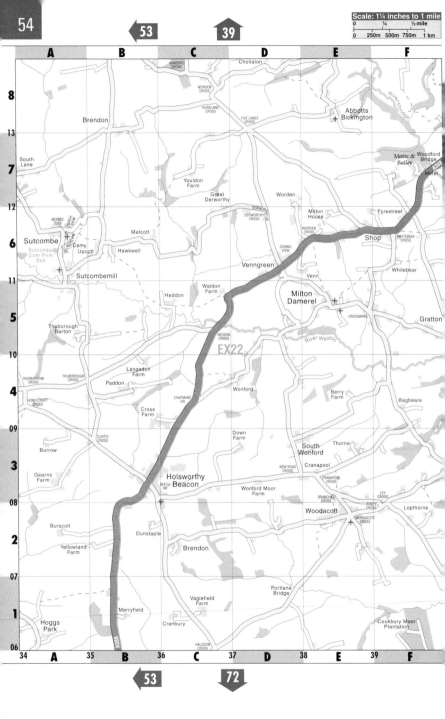

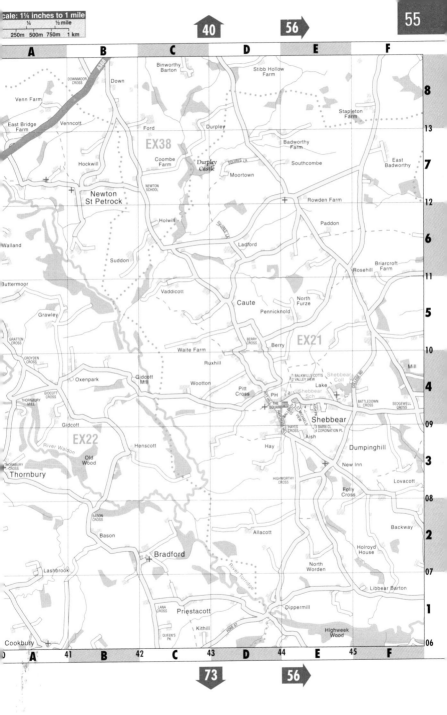

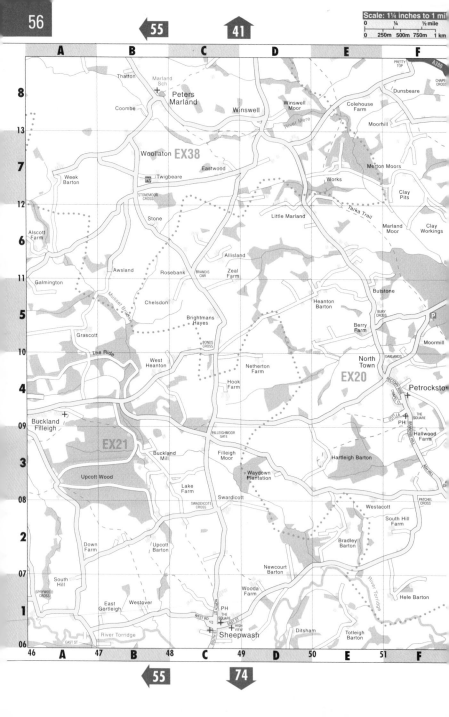

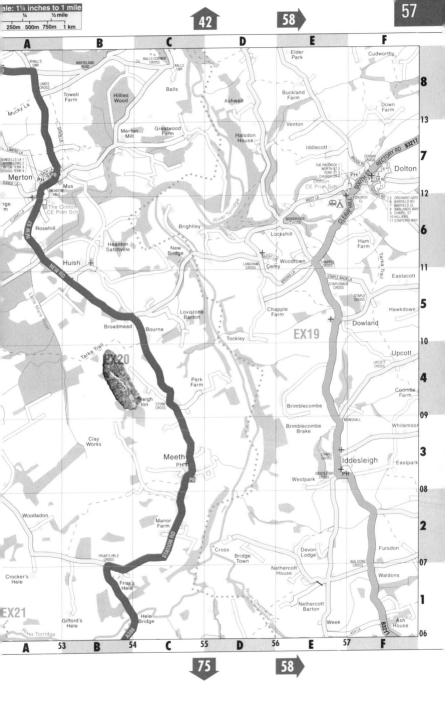

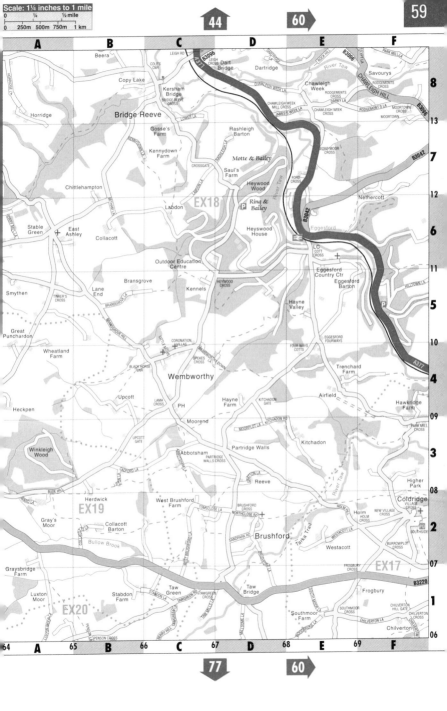

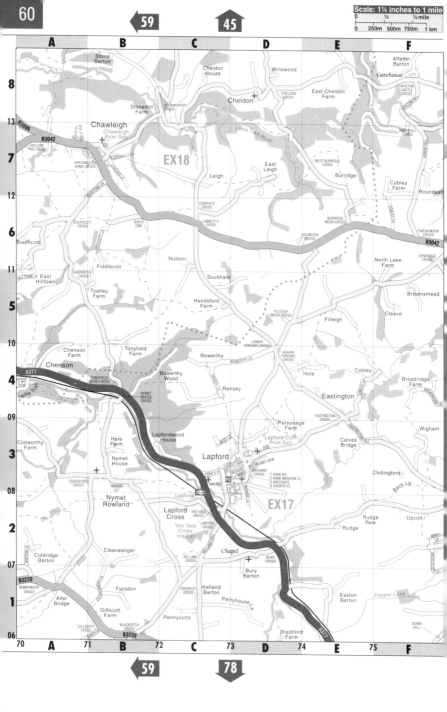

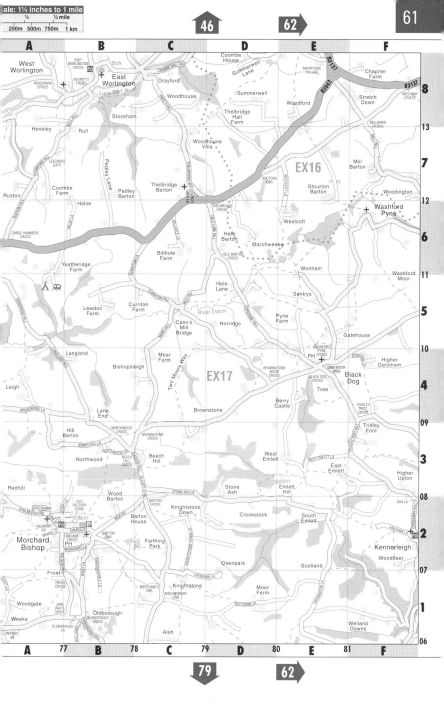

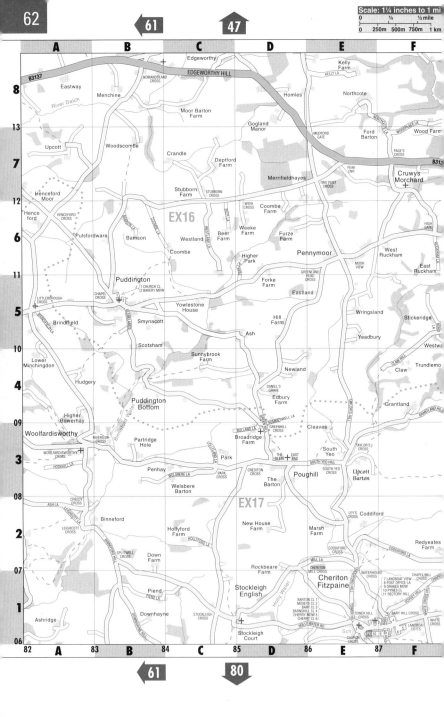

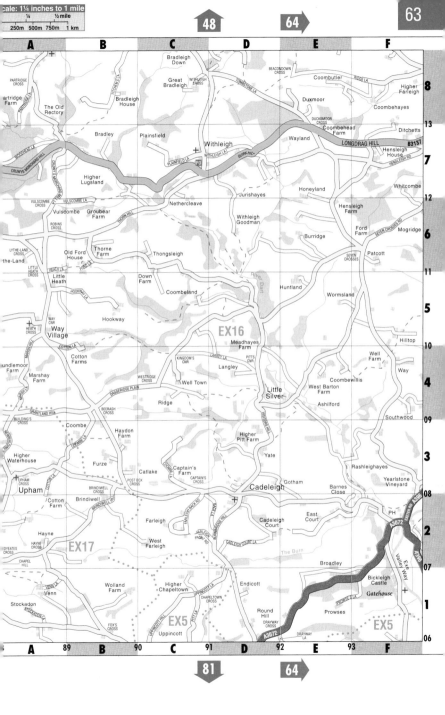

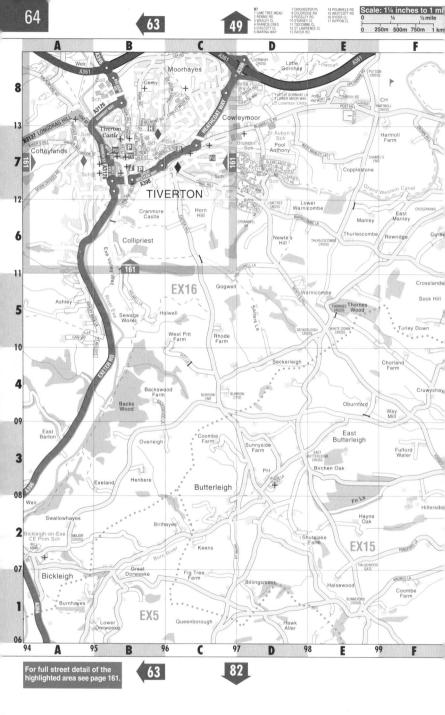

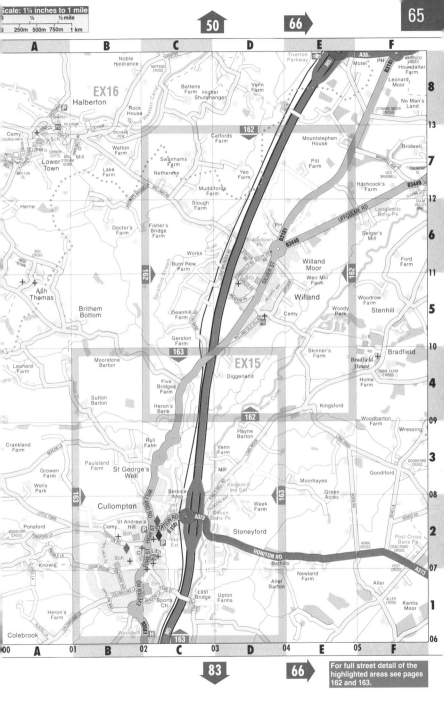

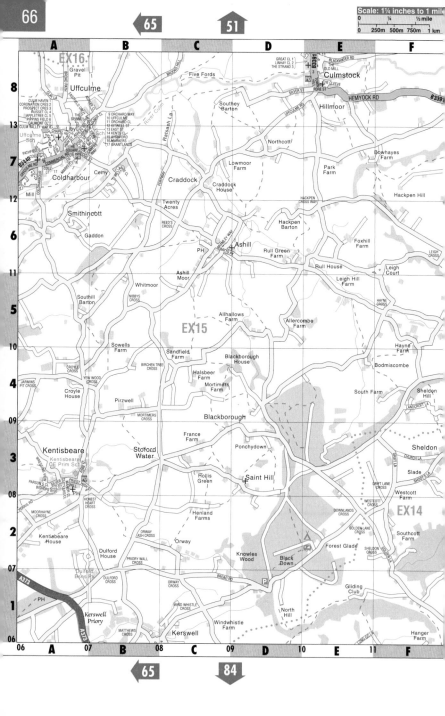

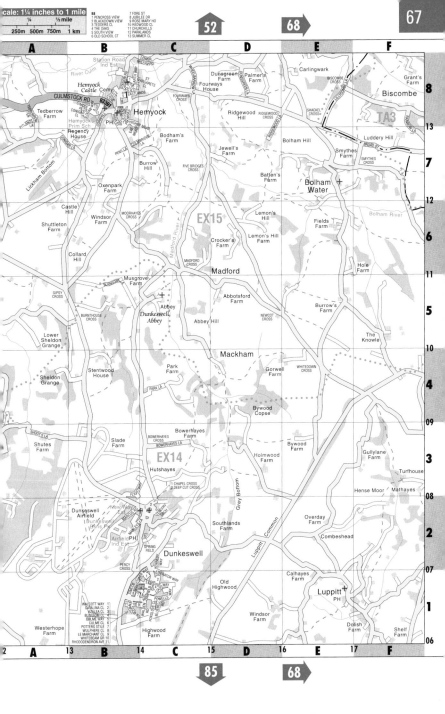

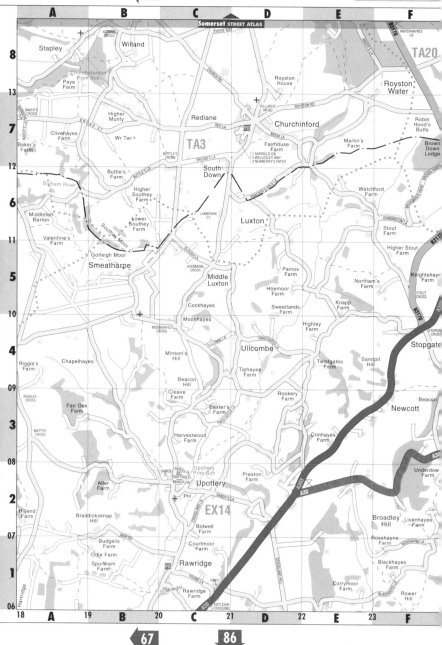

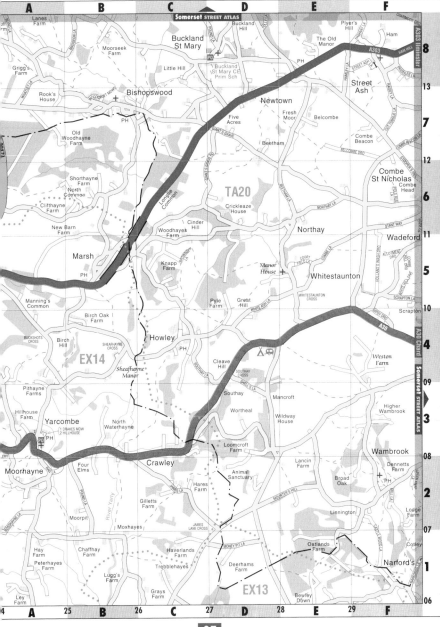

Scale: 1¼ inches to 1 mile
¼ · ½ mile
250m · 500m · 750m · 1 km

A B C D E F

8
13
7
12
6
11
5
10
4
09
3
08
2
07
1
06

Lanes Farm
Grigg's Farm
Rook's House
Moorseek Farm
Little Hill
Buckland St Mary
Buckland Hill
Buckland St Mary CE Prim Sch
The Old Manor
Plyer's Hill
Ham
A303 Ilminster
Street Ash
Bishopswood
PH
Old Woodhayne Farm
Newtown
Fresh Moor
Belcombe
Combe Beacon
Five Acres
Beetham
BELCOMBE DRO
Combe St Nicholas
Combe Head
Shorthayne Farm
North Common
Clifthayne Farm
Longille Common
TA20
Crickleaze House
Northay
Wadeford
New Barn Farm
Cinder Hill
Woodhayes Farm
Knapp Farm
Manor House
Whitestaunton
Scrapton
Marsh
PH
Manning's Common
Birch Oak Farm
Pyle Farm
Great Hill
WHITE ADE LA
WHITESTAUNTON CROSS
A30 Chard
Buckshots Cross
Birch Hill
SHEAFHAYNE CROSS
Howley
PH
Cleave Hill
SOUTHAY CROSS
Weston Farm
EX14
Sheafhayne Manor
Southay
Mancroft
Higher Wambrook
Pithayne Farms
Wortheal
Wildway House
Hillhouse Farm
Yarcombe
PH
North Waterhayne
Loomcroft Farm
Lancin Farm
Wambrook
Dennetts Farm
PH
Moorhayne
Four Elms
Crawley
Animal Sanctuary
Broad Oak
Lodge Farm
Gilletts Farm
Hares Farm
Linnington
Moorpit
Moxhayes
JAMES LANE CROSS
MONEY PIT LA
Hay Farm
Chaffhay Farm
Haverlands Farm
Trebblehayes
Oatlands Farm
Cotley
Narford's
Peterhayes Farm
Lugg's Farm
Deerhams Farm
EX13
Ley Farm
Grays Farm
Bewley Down

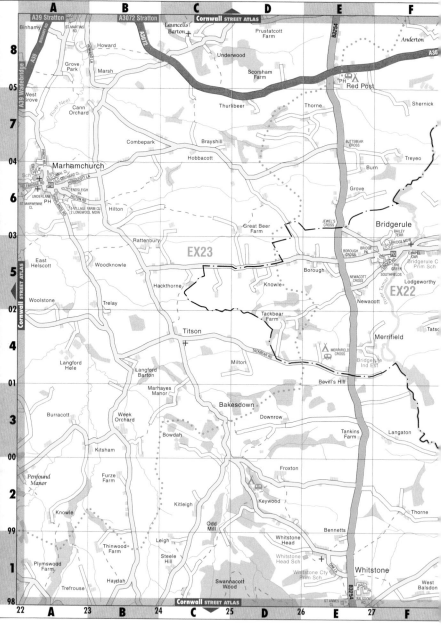

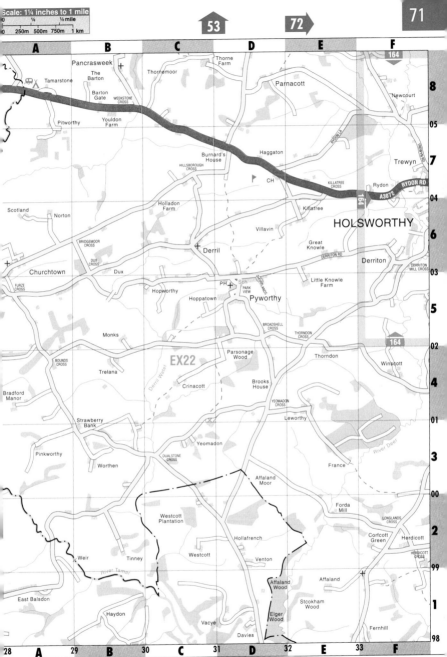

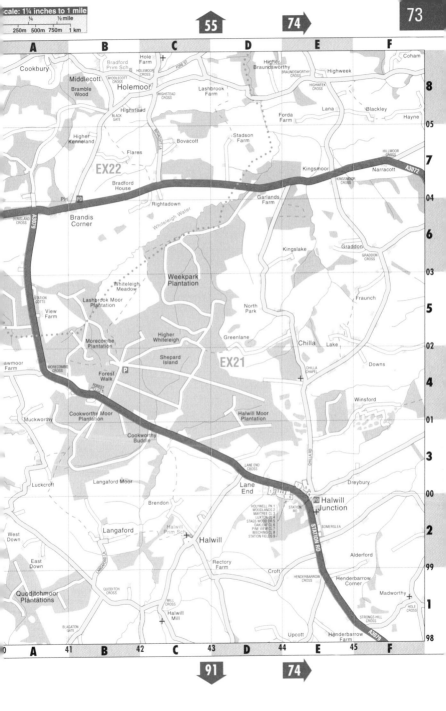

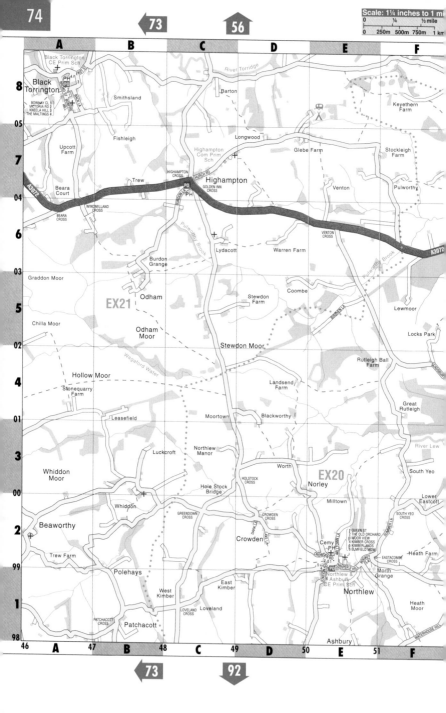

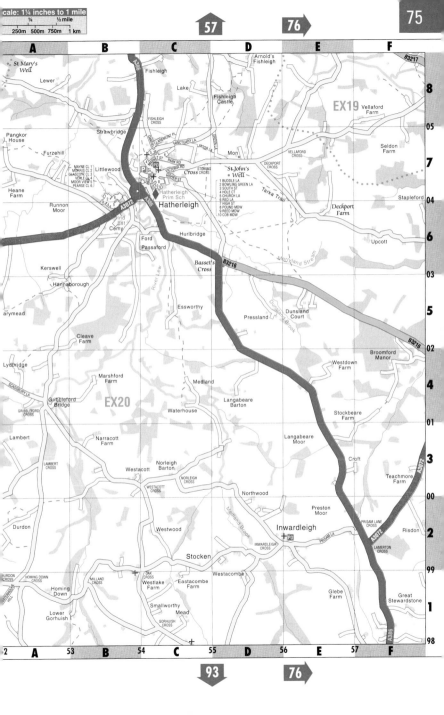

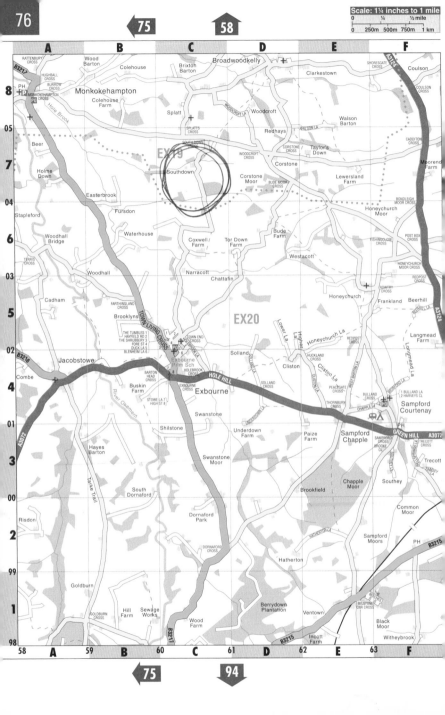

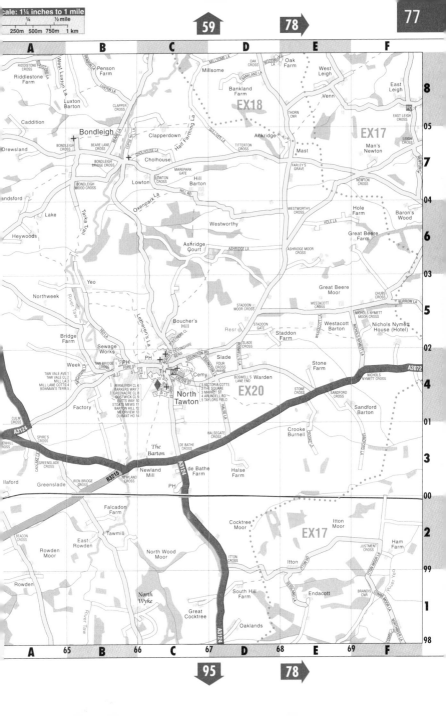

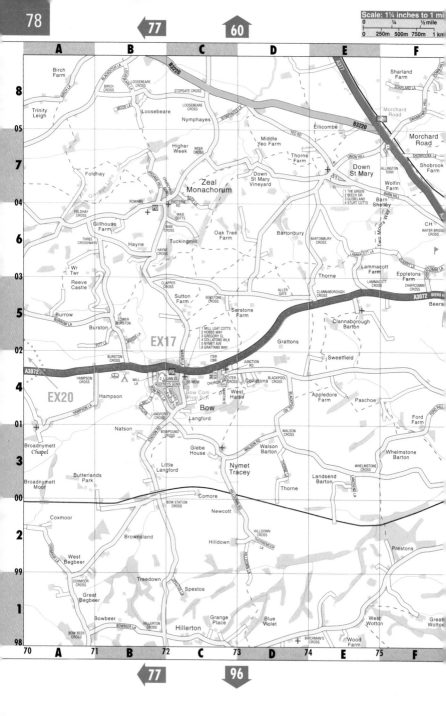

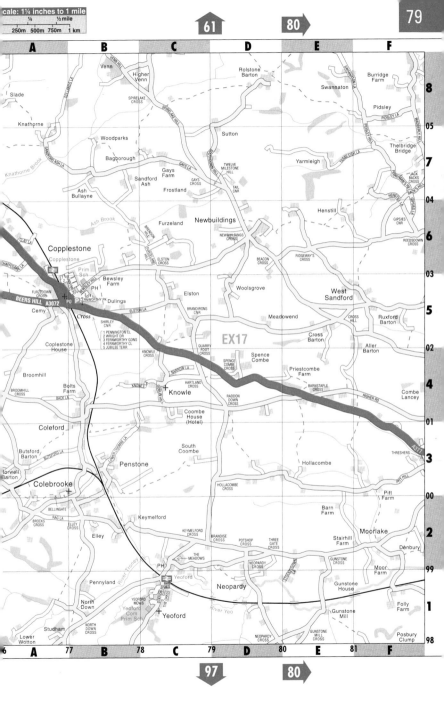

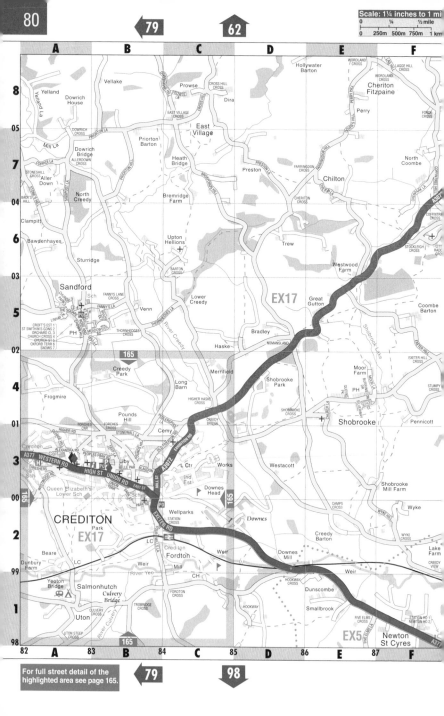

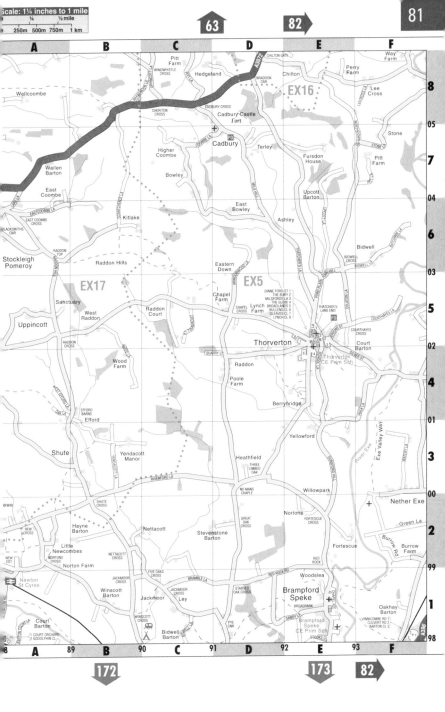

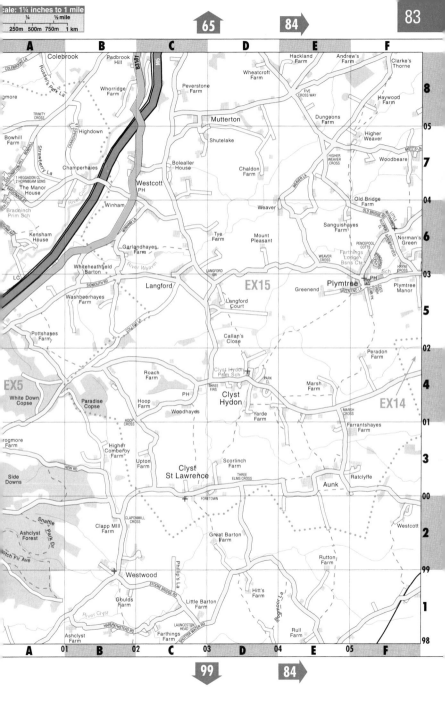

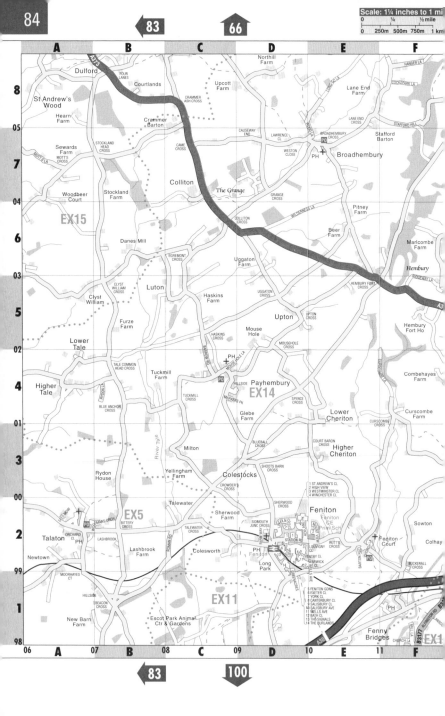

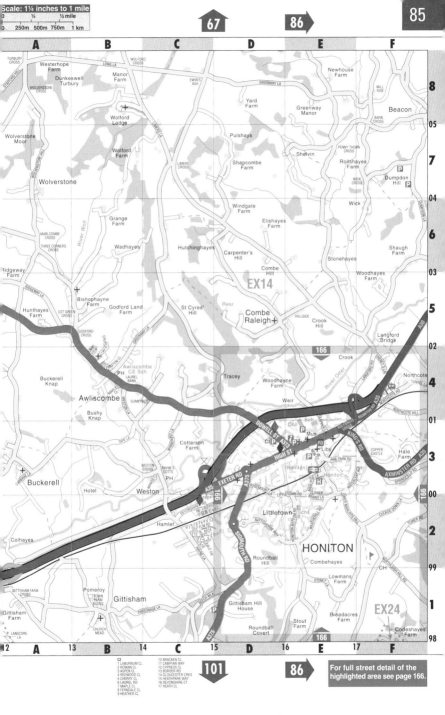

Scale: 1¼ inches to 1 mile

0   ¼   ½ mile
0   250m 500m 750m 1 km

67 86

C2
1 LABURNUM CL
2 ROWAN CL
3 ASPEN CL
4 REDWOOD CL
5 CHERRY CL
6 LAUREL RD
7 MAPLE CL
8 FERNDALE CL
9 HEATHER CL
10 BRACKEN CL
11 CAMPIAN WAY
12 CYPRESS CL
13 BORDER RD
14 GLOUCESTER CRES
15 HEATHPARK WAY
16 DEVONSHIRE CT
17 HEATH CL

101   86

For full street detail of the
highlighted area see page 166.

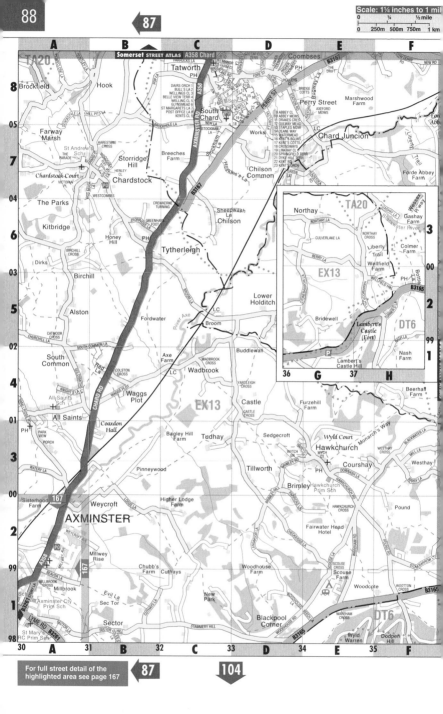

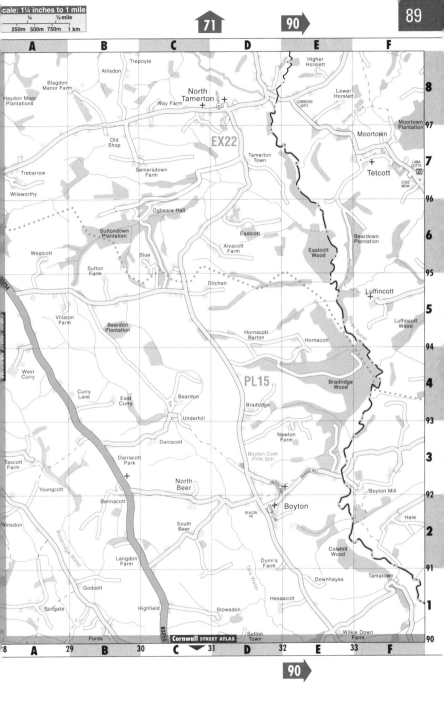

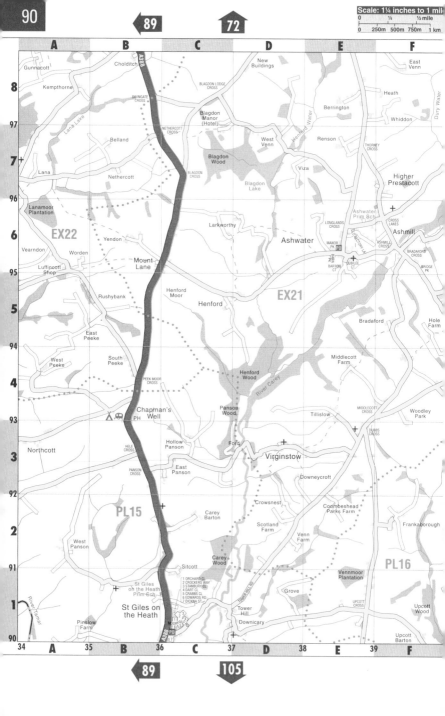

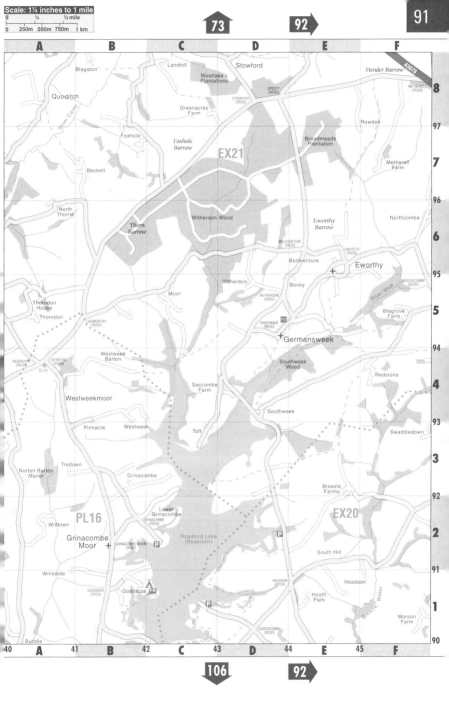

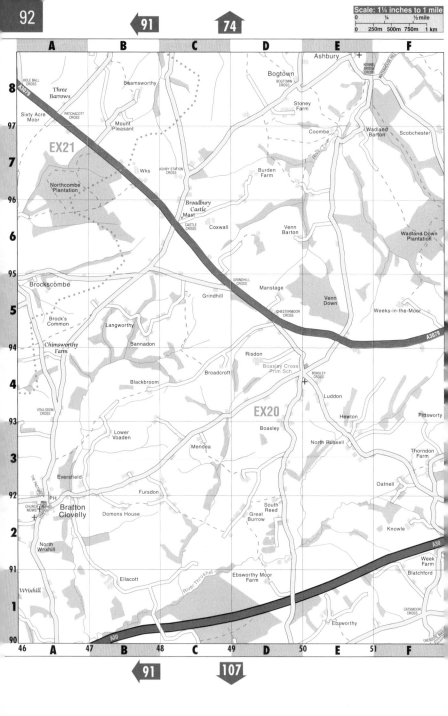

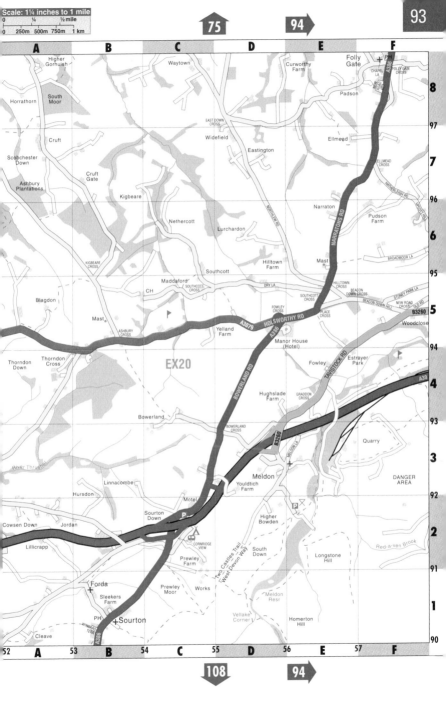

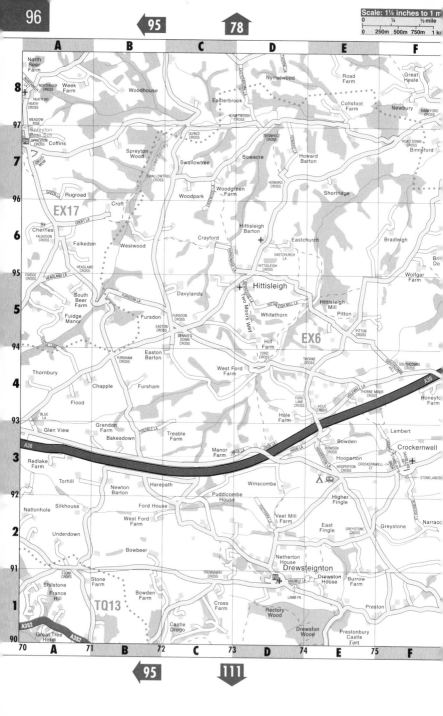

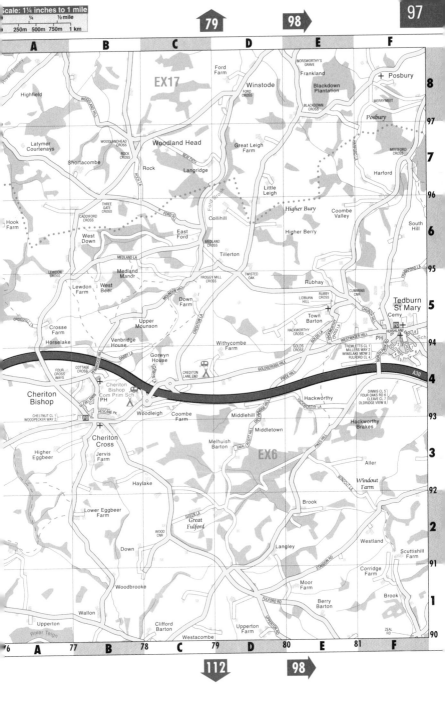

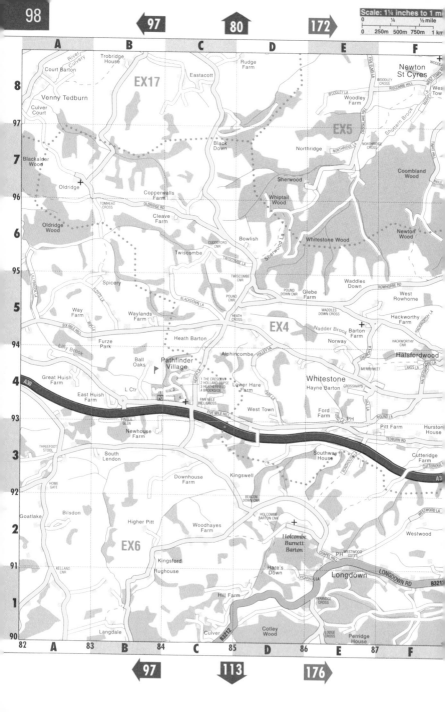

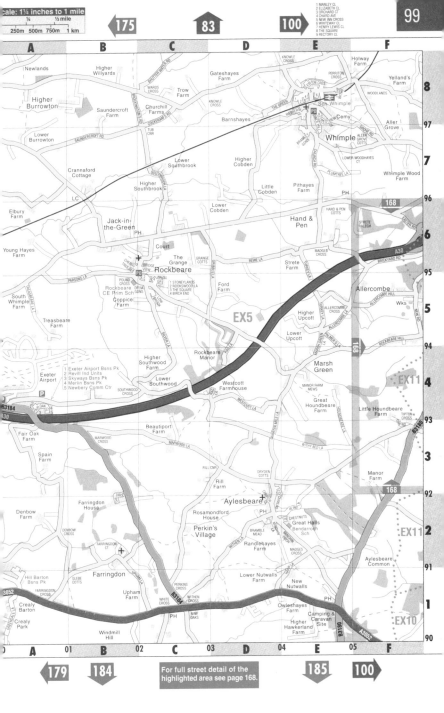

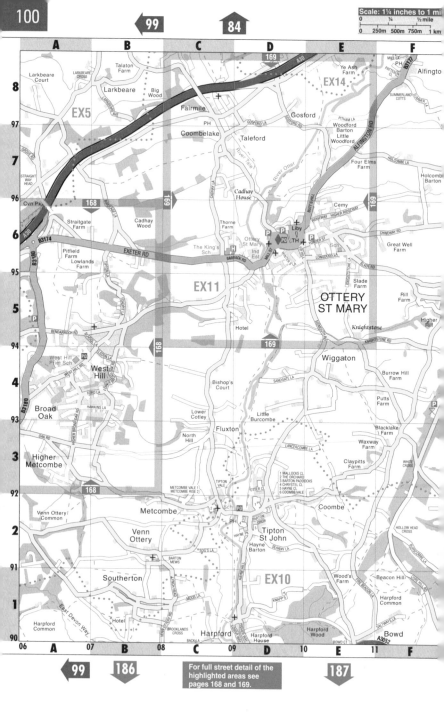

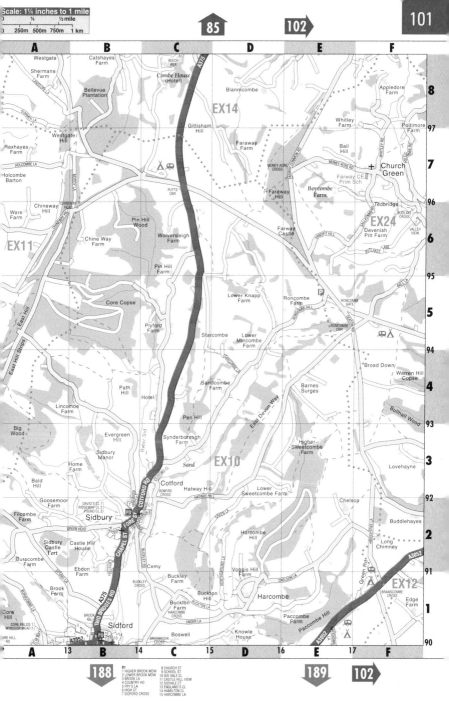

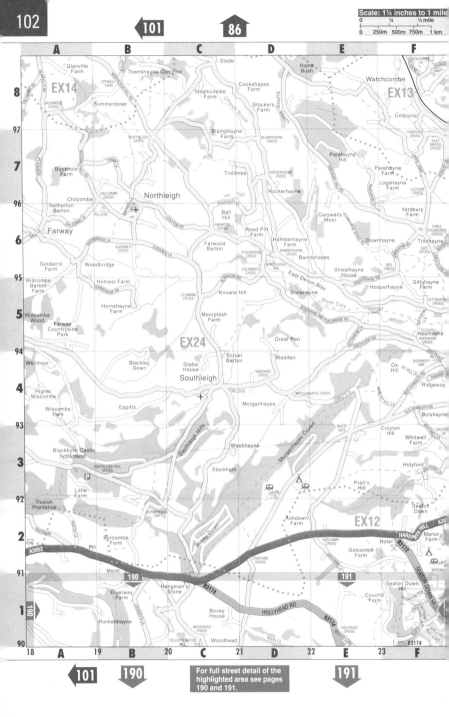

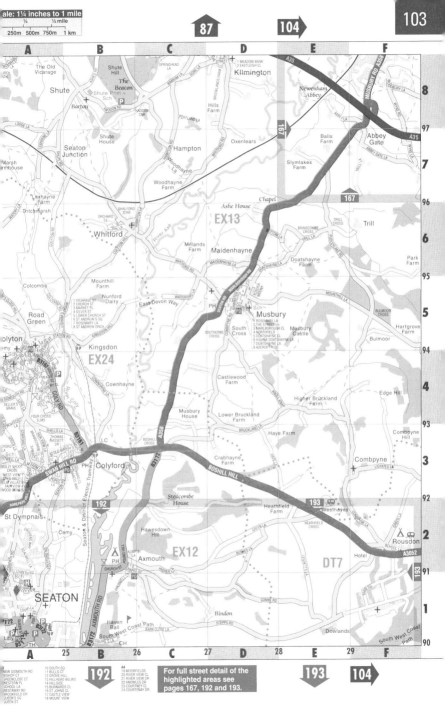

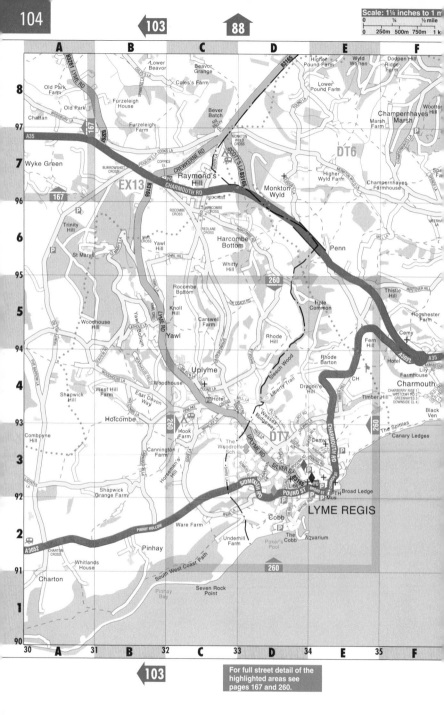

Scale: 1¼ inches to 1 m
0 | ¼ | ½ mile
0 | 250m | 500m | 750m | 1 k

For full street detail of the highlighted areas see pages 167 and 260.

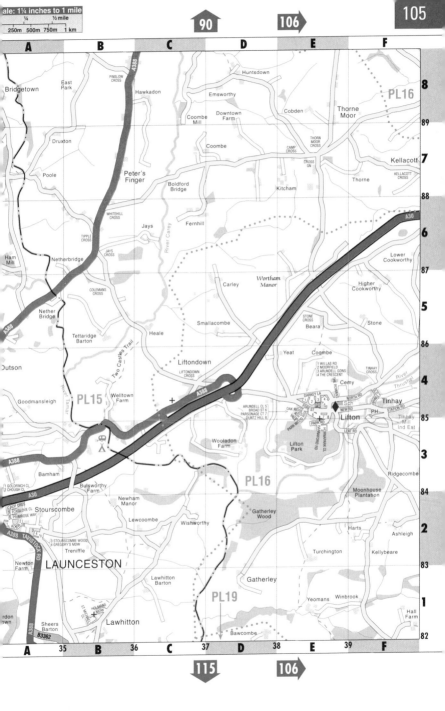

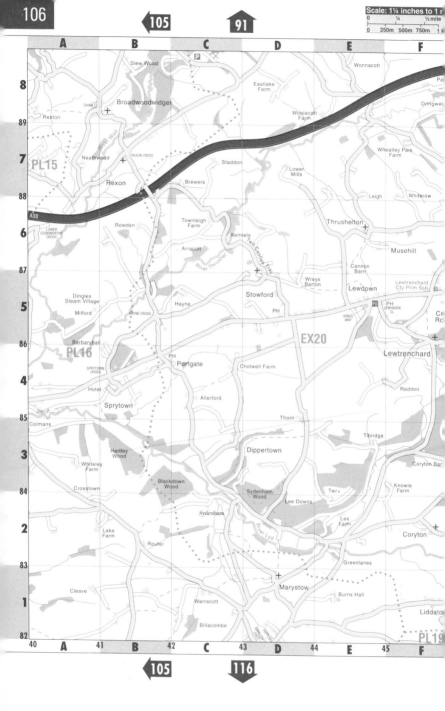

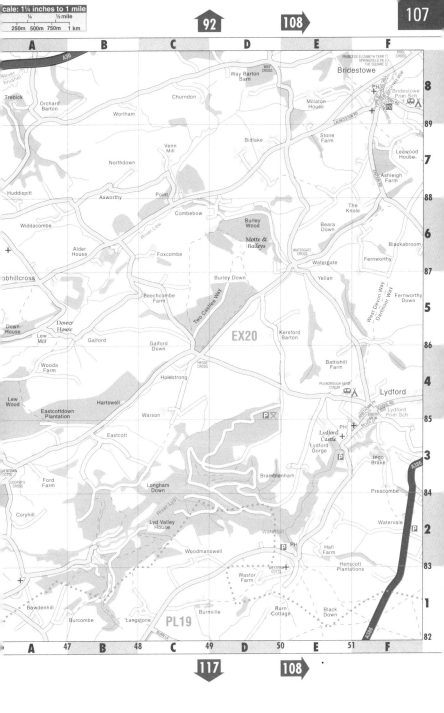

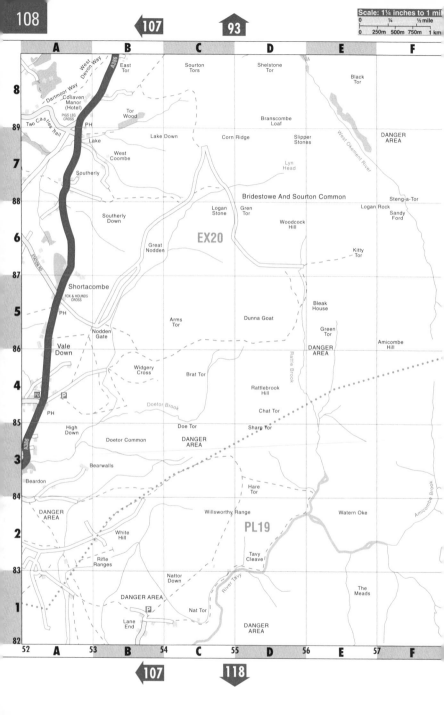

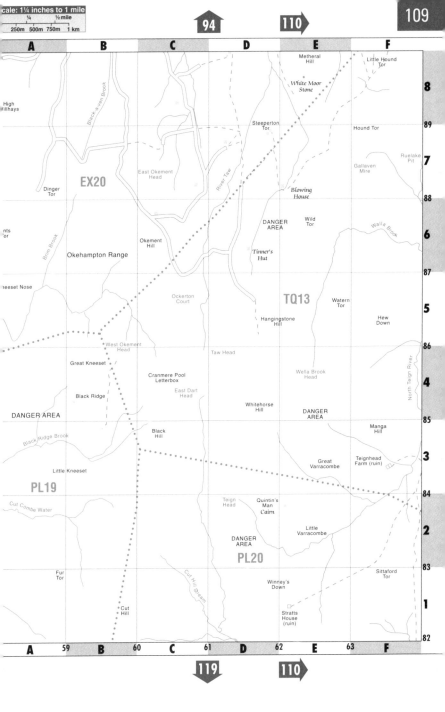

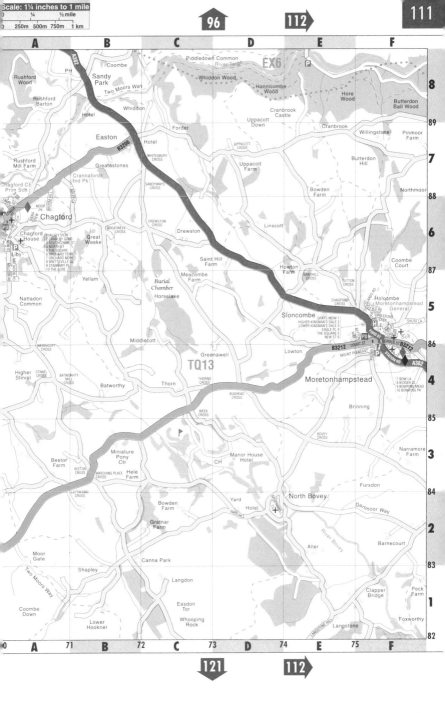

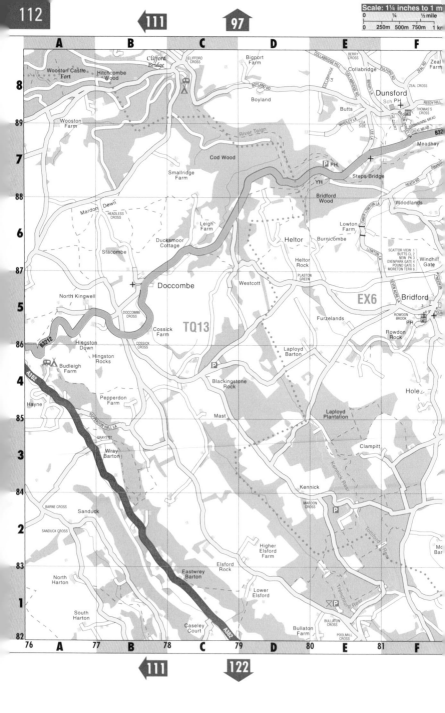

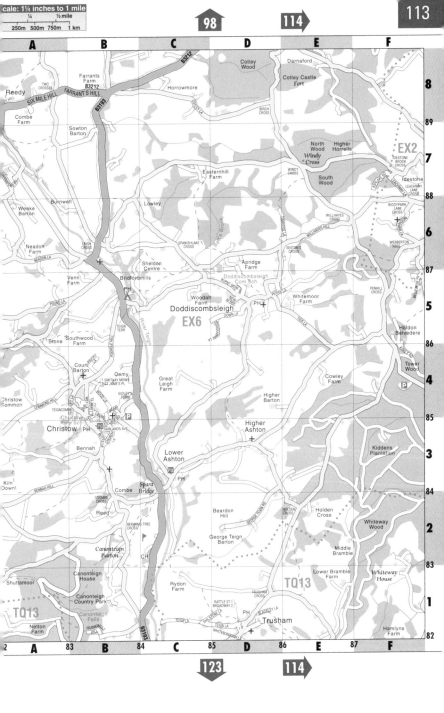

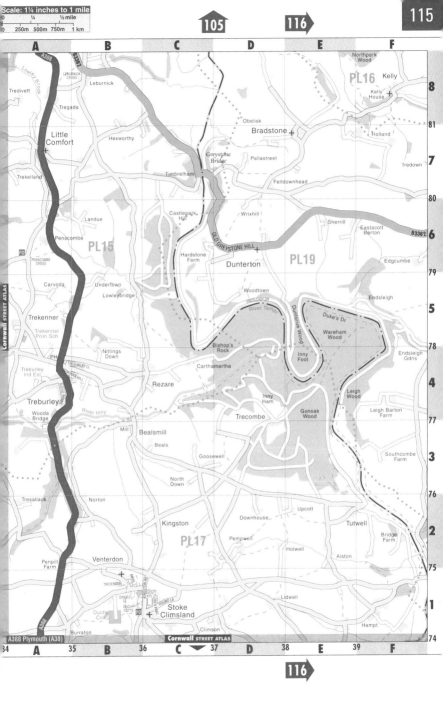

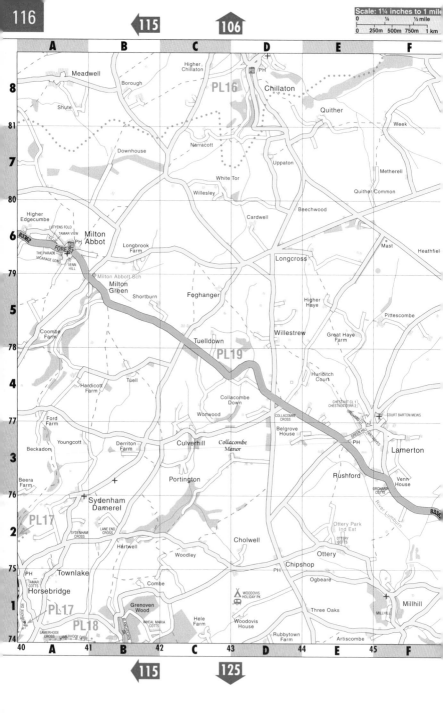

Scale: 1¼ inches to 1 mile

¼   ½ mile
250m 500m 750m 1 km

107   118

A   B   C   D   E   F

Whitstone Farm

Rowden

North Brentor

West Blackdown

Cholwell

Wheal Betsy

Kingsett Down

8

Westcott

Cemy

STATION VIEW
STATION RD

PH

Gibbet Hill

81

Monkstone

Brent Tor

Blacknpr Park

Holyeat

Darmoor Way West Devon Way

Kingsett

7

Hotel

Blackdown

Midlands

PH

80

Brinsabach Farm

STANDARD CT 1
LABURNUM VILLAS 2
CHAPEL LA 3
RODS LA 4
MOOR VIEW 5
GREAT FELLINGFIELD 6
SOUTH VIEW 7
THE OAKS 8
ROUNDSLEYS LA 9

Mary Tavy

Mary Tavy Sch

6

Heathfield

Higher Farm

River Burn

PH

79

The Four Winds

Wallabrook Farm

Burnford

PL19

Smeardon Down

5

Cherrybrook House

Grendon Farm

Heathfield Lodge

PITLAND CNR.

Pitland Farm

River Wallabrook

PH

78

Chaddlehanger

Wringworthy Farm

VILLAGE WAY

Peter Tavy

4

CH

Mana Butts

Kilworthy

River Tavy

Harford Bridge

77

Paisley Mead

3

Hurdwick Farm

Grammerby Wood

Wilminstone

Sowtontown

Langford

171

Hazeldon

PH

76

Tortown

COLLATON LA

2

TAVISTOCK

Weir

Nutley Farm

Collaton

171

75

Kingford Farm

Moorshop

B3357 PORK HILL

Downhouse Farm

Lby Ct

Mount House Sch

B3357 MOUNT TAVY RD

Taviton

Longford

1

Crease

Pennycomequick

74

46   A   47   B   48   C   49   D   50   E   51   F

126   118

For full street detail of the highlighted area see page 171.

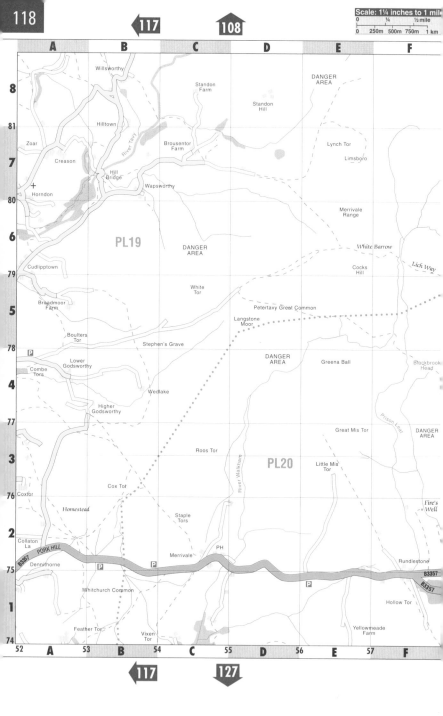

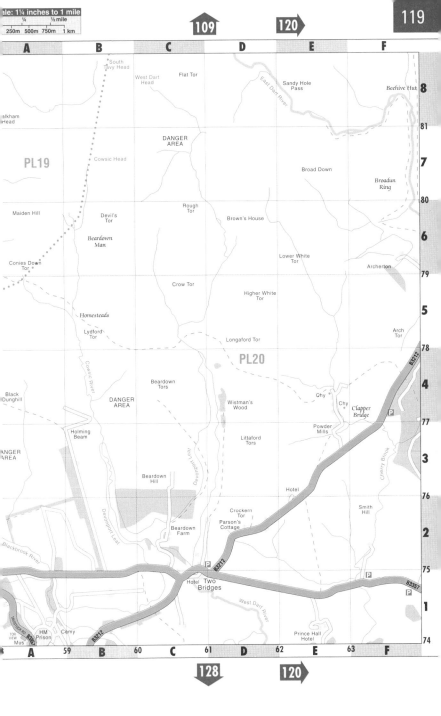

Scale: 1¼ inches to 1 mile
¼ ½ mile
250m 500m 750m 1 km

109
120

A B C D E F

South Tavy Head

West Dart Head

Flat Tor

East Dart River

Sandy Hole Pass

Beehive Hut

8

alkham Head

81

PL19

Cowsic Head

DANGER AREA

Broad Down

Broadun Ring

7

80

Maiden Hill

Devil's Tor

Rough Tor

Brown's House

Beardown Man

Lower White Tor

Archerton

6

Conies Down Tor

Crow Tor

Higher White Tor

79

Homesteads

Lydford Tor

Longaford Tor

PL20

Arch Tor

5

78

B3212

Black Dunghill

Cowsic River

DANGER AREA

Beardown Tors

Wistman's Wood

Chy

Chy

Clapper Bridge

P

4

77

Holming Beam

Powder Mills

ANGER AREA

Devonport Leat

Littaford Tors

Cherry Brook

3

Beardown Hill

Hotel

76

Smith Hill

Crockern Tor

Parson's Cottage

2

Blackbrook River

Devonport Leat

Beardown Farm

P

B3212

75

P

B3557

P

Hotel

Two Bridges

West Dart River

1

TAVISTOCK RD

B3357

TOR VIEW Mus

HM Prison

Cemy

B3212

Prince Hall Hotel

74

A 59 B 60 C 61 D 62 E 63 F

128
120

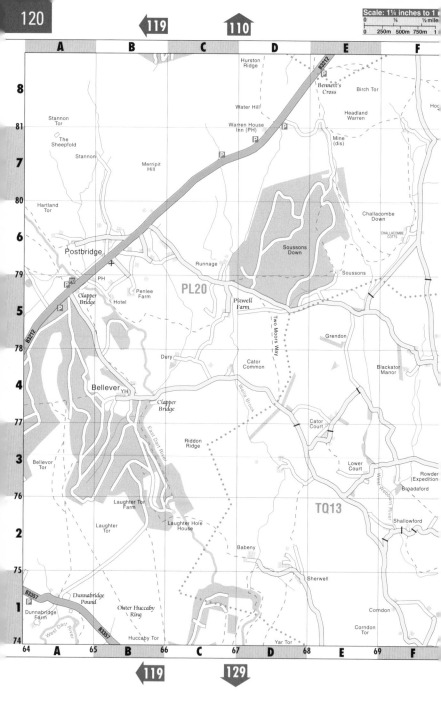

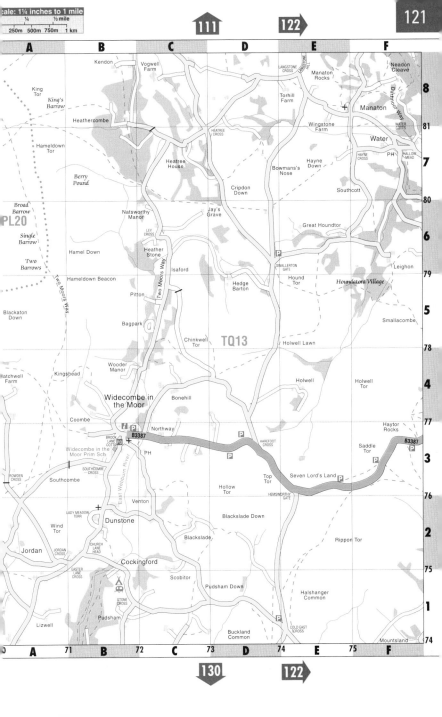

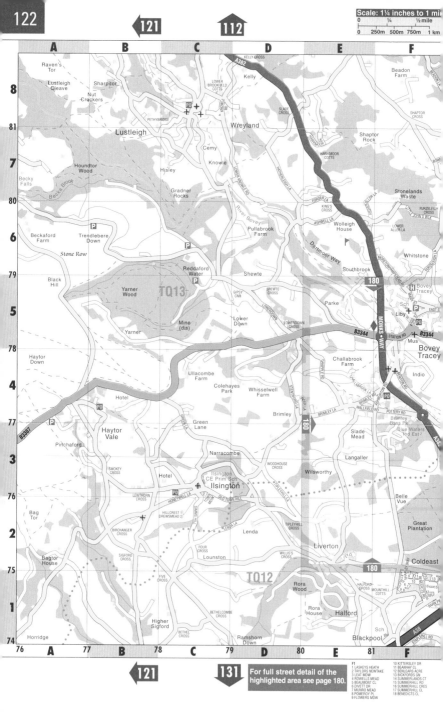

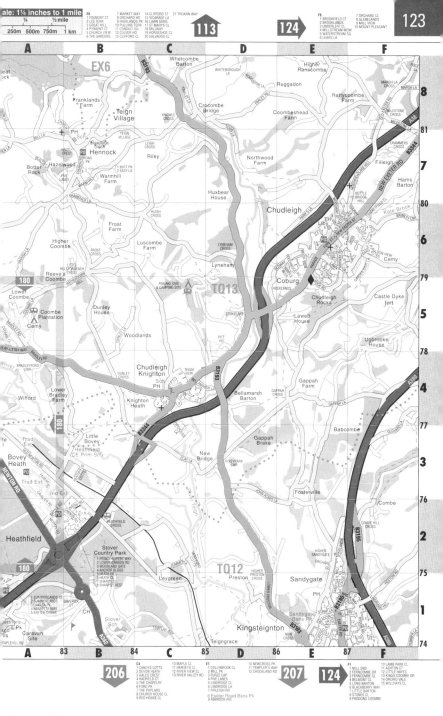

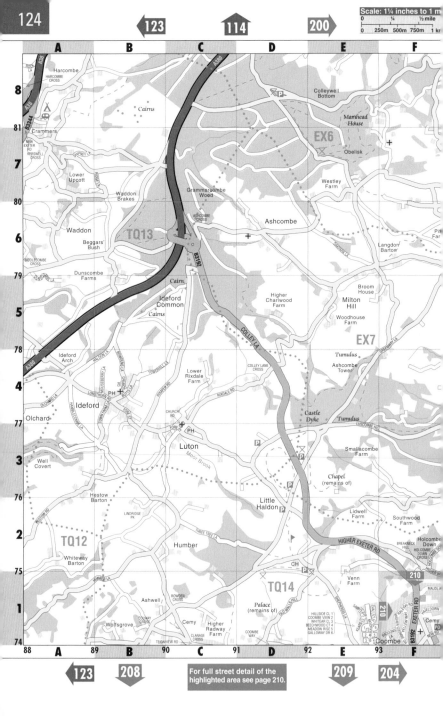

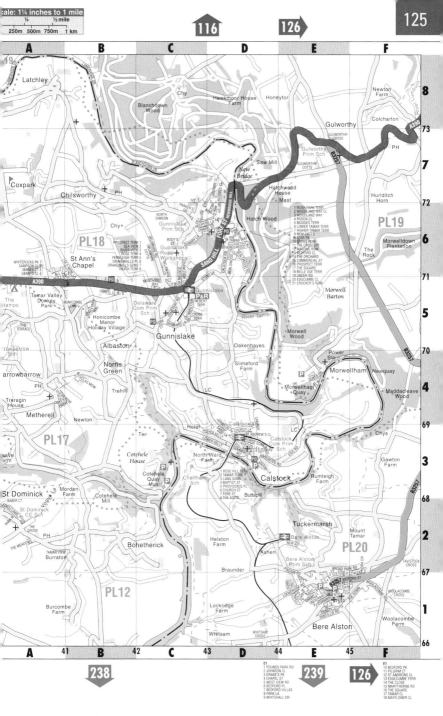

Scale: 1¼ inches to 1 mi
0   ¼   ½ mile
0   250m 500m 750m   1 km

125
117
125
240
241

A   B   C   D   E   F

8
73
7
72
6
71
5
70
4
69
3
68
2
67
1
66

46   47   48   49   50   51

TAVISTOCK

Whitchurch Down
Caseytown
Warren's Cross
Whitchurch
Howell
Middlemoor
Plaster Down
Pennaton
Fullamoor

Parswell
Crowndale
Brook
Rixhill
Works
Shillamill
Tor
Birch Wood
Walreddon
West Devon Way
Woodtown
PL19
Higher Walreddon
Grenofen
Sortridge
Branson Pk 1
Grenofen Cl 2
Birchcleave House
West Down
Bedford Bridge
Grimstone
Horrabridge

F5
1 MADERS VILLAS
2 CHAPEL LA
3 GREENWAY CL
4 KNIGHTON TERR
5 WILLHAM TERR
6 THE GREEN
7 SANDFORD TERR

Broadwell
Double Waters
Bucktor
Weir   NEW PK
PL20
Commercial RD   BEDFORD
Horrabridge Prim Sch

F4
1 RIVERSIDE CL
2 CARADON CT
3 PENCREBER RD
4 CHAPEL LA
5 CHAPEL CL
6 TOWN FARM CL
7 TONBRIDGE VID
8 TOR VIEW
10 PHOENIX CL
10 SOUTH VIEW
11 FILLACE LA

Hocklake Farm
River Tavy
Berra Tor
Alston
Uppaton
Uppaton Farm
Netherton EST
Hotel
The Old Station

F6
1 CLONWAY
3 MORATON CL
3 FEW TOR CL
4 LEATHER TOR LA
5 BRIAR WOOD
6 COX TOR CL
7 BEECH CL
8 LANGTON TERR
9 DEVON TORS

Balstone
Hatch Mill
Coppicetown
St Andrew's CE Prim Sch
Buckland Monachorum
Pound
Roborough Down

TAVISTOCK RD

Denham Bridge
Hunter's Oak
Leigh
Didham Farm

Chapel Mdw 1
Richmond Terr 2
Hillside Clo 3
Cuxton Mdws 4
Hill View 5

MODYT
OLD QUARRY RD
CROSS PARK
Crapstone House

Crapstone Terr 1
Grimstone Terr 2
Woodside 3
The Glade 4

Yelverton Dens Pk
Buckland Terr
Yelverton Paperweight Mus

Crapstone
Axtown
Stokehill
Venton
Mooreland

Buckland Abbey
Hellingtown
CH

Fishacre Wood
Newhouse
Milton Combe
Coombe Farm
Yeoland Farm
Chubb Tor

For full street detail of the highlighted area see page 171.

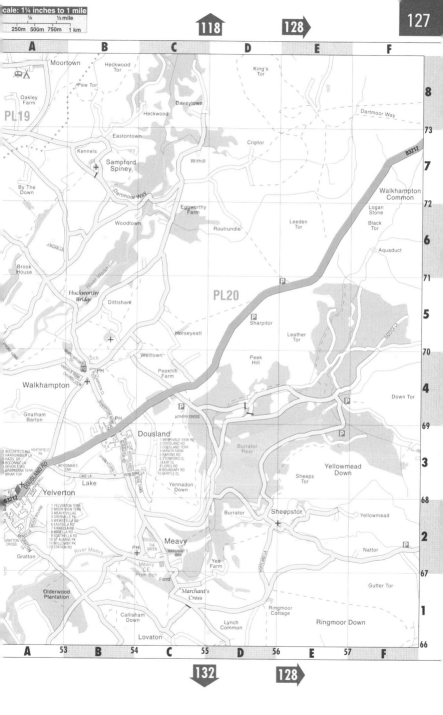

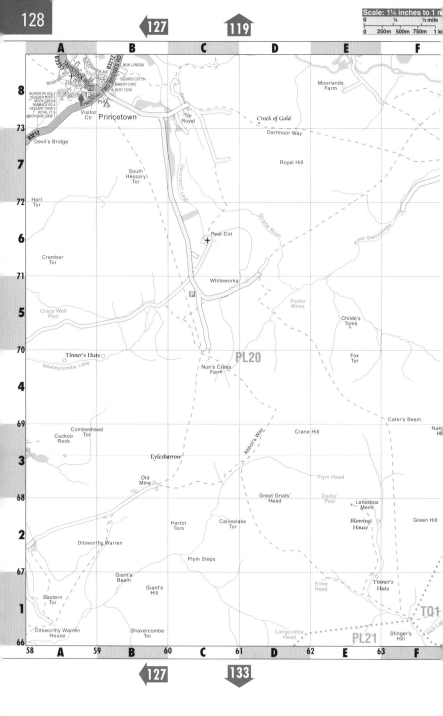

Scale: 1¼ inches to 1 m

| A | B | C | D | E | F |

8

New London

Moorlands Farm

SQUIRES COTTS
BAKERY CRES
ALBERT TERR

73   Crock of Gold

Dartmoor Way

Princetown
Visitor Ctr

Tor Royal

Devil's Bridge

7   Royal Hill

South Hessary Tor

72   Hart Tor

Devonport Leat

River Swincombe

6   Peat Cot

Strane River

Cramber Tor

71   Whiteworks

Foxtor Mires

Childe's Tomb

5   Crazy Well Pool

70   Tinner's Huts   PL20   Fox Tor

Newleycombe Lake   Nun's Cross Farm

4

69   Cater's Beam

Combeshead Tor
Cuckoo Rock   Crane Hill   Nak Hi

3   Eylesbarrow

Abbot's Way

Old Mine   Plym Haed

68   Great Gnats' Head   Ducks' Pool   Letterbox Meml

Green Hill

Hartor Tors   Calveslake Tor   Blowing House

2   Ditsworthy Warren

Plym Steps

67   Giant's Basin   Giant's Hill   Erme Head   Tinner's Huts

1   Elastern Tor   TQ1

Ditsworthy Warren House   Shavercombe Tor   Langcombe Head   PL21   Stinger's Hill

66

| 58 | A | 59 | B | 60 | C | 61 | D | 62 | E | 63 | F |

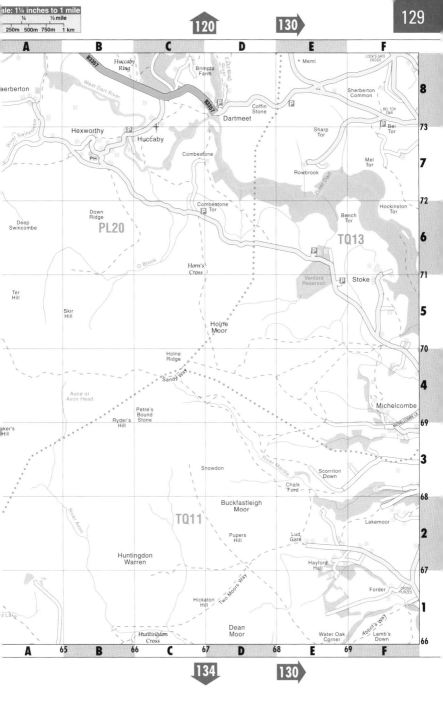

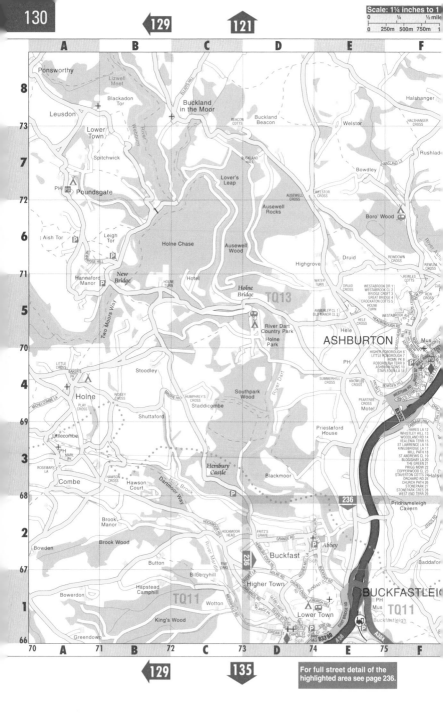

Scale: 1¼ inches to 1
0   ¼   ½ mile
0   250m   500m   750m   1

8
Ponsworthy
Lizwell Meet
Blackadon Tor
Buckland in the Moor
Beacon Cotts.
Buckland Beacon
Halshanger

73
Leusdon
Lower Town
Welstor
Halshanger Cross
Rushlad

7
Spitchwick
Lover's Leap
Buckland Hall
Bowdley

72
PH PO Poundsgate
Ausewell Rocks
Welstor Cross
Ausewell Cross
Boro' Wood

6
Aish Tor
Leigh Tor
Holne Chase
Ausewell Wood
Highgrove
Druid
Rewdown Cross
Rewlpa Cross

71
Hannaford Manor
New Bridge
Holne Turn
Hotel
Holne Bridge
TQ13
Water Turn
Druid Cross
Westabrook Dr 1
Westabrook Cl 2
Biddle Croft 3
Great Bridge 4
Crockaton Cotts 5
Holne Turn
Rewles Cotts.
New Cross

5
River Dart Country Park
Holne Park
ASHBURTON
Amberley Cl 1
Old Manor Cl 2
Hele Cross
Headborough Rd
Westabrook
Hele Turn
Mus

70
Little Cross
Baker's Pk
Stoodley
Southpark Wood
River Dart
Hele
Higher Roborough 6
Little Roborough 7
Home Pk 8
Roborough Terr 9
Ashburn Sons 10
Stapleton La 11
Summerhill Cross
Knowles Cross
PH

4
Michelcombe La
Holne
Redgey Cross
Humphrey's Cross
Staddicombe
Play Cross
Shuttaford
Priestaford House
Peartree Cross
Motel
Western Rd
Bowden Rd

69
Littlecombe
PH
Mare Pk
Rosemary La

3
Combe
Hawson Cross
Hawson Court
Holy Brook
Dartmoor Way
Hembury Castle
Blackmoor
Hares La 12
Whistley Cl 13
Woodland Rd 14
Vealenia Terr 15
St Lawrence La 16
Kingsbridge La 17
Mill Path 18
St Andrews Cl 19
Blogishay La 20
The Green 21
Prigg Mdw 22
Copperwood Cl 23
Staverton Cotts 24
Orchard Rd 25
Church Path 26
Stonepark 27
Stonepark Cres 28
West End Terr 29

68
Brook Manor
Hockmoor Head
Pridhamsleigh Cavern
236

2
Bowden
Brook Wood
Button
Fritz's Grave
Grange Rd
236
Buckfast
Abbey
Baddafor

67
Bilberryhill
Higher Town
Hapstead Camphill
TQ11
Wotton
BUCKFASTLEIGH
Sch
Church Hill
PH
Mus
TQ11

1
Bowerdon
King's Wood
Lower Town
Buckfastleigh
Greendown
Jordan St
Chapel St
Sch
B3380
A38
A384

66

For full street detail of the highlighted area see page 236.

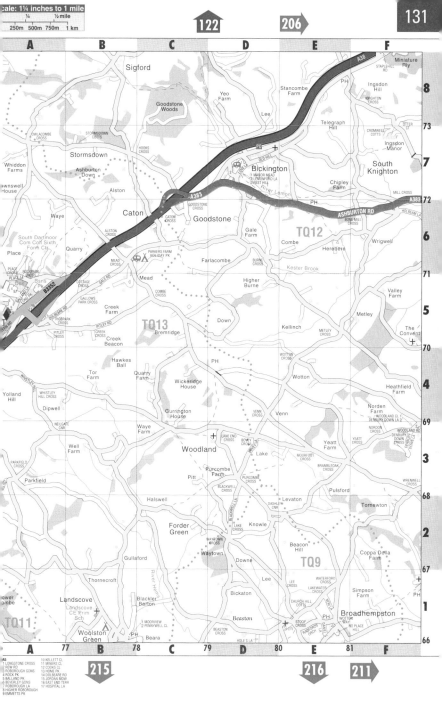

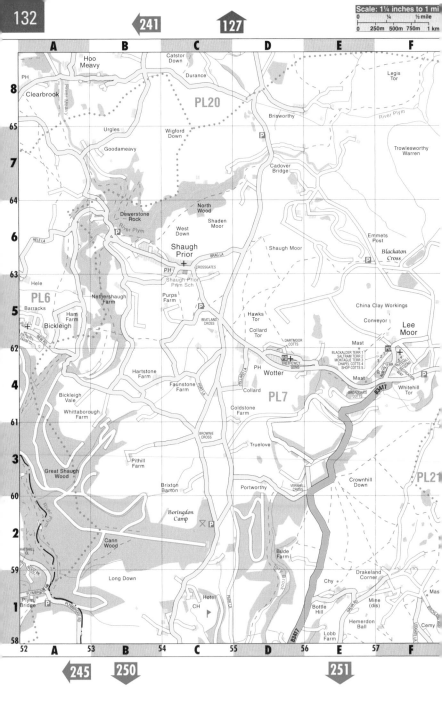

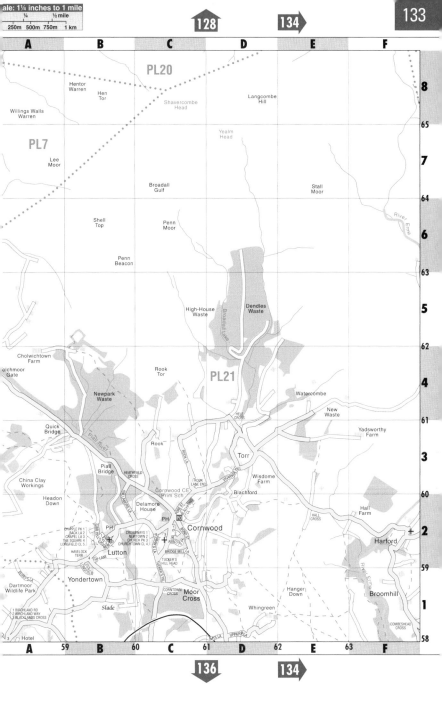

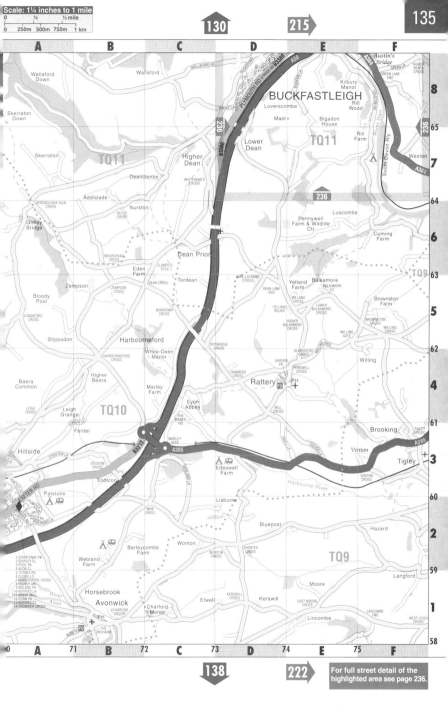

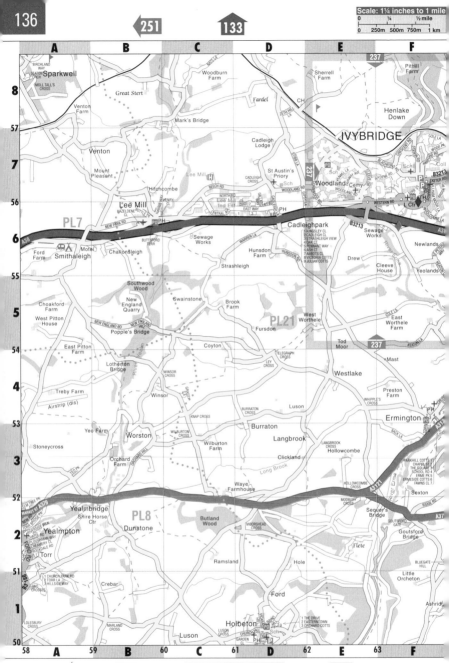

Scale: 1¼ inches to 1 mile
0   ¼   ½ mile
0 250m 500m 750m 1 km

251
133
237

A B C D E F

8
BIRCHLAND WAY
SEATON LOCH
MOLL TALL'S CROSS
Sparkwell
Woodburn Farm
Sherrell Farm
Pithill Farm
Great Start
Fardel
CH
Henlake Down

57
Venton Farm
Mark's Bridge
Cadleigh Lodge
St Austin's Priory
IVYBRIDGE

7
Venton
Mount Pleasant
Lee Mill
Cadleigh Cross
Woodland
B3213
PETER RD
COLE LA

Hitchcombe
BEECH RD
NORTHLAND
Lee Mill
Ind Est
WOODLAND
CADLEIGH
PO
Sch
L Ctr

56
Lee Mill
HAZELDENE POTTS LA
ST HENRY
EAST WAY
CENTRAL
PH

PL7
NEW PARK RD
PH
Cadleighpark
1 KINGSLEY CL
2 CADLEIGH CL
3 STRASHLEIGH VIEW
4 OAK CT
5 PENNANT WAY
6 ASH CT
7 ABBOTS CL
8 VICTORIA COTTS
9 JULIAN COTTS
B3213
Sewage Works
A38

6
A38
Ford Farm
Motel
Smithaleigh
Chaltonsleigh
BUTTSFORD TERR
Sewage Works
WARREN LA
Hunsdon Farm
HUNSDON RD
Strashleigh
Drew
Cleeve House
Newlands
Yeolands

55
Choakford Farm
West Pitton House
Southwood Wood
New England Quarry
Swainstone
Brook Farm
West Worthele
PL21
Fursdon
East Worthele Farm

5
PL21
NEW ENGLAND RD
NEW ENG RD
Popple's Bridge
COLE LA
237
AXEFORD LA

54
East Pitton Farm
Lotherton Bridge
Coyton
LEY CROSS
TELEGRAPH CROSS
Tod Moor
Mast

4
Treby Farm
Airstrip (dis)
WINSOR CROSS
Winsor
KNAP CROSS
Luson
BURRATON CROSS
WHIPPLE'S CROSS
Preston Farm
Westlake

53
Yeo Farm
Worston
WILBURTON CROSS
Wilburton Farm
Burraton
Langbrook
LANGBROOK CROSS
Hollowcombe
Ermington
BACK LA
PH
A3121

3
Stoneycross
Orchard Farm
ORCHARD HILL
Clickland
Long Brook
HOLLOWCOMBE CROSS
PARKHILL COTTS 1 7
CHAPEL ST 2
THE SQUARE 3
SCHOOL RD 4
ERME PK 5
ERMESIDE COTTS 6
FAWNS CL 7

52
ELM TREE PK
MARKET RD
A379
Yealmbridge
Shire Horse Ctr
Dunstone
PL8
Butland Wood
MOORSHEAD CROSS
Waye Farmhouse
MODBURY CROSS
Sexton
Seguer's Bridge
GOUTSFORD GATE
Goutsford Bridge
A37

2
Yealmpton
PL8
Dunstone
Hole
Flete

51
Torr
1 CHURCH PARK RD
2 TORR LA
3 HILLSIDE WAY
Crebar
Ramsland
Ford
BLUEGATE HILL
Little Orcheton

1
IDLESBURY CROSS
TWO CROSSES
MARLAND CROSS
Luson
Holbeton
LUSON CROSS
GARDEN LA
CHURCH PK
PH
1 THE DRIVE
2 EASTERNTOWN
3 ORCHARD COTTS
Ashridge

50
58 A 59 B 60 C 61 D 62 E 63 F

257
141
142

For full street detail of the highlighted area see page 237.

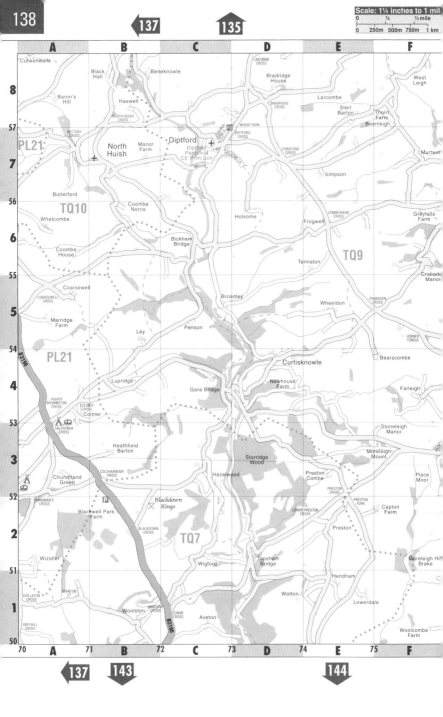

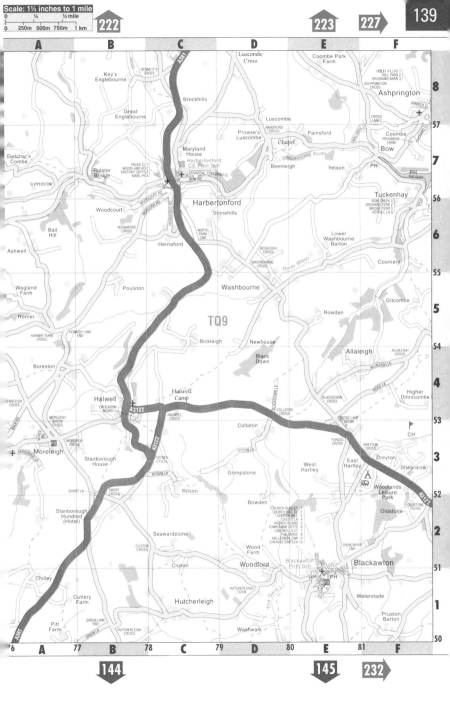

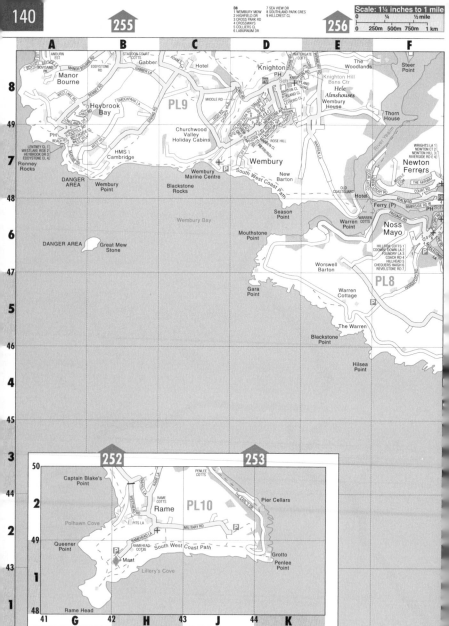

255

256

D8
1 WEMBURY MDW
2 HIGHFIELD DR
3 CROSS PARK RD
4 CROSSWAYS
5 COLLIERS CL
6 LABURNUM DR

7 SEA VIEW DR
8 SOUTHLAND PARK CRES
9 HILLCREST CL

Scale: 1¼ inches to 1 mile

0 ¼ ½ mile
0 250m 500m 750m 1 km

PL9

PL8

PL10

252

253

0   ¼   ½ mile
0   250m 500m 750m 1 km

A   B   C   D   E   F

8

GARDEN CL

WHITEMOOR CROSS

Efford House

Great Orcheton Farm

PL21

Oldaport

Clyng Mill

Shearlangstone

SEVEN STONES CROSS

Cumery

49

PL8

Wastor

Tor Rock

PIPERS CROSS

WASTOR CROSS

Langston

OLDHOUSE LA

Tuffland

7

Pamflete House

River Erme

Torr Down

BLACKPOST CROSS

DOCKS PK

FOUR CROSS

WASTOR PK

Great Torr

LANGSTON CROSS

South Langston

BENTON LA

48

Mothecombe

P

Wonwell Court

Kingston

+PH

CHURCH PK

1 CHURCH PK
2 PARK VIEW COTTS
3 HOME FARM CL
4 YELLANDS PK
5 JARNOLDS CL
6 CHAPEL ROW
7 WESTENTOWN
8 OVERLANGS

MARWELL CROSS

St Ann's Chapel

Holy Well

6

Owen's Hill

Erme Mouth

Wonwell Beach

Malthouse Point

Scobbiscombe

Okenbury

Marwell

BULLHORN CROSS

HILLTOP

PH

P

BIGBURY CT

BOWL...

47

Houghton

Bigbury

5

Pernycombe Beach

Hoist Point

TQ7

Windward Farm

P

46

Beacon Point

South West Coast Path

Westcombe Beach

Ayrmer Cove

Toby's Point

Ringmore

CROSSWAYS

BOWLING GN

4

COASTGUARD COTTS

TAPFIELD CROSS

CH

Hexdow

45

Challaborough

P

3

Warren Point

B3392

POLLY HILL

CLEVELAND OR BURGH ISLAND CSWY
AVON QUILLET

Hotel

Mount Folly

Cockleridge

44

Burgh Island

TQ7

Hotel

Bigbury-on-Sea

P

THE COTTAGES

2

Bantham

43

Butter Cove

1

42

Warren Point

61 A 62 B 63 C 64 D 65 E 66 F

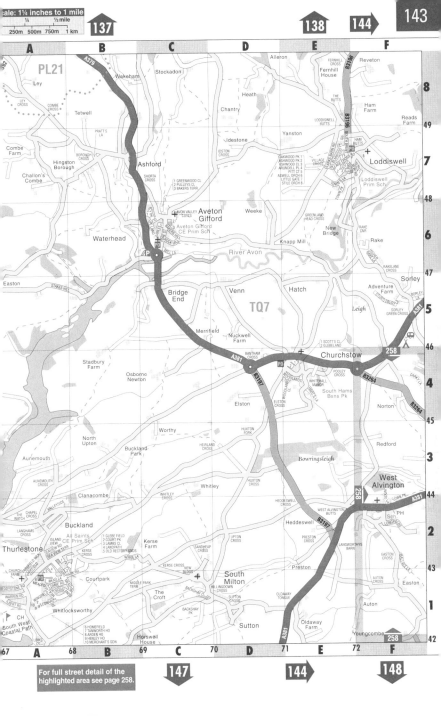

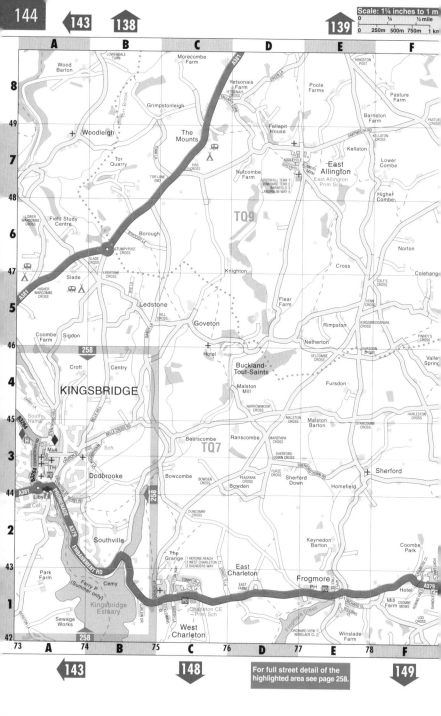

145
233
234

Scale: 1¼ inches to 1 mile
0   ¼   ½ mile
0   250m   500m   750m   1 km

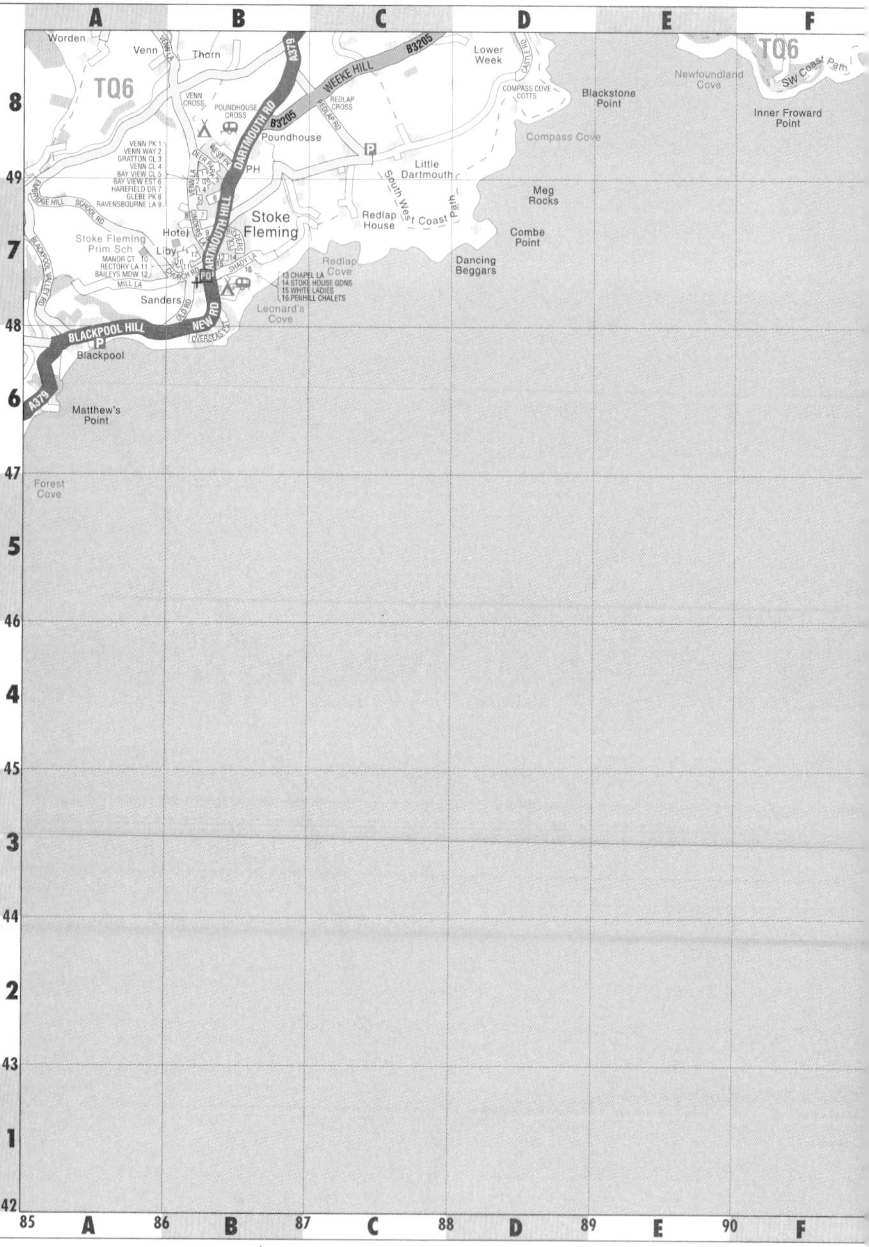

8

Worden

Venn

Thorn

TQ6

Venn
Cross

Poundhouse
Cross

Weeke Hill

Redlap
Cross

Lower
Week

Compass Cove
Cotts

Blackstone
Point

Newfoundland
Cove

TQ6

SW Coast Path

Inner Froward
Point

Poundhouse

Compass Cove

49

VENN PK 1
VENN WAY 2
GRAFTON CL 3
VENN CL 4
BAY VIEW 5
BAY VIEW EST 6
HAREFIELD DR 7
GLEBE PK 8
RAVENSBOURNE LA 9

Little
Dartmouth

Meg
Rocks

7

Stoke Fleming
Prim Sch

MANOR CT 10
RECTORY LA 11
BAILEYS MDW 12

MILL LA

Hotel

Liby

Stoke
Fleming

Redlap
House

Redlap
Cove

Dancing
Beggars

Combe
Point

13 CHAPEL LA
14 STOKE HOUSE GDNS
15 WHITE LADIES
16 PENHILL CHALETS

Sanders

Leonard's
Cove

48

Blackpool Hill

Blackpool

New Rd

Liverpool

6

A379

Matthew's
Point

47

Forest
Cove

5

46

4

45

3

44

2

43

1

42

85   **A**   86   **B**   87   **C**   88   **D**   89   **E**   90   **F**

145

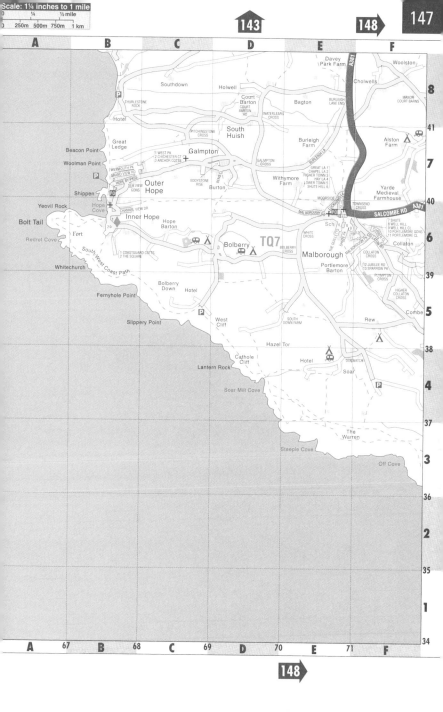

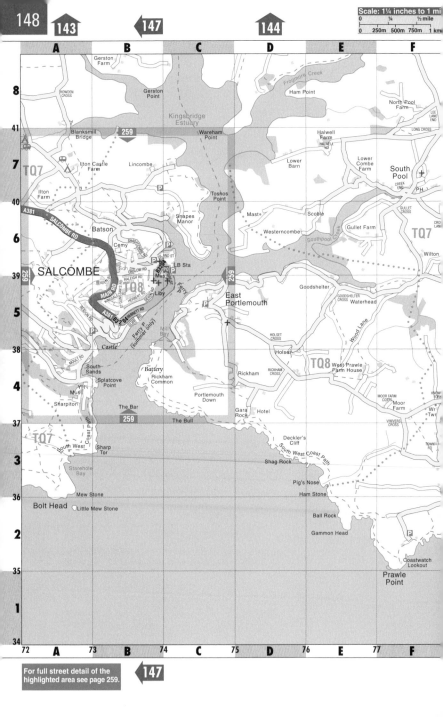

Scale: 1¼ inches to 1 mile

¼ ½ mile
250m 500m 750m 1 km

A 79 **B** 80 **C** 81 **D** 82 **E** 83 **F**

MARBER CROSS
RIDGE CROSS
DURLESTONE CROSS
Molescombe
Widdicombe House
Mast
Hotel

Kernborough
Cotmore
BEESON POOL
BEESON CROSS

Burial Gd
Moyson
Beeson

FORD CROSS
ORCHARD

COUSIN'S CROSS
Ford
Dunstone
DUNSTONE CROSS
HUCKHAM BARN CROSS
Huccombe
THE COUNCIL HOUSES
PH
Beesands

Higher Middlecombe Farm
Tinsey Head

Kellaton
Batton
KELLATON CROSS

TQ7

HILL PK
Muckwell

velstone
Greenstraight

BICKERTON TOP
FORDWORTH COTTS
CHIVELSTONE CROSS
THE MALTINGS
Bickerton
Hotel
Hallsands

South Allington
LANNACOMBE GN
HOLLOWCOMBE HEAD

Down Farm
Masts

Borough
Start Farm
Nestley Point

Woodcombe
Lannacombe Beach
Start Point

East Prawle
PH
RD
Malcombe House
Lannacombe Bay
Raven's Cove

RAVEN

gerstone Point

South West Coast Path

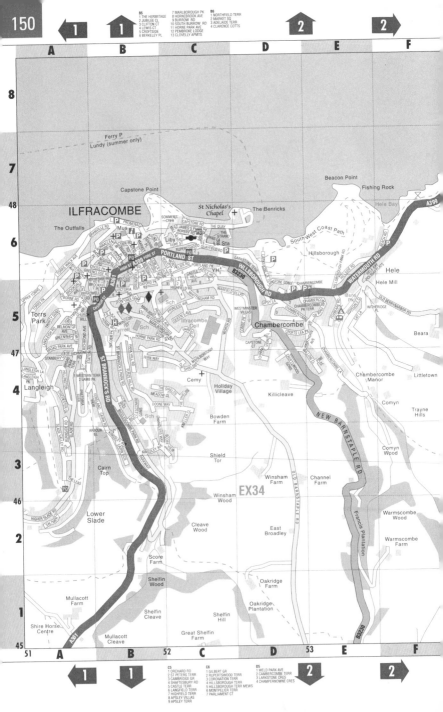

ILFRACOMBE

The Outfalls

Tors Park

Langleigh

St Nicholas's Chapel

The Benricks

Capstone Point

Beacon Point

Fishing Rock

Hele Bay

A399

Southwest Coast Path

Hillsborough

Hele

Hele Mill

Chambercombe

Beara

Chambercombe Manor

Littletown

Ilfracombe Coll

Cemy

Holiday Village

Killicleave

Comyn

Trayne Hills

Bowden Farm

Shield Tor

Comyn Wood

Cairn Top

Winsham Farm

Channel Farm

EX34

Winsham Wood

Warmscombe Wood

Lower Slade

Cleave Wood

East Broadley

Warmscombe Farm

Score Farm

Oakridge Farm

Shelfin Wood

Oakridge Plantation

Mullacott Farm

Shelfin Cleave

Shelfin Hill

Shire Horse Centre

Mullacott Cleave

Great Shelfin Farm

A361

B3230

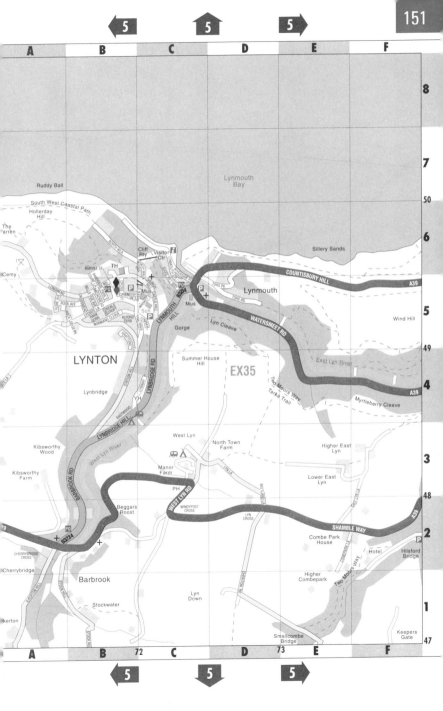

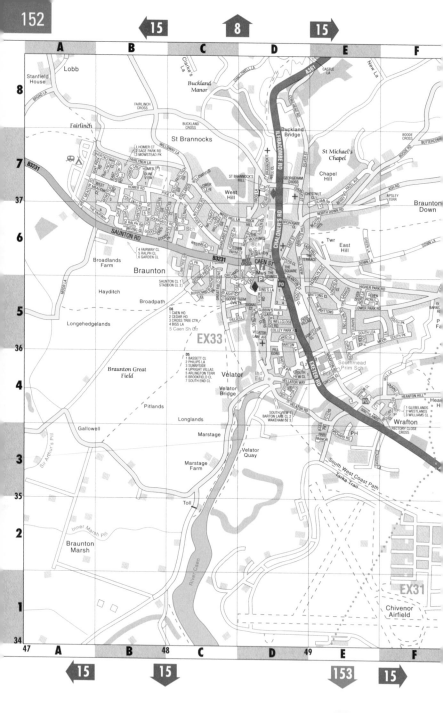

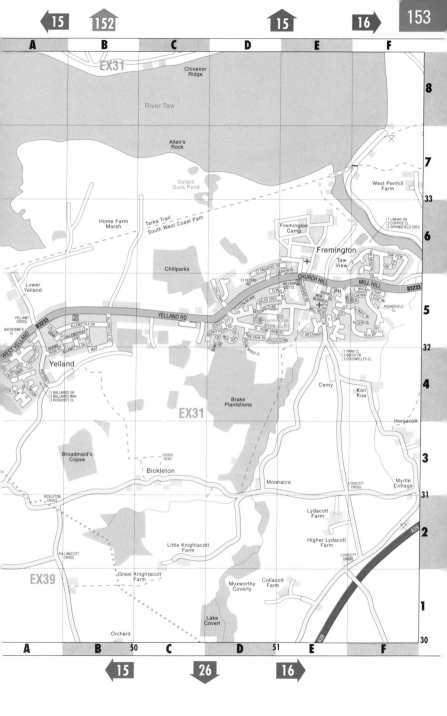

A B C D E F

8
7
33
6
5
32
4
3
31
2
1
30

EX31

Chivenor Ridge

River Taw

Allen's Rock

Saltpill Duck Pond

Home Farm Marsh

Tarka Trail
South West Coast Path

West Penhill Farm

1 LINHAY DR
2 COPPICE CL
3 SPRINGFIELD CRES

Fremington Camp

Fremington

Taw View

Chillparks

ST MICHAELS RD
MANOR CL
ST PETERS RD
CHURCH HILL
MILL HILL
B3233
HILLTOP COTTS
BROAD
STRAP
SOWAY
CLEAVE PK
SPLEA CRES
ELM CL
POUNDFIELD CL
CROSS PARK
ROSEMEADOW RD
SCHOOL LA
BYPARDS CL
REGENT CL
REDLAND
NEW BLDGS
BEECH FIELD RD
PH
Fremington
Prim Sch
1 PARK CL
2 BEECH PK
3 COLDWELLES CL

Lower Yelland

YELLAND RD

KATHERINE'S CL
YELLAND CROSS
B3233
WEST YELLAND
ALLENSTYLE DR
ALLENSTYLE GDNS
ALLENSTYLE WAY
ALLENSTYLE LN
FERN CL
ROOMS LA
BARNFIELD RD
FARM RD
CROSS
BARYTHORN
BLAKE CL
MILL LA
HOME FARM RD
PARK RD
RUSHWOOD CL
GRIGGS GDNS
WESTAWAY

PO

Yelland

1 BALLARDS GR
2 BALLARDS WAY
3 RUSHCOTT CL

1 BALLARDS CRES
BALLARDS
MOON VIEW

Cemy
Kari Koa

Horsacott

Brake Plantations

EX31

Broadmaid's Copse

CROSS HEAD

Bickleton

Moonacre

LYDACOTT CROSS

Myrtle Cottage

BICKLETON CROSS

Lydacott Farm

A39

FULLINGCOTT CROSS

Little Knightacott Farm

Higher Lydacott Farm

LOVACOTT CROSS

EX39

Great Knightacott Farm

Muxworthy Coverty

Collacott Farm

A39

Lake Covert

Orchard

A B 50 C D 51 E F

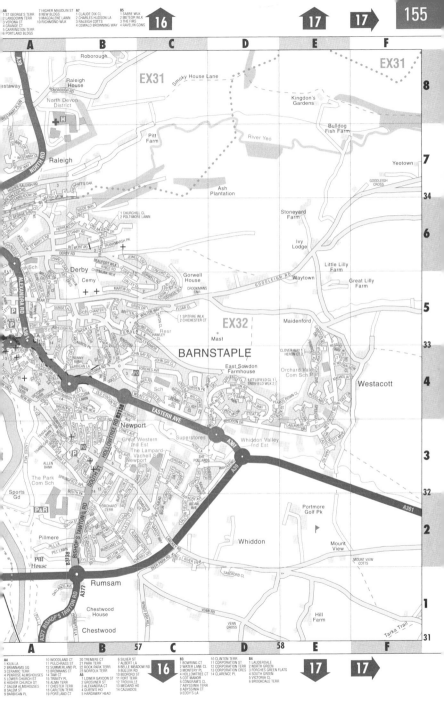

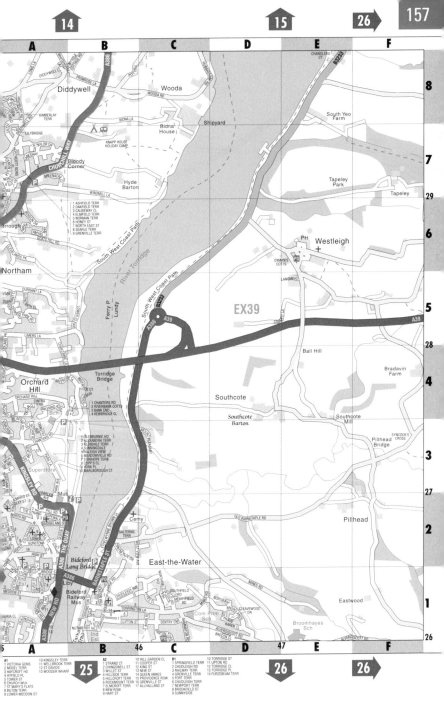

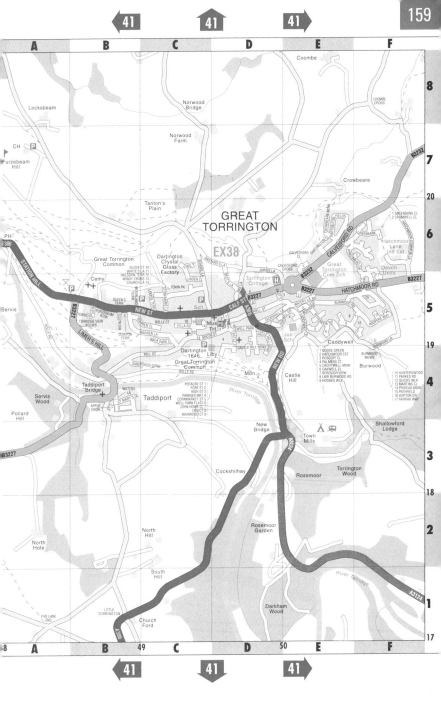

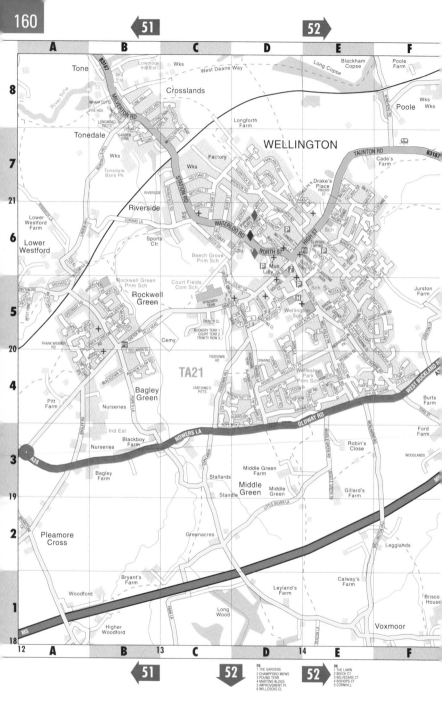

51
52

Tone
Crosslands
Tonedale
Lowmoor Ind Est
Wks
West Deane Way
Long Copse
Blackham Copse
Poole Farm

Poole
Wks
Wks

River Tone
Longforth Farm

WELLINGTON

TAUNTON RD
B3187

Cade's Farm

Tonedale Bsns Pk

Drake's Place
PRIORY CT

Lower Westford Farm

Riverside

Sports Ctr

WATERLOO RD

HIGH ST

Sch

Clifford Mews

Lower Westford

Beech Grove Prim Sch

NORTH ST

Mus
Liby

Jurston Farm

Rockwell Green Prim Sch

Court Fields Com Sch

Sch

HYACINTH TERR

MANTLE ST

Wellington Sch

Rockwell Green

TRINITY CL

ROOKERY TERR 1
COURT TERR 2
TRINITY ROW 3

FRANK WEBBER RD

GILLARDS CL

Cemy

FOXDOWN HO

SWAINS

TA21

Wellesley Park Prim Sch

Bagley Green

FARTHING'S PITTS

Nurseries

Pitt Farm

OLDWAY RD

WEST BUCKLAND RD

Burts Farm

Ind Est

Blackboy Farm

NONERS LA

ROPE WK

Ford Farm

Nurseries

Robin's Close

WOODLANDS

Bagley Farm

Stallards

Middle Green Farm

Gillard's Farm

Standle

Middle Green

Middle Green

LITTLE SILVER LA

MIDDLE GREEN RD

M5

Pleamore Cross

Greenacres

Legglands

Woodford

Bryant's Farm

Leyland's Farm

Calway's Farm

Brisco House

Long Wood

Higher Woodford

Voxmoor

D5
1 THE GARDENS
2 CHAMPFORD MEWS
3 POUND TERR
4 MARTINS BLDGS
5 IMPROVEMENT PL
6 WILLCOCKS CL

D6
1 THE LAWN
2 BEECH CT
3 BELVEDERE CT
4 BISHOPS CT
5 CORNHILL

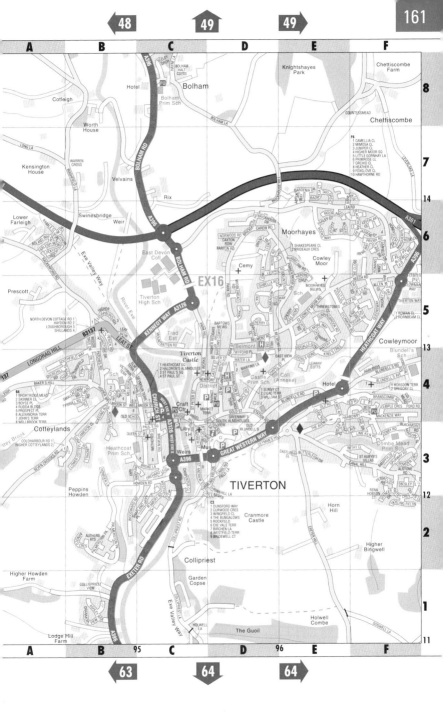

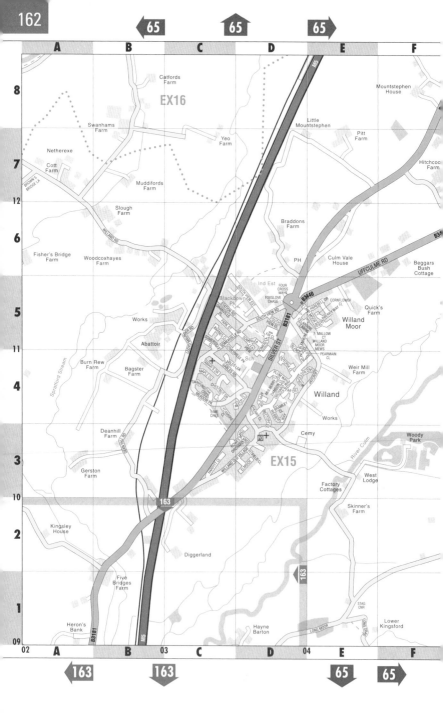

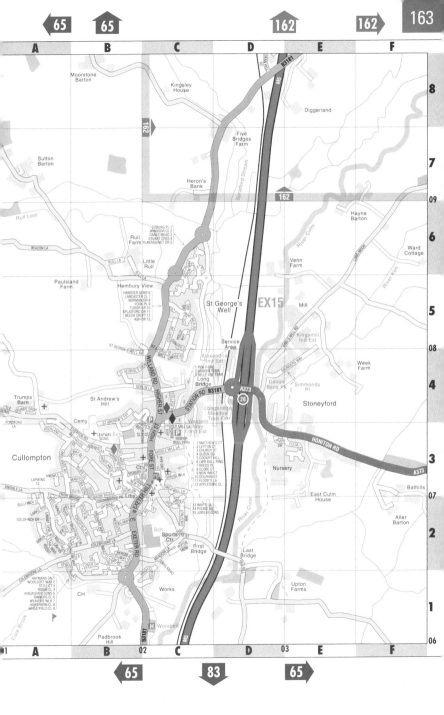

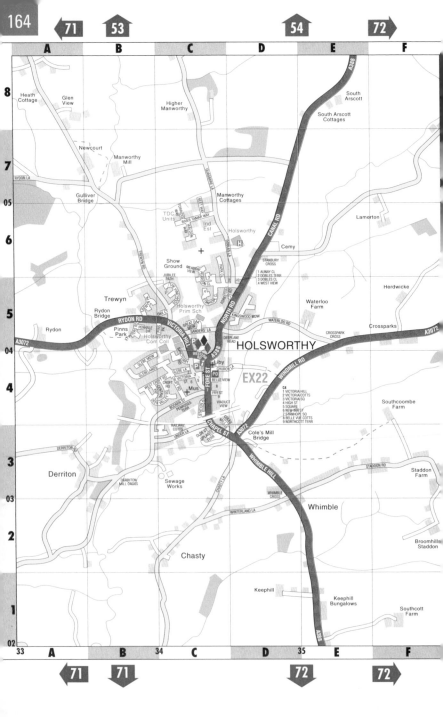

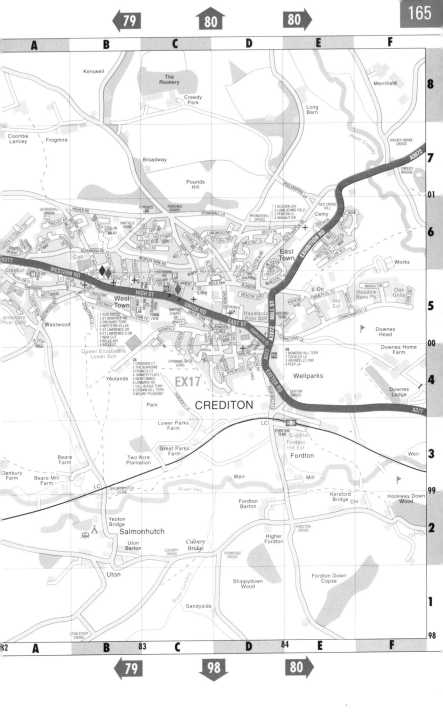

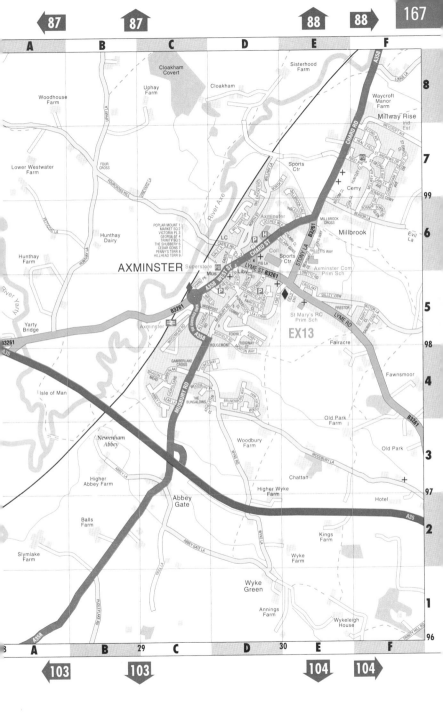

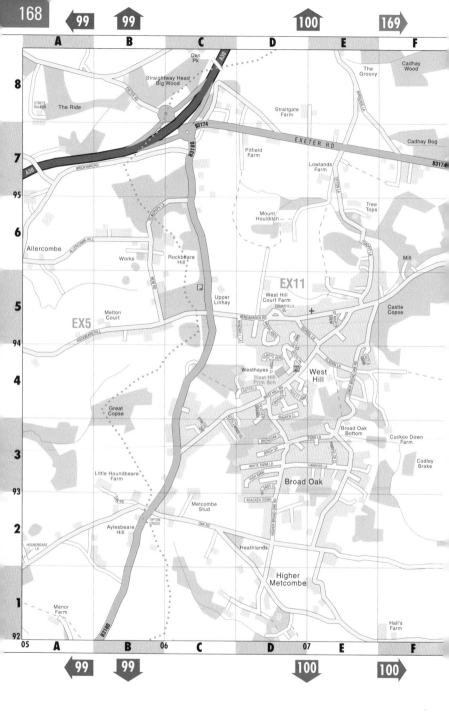

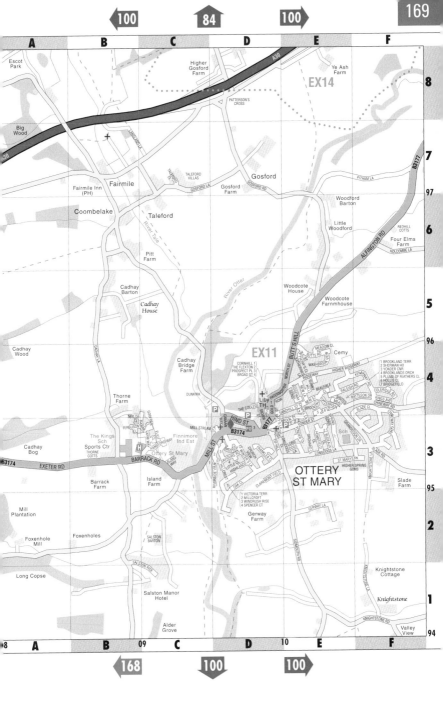

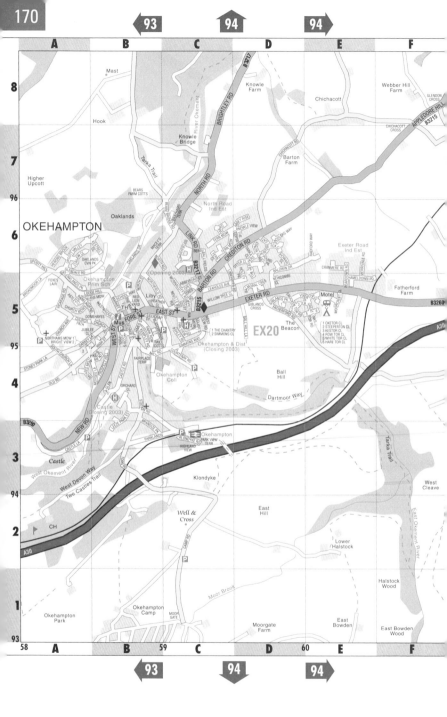

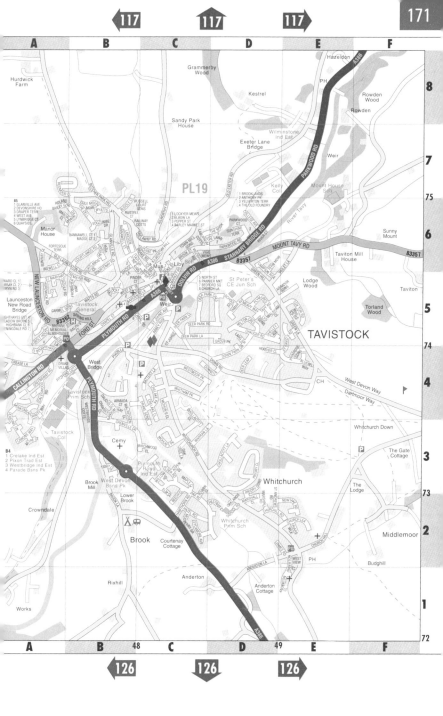

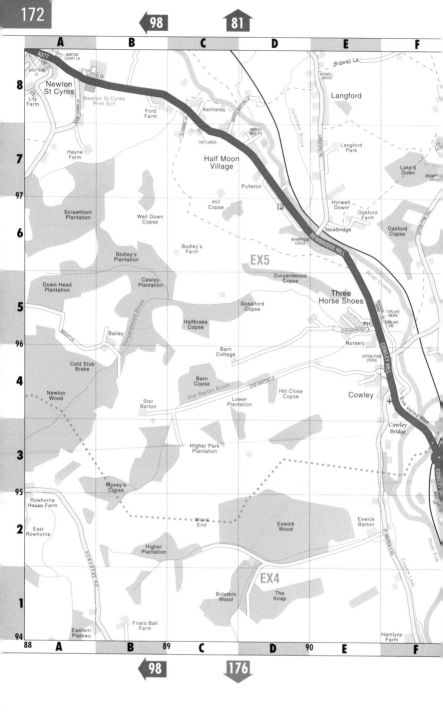

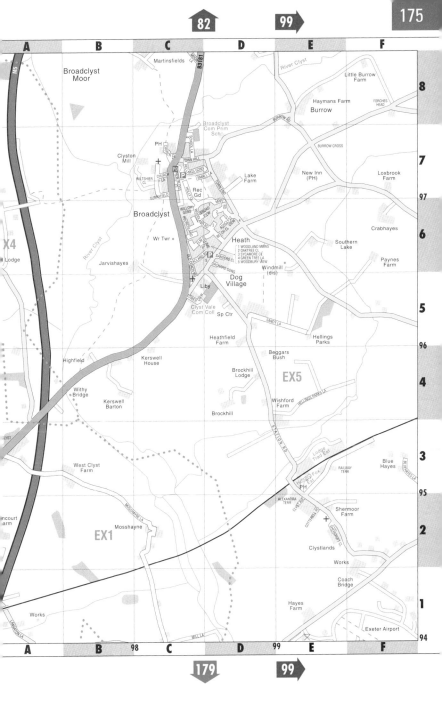

A B C D E F

8
7
97
6
96
5
4
95
3
2
94
1

Broadclyst
Moor

Martinsfields

River Clyst

Little Burrow
Farm

Haymans Farm
Burrow

FORCHES
HEAD

BURROW CROSS

Broadclyst
Com Prim
Sch

PH

Clyston
Mill

WILTSHIER
CL

SUNNYFIELD

TOWN HILL

SCHOOL LA

CHURCH
LA

Lake
Farm

New Inn
(PH)

Loxbrook
Farm

Broadclyst

Rec
Gd

WILLOW GDNS

WOODBURY

ELM
VIEW

Heath

1 WOODLAND MEWS
2 OAKTREE CL
3 SYCAMORE CE
4 GREEN TREE LA
6 WOODBURY VIEW

Crabhayes

Southern
Lake

Paynes
Farm

Wr Twr

Jarvishayes

River Clyst

SANDERS CL

ORCHARD GDNS

Windmill
(dis)

Liby

Dog
Village

Clyst Vale
Com Coll

Sp Ctr

SANDY LA

Hellings
Parks

Heathfield
Farm

Beggars
Bush

EX5

Highfield

Kerswell
House

Brockhill
Lodge

Wishford
Farm

HELLINGS PARKS LA

Withy
Bridge

Kerswell
Barton

Brockhill

Lodge
Trad Est

Blue
Hayes

Railway
Terr

West Clyst
Farm

MOSSHAYNE LA

SLATERS RD

Winged Fox
PH

ALEXANDRA
TERR

CLYST RD

Shermoor
Farm

EX1

Mosshayne

Clystlands

Works

Coach
Bridge

Works

Hayes
Farm

Exeter Airport

MILL LA

A B C D E F
98 99

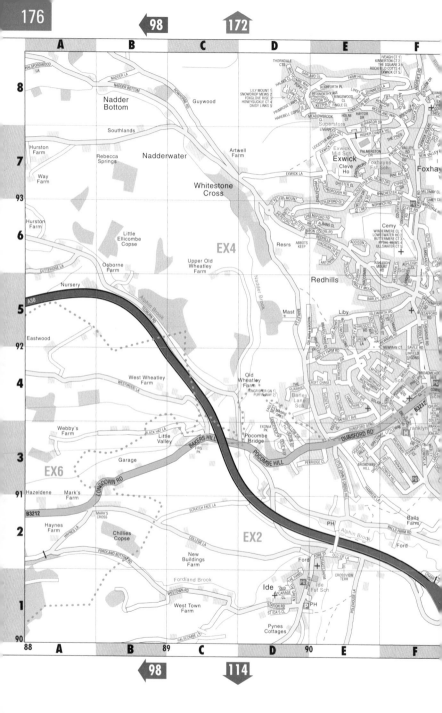

A   B   C   D   E   F

8

HALSFORDWOOD LA

NADDER LA

NADDER BOTTOM

Guywood

THORNDALE CTS

IVEAGH CT 1
KINNERTON CT 2
THE SQUARE 3
ROCKFIELD COTTS 4
EXWICK CT 5

Nadder
Bottom

Hurston
Farm

Rebecca
Springs

Southlands

Nadderwater

Artwell
Farm

GARLAND CL

FARM HILL

GUNNESS LA

LILY MOUNT 1
SNOWDROP MEWS 2
FOXGLOVE RISE 3
HONEYSUCKLE CT 4
DAISY LINKS 5

HALSE CL

BISHORTH PL
REXWORTHY AVE

KINGSWOOD

FINGLE CL

MEADOWBROOK

Superstore

LIVERPOOL HILL

HIGHER EXWICK HILL

THE PINES

7

Way
Farm

Whitestone
Cross

Exwick
Mid Sch

Exwick

Cleve
Ho

Foxhayes
Fst Sch

PALMERSTON
DR

NEW VALLEY

Foxha

93

Hurston
Farm

Little
Ellicombe
Copse

Upper Old
Wheatley
Farm

EXWICK LA

CHESTER CL

BOROUGH RD

MINCHESTER AVE

NORWICH RD

MILDMAY CL

6

CUTTERIDGE LA

Osborne
Farm

EX4

Resrs

ABBOTS
KEEP

Cemy

WINDERMERE CL 1
LOWESWATER HO 2
BUTTERMERE CT 3
RYDAL MEWS 4
ULLSWATER CT 5

Nursery

ADDISON

Redhills

ASHLEIGH
MOUNT

5

A30

TURBURY RD

ALPHIN BROOK

Mast

BARLEY LA

Liby

ISLEWORTH RD

STAFFORD

Eastwood

92

West Wheatley
Farm

WESTWOOD LA

Old
Wheatley
Farm

KINGFISHER GN 1
PUFFIN WAY 2

BARLEY FARM RD

THE
QUARRIES

Barley
Lane Sch

NEWMAN CT

SAVILE RD

4

Webby's
Farm

BLACK HAT LA

Little
Valley

BAKERS HILL

FIRS
PK

EXONIA
PK

DUCK MILL

CROFT CHASE

DUNSFORD RD

3

EX6

Garage

LONGDOWN RD

Pocombe
Bridge

POCOMBE HILL

PERRIDGE CL

LITTLE JOHNS CROSS HILL

BROADWAY
HILL

91

Hazeldene

Mark's
Farm

B3212

MARK'S
CROSS

SCRATCH FACE LA

PH

Alphin Brook

BALLS FARM LA

Balls
Farm

Ford

2

Haynes
Farm

HAMLIN LA

Chillies
Copse

COLLEGE LA

EX2

Ford

OLD IDE LA

CROSSVIEW
TERR

FORDLAND BOTTOM RD

New
Buildings
Farm

WESTOWN RD

Ford

Ide Fst Sch

PH

1

West Town
Farm

STATION RD

Ide

OLD
VICARAGE

PH

ST IDA'S CL

90

88   HALSCOMBE LA   Pynes
Cottages

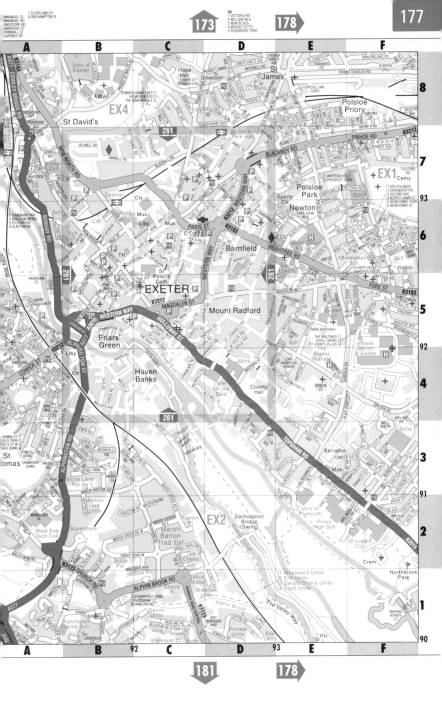

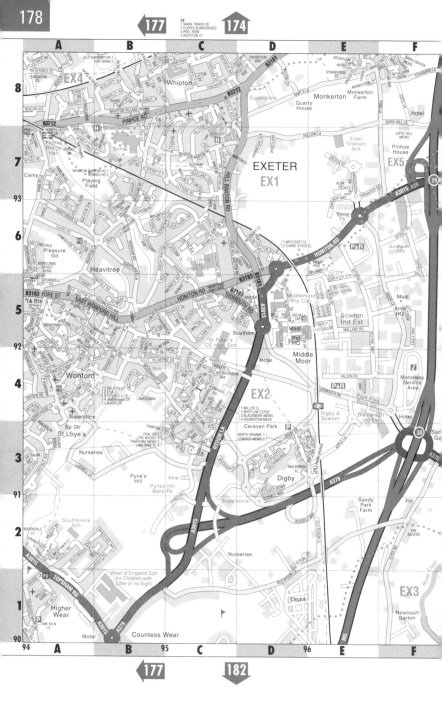

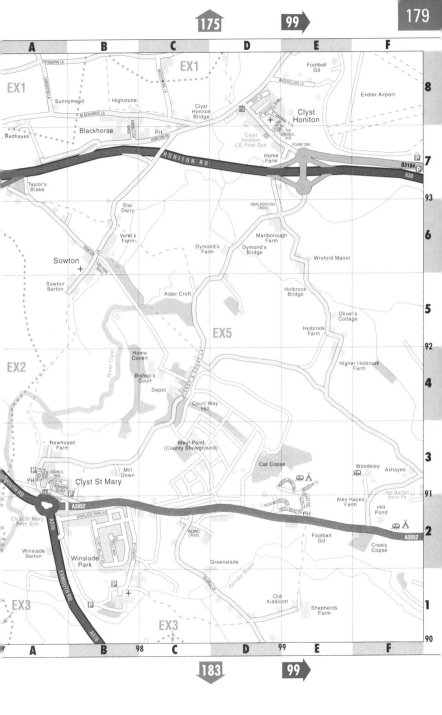

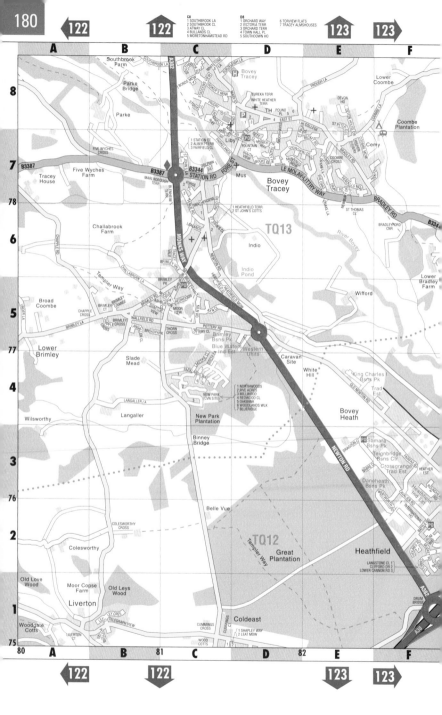

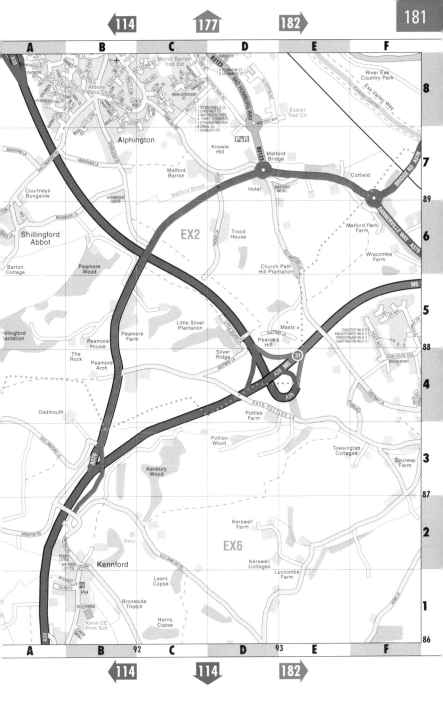

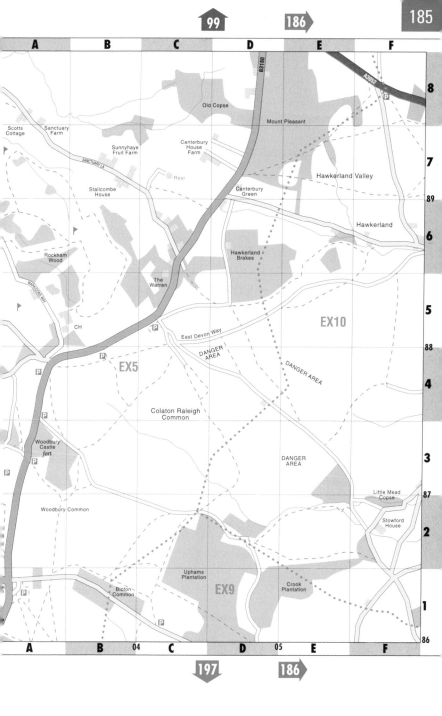

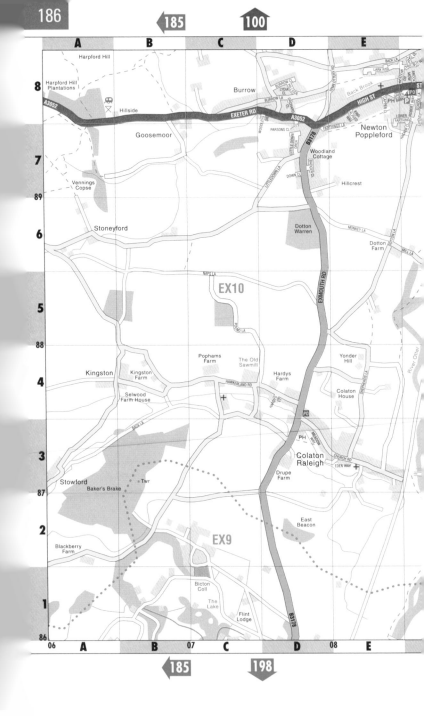

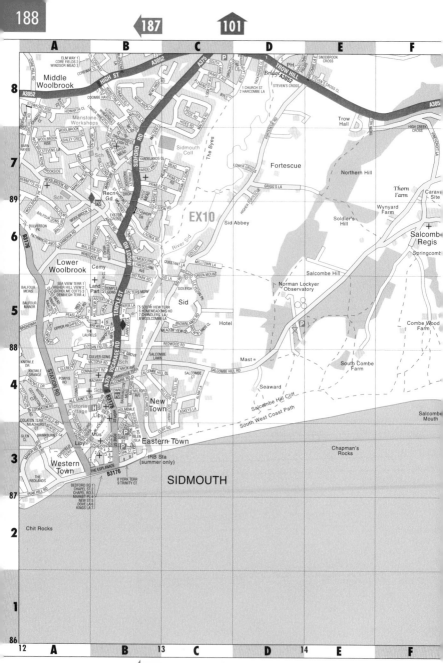

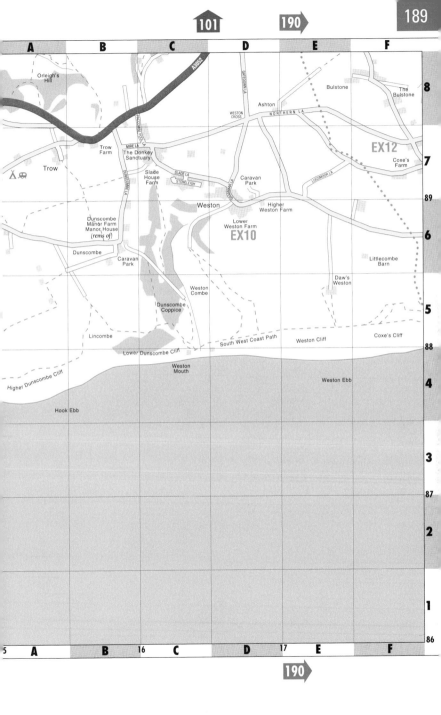

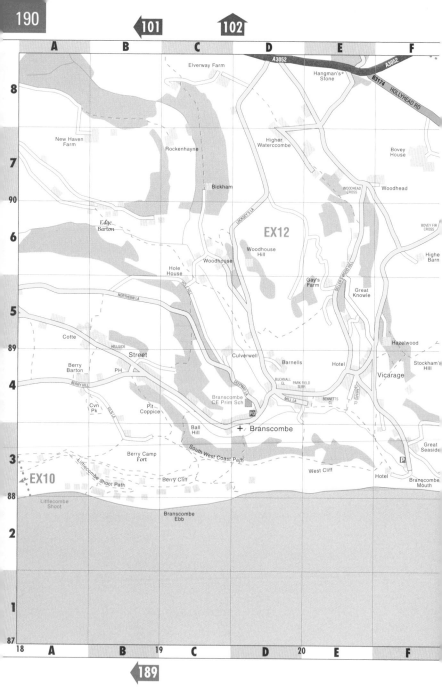

A B C D E F

EX24

HOLLYHEAD RD

Couchill Farm

GATCOMBE LA

HOLLYHEAD CROSS

BOVEY LA

PAIZEN LA

EX12

QUARRY LA

QUARRY COTTS

Beer Quarry Caves

Pecorama Pleasure Gdns

Beer Heights Light Rlwy

PEAZEN FLATS

RATTENBURY COTTS

TOWNSEND

ASH HILL CT

Beer CE Prim Sch

MARE LA

West Underleys

UNDERLEYS

PARK RD

SOUTHDOWN RD

Cemy

LANDS CL

LANGFORD RD

COMMON HILL

LITTLE LA

South Down Farm

BEER HEAD CVN PK

South Down Common

Arratt's Hill

The Hall

South West Coast Path

East Cliff

Hookend Cliff

Under Hookend

Hookend Beach

Sherborne Rocks

Beer Head

Friar's Park Farm

Mast•

B3176

ROMAIN WAY

HONEYBORNE RD

VENBOROUGH CL

CONSTANTINE CL

Upper CHURSTON RISE

CHURSTON RISE

STOWFORD HTS

CHURCHILL RD

MERRIFIELD VW

WEST ACRES

BEER RD

B3174

BUKDA

MARLPIT CL

ALLEYN CT

SANDS CT

HIGHCLYFFE CT

SEAFORTH LODGE

OLD BEER RD

BEER HILL

THE GLEN

Mast•

Seaton Hole

Beer

Beer Roads

NEW RD

B3174

BERRY LA

CAUSEWAY

FORE ST

SEA HILL

SEAVIEW TERR

LONG HILL

HIGHFIELD TERR 1
MARMORA TERR 2
GORDON TERR 3
ROSE COTTS 4
PIONEER COTTS 5
WEST VIEW 6
THE SQUARE 7
BARNARDS FARM 8
BERRY HILL 9

90

89

88

87

8 7 6 5 4 3 2 1

22 23

St Dympna's

HAREPATH HILL A3052

A3052

COMMON LA

SEATON RD

EX24

Axe
Marsh

Stedcombe
House

Stedcombe
Farm

Stedcombe
Wood

B3172

Cemy

Axmouth
Marsh

Hawkesdown
Hill

Seaton Prim Sch

Seaton &
District

RIVERDALE CL

RIVERDALE

THE SALTINGS

EX12

Seaton & District Electric Tramway

Axe
Farm

Axmouth

SOUTHCOMBE
TERR

Higher
Barn

Sewage
Works

Seaton
Marshes

Brook
Terr

PH

CHURCH ST

POUND HILL

STEPPS
CROSS

HIGHER LA

COOMBE
DITCH

HIGHER AXMOUTH
COTTS

GLENWIS

Haven
Farm

COLDHARBOUR LA

SEATON

AXMOUTH RD

Nature
Reserve

Parsonage
Barn

EX12

Haven
Ball

BARN CLOSE LA

South West
Coast Path

STEPS LA

TORY CLOSE LA

B3172
SEATON DOWN RD

THE UNDERFLEET

MANOR RD

THE CLOSE

B3172

P

P

LYME BAY
HOLIDAY VILLAGE

Riverside
Workshops

HARBOUR RD

SQUIRE'S LA

B3172

Old Coastguard
Sta

CH

South West
Coast Path

BEER RD

B3174

B3172

Seaton
Beach

B3172 HARBOUR RD

ESPLANADE

THE SHORELINE

Axmouth
Bridge

Haven Higher
Barn

Haven
Cliff

South West
Coast Path

Seaton Bay

Sparrowbush
Ledge

A4
1 SUNSET HO
2 WEST CLIFF TERR

A5
1 MANOR CL
2 MAJOR TERR
3 THE AVENUE
4 WOODBINE PL
5 BELMONT HO
6 TANYARDS CT
7 THE SQUARE

B4
1 THE BURROW
2 FOSSE WAY CT
3 HOMEBAYE HO
4 HARBOUR CT
5 LYME MEWS
6 BAY CT

103
104

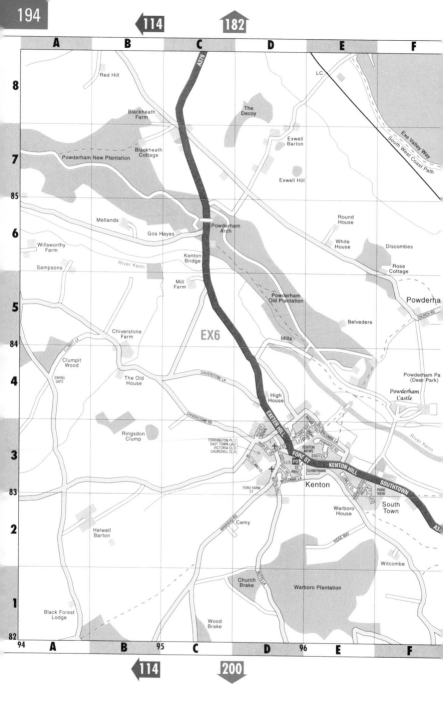

Greenland

Lympstone
Commando

Training
Centre

Lower
Nutwell

PORTER'S LA

PH

STONY LA

Lower
Withhayes

Home
Farm

Gulliford
Farm

EXMOUTH RD

Nutwell
Court

Nutwell Park

Gulliford

EX8

Powderham Sand

HAREFIELD RD

MEETING LA

Thorn
Farm

Belvedere

CHURCHILL
CT

River Exe

Lympstone

Powderham
Pool

CHURCH RD

Powderham
House

Darling's
Rock

Lympstone

PH

OLGA TERR 1
BAKERS COTTS 2
WEST VIEW TERR 3
MEADOW VIEW 4

Sch

CHURCH RD

HAREFIELD COTTS 1
BRIDGE COTTS 2
CHAPEL RD 3
QUAY LA 4

P

LONGMEADOW RD

The Ridge

UNDERHILL

Sowden
Edge

CLAY LA

Sowden

EX6

SOWDEN LA

Sowden
Farm

Exe Valley Way

East Devon Way

Courtlands

West
Lodge

COURT LANDS LA

Painter's
Wood

THE STRAND A379

stile Farm

Staplake
Mount

Lower
Halsdown
Farm

STAPLAKE RISE

COURTENAY CL

arcross

Cockle Sand

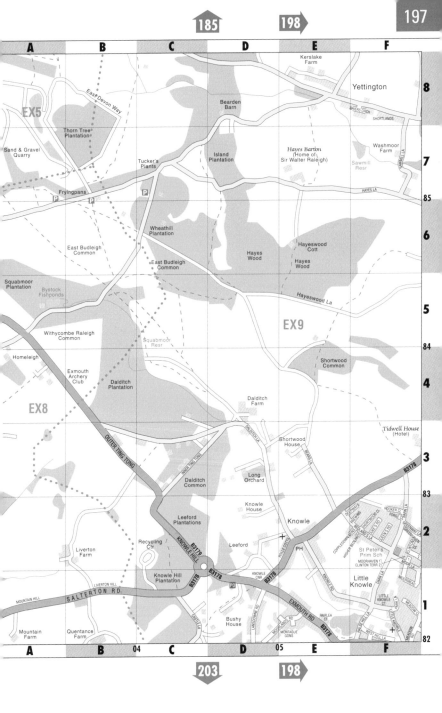

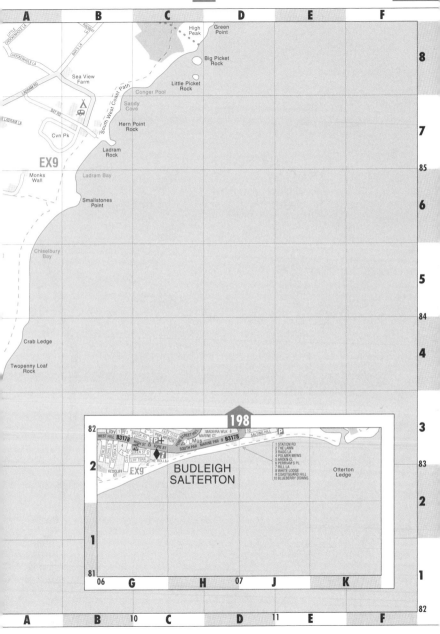

A B C D E F

8

Green Point

High Peak

Big Picket Rock

Little Picket Rock

Sea View Farm

Conger Pool

South West Coast Path

Sandy Cove

Hern Point Rock

85

EX9

Ladram Rock

Monks Wall

Ladram Bay

Smallstones Point

6

Chiselbury Bay

5

84

Crab Ledge

4

Twopenny Loaf Rock

198

3

Liby
WEST HILL B3178
EAST TERR
MADEIRA WLK
SALTING HILL
P

High St
FORE ST
Mus
MARINE PAR B3178
SOUTH PAR

QUEEN ST
THE ROLLE

REDCLIFF CT
EX9

BUDLEIGH
SALTERTON

Otterton Ledge

1 STATION RD
2 THE LAWN
3 RAGG LA
4 POLMER MEWS
5 ARDEN CL
6 PERRIAM'S PL
7 RILL LA
8 WHITE LODGE
9 COASTGUARD HILL
10 BLUEBERRY DOWNS

83

2

2

1

81

06 G H 07 J K 82

A B 10 C D 11 E F

82

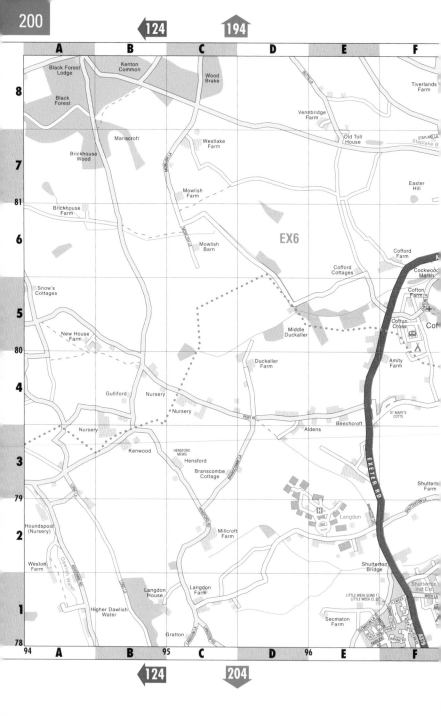

Starcross

A   B   C   D   E   F

8
7
81
6
5
80
4
3
79
2
1
78

Starcross

DREW'S CL 1
COOKSON'S RD 2
BRUNEL RD 3
COURTENAY TERR 4
WARBORO TERR 5
CORONATION TERR 6
CHURCH FLATS 7
CHAPPLE CL 8
BISHOPS CL 9

Jetty

Staplake
STAPLAKE LA
Old Staplake
Farm

Southbrook

PH

THE STRAND

Cockwood Prim Sch

Church Rd

stwood

KENBURY
CRES

Cockwood

South West
Coast Path

Eastdon

ORCHARD LA

DAWLISH WARREN RD

Eastdon
Wood

Eastdon
House

Dawlish
Sands
Holiday
Park

SHUTTERTON LA

SYCAMORE
AVE

HAZELWOOD DR

WILLOW

BRACKEN
WAY

PINE TREE

BEACH

Holiday
Ctr

DEVON
VIEW

Dawlish
Welcome
Holiday
Park

CH

BEACH RD

Dawlish
Warren

First Aid
Post

Visitor
Ctr

iden
nds
iday
ark

Dawlish
Warren

WEEK LA

WARREN

MOUNT PLEASANT

Langstone Cliff
Hotel

River Exe

Ferry P
(summer only)

Dawlish
Warren

Nature
Reserve

The Point

EX8

TRINITY RD 1
SCHOONERS CT 2
ROPEWALK HO 3
SAILMAKERS CT 4
CLIPPER WHARF 5
WINDJAMMER CT 6
PENNANT HO 7
MADISON WHARF 8
PIER HEAD 9
SHELLEY CT 10
MAINHEAD VIEW 11
THE MOORINGS 12

Dock

LB Sta

East Devon Way

Exmouth

Sports
Ctr

ESTUARY

CAMPERDOWN TERR

LANGSMEAD RD

VICTORIA RD

ST ANDREWS RD

MORTON CRES
ESPLANADE

Ctr

EXMOUTH

ALSTON TERR 1
MORTON CRESCENT MEWS 2
ST ANDREWS HO 3
CLINTON SQ 4
SHARPS CT 5
HARBOUR CT 6
SHELLY REACH 7
ELM GR 8
MANCHESTER ST 9
MANCHESTER RD 10
CLEVELAND PL 11

98   99

A6
1 CHAPEL ST
2 MAGNOLIA WLK
3 LOWER FORE ST
4 MARGARET ST
5 UNION ST
6 VICTORIA PL

7 HELENA PL
8 KING ST
9 UPPER CHURCH ST
10 MAGNOLIA HO
11 QUEEN ST
12 QUEEN'S CT
13 TOWER ST

14 CRITERION PL
15 CHAPEL HILL
16 BEACON HILL
17 ALEXANDRA TERR
18 LITTLE BICTON CT

201

196

A7
1 GEORGE ST
2 SHUTE MEADOW ST
3 CHARLES ST
4 STAPLES MEWS
5 GLENARCHY CT
6 ALBION CT

A7
7 HENRIETTA PL
8 HENRIETTA RD
9 ALBION TERR

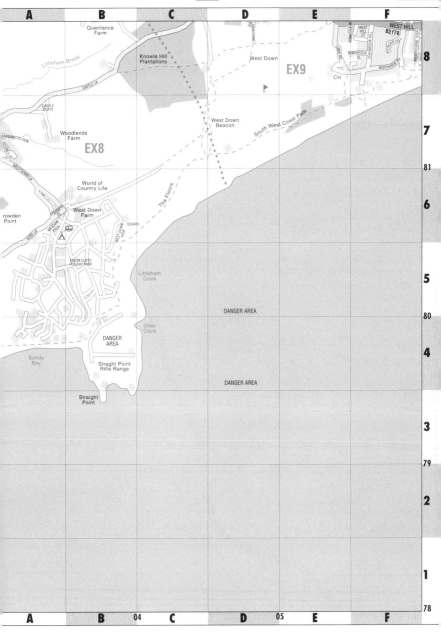

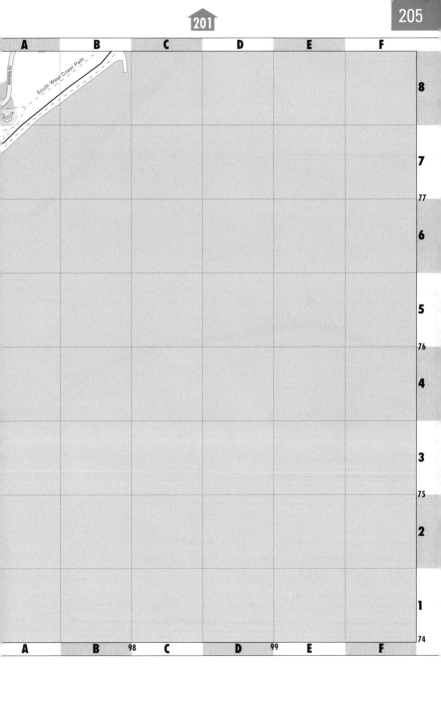

South West Coast Path

WARREN RD

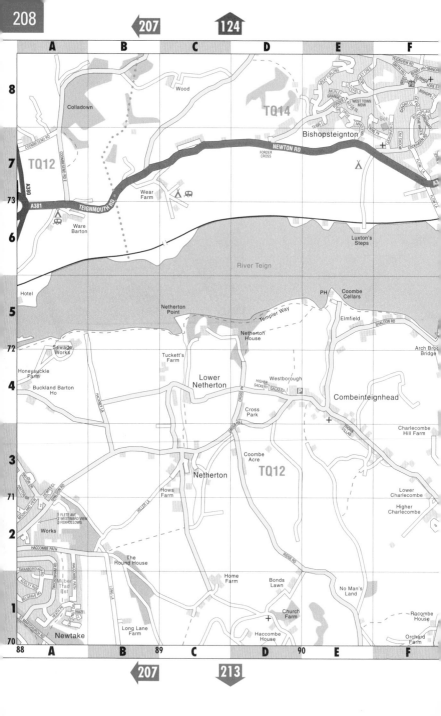

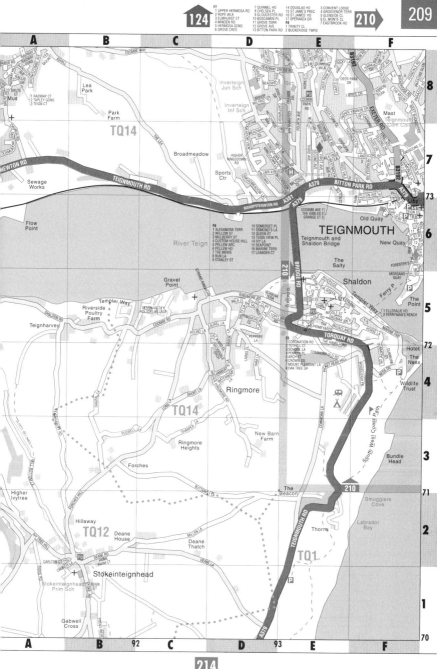

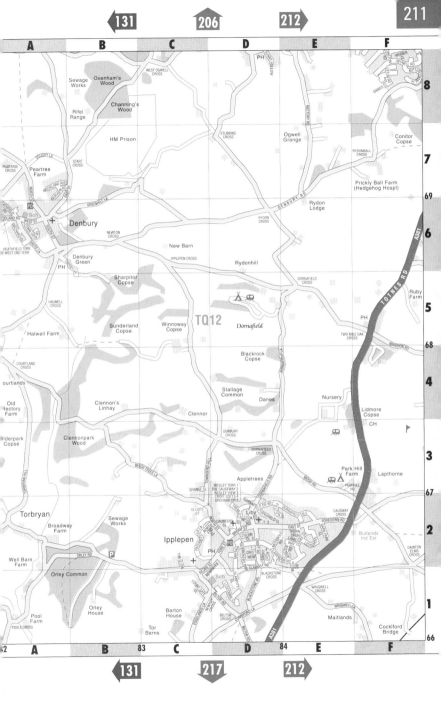

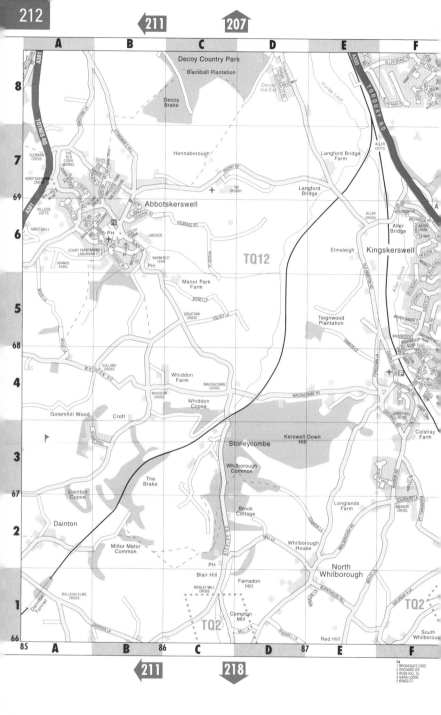

213
209

Lower
Gabwell

TQ12

Higher
Gabwell

Hafod
Farm

WHITEWAY LA

Herring
Cove

Higher
Rocombe
Barton

ASHACRE
CROSS

Ross
Hill

Mackerel
Cove

Blackaller's
Cove

Maidencombe

MAIDENCOMBE
CROSS

TEIGNMOUTH RD

SLADNOR PARK RD

ORESTONE
DR

STEEP

PH

Maidencombe
Beach

SLADNOR
PK

TQ1

Babbacombe Bay

Great
Hill

CLADDON LA

MAIDENCOMBE
HO

Rock
House

ROCK HOUSE LA

South West Coast Path

HELENS
MEAD CL

WATCOMBE HEIGHTS RD

ANSTEY'S WOOD LA

TQ2

MOOR LA

Valley of Rocks

Whitsand
Beach

Watcombe
Head

Sch

Watcombe
Beach

Schs

WHEATCOMBE
CT

STEPS
CROSS

SMALLDON LA

St Augustines

CORNFIELD GN

Smugglers'
Hole

Watcombe

Playing
Field

TORQUAY

Shag
Cliff

HAPPAWAY RD

Ind
Est

GRASMERE CL

Roundhouse
Point

1 STABLE LA
2 MILLY GARDENS RD
3 PETIT WELL LA
4 ST MARYS CT
5 CHARLOTTE CT
6 THE PADDOCK
7 PETITOR MEWS
8 CAMPION CT
9 CHURCH RD

Petit Tor
Beach

Combe
Pafford
Playing
Field

B3199

Petit
Tor

Petit Tor
Point

TEIGNMOUTH RD

ST MARYCHURCH RD

St Marychurch

CH

B3199

B3199

Sch

BRADLEY PARK RD

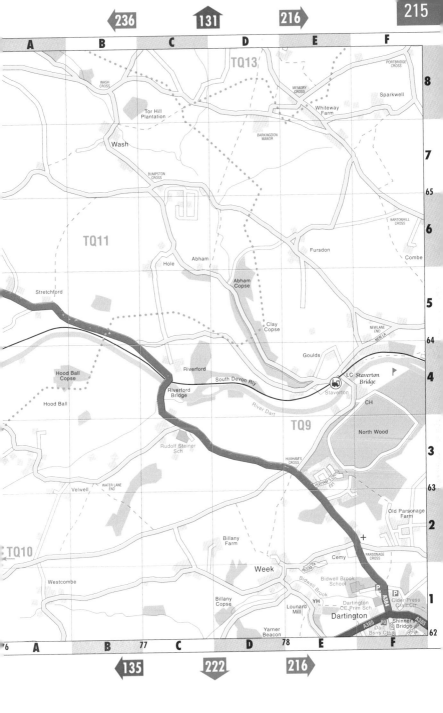

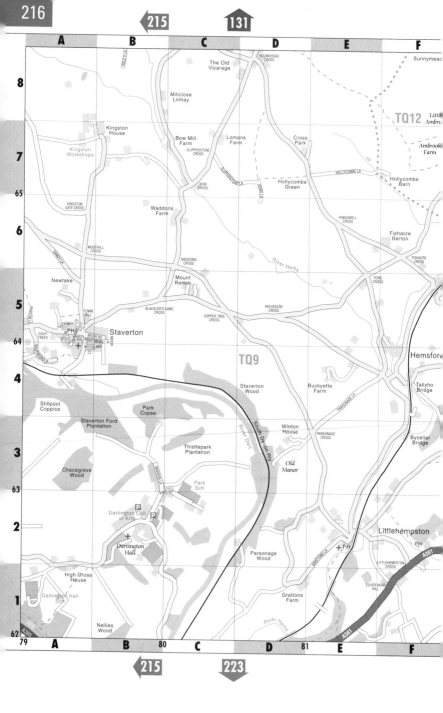

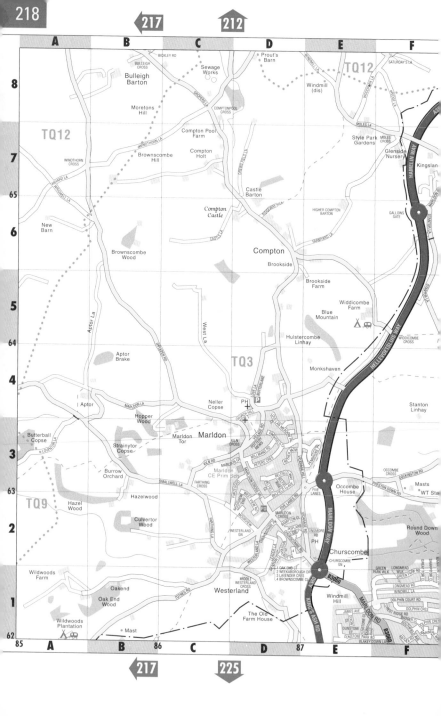

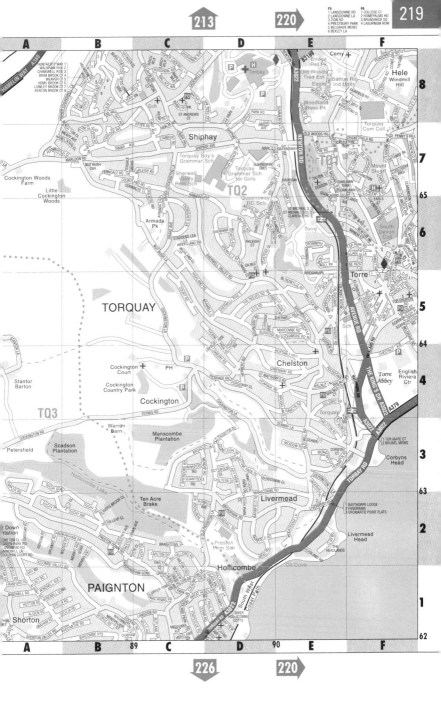

A6
1 TOR DALE
2 SUNBURY TERR
3 ST IVES CT
4 WILNCOTE LO

A7
1 WILLIS CT
2 EMPIRE CT
3 ORCHARD PL
4 HILL VIEW TERR

B5
1 BETHEL TERR
2 ST MICHAEL'S TERR
3 ALBERT CT
4 MYRTLE ROW

B6
1 WELLINGTON PL
2 MOUNT PLEASANT RD
3 WARBERRY VALE
4 ORCHARD RD

B7
1 WARBRO CT
2 PLAINMOOR RD
3 BLYTHSWOOD CRES

D5
1 MANORGLADE CT
2 WELLSWOOD MANOR
3 MAXSTOKE CT
4 UNDERHEATH
5 HAZELWOOD

219
214
219

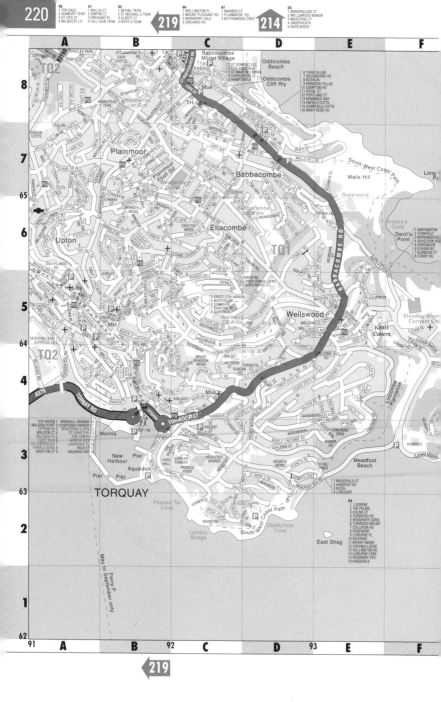

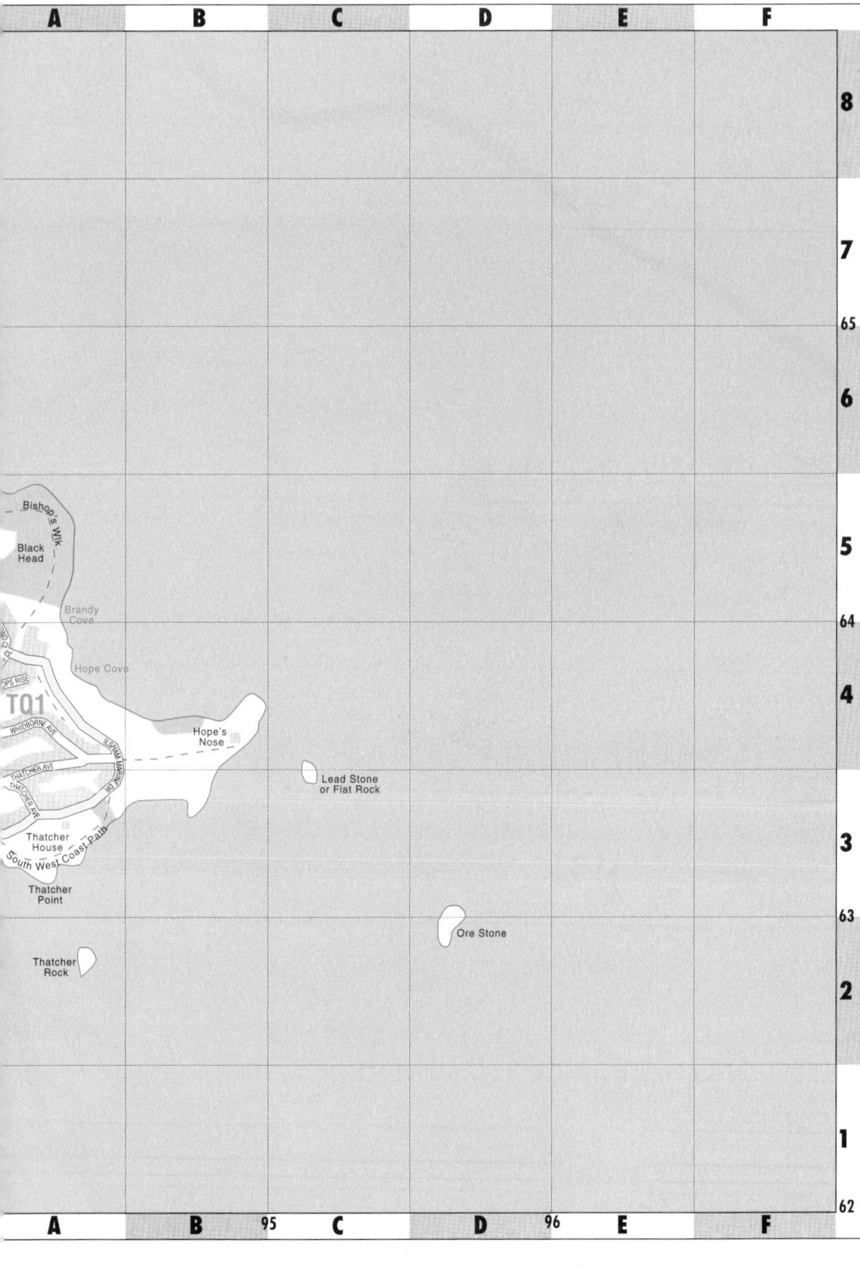

A **B** **C** **D** **E** **F**

8

7

65

6

5

Bishop's Wlk

Black
Head

Brandy
Cove

Hope Cove

TQ1

WHIDBORNE AVE

Hope's
Nose

Lead Stone
or Flat Rock

THATCHER DR

Thatcher
House

South West Coast Path

Thatcher
Point

Thatcher
Rock

Ore Stone

64

4

3

63

2

1

62

A **B** 95 **C** **D** 96 **E** **F**

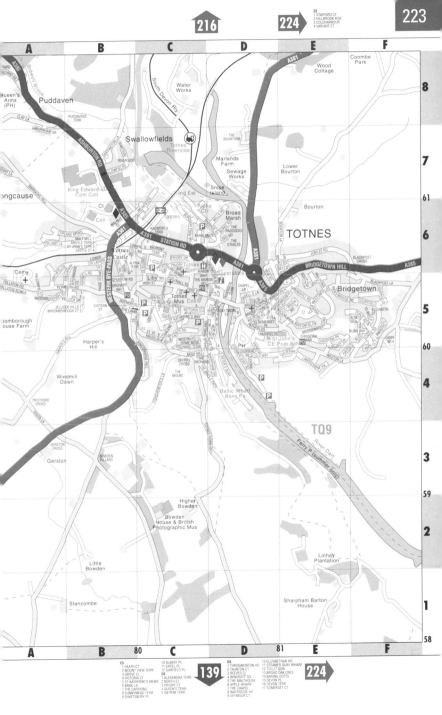

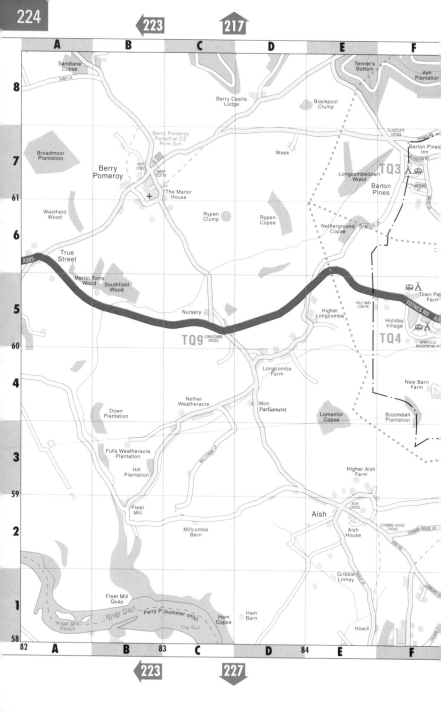

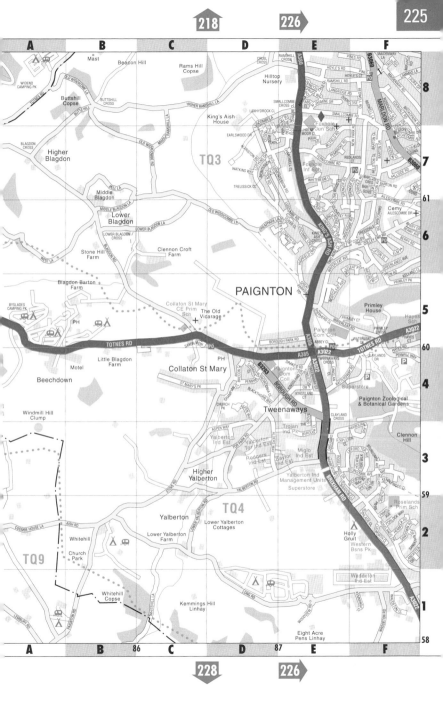

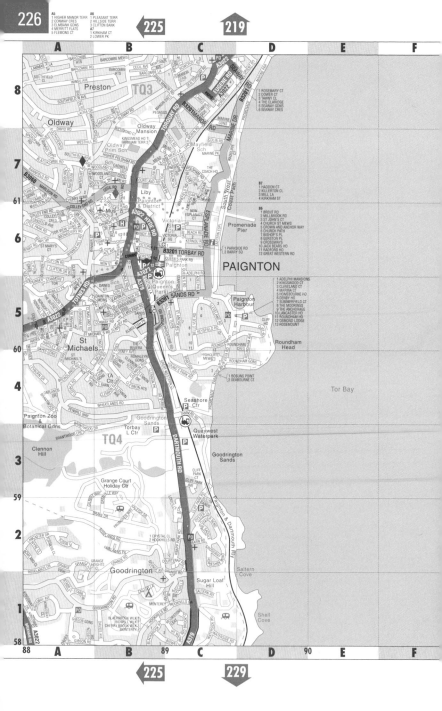

A5
1 HIGHER MANOR TERR
2 CONWAY CRES
3 ELMBANK GDNS
4 MERRITT FLATS
5 FLEMONS CT

A6
1 PLEASANT TERR
2 HILLSIDE TERR
3 CLIFTON BANK
A7
1 KIRKHAM CT
2 LOWER PK

225
219

B7
1 HADDON CT
2 KILLERTON CL
3 MILL LA
4 KIRKHAM ST

B6
1 BRENT RD
2 MILLBROOK RD
3 ST JOHN'S CT
4 CHURCH ST MEWS
5 CROWN AND ANCHOR WAY
6 CHURCH PATH
7 BISHOP'S PL
8 GERSTON PL
9 CROSSWAYS
10 JACK BEARS HO
11 RADFORD HO
12 GREAT WESTERN RD

2 ROSEMARY CT
2 DOWER CT
3 TAWNY CL
4 THE CLARIDGE
5 SEAWAY GDNS
6 SEAWAY CRES

1 ADELPHI MANSIONS
2 KINGSWOOD CT
3 CLEVELAND CT
4 MARINA CT
5 HOMEBOURNE HO
6 DENBY HO
7 SUMMERFIELD CT
8 THE MOORINGS
9 THE ANCHORAGE
10 LANCASTER HO
11 ROUNDHAM HO
12 OSMOND LODGE
13 ROSEMOUNT

1 BOSUNG POINT
2 SEABOURNE CT

1 CRYSTAL CL
2 HOOKHILLS RD

PAIGNTON

Preston

Oldway

Liby
Paignton
& District
Mus

Victoria
Shp

Promenade
Pier

Paignton
Harbour

Roundham
Head

Tor Bay

St
Michaels

Paignton
Queen's
Park

Paignton Zoo
& Botanical Gdns

Clennon
Hill

Torbay
L Ctr

Seashore
Ctr

Quaywest
Waterpark

Goodrington
Sands

Goodrington
Sands

Grange Court
Holiday Ctr

Goodrington

Sugar Loaf
Hill

Saltern
Cove

Shell
Cove

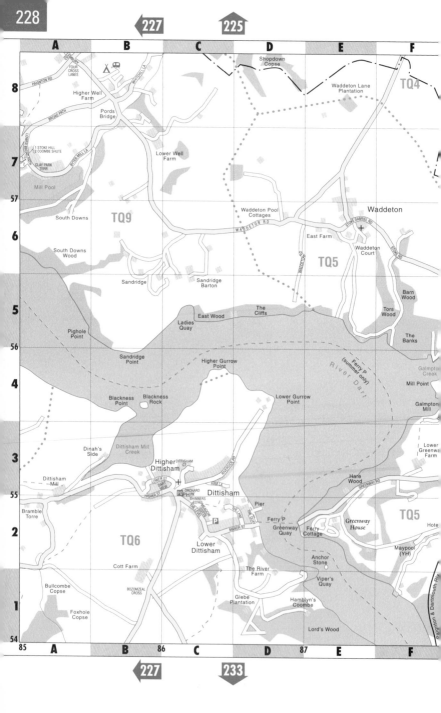

229

C3
1 GARROW CL
2 EVELEIGH CL
3 DOCTORS RD
4 GREENSWOOD RD
5 GLENNON CT
6 MAYFLOWER DR

7 HANOVER CL
8 ORCHARD CL
C4
1 PRINCE WILLIAM CT
2 SAXON HTS
3 VICTORIA TERR
4 TINKERS WOOD CT

5 WATERMILL CT
6 PARKHAM TWRS
7 CHURCHILL CT
8 BOLTON CT
9 WINDMILL CT
10 WREN CT

C5
1 HARBOUR VIEW CL
2 LINDEN CT
3 PROSPECT RD
4 CHURCH ST
5 CHURCH HILL W
6 CHURCH HILL E

7 APTERS HILL
8 MARKET ST
9 UNION LA
10 SOMERSET CT
D5
1 PARADISE PL
2 FURZE LA

3 THE STRAND
4 PUMP ST
5 ST PETER'S HILL
6 TEMPERANCE PL
7 MARINERS CT
8 HEADLAND CT
9 RANSCOMBE CT

BRIXHAM

Tor Bay

Fishcombe Point
Churston Cove
South West Coast Path

Jetty
Outer Harbour
The Breakwater

The Grove
Torbay Holiday Chalets

Breakwater Reach
Shoalstone Point

Brixham Holiday Park
Brixham Cove

Breakwater CT
LB Sta

Wall Park Holiday Ctr

Marina

Landscove Holiday Village

Higher Brixham

Higher Ryddng

St Mary's Holiday Village
St Mary's Bay

Dolphin Holiday Ctr

Mussel Rock

South Bay Holiday Ctr

South West Coast Path

Sharkham Point

Redwells

Southdown Cross

Mill La

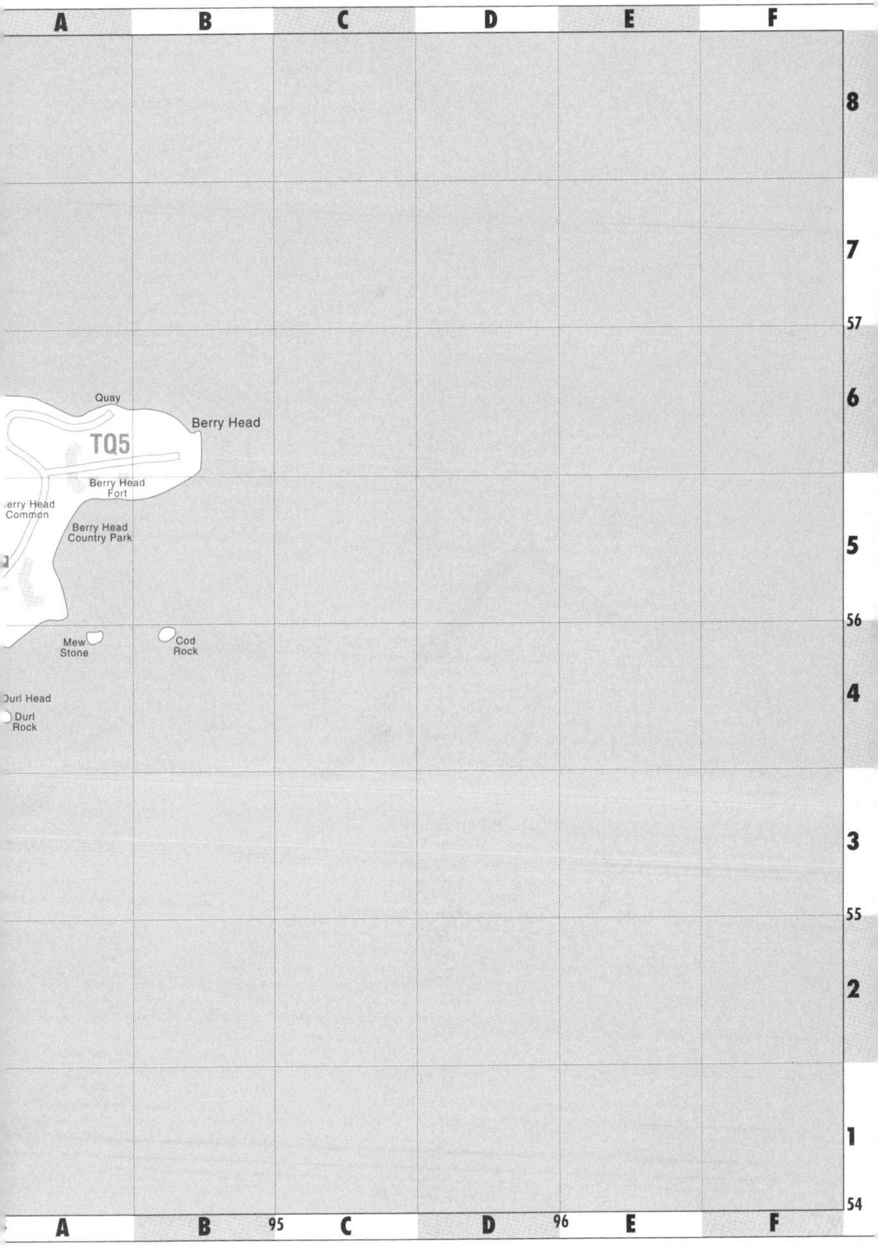

A	B	C	D	E	F

8

7

57

6

Quay

Berry Head

TQ5

Berry Head
Fort

erry Head
Common

Berry Head
Country Park

5

56

Mew
Stone

Cod
Rock

4

Durl Head
Durl
Rock

3

55

2

1

54

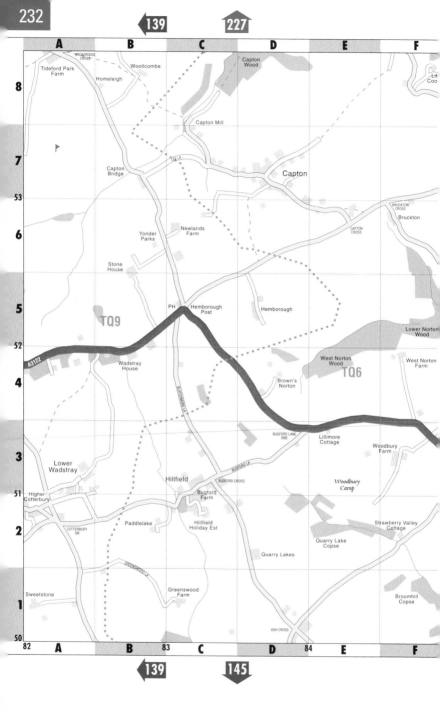

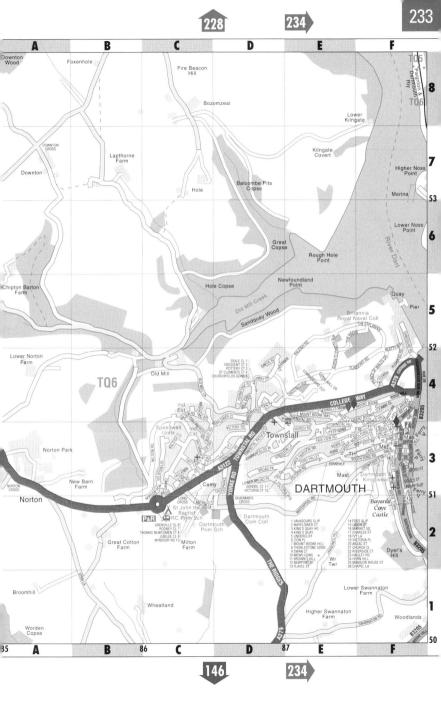

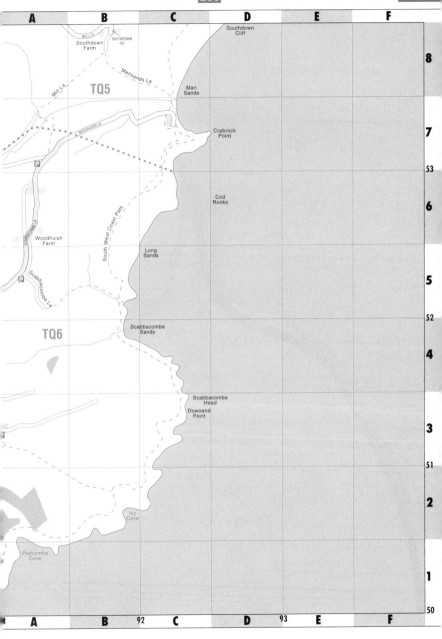

MILL LA
Southdown
Farm
SOUTHDOWN
RD

Mansands La

Southdown
Cliff

8

Mill La

TQ5

Man
Sands

WOODHUISH LA

Crabrock
Point

7

53

South West Coast Path

Cod
Rocks

6

Woodhuish
Farm

Long
Sands

5

Scabbacombe La

52

Scabbacombe La

Scabbacombe
Sands

TQ6

4

Scabbacombe
Head

Downend
Point

3

51

Ivy
Cove

2

Pudcombe
Cove

1

50

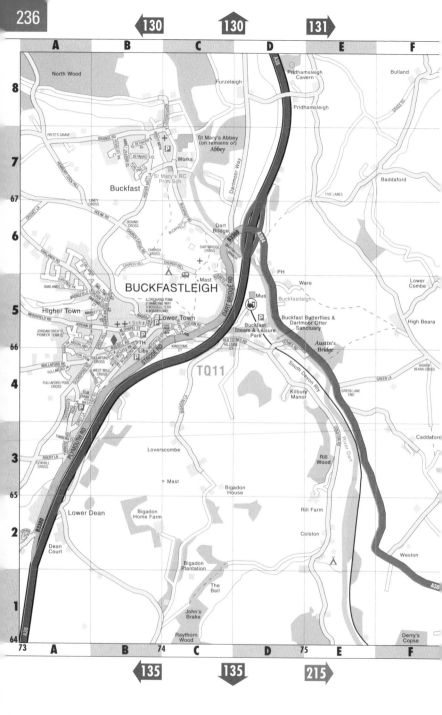

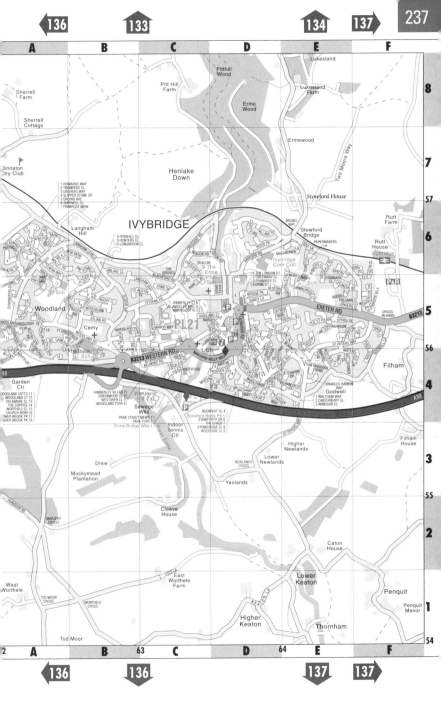

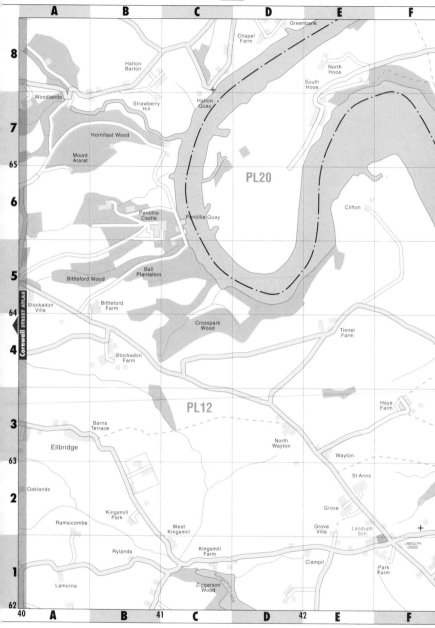

A   B   C   D   E   F

8

Greenbank
Chapel
Farm
Halton
Barton
North
Hooe
South
Hooe
Woodlands
Strawberry
Hill
Halton
Quay

7
Hornifast Wood

65
Mount
Ararat

6
Clifton
Pentillie
Castle
Pentillie Quay

PL20

5
Ball
Plantation
Bittleford Wood

64
Stockadon
Villa
Bittleford
Farm
Crosspark
Wood
Tinnel
Farm

4
Stockadon
Farm

Haye
Farm

PL12

3
Barns
Terrace
North
Wayton
Wayton

63
Ellbridge
St Anns

2
Oaklands
Grove
Kingsmill
Park
Grove
Villa
Landuph
Sch
LANDULPH
CROSS
Ramsicombe
West
Kingsmill

1
Rylands
Kingsmill
Farm
Clampit
Park
Farm
Lamorna
Ziggarson
Wood
Kingsmill Lake

62
40   A   B   41   C   D   42   E   F

Cornwall STREET ATLAS

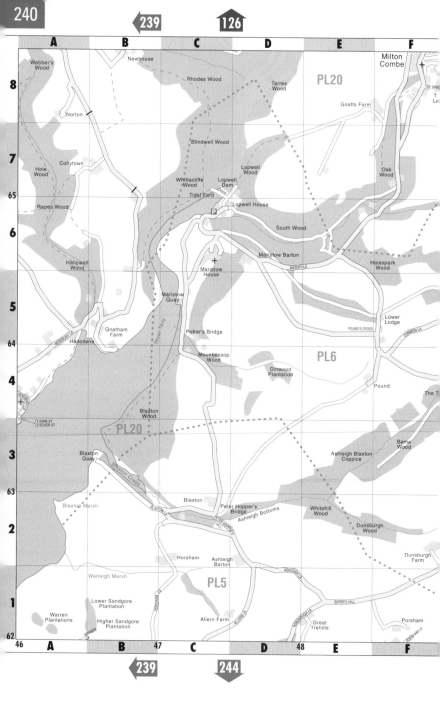

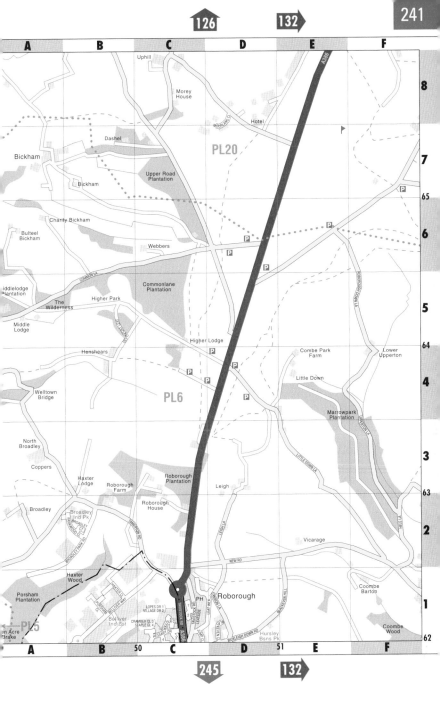

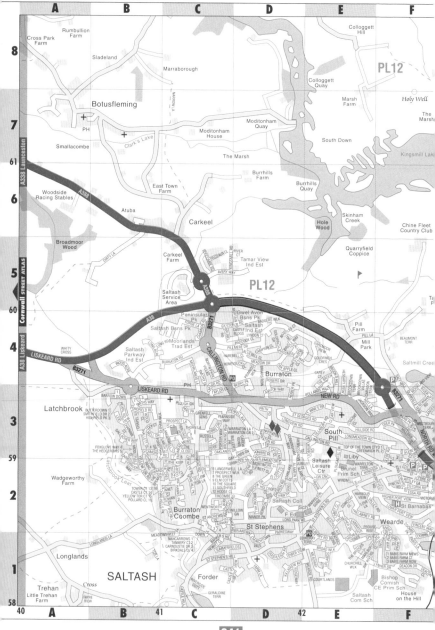

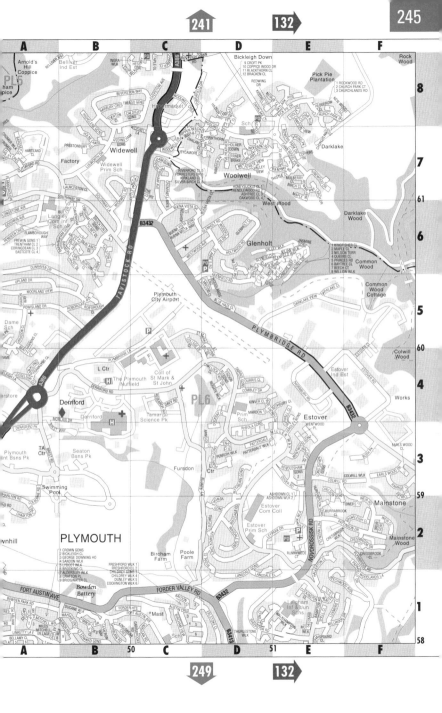

246

242

8

7

57

6

5

56

4

55

3

2

54

1

A B C D E F

40 41 42

Cornwall STREET ATLAS

A374 Lopwell (A387)

PL12

Trehan

Castle Farm

Trematon Castle

Forder Lake

Marsh Coombe

Merryfield View

Wearde Quay

Piers

Shillingham Manor

Antony Passage

Quay

St Germans or Lynher River

Higher Wea Plantati

Shillingham Point

Wivelscombe Lake

Jupiter Point

Jetty

Beggar's Island

Ince Castle

Ince Point

Jupiter Plantation

Bath House

Antony Woodland Garden

Wilderness

Antony House

Tomboy Hill

Great Kithill Plantation

North Wilcove

Wil

Antony Park

Maryfield

Coomb Pk

Bulland Quay

Horson House

Horson Plantation

Mast

Borough Farm House

Sports Gd

1 FISTRAL CL
2 GWITHIAN

Clift Quay

Clift

Bulland

Trevol Bsns Pk

PL11

KERNOW CT 3
TRELAWNEY WAY 4

FROBISHER WAY

HMS Fisgard

Trevol Ho

Longlands Plantation

Cemy

TREVOL RD

Trinaway Plantation

Hay

HMS Raleigh

Rifle Range

West Antony

PO

ABBOTSCOURT LA

HOLLOWGUTTER LA

Sports Gd

Eastdowns Lake

River Tamar Hamoaze

Wolsdon House

Sewage Wks

Efford's Bridge

Deadman's Point

St John's Lake

A374

PL12

Shillingham Manor

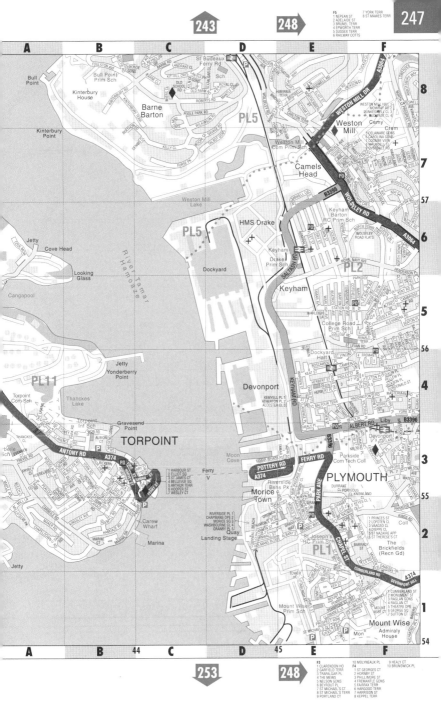

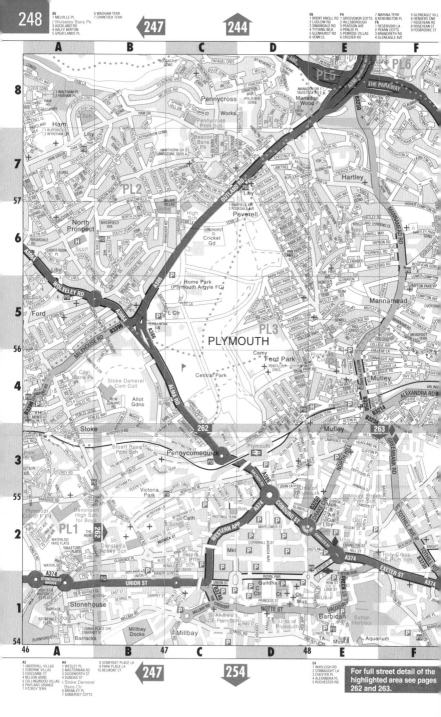

For full street detail of the highlighted area see pages 262 and 263.

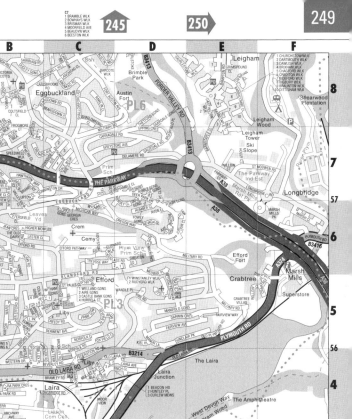
C7
1 BRAMBLE WLK
2 BOWHAYS WLK
3 BRISMAR WLK
4 MOORFIELD AVE
5 BEAUDYN WLK
6 BEESTON WLK

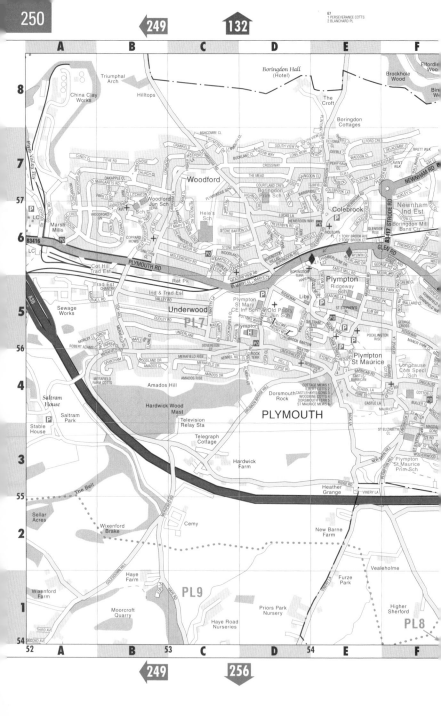

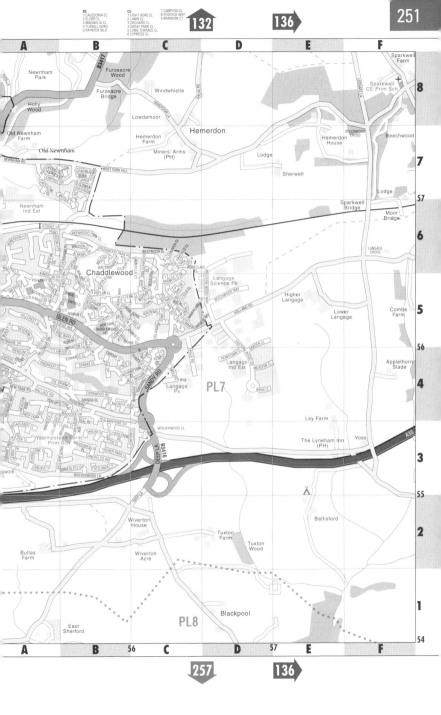

246

St John's Lake

8
Ford
Vanderbands
St John
Vanderbands Farm
PH
CHURCH LA
JACK LA
BUNWELL LA
DODBROOK LA
MONTANA
ANNE LA

Sand Island

7
St John's Down
Mendennick
Penhale
Penhale Lake
Mendennick Hill
PL11

53
B3247
Works

Insworke
CAMPERKNOWLE
OLD RD
WELL RD
SOUTHDOWN RD

6
Sewage Wks
ST PETER RD
TREFUSIS TERR
POTTERY EST
1 HEANTON TERR
2 CLINTON TERR

5
New Barn
Millbrook Resr
Millbrook CE Sch
Blindwell
PRIESTHOOD TERR
MOUNT PLEASANT
PH
GREENLAND
MILL VIEW GDNS

BLINDLE LA
STOKE LA

Withnoe Barton
Higher Hounster Farm
RICHARDS TERR 1
THE PARADE 2
ST ANDREW ST
POST
KING ST
KNILL CROSS
WEST ST

52
Withnoe
CLIFF LA
HOUNSTER HILL
Millbrook
Ande
Cemy

4
Tregonhawke Farm
RADFORD LA
Dadbrook

Tregonhawke
Whitsand Bay Holiday Pk
Mon
Treninnow Grove
Sollac

3
Treninnow
Fourlanesend Com Prim Sch
Treninnow Plantation

MILITARY RD

51
Whitsand Bay
The Hats
TRENINNOW & WIGGLE

2
PL10
Wiggle
Wringford Down
South West Coast Path
TRENCHET LA
Wringford Farm

1
Wiggle Cliff
P
Hotel
Forder
Knatterbury
FORDER LA
DANIELL LA

50
40   A   B   41   C   D   42   E   F

Cornwall STREET ATLAS

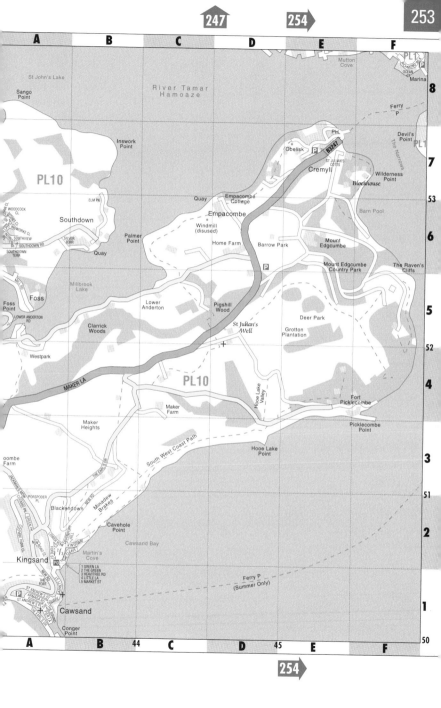

A B C D E F

Mutton Cove

PL1
RICHMOND WALK
P
Marina

8

St John's Lake

River Tamar
Hamoaze

Sango
Point

Ferry
P

Devil's
Point

The Narrows

PL1

7

Inswork
Point

PH.

Obelisk
P
B3247
ST JULIAN'S
CLIFFS

Cremyll

Wilderness
Point

Blockhouse

PL10

Quay

Empacombe
Cottage

Empacombe

Barn Pool

53

ELM PK

WOODCOCK
CL
ISWORKE Q.
SOUTHVIEW
SOUTHDOWN RD

Southdown

Windmill
(disused)

Palmer
Point

Home Farm

Barrow Park

Mount
Edgcumbe

6

SILVER
TERR

Quay

Mount Edgcumbe
Country Park

The Raven's
Cliffs

Foss
Point

Foss

Millbrook
Lake

Lower
Anderton

Pigshill
Wood

St Julian's
Well

Deer Park

Grotton
Plantation

5

LOWER ANDERTON
RD

Westpark

Clarrick
Woods

52

PL10

MAKER LA

Maker
Farm

Hooe Lake
Valley

Fort
Picklecombe

4

Maker
Heights

Picklecombe
Point

oombe
Farm

South West Coast Path

Hooe Lake
Point

3

51

PORSPODER
PL

Blackendown

Minadew
Brakes

THE CLEAVE

Cavehole
Point

2

Kingsand

Martin's
Cove

Cawsand Bay

1 GREEN LA
2 THE GREEN
3 HEAVITREE RD
4 LITTLE LA
5 MARKET ST

THE
FORT

Ferry P
(Summer Only)

ST ANDREW'S LA

Cawsand

Conger
Point

1

B 44 C D 45 E F 50

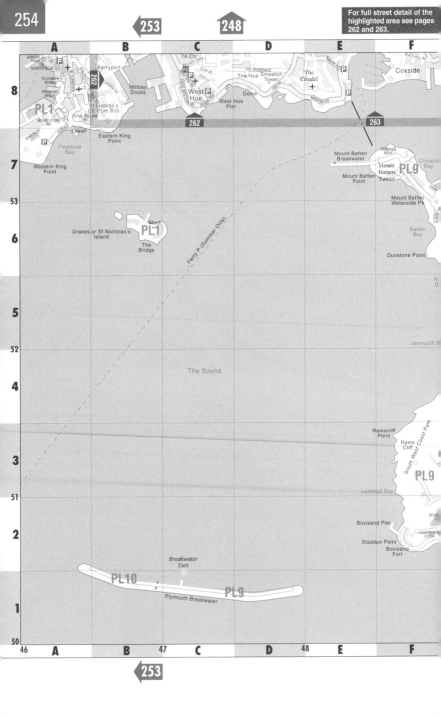

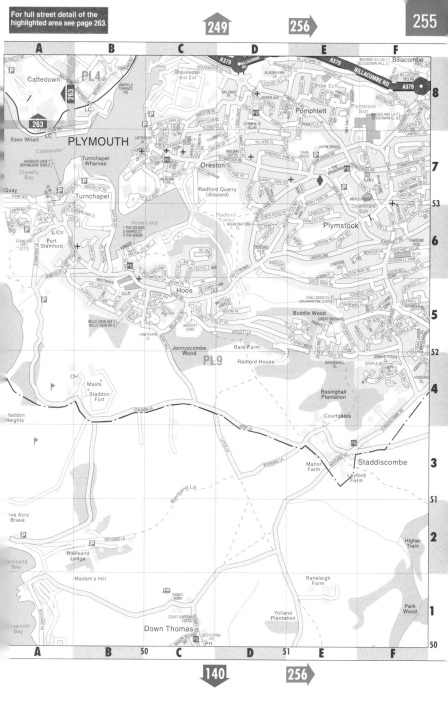

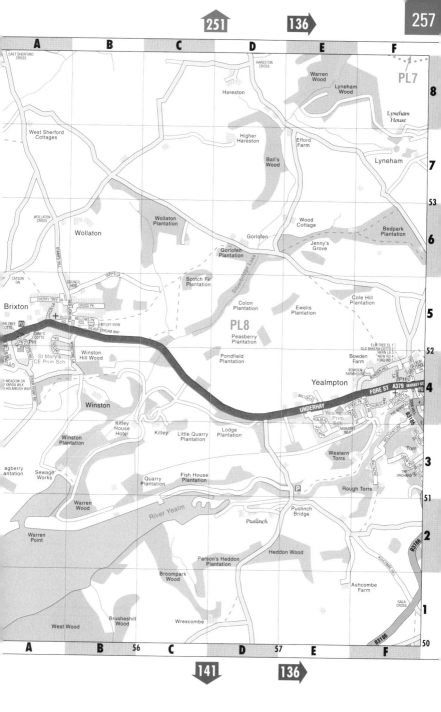

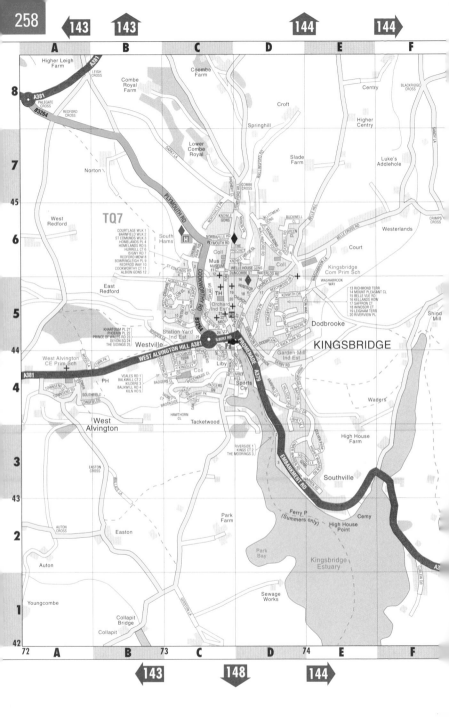

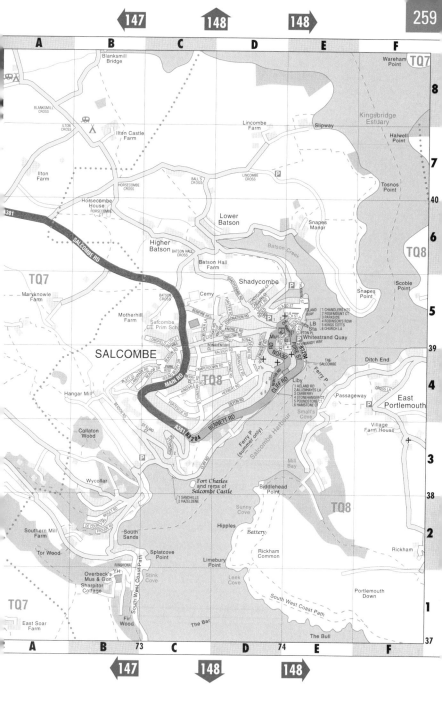

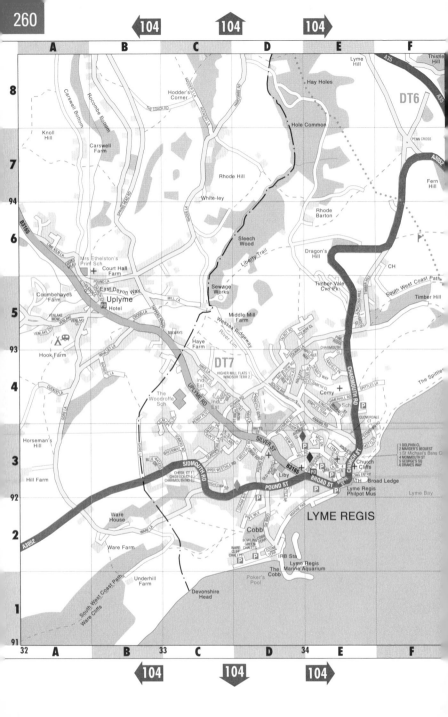

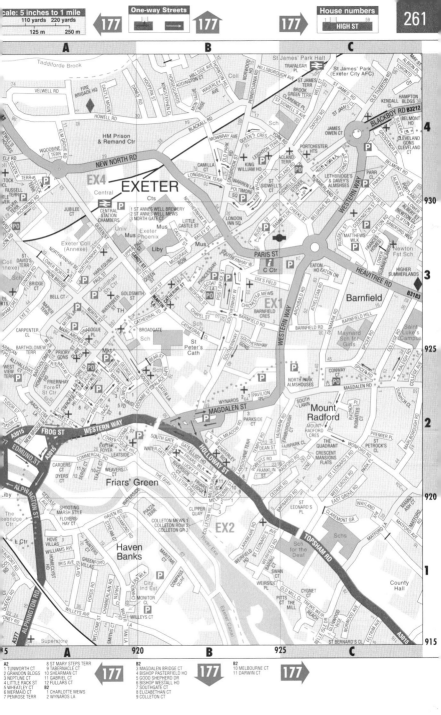

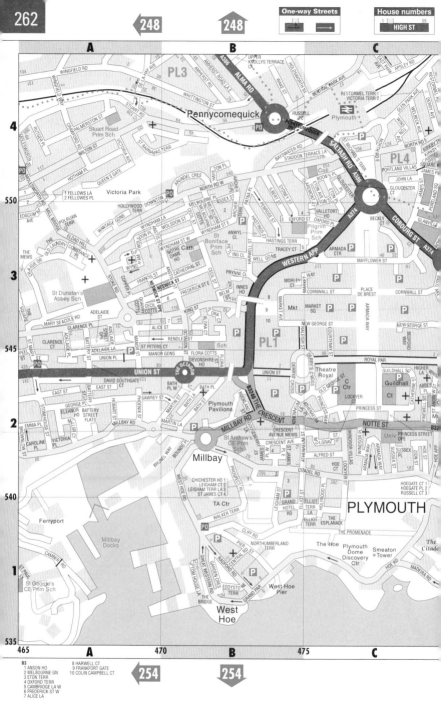

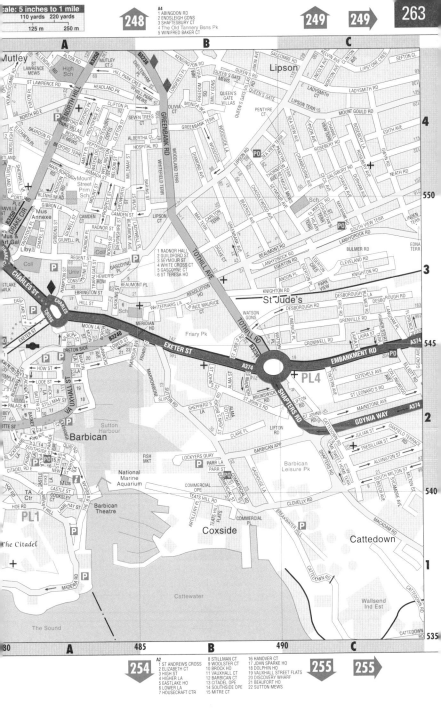

Index

Church Rd **6** Beckenham BR2.........**53** C6

Place name	Location number	Locality, town or village	Postcode district	Page and grid square
May be abbreviated on the map	Present when a number indicates the place's position in a crowded area of mapping	Shown when more than one place has the same name	District for the indexed place	Page number and grid reference for the standard mapping

Public and commercial buildings are highlighted in magenta. Places of interest are highlighted in blue with a star★

Abbreviations used in the index

Acad	Academy	Comm	Common	Gd	Ground	L	Leisure	Prom	Promenade
App	Approach	Cott	Cottage	Gdn	Garden	La	Lane	Rd	Road
Arc	Arcade	Cres	Crescent	Gn	Green	Liby	Library	Recn	Recreation
Ave	Avenue	Cswy	Causeway	Gr	Grove	Mdw	Meadow	Ret	Retail
Bglw	Bungalow	Ct	Court	H	Hall	Meml	Memorial	Sh	Shopping
Bldg	Building	Ctr	Centre	Ho	House	Mkt	Market	Sq	Square
Bsns, Bus	Business	Ctry	Country	Hospl	Hospital	Mus	Museum	St	Street
Bvd	Boulevard	Cty	County	HQ	Headquarters	Orch	Orchard	Sta	Station
Cath	Cathedral	Dr	Drive	Hts	Heights	Pal	Palace	Terr	Terrace
Cir	Circus	Dro	Drove	Ind	Industrial	Par	Parade	TH	Town Hall
Cl	Close	Ed	Education	Inst	Institute	Pas	Passage	Univ	University
Cnr	Corner	Emb	Embankment	Int	International	Pk	Park	Wk, Wlk	Walk
Coll	College	Est	Estate	Intc	Interchange	Pl	Place	Wr	Water
Com	Community	Ex	Exhibition	Junc	Junction	Prec	Precinct	Yd	Yard

Index of localities, towns and villages

A

Abbotsham 156 A2
Abbotskerswell 212 B6
Alfington 100 F8
Alswear 30 C1
Appledore 14 F1
Ashbrittle 50 E8
Ashburton 130 E5
Ashcombe 124 D6
Ashford 16 B6
Ashprington 139 F8
Ashreigney 58 F1
Ashwater 90 D6
Atherington 28 A2
Aveton Gifford 143 C6
Avonwick 135 B1
Awliscombe 85 B4
Axminster 167 C6
Axmouth 192 E7
Aylesbeare 99 D2

B

Bampton 34 C1
Barbrook 151 B1
Barnstaple 155 C4
Beacon 85 F8
Beaford 42 D1
Beare 82 E3
Beer 191 E6
Beesands 149 E7
Belstone 94 D4

Bere Alston 125 E1
Bere Ferrers 239 E3
Berry Pomeroy 224 B7
Berrynarbor 2 E3
Bickington
  (nr Ashburton) 131 D7
Bickington
  (nr Bideford) 154 B4
Bickleigh
  (nr Plymouth) 132 A5
Bickleigh (nr Tiverton) . .64 A1
Bideford 156 E3
Bigbury 142 F5
Bigbury-on-Sea 142 E3
Bishop's Tawton 16 F1
Bishops Nympton 31 A2
Bishopsteignton 208 E7
Bittaford 137 C8
Black Torrington 74 A8
Blackawton 139 F2
Bolham 161 C8
Bondleigh 77 B7
Bovey Tracey 180 D7
Bow 78 C4
Boyton 89 E2
Bradninch 82 F7
Bradworthy 38 E1
Bramford Speke 81 E1
Brandis Corner 73 B6
Branscombe 190 D3
Bratton Clovelly 92 A2
Bratton Fleming 18 A8
Braunton 152 B6
Brayford 18 F5
Brendon 6 A4

Bridestowe 107 F8
Bridford 112 F5
Bridgerule 70 F6
Brixham 230 E3
Brixton 257 A5
Broadclyst 175 C6
Broadhembury 84 E7
Broadhempston 131 F1
Broadoak 168 D3
Broadwoodkelly 76 D8
Broadwoodwidger . . .106 B8
Brushford 33 D4
Buck's Mills 24 C2
Buckfast 236 B7
Buckfastleigh 236 B5
Buckland Brewer 40 C7
Buckland in the Moor . .130 C8
Buckland Monachorum 126 D3
Buckland St Mary 69 C8
Budlake 82 E3
Budleigh Salterton . . .198 A2
Burlescombe 51 B3
Burrington 43 F3
Butterleigh 64 C3

C

Cadbury 81 D7
Cadeleigh 63 D3
Calstock 125 D3
Calverleigh 48 E1
Cargreen 239 A2
Cawsand 253 B2
Chagford 111 A6

Challacombe 11 F3
Chapelton 27 F5
Chard Junction 88 E7
Chardstock 88 B7
Charmouth 104 F4
Chawleigh 60 B7
Cheriton Bishop 97 A4
Cheriton Fitzpaine 62 E1
Chevithorne 49 D2
Chillaton 116 D8
Chillington 145 A2
Chilsworthy 53 E1
Chipstable 35 E6
Chittlehamholt 44 B8
Chittlehampton 28 F5
Christow 113 A3
Chudleigh 123 E6
Chudleigh Knighton . .123 C4
Chulmleigh 44 F1
Churchinford 68 D7
Churchstow 143 E4
Churston Ferrers 229 E4
Clawton 72 B2
Clayhanger 35 C1
Clovelly 23 E3
Clyst Honiton 179 E8
Clyst Hydon 83 D4
Clyst St George 183 C6
Clyst St Lawrence 83 C3
Clyst St Mary 179 B3
Cobbaton 28 D5
Cockwood 201 B5
Coffinswell 213 B6
Colaton Raleigh 186 D3
Coldridge 59 F2

Colebrooke 79 A3
Colyford 103 B3
Colyton 103 A5
Combe Martin 3 B3
Combe St Nicholas . . .69 F6
Combeinteignhead . . .208 E4
Compton 218 D6
Copplestone 79 A6
Cornwood 133 C2
Cornworthy 227 B4
Cove 49 B6
Cowley 172 E4
Crapstone 126 E2
Crediton 165 D4
Crockernwell 96 F3
Croyde 7 E2
Cullompton 163 A3
Culmstock 66 E8

D

Daccombe 213 E5
Dalwood 87 B3
Dartington 215 E1
Dartmouth 233 E3
Dawlish 204 F6
Dawlish Warren 201 A1
Denbury 211 B6
Diptford 138 C7
Dittisham 228 C3
Doddiscombsleigh . . .113 C5
Dolton 57 F7
Dousland 127 C3
Down St Mary 78 E7

Down Thomas 255 C1
Drewsteignton 96 D2
Dulverton 33 E6
Dunchideock 114 A6
Dunkeswell 67 C2
Dunsford 112 F8
Dunterton 115 D6

E
East Allington 144 E7
East Anstey 32 E5
East Buckland 18 D2
East Budleigh 198 A6
East Ogwell 206 E1
East Portlemouth . . .259 F4
East Prawle 149 A3
Ebford 183 C4
Edistone 37 C8
Ermington 136 F4
Exbourne 76 C4
Exebridge 33 F3
Exeter 177 C5
Exeter 261 B4
Exminster 182 B4
Exmouth 202 B7
Exton 183 D2

F
Farway 102 A6
Feniton 84 E2
Filleigh 29 C7
Folly Gate 84 D1
Fremington 153 E6
Frithelstock Stone . . .40 F5
Frogmore 144 E1

G
Galmpton
  (nr Paignton) 229 A6
Galmpton
  (nr Salcombe) . . .147 C7
George Nympton 30 A1
Georgeham 8 B2
Germansweek 91 E5
Gittisham 85 B1
Goodleigh 17 C5
Goodrington 226 B2
Great Torrington . . .159 D6
Greenham 51 B7
Gunnislake 125 C5

H
Halberton 65 B8
Hallsands 149 D5
Halwell 139 B4
Halwill 73 C2
Halwill Junction 73 E2
Harberton 222 D1
Harbertonford 139 C6
Harcombe 101 D1
Harrowbarrow 125 A4
Hartland 22 E3
Hatherleigh 75 C6
Hawkchurch 88 E3
Hawkridge 21 D1
Heasley Mill 19 D3
Heathfield 180 F2
Heddon 29 B7
Hele 82 F5
Hemyock 67 C8
Hennock 123 B7
Hexworthy 129 B7
Heybrook Bay 140 B8
High Bickington 43 B7
Highampton 74 C7
Higher Gabwell . . .214 B7
Hillhead 234 F8
Hittisleigh 96 D5
Hockworthy 50 D6
Holbeton 136 D1
Holcombe 204 D3
Holcombe Rogus 50 F5
Holemoor 73 B8
Hollocombe 58 F6
Holne 130 A4
Holsworthy 164 D5
Holsworthy Beacon . . .54 C3
Holywell Lake 51 E7
Honiton 166 D4
Horns Cross 24 E2
Horrabridge 126 F5
Horsebridge 116 A1

Huish Champflower . . .35 F8
Huntsham 49 F7

I
Iddesleigh 57 F3
Ide 176 D1
Ideford 124 A4
Ilfracombe 150 B6
Ilsington 122 C3
Instow 15 B1
Inwardleigh 75 E2
Ipplepen 211 C2
Ivybridge 237 C6

K
Kennford 181 B2
Kentisbeare 66 A3
Kentisbury 10 E5
Kenton 194 E3
Kilmington 103 D8
King's Nympton . . .44 E6
Kingsbridge 258 E5
Kingskerswell 213 B4
Kingsteignton 207 C8
Kingston 142 C6
Kingswear 234 B3
Knowle 8 D1
Knowstone 32 A2

L
Lamerton 116 F3
Landkey 17 B2
Langford 172 E8
Langtree 40 F2
Lapford 60 C3
Launceston 105 B2
Lee Mill 136 B6
Lee Moor 132 F5
Lewtrenchard 106 F4
Lifton 105 F4
Littleham 202 F7
Liverton 180 A1
Loddiswell 143 F7
Longdown 98 E1
Lustleigh 122 B7
Luton 124 C3
Lutton 133 B2
Lydford 107 F4
Lyme Regis 260 E2
Lympstone 195 E5
Lynmouth 151 D5
Lynton 151 B4

M
Maidencombe 214 D6
Malborough 147 E6
Marhamchurch 70 A6
Mariansleigh 30 D1
Marldon 218 C3
Marsh 69 B5
Mary Tavy 117 E6
Meavy 127 C2
Meeth 57 C3
Membury 87 D6
Merton 57 A7
Meshaw 45 F6
Metherell 125 A4
Millbrook 252 E5
Millmoor 51 E1
Milton Abbot 116 B6
Milton Combe . . .126 C1
Milton Damerel . . .54 D5
Modbury 137 C2
Molland 31 E7
Monkleigh 40 F7
Monkokehampton . . .76 B8
Monkton 86 A5
Morchard Bishop . . .61 A2
Morchard Road 78 F7
Morebath 34 B3
Moretonhampstead . . .111 E4
Morwenstow 36 E2
Musbury 103 D5

N
Nadderwater 176 B7
Newton Abbot . . .207 A2
Newton Ferrers . . .140 F7
Newton Poppleford . . .186 E7

Newton St Cyres . . .172 A8
Newton St Petrock . . .55 B7
Newton Tracey 27 A5
North Brentor 117 C8
North Molton 30 D8
North Tamerton . . .89 C8
North Tawton 77 C4
North Whilborough . . .212 E2
Northam 157 A6
Northleigh 102 B7
Northlew 74 E1
Noss Mayo 140 F6

O
Oakford 48 C8
Offwell 86 B2
Oldways End 32 E3
Otterton 198 F7
Ottery St Mary . . .169 E3

P
Paignton 226 D6
Parkham 39 E8
Parracombe 4 C2
Pathfinder Village . . .98 C4
Payhembury 84 D4
Peter Tavy 117 F4
Peters Marland . . .56 C8
Petrockstow 56 F4
Plymouth 248 C5
Plymouth 262 C1
Plympton 250 E5
Plymstock 255 E6
Plymtree 83 E5
Poltimore 174 F6
Postbridge 120 A6
Princetown 128 B8
Pyworthy 71 D5

R
Rackenford 47 D5
Rame 140 H2
Rattery 135 D4
Rawridge 84 B8
Raymond's Hill . . .104 C7
Rewe 82 A2
Ringmore 142 E4
Roborough (nr Great
  Torrington) 42 F3
Roborough
  (nr Plymouth) . . .241 D1
Rockbeare 99 C6
Rockwell Green . . .160 B5
Rousdon 193 F7
Runnington 51 F8

S
St Dominick 125 A3
St Giles on the Heath . . .90 B1
St John 252 C8
Salcombe 259 B4
Salcombe Regis . . .188 F6
Saltash 242 B1
Sampford Arundel . . .51 E5
Sampford Chapple . . .76 E3
Sampford Courtenay . . .76 F4
Sampford Peverell . . .50 E1
Sandford 80 A5
Saunton 14 F8
Seaton 192 B5
Shaldon 210 B3
Shaugh Prior 132 C6
Shebbear 55 E4
Sheepwash 56 C1
Shillingford 34 E2
Shillingford Abbot . . .181 A6
Shillingford St George . . .114 C7
Shirwell 17 B8
Shobrooke 80 E4
Shop 137 A1
Shute 103 A8
Sidbury 101 B2
Sidford 101 B1
Sidmouth 188 C3
Silverton 82 B5
Simonsbath 13 B2
Skilgate 34 E6
Slapton 145 C4
Sourton 93 B1
South Brent 134 F3
South Molton 158 D3

South Pool 148 F7
South Tawton 95 B5
South Zeal 95 B3
Southleigh 102 C4
Sparkwell 136 A8
Spreyton 95 F7
Staddiscombe 255 F3
Starcross 201 A8
Staverton 216 B5
Stibb Cross 40 C1
Sticklepath 95 A5
Stockland 87 A7
Stockleigh Pomeroy . . .81 A6
Stoke 22 B3
Stoke Canon 173 E8
Stoke Climsland 115 C1
Stoke Fleming 146 B7
Stoke Gabriel 227 F7
Stokeinteignhead . . .209 B1
Stokenham 145 C1
Stopgate 68 F4
Strete 145 E5
Sutcombe 54 A6
Swimbridge 17 D1
Sydenham Damerel . . .116 B2

T
Talaton 84 A2
Taleford 169 C6
Tamerton Foliot 244 B7
Tatworth 88 C8
Tavistock 171 E5
Tedburn St Mary 97 F5
Teigngrace 206 F8
Teignmouth 210 D4
Tetcott 89 F7
Thorverton 81 D5
Throwleigh 95 C1
Thurlestone 143 A2
Tipton St John 100 D2
Tiverton 161 D3
Topsham 182 F5
Torcross 145 D1
Torpoint 247 C3
Torquay 220 B3
Totnes 223 E6
Trebarley 115 A4
Trusham 113 D1
Tuckenhay 139 F7
Twitchen 20 D1

U
Uffculme 66 A8
Ugborough 137 E6
Umberleigh 28 D2
Uploman 50 B2
Uplyme 260 B5
Upottery 68 C2
Upton 34 F8
Upton Pyne 173 A8

V
Venterdon 115 B2
Virginstow 90 D3

W
Walkhampton 127 A4
Wambrook 69 F3
Warkleigh 29 A2
Watercrow 13 F4
Weare Giffard 26 B1
Welcombe 37 A5
Wellington 160 D7
Wembury 140 D7
Wembworthy 59 C4
West Alvington 258 B4
West Anstey 32 C6
West Buckland
  (nr Barnstaple) 18 B2
West Buckland
  (nr Wellington) 52 F7
West Charleton 144 C1
West Down 8 F5
West Hill 168 E4
West Putford 39 C2
West Worlington 41 A8
Westleigh (Bideford) . . .157 E6
Westleigh (Wellington) . . .51 A4
Weston 189 D6
Westward Ho! 156 D8
Westwood 83 C1
Whiddon Down 95 F3

Whimple 99 E7
Whitchurch 171 D3
Whitestone 98 E4
Whitford 103 B6
Whitstone 70 E1
Widecombe in the
  Moor 121 B4
Willand 162 E4
Wilmington 86 D3
Winkleigh 58 E2
Withecombe 46 F1
Withypool 21 C6
Wolverstone 85 A7
Woodbury 184 C3
Woodbury Salterton . . .184 C6
Woolacombe 7 F7
Woolfardisworthy 62 A3
Woolfardisworthy
  or Woolsery 38 E7
Wotter 132 D4
Wrafton 152 F4
Wrangaton 137 D8

Y
Yarcombe 69 A3
Yarnscombe 27 E2
Yealmpton 257 E4
Yelland 153 A4
Yelverton 127 A3
Yeoford 79 C1

Z
Zeal Monachorum 78 C7

A

A-la Ronde* EX8 196 A3
Abbeville Cl EX2 177 E3
Abbey Cl Axminster EX13 167 C4
Bovey Tracey TQ13 180 C7
Crapstone PL20 126 E2
Paignton TQ3 225 E5
Tatworth TA20 88 D8
Teignmouth TQ14 210 C7
Abbey Cross TQ9 227 A4
Abbey Ct Exeter EX2 178 F5
Plymouth PL1 263 A2
Abbey Gate La EX13 167 C2
Abbey Grange Cl TQ11 236 B7
Abbey La EX13 167 B3
Abbey Mdw TQ11 236 B7
Abbey Mews TA20 88 D8
Abbey Pl Plymouth PL1 262 C2
Tavistock PL19 171 C5
Abbey Rd
Barnstaple EX31 154 E6
Bovey Tracey TQ13 180 D7
Cornworthy TQ9 227 A4
Exeter EX4 177 F7
Torquay TQ2 220 A5
Abbey Rise
Okehampton EX20 170 D6
Tavistock PL19 171 C5
Abbey Sch The TQ1 220 C8
Abbeyfield Ho 7 TQ14 210 C5
Abbeyford Ct EX20 170 C5
Abbot Rd PL21 237 A6
Abbot's Cross EX36 31 E6
Abbot's Rd EX4 177 E8
Abbots Cl Lee Mill PL21 136 D6
Woolfardisworthy EX39 38 F8
Abbots Dr EX39 26 A4
Abbots Keep EX4 176 D6
Abbots Mdw EX37 28 F4
Abbotsbury Rd TQ12 207 B4
Abbotsbury Sch TQ12 207 D2
Abbotsbury Way PL2 247 F8
Abbotscourt La PL11 246 A2
Abbotsfield Cl PL19 126 A8
Abbotsfield Cres PL19 126 A8
Abbotsham Cross EX39 25 C4
Abbotsham La EX18 59 C3
Abbotsham Rd EX39 156 E2
Abbotshill TQ12 212 A6
Abbotskerswell Cross
TQ12 212 A7
Abbotskerswell Prim Sch
TQ12 212 B7
Abbotsridge Dr TQ12 206 F1
Abbotswood
East Ogwell TQ12 206 F1
Kingsteignton TQ12 207 F8
Abbotts Hill EX33 152 D6
Abbotts Pk PL21 133 C2
Abbotts Rd PL3 248 E6
Abbrook Ave 9 TQ12 123 E1
Abelia Cl TQ3 225 E8
Aberdeen Ave PL5 244 D2
Abingdon Rd 1 PL4 263 A4
Abney Cres PL6 245 B6
Above Town TQ6 233 F2
Abscott La PL9 255 C5
Abyssinia Ct 8 EX32 155 B3
Abyssinia Terr 7 EX32 155 B3
Acacia Cl Bideford EX39 156 E1
Kingsteignton TQ12 207 F6
Acacia Mews EX6 181 B1
Academic La EX18 44 E1
Acadia Rd TQ1 220 E4
Ackland Pk EX14 84 D2
Acklington Pl PL5 243 E4
Acland Cross EX32 17 B2
Acland Rd
Broadclyst EX5 175 C6
Exeter EX4 261 C4
Ivybridge PL21 237 A6
Landkey EX32 17 B2
Salcombe TQ8 259 D4
Acland Terr EX4 261 C4
Acland Way EX16 161 A6
Aclands EX36 158 D3
Acombe Cross TA3 68 B8
Acre Cl EX39 24 E2
Acre La TQ1 220 E6
Acre Pl PL1 247 F3
Acre Rd EX39 24 E2
Acre The TQ13 111 A6
Ada's Terr EX34 7 F8
Adam's La PL9 140 C8
Adams Cl Plymouth PL5 243 F1
Torpoint PL11 246 F3
Adams Cres PL11 246 E3
Adcroft Rise EX13 103 D5
Adder La EX31 16 B6
Addington Ct EX4 261 B4
Addiscombe La EX6 113 D5
Addison Cl EX4 176 E6
Addison Rd
Newton Abbot TQ12 207 E1
Paignton TQ4 226 A5
Plymouth PL4 263 A4
Addlehole TQ9 144 D7
Adela Rd PL11 247 A3
Adelaide Ct EX2 261 A1
Adelaide La PL1 262 A2
Adelaide Pl PL1 262 A3
Adelaide St
Plymouth PL1 262 A3
2 Plymouth, Ford PL2 247 F5
Adelaide Street Ope
PL1 262 A3
Adelaide Terr 3 EX34 150 B6
Adelphi La TQ4 226 C5
Adelphi Mans TQ4 226 C5
Adelphi Rd TQ4 226 C6
Adit La PL12 242 E3
Adits The PL18 125 D3
Adley La TQ13 111 B7
Admiral's Hard PL1 254 A8
Admirals Ct 5 EX39 156 F7
Admirals Wlk
Exmouth EX8 196 D2
Teignmouth TQ14 210 A8
Admiralty Cotts PL1 254 A7
Admiralty Rd
Plymouth, Millbay PL1 254 A8
Plymouth, St Budeaux PL5 243 C2
Admiralty St
Plymouth, Keyham PL2 247 E6
Plymouth, Millbay PL1 254 A8
Adrian Cl EX39 157 A4
Adworthy La EX17 46 B2
Affeton Castle Cross
EX17 60 F8
Affeton Hill EX17 60 F8
Affeton Moor Cross EX17 46 A2
Agaton Rd PL5 243 E3
Aidan Ave EX32 155 C2
Ailescombe Dr TQ3 225 F6
Ailescombe Rd TQ3 225 F6
Ainslie Terr PL2 247 E7
Aire Gdns PL3 249 B5
Airfield Ind Est EX14 67 B2
Aish Cross TQ9 224 E2
Aish La TQ10 134 E3
Aish Lane End TQ10 134 F2
Aish Pk EX21 55 E4
Aish Rd Paignton TQ4 225 B2
Stoke Gabriel TQ9 224 F2
Alamein Ct PL12 242 E2
Alamein Rd PL12 242 D2
Alandale Cl TQ14 210 C6
Alandale Rd TQ14 210 C6
Alansway EX11 169 C3
Alba Ct EX1 178 E7
Albany Cl EX8 196 E2
Albany Rd TQ3 219 A1
Albany St
3 Newton Abbot TQ12 207 C3
Plymouth PL1 247 E2
Albemarle Villas PL1 247 F3
Albert Ct 3 TQ1 220 B5
Albert La 7 EX32 155 A5
Albert Pl Exmouth EX8 202 A7
10 Totnes TQ9 223 C5
Albert Rd Crediton EX17 165 C5
Plymouth PL2 247 F3
Saltash PL12 243 A2
Torquay TQ1 220 B5
Albert St 17 Dawlish EX7 204 D6
Exeter EX1 261 C4
Albert Terr
Bovey Tracey TQ13 180 C7
Gunnislake PL18 125 C5
7 Newton Abbot TQ12 207 C3
Princetown PL20 128 B8
Alberta Cres EX4 177 F8
Alberta Ct 14 TQ14 210 C5
Albertha Cl PL4 263 B4
Albion Cl EX12 191 F8
Albion Ct
6 Exmouth EX8 202 A7
Torpoint PL11 247 B3
Albion Dr PL2 248 B7
Albion Gdns TQ7 258 C6
Albion Hill Exmouth EX8 202 B7
Newton Abbot TQ12 207 C2
Albion Pl Exeter EX4 261 C4
Exmouth EX8 202 A7
Albion Rd PL11 247 B3
Albion St Exeter EX4 177 A5
Exmouth EX8 202 A7
Teignmouth TQ14 210 A3
Albion Terr 9 EX8 202 A7
Alcester Cl PL2 247 E4
Alcester St PL2 247 F4
Aldborough Ct EX8 202 C6
Alden Wlk PL6 249 B7
Aldens Bsns Ct EX2 181 B8
Aldens Rd EX2 181 B8
Alder Cl
Newton Abbot TQ12 212 F8
Teignmouth TQ14 210 B7
Alder Glade EX31 154 C3
Alder Rd PL19 171 C3
Alderney Rd PL6 244 F7
Alders Way TQ4 225 D3
Aldersley Wlk PL6 245 A1
Alderson Dr EX2 178 D5
Aldridge Mill Hill EX16 48 C6
Aldrin Rd EX4 173 E2
Alexander Rd 23 EX7 204 D6
Alexandra Cl
Crediton EX17 165 A6
Plymouth PL9 256 B8
Alexandra Ct 3 EX32 155 A5
Alexandra Dr PL20 125 F1
Alexandra Ho TQ12 207 E2
Alexandra La TQ1 220 B6
Alexandra Pl
Cornworthy TQ9 227 B4
4 Plymouth PL4 248 E4
Alexandra Rd
Axminster EX13 167 C5
Alexandra Rd *continued*
Barnstaple EX32 155 A5
Crediton EX17 165 B6
1 Newton Abbot TQ12 207 C2
Plymouth, Crownhill PL6 244 F2
Plymouth, Ford PL2 247 F5
Plymouth, Mutley PL4 248 F4
Torquay TQ1 220 B6
Wellington TA21 160 D6
Alexandra Sq PL12 243 A2
Alexandra Terr
Bideford EX39 157 A3
Clyst Honiton EX5 175 E2
Exeter EX4 177 E7
Exmouth EX8 201 F6
Newton Abbot TQ12 207 C2
Plymouth PL2 247 F5
South Molton EX36 158 C5
1 Teignmouth TQ14 210 B4
1 Totnes TQ9 223 C6
Alexandra Way EX17 165 A6
Alexandria Ind Est EX15 163 D4
Alexandria Rd EX10 188 A6
Alexandria Terr 6 EX16 161 B4
Alfington Rd
Alfington EX11 84 F1
Ottery St Mary EX11 169 F6
Alford Cl EX1 178 C7
Alford Cres EX1 178 B7
Alford Terr EX35 151 B5
Alfred Pl PL2 247 F5
Alfred Rd PL2 247 F5
Alfred St PL1 262 C2
Alfriston Rd TQ3 225 D7
Alger Wlk PL6 244 E6
Alice La 7 PL1 262 B3
Alice St PL1 262 A3
Alison Rd TQ3 219 A1
All Hallows Rd TQ3 219 C2
All Saint's Rd EX10 188 A4
All Saints CE Inf Sch
EX10 188 B4
All Saints CE Prim Sch
TQ7 143 A2
All Saints CE Prim Sch
(Marsh) TQ12 207 D3
All Saints Cl EX9 198 B6
All Saints Ct EX14 166 A5
All Saints Pk PL18 125 B5
All Saints Sch EX13 88 A4
All Saints' Rd TQ1 220 C7
Allaleigh Cross TQ9 139 F4
Allaleigh La TQ9 139 F4
Allans Rd PL21 237 D6
Allen Bank EX32 155 A3
Allen Cl EX16 161 F5
Allenby Rd PL2 248 A6
Allendale Rd PL4 263 A4
Allenhayes La TQ8 259 D4
Allenhayes Rd TQ8 259 D4
Allenstyle Cl EX31 153 B5
Allenstyle Dr EX31 153 B5
Allenstyle Gdns EX31 153 B5
Allenstyle Rd EX31 153 B5
Allenstyle View EX31 153 A5
Allenstyle Way EX31 153 B5
Aller Brake Rd TQ12 212 F8
Aller Cl TQ12 213 A6
Aller Cotts TQ12 212 F7
Aller Cross
Chillington TQ7 145 A1
Kentisbeare EX15 65 F1
Kingskerswell TQ12 212 E6
South Molton EX36 29 F7
Aller Gate EX17 78 D5
Aller Grove Cotts EX5 99 F7
Aller Hill
Bishops Nympton EX36 31 A4
Dawlish EX7 204 B5
Aller La EX20 94 F8
Aller Park Rd TQ12 212 F8
Aller Rd Dolton EX19 57 F7
Kingskerswell TQ12 212 F6
Allercombe Cross EX5 99 E5
Allercombe Hill EX5 168 A6
Allercombe La EX5 99 E5
Allerdown Cross EX17 80 A7
Allern La PL5 240 C1
Allerton Wlk PL6 249 B7
Allervale Cl EX2 178 B4
Alley Hill PL20 126 D1
Alleyn Ct EX12 191 F7
Alleyne Gdns PL3 248 E8
Allhalland St 17 EX39 157 A2
Allhallows Ct Exeter EX4 261 A2
1 Honiton EX14 166 C6
Allington Mead EX4 173 A3
Allington Terr EX17 78 F7
Allison La EX17 95 D7
Allotment Dro TA20 69 F5
Allotment Gdns TQ7 258 D6
Allshire La EX16 32 F3
Alma Cotts PL4 263 B2
Alma La EX10 188 C4
Alma Rd Brixham TQ5 230 C5
Plymouth PL3 248 C4
Alma St PL4 263 B2
Alma Terr 16 EX32 155 A4
Almeria Ct PL7 250 D4
Alminstone Cross EX39 39 A7
Almond Ct 3 EX31 154 C2
Almond Dr PL7 251 B6
Almshouse Cross TQ10 135 E4
Alpha Ctr TQ9 223 C6
Alpha Pl 24 EX39 15 A1
Alpha St EX1 177 F6
Alpha Terr TQ9 223 B6
Alphin Brook Rd EX2 177 C1
Alphington Comb Sch
EX2 177 B1
Alphington Rd EX2 177 B3
Alphington St EX2 261 A1
Alpine Rd TQ1 220 B5
Alscott Gdns EX31 27 A4
Alston Cross
Ashburton TQ13 131 B6
Slapton TQ7 145 B5
Alston La TQ5 229 D4
Alston Terr EX8 201 F6
Alstone Rd EX16 161 F3
Alswear New Rd
Alswear EX36 30 C1
South Molton EX36 158 E3
Alswear Old Rd EX36 158 C2
Alta Vista Cl TQ14 210 D7
Alta Vista Rd TQ4 226 C4
Altamira EX3 182 F5
Altamira Cotts EX39 25 D2
Alton Pl PL4 248 E4
Alton Rd PL4 263 A4
Alverdiscott Rd EX39 26 B4
Alvington St PL4 263 C2
Alwin Pk PL6 245 A5
Alwyns Cl 3 TQ14 210 C5
Alwyns Ct 3 TQ14 210 C5
Amacre Dr PL9 255 B6
Amados Cl PL7 250 B4
Amados Dr PL7 250 C4
Amados Rise PL7 250 C4
Ambassador Dr EX1 178 E7
Amberley Cl TQ13 130 E5
American Rd EX33 15 A4
Amershaw Ct EX2 178 A4
Amherst Rd PL3 262 B4
Amherst Road La E PL3 262 B4
Amity Pl PL4 263 A4
Amory Pl EX36 158 C4
Amory Rd Dulverton TA22 33 D6
Tiverton EX16 161 C2
Amyas Way EX39 157 A6
Anchor Bldgs TQ12 123 B2
Anchor Cotts TQ7 147 B7
Anchor Mill EX31 154 E8
Anchorage Cl TQ5 230 E5
Anchorage The TQ4 226 C5
Ander's La TA3 68 E8
Anderton Cl PL19 171 E1
Anderton Ct PL19 171 E2
Anderton La PL19 171 D2
Anderton Rise PL10 252 F4
Andor Ave TQ12 207 D7
Andrew Allan Rd TA21 160 B4
Andrew Cl EX10 187 F8
Andrew Rd EX31 154 E3
Andrew's Hill TA22 33 D6
Andrew's Hill Cross
TA22 33 C6
Andrewshayes La EX13 87 A1
Andurn Cl PL9 256 B6
Andurn Est PL9 140 A8
Angel Ct 2 EX14 166 C6
Angel Hill EX16 161 C4
Angelhill Cross EX36 30 F2
Ann's Pl PL3 248 A4
Anne Cl EX4 173 E1
Anne Cres EX31 154 E3
Annery Kiln Cotts EX39 26 A1
Anning Rd DT7 260 E4
Anson Ho 1 PL1 262 B3
Anson Pl
Plymouth, Devonport PL2 247 F4
Plymouth, St Jude's PL4 263 C3
Anson Rd EX8 196 C2
Anstey Cres EX16 161 F3
Anstey Gate TA22 32 B8
Anstey Way EX39 15 B1
Anstey's Cove Rd TQ1 220 E6
Ansteys Cl TQ1 220 E5
Ansteys Ct EX16 46 E1
Anstis St Plymouth PL1 262 A3
Plymouth PL1 262 B3
Anthea Rd TQ3 218 F1
Anthony Pk PL19 171 D6
Anthony Rd EX1 177 F6
Antonine Cres EX4 176 E6
Antony Gdns PL2 248 C8
Antony Ho* PL11 246 D5
Antony Rd PL11 247 B3
Antony Woodland Gdn*
PL11 246 D6
Antrim Terr 5 TQ9 223 C6
Anvil Cnr EX22 72 D7
Anvil Ct PL17 115 B1
Anwyl Cl PL1 262 B3
Anzac Ave PL5 244 A4
Anzac St TQ6 233 F3
App's La EX39 25 E2
Apple Cl EX8 196 B3
Apple Dr EX15 162 D4
Apple Farm Grange
EX2 178 E3
Apple La EX2 178 E4
Apple Orch EX38 159 B4
Apple Tree Cl
Frogmore TQ7 144 E1
Witheridge EX16 46 E1
Apple Wharf 6 TQ9 223 D5
Applebee Way DT7 260 E4
Appleby Wlk PL5 244 D4
Appledore Cl EX15 163 B3
Appledore Hill EX20 170 F8
Applegarth Ave TQ12 206 E4
Applegarth Cl TQ12 206 E4
Applehayes EX8 202 C5
Applehayes La EX15 52 F2
Applemede EX5 82 B6
Appletree Cl
Barnstaple EX32 155 D4
Uffculme EX15 66 A7
Appletree Mews 5 EX39 15 A1
Appley Cross TA21 51 B8
April Cl EX8 196 B3
Apsley Rd PL4 248 D4
Apsley Terr
Braunton EX33 152 F7
9 Ilfracombe EX34 150 C5
Apsley Villas 8 EX34 150 C5
Apters Hill 7 TQ5 230 C5
Aqualand* TQ1 220 B3
Arbour Cl EX34 150 B3
Arbour The PL6 244 E5
Arcade Rd EX34 150 B6
Arcadia PL9 256 D6
Arcadia Rd PL9 256 C6
Arch St 5 TQ14 210 A3
Arch The EX5 184 B3
Archer Pl PL1 262 B4
Archer Terr PL1 262 B3
Archery Cl TQ7 258 C7
Archibald Rd EX1 261 C3
Archipark EX32 17 E1
Archway Ave PL4 249 B3
Archway Dr TQ6 233 D4
Arcot Gdns EX10 188 B6
Arcot Pk EX10 188 B6
Arcot Rd EX10 188 B6
Arden Cl EX9 199 G2
Arden Dr TQ2 219 D6
Arden Gr PL2 248 C8
Arden Ho TQ7 143 A1
Ardenney Ct EX8 202 C5
Ardwyn TA21 160 D4
Arena Pk EX4 174 B1
Argus Cl EX14 166 E6
Argyle Mews EX4 173 A1
Argyle Terr TQ9 223 B6
Argyll Rd EX4 173 B2
Arimoor Gdns PL19 171 E5
Ark Royal Cl PL5 247 D8
Arkwright Gdns PL5 243 F2
Arley Cl PL6 245 B6
Arlington Pl EX34 8 A6
Arlington Rd
Plymouth PL4 248 F4
Woolacombe EX34 7 F6
Arlington Terr 4 EX33 152 D5
Armada Cl EX12 192 A7
Armada Cres TQ2 219 C6
Armada Ct PL19 171 B4
Armada Ctr PL1 262 C3
Armada Dr TQ14 210 A8
Armada Rd PL10 253 A1
Armada St PL4 263 A4
Armada Way
Plymouth PL1 262 C2
Plymouth PL1 262 C3
Westward Ho! EX39 156 B6
Armourwood La EX5 81 D5
Armstrong Ave EX4 173 D2
Armytage Rd EX9 198 A2
Arnison Cl PL9 255 F5
Arnold Cres EX16 161 B2
Arnold's Cl TQ7 142 C6
Arnold's Point PL4 249 C3
Arnside Cl PL6 245 D3
Arran Cl TQ2 213 E2
Arscott Gdns PL9 255 C5
Arscott La PL9 255 D5
Arthington TQ1 219 F7
Arthur Terr PL11 247 B2
Arthurs Cl EX8 196 D2
Artillery Pl PL4 263 B1
Artisan's Dwellings
EX36 158 D4
Arun Cl PL3 249 C5
Arundel Cl EX2 181 B8
Arundel Cres PL1 262 B4
Arundel Terr PL2 247 F4
Arundell Cl PL16 105 E4
Arundell Gdns PL16 105 E4
Arundell Pl TQ7 143 E7
Arundell Rd EX20 77 C4
Arundells Cnr 3 EX17 165 D5
Ascension Way TQ2 213 F2
Ascerton Cl EX10 188 B5
Ascerton Rd EX10 188 B5
Ash Bridge Cross EX20 95 D1
Ash Cl 7 PL20 126 F3
Ash Cross Bradninch EX5 82 F7
Dartmouth TQ6 232 D1
Halberton EX16 65 A6
Oakford EX16 48 D6
Petrockstow EX20 56 F3
Ash Ct Crediton EX17 165 C6
Lee Mill PL21 136 D6
Ash Dr EX15 163 C5
Ash Farm Cl EX1 174 F1
Ash Gr Exmouth EX8 196 B2
Ivybridge PL21 237 E5
Plymouth PL2 247 F7
Seaton EX12 192 A8
Ash Hill Oakford EX16 48 D6
Petrockstow EX20 56 F3
Ash Hill Cross EX16 48 D6
Ash Hill Ct EX12 191 C5
Ash Hill Rd TQ1 220 A6
Ash La Iddesleigh EX19 57 F1
Withypool TA24 21 F6
Woolfardisworthy EX17 62 A2
Ash Mill Hill EX36 31 B2
Ash Plants Cl EX39 156 D2
Ash Rd Braunton EX33 152 F7
Kingsteignton TQ12 207 E6
Ash Vale PL16 105 E4

sh Way TQ12 207 F1
shacre Cross TQ1 214 B7
shburgh Parc PL12 242 B3
shburn Gdns TQ13 130 F5
shburn Wlk TQ4 229 B8
shburnham Rd PL5 244 A3
shburton & Buckfastleigh Hospl TQ13 131 A5
shburton Cl
Ashburton TQ13 130 F4
Bovey Tracey TQ13 180 C5
shburton Mus* TQ13 130 F4
shburton Prim Sch TQ13 130 F4
shburton Rd
Bickington TQ12 131 F6
Bovey Tracey TQ13 180 C5
Newton Abbot TQ12 206 D4
Totnes TQ9 223 B7
shbury Cross EX20 93 B5
shby Station Cross EX20 92 C7
shclyst View EX5 175 D6
shcombe Cl PL7 250 C7
shcombe Cross EX7 124 C6
shcombe Hill PL8 257 F2
shcombe Rd EX7 204 B8
shculm Hill EX15 52 C2
shdown Cl PL6 245 E3
shdown Cross EX22 38 F3
shdown Wlk PL6 245 E3
sheldon Ho TQ1 220 E5
sheldon Rd TQ1 220 E5
shelford Cnr EX31 10 A3
shery Dr PL9 255 C6
shes Rd Dalwood EX13 87 B1
Shute EX13 103 B8
shfield Cl Ashford EX31 16 B6
Exmouth EX8 196 E1
shfield La EX31 16 B6
shfield Rd TQ2 219 E5
shfield Terr EX39 157 A7
shford Cl PL3 249 A4
shford Cres PL3 249 A4
shford Hill PL4 249 A4
shford Rd Plymouth PL4 248 F4
Topsham EX3 182 E5
Wellington TA21 160 D4
shill TQ14 209 A8
shlake Rd EX6 113 F7
shleigh EX2 181 A8
shleigh Cl Exeter EX4 176 F6
Plymouth PL5 244 C7
Teignmouth TQ14 210 B7
Torquay TQ2 213 F3
shleigh Cres EX32 155 B4
shleigh Ct TQ1 220 D3
shleigh Dr TQ14 210 B7
shleigh La PL5 240 D1
shleigh Mount TQ14 210 B7
shleigh Mount Rd EX4 176 F6
shleigh Pk
Bampton EX16 49 C8
Teignmouth TQ14 210 B7
shleigh Prim Sch EX32 155 A5
shleigh Rd
Barnstaple EX32 155 A5
Exmouth EX8 202 C7
Honiton EX14 166 B6
Kingsbridge TQ7 258 B4
shleigh Rise TQ14 210 B7
shleigh Way
Plymouth PL7 251 C4
Teignmouth TQ14 210 B7
shley Back La EX16 64 A5
shley Brake EX11 168 D4
shley Cl EX15 66 B8
shley Cres EX10 188 A7
shley Ho EX8 202 B6
shley Priors La TQ1 214 C4
shley Rd
Okehampton EX20 170 C5
Uffculme EX15 66 A7
shley Rise EX16 161 B1
shley Terr EX39 156 F1
shley Way EX7 204 F7
shmead Gr EX33 152 C6
shmill Cross EX21 90 F6
shmill Ct TQ12 206 F4
shplants Cl EX19 58 F3
shprington Cross TQ9 139 F8
shridge Gdns
Kingsteignton TQ12 207 F6
Plymouth PL5 244 B2
shridge La EX20 77 D6
shridge Moor Cross EX20 77 E6
shton Cl PL6 245 C6
shton Cres EX33 152 C5
shton Ct 11 TQ12 123 F1
shton Ind Units EX2 177 B2
shton Rd EX2 177 B2
shton Terr TQ1 220 E5
shton Way PL12 242 D3
shtown Cross EX16 34 A3
shtree Cl PL6 245 D7
shtree Gr PL9 256 C8
shwater Prim Sch EX21 90 F6
shwell La TQ13 122 E6
shwood 4 TQ10 134 F3
shwood Cl
Loddiswell TQ7 143 E7
Plymouth PL7 251 B5
shwood Park Rd PL7 251 C6
shwood Pk TQ7 143 E7
shwood Rd EX2 177 B3
spen Cl Exeter EX2 178 C4
Aspen Cl *continued*
3 Honiton EX14 85 C2
Tavistock PL19 171 C3
Aspen Dr TQ12 212 F8
Aspen Gdns PL7 251 B5
Aspen Way Paignton TQ4 225 D3
Tiverton EX16 161 E7
Astley Ct EX20 170 A5
Astor Dr PL4 249 C3
Aswell Orch TQ7 143 F7
Athelstan Cl EX13 167 D4
Athelstan Rd EX1 261 C3
Athenaeum La PL1 262 B2
Athenaeum Pl PL1 262 C2
Athenaeum St PL1 262 B2
Atherton Pl PL2 247 E4
Atherton Way EX16 64 D7
Atkinson Cl EX4 174 A1
Atlantic Village EX39 25 D4
Atlantic Way EX39 156 D7
Attwyll Ave EX2 178 A5
Atway Cl 3 TQ13 180 C8
Atwill's Almshouses EX4 261 A4
Atworthy Cross EX22 38 D3
Auckland Rd 3 PL2 248 A5
Auction Way EX39 38 F8
Audley Ave TQ2 219 F8
Audley Rise TQ12 208 A1
Augustine Cl EX12 191 F8
Aunay Cl EX22 164 D5
Aune Cl TQ10 135 B1
Aunemouth Cross TQ7 143 A3
Ausewell Cross TQ13 130 D7
Austen Cl EX4 178 C8
Austin Ave PL2 248 A6
Austin Cres PL6 245 C1
Austin Farm Prim Sch PL6 249 C7
Authers Hts EX16 161 B2
Auton Cross TQ7 258 A2
Avalon Cl EX4 174 A2
Aveland Rd TQ1 220 C7
Avent Wlk PL7 250 F7
Avenue Cl DT7 260 D3
Avenue Rd
Bovey Tracey TQ13 180 C6
Ilfracombe EX34 150 B6
Kingskerswell TQ12 213 A5
Lyme Regis DT7 260 D3
Torquay TQ2 219 F5
Avenue Terr TQ5 229 E5
Avenue The Exton EX3 183 C1
Newton Abbot TQ12 207 D4
3 Seaton EX12 192 A5
Tiverton EX16 161 E3
Avery Hill TQ12 207 E8
Avery Way PL12 242 C5
Aveton Gifford CE Prim Sch TQ7 143 C6
Aviemore Ind Est EX31 154 D3
Avoca Ave TQ1 219 F6
Avocet Dr EX3 183 C2
Avocet Rd EX2 178 F6
Avon Cl Plymouth PL3 249 D6
South Brent TQ10 135 A2
Avon La EX39 156 D7
Avon Quillet TQ7 142 E3
Avon Rd Bideford EX39 157 C1
Torquay TQ2 219 B7
Avon Valley Cotts TQ7 143 C6
Avondale Ho 9 TQ10 134 F2
Avondale Rd Exeter EX2 178 A5
Exmouth EX8 202 D8
Avondale Wlk 10 TQ10 134 F2
Avranches Ave EX17 165 A6
Awliscombe Prim Sch EX14 85 B4
Axe Cl PL3 249 D6
Axe Vale Cvn Pk EX12 192 B6
Axe Valley Cl EX13 104 C7
Axe Valley Com Coll The EX13 167 D6
Axeford TA20 88 E8
Axeford Mdws TA20 88 E8
Axeview Rd EX12 192 A7
Axminster Com Prim Sch EX13 167 E6
Axminster Hospl EX13 167 D6
Axminster Mus* EX13 167 D5
Axminster Rd
Charmouth DT6 104 F4
Honiton EX14 166 F5
Musbury EX13 103 D5
Offwell EX14 86 A3
Tatworth TA20 88 C7
Axminster Sta EX13 167 C5
Axmouth Rd EX12 192 C5
Axtown La PL20 126 F2
Aycliffe Gdns PL7 251 A3
Aylesbury Cres PL5 244 B5
Aylescott Cross EX37 43 E3
Aylescott Hill EX34 9 A4
Aylescott La EX34 9 A4
Ayleston Cross PL21 137 D2
Ayleston Pk PL21 137 C2
Aylwin Cl PL7 250 E6
Ayres Cl EX39 157 C1
Ayreville Rd PL2 248 B7
Ayreville Residential Pk TQ4 224 F5
Aysha Gdns EX39 156 D8
Ayshford EX15 66 A7
Azalea Cl EX14 67 C1
Azes La EX32 155 A5

B

Babbacombe CE Prim Sch TQ1 220 D6
Babbacombe Cl PL6 249 E8
Babbacombe Downs Rd TQ1 220 D8
Babbacombe Model Village* TQ1 220 C8
Babbacombe Rd TQ1 220 E6
Babbage Rd TQ9 223 D6
Babbages EX31 154 A4
Babblebrook Mews EX1 178 F8
Babeleigh Cl EX39 40 B7
Babeleigh Water EX39 39 E7
Baber Ct PL12 125 A2
Babis Farm Cl PL12 242 F1
Babis Farm Ct PL12 242 F1
Babis Farm Mews PL12 242 F2
Babis Farm Row PL12 242 F1
Babis Farm Way PL12 242 F2
Babis La PL12 242 F1
Babland Cross PL21 137 D2
Bableigh Cross EX32 28 B8
Bableigh Rd EX32 17 B1
Babylon La EX5 82 B5
Back Hill PL12 242 D2
Back Hill Ind Est EX18 44 E1
Back La Abbotsham EX39 156 A1
Bickleigh EX16 63 D2
Black Torrington EX21 74 A8
Bradninch EX5 82 E6
Chittlehampton EX37 28 F4
Chulmleigh EX18 44 E1
Colaton Raleigh EX10 186 B3
Copplestone EX17 79 A4
Ermington PL21 136 F3
Frithelstockstone EX38 40 F5
Lutton PL21 133 B2
Merton EX20 57 A7
Newton Poppleford EX10 186 E8
North Molton EX36 30 D8
Plymouth PL7 250 E4
Sandford EX17 80 A5
Sidmouth EX10 187 C7
Sticklepath EX20 95 A5
Stockland EX14 87 A5
Back Rd Calstock PL18 125 D3
Moreleigh TQ9 139 A3
Newton Abbot TQ12 207 B3
Back St Bampton EX16 34 B1
Modbury PL21 137 B2
Woolfardisworthy EX39 38 F8
Back's Hill Crediton EX17 79 F7
Sandford EX17 80 A7
Backfield 7 EX39 15 A1
Backs The TQ6 233 E5
Backshay Cl TQ7 143 C1
Backshay Pk TQ7 143 C1
Backstone La EX16 47 B6
Backswood La EX16 64 B4
Backways La TA21 51 F6
Backwells Mead EX24 102 B6
Bad Homburg Way EX2 181 D8
Badgaver La EX34 3 B3
Badger Cl
Dartmouth TQ6 233 D4
Exeter EX2 178 D5
Honiton EX14 166 E7
Newton Poppleford EX10 186 D7
Paignton TQ3 218 F1
Badger's Way TQ13 180 D7
Badgers Cl
Ivybridge PL21 237 A5
Kingsbridge TQ7 258 C4
Kingsteignton TQ12 207 D8
Badgers Gn TQ7 258 C4
Badgers Wlk PL12 242 D4
Badlake Cl EX7 204 C7
Badlake Hill EX7 204 C7
Badlake La EX36 32 D6
Badlake Moor Cross TA22 32 D7
Badon Cl EX4 174 A2
Bagley Rd TA21 160 A3
Bagmore Hill EX5 82 F8
Bagshot Ave EX2 177 D3
Bailey La EX5 98 F7
Bailey St EX4 261 B3
Bailey Terr EX22 70 F5
Bailey's Knapp EX16 50 B4
Baileys Mdw TQ6 146 B7
Bainbridge Ave PL3 248 F7
Bainbridge Ct PL7 250 E7
Baker Cl EX10 188 A8
Baker St EX2 177 F5
Baker's Cross TA3 68 A7
Baker's Hill
Newton Abbot TQ12 207 B3
Tiverton EX16 161 A4
Baker's La
Churchinford TA3 68 A7
Wellington TA21 160 E6
Baker's Pk TQ13 130 A4
Bakers Cl PL7 251 C5
Bakers Cotts EX8 195 F5
Bakers Court La EX35 151 B5
Bakers Hill
Aveton Gifford TQ7 143 C6
Brixham TQ5 230 C3
Exeter EX2 176 C3
Bakers Mead EX13 87 A1
Bakers Pl PL1 247 F1
Bakers Terr TQ7 143 C6
Bakers View TQ12 207 A3
Bakery La EX8 202 A7
Bakery Mdw EX16 62 B5
Bakery Way EX32 17 B2
Bal La PL19 117 E6
Bala Brook Cl TQ5 229 F2
Baldwin Dr EX20 170 D6
Balfour Cl EX14 166 E5
Balfour Gdns EX10 188 A6
Balfour Manor EX10 188 A5
Balfour Manor Ct EX10 187 F5
Balfour Mews EX10 188 A5
Balfour Terr
Kilmington EX13 87 C1
Plymouth PL2 247 E4
Balfours EX10 188 A6
Balkwill Ct TQ7 258 C4
Balkwill Rd TQ7 258 C4
Balkwills Cotts EX21 55 E4
Ball Hill EX17 63 A2
Ball Hill La EX20 170 D5
Ball La EX24 101 F5
Ball's Cross TQ8 259 C7
Balland La TQ13 131 A5
Balland Pk 5 TQ13 131 A5
Ballards Cres EX31 153 A4
Ballards Gr EX31 153 A4
Ballards Way EX31 153 A4
Balleroy Cl EX21 55 E4
Ballhill La EX16 49 B8
Balls Cnr Burrington EX37 44 A3
Merton EX20 57 C8
Balls Corner Cross EX20 57 C8
Balls Cross EX36 20 B2
Balls Farm Rd EX2 176 F2
Balls Hill EX37 44 A2
Balmoral Ave PL2 247 F5
Balmoral Cl TQ12 207 E2
Balmoral Cres EX20 170 D5
Balmoral Gdns EX3 182 F5
Balmoral Ho EX31 154 E7
Balmoral La 6 TQ10 134 F3
Baltic Wharf Bsns Pk TQ9 223 D4
Bampflyde Way PL6 244 D6
Bampfylde Cl
Poltimore EX4 174 F6
Tiverton EX16 161 F3
Bampfylde Cross EX36 19 D2
Bampfylde Rd TQ2 219 F5
Bampfylde St EX1,EX4 261 C3
Bampfylde Way PL6 244 E6
Bampton Cl TQ3 218 D2
Bampton Down Rd EX16 49 F7
Bampton Prim Sch EX16 34 B1
Bampton Rd PL6 245 E1
Bampton St EX16 161 D4
Bamson La EX16 62 B6
Banbury Pk TQ2 219 C8
Banfield Way EX14 166 B4
Bank End EX39 157 B4
Bank La Brixham TQ5 230 C5
6 Totnes TQ9 223 C5
Bank Sq TA22 33 D6
Bank St
Newton Abbot TQ12 207 B3
12 Teignmouth TQ14 210 C4
Bankland La EX20 77 D8
Banksia Cl EX16 161 E7
Bankside EX8 196 C3
Bannawell St PL19 171 B6
Bantham Cross TQ7 143 D4
Baptist Chapel Ct EX17 165 C5
Baptist St PL17 125 D3
Bapton Cl EX8 196 B2
Bapton La EX8 196 B1
Bar's La EX9,EX10 199 B8
Barber's La Uplyme DT7 260 B4
West Buckland TA21 52 F7
Barbican App PL4 263 B2
Barbican Cl EX32 155 A4
Barbican Ct Exeter EX4 177 A5
12 Plymouth PL4 263 A2
Barbican La EX32 155 B4
Barbican Leisure Pk PL4 263 C2
Barbican Pl 9 EX32 155 A4
Barbican Rd
Barnstaple EX32 155 A4
Plymouth PL7 250 E4
Barbican Stps
Exeter EX4 177 A6
Exeter EX4 261 A2
Barbican Terr EX32 155 A4
Barbican The PL1 263 A2
Barbican Theatre PL1 263 A1
Barbrook Rd EX35 151 B3
Barbury Cres PL6 245 B8
Barchington Ave TQ2 213 F3
Barcombe Hts TQ3 226 B8
Barcombe La TQ3 226 B8
Barcombe Mews TQ3 226 B8
Barcombe Rd TQ3 226 A8
Barcote Wlk PL6 249 C8
Bardsey Cl PL6 245 A7
Barewell Cl TQ1 220 B8
Barewell Rd TQ1 220 B8
Barfield Cl EX19 57 F7
Barfield Rd EX19 57 F7
Baring Cotts 14 TQ9 223 D5
Baring Cres EX1 177 E6
Baring Ct EX2 261 B1
Baring Flats EX1 177 E6
Baring St PL4 263 B4
Barker's Hill PL12 242 C1
Barkers Way EX20 77 C4
Barkingdon Manor TQ9 215 D7
Barlands Way EX19 57 F7
Barley Cl EX15 163 B2
Barley Farm Rd EX4 176 E4
Barley La EX4 176 D5
Barley Lane Sch EX4 176 D4
Barley Market St PL19 171 C6
Barley Mount EX4 176 F5
Barley Wlk EX6 201 A8
Barleycorn Field 6 EX32 17 B2
Barline EX12 191 D5
Barlow Rd EX31 155 A7
Barn Cl Barnstaple EX32 155 C3
Ivybridge PL21 237 A6
Plymouth PL7 251 D4
Shebbear EX21 55 E4
Whiddon Down EX20 95 F3
Barn Close La EX12 192 E5
Barn Cross EX14 85 F8
Barn Ct TQ5 229 E4
Barn Hayes EX10 187 F7
Barn Hill EX17 78 F7
Barn La EX9 197 F2
Barn Meads Rd TA21 160 E4
Barn Owl Cl TQ2 213 D3
Barn Park Cl TQ12 211 E2
Barn Park Rd
Fremington EX31 153 D5
Plymouth PL3 248 D6
Barn Pk Ashwater EX21 90 E6
Buckfastleigh TQ11 236 A5
Crediton EX17 165 C5
Liverton TQ12 122 F1
Saltash PL12 242 F3
Stoke Gabriel TQ9 227 F8
Wrafton EX33 152 E3
Barn Rd TQ4 226 C2
Barnacott Cross EX39 26 D8
Barnardo Rd EX2 261 C1
Barnards Farm EX12 191 D5
Barnards Hill La EX12 192 A7
Barncroft EX22 39 C1
Barndale Cres PL6 245 B6
Barne Barton Prim Sch PL5 247 D8
Barne Cl PL5 247 C8
Barne Cross TQ13 112 A2
Barne La PL5 243 D1
Barne Rd PL5 247 C8
Barnes Cl Honiton EX14 166 B4
Willand EX15 162 C5
Barnes Close Mead TA22 33 D6
Barnfield Crediton EX17 165 C5
East Allington TQ9 144 D7
Barnfield Ave EX8 202 D7
Barnfield Cl
Braunton EX33 152 E5
Crediton EX17 165 C5
Galmpton TQ5 229 C5
Barnfield Cres EX1 261 B3
Barnfield Dr PL7 251 C5
Barnfield Hill EX1 261 C3
Barnfield Rd
Brixham TQ5 230 D3
Exeter EX1 261 B3
Exeter EX1 261 C3
Paignton TQ3 226 A7
Torquay TQ2 219 D2
Barnfield Terr TQ12 212 B6
Barnfield Wlk TQ7 258 C6
Barnhay 6 EX16 34 B1
Barnhay The TQ9 227 F7
Barnhill Rd TQ12 213 A4
Barningham Gdns PL6 245 A6
Barnmeads Rd TA21 160 E4
Barnpark Cl TQ14 210 C6
Barnpark Rd TQ14 210 C5
Barnpark Terr TQ14 210 C6
Barns Cl Bradninch EX5 82 F6
Kingsteignton TQ12 207 E6
Barns Close Ind Est TA22 33 D6
Barns Rd EX9 198 B1
Barnsclose TA22 33 D6
Barnsclose N TA22 33 D6
Barnsclose W TA22 33 D6
Barnsey Gdns TQ13 130 F5
Barnsfield La TQ11 236 A5
Barnshill Cl EX17 62 F1
Barnsley Cl 1 TQ14 210 C5
Barnsley Dr TQ14 210 C6
Barnstaple C Ctr EX31 154 E5
Barnstaple Cl
Chittlehampton EX37 28 F4
Plymouth PL6 249 E7
Barnstaple Cross
Burrington EX37 43 C3
Crediton EX17 79 E4
Barnstaple Ret Pk EX31 154 F4
Barnstaple St
Bideford EX39 157 B2
South Molton EX36 158 C4
Winkleigh EX19 58 F3
Barnstaple Sta EX31 154 F4
Barnstone Ct EX2 181 A8
Barntown Gate EX19 58 E1
Barntown La EX19 58 D1
Barnwood Cl PL9 255 E5
Barons Pyke PL21 237 E4
Barons Rd PL20 127 B3
Barossa Rd PL11 247 B3
Barpark Cnr EX15 52 E3
Barrack La EX2 114 C7
Barrack Pl PL1 248 A1
Barrack Rd Exeter EX2 177 E4
Modbury PL21 137 B3
Ottery St Mary EX11 169 C3
Barrack St PL1 247 E2
Barracks Hill TQ9 223 A7
Barradon Cl TQ2 214 A4
Barrington Ho TQ1 220 E5

Barrington Mead EX10 ...188 B4
Barrington Rd TQ1 ......220 E5
Barrington St EX16 ....161 D4
Barris 60 C3
Barrow Way EX31 ......154 B1
Barrow Down PL22 ....242 B3
Barrow Rd EX14 ....84 C4
Barrow Way Cross
EX20 ....110 D8
Barrowdale CI EX8 .....196 C3
Barry Sq TQ4 ....226 C6
Bartholomew Rd PL2 ..248 B5
Bartholomew St W EX4 .261 A2
Bartholomew Terr EX4 .261 A2
Barton Ave
Braunton EX33 ....152 D4
Paignton TQ3 ....225 F7
Plymouth PL2 ....247 E5
Barton CI
Cheriton Fitzpaine EX17 ...62 E1
Exton EX3 ....183 C1
Kingsbridge TQ7 ....258 D4
Paignton TQ3 ....225 F7
Parkham EX39 ....39 E8
Plymouth PL7 ....251 C5
Stoke Canon EX5 ....81 F1
Wembury PL9 ....140 D8
Barton Close La EX33 ......8 B4
Barton Cnr EX17 ....61 B2
Barton Cotts EX20 ....95 C1
Barton Court La EX5 ....172 A8
Barton Cres Dawlish EX7 .204 C6
Paignton TQ3 ....225 F7
Barton Cross
East Anstey EX16 ....32 E5
Filleigh EX32 ....29 A6
Heasley Mill EX36 ....15 B2
Morchard Bishop EX17 ...61 C2
Poltimore EX5 ....174 B8
Sandford EX17 ....80 C6
Torquay TQ2 ....213 F4
Barton CI Ashwater EX21 ...90 E6
Exeter EX1 ....178 C7
Parkham EX39 ....39 E8
Barton Dr
Newton Abbot TQ12 ....206 F3
Paignton TQ3 ....225 F7
Barton Gate La 3 EX34 ......3 A3
Barton Gdns TQ3 ....225 F7
Barton Head Cross 76 C4
Barton Hill
Berrynarbor EX34 ....2 E4
Daccombe TQ1,TQ12 ...214 A6
Dawlish EX7 ....204 D6
North Tawton EX20 ....77 C4
Barton Hill Rd TQ2 .....213 F2
Barton Hill Way TQ2 ..213 F2
Barton Ho EX20 ....26 A4
Barton Inf Sch TQ2 ....213 F2
Barton Jun Sch TQ2 ...213 F2
Barton La Berrynarbor EX34 ...2 E4
Bratton Fleming EX31 ...11 D3
Braunton EX33 ....152 D5
Brayford EX32 ....18 F4
Dawlish EX7 ....204 D6
Lapford EX17 ....60 A2
Shillingford Abbot EX2 ..114 C7
Staverton TQ9 ....216 A5
Witheridge EX16 ....46 E1
Barton Lane CI EX33 ...152 D4
Barton Meadow Rd EX37 ...43 E7
Barton Mews Exton EX3 .183 C1
Millbrook PL10 ....252 F6
Parkham EX39 ....39 E8
Tipton St John EX11 ...100 B2
Barton Orch EX10 ....100 D2
Barton Paddocks EX10 .100 D2
Barton Rd
Barnstaple EX32 ....154 D2
Buckland Brewer EX39 ...40 B7
Exeter EX2 ....176 F4
Ilfracombe EX34 ....8 F5
Okehampton EX20 ....170 C5
Paignton TQ3 ....225 F7
Parkham EX39 ....39 E8
Plymouth PL9 ....255 B6
Tiverton EX16 ....161 D6
Torquay TQ2 ....219 E7
Woolacombe EX34 ....7 F6
Barton Rd Ind Units
TQ2 ....219 E8
Barton Rise EX14 ....84 C2
Barton St EX16 ....77 C4
Barton Steep EX35 ....5 A4
Barton Terr EX4 ....204 D6
Barton The TA4 ....35 E8
Barton Tors EX37 ....204 D6
Barton Villas EX7 ....204 C6
Bartonbury Cross EX17 ...78 A6
Bartonhill Cross EX19 .215 F6
Bartows Cswy EX16 .....161 D5
Bartows Mews EX16 ....161 D5
Bartridge Hill EX31 ....27 A5
Barum Arc EX22 ....155 A5
Barum CI TQ12 ....226 C7
Barwick Cross EX19 ......58 B2
Bary CI EX17 ....62 F1
Bary Hill Cross EX17 ....62 F1
Bary La EX17 ....62 F2
Bascombe CI TQ5 ....229 D6
Bascombe Rd TQ5 ....229 D6
Basinghall CI PL9 ....255 E5
Basket Ope PL4 ....263 A2
Bason Cross EX22 ....55 B2

Bassett CI EX39 ....156 F8
Bassetts Farm Prim Sch
EX8 ....196 E1
Bassetts Gdns EX8 .....196 D2
Bastard's La EX38 ....159 D6
Bastard's Park Cnr
PL21 ....137 D3
Batcombe La EX5 ....81 F6
Bate CI EX2 ....177 A1
Bath CI EX14 ....84 D2
Bath Ct EX14 ....156 C7
Bath Hotel Rd EX39 ....156 C7
Bath La Plymouth PL1 ..262 B2
Torquay TQ2 ....219 F5
Bath Meadow Dr EX22 ...33 E6
Bath PI Ilfracombe EX34 .150 B6
Plymouth PL1 ....262 B2
Bath Pl W PL1 ....262 B2
Bath Rd EX8 ....202 A6
Bath St EX1 ....262 B2
Bath Terr 6 Instow EX39 ...15 B1
Teignmouth TQ14 ....210 C4
Batson Cross TQ8 ....259 C5
Batson Gdns TQ4 ....226 B4
Batson Hall Cross TQ8 .259 C6
Batsworthy Cross EX16 ...46 F7
Batsworthy Hill EX16 ....47 A7
Batt's La EX11 ....169 D3
Battens EX14 ....87 A7
Battens Cross EX16 ....65 C8
Batter St PL4 ....263 A2
Batterbridge Hill PL17 .117 E3
Batteridge Hill PL19 ...117 E3
Battershall CI PL9 ......255 F5
Battersway Rd TQ4 .....225 E4
Battery La PL19 ....171 C4
Battery St PL1 ....262 A2
Battery Street Flats
PL1 ....262 A2
Battishorne Way EX14 .166 B4
Battle Rd TQ12 ....180 F2
Battle St EX15 ....52 E1
Battledown Cross EX21 ...55 F4
Battleford La TQ9 ....217 C5
Battleton TA22 ....3 D4
Batts Pk EX15 ....66 C6
Batworthy Mill Cross
TQ13 ....111 A4
Bavent CI EX5 ....173 F8
Baxter CI EX2 ....178 D3
Baxworthy Cross EX39 ...23 A1
Bay Ct EX12 ....192 B4
Bay Rd EX9 ....199 A7
Bay Trees EX14 ....94 C8
Bay View TQ3 ....219 D1
Bay View CI EX39 ....146 B7
Bay View Ct EX39 ....156 F6
Bay View Dr TQ14 ......210 C6
Bay View Rd TQ4 ....146 B7
Bay View Rd
Northam EX39 ....156 F6
Woolacombe EX34 ....7 F6
Bayard's Cove TQ6 .....233 F3
Bayard's Hill TQ6 ....233 F3
Baydon CI PL6 ....245 C1
Bayly's Rd PL9 ....255 B7
Baymount Rd TQ3 ......226 A7
Baynes CI TA21 ....140 A8
Bayside La PL9 ....262 B4
Bayswater Rd PL1 ....262 B4
Baythorpe Lodge TQ2 .219 E2
Baytor Ind Est TQ4 .....225 D3
Baytree CI PL6 ....245 D6
Bayview Gdns PL2 ......248 A7
Bayview Rd EX7 ....260 D4
Baze La EX35 ....6 B4
Bazley Sq EX1 ....178 E8
Beach Rd Croyde EX33 ...7 D2
Dawlish Warren EX7 ....201 B2
Heybrook Bay PL9 ......140 A7
Ilfracombe EX34 ....150 F6
Paignton TQ4 ....226 C6
Seaton EX12 ....192 A5
Torquay TQ1 ....220 D7
Westward Ho! EX39 ....156 D7
Woolacombe EX34 ....8 A6
Beach St 11 EX7 ....204 E6
Beach View Cres PL9 .140 D7
Beacon Ave EX4 ....178 B8
Beacon Bsns Pk PL2 ...248 C7
Beacon Ct PL21 ....237 D6
Beacon Cotts TQ13 ....130 C7
Beacon Cross
Bradninch EX5 ....82 F7
Copplestone EX17 ....79 D6
North Tawton EX20 ....77 A2
South Molton EX36 ......45 C5
Talaton EX5 ....84 F5
Beacon Down Ave PL2 .248 B7
Beacon Down Cnr EX6 ..98 D2
Beacon Down Cross
EX20 ....93 E5
Beacon Down Hill EX20 .93 F5
Beacon Heath EX4 ......174 C1
Beacon Hill Bradninch EX5 .82 F7
10 Exmouth EX8 ....202 A6
Paignton TQ4 ....226 C6
Beacon Hill La EX14 .....87 A5
Beacon Ho PL3 ....248 C7
Beacon Hts EX32 ....152 C6
Beacon La
Bovey Tracey TQ13 .....123 A7
Cullompton EX15 ....65 A3
Exeter EX4 ....178 A8
Kingswear TQ6 ....234 A2
Beacon Park Rd PL2 ....248 B7

Beacon Pk PL15 ....89 D2
Beacon PI EX4 ....202 A6
Beacon Rd Bradninch EX5 .82 F7
Ivybridge PL21 ....237 C6
Kingswear TQ6 ....234 A2
Beacon Rise EX4 ....44 E1
Beacon Terr 4 TQ1 ....134 F2
Beacon The EX8 ....202 A6
Beacon View
Bittaford PL7 ....137 C7
Dartington TQ9 ....168 D2
10 South Brent TQ10 ..134 F2
Beacondown Cross EX4 ...63 E8
Beaconfield Rd PL2 ....248 B7
Beaconpark La EX20 .....95 D3
Beaconsfield Cross EX22 .72 E6
Beadon Dr TQ8 ....259 C4
Beadon La TQ13 ....123 A8
Beadon Rd
Salcombe TQ8 ....259 B4
Salcombe TQ8 ....259 C4
Beaford Com Prim Sch
EX19 ....42 D1
Bealey Court Cross EX18 .45 E2
Bealswood CI PL18 ......125 D6
Bealswood Rd PL18 ....125 D6
Beanhay CI 11 TQ12 ...122 F1
Beara Cross EX20 ....170 A5
Beaple's Moor Cross
EX36 ....47 A8
Bear St Barnstaple EX32 .155 A5
Exeter EX1 ....261 B2
Beara Cross
Bratton Fleming EX31 ...18 A8
Highampton EX21 ....74 A6
King's Nympton EX37 ...44 F6
Roborough EX38 ....42 E6
Beara Head EX36 ....42 E6
Beara Hill EX32 ....19 A5
Beara Hill Head EX36 ...19 A6
Beara La
Bratton Fleming EX31 ...18 A8
Combe Martin EX34 ....3 C3
Beardown Rd EX20 .....170 E5
Beards Rd EX31 ....153 E5
Beare Bridge Rd EX20 .170 C6
Beare Copse La EX19 ...58 F2
Beare Cross EX5 ....82 E3
Beare La EX5 ....82 E4
Bearne's La 8 TQ12 ...207 B3
Bearne's Prim Sch
TQ12 ....207 C3
Bears Cotts EX6 ....181 B2
Bears Farm Cotts EX20 .170 B7
Bears La EX9 ....197 E3
Bearsdown CI PL6 ......249 C8
Bearsdown Rd PL6 .....249 C8
Beaston Cross TQ9 .....131 D1
Beatland Cross PL7 ....132 C5
Beatlands Rd EX10 .....188 B4
Beatrice Ave
Plymouth Keyham PL2 ...247 F6
Plymouth St Jude's PL4 .263 B3
Saltash PL12 ....242 E1
Beatrice Gdns PL12 ....242 E1
Beattie Rd PL5 ....247 B8
Beatty CI PL6 ....245 A4
Beatty Way TQ6 ....233 F4
Beauchamp Cres PL2 .248 C7
Beauchamp Rd PL2 ....248 C7
Beaudyn WIk PL6 ......249 C7
Beaufort CI EX16 ....50 D1
Beaufort Ho 21 PL4 ....263 A2
Beaufort Rd EX2 ....261 A1
Beaufort WIk EX22 .....155 C6
Beauly CI PL7 ....251 A5
Beaumaris Gdns PL3 ..248 F8
Beaumaris Rd PL3 ......248 F7
Beaumont Ave PL4 .....263 A3
Beaumont CI
5 Liverton TQ12 ....122 F1
Torquay TQ2 ....219 D6
Beaumont PI PL4 ....263 A3
Beaumont Rd
Newton Abbot TQ12 ....207 C3
Plymouth PL4 ....263 B3
Beaumont St EX1 ....261 C3
Beaumont Terr PL12 ...242 F4
Beauvale CI EX11 ....169 E4
Beavers Brook CI TQ3 .218 D2
Beavor La EX13 ....167 F6
Beaworthy CI EX2 ......177 A3
Beccott Cross EX31 ......10 D4
Becket Rd TQ13 ....180 E7
Beckets Rd TQ7 ....258 D5
Beckford CI PL7 ....251 A5
Beckford Cross EX13 ...87 D7
Beckham PI PL3 ....249 A6
Beckland CI EX31 ....154 A2
Beckland Cross EX39 ...22 D1
Becky CI PL7 ....132 C3
Becky Falls * TQ13 ....122 A6
Bede Gdns PL5 ....244 C1
Bedford CI PL18 ....125 C6
Bedford Gr PL21 ....237 D5
Bedford Mews PL4 .....263 A4
Bedford Park Villas EX4 .263 A4
Bedford Pk
10 Bere Alston PL20 ...125 A1
Plymouth PL4 ....263 A4
Bedford Rd
Horrabridge PL20 ....126 F4
Plymouth PL9 ....255 E8

Bedford Rd continued
Torquay TQ1 ....220 D8
Bedford Row 15 EX31 .154 F5
Bedford Sq
Sidmouth EX10 ....188 B3
Tavistock PL19 ....171 C5
Bedford St
10 Barnstaple EX32 ....155 A5
Bere Alston PL20 ....125 E1
Exeter EX1 ....261 A2
Plymouth PL2 ....247 F5
Bedford Terr PL4 ....263 A4
Bedford Villas 7 PL20 .125 E1
Bedford Way PL1 ....262 C3
Bedlam La EX13 ....97 F2
Bedland's La EX9 ....197 F2
Beech Ave Exeter EX4 .173 D1
Plymouth PL4 ....263 C2
Beech Barton EX5 ....25 D4
Beech CI Barnstaple EX31 .154 B2
Broadclyst EX5 ....175 D6
Honiton EX14 ....166 A4
Tavistock PL19 ....171 C2
Torpoint PL11 ....247 A3
Totnes TQ9 ....222 F6
Willand EX15 ....162 D4
Beech Croft EX15 ....163 C5
Beech Ct Plymouth PL6 .245 D5
2 Wellington TA21 .....160 D6
Beech Dr
Down St Mary EX17 ......78 E7
Ipplepen TQ12 ....211 E2
Beech Gr
Barnstaple EX33 ....154 F7
Braunton EX33 ....152 C7
Wellington TA21 ....160 C6
Beech Grove Prim Sch
TA21 ....160 C6
Beech Hall EX31 ....160 F5
Beech Hill Cross EX31 ...61 B3
Beech La EX13 ....167 A4
Beech Lea EX18 ....58 F8
Beech Pk Crediton EX17 .165 D6
Fremington EX31 ....153 E5
Holsworthy Beacon EX22 .54 C3
West Hill EX11 ....168 D5
Beech Rd see Mill PL21 .136 C7
Stibb Cross EX38 ....40 D1
Beech Tree Cross TQ12 ...33 C7
Beech Tree Dr EX16 ....161 B5
Beech Tree Mdw EX20 .107 F8
Beech Trees La TQ12 ...211 C3
Beech WIk EX14 ....85 C1
Beechcroft Rd
Plymouth Lower Compton
PL3 ....249 A6
Plymouth, Beacon Park
PL2 ....248 B7
Beeches CI EX5 ....184 B2
Beeches The
Okehampton EX20 ....76 E1
Woolfardisworthy EX39 ...38 F8
Beechfield Ave
Torquay TQ2 ....213 F2
Yelverton PL20 ....127 A3
Beechfield Gr PL3 ....248 E6
Beechfield PI TQ12 .....213 F2
Beechfield Rd EX11 ....163 C6
Beeching CI EX21 ....73 E7
Beechtree La EX10,EX12 .101 F2
Beechway PL6 ....245 A8
Beechwood Ave
Barnstaple EX31 ....154 D4
Newton Abbot TQ12 ....207 E1
Plymouth PL4 ....248 D4
Beechwood CI EX31 ...154 D4
Beechwood Cres EX7 ..201 A2
Beechwood Cross PL7 .251 F7
Beechwood Ct EX14 ....124 E1
Beechwood Dr TQ7 ....258 D5
Beechwood Rd TQ13 ..123 C6
Beechwood Rise PL6 ...245 A8
Beechwood Terr PL4 ...248 D4
Beechwood Way PL7 ...251 D5
Beeley Dvrth Sch 161 C8
Beenleigh Cross TQ9 ..139 D6
Beer CE Prim Sch EX12 .191 C5
Beer Cross EX20 ....90 A6
Beer Head Cvn Pk EX12 .191 D4
Beer Heights Light Rly*
EX12 ....191 C5
Beer Hill Clawton EX22 ...72 B1
Seaton EX12 ....191 B5
Beer La Burlescombe EX16 .51 A2
Dulverton TA22 ....33 B5
Witheridge EX16 ....46 B7
Zeal Monachorum EX17 ...78 C7
Beer Quarry Caves*
EX12 ....191 C6
Beer Rd EX12 ....191 E6
Beerash Cross EX16 ......36 A5
Beere Cross EX36 ....32 A5
Beerhill La EX20 ....76 A6
Beers Hill EX17 ....79 A1
Beesands TQ7 ....149 E7
Beeson Cross TQ7 ......149 C8
Beeson Pool TQ7 ....149 C8
Beeston WIk 6 PL6 .....249 C7
Beetham La EX38 ....151 D2
Beetland La EX35 ....16 A3
Beetor Cross TQ13 ......111 A3
Beggar's Bush TQ10 ...134 F2
Beggars La EX14 ....166 A5
Behind Hayes EX9 ......198 E7
Bekhams Tree Cross
EX6 ....113 B2
Bel Tor Cnr TQ13 ....129 F8
Belair Rd PL2 ....248 C7

Belair Villas PL2 ....248 C7
Belcombe Dro TA20 ....209 E7
Belfield Ave TQ3 ....218 D3
Belfield CI TQ3 ....218 D3
Belfield Rd TQ3 ....225 E7
Belfield Rise TQ3 ....218 D3
Belfield Way TQ3 ....218 D3
Belgrave La PL4 ....248 F4
Belgrave Mews 5 TQ1 .220 B3
Belgrave Rd Exeter EX1 .261 C3
Newton Abbot TQ12 ....207 F1
Plymouth PL4 ....248 F4
Torquay TQ1 ....219 F5
Belgrave Terr
4 Teignmouth TQ14 ....210 C5
Upton Pyne EX5 ....173 A8
Bell CI PL7 ....250 F6
Bell Ct EX4 ....261 A3
Bell La
Bovey Tracey TQ13 .....123 A7
Paignton TQ3 ....225 B7
Bell Mdw EX16 ....64 A2
Bell St EX9 ....198 F7
Bella Vista Rd TQ5 .....230 C6
Belladown Hill EX31 ....27 A6
Bellaire EX31 ....154 E7
Bellaire Dr EX31 ....154 E7
Bellamarsh La TQ13 ...123 C4
Bellamy CI PL6 ....245 A1
Belle Acre CI PL3 ....248 E6
Belle Ave EX17 ....165 B5
Belle Cross Rd TQ7 ....258 E6
Belle CI EX17 ....165 B5
Belle Hill TQ7 ....258 E6
Belle Isle Dr EX2 ....261 C1
Belle Meadow CI EX18
EX32 ....154 F5
Belle Meadow Rd 8
EX32 ....155 A5
Belle Par EX15 ....164 C4
Belle Vue EX22 ....54 F4
Belle View Terr TA20 ...88 C8
Belle Vue EX4 ....60 A7
Belle Vue Ave
Lynton EX35 ....151 B5
Plymouth PL9 ....255 B5
Belle Vue CI EX16 ....114 E4
Belle Vue Cotts 8 EX2 .164 C4
Belle Vue Cross EX38 ...42 A8
Belle Vue Dr PL9 ....255 B5
Belle Vue Rd Exeter EX4 .173 A2
Exmouth EX8 ....202 A8
Kingsbridge TQ7 ....258 D5
Paignton TQ3 ....226 C5
Saltash PL12 ....242 F2
Belle Vue Rise PL9 .....255 B5
Belle Vue Terr
Bideford EX39 ....156 F2
Cullompton EX15 ....163 C4
Gunnislake PL18 ....126 C6
Bellever CI PL20 ....128 B8
Bellever Tor Dr TQ5 ...229 F2
Bellevue Sq PL11 ....247 B2
Bellingate PL7 ....79 A2
Bellingham Cres PL7 ..251 C4
Belliver Ind Est PL6 ....241 B1
Belliver Way PL6 ....241 B1
Bellows Pk PL8 ....257 B5
Bellrock CI TQ2 ....214 B3
Bells CI EX18 ....60 A7
Bellvue Terr EX16 ....114 D4
Belmont EX32 ....155 A5
Belmont Ave
Combe Martin EX34 ......2 F4
Ilfracombe EX34 ....150 A5
Belmont CI
34 Kingsteignton TQ12 ...123 F1
Tiverton EX16 ....161 D5
Belmont Ho Exeter EX4 .261 C4
5 Seaton EX12 ....192 A5
Belmont Hospl EX16 ...161 D5
Belmont PI PL3 ....248 A4
Belmont Rd
Barnstaple EX32 ....155 B6
Brixham TQ5 ....230 C4
Exeter EX4 ....261 C4
Ilfracombe EX34 ....150 A5
Ivybridge PL21 ....237 C6
Tiverton EX16 ....161 D5
Torquay TQ1 ....220 C6
Belmont St PL1 ....262 B3
Belmont Terr
Exmouth EX8 ....196 C1
Totnes TQ9 ....223 C6
Belstone Cr PL5 ....244 A3
Belstone Cnr Cross 76 A1
Belstone Cross EX20 ....94 E4
Beltor Cross TQ12 ......211 D1
Belvedere CI 3 TA21 ...160 D6
Belvedere Ct EX35 ......182 E6
Belvedere CI EX5 ....99 B2
Belvedere Rd
Exmouth EX8 ....202 A7
Ilfracombe EX34 ....150 B6
Newton Abbot TQ12 ....207 F5
Belvedere Rd
Exmouth EX8 ....202 A7
Ilfracombe EX34 ....150 B6
Newton Abbot TQ12 ....207 F5
Belvedere Rd
Ilfracombe EX34 ....154 F7
Belvoir Rd EX19 ....200 D4
Ben Jonson CI PL7 .....251 A4
Ben Venue CI TQ1 ......220 C5
Benbow St PL2 ....247 F5
Bench Tor CI TQ2 ....219 B7
Bendarroch Rd EX11 ...168 D5
Bendarroch Sch EX5 ....99 C2
Bendibus EX22 ....72 E2

Bendibus Hill EX21 ....72 E3
Bendle La EX36 ....30 E8
Bendle Lane Cross EX36 ..30 E8
Bendley Hill EX16 ....46 E1
Benedict CI TQ14 ....210 C7
Benedict Way PL21 ......137 B2
Benedicts CI 18 TQ12 ...122 F1
Benedicts Rd TQ12 .....122 F1
Benleaxs Acre 17 TQ12 ..122 F1
Benley Cross EX18 ....45 D2
Bennah Hill EX6 ....113 A3
Bennets La TQ12 ....242 F3
Bennett CI EX2 ....181 B8
Bennett Rd TQ8 ....259 D3
Bennett Rd EX4 ....178 A8
Bennett St PL1 ....247 E1
Bennett's Cross TQ9 ....139 C8
Bennetts CI TQ12 ......190 E4
Bennetts Hill EX10 .....187 F7
Benns CI TQ7 ....147 D7
Benson CI EX14 ....46 E1
Benson Dr EX39 ....157 A6
Benton Cross EX32 ......18 B7
Benton La EX31 ....18 B7
Benton Rd EX32 ....18 B8
Beraghah Rd TQ1 ......220 B6
Bere Alston Prim Sch
  PL20 ....125 E1
Bere Ferrers Sta PL20 ..125 E2
Bere Hill EX17 ....204 B6
Berea Rd TQ1 ....220 C6
Beresford St PL2 ......248 A4
Berkeley Ave TQ2 .....213 C1
Berkeley Ct EX34 ......150 B5
Berkeley Rise TQ2 .....213 C1
Berkeley Way PL21 ....237 D4
Berkshire Dr Exeter EX4 .176 E4
  Plymouth PL2 ....247 F5
Bernadette CI EX4 .....174 C1
Berner's Cross EX19 ....58 E4
Bernice CI PL4 ....249 B4
Bernice Terr PL4 ......249 B4
Berretts Way TQ12 ....123 A1
Berrow Park Rd PL3 ....248 E6
Berry Ave TQ3 ....225 F6
Berry CI
  Abbotskerswell TQ12 ..212 B6
  Exmouth EX8 ....202 E8
  Salcombe TQ8 ......259 C4
Berry Cross
  Dunsford EX6 ....112 E8
  Shebbear EX21 ....55 D5
Berry Down Cross EX34 ...9 F6
Berry Dr TQ3 ....226 A6
Berry Head Country Pk*
  TQ5 ....231 A5
Berry Head Gdns PL6 ..244 E1
Berry Head Rd TQ5 ....230 E6
Berry Hill Beer EX12 ...191 D5
  Bishopsteignton TQ14 ..208 F8
  Branscombe EX12 ....190 B4
  North Tawton EX20 ....59 C1
Berry La Axminster EX13 ..88 F3
  Beer EX12 ....191 D6
  Combe Martin EX34 ....2 F4
  Exmouth EX8 ....112 E8
Berry Mdw TQ12 ......207 E6
Berry Park CI PL9 .....255 F7
Berry Park Rd PL9 ....255 E7
Berry Pk PL12 ....242 D4
Berry Pomeroy Castle*
  TQ9 ....217 D1
Berry Pomeroy Parochial CE
  Prim Sch TQ9 ......224 B7
Berry Rd Barnstaple EX32 .155 C4
  Braunton EX33 ......152 E7
  Paignton TQ3 ......225 F6
Berry's Ground La EX31 ...4 C5
Berry's La PL7 ....133 A1
Berryball Fields EX20 ..170 C6
Berrybrook Mdw EX6 ...182 B3
Berrydown Cross EX34 ...2 F1
Berrynarbor Prim Sch
  EX34 ....2 E3
Berrys Wood TQ12 ....206 F3
Berthon Rd PL5 ......247 A5
Berwick Ave PL5 ......244 E3
Besigheim Way TQ12 ..207 F4
Besley CI EX14 ....161 C3
Best's La EX38 ....159 D5
Betham Hill EX16 ....46 F2
Betham La EX18 ....59 B6
Bethany Rd TQ12 .....122 F1
Bethel Cross TQ12 .....122 C1
Bethel Terr 11 TQ1 ....220 B5
Bethelcombe Cross
  TQ12 ....122 C1
Betjeman Wlk PL5 .....244 C3
Betjemen Dr EX8 ......196 C3
Betony Rise EX2 ......178 C3
Betton Way TQ13 .....111 F5
Bettys Mead EX4 .....178 A8
Beuvron CI EX39 ....38 F8
Bevan Rd EX2 ....155 A5
Beverley CI EX7 ......178 B4
Beverley Gdns 6 TQ13 .131 A5
Beverley Rd PL3 ......249 C4
Beverley Rise TQ5 ....230 B8
Beverley Way TQ12 ...207 A2
Beverston Way PL6 ....245 A1
Bevil CI EX39 ....157 A1
Beweys Pk PL12 ......242 C2
Bexhill Rd TQ9 ....222 F8
Bewsley Hill EX17 ......79 B5
Bexley La 6 TQ12 .....219 F5
Beyrout PI 6 PL1 .....247 F3
Bhutan CI EX14 ....166 D5
Bibors Hill TA4 ....35 E4

Bicclescombe Gdns
  EX34 ....150 B4
Bicclescombe Park Rd
  EX34 ....150 B4
Bickell Cross EX32 ......28 C6
Bickern Rd PL11 ......247 B3
Bickerton Top TQ7 ....149 C5
Bickfont Hill EX31 ......11 F4
Bickford La 2 TQ14 ...210 C4
Bickfords Gn 8 TQ12 ...88 A5
Bickham La TQ12 ......47 E7
Bickham Park Rd PL3 ..248 D7
Bickham Rd PL5 ......243 D2
Bickingcott Cross EX36 .31 C7
Bickington Hill EX36 ....31 C8
Bickington Lodge EX31 .16 A3
Bickington Rd EX31 ...154 C3
Bickleigh Castle* EX16 ..63 F1
Bickleigh Ct Exeter EX4 .174 D2
  Plymouth PL6 ....245 A1
Bickleigh Down CE Prim Sch
  PL6 ....245 D7
Bickleigh-on-Exe CE Prim
  Sch EX16 ....64 A2
Bickleton Cross EX31 ..153 A2
Bickley Mill Cross TQ12 .212 C1
Bickley Rd TQ12 ......212 C2
Bickwell House La EX10 .187 E5
Bickwell La EX10 .....187 F5
Bickwell Valley EX10 ..187 F4
Bickwill Cross EX36 ....46 D8
Bicton Coll EX9 ......245 D1
Bicton Coll EX9 ......186 C1
Bicton Park Botanical Gdns *
  EX9 ....198 C8
Bicton PI Exeter EX1 ..177 F6
  Exmouth EX8 ....202 A6
Bicton St
  Barnstaple EX32 ....155 A5
  Exmouth EX8 ....202 A6
Bicton Villas EX8 .....202 B6
Bidbrooke La EX36 ......32 A6
Biddacott Cross EX37 ...28 E4
Biddamoor La EX19 ....42 C2
Bidder CI TQ13 ....111 F4
Bidders CI TQ6 ....146 B7
Bidders Ct EX36 ......158 C4
Biddick Dr PL2 ....247 F6
Biddington Way EX14 ..166 A4
Biddlecombe Cross
  TQ12 ....124 A6
Biddypark La EX22 ....113 F6
Biddypark Lane Cross
  EX22 ....113 F6
Bideford & Torridgeside
  Hospl EX39 ....156 F2
Bideford Coll EX39 ...156 E1
Bideford Railway Mus*
  EX39 ....157 B1
Bideford Wlk PL6 ....249 E8
Bidewad Ct EX38 ....206 C7
Bidna La EX39 ....157 B8
Bidwell Brook Dr TQ4 ..226 C1
Bidwell Brook Sch TQ9 .215 F1
Bidwell Cross
  Langford EX5 ....172 E8
  Thorverton EX5 ......81 E6
Bidwell La
  Brampford Speke EX5 ..81 C1
  Thorverton EX5 ......81 F6
Biera View TQ13 .....111 A6
Big Sheep (Farm Pk) The*
  EX39 ....236 C4
Bigadon La TQ11 .....236 C4
Bigbury Way TQ2 ....214 B2
Bigbury Wlk PL6 .....249 E8
Biggin Hill PL5 ......243 F4
Bilbie CI EX15 ....163 B3
Bilbury St PL4 ....263 A2
Billacombe Rd PL9 ...249 E1
Billacombe Villas PL9 ..255 F8
Billhole La EX17 ....61 C6
Billing CI PL6 ....244 D6
Billington CI PL6 .....244 D6
Bilton Terr 11 EX39 ...157 A1
Biltor Rd TQ12 ....211 D1
Bilver Cross TQ12 ....217 C8
Bimbom La EX13 .....103 C8
Bindon Rd EX4 ....174 E2
Binford CI EX1 ....178 B6
Bingfield Ct TQ1 .....220 C5
Bingham Cres EX32 ...155 B4
Binhamy Rd EX23 ......70 A8
Binkham Hill PL20 ....127 A3
Binnamore Cross TQ10 .134 E4
Binneford Cross EX17 ...96 F8
Binneford Hill EX17 ....62 B5
Birch CI PL6 ....245 E7

Bircham View PL6 .....245 C1
Birchanger Cross TQ13 .122 B2
Birchen La
  Highampton EX20,EX21 ....74 E5
  7 Tiverton EX16 ....161 C4
Birchen Tree Cross EX15 ..66 C4
Birchenbeer Cnr EX17 ...61 C1
Birches The PL6 .....245 D6
Birchfield Ave PL2 ...248 B6
Birchill Cross EX13 ....88 A6
Birchland Rd PL7 .....133 A1
Birchland Way PL7 ...136 A8
Birchlea TQ13 ....180 C4
Birchman's Cross EX17 ..78 E1
Birchway La EX20 .....77 B4
Birchwood CI
  Tavistock PL19 .....171 C3
  Totnes TQ9 ....223 B5
Birchwood Gdns PL7 ..251 A7
Birchwood Rd EX16 ...161 E6
Birchy Barton Hill EX1 .178 B6
Birdcage La EX11 ....168 E8
Birdswell La EX34 ......2 E3
Birkbeck CI PL7 .....250 E7
Birkdale CI PL12 .....242 C2
Birkett CI EX2 ....178 C4
Biscombe Cross TA3 ...67 E8
Biscombe Gdns PL12 ..243 A2
Bishmill Gate EX36 ....30 E4
Bishop Cornish CE Prim Sch
  PL12 ....242 F1
Bishop Ct 2 EX24 ....103 A4
Bishop Pasterfield Ho 4
  EX2 ....261 B2
Bishop Westall Ho 6
  EX2 ....261 B2
Bishop Westall Rd EX2 .178 A2
Bishop Wilfrid Rd TQ14 209 D8
Bishop's Clyst EX5 ...179 A3
Bishop's Court La EX5 .179 C4
Bishop's Hill TA21 .....51 B7
Bishop's Nympton Cross
  EX36 ....30 F1
Bishop's Nympton Prim Sch
  EX36 ....16 E1
Bishop's Tawton Prim Sch
  EX32 ....16 B2
Bishop's Tawton Rd
  Barnstaple EX32 ....155 B2
  Bishop's Tawton EX32 ..16 E1
Bishops Ave TQ14 ...208 F8
Bishops CI
  Ivybridge PL21 .....237 E6
  Starcross EX6 ......201 B8
  Torquay TQ12 ......221 A4
Bishops Court Ind Est
  EX2 ....178 E4
Bishops Ct
  Bishopsteignton TQ14 ..208 F8
  4 Wellington TA21 ..160 D6
Bishops Mead 2 TQ10 .134 F3
Bishops Nympton EX36 ..31 C1
Bishops Rise
  Kentisbeare EX15 .....66 A3
  Torquay TQ12 ......221 A4
Bishopsteignton Rd
  TQ14 ....209 D6
Bishopsteignton Sch
  TQ14 ....208 F8
Biss La 4 EX33 .....152 D6
Bitney La TQ12 ......212 C5
Bittadon La EX31 ......9 C4
Bittaford Terr PL21 ...137 C7
Bittaford Wood PL21 ..137 C7
Bittam's La TQ9 ......217 B4
Bittern Ind Units EX2 .178 E5
Bittern Rd EX1 ......179 B6
Bittery Cross EX5 ......84 B2
Bitton Ave TQ14 .....210 B5
Bitton La TQ14 ......210 A5
Bitton Park Rd 10 TQ14 210 B5
Blachford Ct PL21 ....133 C2
Blachford Rd PL21 ....137 B8
Black Dog Cross EX17 ..61 E4
Black Gate EX22 ......73 B8
Black Hat La EX4 ....176 B3
Black Horse Cnr EX18 ..59 C4
Black La Hemyock EX15 ..52 D2
  Holcombe Rogus TA21 ..50 E6
Black Lion Ct 8 EX4 ..166 C6
Black Torrington CE Prim
  Sch EX21 ....74 A8
Blackabrook Ave PL20 .128 A8
Blackacre Rd EX24 ...102 C6
Blackalder Terr PL7 ...132 F4
Blackall Gdns PL6 ....261 A4
Blackall Rd EX4 ......261 B4
Blackaller La EX31 ....33 C1
Blackawton Prim Sch
  TQ9 ....139 C4
Blackball La TQ5 ....230 C6
Blackberry Ct TA21 ..160 D4
Blackberry La
  Bigbury TQ7 ....142 E6
  Plymouth PL9 ......255 E8
Blackberry Way 6
  TQ1 ....123 F1
Blackboy Rd EX1 .....177 E7
Blackbrook Ave TQ4 ..226 B1
Blackbrook CI PL20 ...127 F2
Blackbrook Wlk TQ4 ..226 B1
Blackditch Cross EX17 ..60 B1
Blackdown CI PL21 ...237 E5
Blackdown Cross
  Cornworthy TQ9 .....139 C4
  Loddiswell TQ7 .....138 B2
  Tedburn St Mary EX17 ..97 E8

Blackdown La
  Halwell TQ9 ....139 D4
  Tedburn St Mary EX4 ..98 C5
Blackdown Pk EX15 ...162 C5
Blackdown Rd TA21 ..160 B4
Blackdown View
  2 Hemyock EX15 .....67 B8
  Sampford Peverell EX16 ..50 C1
Blackdown Visitors Ctr*
  EX15 ....52 D3
Blackerway La TQ12 ...213 B7
Blackerton Cross EX16 ..32 E3
Blackett CI PL21 .....237 E4
Blackeven CI PL6 .....241 D1
Blackeven Hill PL6 ...241 E1
Blackfriars La PL1 ...263 A2
Blackgate Cross EX39 ..26 C7
Blackhaven CI TQ4 ...229 B8
Blackhayes La EX14 ...68 F1
Blackhorse La EX5 ...179 B8
Blackler's Land Cross
  TQ9 ....216 B5
Blackley La TQ13 .....113 D1
Blackmoor Rd TA21 ..160 F4
Blackmore Cres PL6 ..244 D6
Blackmore Ct EX8 ...196 E1
Blackmore La EX16 ...188 B4
Blackmore Mews EX2 ..178 C4
Blackmore Rd EX16 ..161 F3
Blackpool CE Prim Sch
  TQ9 ....122 F1
Blackpool Cross EX17 ..78 D4
Blackpool Hill TQ6 ...146 A6
Blackpool Rd EX17 ....78 D4
Blackpool Valley Rd
  TQ6 ....146 A7
Blackpost Cross
  Kingston TQ7 ......142 C7
  Totnes TQ9 ....223 F6
  Totnes, Littlehempston
  TQ9 ....217 A2
Blackpost La TQ9 ....223 F5
Blackridge Cross TQ7 .258 F8
Blacksmith La TQ10 ..137 D8
Blacksmiths Cnr EX17 ..81 A6
Blackstone CI PL9 ....256 B6
Blackstone La EX17 ....61 C1
Blackstone Rd TQ12 ..211 D1
Blackswan PI 10 EX7 ..204 D6
Blackthorn Ave PL6 ..161 F6
Blackthorn CI
  Honiton EX14 ......166 C4
  Plymouth, Honicknowle
  PL5 ....244 B3
  Plymouth, Woolwell PL6 ..245 D8
  Sidmouth EX10 .....187 F8
Blackthorn Cres EX1 ..178 C6
Blackthorn Dr PL21 ...237 E4
Blackthorn Way TQ4 ..225 D4
Blackwalls La EX18 ....60 B7
Blackwater Rd EX15 ...66 E8
Blackwell Cross
  Broadhempston TQ13 ..131 D3
  Strete TQ6 ....146 D3
Blackwell La TQ13 ...131 D2
Bladder La PL5 ......244 A2
Bladon La EX20 ......207 D1
Blagaton Gate EX21 ...73 B1
Blagdon Cross EX21 ...90 C7
Blagdon Hill EX13 .....90 C7
Blagdon Lodge Cross
  EX21 ....90 C7
Blagdon Rd TQ3 .....225 B6
Blagdon Rise EX17 ...165 D6
Blagrove Hill EX17 ....46 C3
Blair Rd PL4 ....237 D5
Blairgowrie Rd PL5 ...244 C3
Blake CI TQ1 ....220 B8
Blake Gdns PL5 .....244 C3
Blakeland Rd EX31 ...153 D5
Blakemore Way TQ9 ..222 A4
Blakes Hill Rd EX32 ...17 B2
Blakewell Cross
  Chittlehampton EX37 ..28 E3
  Umberleigh EX37 .....28 D3
Blakewell Hill EX32 ...28 E4
Blakey Down La TQ3 ..218 F1
Blamphayne Cross
  EX24 ....102 D7
Blanchard PI 2 PL7 ..250 E7
Blandhown Dr PL18 ..125 C7
Blandford Rd PL3 ....249 C6
Blanksmill Cross TQ7 .259 A8
Blatchborough Cross
  EX22 ....38 B1
Blatchcombe Dr TQ3 ..225 F7
Blatchcombe Rd TQ3 ..226 A7
Blatchfords Ct EX20 ..170 B5
Blaxton La PL5 ......241 C6
Blaxton La 2 PL5 ....240 C2
Blenheim CI
  Newton Abbot TQ12 ..207 A5
  Torquay TQ1 ......220 B8
  Willand EX15 ......162 D5
Blenheim Ct EX2 .....177 C1
Blenheim Dr EX15 ...162 D4
Blenheim La EX20 .....76 C4
Blenheim Rd Exeter EX2 177 B2
  Plymouth PL4 ......263 A4
Blenheim Terr TQ13 ..180 C7
Bligh CI TQ14 ....210 A8
Blights Hill EX16,TA22 ..33 F1
Blind Acres La EX33 ...15 A8
Blind La Aylesbeare EX5 ..99 E2

Blind La continued
  Buckland St Mary TA20 ..69 A8
  Pottimore EX5 .....174 B8
Blindwell Ave TQ12 ..207 F7
Blindwell Farm Cotts
  TQ12 ....207 E7
Blindwell Hill PL10 ...252 E5
Blindwell La TA4 .....32 E6
Blindwylle Rd TQ2 ...219 E5
Blogishay La TQ13 ...130 F4
Bloomball CI PL3 ....249 B6
Blossom CI EX14 ......67 C1
Blue Anchor Cross EX14 ..84 B4
Blue Bell TQ7 ....223 C5
Blue Cedar Ct EX8 ...202 B6
Blue Gate TA24 ....19 F8
Blue Haze CI PL6 ....245 D5
Blue La EX17 ....96 A3
Blue Waters Dr
  Lyme Regis DT7 ....260 B3
  Paignton TQ4 .....229 C8
Blue Waters Ind Est
  TQ13 ....180 C5
Bluebell Ave EX16 ...161 F6
Bluebell CI Saltash PL12 242 C2
  Seaton EX12 ......192 B7
Bluebell Rd EX14 ....161 E4
Bluebell Way PL19 ...171 E4
Bluecoat Sch The EX31 .154 F6
Bluegate Hill PL21 ...137 A2
Bluehayes La
  Clyst Honiton EX5 ...175 F3
  Rockbeare EX5 ....100 A5
Blueridge TQ13 ......180 C4
Bluett Rd TQ11 ......160 D4
Blundell's Ave EX16 ..161 F4
Blundell's Rd
  Tiverton EX15 ....64 D8
  Tiverton EX16 .....161 E4
Blundell's Sch EX16 ..161 F4
Blunts La PL6 ....245 C3
Blyth Ct EX39 ....39 E5
Blythswood Cres 3
  TQ1 ....220 B7
Boarden Barn EX48 ..202 B6
Boasley Cross PL16 ...92 E4
Boasley Cross Prim Sch
  EX20 ....92 E4
Bockland CI EX15 ...163 A3
Boconnic La PL20 ....127 A3
Bodley CI EX1 ......178 B7
Bodley Cross EX31 ....4 D1
Bodley La EX31 ......16 C4
Bodmin Rd PL5 ......244 D3
Bodnant Dr EX22 ....164 C4
Body Hayes CI TQ9 ..227 F7
Body's Ct PL18 ......125 C6
Bogmoor Cross EX20 ..92 D8
Bolberry Cross TQ7 ..147 E6
Boldventure PL8 ....257 F3
Boldventure Cross EX9 ..91 E6
Bolham Hall Cotts EX16 161 C8
Bolham La EX16 .....161 C8
Bolham Rd EX16 ....161 C8
Bolt House CI PL19 ..171 A5
Bolton Ct 8 TQ5 ....230 C4
Bolton St TQ5 ......230 C4
Bommerton Cross
  EX36 ....32 A4
Bonair CI TQ5 ....230 C3
Bonaventure CI TQ8 ..259 D5
Bonaventure Rd TQ8 ..259 D5
Bond La EX16 ....62 F5
Bond St Bedford EX19 ..42 D2
  Cornwood PL21 ....133 C2
  Plymouth PL6 .....244 E6
Bondfield Cross EX36 ..30 A5
Bondhouse La EX4 ....98 E3
Bondleigh Bridge Cross
  EX20 ....77 B7
Bondleigh Cross EX20 ..77 B7
Bondleigh Moor Cross
  EX20 ....76 F6
Bonds Cotts EX14 ...166 C4
Bonds Cross
  Chumleigh EX18 .....44 E1
  Petrockstow EX20 ...56 C5
Bonds Mdw TQ13 ...180 C3
Bone Mill Cross TQ12 ..131 F6
Bonehayne & Purlbridge Rd
  EX24 ....102 C5
Bonfire Cross EX14 ...101 C3
Bonfire Hill
  Black Torrington EX21 ..74 A8
  Salcombe TQ8 .....259 C5
Bonford Cross EX14 ...58 E3
Bonhay CI EX16 ......184 C3
Bonhay Rd EX16 .....201 B8
Bonhay Rd Exeter EX4 ..177 A6
  Starcross EX6 .....201 B8
Boniford Cross EX14 ..166 C3
Bonners Cswy EX13 ..167 F7
Bonners Dr EX13 ....167 F6
Bonners Glen EX13 ..167 F6
Bonnicott La EX33 .....7 D1
Bonnington Gr EX1 ...177 F6
Bonny Cross
  Clayhanger EX16 .....34 B3
  Clayhanger EX16 .....35 B1
Bonville CI EX1 ......178 B7
Bonville Cres EX16 ....64 D7

Bonville Rd PL6 . . . . 244 E6
Boobery EX16 . . . . 50 D1
Boode Cross EX33 . . . . . . 152 F7
Boode Rd EX33 . . . . 152 F7
Booklands EX22 . . . . 18 B2
Boon's Pl PL1 . . . . 262 C4
Booth Way EX8 . . . . 196 B2
Borden Gate EX16 . . . . . . 50 B8
Border Rd ▓ EX14 . . . . . . 85 C2
Boringdon Ave PL5 . . . . . 247 D8
Boringdon Cl PL7 . . . . . . 250 D7
Boringdon Hill PL7 . . . . . 250 D7
Boringdon Mill Bsns Ctr
  PL7 . . . . 250 F6
Boringdon Pk PL7 . . . . . 237 A5
Boringdon Prim Sch
  PL7 . . . . 250 D7
Boringdon Rd
  Plymouth, Plympton PL7 . 250 D6
  Plymouth, Turnchapel PL9 . 255 A7
Boringdon Terr
  Plymouth, Plympton PL7 . 250 D6
  Plymouth, Turnchapel PL9 . 255 A7
Boringdon Villas PL7 . . . 250 D6
Borne Cross EX37 . . . . . . 44 B2
Borough Cl TQ4 . . . . 225 E3
Borough Cross
  Aveton Gifford TQ7 . . . . 143 B7
  Bridgerule EX22 . . . . . . 70 E5
  Chilsworthy EX22 . . . . . 53 E2
  Newton Tracey EX31 . . . . 27 A3
  Woolacombe EX34 . . . . . 1 B1
Borough Ct PL11 . . . . . . 246 E4
Borough La TQ9 . . . . 144 B6
Borough Park Rd
  Paignton TQ3 . . . . 225 E5
  Totnes TQ9 . . . . 223 C6
Borough Pk PL11 . . . . . . 246 E4
Borough Rd
  Combe Martin EX34 . . . . . 2 F4
  Great Torrington EX38 . . . 159 E5
  Paignton TQ4 . . . . 225 E4
  Torquay TQ1 . . . . 214 B1
Borough The PL8 . . . . . . 257 F4
Borough View EX38 . . . . 159 E5
Borrowdale Cl PL6 . . . . . 244 D5
Boscastle Gdns PL2 . . . . 248 C8
Boscawen Pl
  Plymouth PL2 . . . . 247 E4
  ▓ Teignmouth TQ14 . . . . 210 B5
Boscundle Row PL12 . . . . 243 A2
Boshill Hill Axmouth DT7 . 193 C8
  Colyford DT7,EX12 . . . . . 103 D3
Bossell Ho TQ11 . . . . . . 236 B4
Bossell Pk TQ11 . . . . . . 236 B4
Bossell Rd TQ11 . . . . . . 236 B5
Bossell Terr TQ11 . . . . . . 236 B5
Bosuns Point TQ4 . . . . . 226 C4
Boswell Cl PL5 . . . . 244 B2
Boswell Way EX12 . . . . . 191 F8
Boswell's La EX20 . . . . . . 77 D4
Boswell's Lane End EX20 . 77 D4
Bottle Bridge Hill TQ13 . . 123 F7
Bottle Pk PL21 . . . . 136 B6
Bottom La EX33 . . . . 10 D5
Bottom's La TQ12 . . . . . 213 E4
Bottompark La TQ2 . . . . 213 F3
Bottoms La EX33 . . . . 8 B2
Bottreaux Mill Cross
  EX36 . . . . 32 A5
Boucher Rd EX9 . . . . 198 B1
Boucher Way EX9 . . . . . . 198 B1
Boucher's La TA4 . . . . . . 35 E4
Bouchiers Cl EX20 . . . . . . 77 C5
Boughmore La EX10 . . . . 187 F3
Boughmore Rd EX10 . . . . 187 F4
Boughhayes Est PL19 . . . 171 A5
Boulden Cl PL7 . . . . 251 C5
Boulter Cl PL6 . . . . 241 C1
Bound The PL10 . . . . 253 A1
Boundary Cl TQ12 . . . . . 212 F5
Boundary Pk
  Bideford EX39 . . . . 26 F4
  Seaton EX12 . . . . 192 A8
Boundary Rd
  Dousland PL20 . . . . 127 B3
  Torquay TQ2 . . . . 219 D5
Bounds Cross EX22 . . . . . 71 A4
Bounds Pl PL1 . . . . 262 B2
Boundy's Cross EX17 . . . . 61 B8
Bounsells La EX20 . . . . . . 57 A7
Bountice La EX34 . . . . 2 D2
Bourchier Cl ▓ EX16 . . . . 34 B1
Bourchier Dr ▓ EX16 . . . . 34 B1
Bourn Rise EX4 . . . . 174 D2
Bourne Bridge Cross
  EX36 . . . . 46 A5
Bourne Cl PL3 . . . . 249 D6
Bourne Ct TQ5 . . . . 229 F2
Bourne Rd TQ12 . . . . . . 213 A5
Bourton La TQ9 . . . . 223 E6
Bourton Rd TQ9 . . . . . . 223 E6
Bourtons The TQ9 . . . . . 223 D7
Boutport St EX31 . . . . . . 154 F5
Boutport St (Mermaid Wlk)
  EX31 . . . . 154 F6
Boutport Street (Mermaid
  Wlk) ▓ EX31 . . . . 154 F6
Bovacott La EX22 . . . . . . 73 C7
Bove Park Rd TQ2 . . . . . 214 A4
Bovemoor's La EX2 . . . . . 178 A4
Bovett St TA21 . . . . 160 C6
Bovey Cross
  Broadhempston TQ13 . . . 131 D3
  Moretonhampstead TQ13 . 111 E3

Bovey Fir Cross EX12 . . . 190 F6
Bovey La EX12 . . . . 191 B7
Bovey Tracey Hospl
  TQ13 . . . . 180 C8
Bovey Tracey Prim Sch
  TQ13 . . . . 180 C8
Bovey Tracey Rd TQ12 . . 206 F6
Boville La PL9 . . . . 256 C7
Bovisand Cir PL9 . . . . . . 254 F2
Bovisand East PL9 . . . . . 140 A8
Bovisand La
  Down Thomas PL9 . . . . . 255 B2
  Staddiscombe PL9 . . . . . 255 D3
Bovisand Pk
  Down Thomas PL9 . . . . . 255 A1
  Heybrook Bay PL9 . . . . . 140 A8
Bovisand Rd PL9 . . . . . . 255 E3
Bow Beer Cross EX17 . . . 78 A1
Bow Com Prim Sch EX17 . 78 C4
Bow Cross TQ13 . . . . . . 139 F6
Bow Cross
  Blackawton TQ9 . . . . . . 145 B8
  Staverton TQ9 . . . . 216 C7
Bow La TQ13 . . . . 111 F4
Bow Mill La EX17 . . . . . . 78 B4
Bow Rd TQ9 . . . . 139 C7
Bow Station Cross EX17 . . 78 C2
Bowbeer La EX17 . . . . . . 78 B1
Bowbridge Cross TQ9 . . . 145 B8
Bowd Cl EX10 . . . . 100 E1
Bowden Cnr EX31 . . . . . . 9 F3
Bowden Cross
  Buckland Brewer EX39 . . 40 B8
  Drewsteignton EX6 . . . . . 96 E3
  Kingsbridge TQ7 . . . . . 144 C3
Bowden Farmhouse
  PL8 . . . . 257 F4
Bowden Gn EX39 . . . . . . 25 E4
Bowden Hill
  Ashburton TQ13 . . . . . . 130 F4
  Crediton EX17 . . . . 165 D5
  Newton Abbot TQ12 . . . . 207 C2
  Yealmpton PL8 . . . . 257 F4
Bowden Hill Terr ▓
  EX17 . . . . 165 D5
Bowden House & British
  Photographic Mus*
  TQ9 . . . . 223 C2
Bowden La TQ13 . . . . . . 123 A7
Bowden Park Rd PL6 . . . . 245 A1
Bowden Pillars TQ9 . . . . 223 B3
Bowden Rd TQ12 . . . . . . 211 E2
Bowdens La
  Ideford TQ13 . . . . 124 B4
  Shillingford EX16 . . . . . . 34 E3
Bowdown Cross TQ10 . . . 135 C5
Bowerhayes Cross EX14 . . 67 C3
Bowerhayes La EX14 . . . . 67 C3
Bowering Ct ▓ EX32 . . . . 155 B3
Bowerland Ave TQ2 . . . . 213 F4
Bowerland Cross EX20 . . . 93 D3
Bowers Cl PL6 . . . . 245 A7
Bowers Park Dr PL6 . . . . 245 A7
Bowers Rd PL2 . . . . 248 B5
Bowerthy La EX17 . . . . . . 60 D4
Bowhay Cl EX21 . . . . 74 A8
Bowhay La
  Combe Martin EX34 . . . . . 3 A3
  Exeter EX4 . . . . 176 E4
Bowhays Wlk ▓ PL6 . . . . 249 C7
Bowhill EX5 . . . . 83 A7
Bowland Cl TQ4 . . . . 226 A2
Bowley Mdw EX5 . . . . . . 82 F6
Bowling Ave EX1 . . . . . . 178 C6
Bowling ▓ Kenton EX6 . . 194 E3
  Willand EX15 . . . . 162 D4
Bramley Gdns EX5 . . . . . 99 E7
Bramley Mdw EX32 . . . . 17 C2
Bramley Rd EX39 . . . . . . 25 D7
Bramley Way EX15 . . . . . 66 C6
Brampford Cross EX5 . . . 172 F7
Brampford Speke CE Prim
  Sch EX5 . . . . 81 E1
Brampton Down Cross
  EX16 . . . . 49 F8
Branches Cross EX22 . . . 54 E3
Brancker Rd PL2 . . . . . . 248 C6
Brand Cl EX14 . . . . 166 C4
Brand Rd PL12 . . . . 242 E1
Brandinam St EX16 . . . . . 161 B4
Branksome Cl TQ3 . . . . . 218 F3
Brannam Cres EX32 . . . . 155 A4
Brannams Sq ▓ EX32 . . . 155 A4
Branscombe CE Prim
  Sch EX12 . . . . 190 D4

Braddons Hill Rd W
  TQ1 . . . . 220 B4
Braddons St TQ1 . . . . . . 220 B4
Bradfield Cl PL6 . . . . 245 E1
Bradfield House Sch
  EX15 . . . . 65 F4
Bradfield Rd EX4 . . . . . . 174 D1
Bradford Cl Exmouth EX8 . 196 C3
  Plymouth PL6 . . . . 249 B7
Bradford Cross EX16 . . . . 47 A3
Bradford Moor Hill EX16 . 47 A3
Bradford Mus Sch EX22 . . 73 B8
Bradham Cl EX8 . . . . 202 D8
Bradham La EX8 . . . . 202 D8
Bradiford EX31 . . . . 154 E7
Bradley Barton Prim Sch
  TQ12 . . . . 206 E3
Bradley Ct ▓ TQ12 . . . . . 207 B3
Bradley La TQ12 . . . . . . 207 A3
Bradley Manor* TQ12 . . . 206 F2
Bradley Park Rd TQ1 . . . 214 B1
Bradley Rd
  Bovey Tracey TQ13 . . . . 180 C7
  Newton Abbot TQ12 . . . . 207 A1
Bradley Rowe Fst Sch
  EX2 . . . . 177 F3
Bradley Rowe Mid Sch
  EX2 . . . . 177 F3
Bradleyford Cnr TQ13 . . . 180 F6
Bradman Way EX2 . . . . . 177 C2
Bradninch Cross EX32 . . . 17 D4
Bradninch Prim Sch EX5 . 83 A6
Bradridge Cross TQ9 . . . 138 D8
Bradstone Rd EX34 . . . . . 150 A5
Bradwell Rd EX34 . . . . . 150 A5
Bradworthy Com Prim Sch
  EX22 . . . . 38 E1
Bradworthy Cross EX22 . . 53 D7
Brady Cl PL7 . . . . 250 E6
Braemar Cl PL7 . . . . 251 C4
Braeside Rd
  Paignton TQ4 . . . . 226 C4
  Torquay TQ2 . . . . 214 A4
Brag La PL7 . . . . 132 C6
Braggs Hill PL15 . . . . . . 89 E3
Braggs' Hill EX37 . . . . . . 43 B7
Brahms Way EX32 . . . . . 155 C5
Brake Ho TQ12 . . . . 207 E2
Brake Rd PL5 . . . . 252 B5
Brake Rd PL5 . . . . 244 E2
Brake Wood Cl EX31 . . . 153 D5
Brakefield TQ10 . . . . 135 A2
Brakeridge Cl PL6 . . . . . 245 E1
Bramble Cl
  Budleigh Salterton EX9 . . 198 C1
  Dartington TQ9 . . . . 222 F8
  Plymouth PL3 . . . . 249 B7
  Sidmouth EX10 . . . . 188 B8
Bramble Mead EX5 . . . . . 99 D2
Bramble Path ▓ EX32 . . . 17 B2
Bramble Wlk
  Barnstaple EX31 . . . . . . 154 B3
  Exeter EX4 . . . . 174 A2
Brambleoak Cross TQ12 . . 131 D4
Brambles The TA21 . . . . 160 D4
Bramdean Sch EX17 . . . . 78 C2
Bramfield Pl PL6 . . . . . . 249 D7
Brandon Rd PL3 . . . . . . 249 C4
Brandreth Rd ▓ PL3 . . . . 248 F6
Brandy Wells EX37 . . . . . 44 E6
Branksome Cl TQ3 . . . . . 218 F3
Brannam Cres EX32 . . . . 155 A4
Brannams Sq ▓ EX32 . . . 155 A4
Branscombe CE Prim
  Sch EX12 . . . . 190 D4
Branscombe Cl
  Colyford EX24 . . . . 103 A3
  Exeter EX4 . . . . 176 E5
  Torquay TQ1 . . . . 220 B7
Branscombe Cross
  EX12 . . . . 101 F1
Branscombe Gdns PL5 . . 244 A3
Branscombe La EX7 . . . . 200 C3

Branscombe Rd EX16 . . . 161 F4
Bransgrove Hill EX18 . . . 59 B5
Bransgrove La EX18 . . . . 59 B5
Branson Cl ▓ PL7 . . . . . . 251 C5
Branson Pk PL19 . . . . . . 126 D6
Brantwood Cl TQ4 . . . . . 226 A4
Brantwood Cres TQ4 . . . 226 A3
Brantwood Dr TQ4 . . . . . 226 A3
Bratton Cross EX31 . . . . . 17 E7
Bratton Fleming Prim Sch
  EX31 . . . . 18 A8
Braundsworthy Cross
  EX21 . . . . 73 E8
Braunton Caen Prim Sch
  EX33 . . . . 152 D6
Braunton Mus* EX33 . . . 152 D6
Braunton Rd EX31 . . . . . 154 D2
Braunton Sch & Com Coll
  EX33 . . . . 152 E4
Braunton Wlk PL6 . . . . . 249 E8
Bray Cl Burlescombe EX16 . 51 B3
  Tavistock PL19 . . . . 171 A5
Bray Hill EX22 . . . . 18 F3
Bray Mill Cross EX37 . . . 29 D4
Brayford Cl PL5 . . . . 244 B3
Brayford Prim Sch EX32 . 18 F5
Brayhams Terr EX20 . . . . 170 C6
Brayley Hill EX32 . . . . . . 18 F6
Brays Cl EX37 . . . . 165 C5
Braytown Cotts EX32 . . . 18 F5
Breach Cotts TA21 . . . . . 51 F5
Breach Hill TA21 . . . . . . 51 F5
Breaka La EX19 . . . . 57 E5
Breakneck Cross EX37 . . . 28 F5
Breakneck Hill
  Chittlehampton EX37 . . . 210 B8
  Manaton TQ13 . . . . 210 B8
Breakwater Ct TQ5 . . . . . 230 E6
Breakwater Hill PL4 . . . . 263 C1
Breakwater Ind Est PL9 . . 255 C8
Breakwater Rd PL9 . . . . 255 C8
Brean Down Cl PL3 . . . . 248 E6
Brean Down Rd PL3 . . . . 248 E6
Brecon Cl Bideford EX39 . 157 D1
  Plymouth PL3 . . . . 249 A7
Bremley Cross EX36 . . . . 31 E3
Brendon Cross EX39 . . . . 39 F6
Brendon Hills EX17 . . . . . 79 C6
Brendon Rd TA21 . . . . . 160 D7
Brendon Two Gates
  TA24 . . . . 13 A6
Brendons Ave TQ2 . . . . 219 C3
Brendons The EX16 . . . . . 50 D1
Brennacott Rd EX39 . . . . 25 E4
Brennans Ct ▓ EX32 . . . . 155 A4
Brent Cl EX5 . . . . 184 C3
Brent Hill PL8 . . . . 136 D1
Brent Knoll Rd ▓ PL3 . . . 248 E5
Brent Mill Bsns Pk TQ10 . 134 F2
Brent Mill Ind Est TQ10 . 134 F2
Brent Rd ▓ TQ3 . . . . 226 B6
Brent Torr * PL19 . . . . . . 117 B7
Brentford Ave PL5 . . . . . 244 B5
Brenton Rd EX6 . . . . 114 B4
Brentor Cl EX4 . . . . 176 F8
Brentor Rd
  Mary Tavy PL19 . . . . . . 249 B2
  Plymouth PL4 . . . . 249 B2
Brest Rd PL6 . . . . 245 A3
Brest Way PL6 . . . . 245 A3
Breton Side PL4 . . . . . . 263 A2
Breton Way EX8 . . . . . . 196 E1
Brett Wlk PL7 . . . . 250 F7
Bretteville Cl EX5 . . . . . 184 C3
Bretteville Ct TQ13 . . . . 111 A6
Brewer Rd EX32 . . . . . . 155 C4
Brewers Hill EX39 . . . . . 39 F8
Brewers La EX39 . . . . . . 38 E8
Brewery Vale TQ13 . . . . 180 B5
Brewin Rd EX16 . . . . . . 161 C3
Brewlands Rd EX4 . . . . . 173 F1
Brewing Wlk EX4 . . . . . . 173 F1
Brian Cl EX33 . . . . 152 C6
Briar Cl Exmouth EX8 . . . 202 D8
Briar Cross PL21 . . . . . . 137 C2
Briar Rd PL3 . . . . 248 F7
Briar Tor PL20 . . . . 127 B3
Briardale Rd PL2 . . . . . . 247 F6
Briarleigh Cl PL6 . . . . . . 245 F2
Briars Row PL12 . . . . . . 242 D4
Briary La TQ1 . . . . 220 B5
Briary Mews ▓ TQ1 . . . . 220 B4
Brick Cross EX9 . . . . . . 198 C7
Brickfield Ho EX16 . . . . . 161 D6
Brickhouse Hill EX16 . . . 161 D6
Brickyard La EX6 . . . . . . 201 A8
Brickyard Rd EX5 . . . . . 168 A7
Bridespring Rd EX4 . . . . 173 F1
Bridespring Wlk EX4 . . . 173 F1
Bridestowe Prim Sch
  EX20 . . . . 107 F8
Bridford Rd EX2 . . . . . . 177 E1
Bridge Cl EX5 . . . . 184 B4
Bridge Cotts
  Chard Junction TA20 . . . . 88 D8
  ▓ Exeter EX4 . . . . 177 E8
Bridge Croft TQ13 . . . . . 130 F4
Bridge Cross
  Ashprington TQ9 . . . . . . 139 F6
  Newton Abbot TQ12 . . . . 34 B1
Bridge Ctr EX4 . . . . 261 A3
Bridge End EX36 . . . . . . 31 D5
Bridge End Rd EX35 . . . . 182 F5
Bridge La Budlake EX5 . . 82 D3
  ▓ Sidmouth EX10 . . . . . 188 B3
Bridge Mill La PL21 . . . . 137 C2
Bridge Pk Ashwater EX21 . 90 F6

Bridge Pk continued
Ivybridge PL21 . . . . 237 D5
Bridge Plats Way EX39 . . 156 E2
Bridge Rd
  Budleigh Salterton EX9 . . 198 B2
  Churston Ferrers TQ5 . . . 229 D5
  Exeter EX2,EX6 . . . . . . 182 A8
  Exmouth EX8 . . . . 202 A8
  Kingswear TQ5,TQ6 . . . 234 B7
  Teignmouth TQ14 . . . . . 210 A3
  Torquay TQ2 . . . . 219 F5
  Totnes TQ9 . . . . 222 F6
Bridge Reeve Cross EX18 . 59 C8
Bridge Ret Pk TQ2 . . . . . 219 E8
Bridge St Bideford EX39 . 157 A1
Bridge St Bideford EX39 . 157 A1
Buckfastleigh TQ11 . . . . 236 C5
Dulverton TA22 . . . . 33 D6
Hatherleigh EX20 . . . . . . 75 C7
Ipplepen TQ12 . . . . 211 D2
Kingsbridge TQ7 . . . . . . 258 D5
Lyme Regis DT7 . . . . . . 260 E3
Sidbury EX10 . . . . 101 B2
Tiverton EX16 . . . . 161 C4
Uffculme EX15 . . . . 66 A7
Bridge Terr
  Ashprington TQ9 . . . . . . 139 F6
  Colyton EX24 . . . . 34 B1
Bridge The PL1 . . . . 262 B1
Bridge View EX5 . . . . . . 99 C6
Bridgefield EX11 . . . . . . 169 E4
Bridgehill Garth EX3 . . . 182 F5
Bridgeman Rd EX5 . . . . . 82 F6
Bridgeland St EX39 . . . . 157 A2
Bridgemoor Cross EX22 . . 71 B6
Bridgend Hill PL8 . . . . . 141 A7
Bridgerule CE Prim Sch
  EX22 . . . . 70 F5
Bridgerule Ind Est EX22 . . 70 E4
Bridges The PL12 . . . . . . 242 E1
Bridgetown TQ9 . . . . . . 223 D5
Bridgetown Hill TQ9 . . . . 223 D6
Bridgetown Hill TQ9 . . . . 223 E6
Bridgewater Gdns TQ9 . . 223 E6
Bridgwater Cl PL6 . . . . . 245 B1
Bridle Cl Paignton TQ4 . . 229 B8
  Plymouth PL7 . . . . 251 B7
Bridle Path The TQ9 . . . . 223 C4
Bridle Way PL12 . . . . . . 242 D6
Bridwell Ave EX15 . . . . . 66 F7
Bridwell La N PL5 . . . . . 247 E8
Bridwell Rd PL5 . . . . . . 247 E8
Brigadier Gdns TQ9 . . . . 223 E6
Bright View EX20 . . . . . . 170 A4
Brightley Cross EX20 . . . . 94 B8
Brightley Rd EX20 . . . . . 170 C6
Brim Brook Ct TQ2 . . . . 219 B8
Brim Hill TQ1 . . . . 214 C5
Brimacombe Rd EX39 . . . 22 E3
Brimford Cross EX39 . . . . 38 A4
Brimhay TQ9 . . . . 222 F8
Brimhill Cl PL7 . . . . 251 B3
Brimhill La Highton PL16 . 117 F6
Brimlands TQ5 . . . . 230 B4
Brimlands TQ5 . . . . 230 B4
Brimley Bsns Pk TQ13 . . 180 A5
Brimley Cnr TQ13 . . . . . 123 F6
Brimley Cross
  Bovey Tracey TQ13 . . . . 180 B5
  Hemyock TA3 . . . . 52 A1
Brimley Ct TQ13 . . . . . . 180 A5
Brimley Dr TQ14 . . . . . . 210 C5
Brimley Gdns TQ13 . . . . 180 A5
Brimley Halt TQ13 . . . . . 180 C5
Brimley La TQ13 . . . . . . 180 A5
Brimley La TQ13 . . . . . . 180 A5
Brimley Pk TQ13 . . . . . . 180 A5
Brimley Rd
  Axminster EX13 . . . . . . 88 D3
  Bovey Tracey TQ13 . . . . 180 B5
Brimley Vale TQ13 . . . . . 180 B5
Brimpenny Rd EX8 . . . . . 196 C3
Brimstone La
  Bratton Fleming EX31 . . . 10 D1
  Membury EX13 . . . . 87 E6
Brinsworthy Cross EX36 . . 19 F1
Brisbane St EX16 . . . . . . 161 D5
Briseham Cl TQ5 . . . . . . 230 D3
Briseham Rd TQ5 . . . . . 230 D3
Brismar Wlk ▓ PL6 . . . . . 249 C7
Britannia Ave TQ4 . . . . . 233 C3
Britannia Pl ▓ PL4 . . . . . 248 F4
Britannia Royal Naval Coll
  TQ6 . . . . 233 F8
Britannia Way EX39 . . . . 156 F4
Briton St ▓ EX16 . . . . . . 34 C1
Briton Streetlane EX6 . . . 112 F8
Brittany Rd EX8 . . . . . . 196 C4
Britten Dr
  Barnstaple EX32 . . . . . . 155 C5
  Exeter EX2 . . . . 178 B5
Britton Cl EX16 . . . . 63 A8
Brixton Rd TQ4 . . . . 226 B6
Brittons The EX13 . . . . . 152 E3
Briwere Rd TQ2 . . . . . . 214 B3
Brixham CE Inf Sch
  TQ5 . . . . 230 D4
Brixham Com Coll TQ5 . . 230 D4
Brixham Cross TQ5 . . . . 229 E4
Brixham Enterprise Est
  TQ5 . . . . 230 D4

rixham Hospl TQ5 ....230 C3
rixham Rd
Haxwirigae TQ2 ....234 B3
Paignton TQ4 ....225 E3
rixham Wlk PL6 ....249 E8
rixington Dr EX8 ....196 D1
rixington Inf Sch EX8 ...196 C2
rixington Jun Sch EX8 ..196 C2
rixington La EX8 ....196 C2
rixton Lodge Gdns
PL8 ....256 F5
Broad Cl Crediton EX17 ..165 A6
North Molton EX36 ......30 E8
road Croft EX13 ....87 E8
Broad La Appledore EX39 ..14 F1
Braunton EX33 ....152 A8
Hawkridge TA22 ....21 D1
Tiverton EX16 ....161 C3
road Lane Head TA22 ....21 D1
road Oak Cres 5 TQ9 ....223 D5
road Park Ave EX34 .....150 A5
road Oak Cres 15 EX33 ..7 E2
Broad Park
Bere Alston PL20 ....125 E2
Exmouth EX8 ....196 C1
Plymouth PL3 ....248 D6
road Park Terr EX34 ....150 A4
Broad Path
Stoke Gabriel TQ9 ......228 A8
Uffculme EX15 ....66 A8
road Pk Dartmouth TQ6 ..233 D3
Plymouth PL9 ....255 C7
road Rd
Kentisbeare EX15 ....66 C1
Kingswear TQ6 ....234 D5
road Reach TQ4 ....229 C7
road St
Black Torrington EX21 ...74 A8
Churchinford TA3 ....21 A5
Ilfracombe EX34 ....150 C6
Lifton PL16 ....105 E4
Lyme Regis DT7 ....260 E3
Modbury PL21 ....137 B2
Ottery St Mary EX11 ....169 D3
South Molton EX36 ......158 C6
Broad View
Broadclyst EX5 ....175 C6
Broadclyst EX5 ....222 F8
road Wlk PL12 ....242 E1
Broadacre Dr TQ5 ....230 D5
Broadclose Hill EX16 ....146 F6
Broadclose Rd EX31 .....154 D3
Broadclyst Com Prim Sch
EX5 ....175 C7
Broaddown Cross PL4 ...96 A1
Broadfield Rd EX32 .....155 B4
Broadfields Rd EX2 .....178 C5
Broadgate
Barnstaple EX31 ....154 E7
Exeter EX1 ....261 A3
Broadgate Cl
Barnstaple EX31 ....154 E7
Exeter EX1 ....152 D6
Broadgate Cres 1 TQ12 ..212 F4
Broadgate La EX17 ......61 B2
Broadgate Rd TQ12 .....213 A4
Broadhayes Cross EX14 ..86 E5
Broadhembury Cross
EX14 ....84 E7
Broadhempton Prim Sch
....................131 E1
Broadland Gdns PL9 ....256 A8
Broadland Rd TQ4 ......255 F8
Broadlands
Bideford EX39 ....157 D1
Northam EX39 ....156 F8
Teignmouth TQ14 ......210 A3
Thorverton EX5 ....81 A4
Broadlands Ave TQ12 ...207 A3
Broadlands Cl PL7 ......251 A3
Broadlands Ct TQ12 ....207 A3
Broadlands Rd TQ4 .....226 A4
Broadleaf Cl EX1 ....178 E8
Broadley Cl PL9 ....241 B2
Broadley Dr TQ2 ....219 C3
Broadley Ind Pk PL6 ....241 B2
Broadley Park Rd PL6 ...241 B2
Broadmead Exmouth EX8 .196 D2
Woodbury EX5 ....184 B3
Broadmead Bglws EX32 ..155 C2
Broadmead Cross EX16 ..48 A5
Broadmead Gdns EX35 ..151 B5
Broadmead Ct TQ12 ....207 D2
Broadmeadow Ave EX4 ..176 F4
Broadmeadow La TQ14 ..209 D7
Broadmeadow View
TQ14 ....209 D7
Broadmoor Cross EX37 ..29 A2
Broadmoor La EX20 ....170 A5
Broadoak Cl EX11 ......168 D3
Broadoak Hill EX31 .....4 C3
Broadoaks Cotts PL7 ...132 E4
Broadpark
Bovey Tracey TQ13 .....180 B5
Brampford Speke EX5 ..81 E1
Broadpark La EX20 .....95 D4
Broadpark Rd
Paignton TQ3 ....226 A7
Torquay TQ2 ....219 D2
Broadparks Ave EX4 ....174 E2
Broadparks Cl EX4 .....174 E2
Broadridge Cl TQ12 ....232 A8
Broadridge La EX17 ....61 A4
Broadsands Bend TQ4 ..229 C7
Broadsands Ct TQ4 ....229 B7

Broadsands Park Rd
TQ4 ....229 C8
Broadsands Rd TQ4 .....229 C7
Broadshell Cross EX22 ..71 C5
Broadstone TQ6 ....233 F4
Broadstone Park Rd
TQ2 ....219 D3
Broadway Exeter EX2 ...176 F3
Fremington EX31 ....153 F5
Sidmouth EX10 ....187 F5
Trusham TQ13 ....113 D1
Woodbury EX5 ....184 C2
Broadway Rd TQ12 .....207 D2
Broadway Hill EX2 ......176 E3
Broadway La EX33 ......7 D3
Broadway Rd TQ12 .....207 C7
Broadway Head EX14,
TA20 ....68 F6
Broadwoodwidger Prim Sch
PL16 ....91 A4
Broady Strap EX31 .....153 F5
Brock Ho 10 PL4 ....263 A2
Brockhole La EX13,TA20 ..88 B7
Brockhurst Pk TQ3 .....218 D2
Brockington's Rd EX5 ...99 C8
Brockley Rd PL3 ....249 C4
Brocks Cross EX17 .....79 A2
Brockscombe Cross
EX21 ....91 F5
Brockton Gdns PL6 .....245 B6
Brodick Cl EX4 ....173 D1
Bromhead Ct PL4 ......249 A8
Bromley Pl 6 PL2 ......248 A4
Bronescombe Ave TQ14 ..209 A8
Bronshill Ho TQ1 ......220 B6
Bronshill Mews TQ1 ....220 B6
Bronshill Rd TQ1 ......220 B6
Bronte Pl PL5 ....244 D1
Brook Cl Exeter EX1 ....178 B8
Ivybridge PL21 ....210 E8
Plymouth PL7 ....251 A3
Sidford EX10 ....101 B1
Brook Ct TQ13 ....154 B3
Brook Green Terr EX4 ...261 C4
Brook Haven Cl TQ12 ..212 F5
Brook La Calverleigh EX16 ..48 F2
Shaldon TQ14 ....209 D5
3 Sidford EX10 ....101 B1
Tavistock PL19 ....171 B2
Brook Lane Cotts TQ13 ..121 B3
Brook Mdw Exmouth EX8 ..196 C1
South Molton EX36 ....158 D4
Brook Orch TQ12 ......212 F4
Brook Rd
Budleigh Salterton EX9 ..199 G2
Cullompton EX15 ......163 B2
Dolton EX19 ....57 F7
Ipplepen TQ12 ....211 D2
Ivybridge PL21 ....237 D5
Brook St Bampton EX16 ..34 B1
Dawlish EX7 ....204 D6
Ottery St Mary EX11 ...169 D3
Slapton TQ7 ....145 C3
Tavistock PL19 ....171 C6
Brook Terr EX12 ....192 D7
Brook The PL12 ....242 E4
Brook View TQ9 ....222 F6
Brook Way TQ12 ....123 E1
Brookdale EX11 ....169 E4
Brookdale Ave EX34 ....150 A5
Brookdale Cl EX10 .....230 B4
Brookdale Ct Brixham TQ5 ..230 B4
Exeter EX2 ....178 A2
Brookdale Pk TQ5 .....230 B4
Brookdale Terr
6 Barnstaple EX32 ....155 B4
18 Dawlish EX7 ....204 D6
Brookdown Terr PL12 ...242 E3
Brooke Cl Saltash PL7 ..243 A2
Sampford Courtenay EX20 ..76 F3
Brooke Rd EX6 ....46 E1
Brookedor TQ12 ....212 F5
Brookfield EX39 ....25 D8
Brookfield Cl
5 Braunton EX33 ......152 D5
Kingsteignton TQ12 ...207 E7
Paignton TQ3 ....226 C8
Plymouth PL7 ....251 B5
Brookfield Dr
7 Colyton EX24 ....103 A4
Tiverton EX16 ....210 C7
Brookfield Gdns EX2 ...177 B1
Brookfield Pl EX34 ....3 A3
Brookfield Rd EX9 .....198 B6
Brookfield St 8 EX39 ...157 B1
Brookfield Terr PL12 ...242 E3
Brookhill TQ6 ....234 B2
Brooking Barn TQ9 ....139 F8
Brooking Way PL12 ....242 C3
Brookingfield Cl PL7 ...250 E5
Brookland Terr EX11 ...169 E3
Brooklands
2 Chudleigh TQ13 ....123 F6
21 Dawlish EX7 ....204 D6
Tavistock PL19 ....171 D6
Totnes TQ9 ....223 D5
Brooklands Cross EX10 ..100 C1
Brooklands Ct PL6 .....244 E3

Brooklands Farm Cl
EX13 ....103 D8
Brooklands La TQ2 .....219 E4
Brooklands Orch EX1 ...169 E4
Brooklands Rd
Exmouth EX8 ....196 D1
Rockwell Green TA21 ...160 B5
Brookleigh Ave EX1 ....178 B5
Brooklyn Pk EX8 ......196 C1
Brooks Hill PL15 ......66 C8
Brooks La PL10 ....252 F5
Brooks Pl TA21 ....160 E6
Brookside
Barnstaple EX31 ......154 A3
Kingsbridge TQ7 .....258 C4
Pathfinder Village EX6 ..98 C4
Brookside Ind Units
EX4 ....188 A7
Brookside Cl
Heybrook Bay PL9 ....140 A7
Teignmouth TQ14 ....210 A5
Brookside Cres EX4 ....174 B2
Brookside Ind Units
EX4 ....174 D1
Brookside Villas 20 EX34 ..3 A3
Brookvale Orch TQ14 ..209 D4
Brookway EX1 ....178 C7
Brookwood Cl 3 TQ10 ..134 F3
Brookwood Rd PL9 ....256 D7
Broom Cl Axminster EX13 ..167 E6
Dawlish EX7 ....204 F8
Exeter EX2 ....178 A5
Broom Hill
Chagford TQ13 ....111 A6
Saltash PL7 ....242 D2
Broom La EX13 ....88 C5
Broom Pk Dartington TQ9 ..215 E1
Broom's La TA3 ....68 A7
Broomball Cross TA22 ..32 F5
Broomball La EX16 ....32 E5
Broomborough Ct TQ9 ..223 B5
Broomborough Dr TQ9 ..223 A5
Broomfield Dr PL9 .....255 C5
Broomhayes Sch EX39 ..157 E1
Broomhayes
Chilsworthy EX22 .....53 B3
Copplestone EX17 ....79 A4
Broomhill Rd EX16 ....161 B4
Broomhill Villas EX32 ..18 E5
Broomhill Way TQ2 ....213 E1
Broomhouse La EX34 ..30 A2
Broomhouse PL11 .....46 E1
Broughton Cl PL3 .....248 F7
Brow Hill TQ12 ....123 B2
Brown Down La TA20 ..68 F7
Brown's Bridge La EX15 ..65 B7
Brown's Ct EX6 ....114 C4
Brown's Hill TQ6 ......233 F3
Brown's Hill Head EX37 ..37 F2
Browne Meml Almshouses
PL5 ....171 A5
Brownhill La EX19 .....140 D8
Brownhills Rd TQ2 ....223 D3
Brownie Cross PL7 ....132 C3
Browning Cl EX2 ......178 A4
Browning Rd PL2 ......248 A5
Brownings End TQ12 ..206 F1
Brownings Mead EX6 ..112 F7
Brownings Wlk TQ12 ..206 F1
Brownlands Cl EX10 ...188 C5
Brownlands Rd EX10 ..188 C5
Browns Bridge Rd TQ12 ..213 D2
Brownscombe Cl TQ3 ..218 D2
Brownsey La TA20 ....69 C5
Brownstone Cross EX17 ..61 D4
Brownstone Rd
Brixham TQ5 ....230 B4
Paignton TQ3 ....225 D8
Plymouth PL7 ....251 B5
Brownston Cross EX17 ..61 C1
Brownston St TQ10 ....135 A8
Brownstone Cross EX17 ..61 D4
Brownstone Moor Cross
EX17 ....61 D4
Broxfords Hill EX17 ...80 C7
Broxton Dr PL9 ....249 E1
Bruckland La EX12,EX13 ..103 D3
Bruckton Cross TQ6 ...232 F6
Brunel Ave Plymouth PL2 ..247 F5
Teignmouth TQ14 ....210 C6
Brunel Cl 16 EX7 ......204 E6
Brunel Ct TQ14 ....177 A7
Brunel Lodge Hospl
PL9 ....207 A1
Brunel Mews TQ2 .....219 F4
Brunel Prim Sch EX2 ..242 E2
Brunel Rd
Newton Abbot TQ12 ..207 D3
Paignton TQ4 ....229 D6
Starcross EX6 ....201 A8
Brunel Terr 3 PL2 .....247 F5
Brunel Way
Ivybridge PL21 ....237 E6
Plymouth PL3 ....248 B3
Brunenburg Way EX13 ..167 D4
Brunswick Pl 4 TQ12 ..207 B8
Brunswick Rd
Dawlish EX7 ....204 E6
16 Newton Abbot TQ12 ..207 B8
Brunswick Rd PL4 .....263 B2
Brunswick Sq 3 TQ1 ..219 F6
Brunswick St EX4 .....177 A5
Brushford Cross TQ2 ..33 E4
Brushford La
Chevithorne EX16 ....49 F3

Brushford La continued
Chulmleigh EX18 ......59 D2
Brushford New Rd TA22 ..33 E4
Brynmoor Cl PL3 ......249 A7
Brynmoor Pk PL3 ......249 A6
Brynmoor Wlk PL3 ....249 A6
Brynsworthy La EX31 ..154 A1
Brynsworthy Lawn
EX31 ....154 A2
Brynsworthy Pk EX31 ..154 B3
Bubbrook La EX6 ......96 F2
Buchanan Cl EX14 ....166 B4
Buckerall Cross EX14 ..84 F2
Buckerell Ave EX2 ....177 E3
Buckeridge Ave TQ14 ..210 B6
Buckeridge Rd TQ14 ..210 B6
Buckeridge Twrs 2 TQ14 ..210 B5
Buckfast Abbey* TQ11 ..236 C7
Buckfast Butterflies &
Dartmoor Otter Sanctuary*
TQ11 ....236 D5
Buckfast Cl
Buckfast TQ11 ....236 D6
Ivybridge PL21 ....237 D4
Plymouth PL2 ....248 A8
Buckfast Rd TQ11 ....236 D6
Buckfast Steam & Leisure
Pk* TQ11 ....236 D5
Buckfastleigh Prim Sch
TQ11 ....236 D5
Buckfastleigh Sta TQ11 ..236 D5
Buckgrove Cotts EX34 ..42 B6
Buckham Cross EX36 ..45 D7
Buckham Hill EX36 ....45 D7
Buckhouse La EX24 ...102 C7
Buckingham Pl PL5 ....244 E2
Buckland Abbey* PL20 ..126 C1
Buckland Brake TQ12 ..207 E2
Buckland Brewer Prim Sch
EX39 ....40 C7
Buckland Cl PL7 ......250 D7
Buckland Cross
Braunton EX33 ....152 C8
Slapton TQ7 ....145 C6
Buckland Hall TQ13 ...130 D7
Buckland Rd
Georgeham EX33 .....8 B3
Newton Abbot TQ12 ..207 F4
Newton Abbot TQ12 ..207 E2
Buckland St Mary CE Prim
Sch TA20 ....69 D8
Buckland Terr TQ12 ...126 F2
Buckland View
Buckland Brewer EX39 ..40 D7
Newton Abbot TQ12 ..207 D4
Buckleigh Cross EX39 ..156 C5
Buckleigh Rd EX39 ...156 C5
Buckley Cross EX16 ...100 C1
Buckley Rd TQ8 ....259 E5
Bucknall Cl EX12 .....190 D4
Bucknill Cl EX6 ....182 A4
Bucknole Cross EX14 ..102 A8
Bucknole Hill Rd EX14 ..102 A3
Bucks Cl TQ13 ....180 D7
Buckshots Cross EX14 ..69 A4
Buckton La EX14 ......101 C1
Buckwell Cl TQ7 ......258 D6
Buckwell Rd TQ7 .....258 D6
Buckwell St PL1,PL4 ...263 A2
Buctor Pk PL19 ....126 A8
Budde Cl Ivybridge PL21 ..237 D5
Plymouth PL9 ....256 A5
Tavistock PL19 ....171 B6
Buddle La Exeter EX4 ..176 E4
Hatherleigh EX20 ....75 C7
Bude St Appledore EX39 ..15 A1
Exeter EX4 ....261 B3
Budge Mdws EX15 ....115 A4
Budgett's Cross TA21 ..52 F6
Budgetts EX11 ....52 F6
Budleigh Cross EX14 ..101 F6
Budlake Cross EX14 ...167 A2
Budlake Units EX5 ....177 C1
Budleigh
Plymouth PL9 ....255 F5
Torquay TQ1 ....220 B6
Budleigh Hill EX9 .....198 B5
Budleigh Salterton Hospl
EX9 ....198 B1
Budshead Gn PL5 .....244 C4
Budshead La PL5 .....244 C5
Budshead Way PL5 ...244 C2
Buena Vista Cl PL6 ...245 D6
Buena Vista Dr PL6 ...245 C6
Buena Vista Way PL6 ..245 C6
Bugford Cross TQ6 ....232 C3
Bugford La TQ6 ....232 D3
Bugford Lane End TQ6 ..232 D3
Bughead Cross TQ13 ..111 D4
Bughole La TA21 .....51 E8
Building's Cross EX17 ..63 A4
Bulford TA21 ....160 D5
Bulford La Kennford EX6 ..181 E1
Wellington TA21 .....160 D5
Bulgis Pk EX36 ....158 A6
Bulkamore Ct TQ10 ...135 E5
Bull Ct EX31 ....154 F5
Bull Hill Barnstaple EX31 ..154 F7
Bideford EX39 ....157 A1

Bull Meadow Rd EX2 ..261 B2
Bull Point Prim Sch
PL5 ....247 B8
Bull Ring TQ13 ....130 F4
Bull's La TQ20 ....88 C8
Bullaford Gate EX34 ..31 E4
Bulland La
Cheriton Fitzpaine EX17 ..62 D3
Sampford Courtenay EX20 ..76 F4
Bullands Cl 4 TQ13 ...180 C8
Bullaton Cross TQ13 ..112 E1
Bulleid Cl PL2 ....247 F7
Bulleigh Cross TQ12 ..218 B8
Bulleigh Elms Cross
TQ12 ....212 A1
Bullen St EX5 ....81 E5
Bullens Cl EX5 ....81 E4
Buller Cl Plymouth PL7 ..250 E4
Plymouth PL11 ....247 A3
Buller Pk PL12 ....242 D3
Buller Rd
9 Barnstaple EX32 ...155 A5
Crediton EX17 ....165 B6
Exeter EX4 ....177 A5
Newton Abbot TQ12 ..207 D2
Torpoint PL11 ....247 B3
Bullfinch Cl EX15 ....163 A2
Bullhead Cross EX19 ..58 B2
Bullhorn Cross TQ7 ...142 F6
Bullow View EX19 ....58 F2
Bulls Ct 11 EX24 .....103 A4
Bully Shoot Cross EX24 ..103 A3
Bulmer Rd PL4 ....263 C3
Bulmoor Cross EX13 ..103 F5
Bulteel Gdns PL6 .....244 C7
Bulverton Pk EX10 ....187 F6
Bulworthy Cross EX16 ..47 E5
Bulworthy Knap EX16 ..47 E5
Bumpston Cross TQ11 ..215 C7
Bun La 8 TQ14 ....210 B4
Bungalows The
Axminster EX13 ......167 C4
4 Tiverton EX16 ......161 C3
Bunkers Farm TQ9 ...144 E7
Bunn Rd EX8 ....196 D4
Bunneford Cross EX15 ..64 E1
Bunson Gate EX18 ...45 A4
Bunting Cl
Newton Abbot TQ12 ..210 A5
Teignmouth TQ14 ....210 A3
Bunts La EX12 ....191 F7
Bunyan Cl PL5 ....244 C2
Burch Cl EX8 ....196 E2
Burch Gdns EX7 ......200 F1
Burches Cross EX16 ..48 A1
Burchill's Hill TA21 ...160 A6
Burchills Cl TA21 ....160 A6
Burcombe Hill EX34 ..158 E8
Burdge La EX24 .....74 C7
Burgage TA21 ....160 D6
Burgh Island Cswy TQ7 ..142 E3
Burgmanns Hill EX8 ..195 D5
Burke Rd TQ9 ....223 D6
Burland Cross EX31 ..9 F4
Burland La EX13 .....88 C2
Burlands The EX14 ...84 D2
Burleigh La
Malborough TQ7 .....147 E7
Plymouth PL3 ....248 D7
Burleigh Lane End TQ7 ..147 E8
Burleigh Manor PL3 ..248 D7
Burleigh Park Rd PL3 ..248 D6
Burleigh Rd TQ2 .....219 C7
Burlescombe CE Prim Sch
EX16 ....51 B3
Burlington Cl EX32 ...155 B3
Burlington Gr EX32 ...155 B2
Burn La Lydford PL19 ..107 C1
North Brentor PL19 ..117 C8
Burn River Rise TQ2 ..219 B8
Burnard Cl PL6 ......244 F5
Burnards Field Rd EX24 ..103 A4
Burnbreach Cnr EX24 ..102 B2
Burnbridge Hill EX16 ..63 D2
Burne Cross TQ12 ....131 D6
Burnet Cl EX2 ....178 C3
Burnet Rd PL6 ....248 F8
Burnham Ct EX12 ....192 A8
Burnham Park Rd PL3 ..248 D6
Burnistone Cl PL7 ....251 A3
Burnley Cl TQ12 .....206 D4
Burnley Rd TQ12 ....206 D4
Burns Ave Exeter EX2 ..177 F3
Plymouth PL5 ....244 C2
Burns Cl EX7 ....204 C6
Burns La PL21 ....137 B2
Burnside EX8 ....196 A3
Burnside Rd EX34 ....150 A3
Burnsome La EX14,EX15 ..67 D8
Burnt Mdw EX6 ......113 D5
Burnthouse Cross EX14 ..167 A8
Burnthouse Hill TQ12 ..212 B6
Burnthouse La EX2 ...177 F3
Burraton Comm Prim Sch
PL12 ....242 C4
Burraton Cross PL21 ..136 C3
Burraton Rd EX16 ....48 C8
Burrator Ave PL20 ...128 A8
Burrator Dr EX4 .....176 E8
Burrator Rd PL20 ....127 B3
Burridge Ave TQ2 ....219 D5

Celandine Gdns PL7 .....251 C5
Celandine Lawns EX15 ..162 D5
Celia Cres EX4 ....174 A2
Cembra Cl EX14 ....166 E5
Cemetery La EX5 ....82 F6
Cemetery Rd PL14 ......125 C5
Centenary Way TQ2 ....213 C2
Centry La Barnstaple EX31 .9 C5
  Parracombe EX31 .....4 D2
Central Ave
  Exeter, Countess Wear
  EX2 ....182 D7
  Exeter, Whipton EX4 .174 B2
  Holsworthy EX22 .....164 B4
  Lee Mill PL21 ....136 C6
  Paignton TQ3 ....226 B7
Central CE Mid Sch
  EX2 ....261 C1
Central Fst Sch EX2 ....261 C1
Central Park Ave PL4 ..262 C4
Central Rd PL1 ....262 B1
Central Sta EX4 ....261 A4
Central Station Chambers
  EX4 ....261 A3
Centre Ct PL21 ....137 C8
Centry Ct TQ5 ....230 E4
Centry Rd TQ5 ....230 E4
Century Dr EX39 ....156 E6
Ceramic Terr 3 EX32 ..155 A4
Chackrell La EX16 .....50 F2
Chad Rd PL9 ....140 A8
Chaddiford La EX31 ...154 D7
Chaddlewood Ave PL7 .263 B3
Chaddlewood Cl PL7 ...251 A4
Chaddlewood Ho PL7 ..251 B5
Chaddlewood Inf Sch
  PL7 ....251 A5
Chaddlewood Prim Sch
  PL7 ....251 A5
Chaffcombe Cross EX17 .78 F5
Chaffcombe La EX17 ...79 A6
Chaffinch Dr EX15 ....163 B2
Chagford CE Prim Sch
  TQ13 ....111 A7
Chagford Cross TQ13 .111 E5
Chagford Wlk PL6 .....249 E8
Chains Rd EX16 ....50 C1
Chaicombe Rocks La
  TA4 ....34 E5
Chalfield Cl TQ2 .....213 F3
Challabrook La TQ13 ..180 B6
Challacombe Cross
  PL20 ....120 F6
Challacombe Cross
  Bratton Fleming EX31 .11 F3
  Chagford TQ13 ......110 F2
  Chulmleigh EX18 ....45 A2
Challacombe Hill EX34 .8 A5
Challacombe Hill Rd EX34 .7 F6
Challenger Cross EX13 .87 E7
Challeycroft Rd TQ5 ..230 A1
Challgood Cl PL9 .....255 F5
Challgood Rise PL9 ...255 F5
Challick La TA4 ......35 F6
Challock Cl PL6 ......245 D4
Challowell La EX33 ...152 D8
Chaloner's Rd EX13 ..152 D6
Chambercombe La
  EX34 ....150 E4
Chambercombe Manor *
  EX34 ....150 E5
Chambercombe Park Rd
  EX34 ....150 E5
Chambercombe Pk Terr
  EX34 ....150 E5
Chambercombe Rd
  EX34 ....150 D5
Chamberlain Rd EX2 ..261 A1
Chamberlayne Dr PL7 .250 E6
Chambers Cl EX10 ....188 A8
Champernhayes La DT6 .104 F7
Champernowne PL21 ..137 B3
  EX34 ....150 D5
Champford La TA21 ...160 D5
Champford Mews 2
  TA21 ....160 D5
Champion Cross TA4 ..35 E3
Chancel Ct EX4 ....174 D1
Chancel La EX4 ....174 D1
Chancellor's Way EX4 .174 A2
Chandlers Gn EX39 ...15 B1
Chandlers Hts TQ8 ...259 D5
Chandlers Wlk EX34 ..150 B3
Chandlers Wlk EX10 ..261 A1
Chandler's La EX10 ..188 B5
Change La TA4 ....34 D6
Channel Park Ave PL3 .249 B5
Channel Sch (Language)
  EX34 ....150 B4
Channel View
  Ilfracombe EX34 ....150 D5
  Ilfracombe EX34 ....1 A2
Channel View Dr TQ7 .147 B6
Channel View Terr PL4 .263 C4
Channon Rd PL12 ....242 C4
Chanter's Ct EX32 ...155 A4
Chanter's Hill EX32 ..155 B5
Chanters Rd EX39 ...157 A3
Chantry Ave EX39 ...157 A3
Chantry Cl PL7 ......251 D5
Chantry Hill TQ7 ....145 D4
Chantry Mdw EX2 ...181 B8
Chantry The EX20 ...170 C5

Chapel Cl
  Gunnislake PL18 ....125 B5
  Halberton EX16 .....65 A8
  6 Horrabridge PL20 .126 F4
  Petrockstow EX20 ...56 F4
Chapel Cnr EX22 .....70 F5
Chapel Cotts PL7 ....132 E7
Chapel Cross
  Dunkeswell EX14 ....67 C2
  Iddesleigh EX19 ....57 E3
  Petrockstow EX20 ...56 F8
  Thorverton EX5 .....81 D5
  Thurlestone TQ7 ....143 A2
  Witheridge EX16 ....62 B5
Chapel Ct
  Stoke Gabriel TQ9 ..227 F8
  Swimbridge EX32 ...28 E8
  Torquay TQ1 ....219 F7
Chapel Down La PL21 .137 F3
Chapel Down Lane End
  PL21 ....137 E3
Chapel Downs Dr EX17 .165 A6
Chapel Downs Rd EX17 .165 A6
Chapel Fields 5 TQ10 .134 F3
Chapel Hill
  4 Budleigh Salterton EX9 .198 A1
  Cheriton Fitzpaine EX17 .62 F1
  Clyst St George EX3 .183 C6
  13 Exmouth EX8 .....202 A6
  Longdown EX6 ......98 E2
  5 Newton Abbot TQ12 .207 B3
  Uffculme EX15 ......66 A7
Chapel Hill Cross EX17 .62 F1
Chapel Ho 4 EX39 ...156 F7
Chapel Knap EX13,EX24 .102 F7
Chapel La
  Combe Martin EX34 ..3 A3
  Dartmouth TQ6 .....233 F3
  Folly Gate EX20 ....93 F8
  4 Horrabridge PL20 .126 F4
  Lutton PL21 ....133 B2
  Malborough TQ7 ....147 E6
  Mary Tavy PL19 .....117 E6
  Ottery St Mary EX11 .193 D4
  Stoke Fleming TQ6 ..226 A7
  Totnes TQ9 ....223 D5
  Yealmpton PL8 ......257 F4
Chapel Mdw PL7 .....126 C3
Chapel Rd
  Brampford Speke EX5 .81 C1
  Bratton Clovelly EX20 .92 A2
  Exeter EX2 ....177 B1
  Lympstone EX8 .....195 D5
  Newton Abbot TQ12 .207 D3
  Parkham EX39 ......39 E8
  Saltash PL12 ....242 B3
  Sidmouth EX10 .....188 B3
  Uplyme DT7 ....136 A2
Chapel Row TQ7 .....142 C6
Chapel St Axmouth EX12 .192 D7
  6 Bere Alston PL20 .125 E1
  Blackawton TQ9 ....139 E1
  Braunton EX33 ......152 D5
  Buckfastleigh TQ11 .236 B5
  Budleigh Salterton EX9 .199 G2
  Dolton EX19 ....57 F7
  Dulverton TA22 .....33 D6
  Ermington PL21 ....136 F4
  Exeter EX1 ....261 B3
  1 Exmouth EX8 .....202 A6
  Georgeham EX33 ....8 A2
  Gunnislake PL18 ....125 D6
  Holsworthy EX22 ....164 C3
  Morchard Bishop EX17 .61 A2
  Plymouth PL4 ....263 A3
  Plymouth, Mount Wise PL1 .247 E2
  Sidbury EX10 ....100 B8
  Sidmouth EX10 .....188 B3
  Tavistock PL19 .....171 B5
  Woolfardisworthy EX9 .38 F7
Chapel The 7 TQ9 ...223 D5
Chapel Way PL3 .....249 A6
Chapeldown Rd PL1 ..247 A2
Chapelry Te 5 TQ13 .123 C4
Chapelton Sta EX37 .28 A4
Chapeltown Cross EX5 .63 C1
Chapman Cr PL12 ....242 B3
Chapmans Ope PL1 ..247 D2
Chapple Cl EX6 ......201 B8
Chapple Cross
  Bovey Tracey TQ13 .180 B5
  Chagford TQ13 .....110 D8
  Dolton EX19 ....57 E6
Chapple Cross Cross
  TQ13 ....110 D8
Chapple Rd
  Bovey Tracey TQ13 .180 A6
  Witheridge EX16 ....46 E1
Chapplecroft Rd EX13 .87 E5
Charberry Rise DT6 ..104 F4
Chard Ave EX5 ......99 E8
Chard Barton PL5 ...244 B3
Chard Rd Axminster EX13 .88 B4
  Plymouth PL5 ....243 D2
Chard St Axminster EX13 .167 D6
  Chardstock EX13 ....87 B7
Chard Stock Cl EX1 ..178 D6
Charfield Dr PL6 ....249 A8
Charford Cross TQ10 .135 B1
Charlacott Cross
  Newton Tracey EX31 .27 B6
  Newton Tracey EX31 .27 B7
Charlemont Rd TQ14 .210 B8

Charles Ave EX39 ....157 A2
Charles Cross
  East Buckland EX32 .18 E3
  Plymouth PL4 ....263 A3
Charles Dart Cres EX32 .155 A4
Charles Hankin Way
  PL21 ....237 C6
Charles Hudson La 2
  EX31 ....155 A7
Charles Rd Honiton EX14 .166 C6
  Kingskerswell TQ12 .213 A2
Charles St
  13 Barnstaple EX32 .154 F6
  Dartmouth TQ6 .....233 F3
  3 Exmouth EX8 .....202 A7
  Plymouth PL1 ....263 A3
Charles Terr PL3 ....247 C1
Charleton CE Prim Sch
  TQ7 ....144 C1
Charleton Way TQ7 ..144 C1
Charlotte Cl TQ2 ....219 F8
Charlotte Ct TQ1 ....214 B1
Charlotte Mews 1 EX2 .261 B2
Charlotte St
  Crediton EX17 ......165 D5
  Plymouth PL2 ....247 E4
  8 Landkey EX32 .....17 B2
  Plymouth PL1 ....263 A3
Charter Cl EX16 .....161 B4
Charton Cross DT7 ..104 A2
Chartwell Cl TQ3 ...225 E7
Chartwell Dr TQ2 ...219 E7
Charwell Mdw EX5 ..82 F6
Chase The Honiton EX14 .166 D7
  Ivybridge PL21 .....237 D4
Chasty La EX22 .....164 C3
Chatsworth Cl PL6 ..243 F3
Chatsworth Gdns PL5 .243 F3
Chatsworth Rd TQ1 .220 B6
Chatto Rd TQ1 ......220 A7
Chatto Way TQ1 ....220 A7
Chattwell La PL21 ..136 F4
Chaucer Ave EX2 ...177 F3
Chaucer Prim Sch PL5 .244 C2
Chaucer Rd PL19 ...171 D5
Chaucer Rise EX8 ..196 C3
Chaucer Way PL5 ..244 C1
Chawleigh Cl PL18 .125 C5
Chawleigh Hill EX18 .59 D8
Chawleigh Prim Sch
  EX18 ....60 D7
Chawleigh Week Cross
  EX18 ....59 E8
Chawleigh Week La
  EX18 ....59 D8
Cheavestone Lea TQ9 .139 F7
Checkridge La EX13 .88 D2
Chedworth St PL4 ..263 A3
Cheeke St EX1 .....261 C3
Cheese La EX10 ....187 F4
Cheglinch Cnr EX34 .8 F5
Cheglinch La EX34 .8 F5
Cheldon Cross
  Chawleigh EX18 .....60 D8
  Chulmleigh EX18 ...45 D2
Chelfham Mill Sch EX12 .17 C4
Chelfham Sch PL20 .125 C3
Chelmer Cl PL7 .....251 A5
Chelmsford Pl PL5 .244 C4
Chelmsford Rd EX4 .176 E6
Chelsea Pl 8 TQ1 ..210 B5
Chelson Gdns PL6 ..245 E2
Chelson La EX11 ...101 C1
Chelston Rd
  Newton Abbot TQ12 .207 B4
  Torquay TQ2 ....219 E2
Cheltenham Cl EX4 .174 A4
Cheltenham Pl PL4 .263 B4
Chene Ct PL21 .....137 B2
Cheney's La EX14 ..166 E8
Chepstow Ave EX6 .182 C8
Chepstow Cl EX2 ..182 B8
Chequers Haigh PL8 .140 F6
Chercombe Bridge Rd
  TQ12 ....206 D3
Chercombe Cl TQ12 .206 E4
Chercombe Valley Rd
  TQ12 ....206 E4
Cheriswood Ave EX8 .196 D1
Cheriswood Cl EX8 .196 D1
Cheriton Bishop Com Prim
  Sch EX6 ....97 A4
Cheriton Cl PL5 ....244 A3
Cheriton Cross
  Cadbury EX5 ....81 C8
  Cheriton Fitzpaine EX17 .80 D7
Cheriton Fitzpaine Prim Sch
  EX17 ....62 E1
Cheriton Hill EX35 ..5 D3
Cheriton Mill Cross EX17 .62 E2

Cheriton Rd EX35 ...151 D1
Cherry Arbour EX32 .155 C3
Cherry Brook Dr TQ4 .229 B8
Cherry Brook Wlk TQ4 .226 B1
Cherry Cl
  Cheriton Fitzpaine EX17 .62 F1
  Exmouth EX8 ....196 C3
  5 Honiton EX14 .....85 C2
  Tiverton EX16 ......161 D5
  Willand EX15 ....162 D4
Cherry Cross TQ9 ..223 C4
Cherry Dr EX12 .....192 A5
Cherry Gdns
  Crediton EX17 ......165 C5
  Exeter EX2 ....178 A4
  Paignton TQ3 ......226 A7
Cherry Gn EX32 ....155 C2
Cherry Gr EX32 ....155 C2
Cherry Mdw TQ12 ..62 F1
Cherry Park Cl TQ2 .219 D2
Cherry Pk Appledore EX39 .14 F1
  Plymouth PL7 ....251 A3
Cherry Tree Cl
  Exeter EX4 ....173 A2
  Rockbeare EX5 .....99 B6
Cherry Tree Dr
  Brixton PL8 ....257 A5
  8 Landkey EX32 ....17 B2
Cherry Tree Gdns EX16 .161 E5
Cherry Tree La PL7 .251 A4
Cherrybridge Cross
  EX35 ....151 A2
Cherryford La EX31 .4 C4
Cherrywood Cl TQ12 .206 E4
Cheshire Dr PL6 ....244 D6
Cheshire Rd EX8 ...196 E2
Chesil Ct DT7 ......260 C3
Chester Cl EX4 .....176 E7
Chester Pl 3 PL4 ..248 E4
Chester Terr 11 EX2 .261 F4
Chesterfield Rd PL3 .249 B4
Chestermoor Cross EX20 .92 D5
Chesterton Cl PL5 ..244 C3
Chestnut Ave
  Cullompton EX15 ...163 C2
  Dartmouth TQ6 .....233 E4
  Exeter EX2 ....178 A3
  Plymouth PL9 ....255 C5
  Torquay TQ2 ....219 F4
Chestnut Cl
  Braunton EX33 .....152 E6
  Cheriton Bishop EX6 .97 B4
  Crediton EX17 ......165 B6
  Exeter EX5 ....196 A3
  Lamerton PL19 .....116 E4
  Saltash PL12 ....242 D4
  Seaton EX12 ....192 A7
  Tavistock PL19 .....171 D2
  Torpoint PL11 ......246 F3
  Wellington TA21 ....160 C5
Chestnut Cres EX5 .173 E8
Chestnut Ct EX2 ...181 B8
Chestnut Dr
  Bideford EX39 ......25 D4
  Brixham TQ5 ....230 A2
  Kingsteignton TQ12 .207 F6
  Newton Poppleford EX10 .186 F8
  Willand EX15 ....162 C4
Chestnut Pk TQ7 ...149 C7
Chestnut Rd
  Plymouth PL3 ....248 D7
  Tiverton EX16 ......161 F5
Chestnut Terr PL19 .116 E3
Chestnut View EX13 .42 B7
Chevithorne Cross
  EX37 ....28 F4

Chilcott Cl 5 EX16 ..64 D7
Chilcott Cross TA22 .33 A7
Chilcott La TA22 ....33 A7
Childrey Gdns PL6 ..245 C1
Childrey Wlk PL6 ...245 C1
Chill Pits La EX13 ..88 B8
Chillan Chapel EX21 .73 E4
Chilla Rd EX21 .....73 E3
Chillaton Cross EX22 .138 A1
Chillpark EX31 .....153 D5
Chiltern Cl TQ2 ....219 D3
Chiltern Cross EX16 .34 B2
Chilton Ave TQ14 ..210 C6
Chilton Cl PL6 .....249 B7
Chilton Gate EX16 .81 D8
Chilton La EX17 ...80 D7
Chilverton Cross EX17 .59 F1
Chilverton Hill Gate EX17 .59 F1
Chilverton La EX17 .59 F1
Chineway Gdns EX11 .169 F3
Chineway Head EX11 .101 B6
Chineway Hill EX11 .101 A6
Chineway Rd EX11 .169 F6
Chingswell St 4 EX39 .157 A2
Chinkwell Rise TQ2 .219 B8
Chinon Pl EX16 ....161 A6
Chipmunk Wlk EX32 .155 B6
Chipple Pk PL21 ...133 B2
Chircombe La EX39 .157 A4
Chiseldon Farm TQ5 .230 B2
Chiseldon Cross TQ5 .230 C2
Chiseldon La EX14 .85 B4
Chiseldon Ho EX14 .173 A1
Chittleburn Cross PL8 .256 E5
Chittleburn Hill PL8 .256 E5
Chittlehampton CE Prim Sch
  EX37 ....28 F4
Chivelstone Cross TQ7 .149 A5
Chivenor Ave PL5 ..243 D4
Chivenor Cross EX31 .15 E5
Chivenor La EX6 ...194 C4
Chivenor Rd EX6 ..194 C4
Chockenhole La EX9 .199 A8
Chockland Rd 6 TQ12 .122 E1
Choakhouse La EX20 .77 C7
Chollacott Cl PL19 .171 C4
Chollacott La PL19 .171 D3
Collaton Cross EX22 .39 E1
Cholloway's Cross EX32 .44 A7
Cholwell Cross TQ9 .222 F4
Chope Rd EX39 ....25 D4
Chopes Cl EX39 ...26 A4
Chough Cl PL15 ...105 A2
Chowns Cross EX5 .82 C8
Christcross La EX5 .82 D7
Christian Mill Bsns Pk
  PL6 ....244 F4
Christina Par TQ9 ..223 F5
Christina Te TQ9 ...223 E5
Christow Cross TQ9 .138 D7
Christow Prim Sch EX6 .113 B4
Christow Rd EX2 ...177 B2
Chrystel Cl EX10 ..100 D2
Chubb Dr PL3 .....248 B4
Chubb Rd EX39 ...26 A4
Chubs Cross EX20 .77 C5
Chubworthy Cross TA4 .35 D5
Chudleigh Cl EX39 .157 B3
Chudleigh CE Com Prim Sch
  TQ13 ....123 E6
Chudleigh Knighton CE Prim
  Sch TQ13 ....123 C4
Chudleigh Rd
  2 Bideford EX39 ....157 B1
  Exeter EX2 ....181 B7
  Kingsteignton TQ12 .207 B8
  Plymouth PL4 ....249 A4
Chudleigh Terr 6 EX39 .157 B1
Chudley Cl EX16 ...196 D1
Chugaton Cross EX37 .28 C5
Chuley Cross TQ13 .130 F3
Chuley Hill TQ13 ..130 F4
Chuley Rd TQ13 ...130 F4
Chulmleigh Hill EX18 .44 E1
Chulmleigh Prim Sch
  EX18 ....44 E1

Church Dr TA21 ....52 F7
Church End Rd TQ12 ...212 F4
Church Farm TQ7 ......143 A1
Church Fields TA21 ....160 E6
Church Flats EX6 ......201 B8
Church Gr EX32 ....155 B3
Church Hill
Awliscombe EX14 ......85 B4
Beer EX12 ....191 D5
Blackawton TQ9 ......139 E1
Brendon EX35 ....5 F4
Buckfastleigh TQ11 ...236 C6
Calstock PL18 ....125 D3
Exeter EX4 ....174 C2
Fremington EX31 ......153 E5
Holbeton PL8 ....136 D1
Honiton EX14 ....166 D5
Ilfracombe EX34 ......150 A5
Kingsower TQ6 ....234 A2
Lynton EX35 ....151 C5
Marldon TQ3 ....218 D4
Milton Combe PL20 ...126 C1
Musbury EX13 ....103 D5
Otterton EX9 ....198 D7
Plymouth PL6 ....245 B1
Tavistock PL19 ....171 E2
Tedburn St Mary EX6 ..97 F5
Winkleigh EX19 ....58 F3
Church Hill Cl TQ9 ....139 E2
Church Hill Cotts TQ9 .131 E1
Church Hill Cross EX20 .94 E7
Church Hill E 6 TQ5 ...230 C5
Church Hill Rd PL9 ....255 A6
Church Hill W 1 TQ5 ..230 C5
Church House Cl 8
TQ13 ....123 C4
Church La Alfington EX11 .84 F1
10 Barnstaple EX31 ..154 F5
Bideford EX39 ....25 C2
Bittaford PL21 ....137 C8
Bridford EX6 ....112 F5
Broadclyst EX5 ....175 C7
Calstock PL18 ....125 D3
Cargreen PL12 ....239 A1
Christow EX6 ....113 B3
Clyst St Mary EX5 ....179 B2
Crediton EX17 ....165 D5
Dunterton TA22 ....33 D6
East Budleigh EX9 ....198 B6
Exeter, Heavitree EX2 .177 F5
Exeter, Pinhoe EX4 ...174 D2
Feniton EX14 ....84 E2
Frithelstockstone EX38 .40 F5
Great Torrington EX38 .159 C5
Hatherleigh EX20 ......75 C7
Holsworthy EX22 ......164 C4
Kentisbeare EX14 .....66 F3
Kingsbridge TQ7 .....258 F2
Langtree EX38 ....40 F2
Membury EX13 ....87 D5
Modbury PL21 ....137 B2
Parracombe EX31 ....4 D1
Salcombe TQ8 ....259 E5
Shobrooke EX17 ....80 E4
St John PL11 ....252 B8
Stokeinteignhead TQ12 .209 B2
Swimbridge EX32 ......28 E8
Tavistock PL19 ....171 C5
Torquay TQ2 ....219 F5
Whitestone EX4 ....98 E4
Winkleigh EX19 ....58 F3
Yealmpton PL8 ....257 F4
Church Lake 8 EX32 ...17 B2
Church Lane Head
TQ13 ....121 B2
Church Lea PL19 ......171 E2
Church Mdw
High Bickington EX37 ..43 B7
Ivybridge PL21 ....237 A4
Landkey EX32 ....17 B2
Church Mdws
Bratton Clovelly EX20 .92 A2
Okehampton EX20 ......93 A6
Church Mead EX14 .....85 B1
Church Mews TQ12 ....207 E6
Church Park Ct TQ9 ...138 C7
Church Park Ct PL6 ...245 E8
Church Park Rd
Newton Ferrers PL8 ...141 A7
Plymouth PL6 ....245 E8
Yealmpton PL8 ....136 A2
Church Parks EX17 ....80 A5
Church Path
Ashburton TQ13 ......130 F4
Barnstaple EX31 ......154 F7
Halberton EX16 ....65 A7
Okehampton EX20 .....170 A5
6 Paignton TQ2 ......226 B6
Shute EX13 ....102 F8
Church Path Rd EX2 ..176 E5
Church Pk Bideford EX39 .25 A3
Cornwood PL21 ....133 C2
Horrabridge PL20 ....126 F4
Kingston TQ7 ....142 C6
Newton Ferrers PL8 ..141 A7
Paignton TQ4 ....225 C2
Church Pool EX34 ....8 F5
Church Quillet TQ9 ...139 E1
Church Rd
Bishopsteignton TQ14 .209 A7
Bovey Tracey TQ13 ...123 B7
Churchinford TA3 .....68 C8
Cockwood EX6 ....201 A6
Colaton Raleigh EX10 .186 E3

Church Rd continued
Dartmouth TQ6 ....233 E3
Exeter, Alphington EX2 ..177 B4
Exeter, St Thomas EX2 .177 A4
Exmouth EX8 ....202 A7
Georgeham EX33 ....8 A2
Highampton EX21 ......74 C7
Ideford TQ13 ....124 B4
Ilfracombe EX34 .....150 A5
Kenton EX6 ....194 F5
Luton TQ13 ....124 C4
Lympstone EX8 ....195 C5
Newton Abbot TQ12 ...207 E6
Plymouth, Plympton PL7 .250 F4
Plymouth, Plymstock PL9 .255 F7
Saltash PL12 ....242 D2
Silverton EX5 ....82 B5
Stoke Fleming TQ6 ...146 B7
Torquay, Barton TQ2 .214 A3
Torquay, St Marychurch
TQ1 ....220 B8
Wembury PL9 ....140 D8
Whimple EX5 ....99 E7
Church Row La PL5 ...244 C6
Church Side EX5 ......179 D7
Church St
Axminster EX13 ......167 D5
Axmouth EX12 ....192 D7
Bradninch EX5 ....83 A7
Braunton EX33 ....152 D7
4 Brixham TQ5 ......230 D5
Buckfastleigh TQ11 ..236 B5
Calstock PL18 ....125 D3
Colyton EX24 ....103 A5
Combe Martin EX34 ....3 A3
Crediton EX17 ....165 D5
Cullompton EX15 ....163 C3
Dawlish EX7 ....204 C6
Dolton EX19 ....57 F7
Ermington PL21 ......136 F4
Exeter EX2 ....177 F5
Exmouth EX8 ....202 A6
8 Honiton EX14 .....166 C6
Ilfracombe EX34 ....150 B5
Kenton EX6 ....194 D3
Kingsbridge TQ7 ....258 D5
Kingsteignton TQ12 .207 E6
Lyme Regis DT7 ......260 E3
Modbury PL21 ....137 B2
Morchard Bishop EX17 ..61 B2
Okehampton EX20 ....170 B5
Paignton TQ3 ....226 B6
Plymouth PL3 ....248 A4
Salcombe TQ8 ....259 E5
Sandford EX17 ....80 A5
Sidbury EX10 ....101 C2
8 Sidford EX10 .....101 B1
Sidmouth EX10 ......188 B3
8 South Brent TQ10 .134 F3
Starcross EX6 ....201 B8
Tiverton EX16 ......161 C4
Torquay TQ2 ....219 F3
Uplyme DT7 ....260 B5
Witheridge EX16 .....46 E1
Church St Mews 4 TQ3 .226 B6
Church Steps Cotts EX5 .184 B3
Church Terr
7 Bampton EX16 ......34 B1
Exeter EX2 ....177 F5
Church View
Bideford EX39 ....26 A1
13 Chudleigh TQ13 ..123 E6
Dawlish EX7 ....204 C6
Kingsteignton TQ12 .207 E6
Ottery St Mary EX11 .169 D3
Sutcombe EX22 ....54 A6
Walkhampton PL20 ...127 B4
Church Way
Newton Abbot TQ12 ..207 E1
Plymouth PL5 ....247 E8
Yealmpton PL8 ......257 F4
Church Ways EX20 ....95 B5
Church Wlk
Avonwick TQ10 ......135 B1
6 Bideford EX39 ....157 A1
Stoke Gabriel TQ9 ...227 F7
Wembury PL9 ....140 D8
Churchfield Rd 5 EX39 .15 A1
Churchfields EX17 ....160 D7
Churchfields Gdns TQ6 .233 D3
Churchfields W TQ6 ..233 D3
Churchford Rd EX33 ...8 A1
Churchgate EX6 ....30 E1
Churchill Ave EX7 ....204 D5
Churchill Cl
Barnstaple EX32 ....155 B6
Kenton EX6 ....194 D3
Churchill Cotts PL21 .137 D6
Churchill Cres EX36 .158 C3
Churchill Ct
4 Brixham TQ5 .....230 C5
Lympstone EX8 ......195 E6
Churchill Dr
Crediton EX17 ......165 B6
Teignmouth TQ14 ...210 C6
Churchill Gdns EX17 .165 B6
Churchill Hill 6 ......10 C4
Churchill La
Axminster EX13 ......88 A5
Calverleigh EX16 ....48 C3
Chulmleigh TA4 .....35 C5
Churchill Rd
Bideford EX39 ....26 A4
Exeter EX2 ....176 F4

Churchill Rd continued
Exmouth EX8 ....196 D2
Tavistock PL19 .....171 D2
Tiverton EX16 ......161 A4
Churchill Way
Appledore EX39 ......14 F1
Northam EX39 ....157 A7
Plymouth PL3 ....248 E6
Churchill Wlk PL12 ..242 E1
Churchills 11 EX15 ...42 F8
Churchills The TQ12 .207 A4
Churchlands EX17 ....78 C4
Churchlands Cl PL6 ..245 E7
Churchlands Rd PL6 .245 E8
Churchstanton Prim Sch
TA3 ....68 B8
Churchstow Wlk PL6 .249 E8
Churchtown Cl PL21 ..137 D6
Churchtown Vale PL12 .242 D1
Churchward Rd TQ3 .226 A8
Churchwater La EX18 .58 D8
Churchway TQ1 ......220 C7
Churchwood Cl TQ1 ..220 C5
Churchyard La EX17 ..61 C7
Churscombe Gn TQ3 .218 E2
Churscombe Pk TQ3 .218 E2
Churscombe Rd TQ3 .218 D2
Churston Broadway
TQ4 ....229 B7
Churston Cl TQ5 ....229 C6
Churston Cross
Churston Ferrers TQ5 .229 E4
West Putford EX22 ...39 B2
Churston Ferrers Gram Sch
TQ5 ....229 C5
Churston Rd TQ5 ....229 C5
Churston Rise EX12 .191 F8
Churston Sta TQ5 ...229 C5
Churston Way TQ5 ..230 B4
Chute St EX1 ....261 C4
Cider Press Craft Ctr*
TQ9 ....215 F1
Cinders La TQ6 .....146 B7
Cintra Terr EX39 ....157 A4
Cistern St TQ9 ......223 B5
Citadel Ope 08 PL1 ..263 A2
Citadel Rd PL1 ......263 A2
Citadel Rd E PL1 ....263 A2
Citadel The* PL1 ....263 A1
City Arc EX4 ....261 A2
City Bsns Pk PL3 ....248 A4
City Coll EX1 ....261 B2
City Mus & Art Gal*
PL4 ....263 A3
City Mus & Art Gal Annexe*
PL4 ....263 A3
Claddon La TQ1,TQ2 .214 A5
Clampet La 2 TQ14 ..210 A3
Clampitts Stile TQ1 .135 C6
Clampitt Cl TQ12 ....211 D1
Clampitt Rd TQ12 ...211 D2
Clampitts EX15 ......163 B2
Clanage Cross TQ14 .124 C1
Clanage St TQ14 ....210 B4
Clannaborough Cross
EX17 ....78 E5
Claponmill Cross EX5 .83 E2
Clapp's La Beer EX12 .191 D5
Seaton EX12 ....192 B5
Clappentail La DT7 ..260 C3
Clappentail Pk DT7 ..260 C3
Clapper Cross
Bondleigh EX20 .....77 A8
Zeal Monachorum EX17 .78 B5
Clapper La EX14 .....66 C7
Clapperbrook La EX2 .177 B1
Clapworthy Cider Mill*
EX36 ....29 D2
Clapworthy Cross EX36 .29 D2
Clara Pl EX3 ....182 E5
Clare Pl PL4 ....161 F6
Clare Pl PL4 ....263 B2
Clare St PL21 ....237 C4
Claredale Rd EX8 ...202 B6
Claremont Ave TQ12 .211 B6
Claremont Field EX11 .169 D3
Claremont Gr Exeter EX2 .261 C1
Exmouth EX8 ....202 A6
Claremont La EX8 ...202 A7
Claremont Pl EX20 ...75 C7
Claremont St PL1 ...262 C4
Clarence Cotts 4 EX34 .150 B6
Clarence Ct PL1 ....262 A3
Clarence Hill TQ6 ..233 F4
Clarence Ho TQ2 ...219 E6
Clarence Pl
14 Barnstaple EX32 .155 B3
Exeter EX4 ....261 C4
Plymouth, Morice Town
PL2 ....247 F4
Plymouth, Stonehouse PL1 .262 A3
Clarence Rd
Budleigh Salterton EX9 .198 A2
Exmouth EX8 ....202 A7
Torpoint PL11 ......247 B3
Clarence St TQ6 ....233 F4
Clarendon Ho 1 PL1 .247 F1
Clarendon Rd
Ipplepen TQ12 .....211 B8
10 Newton Abbot TQ12 .207 B3
Claridge The TQ3 ...226 A8
Clarke Cir EX15 .....65 F7
Clarke Ctr The EX2 .177 C2
Clarke Mead EX7 ...204 D7
Clarks Barn Rd TQ7 .143 E7

Clarks La EX20 ....57 A6
Clatworthy La EX32 ..29 E6
Claude Dix Cl 1 EX31 .155 A7
Claw Cross EX39 ......38 F5
Claw Hill EX16 ....62 F4
Claw Pk EX22 ....72 B2
Clawford Cross EX22 .72 D3
Clawton Prim Sch EX21 .72 B1
Clay La
Chudleigh Knighton TQ13 .123 C3
Colyton EX24 ....103 A4
Copplestone EX17 ....79 A6
Dartington TQ9 .....223 A8
Lympstone EX8 .....195 C4
Teignmouth TQ14 ...210 B5
Uffculme EX15 ......66 A8
Clay Park Terr TQ9 .228 A7
Clayford La TA22 ....33 C5
Clayford Rd TA22 ....33 C5
Clayhidon Crossway
EX15 ....52 E2
Clayland Cross TQ4 .225 E4
Claylands Dr TQ4 ..225 E4
Claylands View EX14 .166 B4
Claymans Pathway
PL21 ....237 A6
Claypark Hill EX16 ..47 D5
Claypits Covert Cross
EX31 ....154 A2
Clayton Pl PL4 ......249 B2
Clayton Rd Exeter EX4 .177 A7
Plymouth PL4 ......249 B2
Clear View PL12 ....242 E3
Clearbrook Ave PL5 .243 E1
Cleave Cl
Barnstaple EX31 ....154 D4
Tedburn St Mary EX6 .97 F4
Cleave Cross EX14 ...86 C3
Cleave Hill Dolton EX19 .57 E6
South Molton EX36 .46 A6
Cleave La
Bishop's Tawton EX32 .27 F7
Burrington EX37 .....44 A2
Chapelton EX32 .....28 A7
Wilmington EX14 ....86 C3
Cleave Lane End EX32 .27 F7
Cleave Rd EX31 .....153 F5
Cleave Rd EX31 .....154 D4
Cleave The PL10 ....253 B2
Cleaveanger La EX17 .62 E5
Cleaveland Rise TQ12 .206 F1
Cleaves Cl EX5 ......81 E5
Cleavewood Dr EX39 .157 D1
Cleeve Dr PL21 .....237 B5
Cleeve Gdns PL2 ...248 A8
Cleeve The EX15 .....66 E8
Clegg Ave PL11 .....246 E3
Clement Rd PL7 ....251 B5
Clement's La EX32 ..28 C6
Clennon Ave TQ4 ...226 B4
Clennon Ct
8 Brixham TQ5 ....230 C3
Torquay TQ2 ......226 B4
Clennon Dr TQ4 ...226 B4
Clennon Gdns TQ4 .226 B4
Clennon Hts TQ4 ..226 B4
Clennon La TQ2 ....214 A2
Clennon Pk TQ4 ...226 B4
Clennon Rise TQ4 ..226 B4
Clennon Summit TQ4 .226 B1
Clerk Cl EX8 ....196 C2
Cleve Rd EX4 ......176 F6
Clevedon Ct EX4 ...173 D1
Clevedon Park Ave PL2 .248 B6
Clevedon Rd EX10 .188 C5
Cleveland Ct Exeter EX1 .261 C4
Exeter EX1 ....261 C4
Cleveland Gdns EX1 .261 C4
Cleveland Pl
8 Dawlish EX7 .....204 E6
Exmouth EX8 ....201 F6
Cleveland Rd
Paignton TQ2 ......226 C5
Paignton TQ4 ......226 C5
Plymouth PL1 ......248 B4
Torquay TQ2 ....219 F6
Cleveland St 7 EX4 .177 A5
Cleveland Terr EX39 .156 C7
Cleveways EX36 .....31 A1
Cleverdon Cross EX22 .53 F8
Cleverhayes La EX14 .86 B4
Cliff Bastin Cl EX2 .178 D8
Cliff Ct 18 EX7 .....204 E6
Cliff Hill TQ6 ......146 B6
Cliff La PL10 ....252 A4
Cliff Park Ave TQ4 .226 C3
Cliff Park Ct TQ4 ..226 C2
Cliff Park Rd TQ4 ..226 C2
Cliff Rd
Budleigh Salterton EX9 .199 G2
Paignton TQ4 ......226 D5
Plymouth PL1 ......263 A1
Salcombe TQ8 ......259 C3
Sidmouth EX10 ....188 C3
Teignmouth TQ14 ..210 B3
Torquay TQ2 ......219 F2
Wembury PL9 ......140 D7
Cliff Terr EX9 ......199 G2
Cliffden Cl 1 TQ14 .210 A3
Cliffden Ct TQ14 ..210 C5
Clifford Cl
10 Chudleigh TQ13 .123 E6
Exeter EX1 ....178 B7
Kingsteignton TQ12 .207 E7
Plymouth PL5 ......243 A3
Teignmouth TQ14 ..210 A3
Clifford Cross EX6 ..112 C8
Clifford Dr TQ12 ...180 F2

Clifford Gdns EX17 .165 D5
Clifford Mews TA21 .160 E6
Clifford Rd EX4 ....177 F8
Clifford St
14 Chudleigh TQ13 .123 E6
Kingsteignton TQ12 .207 E7
Tiverton EX16 .....160 F6
Torquay TQ1 ....220 A5
Cliffside Rd TQ1 ...220 C8
Clifton Ave PL7 ....250 E7
Clifton Bank 3 TQ3 .226 A6
Clifton Cl Paignton TQ3 .225 F6
Plymouth PL7 ......250 E7
Clifton Cres TQ3 ..226 A6
Clifton Ct 3 EX34 .150 B5
Clifton Gdns TQ3 ..226 A6
Clifton Gr TQ3 .....226 A6
Clifton Hill EX1 ...177 E7
Clifton Ho 17 TQ4 .210 C5
Clifton La EX31 .....10 B4
Clifton Pl Dawlish EX7 .204 C6
Plymouth PL4 .....249 A4
Salcombe TQ8 .....259 E5
Clifton Rd Exeter EX1 .261 C3
Paignton TQ3 .....226 A6
Clifton Rise TQ3 ..226 A6
Clifton St
Barnstaple EX31 ...154 F4
Bideford EX39 .....157 B1
Exeter EX1 ....177 E6
Plymouth PL4 .....263 A4
Clifton Terr
Barnstaple EX31 ...154 F4
8 South Brent TQ10 .134 F3
Climsland Rd TQ4 .226 A5
Clinton Ave Exeter EX4 .177 E8
Plymouth PL4 .....249 A4
Clinton CE Prim Sch The
EX20 ....9 E2
Clinton Cl EX9 .....197 F2
Clinton Gdns EX20 .57 A7
Clinton Rd EX32 ....155 B3
Clinton Rise EX12 .191 E6
Clinton Sq EX8 ....201 F6
Clinton St EX4 .....177 A5
Clinton Terr
10 Barnstaple EX32 .155 B3
Budleigh Salterton EX9 .198 A2
Great Torrington EX38 .159 B5
Merton EX20 ....52 F6
Millbrook PL10 ....252 F6
Clipper Quay EX2 ..261 B1
Clipper Wharf EX8 .201 E6
Cliston Ave EX8 ....196 C2
Cliston Cross TQ9 .223 C6
Cliston La EX20 ......76 E4
Clittaford Rd PL6 ..244 F7
Clittaford View PL6 .244 E7
Cliveden Rd EX39 ...26 A4
Cloake Pl PL12 .....239 A2
Clobells 3 TQ10 ...134 F2
Cloggshill Cross EX31 .9 B1
Cloister Rd EX4 ....177 F7
Clonway 1 PL20 ...126 F3
Close The
14 Bere Alston PL20 .125 E1
Brixham TQ5 ......230 C6
Holcombe EX7 .....210 F8
Paignton TQ4 .....229 B6
Rew EX5 ....82 A2
Saltash PL12 ......242 C3
Seaton EX12 ......192 A5
Tiverton EX16 ....161 F6
Cloutman's La EX23 ..7 C2
Clovelly Apmts 2 EX34 .150 B5
Clovelly Cl EX39 ...156 E1
Clovelly Cross EX39 .23 D2
Clovelly Gdns N EX39 .156 C7
Clovelly Gdns S 2 EX39 .156 C7
Clovelly Cross EX39 .23 D3
Clovelly Prim Sch EX39 .23 D3
Clovelly Rd Bideford EX39 .25 D4
Plymouth PL4 .....263 C3
Clovelly Rise
Dawlish EX7 ......204 D5
Paignton TQ3 .....225 E6
Clovelly View PL9 ..255 A7
Clover Dr EX15 ....163 B2
Clover Rise PL6 ...245 E8
Clover Way EX32 ..155 E4
Clover Wlk PL12 ...242 C3
Cloverdale Ct DT7 .260 E3
Clowance Cl PL1 ..247 F1
Clowance La PL1 ..247 F1
Clowance St PL1 ..247 F1
Cluden Cl EX2 .....181 B8
Cluden Rd EX39 ...156 F6
Clumpit La EX6 ...194 A4
Clyde St PL2 ....247 F5
Clydesdale Rd EX4 .173 A1
Clyst Ave Brixham TQ5 .230 A2
Clyst Honiton EX5 .179 E2
Clyst Halt Ave EX2 .178 E3
Clyst Heath EX2 ...178 D3
Clyst Heath CE Prim Sch
EX5 ....179 D7
Clyst Rd Exeter EX3 .178 F2
Topsham EX3 ......182 E5
Clyst St Mary Prim Sch
EX5 ....179 A2
Clyst Units EX2 ...177 D1
Clyst Vale Com Coll
EX5 ....175 D5
Clyst Valley Rd EX5 .179 A2
Clyst William Cross EX15 .84 B5
Clyston Hydon Prim Sch
EX5 ....83 D4
Coach Dr EX39 ......26 D2
Coach Ho The TQ3 .226 A6
Coach House Mews PL9 .256 F6

Coach Pl TQ12 .... 207 C2
Coach Rd
　Newton Abbot TQ12 ...... 207 B1
　Noss Mayo PL8 .... 140 F6
Silverton EX5 .... 82 B6
Coach Rd The DT7 ...... 260 B8
Coarsewell Cross PL21 .. 138 A5
Coastguard Cotts
　Bigbury-on-Sea TQ7 ..... 142 D4
　Dawlish EX7 .... 204 F6
　Down Thomas PL9 ...... 254 F2
　Galmpton TQ7 .... 147 B6
　Stoke EX39 .... 22 B3
　Torquay TQ1 .... 220 D2
Coastguard Hill EX9 .... 199 H2
Coastguard Rd EX9 .... 198 B1
Coates Rd EX2 .... 178 B5
Cob Castle TA21 .... 52 D8
Cob Mdw EX20 .... 75 C7
Cobb La PL9 .... 255 F6
Cobb Rd DT7 .... 260 D2
Cobb Terr DT7 .... 260 D2
Cobb The* DT7 .... 260 D2
Cobbacombe Cross EX16 .49 D6
Cobbaton Combat Collection
　Mus* EX37 .... 28 D5
Cobbaton Cross EX37 .. 28 D6
Cobbett Rd PL5 .... 244 B2
Coblands Cross EX5 .... 82 A7
Cobley La Bideford EX39 . 26 C6
　Lapford EX17 .... 60 E4
　West Worlington EX17 .... 60 F6
Cobourg St PL1 .... 262 C3
Coburg Cl TA21 .... 52 F7
Coburg Pl EX15 .... 163 C6
Coburg Rd EX10 .... 188 A3
Coburg Terr EX10 ...... 188 A3
Cockeram's Rd EX5 ..... 99 C8
Cockhaven Cl TQ14 .... 208 F7
Cockhaven Rd TQ14 .... 208 F7
Cockington Cl PL6 ..... 245 E1
Cockington Country Pk*
　TQ2 .... 219 B4
Cockington La
　Paignton TQ3 .... 219 C1
　Torquay TQ2 .... 219 D4
Cockington Prim Sch
　TQ2 .... 219 F5
Cockington Rd TQ3 .... 219 A3
Cockington Wlk PL6 .... 245 C1
Cockland Hill TA21 ...... 51 C8
Cockle La EX13 .... 48 F3
Cockles La ❶ EX17 .... 165 D5
Cockles Rise EX17 ..... 165 D5
Cockpit Hill EX15 ...... 163 C3
Cockram's La EX37 ..... 43 F7
Cockrams Butt Cross
　EX37 .... 29 B1
Cocks Pk PL21 .... 142 D7
Cockspark La EX14 ..... 84 F8
Cocktree Throat EX20 .. 95 C8
Cockwood Prim Sch
　EX6 .... 201 B6
Codden Cross EX22 .... 28 A8
Codden Hill Cross EX32 . 27 E8
Coddiford Cross EX17 .. 62 E2
Coddiford Hill EX17 .... 62 E1
Coddiford La EX17 ..... 62 F2
Codrington St EX1 .... 261 C3
Coffins La EX6 .... 181 F4
Coffinswell La TQ12 .... 213 A4
Coffintree Cross EX17 .. 80 F6
Coffintree Hill EX17 .... 80 F7
Cofton Hill EX6 .... 201 A5
Cofton La EX6 .... 200 F5
Cofton Rd EX2 .... 177 D1
Coil Cross EX31 .... 10 B6
Coker Ave TQ2 .... 214 A4
Cokers Elm EX14 ...... 87 A7
Cokers Elm Cross EX14 . 87 A7
Colands Ct EX2 .... 181 A8
Colaton La EX5 .... 81 E5
Colaton Terr EX10 ..... 188 A4
Colborne Rd PL6 ...... 245 A2
Colcombe La
　Dalwood EX13 .... 86 F1
　Shute EX13 .... 102 F8
Colcombe Rd EX24 .... 103 A5
Cold East Cross TQ13 .. 121 E1
Coldharbour
　Bideford EX39 .... 157 A2
　❸ Totnes TQ9 .... 223 E5
　Uffculme EX15 .... 66 A7
Coldharbour Cross
　Chilsworthy EX22 ...... 53 E1
　Loddiswell PL21 .... 138 B3
Coldharbour Rd EX16 . 161 A3
Coldrenick St PL5 .... 243 D1
Coldwell La EX12 .... 192 D6
Coldwells Cl EX31 .... 153 E5
Cole La Ivybridge PL21 . 237 C6
　Ivybridge, Higher Keaton
　PL21 .... 237 C1
Cole Moore Mdw PL19 .171 B6
Cole's Cnr EX18 .... 59 C8
Cole's Cotts PL7 ...... 250 E6
Cole's Cross TQ9 ..... 144 F5
Cole's Ct TQ6 .... 233 F3
Cole's La TQ12 .... 212 F5
Colebrook La PL7 .... 250 E7
Colebrook Rd
　Plymouth, Plympton PL7 . 250 E6
　Plymouth, St Budeaux PL5 . 243 D1
Colebrooke La EX15 .. 65 A1
Coleford Hill EX16 .... 48 B6
Coleman Ave TQ14 .... 210 A5
Coleman Dr PL9 ...... 255 F4
Coleman's Cross EX24 .102 D6

Colemans Cross PL15 ..105 B5
Coleridge Ave PL6 .... 244 F2
Coleridge Cl EX8 ..... 196 C4
Coleridge Ct TQ2 ..... 214 A2
Coleridge La EX15 .... 145 A2
Coleridge Rd Exeter EX2 .176 F4
　Ottery St Mary EX11 .. 169 F4
　Plymouth PL4 .... 249 A4
　❶ Tiverton EX16 ...... 64 D7
Coles Mead EX16 .... 161 F4
Coles Mill EX22 ...... 164 C4
Coles's La EX13 ...... 104 B8
Colesdown Hill PL9 .. 250 B1
Colesworthy Cross
　TQ12 .... 180 B2
Colhayne La
　Dalwood EX13 .... 86 F1
　Shute EX13 .... 102 F8
Colin Campbell Ct ❶
　PL1 .... 262 B3
Colin Rd TQ3 .... 226 C7
Coll Ct EX15 .... 66 A7
Coll of St Mark & St John
　PL6 .... 245 C4
Collabear Cnr EX31 .... 27 D8
Collabridge Hill EX6 . 112 E8
Collabridge La EX6 .. 112 E8
Collabridge Rd EX6 .. 112 E8
Collacombe Cross PL19 .116 D4
Collacott Cross EX38 .. 40 F2
Collacotts La EX19 .... 59 B2
Collaford Cl PL7 ...... 251 A4
Collapark TQ9 .... 223 B6
Collard La PL7 .... 132 D4
Collaton Cross
　Halwell TQ9 .... 139 D4
　Malborough TQ7 ...... 147 F6
　Yealmpton PL8 .... 141 B8
Collaton Ct TQ2 ...... 219 C8
Collaton Ho ❶ TQ1 .. 220 D4
Collaton La EX19 .... 117 F2
Collaton Rd
　Malborough TQ7 ...... 147 F6
　Torquay TQ2 .... 219 C8
Collaton St Mary CE Prim
　Sch TQ3 .... 225 C5
Collatons Wlk EX17 .. 78 C4
College TQ13 .... 180 E8
College Ave Exeter EX2 . 261 C2
　Plymouth PL3 .... 248 E5
　Tavistock PL19 .... 171 D6
College Cl EX39 ...... 156 C6
College Ct
　Barnstaple EX31 ..... 154 D3
　❶ Torquay TQ1 ...... 219 F6
College Dean Cl PL6 .. 245 C5
College Gn Bideford EX39 .156 F2
　Uffculme EX15 .... 66 A7
College La
　Clyst Hydon EX5,EX15 . 83 B5
　Ide EX2 .... 176 C2
　Plymouth PL4 .... 248 F4
College Park Pl PL3 . 248 E5
College Rd
　Cullompton EX15 .... 163 C4
　Exeter EX1 .... 261 C3
　Newton Abbot TQ12 .. 207 D2
　Plymouth PL2 .... 247 E5
　Shebbear EX21 .... 55 F4
College Road Prim Sch
　PL2 .... 247 E5
College The EX11 .... 169 D4
College View PL9 ..... 248 C4
College Way TQ6 ..... 233 E4
Collerton Ct ❶ EX2 .. 261 B2
Colleton Cl EX8 ...... 202 C8
Colleton Cres EX2 ... 261 B2
Colleton Gate EX18 .. 44 C1
Colleton Gr EX2 ..... 261 B1
Colleton Hill EX2 .... 261 B1
Colleton Mews EX2 .. 261 B1
Colleton Row EX2 ... 261 B1
Colleton Way EX8 ... 202 C8
Collett Way TQ12 .... 207 E3
Colley Cres TQ3 ..... 226 A6
Colley End Pk TQ3 .. 226 A6
Colley End Rd TQ3 .. 226 A6
Colley La EX17,EX13 . 125 D4
Colley Lane Cross TQ13 .124 D4
Colley Park Rd EX3 .. 152 D5
Colleybrook Cl ❶ TQ12 .123 E1
Collepriest View EX16 .161 B1
Collerton Cl ❶ PL9 .. 140 D8
Collin Cl PL5 .... 243 D1
Collingsdown Cross EX39 .39 F4
Collingwood Ave PL4 . 263 C2
Collingwood Cl
　Dartmouth TQ6 .... 233 C3
　Torquay TQ2 .... 220 C2
Collingwood Rd
　Dartmouth TQ6 .... 233 C3
　Paignton TQ4 .... 226 A5
　Plymouth PL1 .... 248 A3
Collingwood Villas ❶
　PL1 .... 248 A3
Collins Pk EX9 .... 198 B6
Collins Rd Exeter EX4 . 173 E2
　Totnes TQ9 .... 223 B6
Collins La EX16 ...... 161 C1
Collipriest Rd EX16 .. 161 C2
Colliton Cross EX14 .. 84 C6
Colliver Cross EX9 .. 198 E5
Collyland La EX17 .... 62 C3
Collymore Cross PL21 .138 A4
Colne Gdns PL3 ..... 249 B5
Colscott Cross EX22 .. 39 C1
Colston Cl PL6 ...... 245 C8
Colston Cross EX13 .. 88 B4

Colston La EX16 ...... 47 E1
Colston Rd TQ11 .... 236 E3
Coltishall Cl PL5 .... 243 F4
Coltness Rd PL9 .... 256 B5
Coltsfoot Cl PL6 .... 249 B8
Columbjohn Cross EX5 . 82 B2
Colvin Cl EX8 .... 202 D7
Colway Cl DT7 ...... 260 D5
Colway Cross TQ14 .. 124 B1
Colway La
　Chudleigh TQ13 ...... 123 F6
　Lyme Regis DT7 ...... 260 D4
Colwell Rd PL6 ...... 245 E3
Colwill Rd PL6 ...... 245 F3
Colwill Wlk PL6 ..... 245 F3
Coly Rd Colyton EX24 . 103 B4
Colyford Sta EX24 .. 103 A4
Colyton Cross EX14 .. 86 C2
Colyton Gram Sch EX24 .103 A7
Colyton Hill EX13,EX24 . 103 B6
Colyton Prim Sch EX24 .103 A4
Colyton Rd
　Northleigh EX24 ...... 102 C6
　Whitford EX13,EX24 .. 103 A6
Combas La EX13 ...... 7 E2
Combe Beacon La TA20 . 69 F7
Combe Cl EX13 ...... 167 D5
Combe Cross
　Ashburton TQ13 ...... 131 C5
　Aveton Gifford PL21 .. 143 A8
　Ivybridge PL21 .... 137 B6
　Kingsbridge TQ7 ...... 258 D7
　Loddiswell TQ7 .... 138 C1
　Shillingford EX16 ..... 34 D4
　Strete TQ6 .... 145 E7
Combe Hill EX15 ..... 52 C2
Combe Hill Cross TQ12 .123 F2
Combe Mill Dro TA20 . 69 F5
Combe La
　Combe St Nicholas TA20 . 69 E5
　Dulverton TA22 ...... 33 D6
　East Anstey TA22 .... 32 F6
　Galmpton TQ5 .... 229 B3
　North Tawton EX17 .... 77 F1
　Northleigh EX24 ...... 102 B7
　Spreyton EX17 .... 95 F8
　Torquay TQ2 .... 214 A1
Combe Martin Cty Prim Sch
　EX34 .... 2 F4
Combe Martin Wildlife &
　Dinosaur Pk* EX34 . 3 C2
Combe Martin Wildlife Park
　Rly* EX34 .... 3 C2
Combe Mead Prim Sch
　EX16 .... 161 F3
Combe Moor La EX17 .. 77 F1
Combe Pafford Sch
　TQ2 .... 214 B3
Combe Rd
　Axmouth EX12,DT7 .. 193 B6
　Torquay TQ2 .... 214 B2
Combefishacre Cross
　TQ12 .... 217 D8
Combefishacre La TQ9,
　TQ12 .... 217 D6
Combehead Droveway
　EX13 .... 86 E3
Combehead La EX13 .. 86 F3
Combeland La TA22 .. 34 A5
Combepark Cross TQ9 . 217 A1
Comber's Cross EX31 .. 27 E6
Combesdown Cross
　EX22 .... 72 C6
Combeshead Cross
　Cornwood PL21 ...... 133 F1
　Diptford TQ9 .... 138 E6
　Heasley Mill EX36 .... 19 C2
Combeshead La
　Dunchideock EX2 ..... 114 A7
　West Anstey EX36 .... 32 A7
Combley Dr PL6 ..... 245 D4
Combpyne La DT7,EX13 .193 E8
Combpyne Rd EX13 .. 103 D5
Combrew La EX31 .... 16 A3
Combsland Cross EX36 . 31 B4
Combsland New Cross
　EX36 .... 31 B4
Comburg Cl EX8 ..... 196 E3
Comepark La EX35 .. 151 E2
Comer's Cross TA24 .. 21 E6
Comer's Gate TA24 .. 21 E6
Comers La EX34 ...... 3 B3
Comilla Cl EX8 ...... 196 C4
Commanders Cut TQ6 .233 E4
Commercial Ope PL4 . 263 B2
Commercial Pl PL4 .. 263 B1
Commercial Rd
　Barnstaple EX31 ..... 154 F5
　Calstock PL18 .... 125 D3
　Crediton EX17 .... 165 C5
　❶ Dawlish EX7 ...... 204 E6
　Exeter EX2 .... 261 A2
　Horrabridge PL20 .... 126 F4
　Paignton TQ4 .... 226 B6
　Plymouth PL4 .... 263 B2
　Uffculme EX15 .... 66 A7
Commercial St
　Gunnislake PL18 ..... 125 D6
　Plymouth PL4 .... 263 A2
Commin's Rd EX1 .... 177 F7
Commodore Cl EX39 .156 E7
Common Head EX37 .. 43 C3
Common Hill EX12 .. 191 D4
Common La Beer EX12 . 191 D5

Common La continued
　Huish Champflower TA4 .... 35 D7
　Kingskerswell TQ12 .. 212 E2
　Milton Combe PL6 .... 241 B5
　Seaton EX24 .... 192 B8
Common Mews EX39 .. 156 E7
Common Moors La
　EX36 .... 158 A6
Commonmarsh La EX17 .165 E5
Commons Gate EX22 .. 89 E8
Commons Hill EX6 .. 113 A4
Commons La TQ14 .. 210 A2
Commons Old Rd
　Shaldon TQ14 .... 210 A3
　Shaldon TQ14 .... 210 A2
Community College The
　EX18 .... 44 E1
Compass Dr PL7 ..... 251 A7
Compass Quay EX2 .. 261 B1
Compton Ave PL3 .... 249 A5
Compton Castle* TQ3 . 218 C6
Compton CE Prim Sch
　PL3 .... 249 A6
Compton Ho TQ1 .... 220 C7
Compton Knoll Cl PL3 . 249 A6
Compton Leigh PL3 .. 249 A6
Compton Park Rd PL3 . 248 F5
Compton Pl TQ1 ..... 214 B1
Compton Rd TQ7 ... 144 C1
Compton Vale PL3 .. 249 A5
Comptonpool Cross
　TQ3 .... 218 C8
Concord Dr EX32 ... 155 C5
Concorde Rd EX8 ... 196 F1
Condor Dr TQ2 ..... 213 D2
Conduit Sq ❶ TQ13 .. 123 E6
Coney Ave EX32 ..... 155 B3
Coneypark La EX34 ... 3 A3
Congella Rd TQ1 .... 220 C6
Congram's Cl ❻ EX32 .155 B3
Congreve Gdns PL5 .. 244 C1
Conifer Cl EX15 ..... 163 C5
Conifer Mews EX2 .. 178 D3
Conifers The TQ2 ... 214 B3
Conigar Cl EX15 .... 67 A8
Conigar La EX15 .... 67 A7
Conigre Cross EX8 .. 196 B7
Coniston Cl TQ5 .... 230 A2
Coniston Gdns PL6 .. 244 F4
Coniston Rd TQ12 .. 211 F8
Connaught Ave PL4 . 248 F4
Connaught Cl EX10 .. 188 A4
Connaught La ❷ PL4 . 248 E4
Connaught Rd EX10 .. 188 A4
Conniford La TQ12 .. 211 D1
Connybear Cross TQ12 .213 B8
Conqueror Dr PL5 ... 244 E1
Conrad Ave EX4 ..... 178 B8
Conrad Rd PL5 ...... 244 D1
Consort Cl PL5 ..... 244 D3
Constance Pl PL1 ... 262 A3
Constantine Cl EX12 .191 F8
Constantine St PL4 .. 263 A3
Constitution Hill EX32 .155 B4
Contour Hts TQ6 .... 234 A3
Convent Cl
　Barnstaple EX32 ..... 155 C2
　Saltash PL12 .... 242 E3
Convent Fields EX10 . 187 F4
Convent Lodge ❶ TQ14 .210 B6
Convent Rd EX10 .... 187 F4
Conway Cres ❻ TQ4 . 226 A5
Conway Ct EX1 ...... 261 C2
Conway Gdns PL2 ... 248 B7
Conway Rd TQ4 ..... 226 A5
Conybeare Cl EX4 ... 178 B7
Conybeare Dr EX39 .. 156 E6
Conyngham Ct PL6 .. 249 A8
Cooban Ct PL6 ..... 249 A8
Cook Ct PL12 .... 242 B3
Cooke Dr TQ12 ..... 211 E2
Cooks Cl
　❷ Ashburton TQ13 .. 131 A5
　Kingsteignton TQ12 .. 207 F7
Cooks Cross EX36 .. 158 C5
Cooks La EX13 ...... 104 B7
Cooks Mead DT7 .... 260 A6
Cooksley Ct PL1 .... 263 A1
Cookson's Rd EX6 .. 201 A8
Cookworthy Ct TQ7 . 258 C6
Cookworthy Moor Forest
　Wlk* EX21 .... 73 B4
Cookworthy Mus* TQ7 .258 C6
Cookworthy Rd
　Kingsbridge TQ7 ...... 258 C5
　Plymouth PL2 .... 247 F6
Coombe Ave TQ14 ... 210 A5
Coombe Ball Hill
　West Worlington EX17 .. 61 C8
　Witheridge EX16 ..... 46 D1
Coombe Cl
　Bovey Tracey TQ13 .. 180 E7
　Dartmouth TQ6 ...... 233 F4
　Goodleigh EX32 ..... 17 B5
　Honiton EX14 .... 166 C4
Coombe Cross
　Barnstaple EX32 ..... 17 B4
　Bovey Tracey TQ13 .. 180 E7
　Christow EX6 .... 113 B2
　Great Torrington EX38 .159 F8
Coombe Dean Sch PL9 .256 A6
Coombe Down La PL8 . 140 F6
Coombe Dr PL12 .... 239 A2
Coombe Hayes EX10 .. 188 B8
Coombe Hill EX16 .... 47 F1

Coombe House Cross
　TQ9 .... 224 F2
Coombe House La TQ9 . 225 A2
Coombe La
　Axminster EX13 ...... 167 D5
　Bickleigh EX16 .... 63 C3
　Bovey Tracey TQ13 .. 180 F8
　Cadbury EX5 .... 81 C7
　Cargreen PL12 .... 239 A2
　Chulmleigh EX18 ..... 44 E4
　Plymouth PL5 .... 244 D7
　Silverton EX5 .... 82 B7
　Teignmouth TQ14 ... 210 A7
　Tiverton EX16,EX17 .. 63 B3
　Witheridge EX16 ..... 62 B6
Coombe Mdw TQ13 .. 180 E7
Coombe Mdws TQ7 .. 144 F1
Coombe Orch EX12 .. 192 E6
Coombe Park Cl PL10 . 253 A2
Coombe Park La PL5 .. 244 A3
Coombe Park Rd TQ14 .210 A6
Coombe Pk
　Cawsand PL10 .... 253 A2
　Saltash PL12 .... 242 F2
Coombe Rd
　Dartmouth TQ6 ...... 233 F4
　Paignton TQ3 .... 219 C1
　Saltash PL12 .... 243 A2
　Shaldon TQ14 .... 209 C5
Coombe Shute TQ9 .. 227 F7
Coombe St Exeter EX1 . 261 B2
　Lyme Regis DT7 ...... 260 E3
Coombe The
　Dartmouth TQ6 ...... 233 F4
　Galmpton TQ5 .... 229 B5
Coombe Vale EX10 .. 100 D2
Coombe Vale Rd TQ14 . 210 A5
Coombe View
　Plymouth PL2 .... 247 F7
　Teignmouth TQ14 ... 124 E1
Coombe Way
　Bishopsteignton TQ14 .. 209 B8
　Plymouth PL5 .... 243 F1
Coombefield La EX13 . 167 D5
Coombes The ❶ EX31 .. 154 A2
Coombesend Rd
　Kingsteignton TQ12 .. 207 F7
　Kingsteignton TQ12 .. 208 A7
Coombesend Rd E
　TQ12 .... 208 A7
Coombeshead Coll
　TQ7 .... 207 A4
Coombeshead Rd TQ12 .206 F4
Cooper St EX39 ..... 157 A2
Cooper's Cross EX18 .. 60 C6
Cooper's Cross EX20 . 107 A3
Coopers Cross EX37 .. 44 E6
Coopers Dr EX31 ... 154 B2
Coopers Hill EX19 .. 58 F3
Coot Hide EX16 ..... 50 D1
Copland La TQ9 ..... 223 A6
Copland Mdws TQ9 .. 223 B6
Copleston Rd PL4 .. 263 C4
Copley Cl TQ12 ..... 225 F6
Copley Dr EX31 ..... 154 D3
Copp Hill La EX9 ... 198 A2
Copp Path EX7 ..... 204 C5
Copp's Cl EX39 ..... 157 A3
Coppard Mdws PL7 .. 250 B6
Copper Beech Way PL6 .245 C7
Copper Castle EX14 .. 166 C6
Copper Cl EX39 ..... 38 F8
Copper Pl PL1 ...... 262 A3
Copper Tree Cross TQ9 .216 C5
Copperfield Ct EX8 .. 196 E1
Copperfields PL20 .. 126 C5
Coppers Pk EX4 .... 173 C5
Copperthorn Cross TQ9 .222 D4
Copperwood Cl TQ13 . 130 F4
Coppice Cl
　Fremington EX31 ..... 153 F6
　Raymond's Hill EX13 .. 104 B7
Coppice Gate EX32 .. 155 C3
Coppice Gdns PL5 .. 244 E2
Coppice La EX17 .... 80 A7
Coppice The
　Dawlish EX7 .... 204 D4
　Ivybridge PL21 .... 237 A4
Coppice Wood Dr PL6 . 245 C7
Coppledown Gdns EX9 .197 F2
Coppledown Dr EX4 . 173 C1
Copplestone Prim Sch
　EX17 .... 79 B5
Copplestone Rd EX9 . 198 B6
Copplestone Sta EX17 . 79 A6
Copse Cross EX16 .. 62 B6
Copse La EX16 ...... 196 C2
Copse The EX2 ..... 250 D4
Copse Rd PL7 ...... 250 D4
Copstone Hill EX17 .. 62 A6
Copthorne Gdns PL7 .251 F5
Copthorne La EX5 .. 82 D6
Copythorne Cl TQ5 .. 230 A4
Copythorne Pk TQ5 .. 230 A4
Copythorne Rd TQ5 .. 230 A4
Coral Ave EX16 ..... 156 D7

Crossways continued
Tatworth TA20 ....88 D8
4 Wembury PL9 ....140 D8
Whitestone EX4 ....98 E4
Crow Bridge EX15 ....163 B3
Crow Gn EX15 ....163 B3
Crow La EX16 ....47 C3
Crow Pk PL3 ....248 F5
Crow View EX32 ....155 C5
Crowbeare Mdw EX38 ....159 E6
Crowborough Rd EX33 ....8 A2
Crowbridge Pk EX15 ....163 B2
Crowden Cross EX14 ....161 F3
Crowden Cross EX20 ....74 D2
Crowden Rd EX20 ....74 E2
Crowden Cross TQ10 ....135 A2
Crowder Mdw TQ10 ....135 A2
Crowder Pk TQ10 ....135 A2
Crowder's Cross EX14 ....84 C3
Crowdhole Cross EX16 ....46 F4
Crowdhole Hill EX16 ....46 F4
Crown & Anchor Way **5**
TQ3 ....226 B6
Crown Gdns PL6 ....245 A1
Crown Hill Halberton EX16 .....64 F7
West Buckland TA21 ....52 F7
Crown Hill Terr 5 EX15 ......165 C5
Crown Mews TA21 ....52 F7
Crown Sq **6** TQ14 ....210 A3
Crowndale Ave PL3 ....249 A6
Crownhill Cross PL21 ....137 B3
Crownhill Ct
Plymouth PL6 ....244 F3
Torquay TQ2 ....219 E6
Crownhill Fort* PL6 ....244 F3
Crownhill Fort Rd PL6 ....244 F3
Crownhill Pk TQ2 ....219 E6
Crownhill Rd PL5 ....81 C5
Crownhill Rd PL6 ....219 E6
Crownhill Rise TQ2 ....219 E6
Crownley La TQ9 ....227 F8
Crowther's Hill TQ6 ....233 F3
Croyde Rd EX33 ....7 D1
Croyden Cross EX22 ....55 A4
Croydon Gdns PL5 ....245 A6
Croylands Ct EX4 ....202 C6
Croyle Cross EX15 ....66 A4
Crozier Rd **8** PL4 ....248 F4
Cruel Cross TQ3 ....225 D8
Cruffen Cross EX33 ....8 B1
Cruffen La EX33 ....8 B1
Cruwy's Morchard Hill
EX16 ....63 A7
Cruwys Morchard Hill
EX16 ....63 A7
Crystal Cl TQ4 ....226 C2
Cuckoo Down La EX14 ....166 E4
Cuckoo Hill EX17 ....61 C3
Cuckoo La D77 ....260 A4
Cuckoo's La EX32 ....28 B5
Cuddeford Cnr EX4 ....98 C6
Cuddenhay La EX17 ....46 A2
Cuddyford Cross TQ13 ....130 F5
Cudmore Cross EX38 ....41 A1
Cudhill Rd TQ5 ....230 B4
Cudmore Pk EX16 ....264 D6
Cuffe Rd PL3 ....248 C4
Culdrose Cl PL5 ....243 E4
Culford Cross EX17 ....95 E8
Cullompton Com Coll
EX15 ....163 C2
Cullompton Hill EX5 ....83 A7
Culm Cl TQ12 ....219 B8
Culm Cross TQ20 ....77 A4
Culm Haven EX15 ....66 A7
Culm Lea EX15 ....163 E3
Culm Cl EX14 ....67 D1
Culme Rd PL3 ....249 A5
Culm Way EX14 ....67 C1
Culmstock Prim Sch
EX15 ....51 E1
Culver Cl Bradninch EX5 ....83 A6
Plymouth PL6 ....249 A8
Tiverton EX16 ....161 F3
Culver Ct PL12
Rattery TQ10 ....135 E3
Culver Park Cl TQ7 ....258 E3
Culver Rd PL12 ....242 A2
Culver Way PL6 ....249 A7
Culverdale TQ9 ....223 E4
Culverlake La EX14 ....88 G3
Culverland Cl EX4 ....177 D8
Culverland Rd EX4 ....177 D8
Culvert Rd EX5 ....81 F1
Culverwood Cl PL7 ....251 C6
Culvery Cl EX15 ....184 C3
Culvery Cross EX17 ....165 C2
Culvery Gn TQ2 ....219 B8
Cumber Cl Brixham TQ5 ....230 B5
Malborough TQ7 ....147 F6
Cumber Dr TQ5 ....230 B5
Cumberland Cl EX8 ....202 D8
Cumberland Gn TQ5 ....230 B5
Cumberland Rd PL1 ....247 F1
Cumberland St PL1 ....247 E2
Cummings Cross TQ12 ....180 C1
Cummings Ct TQ12 ....180 C1
Cummins Cnr EX6 ....97 E5
Cummins La EX14 ....87 B6
Cundy Cl PL7 ....250 A7
Cunliffe Ave PL9 ....255 A6
Cunningham Ave EX13 ....167 F7

Cunningham Rd
Exmouth EX8 ....196 D2
Plymouth PL5 ....244 C8
Cunningham Way PL12 ....242 D3
Cunningham Way La TQ11 ....187 F3
Cuppers Piece Cross
EX19 ....43 A1
Curledge St TQ4 ....226 B5
Curledge Street Prim Sch
TQ4 ....226 B5
Curlew Cl EX20 ....170 A6
Curlew Dr TQ7 ....258 F1
Curlew Mews PL5 ....243 C4
Curlew Way EX4 ....173 D2
Currington Mdw EX31 ....154 A3
Curlick Cnr EX34 ....20 C4
Curriton Hill EX17 ....61 C5
Curriton La EX17 ....61 B6
Curscombe Cross EX14 ....84 F4
Curscombe La EX14 ....84 F4
Cursons Way PL21 ....237 A5
Curtis Cross EX22 ....54 B3
Curtis St PL1 ....247 E1
Curve Acre EX32 ....152 C5
Curwood Cross **2** EX16 ....161 C3
Cussacombe Cross 20 D1
Cussacombe Gate EX36 ....20 E1
Custance Ho **2** EX14 ....166 C6
Custom House Hill **4**
TQ14 ....210 B4
Custom House La PL1 ....262 B1
Custom La EX16 ....64 B8
Cut Tongue La TA20 ....69 F7
Cuthays La EX13 ....88 B1
Cuthbert Ct TQ1 ....214 A1
Cuthbert Mayne Joint RC &
CE Sch TQ1 ....214 A1
Cutland Cross EX18 ....44 D4
Cutliffe La EX39 ....22 D3
Cutteridge La EX4 ....176 A6
Cutwell Cross TQ10 ....134 E1
Cuxton Mdws PL20 ....126 C3
Cygnet Ct EX2 ....261 C1
Cygnet Units EX2 ....178 E5
Cypress Cl
10 Honiton EX14 ....85 C2
Plymouth PL7 ....251 C5
Cypress Dr EX4 ....176 F7
Cyprus Rd EX8 ....202 B6
Cyprus Terr EX32 ....155 A3

D

D'arcy Ct TQ12 ....207 C4
Dabby La EX6 ....97 B4
Daccabridge Rd TQ12 ....212 F4
Daccombe Cross TQ12 ....213 D5
Daccombe Hill TQ2,
TQ12 ....213 B4
Daccombe Mill La TQ12 ....213 B4
Daddon Hill EX39 ....156 E6
Daddyhole Rd TQ1 ....220 D3
Daggeridge Plain EX16 ....63 B4
Daggers Copse TQ12 ....206 F3
Dagmar Rd TQ1 ....202 A6
Dagmar St TQ14 ....210 B4
Dagra La TQ12,TQ14 ....209 B4
Daimonds La TQ12 ....211 B5
Dainton Elms Cross
TQ12 ....211 F2
Dainton Mews TQ4 ....226 B5
Dairs Orch TQ10 ....135 A2
Dairy Cl EX6 ....182 B3
Dairy Hill TQ2 ....219 C7
Dairy La PL21 ....237 D5
Daison Cots TQ1 ....220 A7
Daison Cres TQ1 ....220 A7
Daisy Links EX4 ....176 D8
Dalbury Ct TQ12 ....206 F3
Dalditch La EX9 ....197 D3
Dale Ave PL6 ....249 C7
Dale Gdns PL4 ....248 D4
Dale Rd PL4 ....248 D4
Daleside Rd EX4 ....173 E1
Daleswood Rd PL19 ....171 A4
Dalton Gdns PL3 ....243 E3
Dalverton Ct TQ5 ....230 C6
Dalwood La EX13 ....87 B3
Dalwood Prim Sch EX13 ....87 A3
Dame Hannah Rogers' Sch
PL21 ....237 B5
Damerel Cl PL1 ....247 F2
Damson Ct EX15 ....163 D4
Danby Heights Cl TQ1 ....220 E4
Danby La EX8 ....202 A7
Danby Terr EX8 ....202 A7
Dandy La EX4 ....174 D5
Daneheath Bsns Pk
TQ12 ....180 F3
West Charleton TQ7 ....144 C1
Danes Cl EX14 ....68 C2
Danes Cross EX15 ....82 C2
Danes Mead EX15 ....163 C4
Danes' Rd EX4 ....261 B4
Daneshay EX39 ....157 A7
Daneshill Cross EX13 ....87 B3
Daneshill Cross EX13 ....87 B3
Danesway EX14 ....174 E2
Daniel's Grave EX16 ....62 D4
Daniel's La
Broadhempston TQ9 ....131 E1
West Charleton TQ7 ....144 C1
Danum Dr PL7 ....250 B7
Danvers Rd TQ2 ....213 F2
Daphne Cl TQ1 ....220 D6
Dare Orch Cross EX16 ....103 A3
Dark La Barnstaple EX31 ....154 F7
Budleigh Salterton EX9 ....197 F1

Dark La continued
Hockworthy EX16 ....50 B8
Modbury PL21 ....137 B3
Northlew EX20 ....74 D2
Sidmouth EX10 ....187 F6
Thorverton EX5 ....81 E5
Wellington TA21 ....160 D5
Dark Street La PL7 ....251 B8
Darkey La Lifton PL16 ....105 E4
Okehampton EX20 ....170 A5
Darkial La PL6 ....245 D8
Darklake La PL6 ....245 D8
Darklake View PL6 ....245 C7
Darky La Chulmleigh EX18 ......59 E8
Kingsbridge TQ7 ....258 C7
Darlick Cnr EX34 ....20 C4
Darnell Cl EX12 ....188 B6
Darracott Cross EX38 ....41 E8
Darracott Hill EX39 ....37 B4
Darran Cl TQ12 ....207 F7
Darran Rd TQ12 ....207 F7
Dart Ave TQ2 ....219 C7
Dart Bridge Rd TQ11 ....236 C6
Dartbridge Cross TQ11 ....236 C6
Dartbridge Manor TQ11 ....236 C6
Dartington CE Prim Sch
TQ9 ....215 F1
Dartington Cl EX38 ....159 C6
Dartington Coll of Arts
TQ9 ....216 B2
Dartington Crystal Glass
Factory* EX38 ....159 C6
Dartington Fields EX38 ....159 C6
Dartington Hall TQ9 ....216 B2
Dartington Hall Sch
TQ9 ....216 A1
Dartington La TQ9 ....223 B7
Dartington Wlk
Exminster EX6 ....181 F5
Plymouth PL6 ....245 E1
Dartmeet* PL20 ....129 D8
Dartmoor Cotts PL7 ....132 D4
Dartmoor Prison Mus*
PL20 ....119 A3
Dartmoor View
Chulmleigh PL18 ....44 E1
Plymouth PL4 ....249 C5
Saltash PL12 ....242 E4
Woolfardisworthy EX17 ....61 E4
Dartmoor Wildlife Pk*
PL7 ....133 A3
Dartmouth & Kingswear
Hospl TQ6 ....233 F3
Dartmouth Castle*
TQ6 ....234 B1
Dartmouth Com Coll
TQ6 ....233 D2
Dartmouth Mus* TQ6 ....146 B7
Dartmouth Rd
East Allington TQ9 ....144 E7
Paignton TQ4,TQ5 ....226 C2
Stoke Fleming TQ6 ....146 B8
Dartmouth Wlk PL6 ....249 E8
Darton Gr TQ9 ....227 F7
Dartridge La EX18 ....44 D1
Dartside TQ9 ....223 B7
Darwin Cres PL3 ....249 D7
Darwin Ct **11** EX32 ....155 B4
Dashley Cnr TQ12 ....131 D2
Dashpers TQ5 ....230 B3
Daucus Cl PL7 ....171 B4
Davenham Cl PL6 ....245 B6
Davey's Cross PL21 ....137 B7
Daveycourt La EX20 ....95 F3
David Cl Braunton EX33 ....152 D5
Plymouth PL7 ....250 F7
David Southgate Ct PL11 .....262 A2
David's Cl EX10 ....101 B2
David's Hill EX33 ....8 A2
Davids La PL21 ....237 E5
Davies Ave TQ4 ....229 A8
Davies Cl PL5 ....82 B6
Davis Ave TQ2 ....213 C3
Davy Cl TQ6 ....233 C3
Davy Rd PL6 ....245 C5
Dawberry Cl PL7 ....211 F8
Dawes Cl TQ12 ....211 E8
Dawes Ct TQ4 ....226 B5
Dawes La Millbrook PL10 ......252 E5
Dawes Mdw TQ12 ....207 F6
Dawlish Com Coll EX7 ....204 D6
Dawlish Mus* EX7 ....204 D6
Dawlish Rd Exeter EX2 ....181 C8
Teignmouth TQ14 ....210 C5
Dawlish St **16** TQ14 ....210 C5
Dawlish Warren Rd EX6 ....201 B4
Dawlish Warren Sta
EX7 ....201 B2
Dawlish Wlk PL6 ....249 E8
Dawn Cl EX1 ....174 F4
Dawn Cl PL6 ....245 D5
Daws Mdw TQ12 ....207 F6
Dawson Cl PL5 ....243 E1
Daymond Rd PL5 ....243 D2

Days-Pottles La EX6,
EX2 ....181 D4
Dayton Cl PL6 ....244 E3
De Bathe Cross EX20 ....77 C3
De Courcy Rd TQ8 ....259 B2
De La Rue Way EX4 ....174 D1
De Tracey Pk TQ13 ....180 D7
De-La-Hay Ave PL3 ....262 A4
Deacon Cl EX2 ....181 B8
Deacon Dr PL12 ....242 F1
Deacons Gn PL19 ....171 A3
Dead La EX15 ....67 F8
Dead Road Cross EX15 ....65 F2
Deadman's Cross TQ6 ....233 D2
Dean Cross
Goodleigh EX32 ....17 C4
Ilfracombe EX34 ....8 E5
Plymouth PL9 ....255 A5
South Brent TQ10 ....135 C5
Dean Cross Rd PL9 ....255 C7
Dean Hill PL9 ....255 E7
Dean Hill Rd EX15 ....162 B3
Dean La Combe Martin EX31 .....3 E1
Ilfracombe EX34 ....8 F5
Luxton EX35 ....52 E5
Dean Lane End TQ10 ....135 D5
Dean Park Rd PL9 ....255 D7
Dean Rd PL7 ....250 D6
Dean St Crediton EX17 ....165 D5
Exeter EX2 ....182 E4
Deane Sleep EX35 ....5 A4
Deane Cl EX33 ....8 D1
Deane La TQ12 ....209 D2
Deane Rd TQ12 ....209 B2
Deane Way TA20 ....88 D8
Deans Cl
Bishopsteignton TQ14 ....208 F8
Northam EX39 ....156 F7
Deans La EX36 ....158 D5
Deans Mead EX36 ....188 A5
Deans Pk EX36 ....158 D5
Debden Cl PL5 ....243 E1
Deckport Cross EX20 ....75 D7
Decoy Country Pk*
TQ12 ....207 C1
Decoy Prim Sch TQ12 ....212 D8
Decoy Rd TQ12 ....207 D1
Deeble Cl PL7 ....251 A5
Deep Cut Cross EX14 ....67 C2
Deep Dene Cl TQ5 ....230 B3
Deep La Crediton EX17 ....165 C6
High Bickington EX37 ....43 D7
Deepdene Pk EX22 ....177 E4
Deeplane Head EX36 ....181 F4
Deepway La EX6 ....181 F4
Deepway
Branscombe EX12 ....190 D4
Exeter EX2 ....181 D4
Exminster EX6 ....182 A4
Deepways EX9 ....192 F2
Deer Leap PL19 ....171 D4
Deer Park Ave TQ14 ....210 A6
Deer Park Cl
Tavistock PL19 ....171 C5
Teignmouth TQ14 ....210 A6
Deer Park La PL19 ....171 C5
Deer Park Cres PL19 ....171 C5
Deer Park Dr
Plymouth PL7 ....249 D7
Teignmouth TQ14 ....210 A6
Deer Park La PL19 ....171 C5
Deer Park Rd
Barnstaple EX32 ....155 C2
Newton Abbot TQ12 ....207 D1
Stoke Fleming TQ6 ....146 B8
Tavistock PL19 ....171 C5
Deer Park Pk Ivybridge PL21 ..237 E5
Saltash PL12 ....242 F3
Deer Valley Rd EX22 ....164 C4
Deerhill La EX36 ....158 C6
Deerpark La TQ12 ....213 E7
Deers Leap PL12 ....242 C5
Defoe Cl PL5 ....244 C1
Delacombe Cl PL7 ....250 F7
Delamere Rd PL6 ....247 D7
Delamore Cl PL21 ....237 A5
Delaware Bsns Ctr
PL18 ....125 C5
Delaware Cotts PL18 ....125 C5
Delaware Cross EX20 ....74 F4
Delaware Ct PL18 ....125 C5
Delaware Gdns PL2 ....247 F7
Delaware Rd PL18 ....125 C6
Delderfield Gdns EX8 ....202 C6
Delia Gdns EX5 ....99 C5
Delius Cres EX2 ....178 C4
Dell The Plymouth PL7 ....250 B6
3 Tavistock PL19 ....171 B5
Delve's Grave Cross
EX38 ....41 F8
Den Brook Cl TQ1 ....220 D6
Den Cross TQ14 ....210 C4
Den Prom TQ14 ....210 C4
Den Rd TQ14 ....210 C4
Den The TQ14 ....210 C4
Denbeigh Terr EX10 ....188 B5
Denbow Cross EX5 ....99 A2
Denbury Cross
TQ12 ....131 D3
Denbury Down La
TQ12 ....131 D3
Denbury Prim Sch
TQ12 ....211 A6
Denbury Rd TQ12 ....211 E6
Dendy Rd TQ4 ....226 B6

Dene Cl EX8 ....196 D1
Denes Cl 2 EX32 ....127 B2
Deneleigh Ct EX7 ....177 E4
Deneridge Cross EX17 ....60 F6
Deneridge Hill EX17 ....61 A5
Denes Rd EX7 ....17 B2
Dengie Cl PL7 ....251 B5
Denham Ct PL5 ....244 C2
Dening Ct EX8 ....202 B8
Denise Cl EX2 ....181 B8
Denmark Rd
Exeter EX1,EX2 ....261 C3
Exmouth EX8 ....202 D8
Denners Way EX15 ....66 A7
Dennington Cross EX32 ....28 D8
Dennington Hill EX32 ....28 D8
Dennington La
Churchinford EX14 ....68 F6
Dulverton TA22 ....33 B4
Dennis Cl PL5 ....247 C7
Dennis Cross EX19 ....57 F7
Dennis's Down Cross
EX6 ....96 C5
Dennysmead Ct EX4 ....173 A1
Densdon Gate EX16 ....46 E6
Densdon Rd EX36 ....46 E6
Densham La EX17 ....61 A4
Denver Cl EX3 ....182 E6
Denver Rd EX3 ....182 E6
Denys Rd Torquay TQ1 ....220 C5
Totnes TQ9 ....223 C5
Deptford Pl PL4 ....263 A4
Deptford Villas **2** EX3 ....154 C3
Derby Rd
Barnstaple EX32 ....155 B6
Kingsbridge TQ7 ....258 C4
Plymouth PL5 ....244 C8
Derick Rd EX16 ....161 B5
Derncleugh Gdns EX7 ....210 F8
Derrell Rd TQ4 ....226 C2
Derriford Hospl PL6 ....245 B4
Derriford Pk PL6 ....245 A3
Derriford Rd PL6 ....245 A4
Derriton Mill Cross
EX22 ....164 B3
Derriton Rd EX22 ....71 E6
Derry Ave PL4 ....263 B2
Derry's Cross PL1 ....262 B2
Derwent Ave PL3 ....249 C5
Derwent Rd TQ1 ....220 B7
Derworthy Cross TQ7 ....154 D6
Derworthy La EX22 ....54 A7
Desborough La PL4 ....263 C3
Desborough Rd PL4 ....263 C3
Deveron Cl PL7 ....251 A5
Devon & Cornwall Pol HQ
(Middlemoor) EX2 ....178 D5
Devon Bsns Pk EX15 ....163 D4
Devon Cliffs Holiday Pk
EX8 ....203 B5
Devon Heath **2** TQ13 ....123 C4
Devon Ho TQ1 ....180 E8
Devon House Dr TQ13 ....180 E8
Devon Pl **18** TQ9 ....223 D5
Devon Rd Exeter EX2 ....177 F8
Salcombe TQ8 ....259 D4
Devon Sq
Kingsbridge TQ7 ....258 C5
Newton Abbot TQ12 ....207 C3
Devon Terr PL4 ....247 C6
Devon Tors EX20 ....221 A3
Devon Tors Rd **8** PL20 ....126 F3
Devon Units Exeter EX2 ....177 F1
Great Torrington EX38 ....159 F6
Devon Valley Holiday Village
TQ14 ....209 C6
Devon View EX7 ....201 B2
Devoncourt TQ5 ....230 E6
Devondale Ct EX7 ....201 B2
Devonia Cl PL7 ....250 E7
Devonport High Sch for Boys
PL1 ....248 A2
Devonport High Sch for Girls
PL2 ....248 A2
Devonport Hill
Cawsand PL10 ....253 A2
Plymouth PL1 ....247 F1
Devonport Leat PL6 ....241 B5
Devonport Rd PL3 ....247 E3
Devonport St **6** EX17 ....165 D5
Devons' Rd TQ1 ....220 C7
Devonshire Ho
Plymouth PL4 ....262 B2
7 Tavistock PL19 ....171 B5
Torquay TQ2 ....220 B4
Devonshire Pl EX39 ....157 A1
Devonshire Pl EX4 ....177 F7
Devonshire St PL4 ....263 A3
Devonshire St PL4 ....263 A3
Dewberry Dr EX31 ....154 B3
Deyman's Hill EX16 ....161 D3
Dial Ho The EX9 ....198 A1
Dial St EX10 ....188 B3
Diamond Ave PL4 ....263 B4
Diamond La TQ10 ....134 D5
Diamond St PL4 ....154 F5
Diamond St **17** EX32 ....154 F5
Diane Cl PL16 ....106 A8
Diane Cl EX8 ....196 D4
Dibbon's La EX34 ....1 D2
Dick Pym Cl EX2 ....178 C4
Dick's Hill EX36 ....46 E8

Dickens Dr EX2 ....177 F3
Dickens Rd PL5 ....244 B1
Dickers Terr TQ12 ....207 E7
Dickiemoor La PL5 ....244 C2
Dickna St PL15 ....90 C1
Dickshill La EX38 ....159 D5
Diddywell CI EX39 ....157 A8
Diddywell Rd EX39 ....157 A8
Dieppe CI PL7 ....247 F2
Digby Dr EX2 ....178 D3
Digby Gr PL5 ....243 F5
Digby Sowton Sta EX2 ...178 E4
Diggerland* EX15 ....163 E8
Diggories La 5 EX14 ....166 B6
Dillons PL8 ....141 A7
Dillybridge Hill EX6 ......97 D4
Dinan Way EX8 ....196 E3
Dinan Way Trad Est
  EX8 ....196 F1
Dince Hill CI EX5 ....99 E2
Dingle CI PL17 ....115 B1
Dingle Rd
  Plymouth, North Prospect
  PL2 ....248 A6
  Plymouth, Plympton PL7 .250 C6
Dingles Steam Village*
  PL16 ....106 A5
Dingwall Ave PL5 ....244 E3
Dinham Cres EX4 ....261 A3
Dinham Rd EX4 ....261 A3
Dinne Ford St EX5 ....81 E5
Dinnis CI EX6 ....97 F4
Dipford Gate EX16 ....48 C3
Dipford La EX16 ....48 C4
Dipford CI TQ4 ....245 D6
Diptford Cross TQ9 ......138 C7
Diptford Parochial CE Prim
  Sch TQ9 ....138 C7
Dirty La PL12 ....242 B5
Discovery Wharf 20 PL4 .263 A2
Distine CI PL3 ....249 B7
District Hospl EX16 ......161 D4
Ditch End Cross EX32 ....18 C7
Ditchett Cross EX16 ......46 E6
Dittiscombe Cross TQ9 ..145 A6
Dittisham Ct TQ6 ....228 C3
Dittisham Wlk PL6 ....249 E8
Ditton Ct PL6 ....249 A8
Divett Dr 5 TQ12 ....122 F1
Dix's Field EX1 ....261 B3
Dixon CI TQ3 ....218 E1
Dixon PI PL2 ....247 F4
Dixon Terr PL8 ....257 F3
Doatshayne CI EX13 .....103 D5
Doatshayne La
  Musbury EX13 ....103 D5
  Musbury EX13 ....103 D6
Dobbin Arch TQ12 ....212 F4
Dobbsmoor Cross EX18 ...44 F3
Dobles CI EX22 ....164 C5
Dobles La EX22 ....164 C6
Dobles Terr EX22 ....164 D5
Dobree Pk TA21 ....160 A4
Doccombe Cross TQ13 ...112 B5
Dock Rd EX8 ....201 E6
Dockeys La TQ7 ....145 D1
Dockray CI PL6 ....245 D4
Dockworthy Cross EX18 ..60 C8
Dockyard Halt PL2 ....247 E4
Docton Mill & Gdns*
  EX39 ....22 B1
Doctors Cnr EX16 ....61 D7
Doctors Rd 3 EX8 ....230 C3
Dodbrooke Ct TQ7 ....258 D5
Doddiscombsleigh Com Sch
  EX6 ....113 D5
Doddridge CI PL9 ....255 F4
Dodscott Cross EX38 .....42 B7
Doe Ct EX38 ....159 D5
Dog Down Cross EX16 ....50 A8
Doggie La EX14 ....1 E2
Dogwatch TQ7 ....147 E4
Doidges Farm CI PL6 ....249 B8
Dokkum Rd EX17 ....165 D4
Dolbeare Rd
  Ashburton TQ13 ....131 A5
  Ashburton TQ13 ....131 A5
Dole Park Cross E EX37 ..43 D5
Dole Park Cross W EX37 ..43 D5
Dolepark La EX37 ....43 D5
Dolphin CI
  Lyme Regis DT7 ....260 E3
  Plymouth PL9 ....255 F6
Dolphin Court Rd
  Paignton TQ3 ....218 F1
  Plymouth PL9 ....255 F6
Dolphin Cres TQ3 ....218 F1
Dolphin Ct Brixham TQ5 .230 C6
  Cullompton EX15 ......163 C3
  Northam EX39 ....156 E7
Dolphin Ho 22 Teignmouth TQ14 ...210 C4
Dolphin Ho 8 PL4 ....263 A2
Dolphin Sch The EX8 ....202 B6
Dolphin Sq
  Bovey Tracey TQ13 ....180 C7
  Plymouth PL9 ....255 F6
Dolphin St EX34 ....103 A5
Dolton CE Prim Sch
  EX19 ....57 E2
Dolvin Rd PL19 ....171 C5
Domehayes EX20 ....170 B5
Donkey La
  Millbrook PL10 ....252 C4
  Ugborough PL21 ....137 D6
Donkey Sanctuary The*
  EX10 ....189 B7
Donnington Dr PL3 ......249 C7
Doomsford La EX37 ....44 B5
Doone Way EX34 ....150 C4
Dorchester Ave PL5 .....244 D4
Dorchester Dr TQ2 ......213 F1
Dorchester Way EX8 .....196 D4
Doreena Rd PL9 ....256 C7
Doriam CI EX4 ....173 C2
Dormy Ave PL3 ....248 F5
Dornafield CI TQ12 ......211 D2
Dornafield Cross
  Abbotskerswell TQ12 ...211 E5
  Ipplepen TQ12 ....211 D3
Dornafield Dr E TQ12 ...211 D2
Dornafield Dr W TQ12 ...211 D2
Dornafield La TQ12 ......211 E4
Dornafield Rd TQ12 .....211 D3
Dornaford Cross EX20 ....76 C2
Dorridge Gate EX37 ......28 D3
Dorset Ave EX4 ....176 E4
Dorset Pk PL15 ....89 D2
Dorset PI 6 EX14 ....166 C6
Dormouth Terr PL7 ......250 C4
Dosson Gr TQ1 ....219 E7
Dotheridge La EX39 ......25 A1
Dotton CI EX1 ....178 D6
Dotton La EX10 ....186 E6
Doughy La TQ12 ....211 A7
Douglas Ave
  Brixham TQ5 ....230 E4
  Exmouth EX8 ....202 C6
Douglas Dr PL9 ....256 A6
Douglas Ho 14 TQ14 ....210 B5
Douglass Rd PL3 ....249 C6
Dousland Ho PL20 ....127 B3
Dousland Rd PL20 ....127 A3
Dousland Terr PL20 .....127 B3
Dove CI Cullompton EX15 .163 A2
  Honiton EX14 ....166 B4
Dove Gdns PL3 ....249 D7
Dove La EX10 ....188 B3
Dove Way EX2 ....176 D3
Dovedale CI EX34 ....150 E5
Dovedale Rd PL2 ....248 A7
Dover Rd PL6 ....245 E3
Dover's Hill EX17 ....80 E8
Dowell St EX14 ....166 B6
Dower Ct TQ3 ....226 C8
Dower Ho The TQ10 .....135 C4
Dower Rd TQ1 ....220 A7
Down CI
  Newton Poppleford EX10 .186 D7
  Saltash PL12 ....242 C2
Down Cross EX16 ....47 A2
Down End EX17 ....165 A5
Down Hill
  Morchard Bishop EX17 ..78 F8
  Rackenford EX16 ....47 A3
Down La Braunton EX33 .152 E6
  Combe Martin EX31 ....10 F6
  Doddiscombsleigh EX6 ..113 D5
  Georgeham EX33 ....8 A4
  Georgeham, North Buckland
  EX33 ....8 B3
  Knowle EX33 ....8 F2
  Molland EX36 ....31 E7
  Rackenford EX16 ....47 A3
  Winkleigh EX19 ....58 F2
Down Park Dr PL19 .....171 D4
Down Rd Instow EX39 ...15 B1
  Plymouth PL7 ....251 C5
  Tavistock PL19 ....171 D4
Down St Mary Vineyard*
  EX17 ....78 D7
Down The PL20 ....125 F1
Down View Rd TQ12 ....211 A6
Downash La EX13 ....88 E3
Downeway La TQ12 .....207 E3
Downeshead La EX17 ...165 E5
Downfield CI TQ5 ....230 A3
Downfield Dr PL7 ....250 D7
Downfield Way PL7 .....250 D6
Downfield Wlk PL7 ......250 D6
Downgate Gdns PL2 ....248 D8
Downham Gdns PL5 ....244 C2
Downham Sch PL9 ......255 F7
Downhayne Hill EX17 ...62 B7
Downhayne Rd EX14 ...102 F6
Downland Cross EX39 ....23 E2
Downlands Cross EX15 ..66 E2
Downlands La TA3 ....52 F1
Downlea PL19 ....171 D4
Downmoor Cross EX38 ..55 B8
Downs Rd EX39 ....15 C1
Downs View EX22 ....54 D6
Downside Ave PL6 ......249 C7
Downside Hill EX10 .....188 A4
Downstow Cross TQ10 ..134 F5
Downton CI PL7 ....262 A4
Downton Cross TQ6 ....233 A7
Dowrich Cross EX17 .....80 A7
Dracaena Ave EX31 ....154 C4
Dragdown Hill EX17 .....95 F7
Dragon Hill EX38 ....40 F2
Dragon's Mead EX13 ...167 C4
Dragon's Tail TQ12 .....181 D3
Dragons Hill DT7 ....260 E5
Dragoon CI TQ12 ......180 E3
Drake Ave
  Teignmouth TQ14 .....210 A8
  Torquay TQ2 ....219 C6
Drake CE Prim Sch EX9 .198 B6
Drake Cir PL11,PL4 ....263 A3
Drake CI EX39 ....156 B6
Drake Dr PL4 ....263 A3
Drake Dr TQ4 ....226 B2
Drake Gdns PL19 ....171 C4
Drake La TQ13 ....180 E7
Drake Prim Sch PL2 ....247 E6
Drake Rd
  Bovey Tracey TQ13 ....180 E7
  Newton Abbot TQ12 ...207 F3
  Salcombe TQ8 ....259 C5
  Tavistock PL19 ....171 C6
Drake Villas PL19 ......171 A4
Drake Way PL9 ....255 E7
Drake's Ave Exmouth EX8 .202 D8
  Sidmouth EX10 ....188 C8
Drake's Cross EX37 .....44 A7
Drake's Pk 3 PL20 ....125 E1
Drake's Pk N PL20 .....125 E1
Drake's Rd TQ4 ....225 E4
Drakefield Dr PL12 .....243 A3
Drakes CI PL6 ....244 F4
Drakes Cres TA20 ....88 D8
Drakes Farm EX2 ....176 E2
Drakes Gdns EX4 ......202 D8
Drakes Mdw
  Cheriton Fitzpaine EX17 ..62 F1
  Yarcombe EX14 ....69 A3
Drakes Pk TA21 ....160 D7
Drakes Pk N TA21 ......160 D7
Drakes Rd EX4 ....177 A8
Drakes Way EX7 ....204 E5
Drakewalls Gdns PL18 ..125 C5
Drakewalls PI PL18 .....125 C5
Draper Terr 3 PL19 ....171 B5
Drapers CI EX14 ....166 B6
Dras Gdns PL6 ....248 E8
Draycott CI EX2 ....178 A4
Drayford Rd EX16 ....46 E1
Drayton Rd PL5 ....244 C1
Drayway Cross EX16 ....63 D1
Draytor La EX16 ....63 E1
Drew St TQ5 ....230 C3
Drew's CI EX6 ....201 A8
Drews Field La TQ3 ....218 D7
Drewsmead TQ13 ......122 C3
Drewston Cross TQ13 ..111 C6
Drewstone Cross EX36 ..30 E6
Dreys Ct EX1 ....177 E6
Dreyton Cross TQ9 .....139 F3
Drift La EX14 ....66 F3
Drift Lane Cross EX14 ...66 F3
Drill The TA20 ....88 E8
Drive The
  Bishopsteignton TQ14 ..208 E8
  Brixham TQ5 ....230 C2
  Dawlish EX7 ....204 E6
  Exeter EX5 ....99 B3
  Holbeton PL8 ....136 D1
  Kingskerswell TQ12 ...213 A4
  Plymouth PL3 ....248 E7
Droridge TQ9 ....222 F8
Droridge La TQ9 ....222 E8
Drove Way TA3 ....54 A4
Drovers Way
  Ivybridge PL21 ....237 A6
  Seaton EX12 ....192 B8
Druid Cross TQ13 ......130 D5
Drum Bridge TQ13 .....180 F1
Drum Way TQ12 ....180 F2
Drummond CI PL7 ......247 F7
Drummond Pl PL7 ......247 F7
Drunken Bridge Hill
  PL7 ....250 D4
Dry La Christow EX6 ....113 B4
  Okehampton EX20 .....93 D5
Drybridge Cross TQ10 ..135 C5
Dryburgh Cres PL2 ....248 A8
Dryden Ave PL5 ....244 C1
Dryden Cotts EX5 ....99 D2
Dryden Rd EX2 ....177 F4
Dulcis Cross EX13 ....87 C2
Dulford Bsns Pk EX15 ..66 B1
Dulford Cross EX15 .....66 B1
Duloe Gdns PL2 ....248 C8
Dulverton Com Sch TA22 .33 D6
Dulverton La TA4 ....35 D7
Dumfries Ave PL5 ......244 D3
Dumpdon La EX14 ....85 F6
Dumpdon View EX14 ....86 A6
Dun Cross TQ9 ....222 C8
Duncan Ho TQ1 ....220 C4
Duncan St PL1 ....247 E1
Duncannon La TQ9 ....227 F7
Duncannon Mead TQ9 .227 F7
Dunclair Pk PL3 ....249 D5
Duncombe Ave PL5 .....244 C3
Duncombe Cross TQ7 ..144 C2
Duncombe St TQ7 .....258 D6
Dundas St 4 PL2 ......248 A4
Dundonald St PL2 ......247 F4
Dune View
  Braunton EX33 ....152 B7
  Westward Ho! EX39 ...156 D7
Dune View Rd EX33 ....152 B6
Dunheved Rd PL12 .....242 F2
Dunkeswell Airfield EX14 .67 B2
Dunkeswell Bsns Pk
  EX14 ....67 B2
Dunkeswell CI PL2 .....247 F8
Dunkirk EX11 ....169 C4
Dunley Cross TQ13 ....123 B4
Dunley CI EX2 ....123 B5
Dunley Wlk PL6 ....245 C1
Dunmere Rd TQ1 ......220 B6
Dunmore Ct TQ14 .....210 B2
Dunmore Dr TQ14 .....210 B2
Dunn La EX39 ....25 E2
Dunn's Hill TA21 ....51 A6
Dunnet Rd PL6 ....244 D7
Dunning Ct EX14 ......166 B6
Dunning Gn 1 EX1 ....154 C3
Dunning Rd TQ14 .....210 A7
Dunning Wlk
  Teignmouth TQ14 .....210 A6
  Teignmouth TQ14 .....210 A7
Dunns CI EX33 ....152 F4
Dunns Close Rd EX6 ...245 A5
Dunrich CI EX2 ....261 C2
Dunscombe La
  Chudleigh TQ13 ....124 A5
  Sidmouth EX10 ....189 B7
Dunscombe Cross EX22 ..53 C3
Dunsford CI EX8 ....202 D6
Dunsford Gdns EX4 ....176 E3
Dunsford Hill EX5 ....81 E3
Dunsford Prim Sch EX6 .112 F8
Dunsford Rd EX2 ....176 E3
Dunsford Way 1 EX16 .161 C2
Dunsgreen La EX15 .....67 D8
Dunsland Cross EX22 ...73 A6
Dunsley Hill EX16,EX36 ..32 D5
Dunster CI PL7 ....251 C4
Dunster Wlk EX6 ....181 B5
Dunsterville Rd PL21 ...237 E6
Dunstone Ave PL9 .....256 A7
Dunstone CI
  Paignton TQ3 ....218 E1
  Plymouth PL9 ....255 F7
Dunstone Cross TQ7 ..149 C7
Dunstone Ct TQ3 ......218 E1
Dunstone Dr PL9 ......255 F7
Dunstone La PL9 ....256 A7
Dunstone Park Rd TQ3 .218 E1
Dunstone Prim Sch PL9 .256 A8
Dunstone Rd
  Plymouth, Plymstock PL9 .255 F7
  Plymouth, St Budeaux PL5 .243 F3
Dunstone Rise TQ3 ....218 E1
Dunstone View PL9 ....256 A7
Dunvegan CI EX4 ......177 A8
Dunwell Cross PL21 ...137 D5
Dural Cross EX22 ....38 B3
Durant Ho EX7 ....204 E6
Durban Rd PL3 ....248 D5
Durbin CI EX14 ....166 D5
Durdon Cross EX20 .....75 A1
Dure La EX36 ....30 E8
Durham Ave PL4 ......263 C4
Durham CI Exeter EX4 .178 C2
  Exmouth EX8 ....196 D4
  Paignton TQ3 ....219 B1
Durham Way EX14 ....166 A4
Durleigh Rd TQ5 ......230 B4
Durlestone Cross TQ7 ..149 B8
Durley Rd EX12 ....191 F7
Durleymoor Cross EX16 ..50 F4
Durnford CI PL1 ....248 A1
Durnford Street Ope
  PL1 ....247 E3
Durrant CI Northam EX39 .157 A5
Durrant La EX39 ....157 A5
Durris CI EX6 ....245 D4
Durris Gdns PL6 ....245 D4
Dursley Way EX39 .....156 E2
Durwent CI PL9 ....256 A5
Duryardwood La EX5 ..172 E4
Dux Cross EX22 ....71 B6
Dyehouse Cnr TA22 ....34 A6
Dyehouse Cross EX16 ..35 A5
Dyehouse La TA22 .....34 A5
Dyers CI Braunton EX33 .152 C6
  West Buckland TA21 ..52 E7
Dyers Ct EX2 ....261 A2
Dyke Hill Terr TA20 ....88 D8
Dymond Rd EX39 ......156 F1
Dynevor CI PL3 ....248 F7

E

Eager Way EX6 ....181 F5
Eagle CI TQ12 ....123 E1
Eagle Cotts EX4 ....177 A5
Eagle Ct TQ2 ....219 E8
Eagle Nest EX2 ....176 D3
Eagle PI TQ13 ....111 F5
Eagle Rd PL7 ....251 C4
Eagle Way EX2 ....178 E5
Eaglewood CI TQ2 .....213 C2
Earl Richard's Rd N EX2 .177 E2
Earl Richard's Rd S EX2 .177 E1
Earl's Acre PL3 ....248 C4
Earl's Dr The
  Cawsand PL10 ....253 A1
  Cawsand, Kingsand PL10 .253 B3
Earl's Dr The PL10 .....140 J2
Earls Ct TQ1 ....219 F6
Earls Mill Rd PL7 ......250 E6
Earls Wood Dr PL6 ....245 F3
Earls Wood Dr PL6 ....245 F3
Earlswood Dr TQ3 .....225 D7
East Allington Prim Sch
  TQ9 ....144 D7
East Anstey Prim Sch
  EX16 ....32 E5
East Ash Cross
  Bradworthy EX22 ......38 F3
  Whiddon Down EX20 ..95 D2
  Whiddon Down EX20 ..95 E1
East Ave EX1 ....177 E6
East Ball Hill EX39 .....22 E3
East Budleigh Rd
  Budleigh Salterton EX9 ..198 B3
  East Budleigh EX9 ....198 C6
East Butterleigh Cross
  EX15 ....64 E3
East Challacombe La EX34 .3 A1
East CI EX16 ....46 E1
East Cliff DT7 ....260 E3
East Cliff Ct EX7 ......204 E7
East Cliff Gdns EX7 ...204 E7
East Cliff Rd EX7 .....204 E7
East Cliff Wlk TQ14 ...210 C2
East Coombe Cross EX17 .81 A6
East Coombe La TA4 ...35 D8
East Devon Bsns Pk
  EX14 ....86 C3
East Devon Coll EX16 .161 C6
East Devon Coll (Annexe)
  EX16 ....161 D4
East Down Cross
  Barnstaple EX34 ....9 F6
  Okehampton EX20 .....93 D8
East Dr EX8 ....196 A1
East End EX17 ....62 D3
East End Terr 10 TQ13 .131 A5
East Farm TQ7 ....144 D1
East Grove Rd EX2 ....261 C2
East Hill EX13 ....152 E6
East John Wlk EX1 ....177 E6
East Lake Cross
  Harberton TQ9 ....222 B1
  Zeal Monachorum EX17 ..77 F8
East Lyn La EX35 .....151 F2
East Mead EX15 ....67 B8
East Meadow Rd EX33 .152 B7
East Mere Cross EX16 ..50 B2
East Moore Cross TQ9 ..133 E1
East Nymph La EX17 ...95 C6
East Pafford Ave TQ2 ..214 B3
East Park Ave PL4 ....262 C4
East Park Rd EX32 ....155 D4
East Pk EX39 ....38 F8
East Pugsley Cross EX37 ..29 B2
East Rowley La EX36 ..45 D5
East Sherford Cross
  PL8 ....257 A8
East St Ashburton TQ13 .130 F5
  Bishop's Tawton EX32 .16 A1
  Black Torrington EX21 ..74 A8
  Bovey Tracey TQ13 ....180 D8
  Braunton EX33 ....152 D6
  Chittlehampton EX37 ..28 F4
  Chulmleigh EX18 ......44 E1
  Crediton EX17 ....165 D5
  Denbury TQ12 ....211 A7
  Great Torrington EX38 .159 D5
  Ipplepen TQ12 ....211 E2
  Newton Abbot TQ12 ..207 C3
  Okehampton EX20 .....170 C5
  Plymouth PL1 ....262 A2
  Sheepwash EX21 ......56 D1
  Sidmouth EX10 ....188 B3
  South Molton EX36 ...158 D4
  Torquay TQ2 ....219 F6
East Terr EX9 ....199 H2
East Tawn La EX6 .....199 F2
East Town La EX6 .....194 D3
East View CI EX5 ......162 F6
  EX16 ....166 C6
East View PI EX16 .....161 E4
East Village Cross EX17 .80 C8
East Way PL21 ....136 D6
East Wonford Hill EX2 ..178 B5
East Worlington Cross
  EX17 ....61 B8
East Worlington Cross
  EX17 ....61 B8

East Youlstone Cross
EX23 ....37 F2
East-the-Water Com Prim
Sch EX39 ....157 C1
Eastacombe Cross
Barnstaple EX31 ....16 81
Northlew EX20 ....74 E2
Eastacombe La EX31 ...15 E6
Eastacombe Rise EX31 ..15 E6
Eastacott Cross EX37 ..28 E2
Eastacott La EX34 ......8 86
Eastbourne Terr EX39 ..156 D7
Eastbrook Ho 6 PL4 ...210 86
Eastbury Ave PL5 ......244 A2
Eastchurch La EX6 .....96 D6
Eastcoombe La EX17 ...81 A6
Eastcote Cl PL6 ....245 86
Eastcott Cross EX23 ...37 D2
Eastdown EX39 ....22 F3
Eastdown Cross TQ9 ..145 D8
Eastella Rd PL20 ......127 A2
Easter Cross EX31 .....154 82
Easter Ct EX31 ....154 B2
Easter Ground La EX34 ..8 F5
Easter Hill EX47 ....28 82
Easter La Berrynarbor EX34 ..2 E3
  Brendon EX35 ....6 84
Easter Lane Cross TQ13 121 B2
Easter St EX32 ....16 E1
Easterbrook La EX6 ....96 D8
Easterdown Cl PL9 .....255 F7
Easterfield La TQ1 ....214 C2
Easterley Terr EX31 ...154 C3
Eastern Ave
  Barnstaple EX32 ....155 C4
  Exeter EX2 ....182 C7
Eastern Espl TQ4 ......226 C6
Eastern Rd
  Ashburton TQ13 ....131 A5
  Zeal Monachorum EX17 ..78 C7
Eastern Wood Rd PL7 ..251 D4
Easterntown PL8 ....136 D1
Eastfield EX11 ....168 D4
Eastfield Ave PL6 .....255 C6
Eastfield Cres PL3 ....249 A6
Eastfield Orch EX15 ...66 A8
Easthay La TA20 ....88 F4
Eastington Cross EX17 ..60 E4
Eastington Hill EX17 ..60 E3
Eastlake Ho 6 PL1 .....263 A2
Eastlake St PL1 ....263 A3
Eastlake Wlk PL1 ......263 A3
Eastlands EX15 ....67 88
Eastleigh Cl EX13 .....103 D8
Eastmoor La TA4 ....34 E8
Easton Cross
  Hittisleigh EX6 ....96 C5
  Kingsbridge TQ7 ....258 B3
Easton La EX33 ....50 D1
Easton Moor Cross EX31 ..27 C1
Eastover La EX36 ....96 C7
Easy Bridge Cross EX13 102 F7
Easy La TQ13 ....123 B7
Eaton Ct TQ14 ....210 87
Eaton Dr EX1 ....261 C3
Eaton Hall Dr TQ6 .....233 E4
Eaton Ho EX1 ....261 C3
Eaton Pl TQ4 ....226 85
Ebberley Lawn EX32 ...155 A5
Ebberly Arms EX38 .....42 F6
Ebberly Cross EX19 ....42 E5
Ebford La EX3 ....183 D4
Ebrington Rd EX2 ......178 B7
Ebrington St
  Kingsbridge TQ7 ....258 D5
  Plymouth PL4 ....263 A3
Eddy's La 9 EX32 ......155 83
Eddystone Cl
  Heybrook Bay PL9 ......140 A7
  Plymouth PL3 ....249 C6
Eddystone Rd
  Down Thomas PL9 ......255 C1
  Thurlestone TQ7 ....143 A1
Eddystone Rise TQ7 ...147 D7
Eddystone Terr PL1 ...262 B1
Eden Cl TQ5 ....230 C3
Eden Gr TQ3 ....225 F7
Eden Park Cty Jun & Inf Schs
  TQ5 ....230 C3
Eden Pk TQ5 ....230 C3
Eden Way EX10 ....186 E3
Edenvale Rd TQ3 ....225 F8
Edgar Terr PL4 ....249 A4
Edgbaston Mead EX2 ...178 C4
Edgcumbe Ave PL1 .....262 A3
Edgcumbe Cl PL10 .....252 F6
Edgcumbe Ct 3 PL3 ...248 A3
Edgcumbe Dr PL19 ....171 86
Edgcumbe Park Rd PL3 248 D6
Edgcumbe Rd PL12 ....242 C5
Edgcombe Way PL18 ...125 B5
Edgcumbe Terr 13
  PL20 ....125 E1
Edgehill Coll EX39 ....156 F2
Edgeland Cross TQ12 ..217 D8
Edgelands La TQ12 ....211 C1
Edgeley Rd TQ2 ....214 A2
Edgerley Cross EX17 ...60 C1
Edgerton Park Rd EX4 177 D8
Edgeworthy Hill EX16 ..62 C8
Edgford Cross EX18 ...45 81
Edginswell La TQ2 ....213 C1
Edginswell La TQ2,TQ2 ..213 A1

Edinburgh Cres EX8 ...195 E6
Edinburgh Dr EX4 .....176 E6
Edinburgh Rd TQ5 .....230 D3
Edinburgh St PL1 .....247 E1
Edith Ave PL4 ....263 C4
Edith St PL5 ....243 D1
Edmonton Cl EX4 .....178 A8
Edmund St EX2,EX4 ....261 A2
Edna Terr PL4 ....263 C3
Edwards Cl PL7 ....251 84
Edwards Cres PL12 ....242 C2
Edwards Dr
  Plymouth PL7 ....251 85
  Westward Ho! EX39 ....156 E7
Edwards Rd PL15 ....90 C1
Edwin Rd EX2 ....177 83
Effingham Cres PL3 ...248 D7
Efford Barns EX17 ....81 84
Efford Cres PL3 ......249 86
Efford La PL3 ....249 85
Efford Pathway
  Plymouth PL3 ....249 C6
  Plymouth PL3 ....249 D5
Efford Rd PL3 ....249 86
Efford Wlk PL3 ....249 86
Egerton Cres PL4 .....263 C3
Egerton Pl PL4 ....263 C3
Egerton Rd Plymouth PL4 263 B3
  Torquay TQ1 ....220 C6
Egg Moor La EX13 ......88 A7
Eggbuckland Com Coll
  PL6 ....249 A8
Eggbuckland Rd PL3 ...249 C7
Eggbuckland Vale Prim Sch
  PL6 ....249 A8
Eggesford Country Ctr*
  EX18 ....59 E6
Eggesford Cross EX17 ..60 A3
Eggesford Fourways
  EX18 ....59 E5
Eggesford Rd EX18 ....58 F3
Eggesford Sta EX18 ....59 E6
Egham Ave EX2 ....177 D3
Egremont Cross EX14 ..84 C6
Egremont Rd EX8 .....202 A7
Egret Cl PL10 ....253 A6
Egypt La EX18 ....44 E1
Eiffel Pl 11 TQ9 .....223 C5
Eight Acre Cl 8 PL7 ..251 C5
Eight Acre La TA21 ...160 E5
Eight Trees TQ9 ......216 A5
El Monte Cl 6 TQ14 ..210 86
Elaine Cl Exeter EX4 ..174 A2
  Plymouth PL7 ....250 85
Elba Cl TQ4 ....226 C1
Elberry La
  Churston Ferrers TQ5 ..229 C5
  Paignton TQ4 ....229 D7
Elbow La PL19 ....171 C6
Elburton Prim Sch PL9 256 C7
Elburton Rd PL9 ......256 88
Elder Cl PL1 ....262 A3
Elder Gr EX17 ....165 E6
Elderberry Way EX15 .162 E5
Eldertree Gdns EX14 ..177 A7
Eleanor Ho PL1 ....262 A2
Elford Cres PL7 ......251 B8
Elford Dr PL9 ....255 C7
Elford Pk PL20 ....226 C6
Elgar Cl Barnstaple EX32 155 C5
  Exeter EX2 ....178 C5
Elgin Cres PL5 ....244 E3
Elim Cl EX10 ....188 85
Elim Ct PL3 ....248 85
Eliot Cl EX11 ....169 C3
Eliot St PL5 ....247 E8
Elizabeth Ave
  Exeter EX4 ....230 A1
  Exeter EX4 ....177 88
Elizabeth Cl
  Barnstaple EX31 ......154 D2
  Ivybridge PL21 ....237 F5
  Lyme Regis DT7 ....260 E4
  2 Whimple EX5 ....99 E8
Elizabeth Ct
  2 Plymouth PL1 ......263 A2
  Torquay TQ2 ....219 F5
  Totnes TQ9 ....223 C5
Elizabeth Dr EX31 ....154 D3
Elizabeth Lea Cl EX22 ..38 E1
Elizabeth Pl PL4 ......263 A4
Elizabeth Rd
  Exmouth EX8 ....196 C2
  Seaton EX12 ....192 A7
Elizabeth Sq 4 TQ12 ..207 F2
Elizabethan Cl 8 EX4 ..261 82
Elizabethan Ho (10) TQ9 223 D5
Elizabethan House (Mus)
  The* PL1 ....263 A2
Elkins Hill TQ5 ....230 D5
Ellacombe Church Rd
  TQ1 ....220 86
Ellacombe Cty Prim Sch
  TQ1 ....220 86
Ellards Cl EX2 ....177 E3
Ellen Tinkham Sch EX1 178 E7
Elleralie Ho TQ14 ....210 83
Ellerslie La EX31 .....33 E4
Ellerslie Rd EX31 ....154 84
Ellesmere TQ1 ....220 C5
Ellesmere Rd TQ1 ....220 85
Elley Cross EX17 ......79 82
Elliot Cl EX32 ....155 C4
Elliot Ho PL1 ....261 82

Elliot Plain TQ11 .....236 C5
Elliot Sq PL11 ....247 83
Elliot St PL1 ....262 81
Elliot Terr PL1 ....262 C1
Elliot Terrace La PL1 ..262 C1
Elliots Hill TQ13 .....130 C8
Elliott Cl Exeter EX4 ..173 C2
  Saltash PL12 ....242 D2
Elliott Ct TQ12 ....211 C2
Elliott Gr TQ5 ....230 84
Elliott Rd PL4 ....249 81
Elliott Way EX2 ......178 D5
Elliott's Hill EX17 ....61 C3
Elliotts Hill PL8 ......257 A4
Ellmead Cross EX20 ...93 F7
Ellwood Rd EX8 ......196 D2
Elm Bridge TQ7 ......258 D4
Elm Cl Broadclyst EX5 175 C6
  Stibb Cross EX38 ......40 D1
  Tavistock PL19 ....171 C3
Elm Cotts Barnstaple EX31 ..16 A3
  Saltash PL12 ....242 C3
Elm Cres PL3,PL4 .....249 A4
Elm Ct EX6 ....201 88
Elm Dr TQ12 ....207 F7
Elm Farm La EX24 ....103 A3
Elm Gdns EX33 ....152 D6
  Exmouth EX8 ....196 D1
  Plymouth PL7 ....250 E5
  Teignmouth TQ14 ....210 88
Elm Grove Ave EX3 ...182 F5
Elm Grove Cl EX7 ....204 E7
Elm Grove Dr EX7 ....204 E7
Elm Grove Gdns EX3 ..182 F5
Elm Grove Rd
  Dawlish EX7 ....204 E7
  Exeter EX4 ....261 A4
  Topsham EX3 ....182 E5
Elm La EX8 ....202 F7
Elm Orch EX12 ....192 D7
Elm Pk Millbrook PL10 ..253 86
  Paignton TQ3 ....225 F6
Elm Rd Brixham TQ5 ..230 A2
  Plymouth PL7 ....250 E5
  2 Newton Abbot TQ12 207 C3
  Plymouth, Glenholt PL6 245 D6
  Plymouth, Mannamead
  PL4 ....248 D6
Elm Terr Honiton EX14 166 D6
  Tiverton EX16 ....161 84
Elm Tree Cl PL8 ......257 F4
Elm Tree Pk PL8 .....136 A2
Elm Units EX2 ....177 D1
Elm Villas EX24 ......103 A3
Elm Way EX10 ....101 A1
Elm Wlk TQ9 ....223 F5
Elmbank Gdns 3 TQ4 226 A5
Elmbridge Gdns EX4 ..177 E8
ElMCroft PL2 ....248 87
Elmcroft Terr 7 EX39 .157 A2
Elmdale Rd EX39 .....157 A3
Elmdon Cl EX4 ....173 D1
Elmfield Gr EX4 ......261 C4
Elmfield Mdw EX20 ....74 E1
Elmfield Rd
  Barnstaple EX31 ....16 A3
  Seaton EX12 ....192 A7
Elmfield Terr EX39 ...157 A7
Elmhirst Dr TQ9 .....223 C5
Elmhurst Ct 13 TQ14 210 85
Elmlea Ave EX31 .....153 E5
Elmore Way EX16 .....161 E5
Elms Rd TA21 ....160 F5
Elms The Colyford EX24 103 A3
  Plymouth PL3 ....248 A3
Elmside
  Budleigh Salterton EX9 ..198 A1
  Exeter EX4 ....177 E7
  Willand EX15 ....163 D3
Elmslie Cl EX4 ....177 E7
Elmsleigh Pk TQ4 ....226 85
Elmsleigh Pk TQ4 ....226 85
Elmstone Rd EX8 .....196 82
Elmton Rd EX4 ....177 A7
Elphinstone Rd PL2 ..248 C7
Elsdale Rd TQ4 ....226 A4
Elsdon La EX11 ....168 E4
Elsdon's La DT6 ......100 E7
Elston Cross
  Chulmleigh EX18 ......44 C3
  Churchstow TQ7 ......143 D4
  Copplestone EX17 .....79 C6
Elston La EX17 ....79 85
Elston Mdw EX17 .....165 A5
Elstone Cross EX18 ...44 C3
Elston Rd EX4 ....177 A7
Elvington Cl EX36 ...158 D5
Elysian Ct EX36 .....158 D5
Elysian Fields EX10 ..188 85
Embankment La PL4 ..249 82
Embankment Rd
  Kingsbridge TQ7 ......258 D6
  Plymouth PL4 ....249 82

Embankment Road La N
  PL4 ....249 82
Emcombe Cross EX32 ..18 F1
Embleford Cres TQ13 ..111 F5
Emblett Dr TQ12 ......206 E4
Emblett Hall View TQ12 206 F1
Embridge Cross PL6 ..146 A7
Embridge Hill TQ6 ....146 A7
Embury Cl TQ12 ......213 A4
Emily Gdns PL4 ......263 84
Emma Pl PL1 ....248 A1
Emma Place Ope PL1 .248 A1
Emmanuel Cl 4 EX4 ..177 A5
Emmanuel Rd 2 EX4 .177 A5
Emmasfield EX8 ......202 D7
Emmetts Pk 9 TQ13 ..131 A5
Emperor Way EX1 ....178 E7
Empire Ct 2 TQ1 ....220 A7
Empire Rd TQ1 ....220 A7
Empsons Cl EX7 .....204 C6
Empsons Hill EX7 ....204 C6
Endfield Cl EX1 ......178 86
Endsleigh Cres EX5 ..179 87
Endsleigh Dr PL15,PL19,
  PL17 ....115 D5
Endsleigh Gdns 2 PL4 263 A4
Endsleigh Park Rd PL3 248 D6
Endsleigh Pk EX23 ....70 A6
Endsleigh Rd PL4 ....263 A4
Endsleigh View PL21 .237 A5
Enfield Cl EX17 ....165 A5
Enfield Cotts TQ1 ....220 D7
Enfield Rd PL4 ....263 B3
England's Cl 6 EX10 ..101 81
Eningdale Rd PL19 ...171 A4
Ennaton Cross PL21 ..137 E7
Ennerdale Gdns PL6 .244 E5
Ennerdale Way EX4 ..174 B1
Ennisfarne Rd EX39 ..156 87
Ensign Ct EX39 ......156 E7
Ensis Cross EX31 .....27 D5
Entrance Cross EX37 ..44 87
Epping Cres PL6 ......249 D7
Epworth Terr 4 PL21 247 F5
Eric Rd Calstock PL18 ..125 E3
  Plymouth PL4 ....263 C3
Erica Dr TQ2 ....213 F3
Erith Ave PL2 ....247 E2
Erle Gdns PL7 ....250 F3
Erlstoke Cl PL6 ......245 D1
Erme Bridge Wks PL21 .237 C4
Erme Ct PL21 ....237 D5
Erme Gdns PL3 ......249 C5
Erme Pk PL21 ....158 A4
Erme Prim Sch The
  PL21 ....237 D5
Erme Rd PL21 ....237 D5
Erme Side PL21 ......237 D4
Ermeside Cotts PL21 ..136 F4
Ermington Prim Sch
  PL21 ....136 F4
Ermington Workshops
  PL21 ....137 A4
Ernborough Ct EX2 ..261 C2
Ernesettle Cres PL5 .243 E3
Ernesettle Gn PL5 ...243 E4
Ernesettle Jun & Inf Sch
  PL5 ....243 E3
Ernesettle La PL5 ....243 D3
Ernesettle Rd PL5 ...243 E3
Ernsbrough Gdns
  EX14 ....166 85
Escot Park Animal Ctr &
  Gdns* EX11 ....84 C1
Eskil Pl EX38 ....159 C6
Esmonde Gdns PL5 ...247 88
Esplanade Exmouth EX8 202 A5
  Seaton EX12 ....192 84
  Teignmouth TQ14 ....226 C6
Esplanade Rd TQ4 ....226 C6
Esplanade The
  Dartmouth TQ6 ......233 F5
  Paignton TQ4 ....226 C5
  Sidmouth EX10 ....188 83
  Woolacombe EX34 ....7 F7
Essa Rd PL12 ....242 82
Essex Cl EX4 ....176 E4
Essex St PL1 ....262 84
Essington Cl EX8 ....196 83
Essington La EX20 ....77 D4
Essinton Ct EX8 .....196 83
Estover Cl PL6 ....245 C3
Estover Com Coll PL6 245 D2
Estover Ind Est PL6 ..245 E4
Estover Prim Sch PL6 245 D4
Estover Rd PL6 ......245 F4
Estuary Bsns Pk EX31 ..15 C3
Estuary Ct EX4 ......201 E6
Estuary View
  Budleigh Salterton EX9 ..198 81
  Northam EX39 ....157 A8
  Yelland EX31 ....15 C2
Ethelston's Cl DT7 ...260 A6
Ethelwynne Brown Cl
  EX39 ....157 82
Eton Ave PL1 ....262 C4
Eton Cl EX39 ....156 F3
Eton Pl PL1 ....262 C4
Eton Rd EX39 ....156 F3
Eton Sq 5 PL1 ....262 C4
Eton Terr 3 PL1 .....262 83
Eugene Rd TQ3 ......226 C8

Eureka Terr
  Bovey Tracey TQ13 ....180 D8
  1 Honiton EX14 ....166 C5
Europa Pk EX34 ....8 86
Evans Pl PL2 ....248 85
Eveleigh Cl 2 TQ5 ...230 C3
Evelyn Pl PL4 ....263 A4
Evelyn St PL5 ....243 D1
Evenden Ct PL11 .....247 A3
Everest Dr EX12 .....192 A7
Everett Pl EX16 ......161 E4
Evergreen Cl EX8 ....196 D3
Evett Cl EX8 ....202 E8
Ewin's Ash EX14 ......85 C8
Eworthy Cross EX21 ...91 E6
Exbourne Cross EX20 ..76 C4
Exbourne Prim Sch EX20 76 C4
Excalibur Cl EX4 .....174 A1
Exchange St PL1 .....263 A2
Exe Cl EX31 ....15 E5
Exe Gdns PL3 ....249 C7
Exe Hill TQ2 ....219 88
Exe St Exeter EX4 ....261 A3
  Topsham EX3 ....182 E5
Exe Units EX2 ....177 D1
Exe Vale Rd EX2 .....178 81
Exe Vale Terr 6 EX3 ..161 C3
Exe View Cotts EX4 ..176 F8
Exe View Rd EX4 ....196 C6
Exebridge Ctr The EX4 261 A1
Exebridge Hill TA22 ...33 F3
Exeter Airport EX5 ....99 A4
Exeter Airport Bsns Pk
  EX5 ....99 A4
Exeter Cl Feniton EX14 84 D2
  Plymouth PL5 ....243 D4
Exeter Coll EX4 ......177 A7
Exeter Coll (Annexe)
  EX4 ....261 A3
Exeter Coll Bishop Blackall
  Annex EX4 ....261 84
Exeter Cross
  Bovey Tracey TQ12 ...123 A1
  Sidmouth EX10 ....188 86
Exeter Foyer EX2 ....261 A2
Exeter Gate EX36 ....158 C3
Exeter Hill
  Cullompton EX15 .....163 82
  Kenton EX6 ....194 D3
  Shobrooke EX17 ......80 F5
  Tiverton EX16 ....161 E2
Exeter Hill Cross EX17 ..80 F4
Exeter Northall Hospl The
  EX2 ....177 E4
Exeter Phoenix EX1 ..261 83
Exeter Rd Braunton EX33 152 E4
  Chudleigh EX11 ....163 D4
  Cullompton EX15 .....163 82
  Dawlish EX7 ....204 C6
  Exmouth EX8 ....202 A6
  Honiton EX14 ....166 A5
  Ide EX2 ....176 D1
  Kennford EX6 ....181 A2
  Kingsteignton TQ12 ..207 D8
  Newton Abbot TQ12 ..207 85
  Newton Poppleford EX10 186 C6
  Okehampton EX20 ...170 85
  Ottery St Mary EX11 ..169 A3
  Rockwell Green TA21 160 83
  Silverton EX5 ....82 85
  South Brent TQ10 ....135 A3
  Teignmouth TQ14 ...210 86
  Topsham EX2,EX3 ....182 D6
  West Hill EX11 ....168 E7
  Whiddon Down EX20 ..95 F3
  Whimple EX5 ....168 88
  Wrington EX37 ....58 F2
Exeter Road Bsns Pk 8
  TQ12 ....123 E1
Exeter Road Ind Est
  EX10 ....188 D6
Exeter Road Prim Sch
  EX8 ....202 A7
Exeter St North Tawton EX20 77 C4
  Plymouth PL4 ....263 A3
  Plymouth PL4 ....263 82
  Teignmouth TQ14 ....210 85
Exeter Trad Ctr EX2 ..181 E8
Exeter YH* EX2 ......182 A8
Exhibition Rd EX17 ...165 E6
Exhibition Way EX4 ..178 D8
Exminster Com Prim Sch
  EX6 ....182 A4
Exminster Hill EX6 ...182 82
Exminster Marshes (Nature
  Reserve)* EX6 ......182 86
Exmoor Gdns TQ12 ..123 D6
Exmoor National Park Visitor
  Ctr* EX35 ....11 C1
Exmoor Steam Rly*
  EX32 ....11 C5
Exmoor View EX36 ...158 C5
Exmoor Zoo* EX31 ....11 83
Exmouth CE Prim Sch
  EX8 ....202 A6
Exmouth Com Coll EX8 202 B8
Exmouth Ct EX8 .....202 87
Exmouth Hospl EX8 ..202 87
Exmouth Mus* EX8 ..202 A7
Exmouth Rd
  Budleigh Salterton EX9 ..197 E1

Exmouth Rd continued
Clyst St Mary EX5 ....179 A1
Exton EX3 ....183 C3
Lympstone EX8 ....195 F7
Newton Poppleford EX10 .186 D5
Plymouth PL1 ....247 F3
Exmouth Sta EX8 ....201 F7
Exonia Pk EX2 ....176 D3
Exton La EX3 ....183 C2
Exton Rd EX2 ....177 C3
Exton Sta EX3 ....183 C1
Exwick Ct EX4 ....176 E8
Exwick Hill EX4 ....176 E7
Exwick Ho EX4 ....176 F8
Exwick La EX4 ....176 D7
Exwick Mid Sch EX4 .....176 E7
Exwick Rd EX4 ....176 F7
Eyewell Gn EX22 ....192 A6
Eymore Dr EX11 ....168 C3
Eyrecourt Rd EX12 ......192 A4

F

Factory Cotts TQ9 ....139 C7
Factory Cross TQ13 ......110 F6
Factory La TA20 ....88 D8
Factory Ope ▪ EX39 .....15 A1
Factory Row
South Molton EX36 ....158 E4
Torquay TQ2 ....220 A5
Fair Isle Cl TQ2 ....213 E2
Fair Oak Cl EX5 ....99 A4
Fair View
Barnstaple EX31 ....154 E6
Colyford EX24 ....103 A3
Fair View La EX24 ....103 A3
Fair View Rd
Dartmouth TQ6 ....233 E3
Honiton EX14 ....166 C5
Fair View Terr EX8 ....202 B7
Fairacre Ave EX32 ....155 C2
Fairfax Gdns EX2 ....177 B2
Fairfax Pl TQ6 ....233 F3
Fairfax Rd TQ12 ....180 F3
Fairfax Terr ▪ PL2 ....247 F4
Fairfax Way EX38 ....159 F5

Fairfield
Bratton Fleming EX31 .....18 A8
Ilfracombe EX34 ....150 C5
Plymouth PL7 ....250 E7
Sampford Peverell EX16 ...50 D1
Fairfield Ave Exeter EX4 .178 C8
Plymouth PL2 ....248 C7
Fairfield Cl
Axminster EX13 ....167 D5
Bovey Tracey TQ13 ....180 C7
Kennford EX6 ....202 B6
Kingsbridge TQ7 ....258 D4
Fairfield Gdns EX14 ......166 C5
Fairfield Gn TA3 ....68 D7
Fairfield Pk DT7 ....260 E4
Fairfield Rd
Crediton EX17 ....165 C6
Exeter EX2 ....181 B8
Exmouth EX8 ....202 B5
Kingskerswell TQ12 ......213 A3
Torquay TQ2 ....219 F8
Fairfield Terr Exeter EX2 .177 A4
Newton Abbot TQ12 .....207 C3
Fairfield Way TQ7 ....145 A1
Fairhazel Dr EX4 ....176 F7
Fairholme Rd EX34 ....7 F6
Fairlands Ave EX6 ....113 B3
Fairlawn Ct EX10 ....188 B5
Fairlawns Pk TQ4 ....226 B2
Fairlea TQ5 ....230 C6
Fairlea Cl EX7 ....200 F1
Fairlea Cres EX39 ....156 F4
Fairlea Ct EX9 ....197 E1
Fairlea Rd EX7 ....200 F1
Fairlinch Cross EX33 .....152 B8
Fairlynch Cl EX33 ....152 B7
Fairlynch Ct EX33 ....152 C7
Fairlynch La EX33 ....152 B7
Fairlynch Mus EX9 ....199 H2
Fairmead EX10 ....187 B8
Fairmead Ct TQ2 ....213 F2
Fairmead Mews PL12 ....242 C3
Fairmead Rd PL4 ....242 C2
Fairpark Cl EX2 ....261 C2
Fairpark Rd EX2 ....261 B2
Fairplace Terr EX20 .....170 B5
Fairview Cl TQ9 ....223 C4
Fairview Ave PL3 ....249 D5
Fairview Rd TQ12 ....211 A7
Fairview Terr EX1 ....174 F1
Fairview Way PL3 ....249 E5
Fairwater Cl TQ12 ....207 F7
Fairwaters TQ12 ....207 E8
Fairway Appledore EX39 .14 F1
Saltash PL12 ....242 C2
Tiverton EX16 ....64 E8
Fairway Ave PL21 ....237 B5
Fairway Cl
Braunton EX33 ....152 B6
Churston Ferrers TQ5 ....229 D5
Fairway The
Braunton EX33 ....152 B6
Exeter EX4 ....173 E1
Newton Ferrers PL8 .....140 F7
Fairways Cl EX37 ....43 B6
Fairways Dr EX37 ....43 A6
Fairways The EX39 ....156 D2
Fairways View EX37 ......43 C6

Fairy La TQ11 ....236 A4
Falcon Ct EX36 ....158 C4
Falcon Rd EX2 ....178 C4
Falcon Units TQ12 ......207 A3
Falkedon Cross EX17 ....96 A6
Falkland Cl EX4 ....173 E2
Falkland Dr TQ12 ....207 F8
Falkland Rd TQ2 ....219 F5
Falkland Way TQ14 ......210 A6
Fallapit Turn TQ9 ....144 C8
Fallow Fields EX32 ....155 C2
Falloway Cl TQ2 ....214 A2
Fallowfield Cl TQ12 .....207 F3
Fallowfields TQ9 ....223 A5
Falmouth Cl TQ2 ....219 B8
Fancy Cross PL21 ....137 A2
Fanny's Cross EX36 ......46 E7
Fanny's La EX17 ....80 B5
Lamerton Cross EX17 ....80 B5
Fanshawe Way PL9 ......255 C6
Far View Rd EX20 ....170 C5
Faraday Mill Bsns Pk
PL4 ....249 B1
Faraday Rd PL4 ....249 B1
Farleigh TQ12 ....206 B5
Farleigh Cross TQ9 ......139 A4
Farleigh Front Rd EX16 ..63 C2
Farleigh Mdws EX16 ....161 A6
Farley Hill TQ13 ....123 D8
Farley La EX35 ....5 E3
Farley's Grave EX20 .....77 E7
Farm Cl Exeter EX2 ......178 C4
Kingskerswell TQ12 .....212 F6
Plymouth PL7 ....250 C7
Farm Hill EX4 ....176 E8
Farm House Rise EX6 ....181 F4
Farm La Plymouth PL5 ...244 B2
Saltash PL12 ....242 D1
Farm Rd DT7 ....193 E6
Farm Way EX14 ....84 D2
Farmer Frank's La EX19 .58 F2
Farmhouse Ave EX1 .....178 F8
Farmyard La TQ3 ....218 E6
Farnham Terr TQ3 ....226 C7
Farnley Cl PL6 ....245 B6
Farpark Hill La EX31 .....9 A1
Farrant's Hill EX6 ......113 B8
Farriel La EX34 ....9 A5
Farringdon Cross
Cheriton Fitzpaine EX17 ..80 E7
Exeter EX5 ....99 A1
Farringdon Ct EX5 ....99 B2
Farringdon Hill EX17 .....80 E7
Farringdon Rd PL4 ......249 B3
Farthing Cross TQ13 ....218 C3
Farthing Down TA21 ....51 E7
Farthing La TQ3 ....218 C2
Farthing Lake Cross
EX32 ....29 A7
Farthing's Pitts TQ1 ....160 C4
Farthingland Cross EX20 .76 B5
Farthings La EX10 ....186 E7
Farthings Lodge Bsns Ctr
EX15 ....83 F6
Farway CE Prim Sch
EX24 ....101 F7
Farway Common Rd
EX14,EX24 ....101 F7
Farway Countryside Pk*
EX24 ....102 A5
Farwell Rd TQ9 ....223 B6
Farwood Cross EX24 ....102 C6
Fatacott Cross EX39 .....22 F5
Fatherford Rd EX20 .....170 D5
Faulkner Cl TQ6 ....233 C3
Fawns Cl PL21 ....136 F4
Fay Rd EX7 ....204 E6
Fayre View PL12 ....242 B1
Fearnside Way PL12 ....242 C3
Featherbed La
Clayhanger EX16 ....35 C1
Exmouth EX8 ....196 B2
Monkton EX14 ....86 D6
Offwell EX14 ....86 B2
Featherstone Rd EX8 ....196 A2
Federation Rd PL3 ....249 C4
Fegan Rd PL5 ....243 B1
Fell Cl PL8 ....141 B8
Fellowes Pl PL1 ....248 A2
Fellows La PL1 ....262 A4
Feltrim Ave EX2 ....261 C1
Feniton CE Prim Sch
EX14 ....84 E2
Feniton Gdns EX14 ......84 D2
Feniton Sta EX14 ....84 D2
Fenten Pk PL12 ....242 F3
Feoffe Cotts EX31 ....159 F7
Ferguson Cl EX11 ....169 B3
Fern Cl Brixham TQ5 ....230 D4
Okehampton EX20 ....170 C6
Plymouth PL7 ....251 C5
Fern Mdw
Okehampton EX20 ....170 C6
Tavistock PL19 ....171 D6
Fern Pk EX34 ....150 B5
Fern Rd TQ12 ....207 F1
Fern Way EX34 ....150 B4
Fernbank Ave PL21 .....237 A4
Ferncombe Cl ▪ TQ12 ..123 F1
Ferncombe Dr ▪ TQ12 ..123 F1
Ferndale
▪ Honiton EX14 ....85 C2
Plymouth PL6 ....245 D8
Ferndale Gdns EX32 ....177 A4
Ferndale Mews TQ2 .....219 B7

Ferndale Rd Exeter EX2 ..177 A4
Plymouth PL2 ....247 F7
Teignmouth TQ14 ....210 B6
Ferndown Cl EX7 ....200 A1
Ferndown Dr EX39 ......156 E2
Ferndown Rd DT7 ....260 E3
Ferne Animal Sanctuary*
TA20 ....69 D2
Fernhill Cl PL21 ....237 B5
Fernhill Cross TQ7 ......143 E8
Fernicombe Rd TQ3 .....225 E7
Fernleigh Cl EX20 ....77 C4
Fernleigh Rd PL3 ....248 F5
Fernleigh Terr PL18 .....125 B5
Fernpark EX2 ....177 F3
Fernworthy Cl
Copplestone EX17 ....79 B5
Torquay TQ2 ....219 A7
Fernworthy Forest Walks*
TQ13 ....110 D2
Fernworthy Gdns EX17 ..79 B5
Fernworthy Pk EX17 ....79 B5
Ferrers Gn TQ5 ....229 E4
Ferrers Rd PL5 ....243 E1
Ferry La PL11 ....246 D5
Ferry Rd Plymouth PL1 ..247 E3
Topsham EX3 ....182 E5
Ferry Slip TQ6 ....233 F3
Ferry St PL11 ....247 C3
Ferryman's Reach
TQ14 ....210 B3
Feversham Pl PL7 ....251 B6
Fiddlecott La EX18 ......60 B6
Field Cl Braunton EX33 ..152 C5
Paignton TQ3 ....219 B2
Field End EX13 ....167 E5
Field La Ashford EX31 ...16 B6
Brannton EX33 ....152 C5
Fillham Moor Cl PL21 ...237 E4
Fillace La PL20 ....126 F4
Filleigh Com Prim Sch
EX32 ....29 C6
Filleigh Mill New Rd
EX32 ....29 D7
Filleigh Moor Cross
EX32 ....60 D5
Fillham Moor La PL21 ...237 D5
Filmer Way EX2 ....177 B3
Fincer Dr PL21 ....237 A4
Finch Cl PL3 ....249 D4
Finch Foundary Mus of Rural
Industry* EX20 ....95 A5
Finches Cl PL9 ....256 C7
Findon Gdns PL6 ....245 D4
Finewell St PL1 ....262 C2
Fingle Cl EX4 ....176 E8
Fingle Glen EX6 ....98 B4
Finlake Cvn & Camping Site
EX6 ....113 B6
Finnigan Rd PL4 ....249 B1
Finnimore Ind Est EX11 .169 C3
Fir Cl Honiton EX14 .....166 B5
Willand EX15 ....162 D5
Fir Terr EX36 ....158 D4
Fir Tree Cl EX8 ....196 E2
Firbank Rd EX7 ....200 F1
Fircroft Rd PL2 ....248 B7
Fire Beacon Cross
Bishop's Tawton EX31 ...27 D7
Sidbury EX10 ....29 B2
Fire Beacon La EX10 ....100 E1
Fire Brigade HQ EX4 ....261 A4
Fire Stone Cross EX10 ..95 C3
Firebeacon Cross EX39 ..37 C7
Firebeacon La
Bolham EX16 ....49 C3
Chittlehampton EX37 ....29 B2
Firestone Cross EX20 ...95 C3
Firestone La TQ12 ......212 A8
Firlands EX14 ....84 D2
Firlands Rd TQ2 ....214 A2
Firleigh Rd ▪ TQ12 .....123 E1
Firs Cross TQ9 ....144 C7
Firs Gr EX32 ....155 B5
Firs Pk EX5 ....176 C3
Firs The
▪ Barnstaple EX32 .....155 B5
Kennford EX6 ....114 D4
Wilmington EX14 ....86 D2
First Ave Axminster EX13 .167 F7
Dawlish EX7 ....204 D5
Exeter, Heavitree EX1 ...177 F6
Exeter, Pinhoe EX1 ......178 F7
Plymouth, Billacombe PL9 .255 E8
Plymouth, Stoke PL2 ....248 A6
Teignmouth TQ14 ....210 A5
Torquay TQ1 ....220 A8
First Dr Teignmouth TQ14 .210 B5
Teignmouth TQ14 ....210 D6
First Raleigh EX39 ......156 D3
Firtree Rise PL21 ....237 D5
Firway Cross EX16 ......34 C3
Fisgard Way PL11 ....246 D3
Fish Mkt PL4 ....263 B2
Fishacre Cl TQ3 ....218 F6
Fishacre Cross TQ9 .....216 F6
Fishchowter's La TQ9 ...223 A4
Fishcombe Rd TQ5 ......230 B6
Fisher Rd
Newton Abbot TQ12 ....207 D2
Plymouth PL2 ....248 A5
Fisher St TQ4 ....226 C6
Fisher's Hill EX17 ....51 D7
Fishers Mead TA22 .....33 D6
Fisherton Cross EX31 ...28 C2
Fishingclose Cross EX20 .76 F6

Fishleigh Cross EX20 ....75 C8
Fishleigh Rd EX31 ....154 B2
Fistral Cl PL11 ....246 F4
Fitzford Cotts PL19 .....171 B4
Fitzroy Rd PL1 ....248 A3
Fitzroy Terr ▪ PL1 ......248 A3
Five Acres TQ13 ....180 C4
Five Barrow La EX13 ....104 A4
Five Barrows Cross EX36 .19 D7
Five Bridges Cross EX15 .67 C7
Five Cross TQ12 ....122 C1
Five Cross Way
Brayford EX31 ....18 F8
Plympton EX15 ....83 E8
West Buckland TA21 ....52 F6
Five Cross Ways TA22 ..32 F7
Five Crosses
Modbury PL21 ....137 A2
Rackenford EX16 ....47 C1
Five Crossway EX36 ....46 D8
Five Elms Cross EX5 ....80 E1
Five Elms La EX5 ....80 E1
Five Hos TA21 ....160 B8
Five Lane End EX38 .....159 A1
Five Lanes
Bovey Tracey TQ13 .....123 B7
Buckfastleigh TQ11 .....236 E7
▪ Kingsteignton TQ12 ..123 E1
Marldon TQ3 ....218 C3
Five Lanes Cross EX22 ..54 D8
Five Lanes Rd TQ3 ......218 D2
Five Mile Hill EX6 ....98 C4
Five Mile Hill Cross EX6 .98 C4
Five Oaks TQ1 ....130 C2
Five Oakes Cross
Brampford Speke EX5 ...81 C1
Burrington EX37 ....43 D4
Five Turnings EX34 .....13 A4
Five Wyches Cross
TQ13 ....180 B7
Flagstaff Rd TQ6 ....233 F4
Flamborough Rd PL6 ...245 A7
Flamborough Way PL6 ..245 A6
Flavel Cross EX15 ....163 C3
Flavel Pl TQ6 ....233 F3
Flavel St TQ6 ....233 F3
Flayes Almshouses ▪
EX4 ....178 C8
Fleet St Plymouth PL2 ...247 E6
Torquay TQ1 ....220 B4
Fleet Wlk TQ2 ....220 B4
Fleming Ave EX10 ......188 C8
Fleming Way EX2 ....177 E4
Flemons Ct ▪ TQ4 ......226 C5
Fletcher Cl TQ2 ....219 E7
Fletcher Cres PL9 ......256 B6
Fletcher Way PL9 ....256 A6
Flete* PL21 ....136 E2
Flete Ave TQ12 ....207 F2
Flete Cl TQ12 ....207 F2
Flete View Terr PL21 ...137 C8
Fletemoor Rd PL5 ......243 E1
Flexapark EX34 ....3 A3
Flexi Units EX7 ....177 C1
Flixton The EX11 ....169 D4
Flightway EX14 ....67 B3
Floaters Rd TQ6 ....233 F4
Flood St TQ9 ....207 F8
Flood's La EX15 ....163 B3
Flora Cotts PL1 ....262 B2
Flora Ct PL1 ....262 B3
Flora St PL1 ....262 B2
Florance Pl TQ12 ......207 D1
Florence Cotts TQ7 ....145 D1
Florence Cross EX36 ...42 B5
Florence St PL5 ....243 D1
Florida Dr EX4 ....173 D2
Florida Gdns PL3 ......249 C6
Florida Rd TQ1 ....220 C6
Flow La TQ14 ....208 F7
Flower Rd EX14 ....84 D2
Flowerpot La EX4 ......177 A5
Flowers Mdw ▪ TQ12 ..122 F1
Floyd Cl PL2 ....247 F7
Floyers-Hay Ct EX2 ....261 A1
Fludes La EX5 ....99 B3
Fluder Cres TQ12 ......213 B3
Fluder Hill TQ12 ....213 B3
Fluder La TQ12 ....213 F5
Fluder Rise TQ12 ......213 B3
Foldhay Cross EX17 ....78 A6
Foliot Ave PL2 ....248 A6
Foliot Rd PL2 ....248 A6
Follafield Pk TQ5 ......230 B2
Follaton Bglws TQ9 ....223 A5
Follaton Gate TQ9 .....222 F5
Follaton Rd TQ9 ....222 F6
Follett Rd Tiverton EX16 .64 D7
Topsham EX3 ....182 E5
Folley La EX34 ....98 D4
Folly Cross TQ10 ......134 C1
Folly Gate Cross EX20 ..93 F8
Folly Gyle Cross EX20 ..93 F8
Folly Hill TQ7 ....144 E6
Folly La
Buckland St Mary TA20 ..69 D8
South Molton EX36 .....30 D4
Football La TQ12 ......207 D1
Footland La
Daccombe TQ12 ....213 F5
Ipplepen TQ12 ....217 F5
Footland Rd TQ4 ....226 A4
Footpark La EX6 ....96 B6
Forbes Cl TQ12 ....180 F2
Forcefield Rd EX15 ....163 B2
Forces Cross TQ9 ......139 E3
Forches Ave EX32 .....155 C4
Forches Cnr EX17 .....165 C6

Forches Cross
Burrington EX37 ....43 F4
Crediton EX17 ....165 C6
Langtree EX38 ....40 F1
Newton Abbot TQ12 ....206 F7
Forches Cross Prim Sch
EX32 ....155 C4
Forches Green Flats ▪
EX32 ....155 B4
Forches Head EX15 ....175 F8
Forches Hill TQ12 ......209 B2
Ford TQ6 ....233 E3
Ford Cl PL21 ....237 A5
Ford Cross EX22 ....53 E8
Ford Cross
Bishops Nympton EX36 ..31 D1
Chawleigh EX18 ....59 E7
Lamerton EX17 ....44 A2
Chillington TQ7 ....149 A7
Columbjohn EX18 ......44 D2
Combe Martin EX31 .....10 D5
Hittisleigh EX6 ....96 D4
Molland EX36 ....31 F7
Meeth EX19 ....58 A3
Oakford EX16 ....48 D5
South Zeal EX20 ....95 A4
Staverton TQ9 ....216 E5
Tedburn St Mary EX17 ..97 D8
Ford Down La EX36 ....158 A3
Ford Farm Ct EX6 .....194 D3
Ford Hill Bow EX17 .....78 F4
Cheriton Bishop EX6,EX17 .97 C6
Combe Martin EX31 .....10 D5
Hartland EX39 ....22 C3
Marldon TQ3 ....248 A5
Thorverton EX5 ....81 E6
Ford La Combe Martin EX31 .10 B5
South Molton EX36 .....158 A8
Tiverton EX16 ....63 B6
West Hill EX11 ....168 B3
Whitestone EX4 ....98 E4
Ford Lane Cross EX6 ....96 D4
Ford Moor Cross EX18 ..59 E7
Ford Orch EX6 ....50 D1
Ford Park La PL4 ......248 C4
Ford Park Rd PL4 ......248 D4
Ford Pk ▪ TQ12 ....123 C4
Ford Plain EX5 ....81 E5
Ford Prim Sch PL2 .....248 A5
Ford Rd
Abbotskerswell TQ12 ...212 B7
Bampton EX16 ....34 C1
Tiverton EX16 ....64 D7
Totnes TQ9 ....223 D6
Wembury PL9 ....140 D8
Yealmpton PL8 ....136 A2
Ford Rise EX39 ....25 F4
Ford St
Moretonhampstead TQ13 .111 F5
Tavistock PL19 ....171 B5
▪ Wellington TA21 .....160 F4
Ford Valley TQ6 ....233 E3
Fordbarn Cross TQ9 ...222 E2
Forde Abbey* TA20 ....88 F8
Forde Cl
Abbotskerswell TQ12 ...212 A7
Newton Abbot TQ12 ....207 D3
Forde Cross EX17 ....80 F8
Forde Gdns TQ12 ......207 D2
Forde Ho TQ12 ....207 E2
Forde La EX36 ....26 D2
Forde Pk TQ12 ....207 D2
Forde Rd TQ12 ....207 D2
Fordens La EX7 ....204 C3
Forder Cross
Bishopsteignton TQ14 ..208 D7
Blackawton TQ9 ....145 C8
Chagford EX20 ....110 D8
Ugborough PL21 ....137 E7
Forder Hill PL10 ....252 F1
Forder Hts PL6 ....245 B1
Forder La
Bishopsteignton TQ14 ..208 E8
Bovey Tracey TQ13 ....122 E7
Cawsand PL10 ....252 F1
Dartington TQ9 ....222 E8
Dartington TQ9 ....207 C3
South Brent TQ10 .....135 B4
Ugborough PL21 ....137 D7
Forder Valley Rd PL6 ...245 A4
Fordishales La EX5,EX15 ..82 F8
Fordland Bottom Rd
EX2,EX6 ....176 B2
Fordlands Cres EX36 ...156 F4
Fordlands Rd TQ13 ....111 F5
Fordmill Cross EX16 ....34 D1
Fordmoor Cross EX16 ..48 C8
Fords Rd EX2 ....261 A1
Fordton Cross EX17 ....165 E2
Fordton Ind Est EX17 ..165 D3
Fordworth Cotts TQ7 ..149 D5
Fore St
Aveton Gifford TQ7 ....143 C6
Bampton EX16 ....34 B1
▪ Bere Alston PL20 ....125 E1
Beer EX12 ....191 D5
Bere Ferrers PL20 .....239 F3
Bishopsteignton TQ14 ..208 F8
Bovey Tracey TQ13 ....180 D7
Bradninch EX5 ....82 F6
Bridestowe EX20 ......107 F8
Brixham TQ5 ....230 C5
Buckfastleigh TQ11 ....236 C5
Budleigh Salterton EX9 .199 G2
Calstock PL18 ....125 D3
Cargreen PL12 ....239 A2
Chagford TQ13 ....110 E2
Cheulleigh TQ13 ....123 E8

Fore St *continued*
Chulmleigh EX18 . . . . .44 E1
Cornwood PL21 . . . . .133 C2
Cullompton EX15 . . . . .163 C3
Culmstock EX15 . . . . .66 E8
Dartmouth TQ6 . . . . .234 A3
Dolton EX19 . . . . .57 F7
Dulverton TA22 . . . . .33 D6
Exbourne EX20 . . . . .76 C5
Exeter EX4 . . . . .261 A2
Exeter, Heavitree EX1 . . . . . . .177 F5
Exmouth EX8 . . . . .202 A6
Great Torrington EX38 . . . . . . .159 D5
Gunnislake PL18 . . . . .125 C5
Gunnislake PL18 . . . . .125 D6
Harberton TQ9 . . . . .222 D2
Hartland EX39 . . . . .22 E3
7 Hemyock EX15 . . . . .67 B8
Holbeton PL8 . . . . .136 D1
Holcombe Rogus TA21 . . . . . . .50 F5
Holsworthy EX22 . . . . .73 C8
Holsworthy EX22 . . . . .164 C4
Ide EX2 . . . . .176 E2
Ideford TQ13 . . . . .124 B4
Ilfracombe EX34 . . . . .150 C6
Ipplepen TQ12 . . . . .211 D2
Ivybridge PL21 . . . . .237 D5
Kentisbeare EX15 . . . . .66 A3
Kenton EX6 . . . . .194 D3
Kingsbridge TQ7 . . . . .258 C6
Kingskerswell TQ12 . . . . .213 A4
Kingsteignton TQ12 . . . . .207 E7
Langtree EX38 . . . . .40 E2
Lifton PL16 . . . . .105 E4
Loddiswell TQ7 . . . . .143 E7
Luton TQ13 . . . . .124 C3
Millbrook PL10 . . . . .252 E5
Milton Abbot PL19 . . . . .116 A6
Morchard Bishop EX17 . . . . . . .61 A2
Moretonhampstead TQ13 . . . .111 F5
North Molton EX36 . . . . .30 D8
North Tawton EX20 . . . . .77 B4
Northam EX39 . . . . .156 F6
Okehampton EX20 . . . . .170 B5
Otterton EX9 . . . . .198 E7
Plymouth, Devonport PL1 . . . . .247 F2
Plymouth, Plympton PL7 . . . . .250 E4
Plymouth, Tamerton Foliot
PL5 . . . . .244 B6
Salcombe TQ8 . . . . .259 E4
Saltash PL12 . . . . .242 F2
Seaton EX12 . . . . .192 B5
Shaldon TQ14 . . . . .210 A3
Shebbear EX22 . . . . .55 D1
Sidbury EX10 . . . . .101 B2
Sidmouth EX10 . . . . .188 B3
Silverton EX5 . . . . .82 B5
5 South Brent TQ10 . . . . . .134 F3
South Tawton EX20 . . . . .95 B5
Tatworth TA20 . . . . .88 D8
8 Teignmouth TQ14 . . . . .210 C4
Tiverton EX16 . . . . .161 D4
Topsham EX3 . . . . .182 F5
Torpoint PL11 . . . . .247 B3
Torquay, Barton TQ2 . . . . .214 A2
Torquay, St Marychurch
TQ1 . . . . .220 B8
Totnes TQ9 . . . . .223 C5
Uffculme EX15 . . . . .66 A7
Ugborough PL21 . . . . .137 D6
Wellington TA21 . . . . .160 D6
Winkleigh EX19 . . . . .58 F3
Witheridge EX16 . . . . .46 E1
Yealmpton PL8 . . . . .257 F4
Fore Street Ctr EX4 . . . . . . .261 A2
Foredown La TQ12 . . . . . . .212 E4
Foredown Rd TQ12 . . . . . . .211 E2
Foreland View EX34 . . . . . .150 B4
Forest Ave PL2 . . . . .248 C7
Forest Hill EX39 . . . . .25 F4
Forest Houses EX21 . . . . . . .73 B4
Forest La TQ7 . . . . .258 A2
Forest Ridge Rd TQ3 . . . . . .218 F1
Forest View PL6 . . . . .245 D7
Forester's Terr TQ14 . . . . . .210 B4
Foresters Rd
Holsworthy EX22 . . . . .164 C5
Plymouth PL9 . . . . .255 D7
Foredown EX15 . . . . .83 D3
Forge Cl EX9 . . . . .197 F2
Forge End EX19 . . . . .58 F2
Forge La Butterleigh EX15 . . .64 A3
Saltash PL12 . . . . .242 E1
Forge Pl TQ13 . . . . .180 C7
Forge Way EX15 . . . . .163 C3
Forges Hill EX15 . . . . .64 F3
Forgeway Cl TQ2 . . . . .219 D4
Fork Cross TQ9 . . . . .222 A5
Forrest Units EX2 . . . . .177 D1
Forresters Dr PL6 . . . . .245 D7
Forster Rd TQ8 . . . . .259 D5
Forsythia Dr PL12 . . . . .242 C3
Fort Austin Ave PL6 . . . . . . .245 C1
Fort Hill Dr EX32 . . . . .155 B5
Fort St EX32 . . . . .155 A5
Fort Terr
1 Barnstaple EX32 . . . . . .155 A5
5 Bideford EX39 . . . . .157 B1
Plymouth PL4 . . . . .244 F3
Fort The PL10 . . . . .253 A1
Fortescue Cl EX13 . . . . .152 E5
Fortescue Cross EX5 . . . . . . .81 E2
Fortescue Pl PL3 . . . . .249 A6
Fortescue Rd
Barnstaple EX32 . . . . .155 B2
Exeter EX2 . . . . .177 B3
Ilfracombe EX34 . . . . .150 B6

Fortescue Rd *continued*
Paignton TQ3 . . . . .219 C1
Salcombe TQ8 . . . . .259 C4
Sidmouth EX10 . . . . .188 D7
Fortescue Terr PL19 . . . . . . .171 A6
Fortfield EX12 . . . . .192 B5
Fortfield Terr EX10 . . . . . . .188 A3
Forth Gdns PL3 . . . . .249 D6
Fortmead Cl EX32 . . . . .155 A5
Forton Rd EX8 . . . . .196 C1
Fortune Way TQ1 . . . . .220 B7
Forward Gn EX5 . . . . .82 E7
Fosbrooke Cl PL3 . . . . .248 F6
Fosketh Hill EX39 . . . . .156 C6
Fosketh Terr EX39 . . . . .156 C6
Foss Slip TQ6 . . . . .233 F3
Foss St TQ6 . . . . .233 F3
Fosse Rd TQ7 . . . . .258 D6
Fosse Way Cl **2** EX12 . . . .192 B4
Fosseway Cl EX13 . . . . .167 D5
Fosterlea EX15 . . . . .163 B3
Foulston Ave PL5 . . . . .247 B8
Foundry Cl **1** TQ13 . . . . . .123 E6
Foundry La PL8 . . . . .140 F6
Fountain Cl TQ13 . . . . .180 D7
Fountain Hill EX9 . . . . .203 F8
Fountains Cres PL2 . . . . . . .248 C8
Four Acres EX39 . . . . .156 D2
Four Acres Cl EX14 . . . . .86 B2
Four Cross
Axminster EX13 . . . . .167 B7
Ilsington TQ12 . . . . .122 C2
Kingston TQ7 . . . . .142 C7
Wilmington EX14 . . . . .86 C4
Four Cross Elms EX24 . . . . .103 A4
Four Cross Lanes TQ9 . . . . .228 A8
Four Cross Way EX32 . . . . . .11 C1
Four Cross Ways
Cheriton Bishop EX6 . . . . . . .97 A4
North Tawton EX20 . . . . .77 D4
Willand EX15 . . . . .162 D5
Winkleigh EX19 . . . . .58 D2
Four Crossways EX18 . . . . . .44 E1
Four Elms
Holcombe Rogus TA21 . . . . . . .51 A6
Sidmouth EX10 . . . . .187 C8
Four Elms Hill EX10 . . . . . . .187 B8
Four Firs EX5 . . . . .185 A1
Four Lanes EX15 . . . . .84 B8
Four Mills La EX17 . . . . .165 D4
Four Oaks EX32 . . . . .17 B2
Four Oaks Cl **1** EX32 . . . . .17 B2
Four Oaks Cross EX32 . . . . . .17 B2
Four Oaks Rd EX6 . . . . .97 F4
Four Views TQ5 . . . . .230 E4
Four Ways Cotts EX18 . . . . . .59 E4
Four Ways Dr EX18 . . . . .44 E1
Four White Gates Cross
EX37 . . . . .29 B4
Fouracre Cl EX4 . . . . .174 A1
Fouracre Way TQ12 . . . . . . .207 F8
Fourcross Hill EX13 . . . . . . .167 B7
Fourlanesend Com Prim Sch
PL10 . . . . .252 F3
Fourth Ave TQ14 . . . . .210 A6
Fourways Cross EX15 . . . . . . .67 C8
Fowelscombe Gate
PL21 . . . . .137 F6
Fowey Ave TQ2 . . . . .219 B8
Fowey Cl EX1 . . . . .177 F7
Fowey Gdns PL3 . . . . .249 D6
Fowey Rd EX31 . . . . .15 E5
Fowler Cl EX6 . . . . .182 A4
Fowey Cross EX20 . . . . .93 D5
Fox & Hounds Cross
EX20 . . . . .108 A5
Fox Cl Okehampton EX20 . . .170 D6
Rockwell Green TA21 . . . . . . .160 A6
Fox Field Cl PL3 . . . . .249 C5
Fox Hill EX39 . . . . .156 F6
Fox Rd EX4 . . . . .174 B2
Fox Tor Cl TQ4 . . . . .229 B7
Fox's Cnr EX14 . . . . .187 F2
Fox's Cross EX17 . . . . .63 B1
Foxbeare Rd EX34 . . . . .150 E5
Foxdown Hill TA21 . . . . .160 A4
Foxdown Rd TA21 . . . . .160 C4
Foxdown Terr TA21 . . . . .160 D4
Foxes Lair EX20 . . . . .170 A6
Foxes' Cross EX38 . . . . .26 E1
Foxglove Chase EX15 . . . . . .162 D5
Foxglove Cl
Barnstaple EX32 . . . . .155 E4
Dunkeswell EX14 . . . . .67 C1
Launceston PL15 . . . . .105 A2
6 Tiverton EX16 . . . . .161 F6
Foxglove Rd EX12 . . . . .192 B7
Foxglove Rise EX4 . . . . .176 D8
Foxglove Way PL12 . . . . . . .242 B4
Foxhayes Fst Sch EX4 . . . . .176 F7
Foxhayes Rd EX4 . . . . .176 F6
Foxhill EX13 . . . . .167 D5
Foxhole Hill EX6 . . . . .113 B4
Foxhole Jun Sch TQ3 . . . . . .225 E7
Foxhole Jun Sch TQ3 . . . . . .225 E8
Foxhole La EX39 . . . . .156 F6
Foxhole Rd Paignton TQ3 . . .225 F7
Torquay TQ2 . . . . .219 D5
Foxholes Hill EX8 . . . . .202 D4
Foxhollows TQ12 . . . . .208 A2
Foxlands Wlk TQ1 . . . . .220 C8
Foxley Cres TQ12 . . . . .206 F3
Foxtor Cl PL5 . . . . .244 B3
Foxtor Rd EX4 . . . . .176 E8
Foxwood Gdns
Plymouth, Plymstock PL9 . . . .255 F5
Plymouth, Southway PL6 . . . .244 E5
Foyle Cl PL7 . . . . .251 A5

Frances Homes EX1 . . . . . .261 C3
Francis Cl EX4 . . . . .176 F4
Francis Court Cotts EX5 . . . . .82 D2
Francis Cres **4** EX16 . . . . . .64 D7
Francis Ct
5 Crediton EX17 . . . . .165 C5
Exeter EX2 . . . . .177 E5
Francis Dr EX39 . . . . .156 C6
Francis St PL1 . . . . .262 A3
Francis Way EX24 . . . . .103 B3
Franeth Cl TQ12 . . . . .207 E8
Frank Webber Rd EX31 . . . . .160 A5
Frankford La EX6 . . . . .97 F5
Frankfort Gate **9** PL1 . . . . .262 B3
Franklea Cl EX11 . . . . .169 D3
Franklin St EX2 . . . . .261 B3
Franklin Ave EX33 . . . . .152 E6
Franklyn Cl EX2 . . . . .176 F3
Franklyn Dr EX2 . . . . .176 F3
Franklyn Hospl EX2 . . . . . . .176 F3
Franklyns Cl PL6 . . . . .245 A4
Frankmarsh Pk EX32 . . . . . .155 B6
Frankmarsh Rd EX32 . . . . . .155 B6
Frankmills Hill EX6 . . . . . . .113 B1
Fraser Dr TQ14 . . . . .210 A6
Fraser Pl PL5 . . . . .244 C7
Fraser Rd Exmouth EX8 . . . .196 D2
Plymouth PL5 . . . . .244 C7
Fraser Sq PL5 . . . . .244 C7
Frederick St E **1** PL1 . . . . .262 B3
Frederick St W PL1 . . . . . . .262 B3
Frederick Terr **10** EX7 . . . .204 D6
Fredington Gr PL2 . . . . .248 B6
Free Cotts EX4 . . . . .261 A3
Freedom Sq PL4 . . . . .263 B4
Freelands Cl EX8 . . . . .202 D8
Freemans Wharf PL1 . . . . . .254 A8
Freestone Rd TQ12 . . . . . . .207 D8
Fremantle Gdns **4** PL2 . . . .247 F4
Fremantle Pl PL2 . . . . .247 F4
Fremington Prim Sch
EX31 . . . . .153 D5
Fremington Rd PL2 . . . . . . .191 F7
French Cl EX5 . . . . .82 B6
French St **7** TQ14 . . . . . . .210 C4
Frensham Ave PL6 . . . . .245 C7
Frensham Gdns PL6 . . . . . . .245 C7
Freshford Cl PL6 . . . . .245 C1
Freshford Wlk PL6 . . . . .245 C1
Freshwater Dr TQ4 . . . . . . .229 B8
Frewin Gdns PL6 . . . . .245 B6
Frewins EX9 . . . . .197 F2
Friar's Hele Cross EX20 . . . . .57 B2
Friars Lodge EX2 . . . . .261 B2
Friars Wlk PL19 . . . . .171 C2
Friars' Gate EX2 . . . . .261 B2
Friars' La PL1 . . . . .263 A2
Friars' Wlk EX2 . . . . .261 B2
Friary Pk EX4 . . . . .263 B3
Friary St PL4 . . . . .263 B3
Friernhay Ct EX4 . . . . .261 A2
Friernhay St EX4 . . . . .261 A2
Frith Rd PL21 . . . . .242 D3
Fritz's Grave TQ11 . . . . .236 A7
Frobisher App PL5 . . . . .244 E2
Frobisher Dr TQ14 . . . . .210 A8
Frobisher Dr PL12 . . . . .242 E2
Frobisher Gn TQ2 . . . . .219 C6
Frobisher La TQ8 . . . . .259 C5
Frobisher Rd EX8 . . . . .196 C2
Frobisher Way
Plymouth PL6 . . . . .226 B2
Tavistock PL19 . . . . .171 B5
Torpoint PL11 . . . . .246 D3
Frog La Bourton EX33 . . . . . .152 D7
Clyst St Mary EX5 . . . . .179 A3
Holcombe Rogus TA21 . . . . . . .50 F5
South Molton EX36 . . . . .158 B5
Frog St Bampton EX16 . . . . . .34 B1
Exeter EX1,EX2 . . . . .261 A2
Woolacombe EX34 . . . . .7 F6
Frogbury Cross EX17 . . . . . . .59 F1
Froggy Mill Cross EX6 . . . . . .97 C5
Frogmore Ave
Plymouth PL6 . . . . .249 B7
Plymouth PL6 . . . . .249 B7
Frogmore Cross EX5 . . . . . . .82 F3
Frogmore Ct PL6 . . . . .249 B7
Frogmore Farm TQ9 . . . . . . .139 F7
Frogmore Rd EX9 . . . . .198 C6
Frogmore Terr TQ7 . . . . .258 C4
Frogstreet Hill EX33 . . . . .8 A2
Frogwell Cross TA4 . . . . .34 D6
Frome Cl PL7 . . . . .251 A4
Frontfield Cres PL6 . . . . .244 E5
Frost Cross
Bovey Tracey TQ13 . . . . .123 B6
Morchard Bishop EX17 . . . . . . .61 B1
Frost's Cnr EX19 . . . . .42 D1
Froude Ave TQ2 . . . . .214 B3
Froude Rd TQ8 . . . . .259 B2
Fry St EX22 . . . . .164 C4
Fryers La **8** EX10 . . . . .101 B1
Fuge Cross TQ6 . . . . .145 E6
Fuidge Cross EX17 . . . . .96 A5
Fuidge La EX17 . . . . .96 A5
Fulda Cres EX17 . . . . .165 D4
Fulford Cl EX6 . . . . .97 F4
Fulford Dr EX15 . . . . .163 A2
Fulford Rd
Cheriton Bishop EX6 . . . . . . .97 D1
Dunsford EX6 . . . . .112 F8
Exeter EX1 . . . . .178 A2
Fulford Way EX5 . . . . .184 C2
Fullaford Cross TQ11 . . . . . .236 B4
Fullaford Rd EX31 . . . . .18 E8

Fullaford Pk TQ11 . . . . .236 A4
Fullaford Pool Cross
TQ11 . . . . .236 A4
Fullars Ct **12** EX2 . . . . .261 A2
Fullerton Rd PL2 . . . . .248 A5
Fullingcott Cross EX39 . . . . .153 A2
Fulton Cl TQ12 . . . . .211 D2
Furland Cl PL9 . . . . .255 C5
Furley Cross EX13 . . . . .87 D6
Furlong Cl TQ12 . . . . .236 B7
Furlong Cotts EX16 . . . . .51 A4
Furneaux Ave PL2 . . . . .248 B5
Furneaux Rd PL2 . . . . .248 B6
Furness Cl TQ4 . . . . .226 A2
Furrough Cross TQ1 . . . . . . .220 C8
Fursdon Cl PL9 . . . . .256 C6
Fursdon Cross
East Allington TQ7 . . . . .144 E4
Hittisleigh EX6 . . . . .96 C5
Fursdon Ho EX5 . . . . .81 E7
Fursdon La EX16 . . . . .96 B5
Fursdon Rd PL9 . . . . .256 C6
Fursham Cross EX6 . . . . .96 B4
Furze Cap **3** TQ12 . . . . . . .123 E1
Furze Cross
Bridgerule EX22 . . . . .71 A5
Chittlehampton EX37 . . . . . . .29 A5
Cornworthy TQ9 . . . . .227 A2
Kingsbridge TQ7 . . . . .144 D3
Furze Gdns EX33 . . . . .37 A1
Furze Hill Rd EX34 . . . . .150 B4
Furze La **2** TQ5 . . . . .230 C5
Furze Park La EX31 . . . . .9 B2
Furze Park Rd EX31 . . . . .18 A8
Furze Pk Totnes TQ9 . . . . . . .223 F5
Woodbury EX5 . . . . .184 C3
Furze Pk Ct EX2 . . . . .251 A7
Furzebeam Row EX38 . . . . . .159 B5
Furzebeam Terr **14**
EX39 . . . . .157 B1
Furzebrook EX11 . . . . .169 E4
Furzedown Cross
Copplestone EX17 . . . . .79 A5
South Zeal EX20 . . . . .95 A6
Furzedown Rd TQ12 . . . . . . .213 A5
Furzegood TQ3 . . . . .218 D3
Furzeham Cl TQ5 . . . . .230 B5
Furzeham Pk TQ5 . . . . .230 B5
Furzeham Prim Sch
TQ5 . . . . .230 C5
Furzehatt Ave PL9 . . . . .256 A6
Furzehatt Park Rd PL9 . . . . .256 A6
Furzehatt Rd PL9 . . . . .256 A6
Furzehatt Rise PL9 . . . . .256 A6
Furzehatt Villas PL9 . . . . . . .255 F6
Furzehatt Way PL9 . . . . .256 A6
Furzehill EX10 . . . . .101 B2
Furzehill Cross TQ9 . . . . . . .227 B3
Furzehill Rd
Heybrook Bay PL9 . . . . .140 A7
Plymouth PL4 . . . . .248 F4
Torquay TQ1 . . . . .220 A6
Furzeland Hill EX17 . . . . .79 C6
Furzeleigh Cross TQ13 . . . . .122 F6
Furzeleigh La TQ13 . . . . . . .180 D8
Furzepark Cross
Bittaford PL21 . . . . .137 C7
Dolton EX19 . . . . .58 A5

G

Gabber La PL9 . . . . .140 B8
Gable Pk TQ1 . . . . .220 C6
Gables La EX15 . . . . .162 C4
Gables Rd EX15 . . . . .162 C4
Gables The
Combe Martin EX34 . . . . .2 F4
Exmouth EX8 . . . . .202 D6
Wellington TA21 . . . . .160 C6
Gabriel Ct **11** EX2 . . . . . . .261 A2
Gabriels Wharf EX2 . . . . . . .177 C3
Gabwell Hill TQ1,TQ12 . . . . .214 C7
Gabwell Rd TQ12 . . . . .214 C7
Gaddacombe Cross EX20 . . . .91 D1
Gains Cross EX22 . . . . .53 C3
Gainsborough Dr EX39 . . . . .156 B6
Gala Cross PL8 . . . . .257 F1
Galahad Cl EX4 . . . . .174 A1
Gale Rd TQ13 . . . . .131 B5
Gales Crest **3** TQ13 . . . . . .123 C4
Galileo Cl EX2 . . . . .230 E6
Gallacher Way PL12 . . . . . . .242 B3
Galleon Way EX39 . . . . .156 E7
Gallery Cl **5** EX14 . . . . . . .166 B6
Galloping La EX39 . . . . .39 B8
Gallops The PL12 . . . . .242 D4
Galloway Dr TQ14 . . . . .124 E1
Gallows Gate TQ13 . . . . . . .218 F6
Gallows Park Cross
TQ13 . . . . .131 B5
Galmpton CE Prim Sch
TQ5 . . . . .229 B5
Galmpton Cross TQ7 . . . . . . .143 B4
Galmpton Ct TQ5 . . . . .229 B5
Galmpton Farm PL8 . . . . . . .143 A4
Galmpton Glade TQ5 . . . . . .229 B5
Galmpton Holiday Pk
TQ5 . . . . .229 B4
Galmpton Rise EX34 . . . . . . .173 E1
Galpin St PL21 . . . . .137 C2
Galsworthy Cl PL5 . . . . .244 C2

For – Geo **281**

Galsworthy Sq EX4 . . . . . . .178 C8
Galva Rd Plymouth PL7 . . . . .251 C8
Sparkwell PL7 . . . . .132 E1
Gamberlake EX13 . . . . .167 C4
Gamberlake Cross EX13 . . . .167 C4
Gamblyn Cross TA4 . . . . .34 F5
Gammaton Moor Cross
EX39 . . . . .26 D3
Gammaton Rd EX39 . . . . . . .26 B4
Gammon Wlk **2** EX32 . . . . .154 F5
Gammons Hill EX13 . . . . . . .87 D1
Ganders Pk (Cvn Pk)
TQ1 . . . . .213 A2
Gandy St EX4 . . . . .261 A3
Ganges Rd PL2 . . . . .248 A5
Ganna Park Rd PL3 . . . . . . .248 D6
Gapemouth Cnr EX13 . . . . . . .87 C1
Gappah Cross TQ13 . . . . . . .123 E4
Gappah La TQ13 . . . . .123 E4
Gara Cl PL9 . . . . .256 B6
Gara Lodge **4** TQ12 . . . . . .212 F4
Gard Cl TQ2 . . . . .214 A3
Garden Cl Braunton EX33 . . .152 B6
Exeter EX2 . . . . .178 C4
Holbeton PL8 . . . . .142 A8
Plymouth PL2 . . . . .251 D5
Garden Cres PL1 . . . . .262 B1
Garden Ct EX9 . . . . .198 A1
Garden La PL9 . . . . .171 B5
Garden Mill Ind Est
TQ7 . . . . .258 D4
Garden Park Cl TQ9 . . . . . . .256 C7
Garden Pk TQ10 . . . . .135 D4
Garden Rd TQ1 . . . . .220 B6
Garden Spot La TQ13 . . . . . .123 F6
Garden St PL2 . . . . .247 E4
Garden Terr
Cullompton EX15 . . . . .163 C4
Wellington TA21 . . . . .160 D7
Garden Village PL9 . . . . .255 F8
Gardenia Dr EX16 . . . . .161 E7
Gardens The
6 Chudleigh TQ13 . . . . . . .123 E6
Dulverton TA22 . . . . .33 D6
Rousdon DT7 . . . . .193 E5
1 Wellington TA21 . . . . . . .160 D5
Gardiner Cl EX5 . . . . .82 A1
Gards La PL5 . . . . .243 E2
Gareth Cres EX4 . . . . .173 F2
Garfield Pl **7** TQ9 . . . . .223 C5
Garfield Rd TQ4 . . . . .226 C6
Garfield Terr PL1,PL3 . . . . . .248 A3
Garland Cl EX4 . . . . .176 E8
Garland Cross EX37 . . . . .45 B5
Garland's La EX16 . . . . .64 A5
Garlandhayes La EX15 . . . . . .52 E2
Garlic Rea TQ5 . . . . .230 D5
Garliford La EX36 . . . . .30 F4
Garners Ct TQ12 . . . . .206 D1
Garners La TQ12 . . . . .206 D1
Garratt Cl EX8 . . . . .196 C3
Garrett St PL10 . . . . .253 A1
Garrick Cl PL5 . . . . .244 C2
Garrison Cl PL1 . . . . .247 E1
Garscombe Rd EX2 . . . . .177 A3
Garston Ave TQ12 . . . . .207 B4
Garston Cl PL9 . . . . .256 A8
Garth Rd TQ2 . . . . .214 A3
Gas La EX38 . . . . .159 D5
Gascoyne Ct PL4 . . . . .263 A3
Gascoyne Pl PL4 . . . . .263 A3
Gashay La EX13 . . . . .88 H3
Gashouse La PL4 . . . . .263 B2
Gasking St PL4 . . . . .263 A3
Gatcombe Cross EX12 . . . . . .162 D2
Gatcombe La Beer EX12 . . . .191 C8
Seaton EX12 . . . . .102 E2
Gate Cl EX13 . . . . .88 C3
Gate Cross EX24 . . . . .102 F6
Gate Field Rd EX39 . . . . . . .156 E2
Gate Tree Cl TQ12 . . . . .207 F7
Gatedown La
Salcombe Regis EX10 . . . . . .101 E1
Sidmouth EX10 . . . . .189 D8
Gatehouse Cl
Cullompton EX15 . . . . .163 B3
Dawlish EX7 . . . . .204 E7
Gatehouse Hill EX7 . . . . . . .204 E7
Gatehouse Prim Sch
EX7 . . . . .204 E8
Gatehouse Rise EX7 . . . . . . .204 E7
Gater La EX1 . . . . .261 B2
Gattery La TQ5 . . . . .229 F1
Gavel The EX36 . . . . .158 D4
Gaverick Ct TQ12 . . . . .123 B1
Gay St PL1 . . . . .262 B2
Gay St TA21 . . . . .160 E6
Gays Cross EX17 . . . . .79 C7
Gays La EX17 . . . . .79 C7
Gaze Hill TQ12 . . . . .206 F5
Gdynia Way PL4 . . . . .263 C2
Geasons La PL7 . . . . .250 E5
Gees La PL21 . . . . .137 C2
Generals Cl EX6 . . . . .201 A7
Generals La EX6 . . . . .201 B7
Geneva Cl EX4 . . . . .3 A3
Geneva Ct EX2 . . . . .177 E4
Geneva Pl EX4 . . . . .177 F4
Geneva Terr EX13 . . . . .115 B6
Gennys Ct PL18 . . . . .125 B6
Gentian Cl TQ3 . . . . .218 D2
George Ave PL7 . . . . .250 F6

George Cross PL7 250 F5
George Downing Ho PL6 245 A1
George Hill EX17 165 B6
George La Kilmington EX13 87 C1
Plymouth PL7 250 F5
George Nympton Cross EX36 30 A2
George Pl PL1 262 A2
George Rd TQ3 219 B1
George Shopping Mews EX36 158 C4
George Sq PL1 247 F1
George St
Axminster EX13 167 D6
11 Barnstaple EX32 154 F6
Exeter EX1 261 A2
1 Exmouth EX8 202 A7
Honiton EX14 166 C6
Newton Abbot TQ12 207 B3
Okehampton EX20 170 B5
Plymouth PL1 247 F1
11 Teignmouth TQ14 210 C4
Wellington TA21 160 D6
George Teign Rd EX6 113 D2
George's Sq DT7 260 E3
Georgeham Cross EX33 152 D7
Georgeham Prim Sch EX33 8 A2
Georgeham Rd
Croyde EX33 7 F2
Woolacombe EX34 8 B5
Georgehill Cross EX17 165 A6
Georgenympton Rd EX36 158 C2
Georges Cl EX1 178 B6
Georgia Cres PL3 249 C6
Georgian Ct TQ1 220 E6
Gerald Dinnis Units EX2 177 D1
Geraldine Terr PL12 242 C1
Gerbestone La TA21 52 E6
Gerrydown Rd EX19 58 D3
Gerston Cross TQ9 223 A3
Gerston La TQ7 258 C1
Gerston Pl 8 TQ3 226 B6
Gerston Rd TQ4 226 B6
Gervase Ave EX2 261 A1
Gerway La EX11 169 E2
Gestridge Cross TQ12 207 D7
Gestridge Rd TQ12 207 D7
Giant's Grave TA20 69 D7
Giant's Grave Rd TA20 69 D7
Gibb Hill PL21 133 B2
Gibbon La PL4 263 A3
Gibbons St PL4 263 A3
Giblands Cross EX20 170 D5
Giblands Pk EX20 170 D5
Gibraltar Rd EX8 195 E6
Gibson Cl EX8 196 E1
Gibson Dr TQ4 226 A1
Gibson Gdns TQ4 226 A1
Gibson Rd TQ4 226 A1
Gidcott Cross EX22 55 A4
Gidley Arms Cross EX36 46 A5
Gidley Cross EX36 46 B4
Gidley's Turn EX6 113 B4
Gidleys Mdw TQ9 222 F8
Gifford Pl PL3 248 D4
Gifford Terrace Rd PL3 248 E5
Gilbert Ave Exeter EX2 178 C4
Teignmouth TQ14 210 A7
Gilbert Cl TQ2 219 D6
Gilbert Ct PL7 251 B6
Gilbert Gr 1 EX34 150 C6
Gilbert La PL2 248 C5
Gilbert Rd TQ12 207 E3
Gilbert Way TQ4 226 A3
Gill Pk PL3 249 B5
Gill's Cross TQ9 222 D2
Gillard Rd TQ5 230 F4
Gillard Way PL21 136 D6
Gillards Cl TA21 160 B4
Gillards Mead TA3 68 D7
Gillscott Cross EX17 60 B1
Gilpin Cl EX7 204 F8
Gilston Rd PL12 242 D4
Gilwell Ave PL9 256 B7
Gilwell Pl PL4 263 A3
Gilwell St PL4 263 A3
Gingaford Cross TQ10 135 A5
Gipsies Cnr EX17 79 F6
Gipsies La EX17 79 F6
Gipsy Cnr Barnstaple EX31 9 C1
Bovey Tracey TQ13 122 D5
Budlake EX5 82 E1
Gipsy Cross EX15 67 A5
Gipsy Dro TA20 69 F4
Gipsy Hill La EX1 178 F8
Gipsy Hill Mews EX1 178 F7
Gipsy La Barnstaple EX31 9 F3
Bideford EX39 25 B4
Buckfastleigh TQ11 236 A4
Exeter EX1 178 F8
Exmouth EX8 202 B8
Ilfracombe EX34 150 D5
Ivybridge PL21 136 D7
Sampford Arundel TA21 51 D5
Girt La EX34 3 B4
Gissage Hill EX17 78 B7
Gissage View 7 EX14 166 B6
Gissons EX6 182 B4
Gissons La EX6 114 D4
Gittisham Cl EX1 178 D6
Gittisham Farm Cross EX14 85 A1
Gittshayne Cross EX24 102 F5
Glade The PL20 126 E2
Gladstone Pl 4 TQ12 207 C3
Gladstone Rd EX1 177 E6
Gladstone Terr
8 Teignmouth TQ14 210 C5
Wellington TA21 160 E6
Glanvill Way EX14 166 B4
Glanville Ave 1 PL19 171 B5
Glanville Rd
Offwell EX14 102 A8
Tavistock PL19 171 B6
Glanville St PL1,PL4 262 C3
Glanville Terr PL12 242 F3
Glanvilles Mill PL21 237 D5
Glanvilles Rd PL21 237 D5
Glascott Cl EX20 75 B6
Glasshouse La EX2 182 B7
Glastonbury Cl EX4 174 A2
Glave Saunders Ave EX2 178 C4
Glazebrook Ct TQ10 134 E2
Glazegate Cross TQ3 224 F7
Glazegate La TQ3,TQ4, TQ9 224 E6
Glazon Way EX39 157 A8
Glebe Ave PL12 242 F3
Glebe Cl Exmouth EX8 202 F7
Lympstone EX8 195 E6
Otterton EX9 198 E7
Upton Pyne EX5 172 F7
Glebe Cotts EX5 99 B1
Glebe Ct EX39 156 F6
Glebe Field TQ7 143 A2
Glebe Hos EX39 156 A1
Glebe La EX22 164 C4
Glebe Land TQ7 143 C6
Glebe Mdw EX22 164 B4
Glebe The
Cheriton Fitzpaine EX17 62 D3
Ipplepen TQ12 211 C2
Thorverton EX5 81 E4
Glebefields EX39 156 F6
Glebeland
Churchstow TQ7 143 E4
Down St Mary EX17 78 E7
Glebeland Villas EX36 31 A2
Glebeland Way TQ2 219 B8
Glebelands
Buckfastleigh TQ11 236 A6
Cheriton Bishop EX6 97 B4
8 Chudleigh TQ13 123 F6
Exminster EX6 182 A4
Holsworthy EX22 164 B4
Lympstone EX8 195 E6
Newton Poppleford EX10 186 F8
Sidmouth EX10 188 A4
Witheridge EX16 62 B5
Wrafton EX33 152 E4
Glebelands Rd EX16 64 D7
Glen Cl Clyst St Mary EX5 179 E2
Sidmouth EX10 188 A3
Glen Farm Cres EX14 166 D5
Glen Gdns EX39 156 F4
Glen Isla EX10 188 B3
Glen Lyn Gorge* EX35 151 C5
Glen Park Ave PL4 262 C4
Glen Park Prim Sch PL7 251 B5
Glen Rd Paignton TQ3 226 B7
Plymouth, Mannamead PL3 248 F5
Plymouth, Plympton PL7 250 F6
Sidmouth EX10 188 A3
Glen The Beer EX12 191 E6
3 Newton Abbot TQ12 207 F2
Okehampton EX20 170 B4
Glen Wlk EX4 173 D2
Glenavon Rd PL3 248 E5
Glenburn Cl PL3 248 E7
Glenburnie Ho EX39 157 A3
Glenburnie Rd EX39 157 A3
Glencarnock Cl TQ1 219 E7
Glencoe EX2 177 E5
Glendale Rd EX20 170 A6
Glendale Terr EX39 157 A3
Glendaragh Rd 12 TQ14 210 C5
Glendon Cross EX20 170 F8
Glendower Rd PL3 248 D5
Gleneagle Ave 4 PL3 248 F6
Gleneagle Rd PL3 248 F6
Gleneagle Villas 5 PL3 248 F6
Glenfield Cl PL6 245 D6
Glenfield Rd
Bideford EX39 157 A4
Plymouth PL6 245 D5
Glenfield Way PL6 245 E6
Glengarth Cl EX39 157 A5
Glenholt Cl PL6 245 D6
Glenholt Rd PL6 245 D6
Glenhurst Rd 5 PL3 248 E6
Glenmore Ave PL2 247 F5
Glenmore Rd
Brixham TQ5 230 C4
Exeter EX2 178 A5
Glennaven Cl PL7 251 C6
Glenorchy Ct 5 EX8 202 A7
Glenside Cl 5 TQ14 210 B6
Glenside Ct TQ1 220 E5
Glenside Rise PL7 250 E6
Glenthorne Cl TQ1 220 D4
Glenthorne Rd EX4 173 A1
Glentor Rd PL3 248 E7
Glentorr Rd EX39 157 A3
Glenview EX14 166 D5
Glenwater Cl EX12 192 D6
Glenwood Rd PL3 248 E6
Glenwood Rise EX2 261 C1
Globe Ct EX15 163 C3
Globe Hill EX5 184 B3
Globe La EX3 182 F4
Globefield EX3 182 F5
Gloster Rd EX32 155 A4
Gloucester Cl
Honiton EX14 166 A5
Torquay TQ2 213 F1
Gloucester Cres EX14 166 A5
Gloucester Ct PL1 262 C4
Gloucester Pl PL1 262 C4
Gloucester Rd
Exeter EX4 176 E7
Exmouth EX8 196 E3
Newton Abbot TQ12 207 C3
9 Teignmouth TQ14 210 B5
Glove Ct EX38 159 C5
Gloyn Pk EX22 53 E1
Glynsmead TA20 88 C8
Gnome Reserve* EX22 39 B2
Goad Ave Plymouth PL4 263 C2
Torpoint PL11 246 E3
Goad Cl PL11 246 F3
Goaman Pk EX39 22 E3
Goaman Rd EX39 26 A4
Goats Hill Rd EX39 157 A6
Goblin Hill EX17 79 C4
Goblin La EX15 163 C4
Godborough View EX39 156 D2
Godding Gdns PL6 244 E6
Godford Cross EX14 85 B5
Godfrey Ave TQ3 219 B2
Godfrey Cl EX11 169 C3
Godfreys Gdns EX17 78 C4
Godhams La TA4 35 A7
Godolphin Cl EX5 81 A1
Godwell La PL21 237 F5
Gogwell La Cove EX16 49 B5
Tiverton EX16 161 F1
Gold Coast Holiday Village EX34 8 C6
Gold St
Ottery St Mary EX11 169 D4
Tiverton EX16 161 D4
Goldburn Cross EX20 76 B1
Golden Cl TQ5 230 B2
Golden Hinde Mus* TQ5 230 D5
Golden Inn Cross EX21 74 C7
Golden Joy EX17 165 D6
Golden La EX14 66 F2
Golden Lane Cross EX14 66 E2
Golden Park Ave TQ2 213 F4
Golden Sq EX14 86 E6
Golden Terr 19 EX7 204 D6
Goldfinch Cl PL15 105 A2
Goldfinch Cres PL12 242 E4
Goldfinch Gr
Cullompton EX15 163 A2
Saltash PL12 242 D4
Golds Cross EX6 97 E4
Golds La EX6 97 E5
Goldscross Hill EX6 97 D4
Goldsmith Gdns PL5 244 D3
Goldsmith St Exeter EX4 261 A3
Exeter, Heavitree EX1 177 F6
Goldsmiths La EX13 88 A4
Goldsmoor Gate EX16 50 E3
Golf Links Rd
South Brent TQ10 134 D1
Westward Ho! EX39 156 D7
Golland La EX37 44 B2
Gollands TQ5 230 B5
Gollands Cl TQ5 230 A5
Gollands La
Copplestone EX17 79 B8
Morchard Bishop EX17 61 B1
Golvers Hill Rd TQ12 207 E7
Good Shepherd Dr 5 EX2 261 B2
Goodacre Cross PL16 91 B1
Goodeve Cl PL9 255 E6
Goodgates Cl EX33 152 C6
Goodgates Cres EX33 152 B6
Goodgates Gr EX33 152 B6
Goodgates Pk EX33 152 C6
Goodgates Rd EX33 152 B6
Goodiford Cross EX15 65 F3
Gooding Rise EX16 161 B4
Goodleigh Cross EX32 155 F7
Goodleigh La EX19 58 E3
Goodleigh Prim Sch EX32 17 B5
Goodleigh Rd EX32 155 D5
Goodridge Cl EX7 204 E8
Goodrington Rd TQ4 226 B1
Goodrington Sands Sta TQ4 226 C4
Goodshelter Cross TQ8 148 E5
Goodstone Cross TQ12 131 C6
Goodstone Way TQ4 225 F3
Goodwells Head EX32 18 C3
Goodwin Ave PL6 245 A6
Goodwin Cres PL2 248 A6
Goodwood Park Rd EX39 157 A5
Goose Moor La EX6 114 B4
Gooseberry La PL1 262 B2
Gooseford Cross EX20 95 D2
Gooseford La PL11 252 C8
Goosewell Hill PL6 249 C8
Goosewell Park Rd PL9 255 F6
Goosewell Prim Sch PL9 255 F6
Goosewell Rd PL9 255 F5
Goosewell Terr PL9 255 F6
Gora La EX34 8 A6
Gordon Ct PL12 242 D2
Gordon Rd Exeter EX1 177 E7
Topsham EX3 182 E6
Gordon Terr Beer EX12 191 D5
Plymouth PL4 248 E4
Gordon's Pl EX1 177 F5
Gore La Exmouth EX8 202 E4
Kilmington EX13 103 C8
Uplyme DT7 260 A4
Gorhuish Cross EX20 75 C1
Gorlegg TA21 51 E5
Gornhay Cross EX16 64 D8
Gorrans Down EX39 22 F1
Gorse La EX8 196 D4
Gorse Way
Ivybridge PL21 237 E4
Sidmouth EX10 187 F4
Gorsey Cl PL5 244 E2
Gorvin Cross EX39 38 B6
Gorway TQ14 210 C6
Gorwell Rd EX32 155 C5
Gorwood Rd EX39 40 B7
Gorwyn La EX6 97 C4
Gosceline Wlk EX14 166 C4
Gosford La EX11 169 C7
Gosford Rd EX11 169 D7
Goshawk Units EX2 178 F6
Goshen Rd TQ2 219 E4
Goss Mdw EX17 78 C4
Gostwick Cl EX20 77 C4
Goswela Cl PL9 255 F5
Goswela Gdns PL9 255 F5
Gothic Rd TQ12 207 B2
Gould Cl EX32 155 B4
Gould Rd
Barnstaple EX32 155 C4
Salcombe TQ8 259 D5
Gourders La TQ12 212 F2
Goutsford Gate PL21 136 F2
Govers Mdw EX24 103 A4
Govetts EX5 184 C3
Gower Ridge Rd PL9 255 D6
Goyle Acre La EX13 87 D4
Grace Par EX2 177 B2
Grace Rd Central EX2 177 C2
Grace Rd W EX2 177 B2
Graddon Cross
Black Torrington EX21 73 F6
Okehampton EX20 93 E4
Grafton Ct TQ1 220 B4
Grafton Hts TQ1 220 C5
Grafton Rd Exeter EX4 173 B1
11 Newton Abbot TQ12 207 B3
Plymouth PL4 248 E4
Torquay TQ1 220 B4
Grafton Terr TQ1 220 B4
Graham Cl EX16 161 D5
Graham Rd TQ3 219 A1
Grainge Rd PL6 245 A1
Grainger Cl EX2 178 C5
Gramercy Hall Sch TQ5 229 E3
Grammar La EX10 189 D7
Grampian Cl TQ4 225 D4
Granary La EX9 198 C1
Granby Ct PL1 247 E2
Granby Gn PL1 247 E2
Granby Pl PL1 247 E2
Granby St PL1 247 E2
Granby Way PL1 247 E2
Grand Hotel Rd PL1 262 B1
Grand Par PL1 262 B1
Grand View Rd TQ7 147 B7
Grand Western Canal (Country Pk)* EX16 50 F2
Grandison Ave TQ14 209 A8
Grandisson Ct EX2 178 A2
Grandisson Dr EX11 169 F3
Grandon Bldgs 2 EX1 261 A2
Grange Ave
Barnstaple EX31 154 C2
Exmouth EX8 202 B8
Paignton TQ4 226 B2
Grange Cl
Bratton Fleming EX32 18 A8
Exmouth EX8 202 B8
Ipplepen TQ12 211 C3
Lympstone EX8 195 F5
Wellington TA21 160 E5
Grange Cotts
Plymouth PL7 250 F4
Rockbeare EX5 99 C6
Grange Cross EX14 84 D7
Grange Ct
4 Barnstaple EX32 155 A6
Teignmouth TQ14 210 A5
Grange Dr TQ14 210 B6
Grange Heights Cl TQ4 226 A1
Grange Hill EX32 18 B8
Grange Hts TQ4 226 A2
Grange La EX20 57 A7
Grange Pk TQ12 212 A6
Grange Rd
Abbotskerswell TQ12 212 B6
Bideford EX39 157 B1
Buckfast TQ11 236 B7
Paignton TQ4 226 B2
Plymouth PL7 251 A4
Torquay TQ1 220 C5
Yelverton PL20 126 F3
Grange The EX33 152 E5
Grange View TQ4 226 A2
Grant's Hill EX16,TA22 33 F2
Grantham Cl PL7 250 B4
Grantland Hill EX16,EX17 63 A4
Grantlands EX15 66 A7
Grantley Gdns PL3 249 A5
Granville Ave EX32 154 F6
Granville Pl EX15 162 C5
Granville Rd EX34 150 B6
Gras Lawn EX2 177 E4
Grasmere Cl
Plymouth PL6 244 E5
Torquay TQ2 214 B2
Grass Rd Ashburton TQ13 131 A3
Buckfastleigh TQ11 236 F8
Grassendale Ave PL2 247 F7
Grasslands Dr EX1 178 F8
Grassmere Way PL12 242 D4
Grasspark Hill EX32 18 E3
Grassy La PL8 136 C4
Grattan La EX31 16 B6
Grattans Way EX17 78 C4
Gratton Cl TQ6 146 B8
Gratton Cross
Shebbear EX22 55 A5
Yelverton PL20 127 A2
Gratton Ct EX31 154 C2
Gratton Dr TQ7 145 A1
Gratton La Barnstaple EX31 9 C5
Brendon EX35 6 A4
Chulmleigh EX18 59 D3
Combe Martin EX31 3 F2
Yelverton PL20 127 A2
Gratton Way EX31 154 C2
Grattons Dr EX35 151 B5
Grattons La TQ9 216 E2
Gravel La EX12 192 B7
Gravel Pit Cross EX36 20 A6
Gravel Wlk EX15 163 C3
Gravesend Gdns PL11 247 B3
Gravesend Wlk PL5 243 D4
Gray Cres PL5 247 C8
Gray's Hill EX15 52 D1
Gray's La EX15 52 D1
Graybridge Rd PL20 126 F4
Graynfylde Dr EX39 157 B2
Grays Ct TQ13 112 B3
Grays Mdw TQ13 111 F5
Great Ambrook Ave TQ12 217 A7
Great Berry Rd PL6 244 F1
Great Bridge TQ13 130 F5
Great Burrow Rise EX39 156 F8
Great Churchway PL9 256 A7
Great Cl EX15 51 E1
Great Fellingfield PL19 117 E6
Great Field Gdns EX33 152 C5
Great Furlong TQ14 208 E8
Great Headland Cres TQ3 219 D1
Great Headland Rd TQ3 219 C1
Great Hele La EX36 158 D2
Great Hill 3 TQ13 123 E6
Great Hill Cross TQ1 213 F5
Great Hill Rd TQ2 213 F4
Great Hill View EX4 173 E2
Great La TQ7 147 E6
Great Lightleigh La EX18 44 F5
Great Links Tor Rd EX20 170 E5
Great Mdw TA22 33 D6
Great Mead EX6 112 F7
Great Mis Tor Cl 5 PL20 126 F3
Great Oak Cross EX5 81 D2
Great Oak Mdw EX22 164 C5
Great Orchard Cl PL9 255 E5
Great Park Cl 4 PL7 251 C5
Great Parks Rd TQ3 225 E5
Great Pitford La EX18 58 D6
Great Rea Rd TQ5 230 D5
Great Ringaton La EX36 32 B6
Great Tor Cl TQ3 218 F1
Great Torrington Bluecoat CE Inf Sch EX38 159 C5
Great Torrington Com Sch EX38 159 E5
Great Torrington Jun Sch EX38 159 E5
Great Western Cl TQ4 226 C4
Great Western Ind Est EX32 155 B3
Great Western Rd
12 Paignton TQ4 226 B6
Plymouth PL1 262 B1
Great Western Way EX16 161 D3
Great Woodford Dr PL7 250 B6
Greatfield Rd PL3 249 B7
Greatlands Cres PL2 248 A6
Greatlands Pl 5 PL2 248 A5
Greatoak Cross TQ12 212 C5
Greatpark La TQ3 225 D6
Greatweek Cross TQ13 111 B6
Greatwood Terr EX3 182 F5
Grebe Cl PL7 250 F5
Grecian Way EX2 178 C4
Greebys The TQ3 226 A6
Green Bank EX10 186 E8
Green Banks Cl TQ7 145 C3
Green Cl Cornworthy TQ9 227 B4
Exmouth EX8 202 C8
Kingsbridge TQ7 258 D6
Green Close La EX31 10 B5
Green End La EX15 83 F5
Green Gate EX16 50 C2
Green Gdns EX39 156 E6
Green Head EX10 101 B2
Green Hill
Cheriton Fitzpaine EX16, EX17 62 D3
Lamerton PL19 116 E3
Sampford Courtenay EX20 76 F3
Tavistock PL19 171 D5
Green Knap La TA20 69 F2

Green La
- Appledore EX39 .... 15 A1
- Axmouth EX12,DT7 ...... 193 B8
- [1] Barnstaple EX31 ...... 154 F5
- Beaford EX19 .... 42 D1
- Bittaford TQ10 .... 137 E8
- Blackawton TQ9 .... 139 B1
- Braunton EX33 .... 153 E6
- Buckfastleigh TQ11 .... 236 F4
- Cawsand PL10 .... 253 A2
- Chard Junction TA20 .... 88 D7
- Chardstock EX13 .... 88 B7
- Cheriton Bishop EX6 .... 97 C2
- Churston Ferrers TQ5 .. 229 E5
- Colyford EX24 .... 103 A3
- East Allington TQ9 .... 144 D8
- Exeter EX4 .... 176 E5
- Exton EX3 .... 183 B2
- Hatherleigh EX20 .... 75 D7
- Ilsington TQ13 .... 122 C4
- Merton EX20 .... 57 A7
- Rackenford EX16 .... 47 C5
- Raymond's Hill EX13 .. 104 C7
- Rewe EX5 .... 82 A2
- Rousdon DT7 .... 193 H8
- Sampford Arundel TA21 .. 51 F4
- Sidbury EX10 .... 101 D2
- Southleigh EX24 .... 102 D3
- Spreyton EX17 .... 96 A7
- Swimbridge EX32 .... 28 B8
- Tavistock PL19 .... 171 E5
- Totnes TQ9 .... 223 A4
- Yelverton PL20 .... 126 F1
Green Lane End
- Blackawton TQ9 .... 139 B1
- Buckfastleigh TQ11 .... 236 E4
Green Lanes Sh Ctr
- EX31 .... 154 F5
Green Mews EX9 ...... 198 A8
Green Mount EX10 .. 188 C6
Green Park Ave PL4 .. 248 C6
Green Park Rd
- Paignton TQ3 .... 218 F1
- Plymouth PL9 .... 255 E5
Green Park Way TQ7 .. 145 A1
Green Park Wlk TQ3 .. 218 F1
Green Pk PL10 .... 253 A2
Green The
- Ashburton TQ13 .... 130 F4
- Bridgerule EX22 .... 70 F5
- Brushford TA22 .... 33 E4
- Cawsand PL10 .... 253 A2
- Down St Mary EX17 ...... 78 E7
- Exmouth EX8 .... 202 F8
- [6] Horrabridge PL20 .. 126 F5
- Ide EX2 .... 176 D1
- Meavy PL20 .... 127 C2
- Milton Combe PL20 .... 240 F8
- Otterton EX9 .... 198 E7
- Plymouth PL9 .... 255 B6
- Saltash PL12 .... 242 C3
- Teignmouth TQ14 ...... 210 A3
- Whimple EX5 .... 99 E8
Green Tree La EX5 .. 175 D6
Greenacre
- Braunton EX33 .... 152 C6
- Torquay TQ1 .... 220 E5
Greenacre Cl
- Bradworthy EX22 .... 53 E8
- North Tawton EX20 ...... 77 C4
- Northam EX39 .... 157 A7
Greenacres Exeter EX4 173 A3
- Plymouth PL9 .... 255 F8
Greenacres Cl EX14 .. 84 D1
Greenaway La EX7 .... 61 A2
Greenaway La TQ12 .. 213 B6
Greenaway Rd TQ12 .. 207 A4
Greenaway Villas [3]
- TQ12 .... 207 B4
Greenbank TQ13 .... 111 D2
Greenbank EX38 ...... 159 F6
Greenbank Ave
- Kingsteignton TQ12 .. 207 D8
- Plymouth PL4 .... 263 B3
Greenbank EX38 ...... 159 F6
Greenbank Rd
- Barnstaple EX32 ...... 155 C4
- Brixham TQ5 .... 230 B4
- Plymouth PL4 .... 263 B4
Greenbank Terr
- Plymouth PL4 .... 263 B4
- Yelverton PL20 .... 127 A3
Greenbanks TQ7 .... 145 C3
Greenclose Cl [3] EX4 103 A4
Greenclose Rd EX34 .. 150 B6
Greendale Cross EX5 .180 F7
Greendale La Exeter EX5 99 A1
- Woodbury Salterton EX5 .184 A8
Greendale Rd PL2 .... 248 A7
Greendown Cross EX20 ..74 C2
Greenfield Dr
- Ivybridge PL21 .... 237 D4
- [7] South Brent TQ10 134 F2
Greenfield Rd
- Paignton TQ3 .... 219 A1
- Saltash PL12 .... 242 D2
Greenfield Terr TA20 .. 88 D8
Greenford Villas EX20 261 A1
Greenhaven EX9 ...... 197 F2
Greenhayes
- Charmouth DT6 .... 104 F4
- Dartington TQ9 .... 222 E8
Greenhays Foot EX13 .. 88 B6
Greenhill
- East Allington TQ9 .... 144 D7
- Teignmouth TQ12 .... 207 E6
Greenhill Ave
- Exmouth EX8 .... 202 C7

Greenhill Ave continued
- Lympstone EX8 .... 195 E5
Greenhill Cl PL9 ...... 255 F5
Greenhill Cross
- Knowle EX13 .... 8 C1
- Knowstone EX36 .... 32 B2
- Sampford Chapple EX20 ..77 A2
- Witheridge EX16 .... 62 C6
Greenhill Gdns TQ12 .. 212 F3
Greenhill Inf Units
- TQ12 .... 207 E6
Greenhill La TQ12 .... 211 B6
Greenhill Rd
- Kingskerswell TQ12 .. 212 F4
- Kingsteignton TQ12 .. 207 E6
Greenhill Terr TQ12 .. 207 F6
Greenhill Way TQ12 .. 207 E6
Greenings Rd EX39 .... 40 C7
Greenlake Cross EX39 ..22 D1
Greenland PL10 ...... 252 F5
Greenland Head Cross
- Churchstow TQ7 ...... 143 E6
- Witheridge EX16 .... 62 E6
Greenlands Ave TQ3 .. 225 F6
Greenlea Cross EX36 .. 31 C8
Greenlees Dr PL7 .... 251 B3
Greenmeadow Dr EX31 155 A7
Greenover Cl TQ5 .... 230 B3
Greenover Rd TQ5 .... 230 B3
Greenpark Ave EX1 .. 178 D7
Greenpark Rd EX8 .... 196 D2
Greenslade Cross EX20 ..77 A3
Greenslade Rd EX16 .. 46 E1
Greenslinch La EX5 .. 82 D6
Greensway Rd PL9 .. 171 A4
Greenswood La TQ6 .. 232 B1
Greenswood Rd [4] TQ5 230 C3
Greenway Crediton EX17 ..165 B5
- Exeter EX4 .... 176 F3
- Halberton EX16 .... 65 A8
- Lyme Regis DT7 .... 260 C3
- Seaton EX12 .... 191 F7
- Woodbury EX5 .... 184 C3
Greenway Cl
- [3] Horrabridge PL20 126 F5
- Ivybridge PL21 .... 237 D5
- Torquay TQ2 .... 214 A1
Greenway Gate EX16 .. 34 E1
Greenway Gdns TQ2 .. 214 A2
Greenway La
- Ashcombe EX7 .... 124 C5
- Awliscombe EX14 .... 85 B5
- Beacon EX14 .... 85 D8
- Budleigh Salterton EX9 198 A2
- Sidmouth EX10 .... 187 B8
- Torquay TQ2 .... 220 B8
Greenway Rd TQ5 .... 229 B4
- Galmpton TQ5 .... 229 B4
- Paignton TQ5 .... 228 E2
- Rockwell Green TA21 .. 160 A5
- Torquay, Chelston TQ2 219 E4
- Torquay, St Marychurch
- TQ1 .... 220 B8
Greenway's Almshouses
- EX16 .... 161 D4
Greenways EX14 .... 150 A5
Greenwich Pl PL12 .. 242 F3
Greenwood
- Aveton Gifford TQ7 .. 143 C6
- Ivybridge PL21 .... 237 C5
Greenwood Dr EX2 .. 178 D5
Greenwood Park Cl PL7 251 B6
Greenwood Park Rd
- PL7 .... 251 B6
Greenwoods The EX39 ..22 E3
Gregory Cl Bow EX17 ..78 C4
- Tiverton EX16 .... 161 F4
Gregory Terr EX39 .... 22 E3
Gregory's Mdw PL15 105 A2
Grenadier Rd EX1 .... 178 B7
Grendon Cl TQ14 .... 210 A5
Grendon La EX16 ...... 46 E4
Grendon Rd EX1 ...... 177 E6
Grenfell Ave PL12 .... 242 D3
Grenfell Gdns PL12 .. 242 C3
Grenofen Cl PL19 .... 126 D6
Grenville Ave Exeter EX4 178 D8
- Teignmouth TQ14 .... 210 A7
- Torquay TQ2 .... 219 D6
Grenville Cl
- Dartmouth TQ6 ...... 233 D3
- Newton Abbot TQ12 .. 207 E3
- Stokenham TQ7 ...... 145 B2
Grenville Coll EX39 .. 156 F2
**Grenville Coll (Moreton
House)** EX39 .... 156 D1
Grenville Ct TQ1 .... 251 C6
Grenville Dr PL19 .... 171 B3
Grenville Est The EX39 ..25 E4
Grenville Estate Cres
- EX39 .... 25 E4
Grenville Pk PL20 .... 127 A2
Grenville Rd
- Exmouth EX8 .... 196 C2
- Plymouth PL4 .... 263 C3
- Salcombe TQ8 .... 259 D4
Grenville Road La S
- PL4 .... 249 B2
Grenville St [8] EX39 .. 157 A2
Grenville Terr
- [4] Bideford EX39 .... 157 B1
- Northam EX39 .... 157 A7
Grenville Way TQ4 .. 226 B3
Gresham Cl PL5 ...... 244 C7
Greycoat La TQ12 .... 206 F7
Greyhill Cross TQ12 .. 138 A1

Greysand Cres [3] EX39 ..15 A1
Greysholt Cross EX32 ..28 B8
Greystoke Ave PL6 .. 249 D7
Greystone Cross EX32 ..96 E2
Greystone Way TQ1 .. 220 C7
Gribble Cl EX32 ...... 155 C4
Gribble La EX5 .... 99 D6
Gribbleford Cross EX20 ..76 B2
Gribblemead EX24 .. 103 A4
Grieg Dr EX32 .... 155 C5
Griffin Way PL9 ...... 256 C6
Grigg's La EX10 ...... 188 D7
Griggs Cl Northam EX39 ..157 A6
- Plymouth PL7 .... 251 B4
Griggs Gdns EX31 .. 153 D5
Grimspound Cl PL6 .. 249 E8
Grimstone Terr EX20 126 E2
Grinacombe Cross PL16 ..91 B2
Grinacombe Moor cross
- PL16 .... 91 B2
Grindhill Cross EX20 .. 92 D5
Grindle Way EX5 .... 179 B2
Grizedale Rd PL6 .... 249 D7
Gronau Cl EX14 ...... 166 C4
Grooms Orch TA21 .. 160 C5
Gropers La
- Ipplepen TQ3,TQ12 .. 218 C8
- North Whilborough TQ12 ..211 A4
Gropy La
- Bishops Nympton EX36 ..31 D1
- South Molton EX36 .... 46 D8
Grosvenor Ave TQ2 .. 213 C1
Grosvenor Cl TQ2 .... 213 C1
Grosvenor Cotts [1] EX4 248 F4
Grosvenor Pl EX1 .... 261 C4
Grosvenor Rd
- Paignton TQ4 .... 226 B5
- Plymouth PL6 .... 244 F2
Grosvenor St [2] EX32 155 A5
Grosvenor Terr
- Paignton TQ4 .... 226 B5
- [7] Teignmouth TQ14 210 B6
Groundhead Rd EX14 ..86 F6
Grove Ave EX12 ...... 210 B5
Grove Cl TQ9 .... 223 C5
Grove Cres [3] EX14 .. 102 A4
Grove Ct EX22 .... 39 D3
Grove Ct Dawlish EX7 204 F6
- Teignmouth TQ14 .... 210 C6
Grove Hill
- Colyton EX24 .... 103 A4
- Topsham EX3 .... 182 F5
Grove Ho EX3 .... 182 F5
Grove La EX36 .... 32 D6
Grove Mdw EX20 .... 94 F5
Grove Pk Tavistock PL19 171 D5
- Plymouth PL7 .... 246 E3
Grove Prim Sch The
- TQ9 .... 223 C5
Grove Rd EX5 .... 99 F7
Grove Terr [1] TQ14 .. 210 B5
Grove The Bittaford PL21 ..137 C8
- Blackawton TQ9 .... 139 E1
- Paignton TQ4 .... 225 E4
- Plymouth, Mannamead PL3 255 D8
- Plymouth, Stoke PL3 .. 248 A4
- Sidmouth EX10 .... 188 A4
- Totnes TQ9 .... 223 C5
- Woolacombe EX34 .... 7 F6
Groves The PL21 .... 237 C6
Gubbin's La EX33 .... 152 D5
Guernsey Cnr EX24 .. 102 F4
Guestland Rd TQ1 .. 220 C7
Guildford Cl Exeter EX4 176 E6
- Plymouth PL5 .... 244 E3
Guildhall St PL4 ...... 263 A3
Guildhall Sh Ctr EX4 263 B3
Guildhall Sq PL1 .... 262 C2
Guildhall Yd TQ9 .... 223 C5
Guinea St EX1 .... 261 A2
Guinevere Way EX4 .. 174 A1
Guinness La EX4 .... 178 C8
Gulland Cross TQ12 .. 212 B4
Gullet Cross TQ7 .... 148 F6
Gulliver La EX20 ...... 77 D7
Gully La EX14 .... 86 C5
Gully Shoot EX24 .... 103 A3
Gullyhole Hill EX36 .. 31 F7
Gulway Mead TA20 .. 88 D8
Gulworthy Cotts PL19 125 E7
Gulworthy Cross PL19 125 E7
Gulworthy Prim Sch
- PL19 .... 125 E7
Gun Cross EX32 .... 17 F3
Gun La EX16 .... 19 D4
Gunnislake Prim Sch
- PL18 .... 125 C6
Gunnislake Rural Workshops
- PL18 .... 125 C6
Gunnislake Sta PL18 .. 125 C5
Gunsdown Villas EX36 ..158 D5
Gunstone Cross EX17 ..79 E2
Gunstone Mill Cross
- EX17 .... 79 E1
Gunswell La EX36 .. 158 B5
Gurnard Wlk PL3 .... 249 C6
Gurney Cl PL11 ...... 246 F3
Gurneys The TQ3 .... 226 A5
Guscott La EX38 ...... 26 E2
Gussiford La EX8 .... 202 B6
Guy Miles Way PL5 .. 244 B3
Guys Rd EX4 .... 176 F6
Gwel Avon Bsns Pk
- TQ11 .... 242 D4
Gwithian Cl PL11 .... 246 F4
Gwyn Rd EX4 .... 263 C4
Gwythers EX36 ...... 158 D4

H

Hacche La EX36 ...... 158 C6
Haccombe Cl EX4 .... 176 E5
Haccombe Cross TQ12 213 E6
Haccombe Path TQ12 208 A2
Hacker Cl EX10 ...... 188 D7
Hackney La
- Kingsteignton TQ12 .. 207 F6
- Newton Abbot TQ12 .. 208 B4
Hackney Marsh (Nature Pk)
- TQ12 .... 207 E5
Hackpen Cross Way
- EX15 .... 66 E6
Hackworthy Cnr EX4 .. 98 F5
Hackworthy Cross EX6 ..97 E5
Hackworthy Cross La
- EX6 .... 97 E5
Hackworthy La
- Nadderwater EX4 .... 98 F5
- Tedburn St Mary EX6 .. 97 E4
Haddacott Cross EX38 ..26 F3
Haddington Rd PL2 .. 247 F4
Haddon Cnr EX14 .. 103 C8
Haddon Ct [3] TQ12 .. 226 B7
Haddon La EX14 .... 34 C7
Haddon Rd EX13 .... 103 C8
Hadfield Ct [3] EX13 .. 123 C4
Hadrian Dr EX4 ...... 176 E6
Hadrians Way EX8 .. 196 D1
Halberton Prim Sch
- EX16 .... 65 A7
Halcyon Cl PL2 ...... 248 A6
Halcyon Rd
- Newton Abbot TQ12 .. 207 B3
- Plymouth PL2 .... 248 A6
Haldene Terr [5] EX32 154 F6
Haldon Ave TQ14 .... 210 C6
Haldon Belvedere*
- EX6 .... 113 F5
Haldon Cl
- [2] Newton Abbot TQ12 207 F2
- Topsham EX3 .... 182 E6
- Torquay TQ2 .... 220 E4
Haldon Ct EX6 .... 196 B2
Haldon La TQ13 ...... 124 B4
Haldon Lodge EX6 .. 114 B5
Haldon Pl PL5 .... 244 A3
Haldon Rd Exeter EX4 177 A6
- Torquay TQ1 .... 220 D4
Haldon Rise [1] TQ12 207 F2
Haldon Terr [6] EX7 .. 204 D6
Haldon View TQ13 .. 123 F6
Haldon View Terr EX2 177 F5
Haldron's Almshouses
- EX14 .... 161 C4
Hale La EX14 .... 166 E6
Haley Barton [4] PL2 248 A5
Haley Cl EX8 .... 196 C2
Half Moon The EX13 ..87 E8
Half Way Cvn Pk TQ4 224 E5
Halford Cross TQ12 .. 212 A4
Halfpenny Cross EX14 ..49 B7
Halfsbury Cross EX37 ..43 E4
Halfway House Flats
- TQ5 .... 230 F6
Hall Cross PL21 ...... 133 E2
Hall Hill EX35 .... 6 D5
Hall La EX7 .... 210 E8
Hall Mus* TQ8 ...... 259 E5
Hall's La TQ12 .... 212 F4
Hall's Mill La EX31 .. 154 E8
Hallamore La PL21 .. 133 B2
Hallerton Cl PL6 .... 245 E2
Hallett Cl PL12 ...... 242 B3
Hallett Ct DT7 .... 260 D4
Halletts Way EX13 .. 167 E6
Halley Gdns PL5 .... 243 E1
Hallow Mead TQ13 .. 121 F7
Halls Cross EX31 ...... 10 E1
Halmpstone Cross EX32 ..28 C7
Halsbury Rd EX16 .. 161 F4
Halscombe La EX2 .. 176 C1
Halsdon Ave EX8 .... 196 A1
Halsdon Cross EX22 .. 54 C1
Halsdon La EX8 ...... 196 A2
Halsdon Rd EX8 ...... 202 A7
Halsdon Terr EX38 .. 159 C5
Halse Hill La EX9 .... 197 F1
Halse La
- North Tawton EX20 ...... 77 D4
- West Worlington EX17 .. 61 B6
Halsegate Cross EX20 ..76 C6
Halses Cl EX4 .... 176 D8
Halsewood Gate EX15 ..64 E2
Halsey Lake Cross EX31 ..10 D1
Halsfordwood La EX4 .. 98 F4
Halshanger Cross TQ13 130 F8
Halstaads Rd TQ2 .. 214 A2
Halswell Cross EX36 .. 29 D2
Halswell Cross
- Denbury TQ12 .... 211 A5
- Halwell TQ9 .... 139 F7
Halwell Ho TQ7 ...... 148 E7
Halwill Prim Sch EX21 ..73 C2
Halyards EX3 .... 182 E5
Ham Butts TQ7 ...... 143 F7
Ham Cl PL2 .... 248 A8
Ham Cross EX3 .... 86 F4
Ham Dr PL2 .... 248 B8
Ham Gn PL2 .... 248 A7
Ham Green Ct PL2 .. 248 A7
Ham Green Ct PL2 .. 248 A7
Ham Green La PL2 .. 248 A7
Ham Hill Asperington EX18 58 E8
- Combe St Nicholas TA20 ..69 F8
Ham Ho PL2 .... 248 A8
Ham La Colyton EX24 .. 103 A4

Ham La continued
- Dittisham TQ6 .... 228 C3
- Plymouth PL2 .... 248 A8
- Shaldon TQ14 .... 209 D4
- Sidmouth EX10 .... 188 B3
- South Molton EX36 .. 158 E4
Ham Rd Dalwood EX13 .. 87 A3
- Wellington TA21 .... 52 D8
Hambeer La EX2 .... 176 E3
Hamber La EX2 ...... 176 E3
Hamberlayne Cross
- EX24 .... 102 C5
Hamble Cl PL3 ...... 249 D7
Hamblecombe La TQ13 124 A4
Hambleton Ho [3] TQ14 210 C5
Hameldown Cl TQ2 .. 219 C3
Hameldown Rd EX20 170 E5
Hameldown Way TQ12 207 D4
Hamelin Way TQ2,TQ3 219 A8
Hamilton Ave EX2 .. 177 F2
Hamilton Cl Bideford EX39 ..25 E4
- [14] Sidford EX32 .... 101 B1
Hamilton Dr Exeter EX2 178 B5
- Newton Abbot TQ12 .. 207 B5
Hamilton Gdns PL4 .. 248 D4
Hamilton Gr EX6 .... 201 B7
Hamilton La EX2 .... 177 F2
Hamilton Rd
- Exmouth EX8 .... 202 D7
- Topsham EX3 .... 182 E6
Hamiltons The TQ4 .. 210 A3
Hamley La TA20 .... 69 E8
Hamlin Gdns EX1 .... 178 A7
Hamlin La EX1 .... 178 A7
Hamlin Way TQ11 .. 236 B5
Hammett Rd EX15 .. 163 B3
Hammetts La
- Barnstaple EX32 ...... 155 B1
- Bishop's Tawton EX32 ..16 E1
Hammond Croft Way
- EX2 .... 181 B8
Hamoaze Ave PL5 .. 247 D8
Hamoaze Pl PL1 .... 247 D2
Hamoaze Rd PL11 .. 247 B2
Hampshire Cl EX4 .. 176 E4
Hampson Cross EX17 ..78 A4
Hampson La EX17 .... 78 A4
Hampton Ave TQ1 .. 220 C8
Hampton Bldgs EX4 261 C4
Hampton La
- Torquay TQ1 .... 220 C8
- Whitford EX13 .... 103 C6
Hampton Rd
- Newton Abbot TQ12 .. 207 C3
- Whitford EX13 .... 103 C7
Hampton St PL4 .... 263 A3
Hams The EX7 .... 176 D1
Hamslade Cross EX16 ..48 D8
Hamslade Hill EX16 .. 48 D8
Hamstone Ct TQ8 .. 259 D4
Hamway La TA20 ...... 69 F8
Hancock Cl PL6 ...... 244 D6
Hand & Pen Cotts EX5 ..99 E6
Hanger La EX14 .... 84 F8
Hanging La EX35 .... 5 A3
Hangman Path EX34 .... 2 F4
Hangman's Cross PL21 138 A2
Hangman's Hill EX16 ..48 D7
Hangman's Hill Cross
- EX16 .... 48 E7
Hangmans Cnr EX17 165 E1
Hankford Cross EX22 ..39 E2
Hannaborrow La EX33 ..14 F8
Hannaford Cross EX32 ..28 C8
Hannaford La EX32 .. 28 D8
Hannaford Rd
- Lifton PL16 .... 105 E3
- Noss Mayo PL8 .... 140 F5
Hannaton Cross EX38 ..24 E8
Hannock Ct EX2 .... 181 D8
Hanover Cl
- [7] Brixham TQ5 .... 230 C3
- Exeter EX1 .... 177 F6
- Plymouth PL3 .... 249 B5
Hanover Ct Exeter EX2 181 C8
- [10] Plymouth PL1 .. 263 A2
Hanover Gdns EX15 .. 163 C5
Hanover Ho TQ1 .... 220 D3
Hanover Rd Exeter EX1 177 F6
- Plymouth PL3 .... 249 C4
Hansetown Rd TA4 .. 34 F8
Hansford Cross
- Ashreigney EX18 .... 44 A1
- Burrington EX37 .... 44 B2
Hansford Way EX11 166 C5
Hansford Way EX11 166 C5
Hanson Pk EX39 ...... 157 A4
Happaway Cl TQ2 .. 214 A2
Happaway Rd TQ2 .. 214 A2
Happaway St TQ4 .. 225 E3
Harbertonford CE Prim Sch
- TQ9 .... 139 C7
Harbour Ave
- Plymouth PL4 .... 263 A2
- Plymouth, Camels Head
- PL5 .... 247 E8
Harbour Ct Exmouth EX8 201 F6
- [4] Seaton EX12 ...... 192 B4
Harbour Rd EX12 .... 192 B4
Harbour St PL11 .... 247 B2
Harbour View
- Plymouth PL9 .... 255 A7
- Saltash PL12 .... 242 E2

Harbour View Cl [1]
TQ5 ....230 C5
Harbourne Ave TQ4 ....225 F3
Harbourneford Cross
TQ10 ....135 B4
Harcombe Cross
  Chudleigh TQ13 ......124 A8
  Raymond's Hill EX13 ..104 C6
  Sidbury EX10 ....101 C1
Harcombe Fields EX10 .188 D8
Harcombe La EX10 ....188 D8
Harcombe La E EX10 ..188 E8
Harcombe Rd
  Raymond's Hill DT7 ...104 D6
  Uplyme DT7 ....260 D8
Hardaway Head [5]
EX32 ....155 A5
Harding Cres EX16 ....196 D3
Hardisworthy Cross EX39 .37 B7
Hardy Cl TQ1 ....220 C2
Hardy Cres PL5 ......244 E1
Hardy Rd EX2 ....178 D5
Hardys Ct EX10 ......146 B4
Hare La 98 D4
Hare Tor Cl EX20 .....170 E5
Harebell Cl PL12 .....242 D4
Harebell Copse EX4 ...176 E8
Harebell Dr EX15 .....162 E5
Haredon Cross PL21 ..137 D6
Harefield Cl EX4 .....177 A8
Harefield Cotts EX4 ..195 D5
Harefield Dr
  Lympstone EX8 ....195 F5
  Newton Abbot TQ6 ...146 B7
Harefield Rd EX8 .....195 F6
Harefoot Cross TQ13 .121 D3
Harepath Hill EX12 ...102 A8
Harepath Rd EX12 ....192 A7
Harepathstead Rd EX5 .83 B1
Harepie Cross EX4 ....27 D6
Hares Gn EX36 ....158 C4
Hares La TQ13 ....130 F4
Haresdown Cross EX36 .47 C7
Hareston Cl PL7 .....251 B3
Hareston Cross PL8 ...257 D8
Harestone Cross EX13 .88 B7
Harewood Cl PL7 .....250 C5
Harewood Cres PL5 ...244 B2
Harewood Rd PL18 ...125 D3
Harford Cross EX32 ..17 C2
Harford La EX6,EX17 .97 F7
Harford Rd
  Ivybridge PL21 ......237 D6
  Landkey EX32 ....17 B2
Hargood Terr [3] PL2 .247 F4
Hargreaves Cl PL5 ...243 F2
Harker La EX6 ....114 B2
Harlech Cl PL3 ....249 A1
Harlequins EX4 ......261 A3
Harleston Cross TQ7 .144 F4
Harley Ct PL21 ......237 D5
Harman Wlk EX37 ...155 C5
Harnorlen Rd PL2 ....248 D7
Haroldsleigh Ave PL5 .244 E2
Harp La 99 E2
Harp's Corner Cross
EX36 ....46 C6
Harper's Hill
  Northlew TQ20 ......74 E2
  Totnes TQ9 ....223 A5
Harpins Ct TQ12 ....213 A6
Harpitt Cl EX15 .....162 C3
Harpson Hill EX36 ...31 F1
Harpson La
  Bishops Nympton EX36 .31 F1
  South Molton EX36 ...46 F8
Harraccott Cross EX31 .27 E6
Harraton Cross PL21 .137 D1
Harrier Way EX2 ....178 E4
Harriers Cl EX12 ....192 A6
Harriet Gdns PL7 ...250 B6
Harringcourt Rd EX4 .174 E2
Harrington Dr EX4 ..174 E2
Harrington Gdns EX4 .174 E1
Harrington La EX4 ...174 D2
Harris La EX14 ......51 A4
Harris Cotts PL21 ...237 C5
Harris Cross EX39 ...38 C8
Harris Ct PL9 ....255 B6
Harris Way PL21 ....136 B6
Harrison St [7] PL2 ..247 F4
Harrowbarrow Sch
PL7 ....125 A4
Harrowbeer La PL20 .126 F3
Harrowby Cl EX16 ..161 F4
Hart Manor St33 ....132 E3
Hart St EX39 ....157 A2
Hart's La Churchstow TQ7 .143 E4
  Exeter EX1 ....178 D8
  Huish Champflower TA4 .35 D7
Hartland Abbey* EX39 .22 C3
Hartland Cl EX4 ....245 A7
Hartland Cross EX17 .79 C4
Hartland Prim Sch EX39 .22 D2
Hartland Quay Mus*
EX39 ....22 A3
Hartland Tor Cl TQ5 .230 A2
Hartland View Rd EX34 .3 A7
Hartley Ave PL3 ....249 A6
Hartley Park Gdns PL3 .248 F6
Hartley Rd Exmouth EX8 .202 A8
  Paignton TQ4 ....226 A5
  Plymouth PL3 ....248 E6
Hartnoll Cross EX16 .64 E8

Harton Cross EX39 ...22 E3
Harton Way EX39 ...22 E3
Hartop Rd TQ1 .....214 B1
Hartop Rd EX4 .....202 A8
Harts Cl Exeter EX1 .178 E8
  Teignmouth TQ14 ...210 A6
Hartwell Ave PL9 ...256 D7
Harvest La EX39 ....156 D2
Harvey Ave PL4 ....249 B1
Harvey St PL11 .....247 B3
Harveys Cl
  [8] Chudleigh Knighton
  TQ13 ....91 D8
  Sampford Courtenay EX20 .76 F4
Harwell Cl [8] PL1 ..262 B2
Harwell St PL1 .....262 B3
Harwood Ave PL5 ..244 C7
Harwood Cl EX8 ....196 D1
Hask La EX4 ....96 D3
Haskins Cross EX14 .84 C5
Haslam Ct TQ1 .....220 A4
Haslam Rd TQ2 ....220 A7
Hastings St PL1 ....262 B3
Hastings Terr PL1 ..262 B3
Haswell Cl PL6 .....249 A8
Hat La PL10 ....252 F2
Hatchcombe La TQ2 .213 F3
Hatcher Cl EX14 ....166 C3
Hatcher St [9] EX4 ..204 D6
Hatchland Rd EX4 ..174 F6
Hatchmoor Common La
EX38 ....159 F6
Hatchmoor Ind Est EX38 .75 B6
Hatchmoor Rd EX38 .159 F5
Hatfield Rd TQ1 ....220 B6
Hatherdown Hill TQ13 .133 B6
Hatherleigh La TQ13 .122 D7
Hatherleigh Prim Sch
EX20 ....75 C2
Hatherleigh Rd
  Exeter EX2 ....177 A2
  Okehampton EX20 ...93 F7
  Winkleigh EX19 .....58 E2
Hatherley La EX20 ..132 F6
Hatshill Farm Cl PL6 .132 A5
Hatway Hill EX1 ....101 C3
Hauley Rd TQ6 .....233 F3
Have's Hill EX17 ...61 C8
Havelock Terr
  Lutton PL21 ....133 B2
  Plymouth PL2 ....247 F3
Haven Cl EX4 ......261 A1
Haven Rd EX2 .....261 A1
Haven Rd TQ14 ....208 F7
Havenview Rd EX12 .192 A5
Hawarden Cotts PL4 .249 B1
Hawcombe La EX33 .8 E1
Haweswater Cl PL6 ..244 E4
Hawkchurch Cross EX13 .88 E2
Hawkchurch Prim Sch
EX13 ....88 E3
Hawkchurch Rd EX13 .88 E3
Hawkerland Rd EX10 .186 C4
Hawkers Ave PL4 ...263 A2
Hawkesdown Cl EX12 .192 D7
Hawkin's La TA4 ....35 E7
Hawkinge Gdns PL5 .243 E4
Hawkins Ave TQ2 ...219 C7
Hawkins Cl PL6 .....245 A5
Hawkins Dr TQ12 ..210 B6
Hawkins La EX13 ...168 E3
Hawkins Rd TQ12 ...207 F3
Hawkins Way EX17 .165 A6
Hawkmoor Cotts TQ13 .122 E7
Hawkmoor Pk TQ13,EX13 .88 H2
Hawkmoor Rd TQ13 .122 E7
Hawkridge Cross
  Hawkridge TA22 ....21 D1
Hawkridge EX14 ....28 C4
Hawkridge Rd EX14 .31 E5
Hawks Pk PL12 .....242 C2
Hawksdown View EX12 .192 A7
Hawkwell Cross EX16 .32 F4
Hawley Cl EX32 ....155 C5
Hawley Cross EX13 .86 F3
Hawley Manor EX32 .155 C5
Hawson Cross TQ11 .130 B3
Hawthorn Ave
  Ilfracombe EX34 ....150 D5
  Torpoint PL11 ....246 F3
Hawthorn Cl
  Cullompton EX15 ...163 B2
  Honiton EX14 ....166 B5
  Kingsbridge TQ7 ...225 C5
  Plymouth, Hooe PL9 .255 C5
  Plymouth, Woolwell PL6 .245 D7
Hawthorn Dr
  Sidmouth EX10 .....187 F8
  Wembury PL9 ......140 D7
Hawthorn Gr
  Exmouth EX8 ....196 E1
  Plymouth PL2 ....248 C7
Hawthorn Park Cl PL9 .140 D7
Hawthorn Park Rd PL9 .140 D7
Hawthorn Pk
  Bideford EX39 ......156 E1
  Lydford EX20 ....107 F4
Hawthorn Rd
  Barnstaple EX32 ....155 C4
  Crediton EX17 ......165 C5
  Exeter EX2 ....177 F3
  Tavistock PL19 .....171 C2
Hawthorn Way
  Exeter EX4 ....181 A8

Hawthorn Way continued
  Plymouth PL3 ....249 B7
Hawthorne Cl TQ12 .212 F8
Hawthorne Rd
  [10] Tiverton EX16 ..161 F6
  Wellington TA21 ....160 F5
Hawthorns PL12 ....242 D2
Haxter Cl PL6 ......241 B1
Haxton Down La EX31 .18 B8
Haxton La EX31 ....18 A8
Hay La TQ7 ....143 E3
Haycroft Rd [3] EX39 .157 A1
Haycross Hill EX21 ..55 D4
Haydn Cl EX23 .....155 C5
Haydon Cross EX14 .48 C4
Haydon Gr PL5 .....243 C1
Haydon Rd EX16 ...161 B5
Haydons Pk EX14 ..166 C5
Hayc Cl DT7 ....260 C4
Haye La
  Colyford DT7,EX13 .103 D3
  Lyme Regis DT7 ....260 D4
Haye Rd PL7,PL9 ...250 C1
Haye Rd S PL9 ....256 C7
Hayes Barton* EX9 .197 F2
Hayes Barton Ct EX4 .177 A5
Hayes Cl
  Budleigh Salterton EX9 .198 A2
  Otterton EX9 ....198 E2
  Totnes TQ9 ....223 E4
Hayes Copse EX32 .17 B2
Hayes Cross EX21 ..55 C4
Hayes Dean TQ11 ..130 C2
Hayes La TQ13 .....130 E4
Hayes Rd Paignton TQ4 .226 B5
  Plymouth PL9 ......255 C7
Hayes Sch TQ4 ....226 C5
Hayes The TQ5 ....229 E5
Hayeswood La EX9 .198 A6
Hayfield Rd EX20 ..76 C5
Hayle Ave TQ4 ....229 B8
Hayley Pk TQ12 ...212 F3
Haymans La EX15 ..163 B2
Haymans Gn EX15 .163 B2
Hayne Cl Exeter EX4 .178 A7
  Tipton St John EX10 .100 D2
Hayne Cross
  Bampton EX16 .....34 B4
  Bishops Nympton EX36 .31 A1
  Cheriton Fitzpaine EX17 .63 A2
  Kentisbeare EX15 ..66 F5
  Lewtrenchard EX20 .106 B5
  Lustleigh TQ13 ....123 D9
  Plymtree EX15 ....83 F6
  Zeal Monachorum EX17 .78 B6
Hayne Hill EX10 ...100 D2
Hayne Ho EX16 ....49 B2
Hayne La Bolham EX16 .49 B3
  Honiton EX14 ......64 C2
  Silverton EX5 .....82 C4
Hayne Pk
  Barnstaple EX32 ...155 B4
  Tipton St John EX10 .100 D2
Hayne Town Cross EX17 .44 B8
Haynes La EX14 ...176 A2
Hayrish Cross EX16 .96 B7
Hayston Pl PL1 ....262 B4
Haytor Ave TQ4 ...225 F3
Haytor Cl Plymouth PL5 .244 B3
  Teignmouth TQ14 ..209 D8
Haytor Dr Exeter EX4 .237 D4
  Newton Abbot TQ12 .208 A3
Haytor Gr TQ12 ...208 A3
Haytor Rd TQ1 ....220 B7
Haytor Terr [11] TQ12 .207 B3
Haytown Pottery* EX22 .39 E1
Haywain Cl TQ2 ...213 B1
Haywards Prim Sch
EX17 ....165 D5
Hazel Ave EX33 ...15 E4
Hazel Cl Kingsbridge TQ7 .258 C4
  Newton Abbot TQ12 .208 A1
  Newton Poppleford EX10 .186 F8
  Plymouth PL6 ......245 B6
  Seaton EX12 ....192 A7
  Teignmouth TQ14 ..210 C8
Hazel Gr
  Dawlish Warren EX7 .201 A2
  Plymouth PL6 ......245 B6
Hazel-Crest TQ13 .123 B7
Hazeldene TQ8 ....259 C3
Hazeldene Cl PL21 .136 B6
Hazeldene Gdns EX8 .196 A1
Hazeldown Prim Sch
TQ14 ....210 B8
Hazeldown Rd TQ14 .210 B8
Hazelmead Rd EX5 .179 E2
Hazelstone EX5 ....82 E2
Hazelwood [5] TQ1 .220 D5
Hazelwood Cl EX14 .166 C4
Hazelwood Cres PL9 .256 D7
Hazel Gr
  Dawlish Warren EX7 .201 A2
  Plymouth PL6 ......245 B6
Hazelbank Rd TQ13 .130 F5
Head Weir Rd EX15 .163 B3
Headborough Rd TQ13 .130 F5

Headgate EX36 ....20 B1
Headingley Cl EX2 .178 C4
Headland Cl EX1 ..178 C7
Headland Cres EX1 .178 C7
Headland Cross EX17 .96 A6
Headland Ct
  [8] Brixham TQ5 ..230 D5
  Woolacombe EX34 .3 F8
Headland Gr TQ13 .219 C1
Headland La EX17 .96 A5
Headland Park Rd TQ3 .219 C1
Headland Pk PL4 ..263 A4
Headland Rd TQ2 .219 E2
Headlands The TQ2 .219 E2
Headlands View Ave EX34 .1 B1
Headless Cross TQ13 .112 B6
Headon Cross EX22 .72 C5
Headon Gdns EX2 .178 A1
Headson Cross EX20 .31 E3
Headstock Rd EX20 .88 E7
Headway Cl TQ14 .209 B7
Headway Cross Rd
TQ14 ....209 D8
Headway Rise TQ14 .209 D8
Heal Park Cres EX31 .153 D5
Heal's Field EX14 ..167 F7
Heale Down La EX31 .4 A3
Healy Cl [8] PL21 .247 F4
Healy Pl PL2 ......247 F4
Heanton Hill EX33 .152 F4
Heanton Hill La EX31 .15 E6
Heanton St EX33 ..152 D5
Heanton Terr PL10 .252 E6
Heard Ave EX8 ...202 C8
Heard Cl TQ6 .....22 E3
Heard Rd PL12 ...242 B3
Hearson Cross EX32 .28 C8
Heasley Cross EX36 .19 C3
Heasley La EX36 ..19 D3
Heath Cl EX16 ....49 C3
Heath Cross
  Spreyton EX17 ....96 A8
  Tedburn St Mary EX4 .98 C5
  Tiverton EX16 .....63 A5
Heath Ct Brixham TQ5 .82 F6
  Exeter EX4 ....261 A4
  Kingsteignton TQ12 .123 E2
  Torquay TQ2 ....213 F1
Heath La Hollacombe EX17 .58 F5
  Tedburn St Mary EX4 .98 C4
  Tiverton EX16 .....63 A6
Heath Pk Brixham TQ5 .230 E5
  Newton Abbot TQ12 .208 A1
Heath Rd Brixham TQ5 .230 E5
  Dunsford EX6 ......112 F7
  Exeter EX4 ....178 F8
  Spreyton EX17 .....96 A8
Heath Rise TQ5 ...230 E5
Heath Terr PL18 ..125 C5
Heathay Cross EX24 .102 F5
Heathbrook Mews EX4 .174 C2
Heathcat Pst Sch EX16 .161 B3
Heathcoat Prim Sch
EX16 ....161 B3
Heathcoat Sq EX16 .161 C4
Heathcoat Way EX16 .161 C3
Heather Cl Exeter EX2 .178 B6
  [3] Honiton EX14 ..85 C2
  Newton Abbot TQ12 .206 F4
  Okehampton EX20 .170 B5
  Seaton EX12 ....192 A7
  Tavistock PL19 ....171 D4
  Teignmouth TQ14 ..210 B7
  [8] Tiverton EX16 ..161 F6
Heather Dr TQ12 ..180 F3
Heather Est TQ12 .180 F3
Heather Grange EX11 .168 D4
Heather Rd TQ10 ..135 A3
Heather Terr PL20 .128 A8
Heather Way TQ5 .230 A4
Heather Wlk TQ7 ..237 D4
Heatherdale EX14 .202 C6
Heatherdene TQ13 .180 C7
Heatherfield EX16 .49 B6
Heathers The
  Okehampton EX20 .170 D6
  Plymouth PL6 ......245 D7
Heathfield CE Prim Sch
TQ12 ....123 B3
Heathfield Cl EX13 .180 C5
Heathfield Cotts TQ12 .123 B3
Heathfield Cross
  Axmouth DT7 ......193 D8
  Bovey Tracey TQ12 .133 C3
  Cornwood PL21 ....184 A7
  Exeter EX5 ....184 A7
  Modbury PL21 .....137 C2
  Poltimore EX4 .....174 D2
Heathfield Ind Est TQ12 .180 F3
Heathfield Mdw TQ12 .180 D5
Heathfield Pk PL20 .127 A3
Heathfield Rd
  Bideford EX39 .....157 C1
  Exeter EX1 ....211 A6
  Plymouth PL3 .....249 B3
Heathfield Terr
  Bovey Tracey TQ13 .180 C6
  Denbury TQ12 ......211 A6
Heathfieldlake Hill
TQ13 ....123 F7
Heathland View EX38 .40 D1
Heathlands Cl TQ14 .210 A8
Heathlands Rise TQ14 .210 A8
Heathpark Ind Est EX14 .166 A5
Heathpark Way [18] EX4 .85 C2

Heaton Lea EX31 ...15 E6
Heatree Cl TQ14 ...210 B8
Heatree Cross TQ13 .121 D7
Heaviside Cl TQ2 ..214 B3
Heaviside Cl TQ2 ..214 B3
Heaviside Gallows EX1 .178 C5
Heavitree Gallows EX1 .178 C5
Heavitree Pk EX1 ..178 A5
Heavitree Rd
  Cawsand PL10 .....253 A2
  Exeter EX1 ....177 E6
Heddeswell Cross TQ7 .143 E2
Heddon Cross
  Heddon EX32 ......29 A7
  Milton Damerel EX22 .54 C5
Heddon Cross EX5 .82 B5
Hedge Cross EX20 .107 C4
Hedgehog Hospl (Prickly Ball
Farm)* TQ12 .....211 F7
Hedgend Rd EX14 .86 B5
Hedgerow Cl
  Crediton EX17 .....165 E6
  Plymouth PL6 ......245 E6
Hedgerows The PL12 .242 B3
Hedingham Ct PL7 .251 C4
Hedingham Gdns PL6 .245 B7
Heggadon Cl EX5 ..83 A7
Heightley Cl EX16 .47 A5
Heirland Cross TQ7 .143 D3
Hele Almshouses PL7 .140 E8
Hele Barton Cross EX17 .61 D6
Hele Bay Holiday Flats
EX34 ....150 E5
Hele Cl Barnstaple EX31 .154 A3
  Bickleigh PL6 ......132 A5
  Torquay TQ2 ....213 F1
Hele Cross
  Ashburton TQ13 ...130 C5
  Bradworthy EX22 ..38 E4
  Cornwood PL21 ....184 D1
  King's Nympton EX37 .44 D7
  St Giles on the Heath PL15 .90 B3
  Torquay TQ2 ....213 F1
Hele Gdns PL7 ....251 A4
Hele Hill EX17 ....61 C5
Hele La Barnstaple EX36 .154 A3
  Frithelstockstone EX38 .40 F5
  Roborough PL6 ....241 A2
  Shaugh Prior PL6,PL7 .132 A6
Hele Lane Hill EX17 .61 D6
Hele Rd Bradninch EX5 .82 F6
  Exeter EX4 ....261 A4
  Kingsteignton TQ12 .123 E2
  Torquay TQ2 ....213 F1
Hele's Ash PL7 ...140 E8
Hele's Sch PL7 ...250 C6
Hele's Terr PL4 ..249 B2
Helebridge Rd EX23 .70 A6
Helena Pl [7] EX8 .202 A6
Helens Mead Cl TQ2 .214 A4
Helens Mead Rd TQ2 .214 A4
Helford Dr TQ4 ...229 B8
Helford Wlk TQ4 ..229 B8
Heligan Dr TQ3 ...225 E8
Hellevoetsluis Way TQ3 .218 F4
Hellier Cl EX14 ...46 C3
Hellinghays La EX16 .46 C3
Hellings Gdns EX5 .175 C7
Hellings Parks La EX5 .175 E4
Helmdon Rise TQ2 .219 B8
Helston Rd TQ2 ...219 F2
Hembury Cock Hill
TQ11 ....236 A7
Hembury Cross
  Holbeton PL8 ......141 F8
  Stibb Cross EX38 ..40 C4
Hembury Fort Cross
EX14 ....84 E5
Hembury Pk TQ11 .236 B8
Hemerdon Hts PL7 .251 A6
Hemerdon La PL7 .250 D5
Hemerdon Way PL7 .250 D6
Hems Brook Ct TQ2 .219 B8
Hems La TQ9 .....216 D7
Hemsworthy Gate TQ13 .121 E3
Hemyock Castle* EX15 .67 B8
Hemyock Prim Sch EX15 .66 E8
Hemyock Rd EX15 .83 A7
Hen St EX5 ....83 A7
Henacre Rd TQ2 ..258 D5
Henacroft Cross EX19 .58 B3
Henbury Cl TQ1 ..220 B6
Henceford Cross EX17 .62 A6
Henderbarrow Cross
EX21 ....73 E1
Henders Cnr [6] PL3 .248 F6
Henderson Pl PL2 .247 F4
Hendon Rd EX16 ..50 D8
Hendwell Cl PL6 ..244 E6
Heneaton Sq EX2 .182 B8
Henlake Cl PL21 ..237 B6
Henley Cl EX13 ...88 C3
Henley Dr PL5 ...244 C7
Henley Ho TQ7 ..143 A1
Henley Rd EX8 ...202 C7
Hennapyn Rd TQ2 .219 E3
Hennock Rd East EX2 .177 D1
Hennock Rd Central
EX2 ....177 C1
Hennock Rd N EX2 .177 C2
Hennock Rd S EX2 .177 B2
Henrietta Pl [8] EX8 .202 A7
Henrietta Rd [2] EX8 .202 A7
Henry Cl PL21 ....136 B6
Henry Lewis Cl [7] PL5 .99 E8
Henry's Way DT7 .260 E4
Hensbury La PL20 .239 E4
Hensford Mews EX7 .200 C3
Hensford Rd EX7 ..200 C3

Hensleigh Dr EX2 . . . . . . 177 E5
Hensleigh Rd EX16 . . . . . . .63 F7
Hensons Dr EX16 . . . . .51 A3
Henstill La EX17 . . . . .79 F7
Henty Ave EX7 . . . . 204 F7
Henty Cl EX7 . . . . 204 F8
Heppenstall Rd EX32 . . . 155 B6
Herbert Ho TA22 . . . . .33 D6
Herbert Pl PL2 . . . . 248 F4
Herbert Rd Exeter EX1 . . . 177 F7
 Salcombe TQ8 . . . . 259 D4
 Torquay TQ2 . . . . 219 D4
Herbert St PL2 . . . . 247 E4
Herdicott Cross EX22 . . . .71 F2
Hereford Cl EX3 . . . . 196 D4
Hereford Rd Exeter EX4 . . 176 D6
 Plymouth PL5 . . . . 244 B5
Heritage Cl PL12 . . . . 242 C3
Hermes Ave EX16 . . . . . . 161 E3
Hermitage Rd
 Dartmouth TQ6 . . . . 233 D4
 Ilfracombe EX34 . . . . . . 150 B6
 Plymouth PL3 . . . . 248 E5
Hermitage The **1** EX34 . 150 B6
Hermosa Gdns **5** TQ14 . 210 B5
Hermosa Rd TQ14 . . . . . . 210 B5
Hern La PL8 . . . . 257 F4
Hernaford Cross TQ9 . . . 139 B6
Hernaford Rd TQ9 . . . . . . 139 C6
Heron Cl PL10 . . . . 252 F6
Heron Ct Barnstaple EX32 155 E4
 Exmouth EX8 . . . . 202 C6
 Heron Ind Units EX2 . . . 178 E5
Heron Rd
 Exeter, Redhills EX2 . . . . 176 D3
 Exeter, Sowton EX2 . . . . 178 E5
 Honiton EX14 . . . . 166 B4
Heron Way
 Cullompton EX15 . . . . . . 163 B2
 Torquay TQ2 . . . . 213 C3
Herons Brook EX20 . . . . . 170 A6
Herons Reach TQ7 . . . . . 144 C1
Herschel Gdns PL5 . . . . . 243 E1
Herschell Rd EX4 . . . . . . 177 E8
Hertland Wlk PL2 . . . . . . 248 A7
Hescane Pk EX6 . . . . .97 B4
Hesketh Cres TQ1 . . . . . . 220 D3
Hesketh Mews TQ1 . . . . . 220 D3
Hesketh Rd TQ1 . . . . 220 D3
Hessary Dr PL6 . . . . 241 C1
Hessary Terr PL20 . . . . . . 128 A8
Hessary View
 Saltash PL12 . . . . 242 E4
 Tavistock PL19 . . . . 171 B6
Hestow Rd TQ12 . . . . 123 F1
Hetling Cl PL1 . . . . 262 B3
Hewer's Row PL4 . . . . . . 263 A3
Hewitt Cl
 Newton Abbot TQ12 . . . . 208 A3
 Saltash PL12 . . . . 242 C1
Hexham Pl PL2 . . . . 248 A8
Hexton Hill Rd PL9 . . . . . 255 B6
Hexworthy Ave EX4 . . . . . 176 E8
Heybrook Ave PL5 . . . . . . 243 D1
Heybrook Dr PL9 . . . . 140 A7
Heydon's La EX10 . . . . . . 188 A4
Heywood Ave EX32 . . . . . 155 C2
Heywood Cl Hartland EX39 .22 E3
 Torquay TQ2 . . . . 219 E7
Heywood Cross EX18 . . . . .59 D5
Heywood Dr EX6 . . . . 201 A8
Heywood Est TQ12 . . . . . 207 D6
Heywood Rd PL9 . . . . 156 F5
Heywoods Cl **11** TQ14 . 210 C5
Heywoods Rd TQ14 . . . . . 210 C5
Hibernia Terr PL1 . . . . . . 247 E8
Hick's La PL4 . . . . 263 A2
Hickory Cl EX14 . . . . 166 E5
Hickory Dr PL7 . . . . 251 B7
Hidden Valley Cvn Pk
 EX34 . . . . .8 D4
Hides Rd EX10 . . . . 188 C8
Hidewood La EX15 . . . . . . .52 F1
Hierns La EX34 . . . . 150 C6
High Acre Dr PL21 . . . . . . 237 A6
High Bank Exeter EX4 . . . 178 B8
 West Hill EX11 . . . . 168 D3
High Bullen EX5 . . . . .82 B6
High Bullen Cross EX16 . . .19 E1
High Bullen La EX35 . . . . . .5 B3
High Cl TQ13 . . . . 180 E7
High Cott EX36 . . . . .19 C8
High Creek Cross EX10 . . 188 F8
High Cross Bampton EX16 .34 A1
 12 Combe Martin EX34 . .3 A5
 High Cross Ho* TQ9 . . . . 216 A1
High Gate EX16 . . . . .62 F6
High House EX7 . . . . 204 D7
High House La TQ7 . . . . . 258 D4
High Mdw EX10 . . . . 188 B7
High Mdws EX4 . . . . 176 E5
High Park Cl EX39 . . . . . . .25 D4
High Rd PL9 . . . . 140 C8
High St Bampton EX16 . . . .34 B1
 Barnstaple EX31 . . . . . . 154 F5
 Bideford EX39 . . . . 157 A2
 Budleigh Salterton EX9 . . 199 G2
 Chagford TQ13 . . . . 111 A6
 Clovelly EX39 . . . . .23 D2
 Combe Martin EX34 . . . . .3 A3
 Crediton EX17 . . . . 165 C5
 Cullompton EX15 . . . . . . 163 C3
 Dawlish EX7 . . . . 204 E6
 Dulverton TA22 . . . . .33 D6
 East Budleigh EX9 . . . . . 198 B6
 Exbourne EX20 . . . . .76 C4
 Exeter EX4 . . . . 261 B3
 Exmouth EX8 . . . . 202 A6

High St continued
 Great Torrington EX38 . . 159 D5
 Halberton EX16 . . . . .65 A7
 Hatherleigh EX20 . . . . . . .75 C7
 Heavy EX15 . . . . .67 B8
 High Bickington EX37 . . . .43 B7
 4 Holsworthy EX22 . . . 164 C4
 Ide EX2 . . . . 176 D1
 Ilfracombe EX34 . . . . . . 150 B6
 Kentisbeare EX15 . . . . . . .66 A3
 Kenton EX6 . . . . 194 D3
 Newton Poppleford EX10 186 E8
 North Tawton EX20 . . . . . .77 C4
 Okehampton EX20 . . . . . 170 B5
 3 Plymouth PL1 . . . . . 263 A2
 Plymouth, Stonehouse PL1 248 A2
 Sidford EX10 . . . . 188 B8
 Sidmouth EX10 . . . . 188 B4
 Silverton EX5 . . . . .82 B6
 Stoke Canon EX5 . . . . . . 173 F8
 Swimbridge EX32 . . . . . . .28 E8
 Topsham EX3 . . . . 182 E6
 Totnes TQ9 . . . . 223 C5
 Uffculme EX15 . . . . .66 A7
 Wellington TA21 . . . . . . 160 C6
 Winkleigh EX19 . . . . .58 F3
High Street & Waterloo
 Street Flats PL1 . . . . . . 248 A1
High View Bideford EX39 . 156 E1
 Feniton EX14 . . . . .84 E1
 Sheepwash EX21 . . . . . . .56 C1
High View Gdns EX8 . . . . 202 B7
High View Terr EX39 . . . . 156 C6
High Wall EX31 . . . . 154 E4
High Way EX16 . . . . .48 D8
Highampton Com Prim Sch
 EX21 . . . . .74 C7
Highampton Cross EX21 . . .74 C7
Highaton Head Cross
 EX36 . . . . .32 C4
Highbank Cl PL19 . . . . . . 171 A4
Highbarrow Cross EX12 . . .54 A4
Highbury Cres PL7 . . . . . 250 D7
Highbury Rd EX39 . . . . . . 157 A8
Highbury Pk EX8 . . . . . . 196 A1
Highbury Rd
 Barnstaple EX32 . . . . . . 155 C3
 Torquay TQ2 . . . . 220 B6
Highclere Gdns PL6 . . . . 245 B8
Highcliff Ct EX7 . . . . 204 E6
Highcliff Rd DT7 . . . . 260 C3
Highcliffe Cl
 Lympstone EX8 . . . . 195 D4
 Seaton EX12 . . . . 191 F6
Highcliffe Cres EX12 . . . . 191 F6
Highcliffe Mews TQ4 . . . . 226 C4
Highcliffe Ct EX12 . . . . . . 191 F6
Highcroft EX4 . . . . 173 A1
Highcross Rd EX4 . . . . . . 177 C8
Highdown Cross EX39 . . . .23 A4
Higher Aboveway EX6 . . . 182 B3
Higher Aller La TQ13 . . . . 122 E6
Higher Alston Farm
 TQ5 . . . . 229 D3
Higher Anderton Rd
 PL10 . . . . 252 F5
Higher Audley Ave TQ2 . . 219 F8
Higher Axmouth Cotts
 EX12 . . . . 192 F6
Higher Barley Mount
 EX4 . . . . 176 E5
Higher Beara Cross
 TQ11 . . . . 236 F4
Higher Bedlands EX9 . . . . 197 F2
Higher Bibbery TQ13 . . . . 180 E7
Higher Brand La EX14 . . . 166 C4
Higher Brimley Rd
 TQ14 . . . . 210 C5
Higher Brixham Prim Sch
 TQ5 . . . . 230 A2
Higher Broad Oak Rd
 EX11 . . . . 168 D2
Higher Brook Mdw **1**
 EX11 . . . . 101 B1
Higher Brook Pk PL21 . . . 237 A5
Higher Brownston Cross
 PL21 . . . . 138 A4
Higher Buckeridge Rd
 TQ14 . . . . 210 B7
Higher Budleigh Mdw
 TQ12 . . . . 206 F3
Higher Bulkamore Cross
 TQ10 . . . . 135 E5
Higher Bull Ring EX15 . . . 163 C3
Higher Bulworthy Cross
 EX16 . . . . .47 E4
Higher Bulworthy La
 EX16 . . . . .47 E4
Higher Buzzacott La EX34 .3 C3
Higher Cadewell La
 TQ2 . . . . 219 C8
Higher Cheglinch La EX34 .8 F6
Higher Church St **6**
 EX32 . . . . 155 A4
Higher Churchway PL9 . . . 256 A7
Higher Clevelands EX32 . . 156 F6
Higher Collaton Cross
 TQ9 . . . . 147 F6
Higher Compton Barton
 TQ3 . . . . 218 F6
Higher Compton Rd
 PL3 . . . . 248 E6
Higher Contour Rd TQ6 . . 234 B3
Higher Coombe Dr
 TQ14 . . . . 210 A3
Higher Coombes TA20 . . . .88 D8
Higher Copythorne TQ5 . . 230 A4

Higher Cotteylands
 EX16 . . . . 161 B3
Higher Cross EX15 . . . . . . .51 C1
Higher Cross Rd EX13 . . . 104 C3
Higher Davis Cl EX32 . . . . .17 F6
Higher Dean TQ11 . . . . . . 135 C7
Higher Dean La EX34 . . . . .3 B3
Higher Doats Hayne La
 TQ13 . . . . 103 D5
Higher Down EX1 . . . . . . 194 D3
Higher Downs Rd TQ1 . . . 220 C8
Higher Dr EX7 . . . . 204 F8
Higher East St EX36 . . . . .30 D8
Higher Edginswell La
 TQ2 . . . . 219 B8
Higher Efford Rd PL3 . . . . 249 B5
Higher Elmwood EX31 . . . 154 C3
Higher Elstone Cross
 EX18 . . . . .44 D3
Higher Erith Rd TQ1 . . . . 220 D4
Higher Exeter Rd TQ14 . . 124 E2
Higher Exwick Hill EX4 . . 176 F8
Higher Forches Cross
 EX17 . . . . .60 D4
Higher Fortescue EX10 . . 188 D7
Higher French Pk TQ12 . . 206 F3
Higher Furzeham Rd
 TQ5 . . . . 230 C6
Higher Gn TQ10 . . . . 135 A2
Higher Green Cross
 TQ7 . . . . 145 C4
Higher Greenway La
 EX10 . . . . 187 E7
Higher Gunstone EX39 . . 157 A2
Higher Haske Cross
 EX17 . . . . 165 F7
Higher Hewish La EX31 . . .9 F4
Higher Hill View EX10 . . . 188 A5
Higher Ho EX38 . . . . .42 B5
Higher Holcombe Cl
 TQ14 . . . . 210 C7
Higher Holcombe Dr
 TQ14 . . . . 210 C8
Higher Holcombe Rd
 TQ14 . . . . 210 C8
Higher Hoopern La EX4 . . 173 C1
Higher Island TQ7 . . . . . . 139 E2
Higher Kelly PL18 . . . . . . 125 D3
Higher King's Ave EX4 . . . 177 D8
Higher Kingsdown Rd
 TQ14 . . . . 209 D7
Higher Kinsman's Dale
 TQ13 . . . . 111 F5
Higher La Axmouth EX12 192 E7
 Plymouth PL1 . . . . 262 C2
Higher Ley EX17 . . . . .60 B3
Higher Lincombe Rd
 TQ1 . . . . 220 E3
Higher Loughborough
 EX16 . . . . 161 B5
Higher Manor Rd TQ5 . . . 230 C5
Higher Manor Terr **1**
 TQ9 . . . . 226 A5
Higher Marley Rd EX8 . . . 196 D4
Higher Maudlin St
 PL4 . . . . 155 A6
Higher Maunders Hill
 EX9 . . . . 198 E7
Higher Mdws Beer EX12 . 191 D5
 High Bickington EX37 . . . .43 B7
Higher Mead EX15 . . . . . . .67 B8
Higher Mill Flats DT7 . . . . 260 D4
Higher Mill La
 Buckfast TQ11 . . . . 236 B7
 Cullompton EX15 . . . . . . 163 C3
Higher Millhayes EX15 . . . .52 B1
Higher Mogworthy Cross
 EX16 . . . . .47 D4
Higher Moor Sq **4**
 EX16 . . . . 161 F6
Higher Mowles PL3 . . . . . 249 B6
Higher Newclose La
 EX31 . . . . .16 B6
Higher Park Cl PL7 . . . . . 251 B3
Higher Park Rd EX13 . . . . 152 E5
Higher Penn TQ5 . . . . . . 230 D3
Higher Pk TQ7 . . . . 149 A3
Higher Polsham Rd
 TQ3 . . . . 226 B7
Higher Port View PL12 . . . 242 F2
Higher Preston Cross
 TQ12 . . . . 123 D1
Higher Rake La TQ7 . . . . . 143 F6
Higher Raleigh Rd EX31 . . 155 A7
Higher Ramshill La TQ3 . . 225 C8
Higher Ranscombe Rd
 TQ5 . . . . 230 D4
Higher Rd Crediton EX17 165 B6
 Fremington EX31 . . . . . . 153 E5
 Woodbury Salterton EX5 . 184 B7
Higher Redgate EX16 . . . . 161 D5
Higher Ridgeway EX11 . . . 169 E4
Higher Ringmore Rd
 TQ14 . . . . 209 D4
Higher Roborough **8**
 TQ13 . . . . 131 A5
Higher Rydons TQ5 . . . . . 230 A4
Higher Sackery TQ12 . . . . 208 F8
Higher Sandygate TQ12 . . 123 E2
Higher Shapter Cl EX3 . . . 182 F4
Higher Shapter St EX3 . . . 182 F4
Higher Slade Rd EX34 . . . 150 A2
Higher Spring Gdns
 EX11 . . . . 169 E3
Higher St Brixham TQ5 . . 230 C5
 Cullompton EX15 . . . . . . 163 C4
 Dartmouth TQ6 . . . . 233 F3
 Dittisham TQ6 . . . . 228 B2

Higher St continued
 Hatherleigh EX20 . . . . . . .75 C7
 Kingswear TQ6 . . . . 234 A3
Higher Stert Terr PL4 . . . . 263 C3
Higher Summerlands
 EX1 . . . . 261 C3
Higher Tamar Terr
 PL18 . . . . 125 D7
Higher Town
 Malborough TQ7 . . . . . . 147 E6
 Sampford Peverell EX16 . 50 C1
Higher Tuckers Pk EX22 . 38 E1
Higher Union La TQ2 . . . . 220 A5
Higher Union Rd TQ7 . . . . 258 C5
Higher Wenn Cross EX32 . 17 A1
Higher Warberry Rd
 TQ1 . . . . 220 D5
Higher Warborough Rd
 TQ5 . . . . 229 B6
Higher Warcombe Cross
 TQ7 . . . . 144 A5
Higher Warren Rd TQ7 . . . 258 E3
Higher Way EX10 . . . . . . 187 A8
Higher Wear Rd EX2 . . . . 182 C7
Higher Weaver Cross
 EX15 . . . . .83 E7
Higher Wellbrook St
 EX16 . . . . 161 B4
Higher Westlake Rd
 4 Barnstaple EX31 . . . 154 A2
 Barnstaple EX31 . . . . . . 154 B2
Higher Westonfields
 TQ9 . . . . 223 E5
Higher Woodfield Rd
 TQ1 . . . . 220 D3
Higher Woodford La
 PL7 . . . . 250 C7
Higher Woodway Cl
 TQ14 . . . . 210 C7
Higher Woodway Rd
 TQ14 . . . . 210 B8
Higher Woolbrook Pk
 EX10 . . . . 187 F7
Higher Yannon Dr TQ14 . . 210 A6
Highermoor Cross EX22 . 53 B1
Highfield Honiton EX14 . . 166 B3
 Lapford EX17 . . . . .60 D3
 Northam EX39 . . . . 156 F6
 Topsham EX3 . . . . 182 F7
Highfield Cl
 Barnstaple EX32 . . . . . . 155 B4
 Brixham TQ5 . . . . 230 A4
 High Bickington EX37 . . . .43 B7
 Plymouth PL7 . . . . 249 C5
Highfield Cres TQ3 . . . . . 225 E6
Highfield Dr
 Kingsbridge TQ7 . . . . . . 258 D4
 2 Wembury PL9 . . . . . 140 D8
Highfield Gdns EX34 . . . . .3 A3
Highfield La EX16 . . . . . . 202 B6
Highfield Pk PL12 . . . . . . 242 B3
Highfield Prim Sch TQ5 . . 249 C5
Highfield Rd
 Dunkeswell EX14 . . . . . . .67 C1
 Ilfracombe EX34 . . . . . . 150 C5
Highfield Terr
 Barnstaple EX32 . . . . . . 191 B1
 2 Ilfracombe EX34 . . . 150 C5
 3 Bishop's Tawton EX32 .16 E1
Highglen Dr PL7 . . . . 251 B7
Highgrove Pk TQ14 . . . . . 210 C2
Highland Cl TQ2 . . . . 219 C6
Highland Rd TQ2 . . . . 219 C5
Highland St PL21 . . . . 237 D5
Highland Terr
 Tiverton EX16 . . . . 161 D4
 Uffculme EX15 . . . . .66 A7
Highlands View EX20 . . . . 170 C3
Highlands EX11 . . . . 169 D3
Highlands Pk **9** TQ13 . . 123 E6
Highridge Cross EX37 . . . .45 B7
Highview Cl PL7 . . . . 251 B3
Highweek Com Prim Sch
 TQ12 . . . . 207 A3
Highweek Cross EX21 . . . .73 E8
Highweek Rd
 Newton Abbot TQ12 . . . . 207 A4
 3 Newton Abbot TQ12 . 207 B3
Highweek St TQ12 . . . . . . 207 B3
Highweek Village TQ12 . . 206 F5
Highweek Way TQ12 . . . . 207 B3
Highwell Rd EX12 . . . . . . 192 A5
Highworthy Cross EX21 . . 55 E3
Hilary Cl EX13 . . . . 167 E6
Hilary Gdns EX13 . . . . . . 167 E6
Hill Barton Bsns Pk
 EX1 . . . . 179 F2
 Exeter EX5 . . . . .99 A1
Hill Barton Cl EX1 . . . . . . 178 C7
Hill Barton La EX1 . . . . . . 178 C7
Hill Barton Rd EX1 . . . . . 178 C7
Hill Budge Terr **7** EX4 . 177 E7
Hill Cl Exeter EX4 . . . . . . 173 D1
 Plymouth PL7 . . . . 250 D4
Hill Cres EX14 . . . . 166 D6
Hill Crest Exminster EX6 . 182 A4
 Kilmington EX13 . . . . . . .87 C1
Hill Crest Rd PL21 . . . . . . 237 D5
 South Tawton EX20 . . . . .95 B5
Hill Crest Sch EX8 . . . . . 196 E1
Hill Cross Cobbaton EX32 .28 B5
 Kingsbridge TQ7 . . . . . . 144 B5
Hill Ct TQ8 . . . . 196 B3
Hill Garden **10** EX39 . . . 157 A2
Hill Gdns PL12 . . . . 239 A2
Hill Head EX37 . . . . .28 F4

Hill Head Cross
 Chittlehampton EX37 . . . .28 F4
 King's Nympton EX37 . . . .44 C5
Hill La Chipstable TA4 . . . .35 C6
 Exeter EX1 . . . . 178 B7
Hill Mdw TQ13 . . . . 130 F5
Hill Park Cl TQ5 . . . . 230 E4
Hill Park Cres EX3 . . . . . . 263 A4
Hill Park Mews PL4 . . . . . 263 B4
Hill Park Rd Brixham TQ5 230 E4
 Newton Abbot TQ12 . . . . 206 F4
 Torquay TQ2 . . . . 220 A7
Hill Park Terr TQ4 . . . . . . 226 D5
Hill Path PL5 . . . . 243 F5
Hill Pk Ashprington TQ9 . 139 F8
 Beesands TQ7 . . . . 149 C6
Hill Rd Bondleigh EX20 . . . .77 C7
 Lyme Regis DT7 . . . . 260 D3
 Newton Abbot TQ12 . . . . 207 B2
Hill Rise Rd DT7 . . . . 260 D3
Hill St PL4 . . . . 263 A3
Hill Top TQ13 . . . . .87 C1
Hill Top Crest PL5 . . . . . . 243 E2
Hill View
 Buckland Monachorum
 PL20 . . . . 126 C3
 Sidmouth EX10 . . . . 188 B5
Hill View Terr **4** TQ1 . . 220 A7
Hill's La EX14 . . . . .86 C5
Hillbrook Rd TQ9 . . . . . . 223 E5
Hillbrook Rise **2** TQ9 . . 223 E5
Hillcliffe Terr **10** EX39 . . .15 A1
Hillcrest Ilsington TQ13 . . 122 C3
 Oakford EX16 . . . . .48 D5
 Ottery St Mary EX11 . . . . 169 D3
Hillcrest Cl Plymouth PL7 251 A5
 9 Wembury PL9 . . . . . 140 D8
Hillcrest Dr PL7 . . . . 251 A4
Hillcrest Pk EX14 . . . . . . 173 C2
Hillcrest Rd
 Barnstaple EX32 . . . . . . 155 B2
 Bideford EX39 . . . . .26 A4
 Silverton EX5 . . . . .82 B6
Hillcroft Terr **5** EX39 . . 157 A2
Hilldale Rd PL10 . . . . 255 E6
Hilldean Cl PL5 . . . . 244 C7
Hilldown TQ20 . . . . 223 C5
Hilldown Cross EX17 . . . . .78 D2
Hilldown Rd EX17 . . . . . . .78 C3
Hilldrop Terr TQ1 . . . . . . 220 B5
Hiller La TQ12 . . . . 208 B2
Hillerton Cross EX17 . . . . .78 B1
Hillesdon Rd TQ1 . . . . . . 220 B4
Hillfield South Zeal EX20 . 95 A4
 Stoke Gabriel TQ9 . . . . . 227 F7
Hillhead Colyton EX24 . . . 103 A4
 Halberton EX16 . . . . .65 A8
 Noss Mayo PL8 . . . . 140 F6
Hillhead Bglws **3** EX24 . 103 A4
Hillhead Cross PL21 . . . . 137 D7
Hillhead Pk TQ5 . . . . 234 E8
Hillhead Terr EX13 . . . . . 167 D5
Hillhouse EX14 . . . . .69 A3
Hilliers EX17 . . . . .57 F7
Hillingdown Cross TQ7 . . 143 D1
Hillington EX34 . . . . 150 A4
Hillmans Rd TQ12 . . . . . . 207 D2
Hillmoor Cross EX21 . . . . .73 F7
Hillrise TQ5 . . . . 229 B5
Hills View
 Barnstaple EX32 . . . . . . 155 A5
 Braunton EX33 . . . . 152 D6
Hillsborough
 2 Plymouth PL4 . . . . . 248 F4
 Torquay TQ2 . . . . 220 B4
Hillsborough Ave EX4 . . . 261 B4
Hillsborough Cross EX17 . .71 C7
Hillsborough Park Rd
 EX34 . . . . 150 C5
Hillsborough Rd EX34 . . . 150 C5
Hillsborough Terr **4**
 EX34 . . . . 150 C6
Hillsborough Terr Mews **5**
 EX34 . . . . 150 C6
Hillsdune Rd PL12 . . . . . . 248 E6
Hillside Branscombe EX12 190 B5
 14 Colyton EX24 . . . . 103 A4
 Honiton EX14 . . . . .85 C5
 Newton Poppleford EX10 186 D8
 Northleigh EX24 . . . . . . 102 B6
 Payhembury EX14 . . . . . .84 C4
 Sidbury EX10 . . . . 101 B2
 South Brent TQ10 . . . . . 134 C6
 Southleigh EX24 . . . . . . 102 C4
 Talaton EX5 . . . . .84 B1
Hillside Ave Exeter EX4 . . 261 B4
 Plymouth PL4 . . . . 248 D4
 Saltash PL12 . . . . 242 F3
Hillside Cl
 Buckland Monachorum
 PL20 . . . . 126 C3
 South Brent TQ10 . . . . . 135 A3
 Teignmouth TQ14 . . . . . 124 E1
Hillside Cotts
 Abbotskerswell TQ12 . . . 212 A6
 Noss Mayo PL8 . . . . 140 F6
Hillside Cres PL9 . . . . . . 255 F8
Hillside Cross TQ7 . . . . . . .72 F4
Hillside Ct TQ11 . . . . 236 C5

Hillside Dr
Kingsbridge TQ7 ....258 D4
Yealmpton PL8 ....257 F3
Hillside Rd Brixham TQ5 .230 C4
Ilfracombe EX34 ....150 E5
Paignton TQ3 ....225 F7
Saltash PL12 ....242 E3
Sidmouth EX10 ....188 C4
Hillside Sch PL5 ....244 B4
Hillside Terr
4 Bideford EX39 ....157 A2
Kingswear TQ6 ....234 A3
2 Paignton TQ3 ....226 A6
Hillside Way PL8 ....136 A2
Hilltop TQ7 ....142 F6
Hilltop Cotts EX31 ....153 E5
Hilltop Rd EX39 ....156 E4
Hiltown Cross
Chittlehampton EX37 ......29 B2
Okehampton EX20 ....93 E5
Rackenford EX16 ....47 D2
Hilton Hill EX36 ....31 C5
Hiltown La EX18 ....59 F5
Hillway La EX10 ....187 A7
Hilly Gardens Rd TQ1 ..214 B1
Hilly Head TA21 ....160 B5
Hillyfield Rd EX1 ....178 C7
Hillymead EX12 ....192 B6
Hilton Ave PL5 ....244 D1
Hilton Cres TQ12 ....219 C1
Hilton Dr TQ3 ....219 C1
Hind St
Marhamchurch EX23 ....70 A6
Monkleigh EX39 ....40 F7
Newton Abbot TQ12 ....207 C3
Hinam Cross TA22 ....33 B7
Hind St
Bovey Tracey TQ13 ....180 D8
Ottery St Mary EX11 .....169 D3
Hindharton La EX39 .....22 E3
Hingston Ct PL6 ....249 A8
Hingston Post TQ9 ......144 E8
Hingston Rd TQ1 ....220 C7
Hirmandale Rd PL5 .....243 F3
Hittisleigh Cross EX6 ...96 D6
Hittisleigh Mill La EX6 ..96 D5
Hittsford La EX36 ....32 A1
Hobart St PL1 ....262 A2
Hobb's Hill EX33 ....7 E2
Hobbacott La EX23 ......70 A6
Hobbs Cres PL12 ....242 C3
Hobbs La EX32 ....18 E2
Hobbs Way EX17 ....78 B4
Hobby Dr The EX39 ......23 E3
Hobby House La EX16 ...30 C1
Hobbymoor Cross EX17 .60 A1
Hockmoor Head TQ11 ...130 C2
Hockmoor Hill TQ11 ....130 C2
Hodder's La EX17 ....260 C8
Hodders Way PL12 ......239 A2
Hodge Cl PL12 ....242 C2
Hodges Wlk EX38 ....159 E5
Hodson Cl TQ3 ....225 F7
Hoe App PL1 ....262 C2
Hoe Ct PL1 ....262 C2
Hoe St PL1 ....262 C2
Hoe The PL2 ....262 C2
Hoegate Ct PL1 ....262 C2
Hoegate Pl PL1 ....262 C2
Hoegate St PL1 ....263 A2
Hofheim Dr EX16 ....161 A6
Hogarth Cl PL9 ....256 B6
Hogarth Wlk PL9 ....256 B6
Hoile La TQ9 ....224 E1
Hoker Rd EX2 ....178 A5
Holbeam Cl TQ12 ....206 E4
Holbeam La
Bickington TQ12 ....131 F6
Newton Abbot TQ12 ....206 A4
Holbeton Sch PL8 ....136 D1
Holborn Pl PL7 ....250 E6
Holborn Rd TQ5 ....230 C6
Holborn St PL4 ....263 B2
Holbrook Terr TQ7 ......145 B1
Holcombe Barton Cnr
EX6 ....98 D2
Holcombe Cross EX7 ...210 F8
Holcombe Down Cross
TQ14 ....124 F2
Holcombe Down Rd
EX7,TQ14 ....204 A4
Holcombe Dr
Holcombe EX7 ....210 F8
Plymouth PL9 ....255 F5
Holcombe La
Ottery St Mary EX11 .....100 F7
Uplyme DT7 ....104 B4
Holcombe Rd TQ14 .....210 E8
Holcroft Cl PL12 ....97 C2
Holden Cross EX6 ....113 E2
Holdridge La EX36 ....30 D8
Holdstone Way EX34 ....3 B2
Holdsworth St PL4 ......262 B4
Hole Ball Cross EX21 ...92 A8
Hole Cleave Rd EX33 ....8 A1
Hole Cross Halwill EX21 .73 F1
Hittisleigh EX6 ....96 E4
Yelverton PL20 ....239 E7
Hole Ct EX20 ....75 C7
Hole Hill
Branscombe EX12 ....190 C5
Exbourne EX20 ....76 C4
Witheridge EX16 ....46 F2
Hole La Chulmleigh EX18 ..45 B3

Hole La continued
Combe Martin EX31 ....10 B6
Croyde EX33 ....7 F1
North Tawton EX20 ....77 E6
Hole's La
Broadhempston TQ9 ......131 D1
Staverton TQ9 ....216 B8
Holebay Cl PL9 ....256 A5
Holebrook Cross EX6 ...76 C4
Holebrook La EX20 ....76 C5
Holemoor Cross EX22 ...73 C8
Holemore Cross EX14 ...68 C5
Holestone La EX10 .....187 A1
Holewater Cross EX32 ..19 A6
Holewater Hill EX32 .....19 A6
Holewell La EX6 ....96 E4
Hollacombe Brake PL9 .256 C1
Hollacombe Cross
Holsworthy EX22 ....72 D6
Ilfracombe EX34 ....79 D3
Hollacombe La TQ3 ....219 D1
Hollam Cross TA22 ....33 E7
Hollam Dr TA22 ....33 D6
Hollam La TA22 ....33 D7
Holland Way TQ12 ......207 F8
Holland Copse EX6 ......98 C4
Holland Rd Exeter EX2 .176 F4
Exmouth EX8 ....196 D1
Plymouth, Chaddlewood
PL7 ....251 D5
Plymouth, Peverell PL3 .248 E6
Plymouth, Plymstock PL9 .255 F6
Holland St **4** EX31 .....154 F5
Holland Wlk **3** EX31 ..154 F5
Holland's La TA4 ....35 E8
Holland's Wash Dro TA20 .69 F5
Hollands Park Ave EX34 ..3 A3
Hollands Rd **4** TQ14 ..210 C4
Holley Cl EX6 ....182 A4
Holley Pk EX20 ....170 D6
Holleys Cl TA20 ....88 D8
Hollies The EX31 ....154 B3
Hollingarth Way EX15 ...67 B8
Hollington Ho **10** TQ1 ...220 D4
Hollis Ct EX11 ....169 E4
Hollocombe Cnr EX18 ...58 D6
Hollocombe Moor Gate
EX18 ....58 D7
Hollocombe Moor Head
EX18 ....58 D7
Hollow Head Cross
EX10 ....100 F2
Hollow La EX1 ....178 E7
Hollow Pits Ct EX2 .....181 B8
Hollow Tree Cross EX8 ..60 A7
Hollowtree Rd EX32 ....155 B3
Holly Cl Broadclyst EX5 .175 C7
Honiton EX14 ....166 C4
Tiverton EX16 ....161 E5
Holly Ct PL6 ....249 E7
Holly Park Cl PL5 ....244 A5
Holly Park Dr PL5 ....244 A5
Holly St **2** EX33 ....152 F4
Holly Tree Cl EX15 ....67 B8
Tiverton EX16 ....161 E5
Holly Villas TQ9 ....139 F8
Holly Water Rd EX17 ....62 E1
Holly Way EX15 ....163 C5
Holly Wlk EX8 ....196 C3
Hollycombe Cross EX20 ..95 E4
Hollycombe La TQ7 .....216 E7
Hollycroft Rd PL3 ....249 A7
Hollyford La EX17 ....62 C2
Hollyhead Cross EX12 .191 B8
Hollyhead Rd EX32 ....19 A8
Hollymount Cl EX8 ......196 C3
Hollywater Cl TQ1 ......220 D5
Hollywood Terr PL1 .....262 A3
Holman Cl Exeter EX4 ..174 F1
Tiverton EX16 ....59 F2
Holman Hill EX17 ....59 E7
Holmacott Cross EX39 ..26 C7
Holman Cl EX7 ....204 F8
Holman Ct PL2 ....248 C8
Holman Way
Ivybridge PL21 ....237 A6
Topsham EX3 ....182 F5
Holmans Bldgs PL14 ...247 D2
Holmans Mdw PL15 ....105 B1
Holmbush Way PL8 ......257 A4
Holmdale EX10 ....188 C6
Holme Ct **3** TQ1 ....220 D4
Holmead La EX16 ....48 B3
Holmer Down PL6 ....245 D7
Holmes Ave PL3 ....249 B5
Holmes Rd TQ3 ....180 F2
Holmleigh Rd TQ7 ......145 D6
Holmsleigh Cross EX14 ..86 B2
Holmwood Ave PL9 .....255 E5
Holne Chase PL6 ....245 A8
Holne Ct EX4 ....176 E8
Holne Moor Cl TQ3 .....225 E7
Holne Rd TQ11 ....230 B4
Holne Rise EX2 ....178 B4
Holne Turn
Ashburton TQ13 ....130 E5

Holne Turn continued
Holne TQ13 ....130 B5
Holset Cross TQ8 ....148 D5
Holsome La TQ9 ....138 D7
Holstock Cross EX22 .....74 D3
Holsworthy Com Coll
EX22 ....164 C5
Holsworthy Hospl EX22 ..164 C4
Holsworthy Mus* EX22 .164 C4
Holsworthy Prim Sch
EX22 ....164 C5
Holsworthy Rd EX20 .....93 D5
Holt The
10 Appledore EX39 ....15 A1
Honiton EX14 ....166 E7
Holtwood Dr PL21 ....237 A5
Holtwood Rd PL6 ....245 D6
Holway TA20 ....88 D8
Holwell Cl PL6 ....256 A5
Holwell La EX16 ....64 B5
Holwell Rd TQ5 ....230 B4
Holwill Dr EX38 ....159 D5
Holwill Tor Wlk TQ4 ....225 F3
Holy Cross RC Prim Sch
PL4 ....263 A3
Holy Moor Cross EX36 ..32 C1
Holy Moor La EX36 ......32 C1
Holyford La EX24 ....102 F3
Holyoake St TA21 ....160 C7
Holyrood Pl PL1 ....262 C2
Holyshute Cross EX14 .166 D6
Holywell CE Prim Sch
EX31 ....27 D8
Holywell Cross EX36 .....19 F2
Holywell Pk EX21 ....73 F5
Home Cl Brixham TQ5 ...230 C3
Chillington TQ7 ....145 A1
Home Farm Cl Croyde EX33 ..7 E2
Kingston TQ7 ....142 C6
Home Farm Cres EX15 ...65 F4
Home Farm Ct TQ12 ....209 B2
Home Farm Rd
Fremington EX31 ....153 D5
Plymouth PL9 ....255 E8
Home Gate EX6 ....98 A3
Home La EX34 ....1 C3
Home Mdw TQ7 ....223 C5
Home Orch TQ12 ....227 E7
Home Park PL3 ....248 E6
Home Park Rd PL12 ....242 E3
Home Pk Ashburton TQ13 .130 F5
Plymouth PL2 ....247 E8
Home Sweet Home Terr
PL4 ....263 C2
Homebaye Ho **3** EX12 .192 B4
Homebourne Ho TQ4 ..226 C5
Homeclose La EX13,TA20 ..88 A8
Homeclyst Rd EX2 ....261 A1
Homecourt Ho EX4 ....261 A3
Homedown Cross EX37 ..28 F4
Homefield
Thurlestone TQ7 ....143 A1
Wellington TA21 ....160 E4
Homefield Cl EX11 ......169 D3
Homefield Cotts TQ1 ...220 D7
Homefield Rd EX1 ....177 F6
Homelace Ho EX14 ......166 C7
Homelands Pl TQ7 ......258 C6
Homelands Rd TQ7 ......258 C6
Homemeadows Ho
EX10 ....188 A5
Homepalms Ho **2** TQ1 .219 F6
Homer Cl EX31 ....152 B7
Homer Cres EX33 ....152 B7
Homer Dr EX33 ....152 B7
Homer La Seaton EX12 .191 F8
Seaton EX12 ....192 A6
Homer Park La S PL9 ...255 C5
Homer's Cross PL21 ....137 D7
Homer Rise PL9 ....256 B7
Homers Cl TQ12 ....207 D6
Homers Cres TQ12 ......207 D6
Homers La EX17 ....78 B2
Homershill Cross PL21 ..137 B6
Homesleigh Rd EX14 .....86 A5
Homestead Rd TQ1 .....220 A8
Homestead Terr TQ1 ...220 A8
Homeyards The TQ14 ..210 A3
Homing Down Cross
EX20 ....75 A1
Honcray PL9 ....255 D8
Hone Cross EX16 ....34 F5
Honest Heart Cross EX15 ..66 A3
Honestone St EX39 .....157 A1
Honey Ditches Dr EX12 .191 F8
Honey La
Daccombe TQ1,TQ12 .....213 F5
Exeter EX4 ....174 F2
Woodbury Salterton EX5 .187 C7
Honey Park Rd TQ9 ......139 B2
Honey St EX39 ....157 A1
Honeybeetle Cross EX37 ..29 A5
Honeychurch Moor Cross
EX20 ....76 F6
Honeycroft Cross EX14 ...54 A4
Honeylands Childrens Ctr
(Hospl) EX4 ....178 A7
Honeylands Dr EX4 ......178 A7
Honeylands Way EX4 ...178 A7
Honeymoor La EX16 ......48 E7
Honeysuckle Cl
2 Barnstaple EX32 ....154 B3

Honeysuckle Cl continued
Paignton TQ3 ....225 E8
Plymouth PL6 ....245 E7
Saltash PL12 ....242 D3
Tiverton EX16 ....161 F6
Honeysuckle Ct EX14 ...176 D8
Honeysuckle Dr EX14 ....85 C2
Honeywell TQ12 ....207 E6
Honeywell La EX32 ....32 B2
Honeywell Rd TQ12 .....207 E6
Honeywins Cross EX36 ..19 C2
Honicknowle Gn PL5 ....244 B2
Honicknowle La PL5 .....244 B1
Honiton La EX14 ....166 E7
Honiton Rd PL7 ....125 E5
Honicombe Manor Holiday
Village PL17 ....125 B5
Honiton Bottom Rd
EX14 ....166 C4
Honiton Bsns Pk EX14 ...166 A6
Honiton Com Coll EX14 .166 C6
Honiton Cross EX36 ......29 F3
Honiton Hospl EX14 .....166 C5
Honiton La EX36 ....29 E3
Honiton Mus* EX14 ......166 C6
Honiton Prim Sch EX14 .166 C6
Honiton Rd
Clyst Honiton EX5 ....179 C7
Cullompton EX15 ....163 E3
Exeter EX1 ....178 C5
Tiverton EX14 ....166 C5
Honiton Wlk PL5 ....244 B4
Honors Farm EX5 ....173 F8
Hooda Cl EX23 ....17 E1
Hoodown La TQ6 ....234 B4
Hoo Meavis La PL8 ....255 F5
Hooe Hill PL9 ....255 C5
Hooe Lake Rd PL9 ....255 D3
Hooe Prim Sch PL9 ......255 B5
Hooe Rd PL9 ....255 C5
Hook Cross EX13 ....87 D2
Hook Farm Cvn & Camping
Pk DT7 ....260 A5
Hooker Cl EX17 ....197 F2
Hookhill La EX17 ....62 A3
Hookhills Dr TQ4 ....226 C1
Hookhills Gdns TQ4 ....229 E8
Hookhills Gr TQ4 ....226 C1
Hookhills Rd TQ4 ....226 B1
Hookmoor Cross PL21 ..137 E7
Hooks Cross TQ12 ....131 C7
Hooksbury Ave PL7 .....251 B3
Hookway EX17 ....80 D1
Hookway Cross EX5 ....80 D1
Hookway La EX16 ....63 B5
Hookwell Down La EX36 ..30 A8
Hooperhayne Rd EX24 .102 E5
Hoopern Ave EX4 ....173 D1
Hoopern La EX4 ....177 C8
Hoopern St EX4 ....261 A4
Hoopern Terr **4** EX4 ...261 A4
Hoopers Cross EX16 ......34 D3
Hoopers La PL18 ....125 C6
Hoopers Way EX38 .....159 F5
Hooperton Cross EX6 ....96 E3
Hope Cl TQ9 ....223 F5
Hope Rd EX2 ....178 A5
Hope Wlk TQ9 ....223 F5
Hope's Cl TQ12 ....210 A6
Hopkins Cl **10** TQ12 ....207 C3
Hopkins La TQ12 ....207 C3
Hopperstyle EX31 ....154 B3
Hopton Cl PL6 ....248 F8
Hopton Dr EX38 ....159 F5
Horace Rd TQ12 ....213 F2
Hore Down Gate EX34 ...9 B6
Hore's Cross PL21 ....137 D7
Horestone Cross EX16 ...47 F4
Horn Cross
Kentisbeare EX15 ....65 F2
Plymouth PL9 ....255 E7
Horn Cross Rd PL9 .....255 F7
Horn Hill TQ6 ....233 F3
Horn Hill EX17 ....257 A5
Horn La Braunton PL8 ..257 A5
Horn Lane Flats PL9 .....255 F7
Horn Rd EX15 ....163 C3
Hornapark Cl PL16 ......105 E3
Hornbeam Cl
Honiton EX14 ....166 A4
Tiverton EX16 ....161 F5
Hornbeam Gdns EX5 .....43 A2
Hornbeam Hollow **1**
EX31 ....154 C2
Hornbrook Gdns PL6 ...244 D6
Hornby St **2** PL2 ....247 F4
Hornchurch La PL5 ......243 E5
Hornchurch Rd PL5 .....243 E5
Horne Park Ave **11**
EX34 ....150 B5
Horne Rd EX34 ....150 B5
Hornebrook Ave **8**
EX34 ....150 B5
Horner Tongue TQ9 ....138 F5
Horner Turn Cross TQ9 .138 F5
Horns Pk TQ12 ....211 D2
Hornshayes Knap Cross
EX14 ....176 F5
Hornshayne Rd EX24 ...102 B5
Horrabridge Prim Sch
PL20 ....126 E3
Horridge La EX18 ....59 A8
Horry Mill La EX18 ....59 A6
Horsdon Rd EX16 ....161 F4

Horsdon Terr EX16 ......161 F4
Horse Hill EX17 ....60 F7
Horse Hill Cross EX22 ...38 F1
Horse La TQ14 ....210 B3
Horsecombe Cross TQ8 .259 B7
Horseguards EX4 ....261 B4
Horsehill Cross EX17 .....60 F7
Horsepond Mdw EX36 .158 C3
Horsepool St TQ5 ....230 B3
Horseshoe Bend TQ4 ..226 C2
Horseshoe Cl **10** TQ13 .123 E6
Horsham La
Plymouth, Honicknowle
PL5 ....244 C2
Plymouth, Tamerton Foliot
PL5 ....244 A8
Horslears EX13 ....167 C4
Horswell Cl PL7 ....251 B5
Horton Cross EX22 ....38 C3
Horwood & Newton Tracey
Prim Sch EX31 ....27 A6
Horwood Cross EX39 .....26 D7
Horwood Sq **11** EX31 ..154 F5
Hosegood Way TQ12 ...207 D7
Hosford Cl PL9 ....256 A4
Hoskings Ct TQ11 ....236 B5
Hospital Hill EX7 ....204 D6
Hospital La
11 Ashburton TQ13 .....131 A5
Exeter EX15 ....178 C5
Hospital Rd PL4 ....263 B4
Hostle Park Rd EX34 ...150 C6
Hostle Pk EX34 ....150 C6
Hotham Pl PL1 ....262 A4
Hothill La
Ashprington TQ9 ....139 F6
Cornworthy TQ9 ....227 A4
Houghton La EX10 ......187 A5
Houldsworth Rd PL9 ...255 C7
Hound Tor Cl TQ4 ....229 B7
Houndbeare La
Aylesbeare EX5 ....99 E4
West Hill EX5 ....168 A2
Houndhead Cross TQ9 .216 D8
Houndiscombe Rd PL4 .248 E4
Hounster Dr PL10 ....252 D4
Hounster Hill PL10 ......252 D4
Housecraft Ctr **7** PL4 ..263 A2
Housman Cl PL5 ....244 D3
Hove Villas EX2 ....261 A1
How St PL4 ....263 A2
Howard Ave EX32 ....155 B4
Howard Cl Exeter EX4 ...176 F8
Okehampton EX20 ....70 D6
Plymouth PL5 ....243 F2
Saltash PL12 ....242 D3
Tavistock PL19 ....171 A5
Teignmouth TQ14 ....210 A7
Torquay TQ2 ....219 D6
Howard Cross EX6 ....96 D7
Howard La EX22 ....92 D7
Howard La Hittisleigh EX6 .96 D7
Marhamchurch EX23 ....70 B8
Howard Rd Plymouth PL9 .255 E8
Wellington TA21 ....160 D7
Howards Cl EX36 ....158 C2
Howards Way
Ivybridge PL21 ....237 A6
Newton Abbot TQ12 ......207 F4
Howarth Cl EX10 ....188 A8
Howden La EX16 ....161 B3
Howden Rd EX16 ....161 B3
Howell Rd Exeter EX4 ...177 A7
Exeter EX4 ....261 A4
Howton La TQ12 ....206 B5
Howton Rd TQ12 ....206 C6
Hoxton Rd TQ1 ....220 B5
Hoyle's Cl TQ3 ....225 F8
Hoyle's Rd TQ3 ....225 E8
Hoyles Rd TQ3 ....225 E8
Hoyles Rd TA21 ....160 E4
Hubbastone Rd EX39 ...157 C8
Huccaby Cl TQ5 ....229 F2
Huckham Barn Cross
TQ7 ....147 C7
Huckham La EX31 ....10 F3
Huckland Cross EX20 ....76 E4
Huddisford Cross EX39 ..38 D7
Hudley Mill Hill EX22 .....29 D2
Hudson Cross EX22 ....53 B4
Hue La EX33 ....8 A1
Hugh Squier Ave EX36 .158 D5
Hughball Cross EX19 .....76 A8
Hughes Ave EX32 ....155 B5
Hukeley Head Cross EX16 .34 D3
Hulham Rd EX8 ....196 C3
Hulk La EX5 ....81 F4
Humber Cl PL3 ....249 D6
Humber La TQ12,TQ14 .207 F8
Hume Ave EX35 ....151 A5
Hummingbird Cl EX14 ..174 E1
Humphry's Cross
TQ13 ....130 C4
Humphreys Rd TQ12 ....160 E7
Humphries Pk EX8 ....196 D1
Hungerford Rd PL2 ......248 B5
Hungry Fox Est EX5 ......175 E3
Huniver's La EX17 ....165 C4
Hunivers Pl EX17 ....165 D4
Hunsdon Rd
Plymouth PL3 ....237 A2
Torquay TQ1 ....220 C4
Hunstone Cross EX36 ...19 B2
Huntacott Way TQ2 ....219 B8

Hunter Cl PL6 ....244 F2
Hunter La EX34 ....7 F6
Hunter's Hill EX15 ....51 E1
Hunter's Way EX15 ....51 E1
Hunters Cl PL21 ....237 B5
Hunters Ct TQ3 ....224 F7
Hunters Gate EX20 ....170 D6
Hunters Moon TQ9 ....222 F7
Hunters Tor Dr TQ4 .....229 B7
Hunter's Oak PI Q2 ......126 A2
Hunterswell Rd TQ12 ....207 A3
Hunterswood EX38 ....159 F5
Hunthay La EX13 ....167 B6
Huntingdon Gdns PL5 ...244 D4
Huntley Cl EX13 ....167 F7
Huntley La EX13 ....188 A8
Huntley Pl PL3 ....249 C4
Hunton Cl EX8 ....195 F5
Hunts Cross EX31 ....137 B1
Huntshaw Cross EX31 .....27 C7
Huntshaw Moor Cross
EX38 ....26 F2
Hurdwick Rd PL19 ....171 A5
Hurrabrook Cl PL6 ....245 E2
Hurrabrook Gdns PL6 ....245 E2
Hurrell Cl PL6 ....244 D6
Hurrell Ct
  Kingsbridge TQ7 ....258 C5
  Plymouth PL3 ....249 C5
Hurrell Rd TQ7 ....258 C5
Hursley Bsns Pk PL6 .....241 D1
Hurst Ave EX3 ....178 B4
Hurst Cl PL9 ....255 F5
Hussey's La EX14 ....86 F6
Husseys Cross EX14 ....86 F6
Hutcherleigh Cross TQ9 .139 B1
Hutcherleigh Turn TQ9 ...139 D1
Hutchings Cl PL6 ....244 D6
Hutchings Mead EX1 .....178 F8
Hutchings Way TQ14 .....209 D8
Hutgate Rd EX14 ....86 A4
Hutton Rd TQ3 ....219 A1
Huxford Cross EX37 ....44 F7
Huxford La EX37 ....44 F7
Huxham Cl PL6 ....249 A8
Huxham's Cross TQ9 .....215 E3
Huxham's Cross Est
  TQ9 ....215 E3
Huxley Cl PL7 ....250 F7
Huxley Vale TQ12 ....212 F3
Huxnor Cross TQ12 ....212 F2
Huxton Rd TQ12 ....212 F3
Huxtable Hill TQ2 ....219 E4
Huxtable La EX32 ....18 C2
Huxton Cross TQ7 ....143 D3
Huxton Fork TQ7 ....143 D3
Hyacinth Terr TA21 ......160 C5
Hyde Park Jun & Inf Schs
  PL3 ....248 E5
Hyde Park Rd PL3 ....248 E5
Hyfield Rd TQ4 ....226 B6
Hyfield Gdns TQ1 ....220 B4
Hylbert Rd Kingsbridge TQ7 258 C5
Hylands Cl EX11 ....168 D3
Hylton Gdns EX4 ....176 F6
Hynetown Rd TQ6 ....145 E5
Hynicombe La TA4 ....35 D6

Ibex Ct EX39 ....15 A1
Ice House La EX10 ....187 F7
Icy Pk TQ7 ....143 C6
Iddesleigh Cross EX19 ....57 E3
Iddesleigh Rd EX4 ....177 E8
Iddesleigh Terr 10 EX7 ..204 E6
Ide Fst Sch EX2 ....176 E1
Ide La EX2 ....177 A1
Idestone Brook Cross
  EX2 ....113 F7
Idestone Cross EX2 ....114 A7
Idewell Rd TQ2 ....214 B2
Idston Cross TQ7 ....143 D7
Ilbert Cotts PL7 ....250 E4
Ilbert Rd Kingsbridge TQ7 258 C5
  Thurlestone TQ7 ....143 A1
Ilbert St PL1 ....262 B4
Ilex Cl Exeter EX4 ....174 B2
  Shillingford St George EX2 114 C6
Ilfracombe CE Jun Sch
  EX34 ....150 C5
Ilfracombe Coll EX34 .....150 C5
Ilfracombe Inf Sch
  EX34 ....150 B5
Ilfracombe Mus* EX34 ..150 B5
Ilfracombe Rd
  Braunton EX33 ....152 D7
  Ilfracombe EX34 ....8 F5
Ilkerton Hill EX35 ....151 A1
Ilsham CE Prim Sch
  TQ1 ....220 E5
Ilsham Cl TQ1 ....220 F5
Ilsham Cross TQ1 ....220 D4
Ilsham Ho TQ1 ....220 E5
Ilsham Marine Dr TQ1 ...221 A4
Ilsham Rd TQ1 ....220 F5
Ilsington CE Prim Sch
  TQ13 ....122 C3
Ilton Cross TQ7 ....259 A7
Ilton Way TQ7 ....258 D5
Immenstadt Dr TA21 ....160 D4
Imperial Bldgs TQ12 ....207 D8
Imperial Ct TQ1 ....220 A4
Imperial Mews 5 TQ12 .207 C3
Imperial St EX4 ....201 F6
Imperial St EX4 ....176 F5

Improvement Pl 6
  TA21 ....160 D5
Ince Cl PL11 ....246 F4
Inchcoulter EX8 ....202 C5
Inchkeith Rd PL6 ....244 F7
Inckledon Hill EX33 ....8 A3
Ind Units EX34 ....3 A3
Indicombe La EX32 ....18 B2
Indio Rd TQ13 ....180 C6
Ingleside EX32 ....167 E6
Ingleside EX29 ....198 A1
Ingra Rd PL3 ....249 A6
Ingra Tor Cl 4 PL20 ......126 F3
Ingsdon Hill EX8 ....245 B8
Inner Ting Tong EX9 .....197 C3
Innes Ho PL1 ....262 B3
Instaple Cross EX22 ....53 D6
Instow Ho 4 EX39 ....15 B1
Instow Prim Sch EX39 ...23 C1
Instow Signal Box Mus*
  EX39 ....15 B1
Instow Wlk PL5 ....244 A3
Inswell Ct PL9 ....171 A6
Insworke Cl PL10 ....253 A6
Insworke Cres PL10 ......252 F6
Insworke Pl PL10 ....253 A6
International Ho TQ12 ...180 F2
Inverdene PL3 ....248 D5
Inverteign Dr TQ14 ......210 A5
Inwardleigh Cross EX20 ..75 D2
Iolanthe Dr EX4 ....196 A2
Iona Ave EX8 ....196 A2
Ipplepen Bsns Pk TQ12 .217 D8
Ipplepen Cross TQ12 ....211 C6
Ipplepen Prim Sch
  TQ12 ....211 D3
Ipplepen Rd TQ3 ....218 C4
Irene Way EX16 ....244 C4
Irsha St EX39 ....15 A1
Irving Cl EX33 ....152 B6
Isaac Cl EX9 ....198 E7
Isaacs Rd TQ2 ....214 A2
Isabella Rd EX16 ....161 D5
Isambard Ct TQ2 ....214 B3
Isambard Par EX4 ....177 A7
Isca Rd Exeter EX2 ......261 A1
  Exmouth EX8 ....202 C5
Isigny Rd TQ7 ....258 C5
Isis Ct EX14 ....166 E7
Island Quay TQ8 ....259 E5
Island St TQ8 ....259 E5
Island View TQ7 ....143 A2
Isleworth Rd EX4 ....176 E6
Iter Cirr EX7 ....78 C4
Iter Cross EX17 ....78 C4
Iter Pk EX17 ....78 C4
Itton Cross EX20 ....77 D2
Itton Moor La EX17 ....77 F2
Itton Rd EX17 ....77 E2
Ivanhoe Rd PL5 ....243 D2
Ivatt Rd TQ6 ....233 C3
Iveagh Ct EX4 ....176 F8
Ivy Cl Exeter EX2 ....178 A4
  Sidmouth EX10 ....188 B7
Ivy Cotts EX18 ....125 C6
Ivy Cross TQ13 ....180 C6
Ivy Cross TA21 ....51 D7
Ivy Ct 2 EX39 ....15 A1
Ivy Ho TQ1 ....160 C6
Ivy La Dartmouth TQ6 ...233 F3
  Teignmouth TQ14 ....210 B4
Ivy Tree Hill TQ12 ....209 A2
Ivybridge Com Coll
  PL21 ....237 D6
Ivybridge Sta PL21 ......237 F6
Ivycombe Hill TQ7 ....149 B5
Ivydale EX8 ....196 D3
Ivydale Rd PL4 ....248 F4
Ivydene Rd PL21 ....237 C5
Ivyhouse Cross PL16 .....91 A4

Jack Backs Cross EX17 ...79 F7
Jack Bears Ho 10 TQ4 ...226 B6
Jackets La EX39 ....156 F7
Jackett's TQ13 ....213 F3
Jackets Cl EX9 ....198 E7
Jacketts Cotts EX9 ....198 E7
Jackman's La TQ9 ....222 F4
Jackman's Mdw PL20 ...253 A3
Jackmans Cl TQ9 ....222 E6
Jackson Cl PL5 ....247 F8
Jackson Pl PL2 ....247 F4
Jackson Way TQ12 ......207 A3
Jacob's Pool EX20 ....170 B5
Jacobs Field EX39 ....39 E8
Jacolind Wlk TQ5 ....230 D5
Jago Ave PL11 ....247 B3
James Ave TQ3 ....218 E1
James Cl PL9 ....256 B6

James La EX14 ....69 C2
James Lane Cross EX13 ..69 C2
James Owen Ct EX4 .....261 C4
James PI PL4 ....262 C4
James Rd PL19 ....171 E2
James St Plymouth PL1 ..262 C4
  Plymouth, Mount Wise PL1 247 E1
James's Week La EX18 ...59 E8
Jane Way's Grave EX17 ..61 B1
Jardine PL EX2 ....177 C1
Jarmins Pitt Cross EX15 ..66 A4
Jarvis Cl EX8 ....202 E7
Jasmine Cl EX16 ....161 F6
Jasmine Gdns
  Plymouth, Chaddlewood
  PL7 ....251 B5
  Plymouth, Glenholt PL6 ..245 E6
Jasmine Gr TQ3 ....225 E8
Jawbones Hill TQ6 ....233 E2
Jaycroft EX15 ....162 E4
Jays Cross PL15 ....105 B6
Jean Cres PL1 ....249 B6
Jedburgh Cres PL2 ....248 A8
Jeffery Cl PL6 ....244 D6
Jefford Ho EX4 ....173 A1
Jeffrey Cl EX39 ....22 E3
Jeffs Way EX15 ....167 E6
Jellicoe Rd PL5 ....244 E1
Jellicoe Vills TQ9 ....223 B5
Jenker's Hill EX33 ....8 B2
Jenkins Cl PL9 ....256 A5
Jennifer Cl EX2 ....177 E3
Jenns Cross EX22 ....53 D7
Jenny's Portion EX5 ......82 A6
Jennycliff La PL9 ....255 A6
Jenny Combe Cl PL9 .....255 F4
Jenwood Rd EX14 ....67 B1
Jephson Rd PL4 ....249 B3
Jericho St EX5 ....81 E5
Jerrard Ct EX14 ....166 C5
Jerrard Cres EX14 ....166 C5
Jesmond Rd EX1 ....177 E7
Jessops PL7 ....250 D7
Jesu St EX11 ....168 D3
Jetty Marsh Rd TQ12 ...207 B5
Jewel's Cross PL16 ....90 E6
Jewell Cres EX14 ....155 C6
JHTaylor Dr EX39 ....157 A7
Jingles La EX32 ....17 B8
Joan Spry Cl EX16 ....46 E1
Jobble's La EX24 ....102 E4
Jocelyn Mead EX17 .....165 B6
Jocelyn Rd EX9 ....198 A2
Jockey Hill EX4 ....166 C5
John Acres La TQ12 .....123 D3
John Gay Cl EX32 ....155 C5
John Gay Rd EX32 ....155 C5
John Grinter Way TA21 ..160 D4
John Howe Cl EX38 ......159 D5
John Kitto Com Coll
  PL5 ....244 B1
John La PL4 ....262 C4
John Nash Dr EX7 ....204 C4
John Penrose Rd EX31 ..154 B2
John Smale Rd EX31 ....154 C4
John Sparke Ho 17 PL1 ..263 A2
John St Exeter EX1,EX4 ..261 A2
  Plymouth PL1 ....247 E3
  Tiverton EX16 ....161 C6
John Stocker Mid Sch
  EX4 ....176 F4
John's Terr 7 EX16 ......161 B4
John's Cl EX34 ....150 B5
Johnson Pk PL18 ....125 D3
Johnstone Dr EX16 ......161 B5
Johnstone La EX36 ....30 D4
Jones's Hill EX33 ....7 E2
Jonida Cl TQ1 ....220 A2
Jordan Cl EX32 ....155 C3
Jordan Cross TQ13 ......121 A2
Jordan Dr TQ14 ....209 D8
Jordan La
  Horrabridge PL20 ......126 F5
  Walkhampton PL20 ....127 A6
Jordan Mdw 15 TQ13 ..131 A5
Jordan Orch TQ11 ....236 A5
Jordan St TQ11 ....236 A5
Jordans Brook TQ9 ......222 E6
Jose's Cross EX37 ....44 F8
Jose's La EX31 ....4 B5
Joslin Cl TQ12 ....207 D8
Joslin Rd EX14 ....166 B5
Joy St EX31 ....154 F5
Jubilee Cl
  Dartmouth TQ6 ....233 C3
  Exminster EX6 ....182 B4
  2 Ilfracombe EX34 .....150 B5
  Ivybridge PL21 ....237 D6
  Newton Abbot TQ12 ...207 F3
  Saltash PL12 ....242 D2
Jubilee Ct Ashwater EX21 ..90 E6
  Exeter EX4 ....261 A3
  Torquay TQ1 ....220 B5
Jubilee Dr Exmouth EX8 196 C3
  4 Hemyock EX15 ....67 B8
Jubilee Gdns
  Cullompton EX15 ....163 C2
  North Molton EX36 ....30 D8
Jubilee La EX8 ....196 C3
Jubilee Path EX17 ....62 E2
Jubilee Rd Appledore EX39 ..14 F1
  Exeter EX1 ....177 E7
  Malborough TQ7 ....147 F6
  Newton Abbot TQ12 ...207 B2
  Plymouth PL5 ....243 F3

Jubilee Rd continued
  Totnes TQ9 ....223 E6
Jubilee St TQ7 ....143 C6
Jubilee Terr
  Copplestone EX17 ....79 B5
  Kingswear TQ6 ....234 B3
  Paignton TQ3 ....226 A6
Julian Cl PL4 ....249 B2
Julian Cotts PL21 ....136 D6
Julian Rd PL21 ....237 B5
Julian St PL4 ....263 C2
Julian Wlk PL6 ....245 E6
Jump Cl PL6 ....241 C1
Junction Rd EX17 ....78 C4
Juniper Cl Exeter EX4 ...174 B2
  3 Honiton EX14 ....166 A4
  3 Tiverton EX16 ....161 F6
Juniper Cl EX31 ....154 C3
Juniper Way PL7 ....251 B5
Junket St EX37 ....43 B7
Jupes Cl EX6 ....182 B3
Juries La EX38 ....159 D6
Jurston Cross TQ13 ....110 F4
Jurston La
  Wellington TA21 ....160 E6
  Wellington TA21 ....160 F5
Jury Cross TA22 ....33 C6
Jury Hill TA22 ....33 E6
Jury Pk EX36 ....158 B4
Jury Rd TA22 ....33 C6
Jurys Cnr TQ12 ....213 A4
Jurys Corner Cl TQ12 ...213 A4
Justment Cross EX17 .....77 F7

Kabale Cl EX16 ....161 A6
Kala Fair EX39 ....156 E7
Karen Cl EX39 ....157 D1
Katherines La EX14 .....166 C5
Kathleaven St PL5 ....243 D1
Kay Cl Exmouth EX8 .....202 C8
  Plymouth PL7 ....250 F7
Keals Croft EX35 ....151 B5
Keat St PL2 ....248 A4
Keatings La TQ14 ....210 A5
Keaton Barns PL8 ....141 E6
Keaton La PL21 ....237 D1
Keaton Rd PL21 ....237 D1
Keats Cl Exmouth EX8 ..196 C4
  Teignmouth TQ14 ....124 E1
Kedlestone Ave PL5 .....244 A3
Keep Cotts TQ7 ....144 B7
Keep Gdns The TQ6 .....233 E3
Keep La TQ8 ....233 E4
Keep The EX22 ....242 C2
Keepers Cross EX16 ......49 A2
Kellacott Cross PL16 ....105 F7
Kelland Cl TQ3 ....226 A5
Kelland Cnr EX14 ....98 A1
Kelland Cross EX17 ......60 C2
Kelland Rd TQ3 ....226 A5
Kellands Row TQ7 ....258 D5
Kellaton Cross
  Beesands TQ7 ....149 C6
  East Allington TQ9 .....144 C5
Kellett Cl 10 TQ13 ......131 A5
Kellock Dr TQ9 ....223 B5
Kelly Cl Plymouth PL5 ..247 E8
  Torquay TQ2 ....220 C2
Kelly Coll PL19 ....171 D7
Kelly Cross TQ13 ....122 D8
Kelvin Ave PL4 ....263 C4
Kelvin Ho EX4 ....175 B1
Kelvin Ct Brixham TQ5 ..230 D5
  Torquay TQ1 ....214 C1
Kelway Rd TA21 ....160 E7
Kemmings Cl TQ4 ....225 F1
Kemp's La EX12 ....192 D7
Kempe Cl PL2 ....247 F6
Kempland La EX16 ....45 B2
Kempley Rd EX20 ....170 B5
Kemps Way TA22 ....33 D6
Kempton Terr PL11 .....247 B2
Kempshill PI PL2 ....247 E4
Kenbury Cres EX6 ......201 B6
Kenbury Dr EX2 ....181 C8
Kendal Pl PL5 ....244 E4
Kendall Cl EX4 ....261 C4
Kendall Rd EX10 ....188 B3
Kendall Ho EX14 ....166 C5
Kendlewood EX14 ....225 F3
Kenilworth Cl PL2 ....248 B7
Kenilworth Rd PL2 ......248 A8
Kenley Gdns PL5 ....243 F4
Kenmare Dr PL7 ....251 A5
Kenn CE Prim Sch EX6 ..181 B1
Kenn La PL4 ....244 B3
Kenn La Exeter EX6 .....181 F1
  Exminster EX6 ....182 A2
Kennacott Cross EX21 ...72 B1
Kennaway Rd EX11 .....169 F4
Kennedy Way
  Dunkeswell EX14 ....67 C2
  Tiverton EX16 ....161 C5
Kennel Bridge Cross
  EX20 ....92 E8
Kennel Hill PL7 ....250 D4
Kennel Hill Cl PL7 ....250 C4
Kennel La Georgeham EX33 ..8 A2
  Ivybridge PL21 ....237 B5
Kennels Rd TQ5 ....229 C4
Kennels The PL21 ....237 B6
Kennerland Cross EX39 ..38 E8
Kennerley Ave EX4 ......178 B8
Kennett Cl PL3 ....249 B6
Kenneth Ct TQ2 ....219 C8
Kennford Rd EX2 ....177 B3

Kennicot House King Edward
  VI Com Coll TQ9 ....223 B6
Kenniford Cross EX5 ....183 D8
Kennydown La EX18 .....59 B7
Kensall Cross EX36 ....20 B1
Kensey Cl TQ1 ....220 E6
Kensham Ave EX5 ....83 A6
Kensham Cl EX5 ....82 F6
Kensington Pl 8 PL4 ....248 F4
Kensington Rd PL4 .....263 B4
Kensington St EX5 ....82 B5
Kent Cl EX2 ....178 A4
Kent Rd Plymouth PL2 ..247 F5
  Tatworth TQ20 ....88 D8
Kent's Bglws TA20 ....88 D8
Kent's Cotts TA20 ....88 D8
Kent's La TQ1 ....220 E5
Kent's Orch TA20 ....88 D8
Kent's Rd TQ1 ....220 D5
Kentisbeare CE Prim Sch
  EX15 ....66 A3
Kentisbury Cty Prim Sch
  EX31 ....10 E6
Kenton Brook Ct TQ2 ...219 B8
Kenton Hill EX6 ....194 D3
Kenton Mews EX6 ....194 D3
Kenton Pl EX2 ....177 C2
Kenton Prim Sch EX6 ...194 D3
Kents Cavern* TQ1 ......220 E5
Kents Cl Tatworth TA20 ..88 C8
  Uffculme EX15 ....66 A7
Kents La TA20 ....88 D8
Kenwith Dr TQ2 ....258 D5
Kenwith Rd EX39 ....156 F4
Kenwith Terr EX39 ......156 F3
Kenwith View EX39 .....156 E3
Kenwyn Rd TQ1 ....220 C6
Keppel Pl PL2 ....247 F4
Keppel St PL2 ....247 F4
Keppel Terr 3 PL2 ....247 F4
Ker St PL1 ....247 E1
Ker St Ope PL1 ....247 E1
Kernou Rd TQ4 ....226 C5
Kernow Cl PL11 ....246 E3
Kinkin Ave PL6 ....246 E3
Kernstone Cross EX39 ...22 B2
Kerria Cl TQ3 ....225 E8
Kerries Cl TQ10 ....135 A2
Kerries La TQ10 ....135 A2
Kerries Rd TQ10 ....135 A2
Kersbrook La EX9 ....198 A3
Kerscott EX32 ....28 F8
Kerse Cross
  Thurlestone TQ7 ......143 B2
  Thurlestone, South Milton
  TQ7 ....143 C2
Kerse La TQ12 ....213 C6
Kerslake's Ct 9 EX14 ..166 C6
Kerswell Cross TQ13 ...124 A7
Kerswell La
  Kingskerswell TQ12 ...213 A5
  Molland EX36 ....31 C8
Kerswill Cross TQ9 ......135 D1
Kerswill Rd EX4 ....176 F4
Kestell Rd EX10 ....188 C4
Kester Cross PL21 ....170 D5
Kestor Dr Exeter EX4 ...178 A8
  Paignton TQ3 ....219 A1
Kestral Units PL5 ....244 A1
Kestrel Cl
  Okehampton EX20 ......170 B6
  Plymouth PL6 ....245 D8
Kestrel Way
  Barnstaple EX32 ....155 C5
  Exeter EX2 ....178 E5
Keswick Cres PL6 ....245 D2
Keveral Rd EX8 ....196 A1
Kew Ct EX2 ....176 E4
Kewbridge Cl EX39 .....157 B4
Keyberry TQ12 ....207 D1
Keyberry Pk TQ12 ......207 D1
Keyberry Rd TQ12 ......207 D1
Keyes Cl PL1 ....247 F2
Keyham Barton RC Prim Sch
  PL2 ....247 F6
Keyham Rd PL2 ....247 F6
Keyham St PL5 ....247 F6
Keyham Sta PL2 ....247 E6
Keymelford Cross EX17 ..79 C2
Keysfield Rd TQ4 ....226 C5
Khartoum Pl TQ1 ....220 B5
Khyber Cl PL11 ....247 A3
Kiddicott EX17 ....165 B5
Kidland La
  Bishops Nympton EX36 ..31 E1
  Molland EX36 ....46 E8
Kidwelly Cl PL7 ....251 B6
Kiel Pl PL1 ....249 D5
Kigbeare Cross EX20 ....93 B6
Kilb Arran Rise EX4 .....177 C8
Kilbury Terr TQ7 ....258 C4
Killarney Springs Leisure
  Pk* EX23 ....37 E1
Killatree Cross EX22 .....71 E7
Killerton Cl TQ3 ....226 B7
Killerton Ho 3 EX5 ......82 F6
Killigrew Ave PL12 .....242 D1
Killington Cross EX31 ....4 D2
Kilmorie TQ1 ....220 F3
Kilmorie Cl TQ1 ....220 F3
Kiln Cl Bovey Tracey TQ13 180 C5
  Plymouth PL9 ....255 E2
Kiln Close La 3 EX39 ...157 B1

Kiln Cross TQ3 ....218 D3
Kiln Ho TQ7 ....258 C4
Kiln La
1 Barnstaple EX32 ....155 A4
Branscombe EX12 .....190 B4
Combe Martin EX34 ......3 B2
Stokenham TQ7 ....145 B1
Kiln Orch TQ2 ....206 F3
Kiln Path TQ5 ....230 C4
Kiln Rd
Bovey Tracey TQ13 ....180 C5
Marldon TQ3 ....218 C3
Kilnford Rd TQ12 .....207 F7
Kilnwood Pk EX31 .....154 A3
Kilworthy TQ 220 B8
Kilworthy Hill PL19 ...171 C6
Kilworthy Rd PL19 ....171 C6
Kimber Cross EX20 .....74 E2
Kimberlands EX20 ......74 E2
Kimberley Terr EX39 ...157 A8
Kimberley Ct PL21 .....237 D5
Kimberley Rd EX2 .....261 B2
Kimberley Villas PL21 .237 C4
Kimberly Dr PL6 ....245 B1
Kimbland Cross EX32 ...18 C5
Kinevor CI EX34 ....7 F8
King Alfred Way EX2 ...186 E8
King Arthur's Rd EX4 ..174 A1
King Charles I Bsns Pk
TQ12 ....180 E4
King Edward Rd
Axminster EX13 ....167 C5
Saltash PL12 ....242 F2
King Edward St
12 Barnstaple EX32 ...154 F6
Exeter EX4 ....173 A1
King Edward Vi Com Coll
TQ9 ....223 B7
King Henry's Rd EX2 ...177 E3
King St 12 Bideford EX39 .157 A2
Brixham TQ5 ....230 D5
Colyton EX24 ....103 A5
Combe Martin EX34 .....3 A3
10 Dawlish EX7 ....204 D6
Exeter EX1,EX4 ....261 A2
8 Exmouth EX8 ....202 A6
Gunnislake PL18 ......125 D6
Honiton EX14 ....166 C6
Millbrook PL10 ....252 E5
Newton Abbot TQ12 ...207 C3
Plymouth PL1 ....262 B3
Silverton EX5 ....82 B6
South Molton EX36 ....158 C4
Tavistock PL19 ....171 B6
Tiverton EX16 ....161 C3
Torpoint PL11 ....247 C3
King William Ho EX4 ...261 B4
King William St EX4 ...258 D6
King's Ash Cross TQ3 ..225 E6
King's Ash Rd TQ3 ....225 E6
King's CI EX2 ....155 C2
King's Cnr TA22 ....33 D6
King's Cres EX16 ......161 E4
King's Cross TQ13 ....122 E6
King's Dr The TQ2 ....219 F4
King's Gdns EX14 .....166 C6
King's La
Bishop's Tawton EX32 ...27 F7
Lynton EX31 ....4 B5
King's Mill Rd EX15 ...163 C5
King's Nympton Prim Sch
EX37 ....44 E6
King's Nympton Station TA37 ..44 C5
King's Quay TQ6 ......233 F4
King's Quay Ho TQ6 ...233 F4
King's Rd Exeter EX4 ..177 E8
Honiton EX14 ....166 D6
Kennford EX6 ....114 A4
Plymouth PL1 ....248 A2
King's Tamerton Rd PL5 .248 F2
Kingdom Mews EX4 ....177 A7
Kingdom's Cnr EX16 ...63 C4
Kingdon Ent Pk EX39 ...25 D4
Kingfisher CI
Plymouth PL6 ....245 E6
Torquay TQ2 ....213 D2
Kingfisher Ct EX4 .....174 D1
Kingfisher Dr
Barnstaple EX32 ......155 E4
Exeter EX4 ....173 D2
Kingfisher Gdns EX15 .163 B2
Kingfisher Gn EX2 ....176 D3
Kings Ave
Ottery St Mary EX11 ...169 F4
Paignton TQ3 ....226 C7
Kings Coombe Dr 16
TQ12 ....123 F1
Kings Cotts
6 Newton Abbot TQ12 ..207 C3
Salcombe TQ8 ....259 E5
Kings Ct Honiton EX14 ..166 C6
Kingsbridge TQ7 ......258 D3
6 Kingskerswell TQ12 .212 F4
Kingsteignton TQ12 ...207 F6
Plymouth PL1 ....248 A3
Kings Farm La EX19 ....58 F3
Kings La EX10 ....188 B3
Kings Mdw TQ12 ......212 F4
Kings Meadow Dr EX19 ..58 F3
Kings Orch TQ9 ....223 E5
Kings Pk EX18 ....44 E1
Kings Rd Barnstaple EX32 .155 B6
Paignton TQ3 ....226 C7
Plymouth, Devonport PL1,PL2 .247 E3
Plymouth, West Park PL5 .243 F3

Kings Rydon CI TQ9 ...227 F8
Kings Sch PL3 ....248 E6
Kings Sch The EX11 ....169 B3
Kings Terr EX14 ....166 C6
Kings Way EX20 ....106 E5
Kingsacre EX33 ....152 C6
Kingsacre Prim Sch
EX33 ....152 C6
Kingsale Rd TQ8 ......259 C4
Kingsbridge Com Coll
(Tressilian Campus)
TQ7 ....258 CG
Kingsbridge Com Coll
(Westville Campus)
TQ7 ....258 C4
Kingsbridge Com Prim Sch
TQ7 ....258 E6
Kingsbridge Hill TQ9 ..223 C4
Kingsbridge La TQ13 ..130 F4
Kingsbridge Rd TQ10 ..137 E8
Kingsbridgefork Cross
TQ9 ....144 E5
Kingscott Hill EX38 ....42 B4
Kingsdale TQ16 TQ 220 D4
Kingsdon Hill EX24 ...103 B5
Kingsdown CI
Dawlish EX7 ....204 E7
Teignmouth TQ14 .....209 D7
Kingsdown Cres EX7 ..204 E7
Kingsdown Rd TQ14 ...209 D7
Kingsgate EX4 ....177 D8
Kingsgate Bsns Units 5
EX14 ....166 A4
Kingsgate CI TQ2 .....213 A4
Kingsholme EX24 .....103 B3
Kingshurst Dr TQ3 ....226 B8
Kingskerswell CE Prim Sch
TQ12 ....213 A5
Kingskerswell Cross
TQ12 ....213 C3
Kingskerswell Rd
Newton Abbot TQ12 ...212 D7
Torquay TQ2 ....213 D3
Kingslade La EX10 ....187 B2
Kingslake Ct EX8 .....202 A8
Kingslake Rise EX8 ...202 A8
Kingsland Ct TQ4 .....225 E4
Kingsland Dr TQ4 ....225 E4
Kingsland Gardens CI
PL3 ....248 E6
Kingsleigh Manor TQ1 ..220 C5
Kingsley Ave
10 Appledore EX39 .....15 A1
8 Barnstaple EX32 ....154 F6
Exeter EX4 ....177 B8
Ilfracombe EX34 ......150 B3
Torpoint PL11 ....247 B2
Kingsley CI PL21 .....136 D6
Kingsley Pk EX39 .....156 E7
Kingsley Rd
Bideford EX39 ....157 A3
Kingsbridge TQ7 .....258 C4
Plymouth PL4 ....248 E4
Westward Ho! EX39 ...156 C6
Kingsley Terr EX39 ...157 A1
6 Combe Martin EX34 ..3 A3
Kingsmead Dr EX38 ...159 E6
Kingsmead Ho TQ3 ...226 B7
Kingsmill Ind Est EX15 .163 E5
Kingsmill Rd PL12 ....242 C5
Kingsmoor Cross EX21 ..73 E7
Kingsteignton Rd TQ12 .207 C4
Kingstephen CI EX4 ...261 B4
Kingston Ave 4 EX34 ...3 A3
Kingston CI
Kingskerswell TQ12 ...213 A5
Plymouth PL7 ....251 A5
Kingston Dr PL7 ......251 B5
Kingston Gate Cross
TQ9 ....216 A6
Kingston La TQ6 ......233 E3
Kingston Rd
Exmouth EX8 ....202 C7
Stoke Climsland PL17 .115 C1
Kingston Workshops
TQ9 ....216 A7
Kingsteynton Rd TQ5 ..230 C5
Kingsway Cawsand PL10 .253 B2
Kingsway EX4 ....177 F5
Lyme Regis DT7 ......260 E4
South Molton EX36 ...158 C3
Teignmouth TQ14 .....209 D7
Kingsway Ave TQ4 ....226 A1
Kingsway Ct TQ4 .....226 A1
Kingsway CI TQ4 .....226 A1
Kingsway Dr TQ4 .....226 A1
Kingsway Gdns PL6 ...244 F3
Kingsway Pk TQ7 .....258 C4
Kingswear Cres PL6 ...245 B1
Kingswear Prim Sch
TQ6 ....234 B3
Kingswear Rd TQ5 ....234 F8
Kingswear Sta TQ6 ...234 F8
Kingswood Ct EX4 ....176 E8
Kingswood Cross EX34 ..3 A3
Kingswood Mdw EX22 ..164 D5
Kingswood Park Ave
PL3 ....248 D6
Kingswood Rd PL18 ...125 D6
Kinlacey Ct TQ1 ......220 C6
Kinnaird Cres PL6 ....244 F7
Kinnard Cres PL6 .....244 F7
Kinnerton Cross EX4 ..176 F8
Kinnerton Way EX4 ...176 E8
Kinross Ave PL4 ......249 A4
Kinsale Rd EX4 ......243 F3

Kinscombe Ct TQ11 ...236 C5
Kinsford Gate Cross
TA24 ....19 D7
Kinsford Hill TA24 ....19 E7
Kinterbury Rd PL5 ....247 B8
Kinterbury St PL1 .....263 A2
Kinterbury Terr PL1 ...247 B8
Kintyre CI TQ2 ....213 E2
Kinver CI PL6 ....245 D4
Kipling Ct EX39 ......156 C6
Kipling Dr EX2 ....177 F4
Kipling Gdns PL5 ....244 D2
Kipling Terr EX39 ....156 C6
Kipscombe Cross EX35 ...6 A6
Kipscombe Hill EX31 ..11 D2
Kirby CI EX13 ....167 D5
Kirby PI PL4 ....262 C4
Kirby Terr PL4 ....262 C4
Kirkdale Gdns PL2 ...248 B7
Kirkella Rd PL20 .....127 A8
Kirkham Ct 1 TQ3 ...226 A7
Kirkham House Mus*
TQ3 ....226 B6
Kirkham St 4 TQ3 ....226 B7
Kirkland CI PL6 ......245 E7
Kirkstall CI PL2 ......248 A8
Kirkstead CI TQ2 ....219 E8
Kirkwall Rd PL5 ......244 E3
Kirton La EX16 ....48 A1
Kirton PI PL3 ....249 B5
Kirtons Rd TQ12 .....214 B7
Kismeldon Cross EX22 ..39 B3
Kissing Gate Cross EX16 .48 D5
Kit Hill Cres PL5 .....247 C8
Kitchadon Gate EX18 ...56 D4
Kitchadon Rd EX18 ...59 D3
Kitcott Cross EX36 ....45 F6
Kitcott Hill EX36 ......45 F6
Kitley View PL8 ......257 B5
Kitley Way PL5 ....243 D1
Kitridge La TA24 ......21 B7
Kits CI TQ13 ....123 F6
Kitter Dr PL9 ....256 A5
Kitterford Cross PL21 .137 F7
Kittersley Dr 10 TQ12 .122 F1
Kitts TA21 ....160 D4
Kitts Cross EX10 .....187 A7
Kitts La EX10 ....187 B6
Kitwell St EX5 ....66 A7
Kitty Wlk PL6 ....170 D2
Knacker's Hole La TA3 ..68 A6
Knackershole La EX17 ..61 B2
Knap Cross PL21 .....136 C4
Knap Down La EX34 ....3 B4
Knapp Hill EX10 .....188 A5
Knapp House Holiday Camp
EX39 ....15 B1
Knapp Park Rd TQ4 ..226 C2
Knapp's La EX10 ......100 D1
Knapps CI PL9 ....256 C6
Knaves Ash Cross TQ9 .217 A5
Kneela Hill EX21 ......54 B4
Kneele Gdns PL3 .....248 E8
Kneller CI EX34 ......150 C4
Knick Knack La TQ5 ..230 C3
Knight's La EX11 .....69 A4
Knightacott Cross EX32 .11 C2
Knighthayes Wlk EX6 .181 F5
Knightley Rd EX2 ....177 E3
Knighton Cross TQ12 .131 F8
Knighton Hill Bsns Ctr
PL9 ....140 E8
Knighton Rd
Plymouth PL4 ....262 C3
Wembury PL9 ....140 D8
Knighton Terr 4 PL20 .126 F3
Knights Cres EX2 .....178 D3
Knights Field Way EX39 .157 A8
Knights Rd TA21 ......52 D8
Knightstone Down La
EX17 ....61 C2
Knightstone La
Ottery St Mary EX11 ...169 F1
Ottery St Mary EX11 ...169 F1
Knightstone Rd EX11 ..169 F1
Knightswood EX15 ...163 C2
Knights CI PL6 ....252 E5
Knockworthy Cross EX38 .26 F1
Knoll Knap EX13 .....103 E4
Knoll The PL7 ....250 B6
Knowland CI PL1 .....247 F3
Knowle Ave PL2 .....247 E6
Knowle CI
Ashburton TQ13 .....130 E4
Cullompton EX15 .....163 A3
Lamtey EX32 ....166 C6
Lindley EX32 ....17 B2
Knowle Cnr EX9 .....197 D1
Knowle Cross
Bovey Tracey TQ13 ...123 C8
Copplestone EX17 ....79 C4
Knowle CI TQ8 ....259 D5
Knowle Dr Exeter EX4 .176 F7
Sidmouth EX10 ....188 A4
Knowle Fork TQ2 ....148 F4
Knowle Gdns
Combe Martin EX34 ....3 A3
Kingsbridge TQ7 .....258 C6
Sidmouth EX10 ....187 F4
Knowle Grange EX10 ..188 A4
Knowle Gr TQ2 ......148 F4
Knowle Ho (Fire Service HQ)
EX2 ....183 B6
Knowle House CI TQ2 .258 D6
Knowle La
Butterleigh EX15 ......64 F1
Copplestone EX17 .....79 C4

Knowle La continued
Drewsteignton EX6 ....96 D1
Knowle Prim Sch PL5 .244 A4
Knowle Rd
Budleigh Salterton EX9 .197 E1
Lustleigh TQ13 ....122 C8
Salcombe TQ8 ....259 D5
Knowle Terr PL20 ....127 B4
Knowle View EX20 ....58 D6
Knowles Cross TQ13 ..130 E4
Knowles Dr 22 EX24 ..103 A4
Knowles Hill Rd TQ12 .207 B4
Knowles Hill Sch
Newton Abbot TQ12 ...207 A4
Newton Abbot TQ12 ...207 B4
Knowstone Cross EX16 .47 D6
Knowstone Moor Cross
EX36 ....47 B8
Kyl Cober Parc PL17 ..115 C1
Kynance CI PL11 .....246 F4
Kynock Ind Est EX39 ..25 F4

L

Labbett's Cross EX18 ..60 C6
Laboon La EX18 ......59 C7
Laburnam Ct TQ12 ...212 B6
Laburnam Terr TQ12 ..212 B7
Laburnam Gr TQ9 ....223 A7
Laburnum CI
Exmouth EX8 ....196 D3
1 Honiton EX14 ....85 C2
Laburnum Cotts PL19 .171 C6
Laburnum Dr
Barnstaple EX32 .....155 E3
6 Wembury PL9 ......140 D8
Laburnum Rd Exeter EX2 .177 F3
Newton Abbot TQ12 ...207 E1
Wellington TA21 .....160 E5
Laburnum Row 4 TQ2 .219 F6
Laburnum St TQ2 ....219 F5
Laburnum Villas PL19 .117 E6
Laburnum Way TQ9 ..144 E7
Lace Wlk EX14 ....166 C6
Lackabourough Ct EX22 .181 A8
Lacy Rd TQ3 ....219 A1
Ladder La EX34 ....3 B3
Ladies Mile EX31 .....A4 A4
Ladies' Mile EX32 ....165 B6
Ladram Rd EX9 ......199 A8
Lady Harriet Acland's Dr
TA22 ....34 A8
Lady Meadow Terr
PL20 ....121 B2
Landrake CI PL5 .....244 D2
Lady La PL9 ....255 F7
Lady Park Rd TQ2 ....219 D3
Lady Seawards Prim Sch
EX3 ....183 C6
Lady St TA22 ....33 D7
Lady Victoria's Dr TA22 .33 E6
Ladymead EX10 .....187 F8
Ladysmith CI PL4 ....263 C4
Ladysmith Fst Sch EX1 .177 F7
Ladysmith Rd Exeter EX1 .177 F7
Plymouth PL4 ....249 B3
Ladywell PI PL4 .....263 B3
Lag Hill EX17 ....62 F1
Lagge Hill Cross EX17 .85 B4
Laggan View EX31 ...153 A4
Lahteglos CI PL21 ....137 C7
Laira Ave PL3 ....249 D4
Laira Bridge Rd PL4 ..249 B1
Laira Gn EX9 ....
Laira Green Prim Sch
PL3 ....249 C4
Laira Park Cres PL4 ..249 B4
Laira Park PI PL4 ....249 B4
Laira Park Rd PL4 ....249 B4
Laira PI PL4 ....249 C2
Laira St PL4 ....249 B2
Laity Wlk PL6 ....244 D6
Lake Ave TQ14 ......210 A7
Lake CI EX14 ....166 C5
Lake Cross TQ9 .....131 D2
Lake La EX34 ....166 C6
Lake St TQ6 ....233 F3
Lake View EX17 .....165 E6
Lake View CI PL5 ....244 B6
Lakelands Ct EX16 ...46 C1
Lakelands Dr EX4 ...176 F6
Lakenham Cotts EX39 .156 F7
Lakenham Hill EX39 ..156 F7
Lakes CI TQ5 ....230 A5
Lakes Cross EX20 .....57 A8
Lakes La EX4 ....230 A4
Lakes Rd TQ5 ....230 A4
Lakeside
Abbotskerswell TQ12 .212 B6
Buckland Monachorum PL20 .126 C3
Great Torrington EX38 .58 F7
Newton Abbot TQ12 ...207 E2
Northlew EX20 ....74 D2
Stockleigh Pomeroy EX17 .81 A7
Lakeside Ave PL6 ....182 B8
Lakeside CI TQ13 ....180 C4
Lakeside Dr PL5 .....243 E5
Lakeview Dr PL5 .....244 B6
Lakewater Cross TQ9 .131 E1
Lalebrick Rd PL9 ....255 B5
Lama Cross EX14 .....59 C4
Lamacraft CI EX7 ....204 F8
Lamacraft Dr EX4 ....178 A7

Lamaton Pk EX36 .....158 D3
Lamb Park CI 10 TQ12 .123 F1
Lamb Pk Chagford TQ13 .111 A6
Drewsteignton EX6 ....96 D1
Ilfracombe EX34 .....150 A4
Lamb The TQ9 ....223 B5
Lambert CI EX7 ......204 F8
Lambert Cross EX20 ..75 A3
Lambert La EX6 ....9 B7
Lambert Rd PL5 ......244 B6
Lambert's La TQ14 ...209 D4
Lambhay Hill PL1 ....263 A1
Lambhay St PL1 ......263 A1
Lambpark Ct TA3 ....68 A8
Lambs CI TQ7 ....143 A2
Lambscombe Cross EX31 .34 A8
Lambscombe Hill EX36 .31 A8
Lamejohns Field EX17 .165 D6
Lamerhooe Cross PL19 .116 A1
Lamerhooe Dr PL19 ..116 A1
Lamerton Cross EX20 ..75 F2
Lammacott La EX17 ...78 E6
Lammacott La EX17 ...78 E6
Lammas La TQ1 ......220 B4
Lamonaby Rd TQ8 ...246 E4
Lampard-Vachell Sch The
EX32 ....155 C3
Lamplough Rd EX8 ...196 A3
Lana Cotts EX22 ......89 F7
Lana Cross EX22 ......55 C1
Lanbridge Cross TQ9 .222 F1
Lancaster CI
Cullompton EX15 ....163 C5
Exeter EX2 ....178 B5
Lancaster Dr TQ4 ...226 A2
Lancaster Gdns PL5 .244 D4
Lancaster Ho TQ4 ...226 C5
Lancelot Rd EX4 .....174 A2
Lancer CI TA21 ......160 D6
Lancercombe La EX10 .100 D3
Lanchitt Cross EX36 ...19 B2
Lancock St TA21 .....160 A5
Land Pk EX18 ....44 E1
Landacre La TA24 ....21 A7
Landboat Cotts EX17 ..62 F1
Landboat View EX17 ..62 F1
Landcroft La EX15 ....66 F4
Lander Rd PL2 ....242 F3
Landhayes Rd EX4 ...176 F5
Landkey Prim Sch EX32 .17 B2
Landkey Rd EX32 ....155 C2
Landlord's Hill TA21 ..51 E7
Landmark Rd TQ8 ...259 B4
Landpath TQ7 ....143 A2
Landrake CI PL5 .....244 D2
Lands Rd Brixham TQ5 .230 F6
Exeter EX4 ....174 D1
Landscore EX17 .....165 B5
Landscore CI
Crediton EX17 ......165 B5
Teignmouth TQ14 ...210 B5
Landscore Rd
EX17 ....165 A5
Landscove Rd
8 Exeter EX4 ....177 A5
Teignmouth TQ14 ...210 B5
TQ13 ....131 B1
Landsdowne Pk TQ9 .223 E4
Landsend La EX17 ...78 E6
Landulph Cross PL12 .238 F1
Landulph Gdns PL5 ..247 C8
Landuph Sch PL12 ...238 F1
Lane Cross EX22 .....53 F7
Lane End Cross
Broadhembury EX14 ..84 E8
Broadhempston TQ13 .131 D3
Halwill EX21 ....73 D3
Lane End Rd EX24 ...103 A4
Lane End Bro La EX32 .155 D4
Lane End Pool TQ9 ..227 B3
Lane End Rd EX39 ....15 B1
Lane Field Rd EX39 ..156 D2
Lane Head CI EX33 ...7 F2
Lane The Ottisham TQ6 .228 D2
Lutton PL21 ....133 B2
Lanehead Rd EX22 ...191 D5
Lanepark La EX39 .....37 A5
Lang Gdns PL18 .....125 D3
Lang Gr Plymouth PL9 .256 C7
Tavistock PL19 ......171 D4
Lang Way TQ12 ....211 E2
Langaford La EX21 ....73 B2
Langage Cross PL7 ...251 F6
Langage Ind Est PL7 .251 D4
Langage Pk PL7 .....251 C4
Langage Science Pk
PL7 ....
Langaller CI TQ13 ....180 B5
Langaller Hill TQ22 ..33 D4
Langaller La TQ13 ...180 B4
Langarron Pk EX32 ..155 B5
Langdale Gdns EX1 ..174 F1
Langaton La EX1 .....175 A1
Langbrook Cross EX21 .245 D1
Langdale CI PL6 .....245 D1
Langdale Gdns PL6 ..245 D1
Langdon Cross PL21 .137 F1
Langdon Ct PL21 .....256 B6
Langdon Down Way
PL5 ....246 E3
Langdon Fields TQ5 .229 B6
Langdon Hospl EX7 ..200 E2
Langdon La Dawlish EX7 .204 C8
Galmpton TQ4,TQ5 ...229 B6

Langdon Rd
  Bradworthy EX22 ....38 E1
  Dawlish EX7 ....204 D8
  Paignton TQ3 ....219 C1
Langdons Way TQ10 ....88 C8
Langerwehe Way EX8 ....201 F6
Langerwell Cl PL12 ....242 C3
Langerwell La PL12 ....242 C3
Langfield Terr ⑥ EX34 ....150 C5
Langford Ave EX14 ....166 D6
Langford Cres TQ2 ....213 F3
Langford Cross EX17 ....78 B4
Langford Gate PL21 ....137 F8
Langford Gn EX15 ....83 D5
Langford Rd
  Honiton EX14 ....166 D7
  Honiton EX14 ....166 E8
  Langford EX5 ....172 E7
Langham Cross EX19 ....57 D6
Langham La EX17 ....61 F2
Langham Levels PL21 ....237 B6
Langham Pl PL4 ....263 C3
Langham Way PL21 ....237 C5
Langhill Rd PL3 ....248 D5
Langland Hill EX17 ....61 A4
Langland La EX13 ....169 B7
Langlands Bsns Pk EX15 ....65 F6
Langlands Cl TQ4 ....225 E4
Langlands Cross EX14 ....87 A6
Langlands Rd EX15 ....163 A3
Langleigh La EX34 ....150 A4
Langleigh Pk EX34 ....150 A4
Langleigh Rd EX34 ....150 A5
Langley Ave TQ5 ....230 C4
Langley Cl Brixham TQ5 ....230 C4
Langley Com Inf Sch
  PL6 ....245 A6
Langley Cres PL6 ....244 F7
Langley Cross EX37 ....27 F3
Langley Gdns EX18 ....44 E1
Langley La EX18 ....44 E1
Langmead EX39 ....157 E5
Langmead Cl PL6 ....249 C8
Langmead Rd PL6 ....249 C8
Langmoor La EX13 ....88 D2
Langmore Cl PL6 ....249 A7
Langridge Cross EX37 ....27 F1
Langridge Rd TQ3 ....225 E8
Langs Rd TQ3 ....226 A8
Langsfield EX33 ....7 D1
Langsford Rd PL19 ....117 E3
Langston Cross PL21 ....142 D7
Langstone Cl
  Heathfield TQ12 ....180 F2
  Torquay TQ1 ....220 D6
Langstone Cross TQ13 ....121 E8
Langstone Dr EX8 ....196 C1
Langstone Hill
  Lustleigh TQ13 ....121 E8
  Moretonhampstead TQ13 ....111 C1
Langstone Rd TQ2 ....248 C7
Langstone Terr EX34 ....248 C7
Langton Rd ⑧ PL20 ....126 F3
Langtree Com Prim Sch
  EX38 ....40 F2
Langwells Ct TQ9 ....139 E1
Langworthys Barn TQ7 ....143 E2
Lanherne EX7 ....204 E6
Lanherne Sch EX7 ....204 D6
Lanhydrock Cl TQ3 ....225 D8
Lanhydrock Rd PL4 ....249 B2
Lannacombe Gn TQ7 ....149 C5
Lanscore La EX14 ....101 A8
Lansdown Terr ② EX34 ....155 A6
Lansdowne EX22 ....178 B4
Lansdowne La ② TQ2 ....219 F5
Lansdowne Pk EX39 ....156 F8
Lansdowne Rd
  Budleigh Salterton EX9 ....197 D1
  Plymouth PL6 ....244 F2
  ① Torquay TQ2 ....219 F5
Lansdowne Terr
  Bideford EX39 ....156 F1
  Exeter EX2 ....261 B2
Lapford Com Prim Sch
  EX17 ....60 D3
Lapford Cross EX17 ....60 C2
Lapford Sta EX17 ....60 C2
Lapthorn Cl PL9 ....255 C7
Lapwing Cl EX15 ....163 A3
Larch Cl Exmouth EX8 ....196 D3
  Saltash PL12 ....242 C3
  Seaton EX12 ....192 A8
  Teignmouth TQ14 ....210 B8
Larch Dr PL6 ....245 E7
Larch Rd EX4 ....176 F3
Larch Wlk TQ2 ....219 C8
Larcombe End TQ9 ....135 F1
Lark Cl EX4 ....173 D1
Lark Hill PL2 ....248 A6
Lark Rise
  ⑤ Barnstaple EX31 ....154 A2
  Newton Poppleford EX10 ....186 E8
Larkbeare Ave EX5 ....100 B8
Larkbeare Cross EX5 ....100 B8
Larkbeare Rd EX2 ....261 B1
Larkey La EX16 ....63 D4
Larkhall Rise PL3 ....249 B5
Larkham Cl PL7 ....250 C6
Larkham La PL7 ....250 C6
Larks Cl TQ14 ....209 D4
Larks Mdw EX15 ....163 A2
Larkshayes Cross EX13 ....86 E3
Larkshayes Droveway
  EX13 ....86 F3
Larkshayes Knap EX13 ....86 F3

Larksmead Cl TQ12 ....207 A1
Larksmead Way TQ12 ....207 A1
Larkspur Gdns EX32 ....155 E4
Larkstone Cres ⑥ EX34 ....150 D5
Larkstone Gdns EX34 ....150 D5
Larkstone La EX34 ....150 D6
Larkstone Terr EX34 ....150 D6
Lashbrook EX5 ....84 B2
Lashingcott Cross EX31 ....27 B3
Lashingcott Lane End
  EX31 ....27 B2
Laskeys Heath ① TQ12 ....122 F1
Laskeys La EX10 ....188 B6
Latch La EX38 ....40 E2
Latches Wlk EX14 ....167 D6
Latchgate Cross EX36 ....31 F7
Latchgate Hill EX36 ....31 F7
Latham Cl PL4 ....249 A7
Latimer Cl PL7 ....251 B5
Latimer La EX16 ....178 A8
Latimer Wlk PL4 ....244 E7
Lauder La EX31 ....154 C1
Lauderdale ⑤ EX32 ....155 B4
Lauderdale Dr EX32 ....155 B4
Launceston Cl PL6 ....245 B7
Launceston Head EX5 ....83 C1
Launceston Rd EX20 ....107 E8
Laura Ave TQ3 ....226 A8
Laura Gr TQ3 ....226 A8
Laurel Ave EX39 ....156 E1
Laurel Bank EX14 ....85 B4
Laurel Cl PL2 ....247 F8
Laurel Dene PL7 ....248 A7
Laurel Dr PL6 ....245 E6
Laurel La TQ14 ....209 D5
Laurel Rd EX2 ....177 F3
  ① Honiton EX14 ....166 A4
  Plymouth PL2 ....248 A7
Laurel Rise EX8 ....202 D8
Laurels The
  Barnstaple EX31 ....154 B2
  Sidmouth EX10 ....188 A5
Laurston Rd TQ12 ....207 C2
Laurie Ave TQ12 ....206 F4
Lauriston Cl TQ12 ....220 A5
Lavender Cl TQ5 ....230 A4
Lavender Cres TQ3 ....218 D2
Lavington Cl PL7 ....251 B5
Lavinia Dr PL7 ....250 C5
Law Wlk PL6 ....244 D6
Lawn Cl ② Plymouth PL7 ....251 A5
  Torquay TQ2 ....213 F4
Lawn Dr TQ13 ....123 C6
Lawn Gdns ⑩ TQ13 ....123 C6
Lawn Hill ③ EX7 ....204 E6
Lawn Rd EX8 ....202 A7
Lawn Terr ② EX7 ....204 D6
Lawns The
  ⑤ Budleigh Salterton EX9 ....198 A1
  Tavistock PL19 ....171 D6
  ① Wellington TA21 ....160 D6
Lawns The Plymouth PL5 ....188 B5
  Torpoint PL11 ....247 A4
Lawrence Ave EX4 ....177 A5
Lawrence La Bittaford PL21 ....137 C8
  Combe Martin EX34 ....3 C2
Lawrence Pl TQ2 ....220 B4
Lawrence Rd PL9 ....255 A6
Lawson Gr PL9 ....255 C7
Laxton Ave EX1 ....178 C6
Layne Cl EX6 ....113 B4
Layne Fields EX6 ....113 B4
Laywell Cl TQ5 ....230 B2
Laywell Rd TQ5 ....230 A3
Lazenby Rd EX16 ....161 F3
Le Locle Cl EX10 ....187 F8
Le Marchant Cl EX34 ....67 B1
Le Molay-Littry Way
  TQ13 ....180 C7
Lea Combe EX13 ....167 D5
Lea La EX9 ....198 C4
Lea Mount TQ14 ....209 A8
Lea Mount Cl EX7 ....204 D5
Lea Mount Dr EX7 ....204 D5
Lea Mount Rd EX7 ....204 E5
Lea Rd Otterton EX9 ....198 E2
  Tiverton EX16 ....161 F6
  Torquay TQ2 ....214 B3
Lea Side EX6 ....112 E8
Lea Terr EX39 ....15 A1
Lea The TQ14 ....207 A3
Lea Vale Rd TQ12 ....207 A3
Lea View EX15 ....162 D5
Leaches La EX18 ....60 B7
Leachway La EX2 ....113 F7
Leachway Lane Cross
  EX2 ....113 F7
Leadengate Cl EX33 ....7 E1
Leadengate Fields EX33 ....7 D1
Leader La TQ3 ....218 D2
Leaholes Ave EX20 ....170 C5
Lealands TQ13 ....180 C6
Leander Cl ⑤ TQ12 ....210 B4
Leander Way PL5 ....244 D2
Leanway PL12 ....242 E2
Lear La EX15 ....167 C4
Lear Pk EX15 ....83 A5
Lears La ⑥ TQ13 ....123 F6
Leary Cross EX12 ....29 B8
Leas Rd EX9 ....198 A1
Leas The EX34 ....150 A3
Lease Cotts EX5 ....82 D4
Lease Cotts Rd EX5 ....82 E4
Leat Cl PL20 ....127 B3
Leat Mdw
  ③ Liverton TQ12 ....122 F1
  Tiverton EX16 ....161 B5

Leat Rd PL16 ....105 F3
Leat St EX16 ....161 B5
Leat View PL12 ....242 B3
Leat Wlk Plymouth PL3 ....248 E6
  Roborough PL6 ....241 D1
Leather Cl PL6 ....244 F4
Leather Cl PL6 ....244 F4
Leather Tor Cl ④ PL20 ....126 F3
Leatside Exeter EX2 ....261 C1
  Roborough PL6 ....241 C1
Leatside Hospl TQ12 ....207 A3
Leatway Gdns EX15 ....163 B3
Leaves Yd PL3 ....249 B7
Leaway Cotts EX15 ....163 E4
Leaze Rd TQ12 ....207 D8
Lebanon Cl EX4 ....173 E1
Leburnick Cross PL15 ....115 B8
Ledgate La Plymouth PL7 ....251 F8
  Sparkwell PL7 ....132 F1
Ledsgrove TQ12 ....211 E2
Ledstone Cross TQ7 ....144 B5
Lee Ave EX39 ....25 F1
Lee Ball Cross EX31 ....11 E3
Lee Ball Hill EX31 ....11 D3
Lee Cl EX5 ....99 F8
Lee Cross
  Broadhempston TQ9 ....131 E1
  Great Torrington EX37 ....42 F7
  North Molton EX36 ....30 B8
  Woolacombe EX34 ....1 C1
Lee Ct TQ5 ....230 E4
Lee La
  Bishops Nympton EX36 ....31 F6
  Dartmouth TQ6 ....232 C2
  Hartland EX39 ....22 E7
Lee Lane End TQ7 ....148 F8
Lee Mill Hospl PL21 ....136 C6
Lee Mill Ind Est PL21 ....136 C6
Lee Pk TA21 ....52 F7
Lee Rd EX35 ....151 B5
Lee Terr ① TQ13 ....123 E6
Leechwell La TQ9 ....223 C5
Leechwell St TQ9 ....223 B5
Leecross Gate EX17 ....61 A7
Leeford La EX35 ....6 B5
Leeford Ho EX35 ....6 B5
Lees Mdw EX5 ....84 A2
Leeward La TQ2 ....213 E3
Leeze Park Est EX20 ....170 B4
Leggetts La PL7 ....251 A5
Legion La PL8 ....257 A5
Legion Way EX2 ....177 B2
Legis Wlk PL6 ....245 B8
Leicester Mead EX4 ....176 E7
Leigh Cl PL21 ....137 C8
Leigh Cross
  Bittaford PL21 ....137 D8
  Bovey Tracey TQ13 ....123 C7
  Chulmleigh EX18 ....59 C8
  Doddiscombsleigh EX6 ....113 B6
  Kentisbeare EX15 ....66 B5
  Modbury PL21 ....137 F3
  South Brent TQ10 ....135 A4
  Zeal Monachorum EX17 ....77 F7
Leigh Cross Rd ⑥ EX14 ....249 A8
Leigh La Bittaford PL21 ....137 C8
  Combe Martin EX34 ....3 C2
  Roborough PL6 ....241 D2
Leigh Rd Bideford EX39 ....156 E1
  Chulmleigh EX18 ....44 D1
  Marldon TQ3 ....218 D3
Leigh Villas EX18 ....44 E1
Leigham Ct
  ⑦ Dawlish EX7 ....204 E6
  Plymouth PL1 ....262 B2
Leigham Inf & Jun Schs
  PL6 ....245 E1
Leigham St PL1 ....262 B1
Leigham Terr ① PL1 ....258 C5
Leigham Terrace La
  PL1 ....262 B2
Leighcott Cross EX17 ....62 A2
Leighcott La EX17 ....62 A2
Leighmoor Cross PL21 ....137 F3
Leighton Rd TQ3 ....248 F8
Leighton Terr EX4 ....261 B4
Leighty Water EX38 ....42 A6
Leland Gr PL7 ....237 D4
Lembury Rd PL21 ....225 A1
Lemon Pl TQ12 ....207 C2
Lemon Rd TQ12 ....207 C3
Lemonford La TQ12 ....131 D7
Lenards Rd EX39 ....156 F6
Lenda La TQ12 ....122 C2
Lendon Way EX19 ....58 F2
Lennard Rd ⑧ TQ12 ....165 C5
Lennox Ave EX10 ....188 B4
Lentney Cl PL9 ....140 A8
Lenton La EX37 ....44 C6
Lenwood Ctry Club
  EX39 ....156 C5
Lenwood Pk EX39 ....156 D6
Lenwood Rd EX39 ....156 D6
Leofric Rd EX16 ....161 D6
Leonard Moor Cross
  EX15 ....65 F8
Leonards Cl TQ7 ....143 A1
Leonards Rd PL21 ....137 C2
Lerwell Beech Tree Cross
  EX37 ....29 A5
Leslie Rd EX8 ....202 A8
Lescove Cl PL7 ....249 B6
Lestock Cl EX8 ....202 F7
Lethaby Rd EX22 ....155 B6
Lethbridge Rd EX2 ....178 B4

Lethbridge's & Davey's
  Almshouses EX1 ....261 C4
Lettaford Cross TQ13 ....111 B3
Level The TQ6 ....228 C2
Leverlake Cl EX16 ....161 F6
Leverlake Cl EX16 ....161 F6
Leverlake La EX16 ....161 F7
Lewdon Cross EX6 ....97 A5
Lewes Gdns PL5 ....244 C4
Lewhaven Cl EX20 ....106 E5
Lewis Ave EX16 ....161 E4
Lewis Cres EX2 ....178 D3
Lewis Cl ④ EX34 ....150 B5
Leworthy Cross EX39 ....39 B6
Leworthy Hill EX31 ....11 D1
Leworthy Post EX32 ....11 C1
Lewsley Cross EX13 ....87 E4
Lewsley La EX13 ....87 E4
Lewthorn Cross TQ13 ....122 B3
Lewtrenchard Cty Prim Sch
  EX20 ....106 F5
Lexhayne La EX13 ....103 A7
Ley Cl TQ12 ....180 B1
Ley Cres TQ12 ....180 B1
Ley Cross Ashreigney EX18 ....58 F8
  Aveton Gifford PL21 ....143 A8
  Ermington PL21 ....136 D4
  Holsworthy Beacon EX22 ....54 B6
  North Molton EX36 ....30 F8
  Widecombe in the Moor
  TQ13 ....121 C6
Ley La Bere Ferrers PL20 ....239 D6
  Combe Martin EX31 ....10 D6
  Kingsteignton TQ12 ....207 D8
Ley Meadow Dr EX31 ....154 A3
Ley's Cross EX17 ....62 E2
Ley's La EX31 ....4 C1
Leyburn Gr TQ4 ....226 A4
Leyfield Wlk EX7 ....204 E7
Leyford Cl PL9 ....140 D8
Leyland Cross EX22 ....53 E8
Leypark Cl PL7 ....178 C7
Leypark Cres EX1 ....178 C7
Leypark Dr PL6 ....245 E2
Leypark Rd EX1 ....178 C7
Leypark Wlk EX1 ....178 C7
Leys Rd TQ2 ....219 D5
Leyton Ct EX15 ....163 C3
Leywood EX14 ....86 D2
Librator Way EX14 ....67 C1
Liberty Stile EX39 ....22 C2
Libra Gdns EX4 ....2 F4
Lichfield Ave TQ2 ....214 A1
Lichfield Cl TQ5 ....230 A4
Lichfield Dr TQ5 ....230 A4
Lichfield Rd EX4 ....176 D6
Lichgate Rd EX2 ....181 C8
Lidburn Hill EX6 ....97 E5
Lidford Tor Ave TQ4 ....225 F3
Lidgates La DT7,EX13 ....103 F3
Liffey Rise EX4 ....176 E8
Lifton La EX19 ....59 B3
Lifton Prim Sch PL16 ....105 E4
Lifton Rd PL4 ....249 A4
Littondown Cross PL16 ....105 C4
Light La TQ5 ....229 B4
Lighthouse Cross EX39 ....23 B3
Lightleigh Cross EX18 ....44 F5
Lilac Cl PL9 ....255 C5
Lilac Rd Exeter EX2 ....177 E3
  Tiverton EX16 ....161 F5
Lilac Terr EX16 ....161 D4
Lilian Cl EX17 ....78 B4
Lillagey La EX19 ....198 A6
Lillebonne Cl TA21 ....160 F6
Lilliscrap La EX20 ....170 B5
Lillybrook La EX4 ....98 A5
Lillycombe La TA3,EX15 ....67 E8
Lily Cl EX39 ....157 A7
Lily La EX5 ....172 A8
Lily Mount PL4 ....176 D8
Lilybridge EX39 ....157 A7
Lilylake Cross EX24 ....102 F7
Lime Ave TQ2 ....219 F5
Lime Cl Broadclyst EX5 ....161 F5
  Honiton EX14 ....161 F5
Lime Cres EX15 ....162 C4
Lime Gr Bideford EX39 ....156 F2
  Exminster EX6 ....182 A5
  Ilfracombe TQ7 ....258 C5
Lime Kiln La Exeter EX2 ....178 A1
  Uplyme DT7 ....260 A6
Lime Kiln Rd EX16 ....161 F3
Lime St ① EX5 ....99 E2
Lime Tree Cl EX7 ....178 C3
Lime Tree Mead ① EX16 ....64 D7
Lime Tree Wlk TQ12 ....207 E1
Lime Way EX14 ....192 A7
Limegrove Rd EX4 ....176 E7
Limehayes Rd EX20 ....170 C5
Limekiln La EX31 ....16 A6
Limer's Hill EX36 ....159 B5
Limer's La EX36 ....158 B2
Limer's Lane Cross
  EX36 ....158 B2
Limerick Pl PL4 ....263 C3
Limers Cross
  Chittlehampton EX37 ....29 A4
  Wolverstone EX14 ....85 C7
Limers La Merton EX20 ....57 A7
  Northam EX39 ....157 A5
  Wolverstone EX14 ....85 C7
Limes Cotts EX5 ....182 A4
Limes The PL6 ....244 F2
Limetree Cross EX16 ....64 D6

Limetree Gr EX33 ....152 C6
Limetree Rd PL3 ....248 D7
Linacre La TQ12 ....213 C6
Linacre Rd TQ2 ....213 F4
Linch Cross PL12 ....242 C6
Lincoln Cl Exmouth EX8 ....196 E4
  Fenton EX14 ....84 D2
Lincoln Gn TQ2 ....214 A1
Lincoln Rd EX4 ....176 E6
Lincombe Cross
  Digtford TQ9 ....138 C8
  Salcombe TQ8 ....259 D7
Lincombe Dr TQ1 ....220 E3
Lincombe Hill Rd TQ1 ....220 E4
Linda Cl EX1 ....178 B5
Linden Cl
  Cullompton EX15 ....163 C4
  Dawlish EX7 ....204 D5
Linden Terr
  Newton Abbot TQ12 ....207 A3
  Plymouth PL4 ....263 C3
Lindisfarne Way TQ12 ....213 B2
Lindridge Cl ⑧ TQ12 ....123 E1
Lindridge Hill TQ12 ....123 F1
Lindridge La ⑥ TQ12 ....123 E1
Lindridge Pk TQ14 ....124 B2
Lindridge Rd TQ1 ....220 C8
Lindsay Rd TQ3 ....219 A2
Lindthorpe Way TQ5 ....230 B4
Liney Cross TQ11 ....236 A6
Linfield Gdns EX34 ....176 F4
Linhay Bsns Pk TQ13 ....131 A5
Linhay Cl Brixham TQ5 ....234 F8
  Honiton EX14 ....166 C4
  Millmoor EX15 ....51 E1
Linhay Dr EX31 ....153 F6
Linhay Pk EX17 ....80 A5
Linhay Cl TQ7 ....258 D4
Link House Cl EX14 ....67 C1
Link Rd EX20 ....170 C6
Linkadells PL7 ....250 D5
Linketty La PL6 ....250 C5
Linketty La E PL6 ....245 A1
Linketty La W PL6 ....268 F8
Linkhay TA20 ....88 D8
Linkhay Cl TA20 ....88 D8
Links Cl
  Churston Ferrers TQ5 ....229 C6
  Exmouth EX8 ....202 C8
Links Ct TQ1 ....143 A1
Links Rd EX9 ....203 E8
Links The EX9 ....156 E7
Linnet Cl EX4 ....173 D2
Linnet Dene EX15 ....163 A2
Linscott Cres EX31 ....153 A4
Linton Cl PL5 ....244 C8
Linton La EX39 ....37 B5
Linton Rd PL4 ....263 C4
Linton Sq PL5 ....244 C8
Lion Cl TQ7 ....258 C5
Lion's Close Hill EX24 ....103 A5
Lion's Rump EX32,EX36 ....18 F1
Lions Mill EX31 ....154 E7
Lippell Dr PL9 ....255 E6
Lipson Ave PL4 ....263 C4
Lipson Com Coll PL4 ....249 C4
Lipson Rd PL4 ....263 B3
Lipson Rd PL4 ....263 B4
Lipson Vale PL4 ....263 C4
Lipson Vale Prim Sch
  PL4 ....249 A4
Lipstone Cres PL4 ....263 C4
Lisa Cl EX2 ....178 A4
Lisburne Cres ⑭ TQ1 ....220 D4
Lisburne Pl ⑨ TQ1 ....220 D4
Lisburne Sq TQ1 ....220 D4
Liscawn Terr PL11 ....247 B3
Liscombe Cl PL18 ....125 D7
Lisham's Drain EX24 ....103 A5
Lishaperhill Cross EX22 ....53 B2
Liskeard Rd PL14 ....242 B3
Lisson Gr PL4 ....248 F4
Lister Cl PL7 ....251 D5
Litchardon Cross EX31 ....26 F8
Litchaton Cross PL7 ....250 B7
Litchaton Cross
  East Buckland EX32 ....18 F1
  North Molton EX36 ....30 A8
Litchaton Hill
  East Buckland EX36 ....18 F1
  North Molton EX36 ....30 A8
Litchaton Way PL7 ....250 B7
Litchdon La EX32 ....155 A4
Litchdon St EX32 ....155 A4
Litchfield Cl PL7 ....251 B6
Litelbury Rd EX17 ....64 D7
Littabourne EX31 ....154 F7
Little Ash Gdns PL5 ....243 B1
Little Ash Rd PL5 ....243 B1
Little Barton ⑦ TQ12 ....123 F1
Little Bicton Ct ⑱ EX8 ....202 A6
Little Bicton Pl EX8 ....202 A6
Little Bossell La TQ11 ....236 B4
Little Bray Cross EX31 ....18 C8
Little Butts PL9 ....255 C6

Little Castle St EX4 ....261 B3
Little Chockenhole La
EX9 ....199 A8
Little Cl
Kingsteignton TQ12 ......207 E8
Ottery St Mary EX11 .....169 D3
Little Cross TQ13 ....130 A4
Little Dock La PL5 ....244 B2
Little Down La PL6 ....241 E3
Little Down Orch EX10 ...186 D7
Little Esworthy La EX16 ..48 A1
Little Fancy Cl PL6 ....245 C7
Little Field EX39 ....156 D2
Little Gate TQ7 ....143 F7
Little Gornhay La
Chevithorne EX16 ....49 D1
Tiverton EX15 ....64 D8
5 Tiverton EX16 ....161 F6
Little Hayes 12 TQ12 .....123 F1
Little Hayes La EX18 ......58 D8
Little Heath Cross EX16 ..63 A6
Little Helstonbench Cross
TQ13 ....123 B6
Little Hill TQ8 ....259 C5
Little Hill Cl TQ12 ....123 F1
Little John's Cross Hill
EX2 ....176 E3
Little John's Wlk TQ13 ...122 F6
Little Knowle La EX9 ......197 F1
Little Knowle Ct EX9 ......197 F1
Little La Beer EX12 ....191 D4
Cawsand PL10 ....253 A2
Staddiscombe PL9 ....255 D3
Little Mdw EX8 ....196 E3
Little Mdws EX18 ....59 C4
Little Meadow Way
EX39 ....156 E2
Little Normans EX15 ......83 F6
Little Park Rd TQ3 ....226 A6
Little Point Cres PL10 ....252 F5
Little Queen St EX4 ....261 B3
Little Rack St 4 EX1 ......261 A2
Little Rackenford La
EX16 ....47 E5
Little Raddon Cross EX17 ..80 A4
Little Roborough TQ13 ....130 F5
Little Silver Exeter EX4 ...261 A4
Tiverton EX16 ....161 D3
Little Silver La
Exeter EX2 ....181 D5
Wellington TA21 ....160 D2
Little Torns EX15 ....64 A5
Little Torrington EX38 ....159 B1
Little Week Cl EX7 ....200 F1
Little Week Gdns EX7 .....200 F1
Little Week Rd EX7 ....200 F1
Little Wiveliscombe La
TA4 ....35 D6
Littleborough Cross
EX17 ....62 A5
Littlebray La EX32 ....18 E6
Littlebridge Mdw EX22 ....70 F5
Littledown Cl EX38 ....202 F7
Littledown La EX10 ....186 D7
Littlefield TQ14 ....208 E8
Littlefield Cl
Barnstaple EX32 ....155 D4
Torquay TQ2 ....213 D1
Littlefields EX12 ....192 A7
Littleford Cross EX22 .....53 E8
Littlegate Rd TQ3 ....226 B6
Littleham CE Prim Sch
EX8 ....202 F7
Littleham Cross EX38 .....202 F7
Littleham Rd EX8 ....202 E7
Littlehempston Cross
TQ9 ....216 F2
Littlejoy Rd TQ12 ....206 C4
Littlemead La EX8 ....196 B3
Littlemoor Cl EX31 ....153 A4
Littleton Pl PL2 ....247 F4
Littletown Rd EX14 ....166 B4
Littleham Villas EX14 .....166 C4
Littleway EX2 ....176 F3
Littleweek La EX7 ....200 F1
Littlewood Cl PL7 ....251 A4
Livarot Wlk EX36 ....158 B4
Livaton Cross EX20 ....95 D4
Livermead Hill TQ2 ....219 E2
Livermore Rd EX14 ....166 C5
Liverpool Hill EX4 ....176 E7
Liverton Bsns Pk EX8 .....196 F4
Liverton Ct EX12 ....202 E8
Liverton Cl TQ12 ....180 A1
Liverton Hill EX8 ....197 B1
Livery Dole Almshouses
EX2 ....177 E5
Livingshayes Rd EX5 ......82 C6
Livingstone Ave PL4 ......18 A8
Livingstone Rd EX14 .....210 C6
Livonia Rd EX10 ....188 B6
Lixton Pk PL21 ....137 F1
Lizard Cl PL6 ....244 F7
Lizard Wlk PL6 ....245 A7
Lloyd Ave TQ2 ....219 D7
Lloyd Maunder Rd EX15 .162 C5
Lloyds Cres EX1 ....178 C8
Lloyds Ct EX1 ....178 C8
Loatmead Cross EX22 .....38 B3
Lobthorn Stile EX33 ....8 B1
Locarno Ave TQ2 ....219 D1
Locarno Rd EX4 ....176 F4
Lock La EX31 ....10 E4
Lock Lane Cross EX31 ....10 F3

Lock's Gate Cross
TQ13 ....129 F8
Lockeridge Rd PL20 ......125 E1
Lockfield Ct EX2 ....177 B1
Lockington Ave PL3 ......248 F7
Locks Cl Braunton EX33 ..152 D5
Torquay TQ1 ....220 D7
Locks Hill TQ1 ....220 D7
Locks Wlk PL1 ....247 E1
Locksey's La EX12 ....190 D6
Locksley Cl Exeter EX2 ...182 A8
Torquay TQ1 ....220 B7
Locksley Grange TQ1 .....220 A7
Lockyer Ave EX10 ....188 C8
Lockyer Cres EX16 ....161 F6
Lockyer Ct PL1 ....262 C2
Lockyer Mews PL19 ......171 C6
Lockyer Rd PL3 ....248 E5
Lockyer St PL1 ....262 C2
Lockyer Terr PL12 ....183 A3
Lockyers Quay PL4 ....263 B2
Loddiswell Butts TQ7 ....143 E8
Loddiswell Prim Cross
TQ7 ....143 F7
Lodge Cl TA21 ....160 D6
Lodge Cnr EX31 ....27 D8
Lodge Cross
Chulmleigh EX18 ....45 A1
Longdown EX6 ....98 E1
Lodge Gdns PL6 ....244 E3
Lodge Hill Exeter EX4 ....177 A8
Okehampton EX20 ....170 B5
Lodge La Axminster EX13 ..88 B2
Bratton Fleming EX31 .....18 E8
Brixton PL8 ....255 F6
Shute EX13 ....103 A8
Lodge Rd EX16 ....161 E4
Lodge Trad Est EX5 ......175 E3
Lofoten Cl PL1 ....247 E2
Loftus Gdns PL5 ....243 C2
Logan Rd TQ3 ....225 E7
Logan Way EX14 ....67 B8
Lolesbury Cross PL8 ......136 A1
Lollabury Rd PL12 ....242 E3
Lombard Cl EX39 ....25 D4
London Ct The PL21 ......237 D5
London Inn Sq EX1 ....261 B3
Long Acre PL12 ....242 B4
Long Barton 5 TQ12 ......123 F1
Long Bridge Cross EX13 ..87 B8
Long Copp EX9 ....198 A2
Long Cross
Dartmouth TQ6 ....233 C3
South Pool TQ7 ....148 F7
Long Cswy EX8 ....202 B6
Long Down Gdns PL6 .....245 E3
Long Drag EX15 ....65 C3
Long Entry DT7 ....260 E3
Long Hill EX12 ....191 D5
Long Holcombe Cross
EX36 ....35 D6
Long La Appledore EX39 ..14 F1
Ashford EX31 ....16 B6
Barnstaple EX31 ....154 A8
Calverleigh EX16 ....48 D2
Combe Martin EX31,EX34 ..3 D1
Dawlish EX7 ....200 B1
Exmouth EX8 ....202 C6
Georgeham EX33 ....8 B1
Modbury PL21 ....147 B8
Newton Abbot TQ12 ......208 B1
Northam EX39 ....157 A8
Shaldon TQ14 ....209 D4
Tiverton EX16 ....161 A7
Wolverstone EX14 ....85 B8
Long Ley PL3 ....249 B6
Long Mdw Plymouth PL7 ..250 D7
South Brent TQ10 ....134 F3
Long Meadow Dr EX32 ...155 B6
Long Moor
Cullompton EX15 ....163 F6
Willand EX15 ....162 E1
Long Orch PL20 ....125 E1
Long Park Cl PL9 ....255 F5
Long Park Dr PL6 ....245 D7
Long Park Rd PL12 ....242 D2
Long Pk Ashburton TQ13 ..131 A5
Modbury PL21 ....147 B8
Woodbury EX5 ....184 C3
Long Rd Paignton TQ4 ...225 D1
Saltash PL12 ....242 B4
Long Rowden PL3 ....248 E6
Long Rydon TQ9 ....227 F8
Long Terrace Cl 6 PL7 ...251 C5
Long Walk Dr EX31 ....16 B7
Long Wools TQ4 ....229 D7
Long-Go La EX14 ....84 E8
Longacre PL7 ....250 B7
Longbridge Cl PL6 ....249 F6
Longbridge Meadow Trad Est
EX15 ....163 D4
Longbridge Rd
Plymouth, Laira PL3 ......249 C4
Plymouth, Longbridge PL6 ..249 E7
Longbrook TQ7 ....145 A1
Longbrook Barton PL7 ...250 D6
Longbrook Cl PL21 ....237 B5
Longbrook La EX5 ....195 F4
Longbrook Rd PL21 ......237 B5
Longbrook St Exeter EX4 ..261 B4
Plymouth PL7 ....250 D6
Longbrook Terr EX4 ......261 B4
Longcause PL7 ....250 F4
Longcause Com Specl Sch
PL7 ....250 F4
Longcombe Cross TQ9 ....224 C5
Longcroft Ave TQ5 ....230 B3
Longcroft Dr TQ5 ....230 B3
Longdogs La EX11 ....169 E3

Longdogs La EX11 ....169 E3
Longdown Rd EX2,EX6 ...176 B3
Longdrag Hill EX16 ....161 A4
Longfield
11 Appledore EX39 ....15 A1
Lutton PL21 ....133 B1
Longfield Ave TQ12 ......207 F8
Longfield Cl
Braunton EX33 ....152 E5
Lutton PL21 ....133 B2
Longfield Dr TQ8 ....259 C5
Longfield Est EX6 ....201 A8
Longfield Pl PL4 ....263 B4
Longfield Villas PL9 ......255 D8
Longfields TQ7 ....258 D3
Longford Cross TQ12 .....207 E8
Longford Down Head
PL21 ....137 F6
Longford La TQ12 ....207 E8
Longford Pl TQ12 ....207 F8
Longford Rd TQ12 ....207 E8
Longland Cl EX32 ....17 B5
Longland Cross TQ9 ......227 C3
Longland La EX33 ....8 A2
Longlands Dawlish EX7 ...204 D6
Plymouth PL4 ....255 D8
Longlands Cross
Ashwater EX21 ....90 E6
Holsworthy EX22 ....71 F2
Longlands Dr PL9 ....140 A8
Longlands La PL21 ....58 F7
Longmead EX15 ....151 A5
Longmead Cl TA21 ....160 B8
Longmead Cotts TA21 ....160 B8
Longmead Rd TQ3 ....218 F1
Longmead Wlk TQ3 ......218 F1
Longmeadow Budleigh EX5 ..82 E1
Tiverton EX16 ....161 D5
Longmeadow Rd
Woodbury EX5 ....184 C3
Longmeadow Cl PL7 .....250 F7
Longmeadow Rd
Lympstone EX8 ....195 F5
Saltash PL12 ....242 E3
Longmeadows EX17 ....165 D6
Longpark Hill TQ1 ....214 C6
Longstone Ave PL6 ......245 A6
Longstone Cross 1
TQ13 ....131 A5
Longstone Rd TQ4 ....225 E4
Longthorn Rd TQ13 ....124 B4
Longview Terr PL3 ....249 D7
Longview Terr PL3 ....249 B7
Longwood Cl PL7 ....251 A4
Longwood La TA21 ....51 C4
Longwood Mdw EX23 .....70 A6
Lonsdale Rd Exeter EX1 ..178 B5
Newton Abbot TQ12 ......207 D2
Loo Cross TQ7 ....144 F1
Looe Rd EX4 ....177 A7
Looe St PL4 ....263 A2
Looseall La TA22 ....33 D8
Loosebeare Cross
Zeal Monachorum EX17 ...78 C8
Zeal Monachorum EX17 ...78 C8
Loosebeare La EX17 ....78 B8
Losedon Cross EX19 ....58 B4
Loseland Cross EX16 ......47 D1
Loosleigh Cl PL6 ....245 A4
Loosleigh La PL6 ....244 F5
Lopes Cres EX20 ....170 C5
Lopes Dr PL6 ....241 C1
Lopes Rd Dousland PL20 ..127 B3
Plymouth PL2 ....248 B6
Lopwell Cl PL6 ....244 F5
Loram Way EX2 ....181 C8
Lord Louis Cres PL9 ......254 F6
Lord Mamhead Homes
EX2 ....177 E4
Lords Meadow La 6
EX16 ....34 B1
Lords Pl TQ1 ....220 B6
Lords Way EX2 ....178 C4
Loretto Rd EX13 ....167 E5
Loring Rd TQ8 ....259 D4
Lorrie Dr TQ14 ....210 B6
Lorrimore Ave PL2 ....247 F5
Lotherton Cl PL7 ....251 B3
Loughboro Rd PL5 ....243 C1
Loughborough EX16 ......161 B5
Loughwood La EX13 ......87 B2
Louis Way EX14 ....67 C1
Louisa Gate TA22 ....33 F7
Louisa Pl EX8 ....202 A5
Louisa Terr EX8 ....202 A5
Louise Terr EX38 ....159 C5
Louvigny Cl EX14 ....84 E2
Louville Cl TQ4 ....226 C2
Lovacott Cross EX31 .....153 F7
Lovacott School Cross
EX31 ....27 A6
Love La Ashburton TQ13 ..130 F4
Bickington TQ12 ....127 F5
Crediton EX17 ....165 E1
Colyton EX24 ....103 A4
Marldon TQ3 ....218 D4
Saltash PL12 ....242 E2
Low Lane Cl TQ12 ....218 D4
Lovelace Cres EX8 ....202 D8
Lovelace Gdns PL2 ....181 B8
Loveland Cross EX20 .....74 C1
Lovell Cl EX8 ....196 C3
Lovell Pl PL3 ....248 F6
Loventor La TQ3,TQ9 ....217 F3
Lover's La EX39 ....41 F1
Loveridge La PL20 ....88 D8
Lovering Ct EX31 ....153 F5
Loverings Ct 3 EX31 .....154 F5

Low Brook EX5 ....99 C5
Low Meml Ho 4 EX32 ....16 E1
Lower Albert St EX1 ......261 C3
Lower Aller La TQ13 ......122 E6
Lower Almshouses 2
EX31 ....154 F6
Lower Anderton Rd
PL10 ....252 F5
Lower Argyll Rd TQ2 .....173 A2
Lower Audley Rd TQ2 ....219 F8
Lower Ave EX1 ....177 F6
Lower Biteford Cross
EX39 ....38 B6
Lower Blagdon Cross
TQ3 ....225 B6
Lower Blagdon La TQ3 ...225 B6
Lower Brand La EX14 ....166 C4
Lower Brimley Cl 2
TQ14 ....210 C5
Lower Brimley Rd TQ14 ..210 C5
Lower Broad Oak Rd
EX11 ....168 E4
Lower Broad Path TQ9 ...228 A2
Lower Broad Rd TQ6 .....233 D3
Lower Brook Mdw 2
EX10 ....101 B1
Lower Brook Pk TQ1 .....237 A5
Lower Brook St 13
TQ14 ....210 C5
Lower Brookfield Cotts
TQ13 ....122 C8
Lower Budleigh Ave EX9 ..198 B5
Lower Budleigh Mdw
TQ12 ....206 F3
Lower Bulkamore Cross
TQ10 ....135 E5
Lower Bulworthy Gate
EX16 ....47 D4
Lower Bulworthy La
EX16 ....47 D4
Lower Burston EX17 ......78 B5
Lower Burwood Rd
EX38 ....159 E5
Lower Cannon Rd
Bovey Tracey TQ12 ....123 B2
Heathfield TQ12 ....180 F2
Lower Church St
6 Barnstaple EX32 ....155 A4
Colyton EX24 ....103 A5
Lower Cl EX16 ....44 A8
Lower Claypark EX34 ......7 F7
Lower Cleave EX39 ....157 B5
Lower Cleve EX33 ....152 C7
Lower Cobbaton EX37 ....26 B8
Lower Collapark TQ9 .....223 B6
Lower Collins Rd TQ9 ....223 B6
Lower Compton Rd PL3 ..248 F5
Lower Congella Rd TQ1 ..220 C6
Lower Contour Rd TQ6 ...234 B3
Lower Cookworthy Cross
PL16 ....106 A6
Lower Coombe La EX17 ...79 B3
Lower Coombe Rd TQ12 ..207 F2
Lower Coombe St 4 EX1 ..261 A2
Lower Coombses TA20 ....88 D8
Lower Cotteylands
EX16 ....161 B3
Lower Court Rd PL8 ......140 F7
Lower Cross EX15 ....83 C1
Lower Cross St EX31 .....154 B4
Lower Dawlish Water Rd
EX7 ....204 A7
Lower Dean Cross EX31 ...3 F2
Lower Dean La EX31 ....3 B2
Lower Dr EX7 ....204 F8
Lower Duck St EX16 ......182 B3
Lower East St EX36 ......30 E8
Lower Ellacombe Church Rd
TQ1 ....220 C6
Lower Erith Rd TQ1 ......220 D4
Lower Fairview Rd TQ9 ..233 E3
Lower Farm Rd PL7 ......251 A4
Lower Farthings EX10 ....186 F8
Lower Ferry Rd TQ12 ....212 F8
Lower Forches Cross
EX17 ....60 D4
Lower Fore St
11 Exmouth EX8 ....202 A6
Saltash PL12 ....243 A2
Lower Fowden TQ4 ....229 D6
Lower Foxmoor Rd
TA21 ....160 B5
Lower French Pk TQ12 ...206 F3
Lower Fyldon Cross
EX36 ....29 D4
Lower Gaydon St 1
EX32 ....155 A5
Lower Green Cross TQ7 ..145 C4
Lower Griggs EX10 ....188 D7
Lower Gunstone EX39 ...157 A2
Lower Harrington La
EX4 ....174 E1
Lower Hill Barton Rd
EX1 ....176 C6
Lower Hollicombe Cotts
TQ3 ....219 D1
Lower Kelly PL18 ....125 D3
Lower King's Ave EX4 ....177 D8
Lower Kingsdown Rd
TQ14 ....209 D7
Lower Kinsman's Dale
TQ13 ....111 F5
Lower Knowle Rd TQ12 ..122 D7
Lower La Chulmleigh EX18 ..59 C8
Dalwood EX13 ....87 B2
Ebford EX3 ....183 C4
6 Plymouth PL1 ....263 A2
Lower Ladram La EX9 ....199 A7

Lower Lodfin EX16 ....34 B2
Lower Lowton La EX6 ....112 E6
Lower Manor Rd TQ5 ....230 C5
Lower Marlpits Hill
EX14 ....166 D4
Lower Meadow Rise
EX7 ....204 C6
Lower Meddon St 9
EX39 ....157 A1
Lower Mill La EX15 ......163 C3
Lower Millhayes EX15 ....67 C8
Lower Moor EX22 ....155 D4
Lower Moor Way EX15 ...64 D8
Lower North St EX4 ......261 A3
Lower Northcote Rd
EX14 ....166 E7
Lower Park Dr PL9 ....255 F4
Lower Park Rd EX33 .....152 C5
Lower Penns Rd TQ3 ....219 C1
Lower Pk
2 Paignton TQ3 ....226 A7
Umberleigh EX37 ....28 D2
Lower Polsham Rd TQ3 ..226 C7
Lower Port View PL12 ....242 F2
Lower Preston TQ12 ......123 D1
Lower Preston Cross
TQ9 ....138 E2
Lower Raleigh Rd EX31 ..155 A7
Lower Rd EX5 ....184 B7
Lower Rea Rd TQ5 ....230 D5
Lower Ridings PL7 ....251 B7
Lower Row PL10 ....253 A2
Lower Saltram PL9 ....255 C7
Lower Shapter St TQ3 ...182 F4
Lower Shirburn Rd TQ1 ..220 A4
Lower St Chagford TQ13 ..111 A6
Dartmouth TQ6 ....233 F3
Dittisham TQ6 ....228 B3
Plymouth PL4 ....263 A3
West Alvington TQ7 ......258 A4
Lower St German's Rd
EX4 ....177 C8
Lower Summerlands
EX1 ....261 C3
Lower Tamar Terr PL18 ..125 D7
Lower Terr EX22 ....38 E1
Lower Thurlow Rd TQ1 ..220 A5
Lower Tidderson Cross
EX16 ....47 E4
Lower Town
Halberton EX16 ....65 A7
Malborough TQ7 ....147 E6
Sampford Peverell EX16 ..50 D1
Winkleigh EX19 ....58 A7
Woolfardisworthy EX39 ...38 F7
Lower Union La TQ2 .....220 B5
Lower Warberry Rd TQ1 ..258 C5
Lower Warberry Rd
TQ1 ....220 C4
Lower Warcombe Cross
TQ7 ....144 A6
Lower Warren Rd TQ7 ...258 D3
Lower Way EX10 ....187 A8
Lower Wear Rd EX2 ......182 B8
Lower Westlake Rd
EX31 ....154 A2
Lower Wheathill EX10 ...188 B8
Lower Winsham Rd EX33 ..8 D1
Lower Woodfield Rd
TQ1 ....220 C4
Lower Woodhays Ct
EX5 ....99 E2
Lower Yalberton Rd
TQ4 ....225 C2
Lowerdale Turn TQ9 .....144 B8
Lowerdown TQ13 ....122 D5
Lowerside PL2 ....248 A8
Lowertown Cotts EX20 ...107 A3
Lowery Cross PL20 ....127 D4
Loweswater Ho EX4 ......176 F6
Lowley Brook Ct TQ2 ....219 B8
Lowman Cross EX16 ......50 B1
Lowman Units EX16 ....64 D8
Lowman Way EX15 ....64 D8
Lowman Terr EX16 ....64 D8
Lowman Ind Est TA21 ...160 B8
Lownard Cross TQ9 ......222 E8
Lowton Cross EX20 ....77 C7
Lowton La PL6 ....112 E6
Lowtrow Cross TA4 ....35 A8
Loxbury Rd TQ2 ....219 D4
Loxbury Rise TQ2 ....219 D5
Loxdown Rd EX39 ....41 A7
Loxhore Cross EX31 ....17 D7
Loxton Cl EX39 ....24 E8
Lucas La PL7 ....250 D6
Lucas Terr PL4 ....249 B2
Lucerne 1 TQ1 ....220 D4
Lucius St TQ2 ....220 A4
Ludgate Cl TQ12 ....147 E6
Ludbrook Gate PL21 .....137 C5
Ludlow Rd 2 PL2 ....248 E6
Ludwell La EX2 ....178 A3
Lugsmoor La EX10 ....188 E2
Lugworthy Cross EX21 ...91 B5
Luke St EX16 ....34 B1
Lulworth Cl TQ4 ....225 F2
Lulworth Dr PL6 ....245 B7
Lumley Cl EX6 ....194 E3
Lummaton Cross TQ2 ....214 A2
Lummaton Pl TQ2 ....214 A3
Lundy Cl Barnstaple EX32 ..155 C5
Plymouth PL6 ....244 F7
Lundy Cross EX39 ....156 E6
Lurley Cross EX16 ....48 E2
Luscombe Cl
Ipplepen TQ12 ....211 D1

Luscombe Cl continued
Ivybridge PL21 ....237 A4
Luscombe Cres TQ3 ....225 E6
Luscombe Cross TQ9 ..139 D8
Luscombe Hill
Dawlish EX7 ....204 A6
Teignmouth EX7 ....124 E3
Luscombe La TQ3 ......225 D8
Luscombe Rd TQ3 ......225 E6
Luscombe Terr 11 EX7 ..204 D6
Luson Cross PL8 ....136 C1
Lustleigh Cl EX2 ....181 C8
Lutehouse La EX19 .....58 E3
Lutsford Cross EX39 ...37 D6
Lutterburn St PL21 ....137 D6
Lutyens Dr TQ1 ....225 D7
Lutyens Fold PL19 .....116 A6
Luxmore Cl PL6 ....245 E1
Luxton Cl EX21 ....73 E3
Luxton La EX20 ....77 B8
Luxton Moor La EX20 ..59 A1
Luxton Rd TQ12 ....211 F8
Lwr Bull Ring EX15 ....163 C3
Lych Cl PL9 ....255 A6
Lyd Gdns PL19 ....171 D5
Lydacott Cross EX31 ..153 F3
Lydcot Wlk PL6 ....245 A1
Lyddicleave EX31 ......154 A3
Lyddon Cl TA21 ....160 D4
Lydford Castle* EX20 ..107 E3
Lydford Cl PL21 ....237 D4
Lydford Gorge* EX20 ..107 E3
Lydford Ho TQ12 ....207 D4
Lydford Park Rd PL3 ..248 D5
Lydgates Rd EX12 .....192 A6
Lydia Cl EX10 ....186 D8
Lydia Way PL4 ....248 E4
Lydiate La Lynton EX35 ..151 B5
Lynton EX35 ....5 A5
Lydon La TA4 ....35 D5
Lydwell Park Rd TQ1 ..220 E5
Lydwell Rd TQ1 ....220 D6
Lye La EX14 ....87 A8
Lym Cl DT7 ....260 E3
Lyme Bay Holiday Village
EX12 ....192 B5
Lyme Bay Rd TQ14 ....210 C7
Lyme Cl EX13 ....167 D5
Lyme Mews 5 EX12 ..192 B4
Lyme Rd Axminster EX13 ..167 E5
Uplyme DT7 ....104 B5
Lyme Regis Ind Est DT7 ..260 C4
Lyme Regis Marine
Aquarium* DT7 ....260 D2
Lyme Regis Philpot Mus*
DT7 ....260 E3
Lyme St EX13 ....167 D6
Lyme View Cl TQ1 .....220 D7
Lyme View Rd TQ1 ....220 D7
Lymeborne Ave EX1 ..188 B6
Lymebourne Ave EX10 ..188 B6
Lymebourne La EX10 ..188 B6
Lymebourne Pk EX10 ..188 B6
Lymington Rd TQ1 ....220 A6
Lympne Ave PL5 ....243 F5
Lympstone CE Prim Sch
EX8 ....195 E5
Lympstone Commando Sta
EX8 ....195 C8
Lympstone Sta EX8 ...195 D5
Lyn Cross PL5 ....151 D2
Lyn Gr TQ12 ....212 F6
Lyn La EX35 ....151 D3
Lynbridge Cl 5 PL19 ..171 B5
Lynbridge Hill EX35 ..151 C3
Lynbridge Rd EX35 ...151 C4
Lynbro Rd EX31 ....154 F7
Lynch Cl EX5 ....81 E5
Lynch Head EX10 .....100 C1
Lyncombe Cl EX4 .....173 E1
Lyncombe Cres TQ1 ..220 E3
Lyncourt TQ1 ....220 D3
Lyndale Rd TQ12 .....207 D8
Lyndhurst Ave TQ12 ..213 A5
Lyndhurst Cl
Kingskerswell TQ12 ..213 A6
Plymouth PL2 ....248 C6
Lyndhurst Rd Exeter EX2 ..177 E5
Exmouth EX8 ....202 A8
Plymouth PL2 ....248 C6
Lyndon Cl PL12 ....242 D4
Lyndrick Rd PL3 ....248 D7
Lyneham Cross TQ13 ..123 D6
Lyngrove Ct TQ12 ....212 F6
Lynhayes EX13 ....87 C1
Lynher Dr PL12 ....242 F1
Lynher St PL5 ....243 D2
Lynhurst Ave EX31 ...154 C4
Lynmouth Ave TQ4 ..225 F2
Lynmouth Cl PL7 .....250 C7
Lynmouth Hill EX35 ..151 C5
Lynmouth St EX35 ...151 C5
Lynton & Exmoor Mus*
EX35 ....151 C5
Lynton & Lynmouth Cliff
Rlwy* EX35 ....151 C6
Lynton CE Prim Sch
EX35 ....151 C5
Lynton Cross EX34 ...9 B6
Lynton YH* EX35 ......151 C4
Lynway Lynton EX35 ..151 C4
Lynton EX35 ....151 C4
Lynway Ct TQ1 ....220 B6
Lynwood TQ12 ....206 F4
Lynwood Ave Exeter EX4 ..177 A5
Plymouth PL7 ....250 B6
Lyte La TQ7 ....144 C1
Lyte's Rd TQ5 ....230 D4

Lythe-Land Cross EX16 ..63 A6
Lytton Ho TQ2 ....220 A4

M

Mabel Pl TQ4 ....226 B5
Macadam Rd PL4 .....263 C1
Macandrew Wlk PL21 ..237 E6
Macaulay Cres PL5 ...244 C1
Macauley Cl EX14 ....166 E6
Macey St PL11 ....247 C3
Macey's Terr EX20 ...170 B6
Machine Cross TA22 ..33 F6
Mackenzie Pl PL5 ....243 C2
Mackenzie Way EX16 ..161 F4
Mackrell's Almshouses
TQ12 ....207 A2
Maclins Cl EX36 ......158 C4
Macwood Dr EX12 ...192 A6
Madagascar Cl EX8 ..202 E8
Maddacombe Cross
TQ12 ....212 C4
Maddacombe Rd TQ12 ..212 D4
Madden Rd PL1 ....247 F2
Maddock Cl PL7 ......261 A4
Maddock Dr PL7 ......251 B4
Maddocks Cross EX22 ..38 D2
Madeira Cl EX8 ....202 B5
Madeira Pl TQ2 ....220 A5
Madeira Rd PL1 ....263 A1
Madeira Villas EX8 ..202 A7
Madeira Wlk EX9 .....199 H2
Madeirs Villas 1 PL20 ..126 F5
Madford Cross EX15 ..67 C6
Madge Ct PL19 ....171 B6
Madge La PL19 ....171 B6
Madgeon La EX20 ...69 B8
Madges Cross
Aylesbeare EX5 ....99 E2
Rockbeare EX5 ....99 E6
Madicks Orch TQ9 ..227 F8
Madison Ave EX1 ....178 A6
Madison Cl EX5 ......173 F8
Madison Wharf EX8 ..201 E6
Madrepore Rd TQ1 ..220 B4
Maer Bay Ct EX8 .....202 A5
Maer La EX8 ....202 E5
Maer Rd EX8 ....202 C5
Maer Top Way EX31 ..155 A7
Maer Vale EX8 ....202 C6
Magdala Rd EX31 ...154 A3
Magdalen Bridge Ct 3
EX2 ....261 B2
Magdalen Court Sch
EX2 ....177 E5
Magdalen Gdns
Exeter EX2 ....177 E5
Plymouth PL7 ....250 F3
Magdalen Rd EX2 ...261 C2
Magdalen St EX1,EX2 ..261 B2
Magdalen Way EX4 ..155 A6
Magdalene Lawn 9
EX32 ....155 A6
Magdalene Rd TQ1 ..220 A6
Magnolia Ave
Exeter EX2 ....178 A3
Exmouth EX8 ....202 E8
Magnolia Cl
Barnstaple EX32 ......155 E4
3 Plymouth PL7 ....251 B5
Magnolia Ct EX16 ...161 E7
Magnolia Ho 1 EX6 ..202 B8
Magpie Hill TQ13 ....130 C4
Maida Vale Terr PL4 ..248 F4
Maiden St 4 EX11 ...154 F5
Maidencombe Cross
TQ1 ....214 C6
Maidencombe Ho TQ1 ..214 C4
Maidenhayne La EX13 ..103 D6
Maidenhead Cross EX16 ..51 C2
Maidenway La TQ3 ..225 F8
Maidenway Rd TQ3 ..225 F8
Maidstone Pl PL5 ....243 E4
Main Ave TQ1 ....220 A8
Main Rd Exeter EX4 ..174 E2
Main St TQ9 ....139 E1
Maine Cl EX39 ....156 D2
Maine Gdns PL2 .....247 F7
Mains Down La EX33 ..8 A4
Mainstone Ave PL4 ..263 C2
Maire Rd EX36 ....46 E5
Maitland Dr PL3 ......248 F8
Major Cross EX16 ...64 A2
Major Terr 2 EX12 ..192 A5
Majorfield Rd EX3 ...182 F5
Mallands Mdw TQ12 ..212 A7
Mallard Cl Plymouth PL7 ..250 F5
Torquay TQ2 ....213 D2
Mallard Rd EX2 ......178 E5
Mallet Rd EX16 ......237 A6

Malletts La EX32 .....155 A5
Mallingbrook Cross EX18 ..44 E1
Mallison Cl EX4 ......176 F8
Mallock Rd TQ2 .....219 E5
Mallocks Cl EX10 ...100 D2
Mallow Ct EX15 .....162 D5
Malmesbury Cl PL2 ..248 B8
Malory Cl PL5 ....244 D2
Malson La EX16 ....47 B4
Malston Cross TQ7 ..144 D4
Malt Field EX8 ....195 F5
Malt Mill TQ9 ....223 B6
Malthouse The
Noss Mayo PL8 ......141 A7
1 Totnes TQ9 ....223 D5
Malting Cl 1 EX7 ...204 E6
Maltings The
21 Appledore EX39 ..15 A1
Black Torrington EX21 ..74 A8
Crediton EX17 ....165 D5
East Prawle TQ7 ......149 B5
Exeter EX2 ....177 F5
Malvern Gdns EX2 ..178 A4
Malvern Rd EX10 ...188 B6
Malvern Way EX14 ..156 D2
Malvernleigh TQ1 ...220 D8
Mambury Cross EX22 ..39 D3
Mamhead View EX8 ..201 E6
Mamhead Rd Exeter EX2 ..178 C4
Kenton EX6 ....194 C2
Mamhead Rd PL5 ...244 D5
Manadon Dr PL5 ....244 E1
Manadon Hill PL5,PL6 ..244 E1
Manadon Vale Prim Sch
PL5 ....248 E8
Manaton Cl EX2 .....181 C8
Manaton Ct EX2 .....181 C8
Manaton Tor Rd TQ3 ..218 F1
Manby Gdns PL5 ....243 F5
Manchester Rd EX8 ..201 F6
Manchester St EX10 ..201 F6
Mandrake Cl EX2 ...177 B1
Mandrake Rd EX2 ...177 A1
Manifold Gdns PL3 ..249 D5
Manitoba Gdns PL5 ..163 B3
Manley Cl 1 EX5 ....99 E8
Manley La EX14 .....67 B2
Manna Ash Ct EX2 ..261 C1
Mannacott La EX31 ..4 C4
Mannacott Lane Head
EX31 ....4 C4
Mannamead Ave PL3 ..248 F5
Mannamead Rd PL3 ..248 F6
Manning Ave EX15 ..163 A2
Mannings Mdw TQ13 ..180 D7
Mannings Way EX31 ..154 F7
Manor Ave
Lyme Regis DT7 ......260 D4
Paignton TQ3 ....226 C8
Manor Bend TQ5 ....229 C5
Manor Bourne Rd
Down Thomas PL9 ...255 C1
Heybrook Bay PL9 ...140 A8
Manor Cl
Abbotskerswell TQ12 ..212 A7
Awliscombe EX14 ....85 C3
Barnstaple EX31 ......154 C3
Dawlish EX7 ....204 D6
Fremington EX31 .....153 E6
Ivybridge PL21 ....237 C5
Kentisbeare EX15 ....66 A3
Kingskerswell TQ12 ..213 A3
Sidmouth EX10 ....188 B3
Tavistock PL19 ....171 A6
Uffculme EX15 ....66 A8
Wrafton EX33 ....152 E4
1 Seaton EX12 ....192 A5
Manor Cotts
8 Newton Abbot TQ12 ..207 B3
Rackenford EX16 .....45 C6
Manor Court Barns TQ7 ..147 F8
Manor Cres
Honiton EX14 ....166 C4
Paignton TQ3 ....226 C8
Manor Ct Galmpton TQ5 ..229 A5
Kingskerswell TQ12 ..213 A3
Landkey EX32 ....17 B2
Seaton EX12 ....192 A5
8 South Brent TQ10 ..134 F3
Stoke Fleming TQ6 ...146 B7
Torquay TQ2 ....219 F6
Manor Dr Chagford TQ13 ..110 F6
Ivybridge PL21 ....213 A3
Kingskerswell TQ12 ..213 A3
Manor Farm PL20 ...127 B3
Manor Farm Cl TA20 ..88 C8
Manor Farm Mews EX5 ..99 E4
Manor Gdn TQ1 ......220 E3
Manor Gdns
Horrabridge PL20 ....126 C4
Kingskerswell TQ12 ..213 A3
Paignton TQ3 ....226 C8
Manor Gn EX14 ......68 C2
Manor Ho The TQ9 ..223 D5
Manor Ho TQ13 ......131 D7
Manor Mill Rd EX33 ..8 D1
Manor Park Cl PL7 ..251 A4
Manor Park Dr PL7 ..251 A4
Manor Pk Ashwater EX21 ..90 E6
Barnstaple EX31 ......154 C3
Bradworthy EX22 .....53 D8
Clyst St Mary EX5 ....179 A3
Dousland PL20 ....127 B3

Manor Pk continued
Kingsbridge TQ7 .....258 D6
Saltash PL3 ....242 D2
Manor Prim Sch PL21 ..237 C5
Manor Rd
Abbotskerswell TQ12 ..212 B7
Bishopsteignton EX9 ..208 F8
Chagford TQ13 ....110 F6
Exeter EX4 ....177 A5
Landkey EX32 ....17 B2
Newton Abbot TQ12 ..206 F3
Paignton TQ3 ....226 C8
Plymouth PL9 ....255 E8
Seaton EX12 ....192 A5
Sidmouth EX10 ....188 A5
Tavistock PL19 ....171 B6
Torquay TQ1 ....220 C8
Manor St Dittisham TQ6 ..228 D2
Plymouth PL1 ....262 A3
Manor Terr Brixham TQ5 ..230 C5
Paignton TQ3 ....226 A5
Manor Vale Rd TQ5 ..229 C5
Manor View TQ12 ...207 A3
Manor Way
Ivybridge PL21 ....237 C5
Totnes TQ9 ....223 C6
Manorglade Ct 1 TQ1 ..220 D5
Manosbridge Rd TQ9 ..223 E5
Manscombe Cl TQ2 ..219 D3
Manscombe Rd TQ2 ..219 D3
Mansfield Rd EX4 ...177 E8
Mansfield Terr EX9 ..198 B2
Mansion King Edward VI Com
Coll The TQ9 ....223 D5
Manston Terr 3 EX34 ..3 A3
Manston Cl PL15 ....243 E5
Manston Ct EX2 .....181 C8
Manston Ct TQ1 .....220 C2
Manston Rd EX1 .....177 E7
Manston Terr EX2 ...177 F5
Manstone Ave EX10 ..188 A7
Manstone Cl EX10 ...188 B7
Manstone La EX10 ...188 B7
Manstone Mead EX10 ..188 B8
Manstone Workshops
EX10 ....188 B8
Manstree Cross PL12 ..114 A6
Manstree Rd EX2 ....114 A6
Manstree Terr EX2 ..114 C6
Mantle Gdns PL5 ....247 D8
Mantle St TA21 ....160 C5
Maple Ave PL6 ....247 A3
Maple Cl Brixham TQ5 ..230 A2
16 Chudleigh Knighton
TQ13 ....123 C4
7 Honiton EX14 ....85 C2
Kingsteignton TQ12 ..207 E6
Plymouth PL6 ....245 E6
Seaton EX12 ....192 A7
Tavistock PL19 ....171 C3
Willand EX15 ....162 C4
Maple Dr EX8 ....196 D3
Maple Gr
Barnstaple EX31 ......154 C3
Plymouth, Mutley PL4 ..248 F4
Plymouth, Plympton PL7 ..250 B5
Tiverton EX16 ....161 D4
Maple Rd Brixham TQ5 ..230 A2
Broadclyst EX5 ....175 D6
Exeter EX4 ....177 A5
Maple Way PL6 ....245 E7
Maple Wlk TQ2 ....219 C8
Mapledene CI TQ9 ...227 F8
Maples Ct 6 EX2 ....154 F6
Mapleton Cl TQ12 ...206 F4
Marber Cross TQ7 ...149 A8
Marchant's Cross PL20 ..127 C1
Marchant's Way PL20 ..127 C2
Marcom Cl EX4 ....196 D3
Marcombe Rd TQ2 ..219 E5
Marcus Rd
Dunkeswell EX14 ....67 B2
Exmouth EX8 ....196 D1
Marder's Bequest DT7 ..260 E3
Mardle Way TQ11 ...236 B5
Mardon Cl PL6 ....245 D4
Mardon Hill EX4 .....173 B1
Mare Hill EX17 ....61 C5
Mare La Barnstaple EX31 ..9 B1
Beer EX12 ....191 B5
Marepark Cross TQ7 ..144 D3
Marepark Gate EX20 ..77 C7
Maret Rd PL5 ....243 C1
Margaret Cl
East Ogwell TQ12 ....206 F1
Kingsteignton TQ12 ..207 E7
Margaret Gdns TQ12 ..207 F2
Margaret Pk PL3 .....248 F8
Margaret Rd
East Ogwell TQ12 ....206 F1
Exeter EX4 ....173 E1
Kingsteignton TQ12 ..207 E7
Margaret St 8 EX9 ..202 A6
Margarne Terr 9 EX32 ..154 F6
Marguerite Cl TQ12 ..206 F4
Marguerite Rd EX16 ..161 F6
Marguerite Way TQ12 ..206 F4
Mariansleigh Cross EX36 ..31 A3
Marina Ct TQ5 ....230 E5
Marina Ct Brixham TQ5 ..230 E5
2 Paignton TQ3 ......226 B6
23 Teignmouth TQ14 ..210 C4
Marina Dr Brixham TQ5 ..230 E5

Marina Rd continued
Plymouth PL5 ....243 F3
Marina Terr 7 PL4 ...248 F4
Marina Way 6 EX6 ...64 D7
Marine Cres EX12 ...192 A4
Marine Ct
Budleigh Salterton EX9 ..199 H2
Instow EX39 ....15 B1
Torpoint PL11 ....247 B2
Marine Dr
Bigbury-on-Sea TQ7 ..142 E3
Heybrook Bay PL9 ....140 A7
Paignton TQ3 ....226 C7
Torpoint PL11 ....247 B2
Marine Gdns TQ3 ....226 C8
Marine Par
Appledore EX39 ....15 A1
Budleigh Salterton EX9 ..199 H2
Dawlish EX7 ....204 E5
Instow EX39 ....15 B1
Lyme Regis DT7 ......260 D2
Paignton TQ3 ....226 D8
Teignmouth TQ14 ....210 B3
Marine Pk TQ3 ....226 C7
Marine Pl
Ilfracombe EX34 ......150 B6
Seaton EX12 ....192 A4
Marine Terr 16 TQ14 ..210 B4
Marine Way EX8 .....202 A8
Mariner's Way EX39 ..15 A1
Mariners Ct
5 Brixham TQ5 ....230 D5
18 Dawlish EX7 ....204 E6
Mariners Way TQ1 ..218 F1
Marino The EX10 ....187 F3
Marions Way EX8 ...196 D2
Marist Way EX22 ...155 C3
Maristow Ave
Exmouth EX8 ....196 B2
Plymouth PL2 ....247 F5
Marjery Cross PL21 ..244 F5
Marjorie Kelly Way
PL21 ....237 D4
Marjory Wlk PL8 .....257 E3
Mark Twain Ho 8 EX4 ..178 C8
Mark's Cross EX31 ..166 C4
Marker Way EX14 ...166 C4
Markers EX15 ....66 A7
Markers Pk EX14 ....66 A7
Markers Rd EX15 ....66 A7
Market Cl
4 Bampton EX16 ....34 B1
Brushford PL22 ....33 E4
Buckfastleigh TQ11 ..236 B5
Plymouth PL1 ....248 A1
Market Pl Bideford EX39 ..157 A2
Burlescombe EX16 ...51 B3
Colyton EX24 ....198 B3
Sidmouth EX10 ....188 B3
Market Rd Plymouth PL7 ..250 D5
Tavistock PL19 ....171 C5
Market Sq
Axminster EX13 ......167 D6
Dartmouth TQ6 ....233 F3
Lynton EX35 ....151 C5
Newton Abbot TQ12 ..207 B3
Market St
2 Appledore EX39 ..15 A1
5 Barnstaple EX31 ..154 F5
2 Crediton EX17 .....165 D5
Buckfastleigh TQ11 ..236 B5
Cawsand PL10 ....253 A2
Crediton EX17 ....165 D5
Dartmouth TQ6 ....233 F3
Exeter EX1 ....261 A2
Exmouth EX8 ....202 A6
Hatherleigh EX20 ....75 C7
Ilfracombe EX34 ......150 B6
Newton Abbot TQ12 ..207 B3
North Tawton EX20 ...77 C4
Okehampton EX20 ...170 B5
Plymouth PL1 ....262 B2
Salcombe TQ8 ....259 E5
South Molton EX36 ..158 C4
Tavistock PL19 ....171 C5
Torquay TQ1 ....220 B5
Yealmpton PL8 ....257 F4
Market Way
7 Barnstaple EX32 ..155 A5
Plymouth PL1 ....248 A1
Market Wlk 7 TQ12 ..207 B3
Markham Cross EX2 ..177 B1
Markham La Exeter EX2 ..181 B7
Ide EX2 ....177 A1
Markwood Pl EX14 ..166 D6
Marl Pk
Harbertonford TQ9 ...130 A3
Holne TQ13 ....130 A3
Marland Cross PL8 ..136 B1
Marland Sch EX38 ..56 B8
Marland Terr EX38 ..56 B8
Marlborough Cl TQ1 ..220 D5
Marlborough Cross
EX5 ....179 D6

Marlborough Ct
Bideford EX39 . . . . .157 A3
Exeter, Alphington EX2 . . .181 C8
Exeter, Heavitree EX2 . . . .177 E5
Marlborough Pk 7
EX34 . . . . .150 B5
Marlborough Pl TQ12 . . . .207 A4
Marlborough Prim Sch
PL1 . . . . .247 E2
Marlborough Rd
Exeter EX2 . . . . .261 C2
Ilfracombe EX34 . . . . .150 C5
Musbury EX13 . . . . .103 D5
Plymouth PL4 . . . . .263 A4
Marlborough Row PL1 . .247 E2
Marlborough St PL1 . . . .247 E2
Marlborough Terr TQ13 .180 C7
Marlborough Way EX34 .150 C4
Marlcombe Cross EX14 . .85 A6
Marldon Ave TQ3 . . . . . .226 A6
Marldon CE Prim Sch
TQ3 . . . . .218 D3
Marldon Cl PL5 . . . . .244 B3
Marldon Cross TQ3 . . . .218 D2
Marldon Cross Hill TQ3 .218 D3
Marldon Gr TQ3 . . . . . . .218 D3
Marldon La TQ3 . . . . . . .218 B4
Marldon Rd
Paignton TQ3 . . . . .225 F8
Torquay TQ2 . . . . .219 B7
Marldon Way TQ3 . . . . .218 E2
Marlen Ct EX39 . . . . .25 F4
Marlers Cl EX14 . . . . . . .43 B4
Marles The EX8 . . . . . . .196 C2
Marley EX8 . . . . .196 C4
Marley Dr EX8 . . . . .196 C3
Marley Head TQ10 . . . . .135 C3
Marley Rd EX8 . . . . .196 C3
Marlow Cres PL16 . . . . . .106 D1
Marlow Gdns PL9 . . . . . .255 F5
Marlowe Cl TQ2 . . . . . . .219 D7
Marlpit Cl EX12 . . . . .191 F7
Marlpit Cross EX14 . . . . .87 A6
Marlpit La EX12 . . . . . . .192 A5
Marlpits La EX14 . . . . . . .166 C5
Marlpool Hill EX8 . . . . . .202 B7
Marmora Terr EX12 . . . .191 D5
Marnham Rd TQ1 . . . . . .220 B7
Marpool Cres EX8 . . . . . .202 C8
Marpool Hill EX8 . . . . . .202 B7
Marpool Prim Sch EX8 . .202 C8
Marridge Cross PL21 . . .137 F5
Marrowbone Slip PL4 . . .263 B2
Marryat Gdns PL5 . . . . . .244 E1
Mars Hill Way EX35 . . . .151 C5
Marsh Barton La EX5 . . .172 D8
Marsh Barton Rd EX2 . . .177 C1
Marsh Barton Trad Est
EX2 . . . . .177 C2
Marsh Cl PL6 . . . . .249 F6
Marsh Cross EX15 . . . . . .83 E4
Marsh Dro EX13 . . . . .87 B2
Marsh End EX17 . . . . . . .165 F5
Marsh Green La EX5 . . . .99 E5
Marsh Green Rd N EX2 . .177 C2
Marsh Green Rd N EX2 . .177 C2
Marsh Green Rd W EX2 . .177 C2
Marsh Hill Dulverton TA22 . .33 C8
Tiverton PL16 . . . . .63 A4
Marsh La Bow EX17 . . . . . .78 B5
Calstock PL18 . . . . .125 D3
Chudleigh TQ13 . . . . .123 F8
Clyst St George EX3 . . . . .183 B6
Crediton EX17 . . . . .165 E5
Instow EX39 . . . . .15 B1
Newton St Cyres EX5 . . . . .98 F8
North Molton EX36 . . . . . .30 C6
Seaton EX12 . . . . .192 B7
South Molton EX36 . . . . . .158 F7
Tiverton EX16 . . . . .161 A6
West Charleton TQ7 . . . . .144 C1
Marsh La Cross TQ13 . . .123 F8
Marsh Mill Ct EX5 . . . . .172 D7
Marsh Mills PL6 . . . . . . .249 F7
Marsh Mills Pk PL6 . . . .249 F6
Marsh Mills Ret Pk PL6 . .249 E7
Marsh Rd Crediton EX17 . .165 E5
Newton Abbot TQ12 . . . . .207 C3
Newton Abbot TQ12 . . . . .207 C4
Seaton EX12 . . . . .192 B5
Marshall Cl
Tavistock PL19 . . . . .171 D2
Tiverton EX16 . . . . .161 F3
Marshall Dr PL21 . . . . . .237 D4
Marshall Rd
Plymouth PL7 . . . . .250 A5
Tavistock PL19 . . . . .171 D3
Marshalls Field PL21 . . .237 E5
Marshalls Mead EX19 . . .42 D1
Marshbridge Cross TA22 .33 C7
Marshclose Hill TA22 . . . .21 E2
Marston Cl EX7 . . . . .204 F7
Mart The EX20 . . . . .170 B5
Martin La
Plymouth, Barbican PL4 . . .263 A2
Plymouth, Millbay PL1 . . . .262 B2
Martin Rd EX32 . . . . .155 A5
Martin St PL1 . . . . .262 B2
Martin's La EX1,EX4 . . . .261 B3
Martins Bldgs 4 TA21 . . . .4 E3
Martins Cl
Great Torrington EX38 . . . .159 F5
Wellington TA21 . . . . .160 D5
Martins Rd EX8 . . . . .196 E2

Martlesham Pl PL5 . . . . .243 F4
Marwell Cross TQ7 . . . . .142 E6
Marwood Cross EX5 . . . . .99 B3
Marwood Ct EX38 . . . . . .159 D5
Marwood Ave EX12 . . . . . .99 C3
Marwood Prim Sch EX31 . . .9 D1
Marwood's Cross
TQ10 . . . . .133 A8
Mary Arches St EX4 . . . .261 A3
Mary Cross PL21 . . . . . .137 C3
Mary Dean Ave PL5 . . . .244 C7
Mary Dean Cl PL5 . . . . .244 C7
Mary Dean's CE Prim Sch
PL5 . . . . .244 C7
Mary Newman's Cottage*
PL12 . . . . .243 A2
Mary Rose Ho TQ1 . . . . .220 B3
Mary Seacole Rd PL1 . . .262 A3
Mary St TQ13 . . . . .180 D8
Mary Tavy Sch PL19 . . . .117 E6
Maryfield Ave EX4 . . . . .177 D8
Maryland Gdns PL2 . . . .247 F7
Marypole Rd EX4 . . . . . .173 F1
Marypole Wlk EX4 . . . . .173 F1
Marythorne Rd 10 PL20 . .125 E1
Masefield Ave EX31 . . . .154 F7
Masefield Gdns PL5 . . . .244 E1
Masefield Rd EX4 . . . . . .178 C8
Masey Rd EX8 . . . . .202 D8
Masons Row PL18 . . . . . .125 C6
Masterman Rd PL2 . . . . .247 F4
Matford Ave EX2 . . . . . .177 E4
Matford La EX2 . . . . .261 C1
Matford Mews EX2 . . . . .181 D7
Matford Park Rd EX2 . . .181 D8
Matford Rd EX2 . . . . . . .177 E4
Mathews Cl EX14 . . . . . .166 B4
Mathill Cl TQ5 . . . . .230 B3
Mathill Rd TQ5 . . . . .230 B3
Maton Cl PL21 . . . . .237 D4
Matthew's Ct EX15 . . . . .163 D2
Matthews Cross EX15 . . . .66 B1
Matthews Ct EX4 . . . . . .177 A3
Mattiscombe Cross TQ7 .145 B1
Mattys Cross EX14 . . . . . .68 A3
Maudlin Dr TQ14 . . . . . .210 B8
Maudlin Rd TQ9 . . . . . . .223 C5
Maudlins La PL19 . . . . . .171 A5
Maunder's Hill EX9 . . . . .198 E7
Maunsell Cl PL2 . . . . . . .247 F7
Maurice Ct PL7 . . . . .250 F4
Mawes Ct PL18 . . . . .125 A5
Maxstoke Ct 3 TQ1 . . . .220 D5
Maxwell Rd PL4 . . . . . . .255 B8
May Terr Plymouth PL4 . .263 B3
Sidmouth EX10 . . . . .188 B4
Maybank Rd PL4 . . . . . . .263 C3
Maybrook Dr PL12 . . . . .242 D2
Mayers Way PL9 . . . . . . .255 D6
Mayfair EX16 . . . . .64 E8
Mayfair Cres PL6 . . . . . .245 B1
Mayfair Rd TQ12 . . . . . .211 D2
Mayfield PL21 . . . . .237 A4
Mayfield Cres TQ12 . . . .206 F3
Mayfield Rd EX8 . . . . . . .202 D6
Mayfield Rd
Exeter, Pinhoe EX4 . . . . . .174 E1
Exeter, Wonford EX2 . . . . .178 A5
Mayfield Sch TQ3 . . . . . . .226 C7
Mayflower Ave
Exeter EX4 . . . . .173 D2
Newton Abbot TQ12 . . . . .207 F2
Mayflower Cl
16 Bere Alston PL20 . . . .125 E1
Chittlehampton EX37 . . . . .28 F4
Dartmouth TQ6 . . . . .223 D4
Dawlish EX7 . . . . .204 E6
Plymouth PL9 . . . . .255 F7
Mayflower Ct TQ6 . . . . . .233 F4
Mayflower Dr
6 Brixham TQ5 . . . . . . .230 C3
Plymouth PL9 . . . . .248 B5
Mayflower St PL1 . . . . . .262 C3
Maynard Pk PL20 . . . . . .125 E1
Maynard Sch for Girls
EX1 . . . . .261 C3
Maynarde Cl PL7 . . . . . .251 B5
Mayne Cl EX20 . . . . .75 B7
Mayor's Ave TQ6 . . . . . . .233 F4
Maytree Cl EX21 . . . . .73 E3
Mazard Tree Hill
Bishops Nympton EX36 . . . .31 C1
South Molton EX36 . . . . . .46 C8
Mazzard Cl 9 EX32 . . . . .17 B2
Mead Cl Cullompton EX15 .163 B2
Ivybridge PL21 . . . . .237 A6
Paignton TQ3 . . . . .226 C7
Mead Cnr EX39 . . . . .37 A4
Mead Cotts EX8 . . . . . . .202 F7
Mead Cross TQ13 . . . . . .131 B6
Mead Dr TQ7 . . . . .143 A1
Mead La Paignton TQ3 . . .226 C7
Thurlestone TQ7 . . . . .143 A1
Mead Park Cl EX13 . . . . . .16 A3
Mead Rd EX31 . . . . .16 B4
Mead Rd TQ2 . . . . .219 D7
Mead The Plymouth PL7 . .250 D7
Silverton EX5 . . . . .82 B5
Mead View Rd EX14 . . . .166 C5
Mead Way EX12 . . . . . . .192 A6
Meadcombe Rd TQ7 . . . .143 A1
Meadfoot TQ7 . . . . .143 A1
Meadfoot Cl TQ1 . . . . . . .220 D3
Meadfoot Ct EX14 . . . . . .220 D3
Meadfoot Grange TQ1 . .220 C3
Meadfoot La TQ1 . . . . . . .220 D3

Meadfoot Rd TQ1 . . . . . .220 C3
Meadfoot Sea Rd TQ1 . .220 D3
Meadfoot Terr PL4 . . . . .248 F5
Meadhurst Ct EX10 . . . . .188 A3
Meadow Ave EX12 . . . . .192 A6
Meadow Bank EX13 . . . . .87 D1
Meadow Brook PL19 . . . .171 A4
Meadow Bsns Pk EX17 . . .165 F5
Meadow Cl
Bratton Fleming EX31 . . . . .18 A8
Bridford EX6 . . . . .113 A5
Cheriton Fitzpaine EX17 . . .62 F7
Clyst St Mary EX5 . . . . . . .179 E3
Harberton TQ9 . . . . .222 D2
Ilfracombe EX34 . . . . .150 B4
Kingskerswell TQ12 . . . . . .212 F6
Landkey EX32 . . . . .17 C1
Lympstone EX8 . . . . .195 F5
Newton Ferrers PL8 . . . . . .141 A7
Ottery St Mary EX11 . . . . .169 E4
Plymouth PL7 . . . . .251 D4
Saltash PL12 . . . . .242 F3
Seaton TQ9 . . . . .223 F5
Meadow Crts TQ6 . . . . . .228 C2
Meadow Cres EX8 . . . . . .203 A6
Meadow Ct Barns TQ7 . .145 B1
Meadow Dr Brixton PL8 . .257 A4
Newton Poppleford EX10 . .186 F8
Saltash PL12 . . . . .242 D4
Meadow Gdns EX17 . . . .165 D5
Meadow Halt TQ12 . . . . .207 A4
Meadow La Croyde EX33 . . .7 E2
Cullompton EX15 . . . . .163 C2
Instow EX39 . . . . .15 B1
Meadow Lea EX5 . . . . . . .82 B6
Meadow Park Dr EX37 . . .43 F3
Meadow Pk
Barnstaple EX31 . . . . .154 B2
Bideford EX39 . . . . .157 A3
Brixham TQ5 . . . . .230 B5
Dawlish EX7 . . . . .204 C7
Marldon TQ3 . . . . .218 B3
Okehampton EX20 . . . . . . .93 D6
Plymouth PL9 . . . . .255 C5
South Molton EX36 . . . . . .158 C3
Willand EX15 . . . . .162 C4
Meadow Rd
Barnstaple EX31 . . . . .154 E7
Budleigh Salterton EX9 . . .197 F2
Seaton EX12 . . . . .192 A5
Torquay TQ2 . . . . .219 E3
Meadow Rise
Dawlish EX7 . . . . .204 C7
Plymouth PL7 . . . . .251 A4
Spreyton EX17 . . . . .96 A7
Teignmouth TQ14 . . . . . . .124 E1
Meadow St EX8 . . . . .202 A7
Meadow Vale EX20 . . . . .170 A5
Meadow View
2 Bampton EX16 . . . . . .34 B1
Bishops Nympton EX36 . . . .30 F2
East Ogwell TQ12 . . . . . . .206 F1
Hartland EX39 . . . . .22 E3
Kentisbury EX22 . . . . .164 C6
Lympstone EX8 . . . . .195 F5
Rackenford EX16 . . . . .47 D5
Uffculme EX15 . . . . .66 A7
Meadow View Cl EX10 . .188 C5
Meadow View Rd PL7 . . .250 D5
Meadow Way
Colaton Raleigh EX10 . . . .186 D3
Exeter EX2 . . . . .177 F5
Plymouth PL7 . . . . .250 D7
Meadowbrook Cl EX4 . . .176 E8
Meadowcroft Dr TQ12 . . .123 E2
Meadowfell Pl PL7 . . . . .251 B3
Meadowlands
Newton St Cyres EX5 . . . . .98 F8
Plymouth PL6 . . . . .245 D7
Meadows Cres EX14 . . . .166 B6
Meadows The
Beer EX12 . . . . .191 D5
Kingsteignton TQ12 . . . . .207 F6
St Dominick PL12 . . . . . . .125 A2
Torpoint PL11 . . . . .246 E4
Yeoford EX17 . . . . .79 C2
Meadowside Ashford EX31 .16 B6
Chillington TQ7 . . . . .145 A1
Newton Abbot TQ12 . . . . .207 A3
Plymouth PL9 . . . . .255 F7
Rockwell Green TA21 . . . .160 B5
Meadowside Rd EX17 . . .80 B5
Meadowstone Cl EX18 . . .40 A5
Meadowsweet La 3
EX31 . . . . .154 B3
Meadowsweet Pk PL12 . .242 C2
Meadowview Rd EX6 . . . .196 C2
Meadowview Wlk EX6 . . .157 A3
Meadway
Newton Abbot TQ12 . . . . .212 D8
Saltash PL12 . . . . .242 E1
Sidmouth EX10 . . . . .188 B6
Mear Top EX31 . . . . .154 F7
Measbury Moor Cross
EX18 . . . . .45 A6
Meatherel Cl PL21 . . . . . .237 B4
Meavy Ave Plymouth PL5 .244 D2
Torquay TQ2 . . . . .219 B7
Meavy Bourne PL20 . . . .127 C2
Meavy CE Prim Sch
PL20 . . . . .127 C2
Meavy La PL20 . . . . .127 C2
Meavy Villas PL20 . . . . . .127 C2
Medard Ho 18 EX32 . . . .155 A5
Meddon Cross
Edistone EX39 . . . . .37 F5

Meddon Cross continued
Welcombe EX39 . . . . .37 F4
Meddon St EX39 . . . . . . .157 A1
Mede The Exeter EX4 . . . .178 B8
Topsham EX3 . . . . .182 E5
Medland Cres PL6 . . . . . .244 D6
Medland Cross EX6 . . . . .97 C6
Medland La EX6 . . . . .97 B6
Medway Pl PL3 . . . . .249 D6
Medway Rd TQ2 . . . . . . .214 B2
Meeches The EX16 . . . . . .48 F2
Meeks Row PL18 . . . . . . .125 D6
Meerhay La DT6 . . . . . . .104 F6
Meetford Cross TQ6 . . . . .97 F7
Meeting La EX34 . . . . . . .150 C8
Meeting St EX36 . . . . . . .195 E6
Meeting St
Appledore EX39 . . . . .15 A1
Exmouth EX8 . . . . .202 A7
Melbourne Cotts PL1 . . .262 B3
Melbourne La
Plymouth PL1 . . . . .262 B4
Melbourne St Exeter EX2 .261 B2
Plymouth PL1 . . . . .262 B3
Tiverton EX16 . . . . .161 B4
Melbury Rd EX39 . . . . . . .39 E8
Melcot Cl TQ12 . . . . .207 C7
Meldon La EX20 . . . . .93 E3
Meldon Rd TQ13 . . . . . . .111 A6
Meldrum Cl EX7 . . . . . . .204 E6
Melhuish Cl EX16 . . . . . . .46 E1
Mellons Cl TQ12 . . . . . . .206 D4
Mellons Wlk TQ12 . . . . . .206 D4
Mellows Mdw TQ12 . . . .206 F3
Melrose Ave TQ2 . . . . . . .248 C8
Melville La TQ1 . . . . .220 B4
Melville Pl 2 PL2 . . . . . .248 A5
Melville Rd PL2 . . . . .248 A5
Melville St TQ1 . . . . .220 B4
Membury Cl EX11 . . . . . .169 D6
Membury Com Sch EX13 .87 D6
Membury Rd EX13 . . . . . .87 E5
Memory Cross TQ13 . . . .215 E8
Mena Park Cl
Paignton TQ4 . . . . .225 F2
Plymouth PL9 . . . . .256 B7
Mena Park Rd PL9 . . . . . .256 B7
Mendip Rd TQ2 . . . . .219 D3
Merafield Cl PL7 . . . . . . .250 B5
Merafield Dr PL7 . . . . . . .250 C4
Merafield Farm Cotts
PL7 . . . . .250 B4
Merafield Rd PL7 . . . . . . .250 C4
Merafield Rise PL7 . . . . .250 C4
Mercer Ct EX2 . . . . .177 D8
Merchant's Gdn TQ7 . . . .143 A1
Merchants Cnr EX7 . . . . .204 E6
Merchants House (Mus)*
PL1 . . . . .262 C2
Mere La 15 TQ14 . . . . . .210 C5
Meredith Rd PL2 . . . . . . .248 C6
Meresyke EX8 . . . . .202 C6
Meriden TQ14 . . . . .210 C2
Meridian Ho PL4 . . . . . . .263 A3
Meridian Pl EX34 . . . . . . .150 B6
Merivale Cl TQ12 . . . . . . .210 C7
Merley Rd EX39 . . . . .156 B7
Merlin Bsns Pk EX5 . . . . .99 A4
Merlin Cl PL6 . . . . .245 E8
Merlin Cres EX14 . . . . . .174 A1
Merlin Way TQ2 . . . . . . .213 D2
Mermaid Ct 6 EX1 . . . . .262 A4
Mermaid Yd EX1 . . . . . . .261 A2
Merrifield Cross
Bridgerule EX22 . . . . .70 E4
Slapton TQ7 . . . . .145 C6
Merrifield Rd TQ11 . . . . .130 C1
Merrifields La EX16 . . . . .64 D3
Merritt Flats 4 TQ3 . . . .226 A5
Merritt Rd TQ3 . . . . .226 A5
Merrivale Cl TQ2 . . . . . . .214 B4
Merrivale Rd Exeter EX4 . .176 E4
Okehampton EX20 . . . . . . .170 E6
Plymouth PL2 . . . . .247 F6
Merrivale View Rd PL20 .127 B3
Merrow Down Dr EX12 . .191 F8
Merryfield Cl EX13 . . . . . .27 C6
Merryfield La EX6 . . . . . . .95 F2
Merryfield Rd EX19 . . . . .157 C1
Merryland Cl TQ3 . . . . . .226 B7
Merryland Gdns TQ3 . . .219 B2
Merrymeet
Tedburn St Mary EX17 . . . .97 F8
Whitestone EX4 . . . . .98 B4
Merryside Villas EX16 . . .61 D8
Merryvale Rd EX13 . . . . .153 D5
Merrywood TQ12 . . . . . . .211 C2
Mersey Cl PL3 . . . . .249 D6
Merstone Cross Rds EX36 . .46 A5
Meshaw Moor Cross
EX36 . . . . .46 A5
Meshaw Rectory Cross
EX36 . . . . .46 A5
Metcombe Cross EX31 . . .48 E2
Metcombe La EX31 . . . . . .9 B1
Metcombe Rise EX11 . . .100 C2
Metcombe Vale EX11 . . . .100 C2
Meteor Wlk 2 EX2 . . . . .155 B5
Metherell Ave TQ5 . . . . .230 D3

Metherell Avenue Ind Est
TQ5 . . . . .230 C3
Metherell Cross EX21 . . . .91 F8
Metherell Rd EX39 . . . . .156 F1
Metley Cross TQ12 . . . . .131 C5
Mettaford Cross EX39 . . .22 F3
Mews Ct 20 EX7 . . . . . . .204 E6
Mews Gdns TQ6 . . . . . . .233 F3
Mews The Bittaford PL21 .137 C8
Dawlish EX7 . . . . .204 E6
Exmouth EX8 . . . . .196 F3
Plymouth, Devonport PL1 . .248 A3
Plymouth, Stonehouse PL1 .262 A3
7 Teignmouth TQ14 . . . .210 B4
Mewstone Ave PL9 . . . . .140 D8
Meyrick Rd TQ1 . . . . . . .220 C7
Mezidon-Canon Ave
EX14 . . . . .166 D5
Michael Rd PL3 . . . . .249 A5
Michelcombe La TQ13 . . .130 A4
Michigan Way
PL1 . . . . .173 C2
Mid Churchway PL9 . . . .256 A7
Middle Blagdon La TQ3 .225 B6
Middle Budleigh Mdw
TQ12 . . . . .206 F3
Middle Combe Dr EX31 . .154 A5
Middle Down Cl PL9 . . . .256 A5
Middle Green Rd TA21 . .160 E3
Middle Leigh PL8 . . . . . .140 F7
Middle Lincombe Rd
TQ1 . . . . .220 D3
Middle Mill La EX15 . . . .163 C3
Middle Park Terr TQ7 . . .143 B1
Middle Ramshill La TQ3 .225 C7
Middle Rd PL9 . . . . .140 D8
Middle St Brixham TQ5 . . .230 C5
East Budleigh EX9 . . . . . . .198 B6
Teignmouth TQ14 . . . . . . .220 A8
Middle Warberry Rd
TQ1 . . . . .220 D5
Middle Westerland Cross
TQ3 . . . . .218 D1
Middleborough La EX33 . .7 D3
Middlecombe La PL8 . . . .140 F6
Middlecott Cross
Holemoor EX22 . . . . .73 B8
Virginstow EX21 . . . . .90 E4
Middlecott Hill EX32 . . . .18 D3
Middlecott La EX17 . . . . . .60 F2
Middlefield Rd PL6 . . . . .244 B2
Middlefield Cl PL12 . . . . .242 B2
Middlemead Rd EX16 . . .161 D5
Middlemoor Cross EX37 . .43 C3
Middlemoor Police Training
Coll EX2 . . . . .178 D5
Middleton Rd EX39 . . . . .156 F3
Middleton Wlk PL5 . . . . .243 D4
Middletown La EX9 . . . . .198 B6
Middlewood Hill EX6 . . . .201 A5
Midella Rd PL20 . . . . . . .127 A2
Midlands Cvn Pk EX31 . .154 A8
Midvale Rd TQ4 . . . . .226 B5
Midway Exmouth EX8 . . . .202 E8
Kingskerswell TQ12 . . . . . .212 F6
Midway Cl EX2 . . . . .177 A1
Midway Terr EX2 . . . . . . .177 A1
Miers Cl PL5 . . . . .247 C8
Miglo Ind Est TQ4 . . . . . . .225 E3
Milber Com Inf Sch
TQ12 . . . . .207 F3
Milber Com Jun Sch
TQ12 . . . . .207 F3
Milber La TQ12 . . . . .207 D2
Milber Trad Est TQ12 . . . .208 A1
Milbury Cl EX6 . . . . .182 B4
Milbury La EX6 . . . . .182 B4
Mildmay Cl EX4 . . . . .176 F7
Mildmay St PL4 . . . . .263 A4
Mile End Rd TQ12 . . . . . .206 E5
Mile Gdns EX4 . . . . .173 F2
Mile La EX4 . . . . .174 A1
Milehouse Rd PL2 . . . . . .248 A5
Miles Mitchell Ave PL6 . .245 A1
Miles Mitchell Village
PL6 . . . . .245 A1
Milestone Cross TQ13 . . .123 F8
Milestone La TQ12 . . . . .123 F8
Milford Ave EX10 . . . . . .188 B4
Milford Cl TQ14 . . . . .210 A5
Milford Cotts EX6 . . . . . .181 B2
Milford Cross EX39 . . . . .22 E1
Milford La EX6 . . . . .181 B2
Milford Rd EX10 . . . . . . .188 B4
Military Rd
Millbrook PL10 . . . . .252 C3
Plymouth PL3 . . . . .249 E6
Plymouth PL4 . . . . .263 A3
Milizac Cl PL8 . . . . .257 E4
Milk Hill EX5 . . . . .81 D7
Milkaway La EX33 . . . . . . .7 E1
Milky Way Adventure Pk*
EX39 . . . . .37 E6
Mill Bottom La TQ12 . . .209 A3
Mill Bridge PL1 . . . . .262 A3
Mill Cl Lee Mill PL21 . . . .136 D6
Newton Abbot TQ12 . . . . .206 F4
Mill Cotts
Okehampton EX20 . . . . . . .170 B5
Stoke Canon EX5 . . . . .173 F7
Mill Cross
Ashwater EX21 . . . . .90 D4
Mill Dr TQ14 . . . . .177 F1

Mill End ☐ TQ12 .... 123 F1
Mill Ford Sch PL5 .... 243 F4
Mill Gn D17 .... 260 E3
Mill Head EX14 .... 150 C6
Mill Hill Barnstaple EX31 ...16 A3
  Fremington EX31 .... 153 F5
  Stoke Gabriel TQ9 .... 227 F7
  Witheridge EX16 .... 61 F7
Mill Hill Ct TQ9 .... 227 F7
Mill La Alfington EX11 .... 84 F1
  Aveton Gifford TQ7 .... 143 C6
  Axminster EX13 .... 88 F3
  Barnstaple EX31 .... 154 E6
  Berrynarbor EX34 .... 2 D4
  Bow EX17 .... 78 B4
  Branscombe EX12 .... 190 D4
  Bratton Fleming EX31 .... 11 E3
  Brayford EX32 .... 18 B6
  Brixham TQ5 .... 230 A1
  Burrington EX37 .... 44 A2
  Charmouth DT6 .... 104 F6
  Cheriton Fitzpaine EX17 ....62 E2
  Clyst Honiton EX1 .... 175 C1
  Croyde EX33 .... 7 E2
  East Buckland EX32 .... 18 E2
  East Ogwell TQ12 .... 206 D1
  Galmpton TQ5 .... 229 A4
  George Nympton EX36 ......30 A1
  Loddiswell TQ7 .... 138 C7
  Lyme Regis DT7 .... 260 E3
  Newton Poppleford EX10 ..186 F6
  North Tawton EX20 .... 77 B4
  North Whimbourough TQ12 ...212 D2
  North Whimbourough TQ2 .... 212 D1
  Offwell EX14 .... 86 B1
☐ Paignton TQ3 .... 226 B7
  Sandford EX17 .... 80 B5
  Shirwell EX31 .... 17 F8
  South Molton EX36 .... 45 F7
  Stockland EX13 .... 87 B7
  Stoke Fleming TQ6 .... 146 A7
  Teignmouth TQ14 .... 209 D7
  Torpoint PL11 .... 247 A2
  Torquay TQ2 .... 219 C5
  Uplyme DT7 .... 260 C5
  Wambrook TA20 .... 69 F2
  Woolacombe EX34 .... 7 F6
  Wrafton EX33 .... 152 F4
Mill Lane Cotts EX20 .... 77 B4
Mill Leat Cotts EX17 ....78 B4
Mill Mdw
☐ Combe Martin EX34 ......3 A3
  Ivybridge PL21 .... 237 D5
Mill Park Ind Est EX5 .... 184 E8
Mill Path TQ13 .... 130 F4
Mill Pk TQ12 .... 123 E1
Mill Rd Barnstaple EX31 ...154 E5
  Bradworthy EX22 .... 38 E1
  Exeter EX2 .... 177 F1
  Fremington EX31 .... 153 E5
  High Bickington EX37 .... 43 B7
  Landkey EX32 .... 17 B1
  Millbrook PL10 .... 253 A5
  Okehampton EX20 .... 170 B4
  Tiverton EX16 .... 222 E8
Mill Rise EX14 .... 85 F8
Mill St Bideford EX39 .... 157 A2
  Chagford TQ13 .... 110 F6
  Crediton EX17 .... 165 D5
  Great Torrington EX38 ...159 C4
  Honiton EX14 .... 166 B5
  Kingsbridge TQ7 .... 258 C5
  Ottery St Mary EX11 .... 169 C3
  Sidmouth EX10 .... 188 B4
  South Molton EX36 .... 158 D4
  Uffculme EX15 .... 66 B7
Mill Steep Molland EX36 ...31 C8
  Twitchen EX36 .... 20 C1
Mill Stream Ct EX11 .... 169 D3
Mill Stream Gdns
  Halberton EX16 .... 65 A7
  Wellington TA21 .... 160 B7
Mill Tail TQ9 .... 223 D5
Mill The EX2 .... 261 C1
Mill View ☐ TQ13 .... 123 F6
Mill View Gdns PL10 .... 252 F5
Mill View Rd PL10 .... 252 F5
Mill-Leat Gdns EX32 .... 17 B2
Mill-on-the-Mole EX36 ...158 E4
Milland Cross EX20 .... 75 B1
Millards Hill ☐ EX39 .... 15 B1
Millbarn Cross EX16 .... 61 F8
Millbay Rd PL1 .... 262 A2
Millbrook CE Sch PL10 ...252 E5
Millbrook Cross EX33 .... 167 C6
Millbrook Dale EX13 .... 167 C6
Millbrook Lea EX17 .... 177 F2
Millbrook Park Rd TQ2 ...219 E5
Millers Brook PL2 TQ3 .... 226 B6
Millcombe Cnr TQ9 .... 139 C1
Millcombe La TQ9 .... 139 C1
Millcroft EX11 .... 169 D3
Milldale Cres EX14 .... 166 B5
Millen La TQ12 .... 209 C2
Millennium Way EX39 ...156 E7
Miller Ct EX2 .... 178 C4
Miller Cres EX32 .... 155 A5
Miller Ct PL1 .... 262 A2
Miller Way Exminster EX6 .181 F5
  Plymouth PL6 .... 245 E3
Millers Way
  Honiton EX14 .... 166 B5
  Tedburn St Mary EX6 ......97 F4
Milletts Cl EX6 .... 182 A4

Millgreen La EX13 .... 87 D1
Milham La TA22 .... 33 D6
Millhayes Cross EX14 ....86 F6
Millhayes Rd EX14 .... 86 F6
Millhead Rd EX14 .... 166 B5
Millhill PL19 .... 116 F1
Millhouse Pk PL11 .... 247 A2
Millmans Rd TQ3 .... 218 D3
Millmoor Cross EX37 .... 44 B2
Millmoor La EX10 .... 188 C6
Millmoor Vale EX10 .... 186 F8
Millpool Head PL10 .... 252 E4
Millpool Rd PL10 .... 253 A6
Mills Rd PL1 .... 247 F2
Millsome La
  Bondleigh EX18 .... 77 C8
  North Tawton EX18 .... 59 D1
Millstream Mdw ☐
  TQ13 .... 123 F6
Milltown Hill EX36 .... 45 F7
Milltown La
  Northlew EX20 .... 74 E2
  Sidmouth EX10 .... 188 C6
Millway Bradninch EX5 ...82 F6
☐ Chudleigh TQ13 .... 123 E6
Millway Gdns EX5 .... 82 F6
Millway Pl PL9 .... 255 D8
Millwey Ave EX13 .... 167 F7
Millwood TQ13 .... 180 C4
Millwood Bsns Pk TQ12 ...207 E3
Millwood Pl PL8 .... 245 E1
Millwood Terr EX37 .... 28 C2
Milne Pl PL1 .... 247 F3
Milsfords La EX5 .... 81 E5
Milton Abbott Sch PL19 ...116 B5
Milton Ct Brixham TQ5 ...230 B2
  Plymouth PL5 .... 244 D2
Milton Cres Brixham TQ5 ...230 B2
  Tavistock PL19 .... 171 D5
Milton Ct
☐ Newton Abbot TQ12 .... 207 C2
  Plymouth PL4 .... 249 B1
  Plymouth PL4 .... 263 C2
Milton Fields TQ12 .... 230 A2
Milton La TQ6 .... 233 C2
Milton Pk TQ5 .... 230 B2
Milton PI PL19 .... 156 F1
Milton Rd Exeter EX2 .... 177 F3
☐ Newton Abbot TQ12 .... 207 B4
Milton St TQ5 .... 230 A2
Milverton Rd TQ1 .... 160 B8
Mimosa Cl ☐ EX16 .... 161 F6
Minacre La TQ12 .... 212 E1
Mincent Cl TQ2 .... 214 A3
Mincent Hill TQ2 .... 214 A3
Minchin La EX5 .... 99 D2
Minchin Orch EX5 .... 99 E2
Mincinglake Rd EX4 .... 173 F1
Minden Rd ☐ TQ14 .... 210 B5
Minehead La TA22 .... 34 A7
Miners Cl ☐ TQ13 .... 151 A5
Minerva Cl PL7 .... 251 A5
Minerva Way TQ12 .... 207 E3
Mines Rd Bideford EX39 ...157 C1
  Bideford EX39 .... 157 D1
Miniature Pony Ctr*
  TQ13 .... 111 B3
Minifie Rd EX14 .... 166 B6
Minniemoor Cross EX31 ...4 B1
Minniemoor La EX31 ......4 C1
Minses Cl PL9 .... 256 C7
Minster Rd EX6 .... 182 B5
Mint Park Rd EX33 .... 152 B7
Mirador Pl PL4 .... 249 C3
Mire La EX10 .... 189 B7
Mirey La EX5 .... 184 C3
Misterton Cl PL9 .... 256 B8
Mitchell Ho EX4 .... 177 D8
Mitchell St TA21 .... 160 C7
Mitre Cl TQ14 .... 208 E8
Mitre Ct ☐ Plymouth PL1 ...263 A2
  Tavistock PL19 .... 171 A3
Mitre La EX4 .... 261 A3
Moat Hill TQ9 .... 223 C4
Mockham Down Gate
  EX32 .... 18 C7
Modbury Ct PL5 .... 244 B3
Modbury Cross PL21 .... 136 E2
Modbury Prim Sch
  PL21 .... 137 B2
Model Terr ☐ EX39 .... 157 A1
Modred Cl EX14 .... 174 A1
Modryford Wlk PL20 .... 126 C3
Mogworthy La EX16 ......47 D3
Mohun's Cl PL19 .... 171 C4
Mohun's Pk PL19 .... 171 C3
Mole Bridge La EX36 ...158 E4
Mole Ridge Way EX36 ...158 C5
Moles Cross TQ3 .... 218 E2
Moles La
  Kingskerswell TQ12 .... 212 E1
  Paignton TQ3 .... 218 E8
  Torquay TQ3 .... 219 A7
Molesworth Rd
  Plymouth, Plympton PL7 ...250 C6
  Plymouth, Stoke PL1,PL3 ...248 A3
Molesworth Terr PL10 ...252 F5
Moll Tall's Cross PL7 ...136 A8
Molland Cross
  Brayford EX36 .... 19 B4
  Chulmleigh EX18 .... 45 E3
Molland Hill EX32,EX36 ...19 A5
Mollison Rd PL5 .... 243 E2
Molyneaux Pl ☐ PL1 .... 247 F3
Monastery Rd TQ3 .... 226 A6
Mondeville Way
  Northam EX39 .... 156 F6

Mondeville Way continued
☐ Northam EX39 .... 156 F7
Money Acre Cross EX34 ...101 E7
Money Acre Rd EX24 .... 101 E7
Money Pit La EX13 .... 69 D1
Monica Wlk PL4 .... 263 B4
Monitor Cl EX2 .... 261 A1
Monk's Rd EX4 .... 177 F7
Monkerton Ct EX1 .... 178 E8
Monkerton Dr EX1 .... 178 E8
Monkey La EX10 .... 186 E6
Monkleigh Mill La EX39 ...40 D8
Monkleigh Prim Sch
  EX39 .... 40 F7
Monkokehampton Cross
  EX19 .... 76 A8
Monks Cl EX39 .... 156 E6
Monks Hill PL15 .... 115 A4
Monks Orch TQ12 .... 212 A6
Monks Way TQ13 .... 180 C6
Monksbridge Rd TQ5 .... 230 B3
Monksmead PL19 .... 171 A4
Monkswell Rd EX4 .... 177 E8
Monkton Rd EX14 .... 166 E7
Monkton Wyld Cross
  DT6 .... 104 C7
Monkton Wyld La DT6 ...104 F7
Monmouth Ave EX3 .... 182 F4
Monmouth Gdns PL5 .... 244 C4
Monmouth Hill EX3 .... 182 F4
Monmouth St
  Lyme Regis DT7 .... 260 E3
  Topsham EX3 .... 182 F4
Monmouth Way EX14 ...166 D5
Monro Mead ☐ TQ12 .... 122 F1
Mons Terr ☐ TQ10 .... 134 F3
Monshall EX17 .... 57 E3
Mont Le Grand EX1 .... 177 E6
Montacute Ave PL5 .... 244 B2
Montagu Rd TQ7 .... 258 C5
Montague Gdns EX9 .... 197 E1
Montague Pl EX39 .... 156 F1
Montague Rise EX14 .... 261 B4
Montague Terr PL7 .... 132 F4
Monterey TQ4 .... 226 C1
Monterey Ct TQ2 .... 214 A3
Monterey Gdns EX14 .... 173 E1
Montery Pl ☐ EX32 .... 155 B3
Montessori Cl TQ12 .... 225 D7
Montessori Rd TQ13 .... 225 D7
Montgomery Cl
  Ivybridge PL21 .... 237 E5
  Saltash PL12 .... 242 D3
Montgomery Comb Sch
  EX4 .... 177 A5
Montpelier Ct
  Exeter EX4 .... 177 A7
  Paignton TQ3 .... 219 B1
Montpelier Jun & Inf Schs
  PL2 .... 248 B6
Montpelier Rd
  Exeter EX4 .... 150 C6
  Plymouth PL2 .... 248 C7
Montpelier Terr ☐
  EX34 .... 150 C6
Montpellier Rd
  Exeter EX4 .... 202 A6
  Torquay TQ1 .... 220 B4
Monument Cl TA21 .... 160 E4
Monument Rd TA21 .... 160 E3
Monument St PL1 .... 247 E1
Moon Hill Cl EX2 .... 181 C8
Moon La Modbury PL21 .... 137 B2
  Plymouth PL4 .... 263 A3
Moon St PL4 .... 263 A3
Moon's Cross EX20 .... 95 B5
Moonhayes Cross EX14 ...68 C4
Moonridge EX2 .... 182 C7
Moor Cl TQ14 .... 210 C7
Moor Cres PL20 .... 128 A8
Moor Farm Cotts TQ8 ...148 F4
Moor Gate EX20 .... 170 C6
Moor La Barnstaple EX31 ...9 C5
  Bovey Tracey TQ13 .... 180 C5
  Braunton EX33 .... 152 A5
  Broadclyst EX5 .... 175 C8
  Brushford TA22 .... 33 F2
  Budlake EX5 .... 82 E1
  Budleigh Salterton EX9 ...197 F2
  Churchinford TA3 .... 68 D7
  Croyde EX33 .... 7 D2
  Exeter EX2 .... 181 C8
  Hatherleigh EX20 .... 75 D7
  Molland EX36 .... 31 E7
  Newton Poppleford EX10 ...100 C1
  Plymouth PL5 .... 243 E1
  Poltimore EX4 .... 174 F7
  Shobrooke EX17 .... 80 F4
  Staverton TQ9 .... 216 B5
  Torquay TQ2 .... 214 B3
  Yarnscombe EX31 .... 27 E2
  Zeal Monachorum EX17 ...78 B8
Moor Lane Cl TQ2 .... 214 A3
Moor Lane Cross EX36 ...31 E8
Moor Lea EX33 .... 152 F5
Moor Park Cl EX33 .... 7 D2
Moor Pk Chagford TQ13 ...111 A6
  Honiton EX14 .... 166 B3
  Teignmouth TQ14 .... 212 F6
Moor Rd Ipplepen TQ12 ...211 E3
  Staverton TQ9 .... 216 B5
Moor View
  Bovey Tracey TQ13 .... 180 C5
  Chudleigh TQ13 .... 123 E6
  Hatherleigh EX20 .... 75 B6
  Mary Tavy PL19 .... 117 E6
  Northlew EX20 .... 74 E2
  Plymouth, Keyham PL2 .... 247 F5

Moor View continued
  Plymouth, Laira PL3 .... 249 C4
  Torpoint PL11 .... 247 B3
  Whitchurch EX16 .... 62 E6
Moor View Cl EX10 .... 187 F7
Moor View Terr
  Plymouth PL4 .... 248 E4
  Yelverton PL20 .... 127 A2
Moorcourt Cl EX10 .... 187 F3
Moorcourt Cross EX13 ...86 E2
Moorcroft Cl
  Okehampton EX20 .... 170 C5
  Plymouth PL9 .... 256 A7
Moore Cl TQ12 .... 212 F8
Moore Ct EX17 .... 165 C5
Mooredge La EX5 .... 82 E1
Moorfield PL16 .... 105 E4
Moorfield Ave ☐ PL6 .... 249 C7
Moorfield Cl EX8 .... 202 C8
Moorfield Gdn TA24 .... 21 C6
Moorfield Rd
  Exmouth EX8 .... 202 C8
  St Giles on the Heath PL15 ...90 C5
Moorfields
  Bittaford PL21 .... 137 C8
☐ Colyton EX24 .... 103 A4
Moorfoot Cross TQ12 ...131 E3
Moorhaven EX9 .... 197 F2
Moorhayes TQ13 .... 180 D7
Moorhayes Bglws EX16 ...161 E5
Moorhayes Cross EX15 ...67 B6
Moorhayes Ct EX5 .... 84 A1
Moorhayne Cross EX15 ...66 A2
Moorhouse La TA4 .... 35 A8
Moorings Reach TQ5 .... 230 D5
Moorings The
  Braunton EX33 .... 152 D6
  Kingsbridge TQ7 .... 258 C6
  Kingston TQ7 .... 142 D4
  Plymouth TQ4 .... 226 C5
Moorland Ave
  Denbury TQ12 .... 211 A7
  Plymouth PL7 .... 250 F6
Moorland Cl
  Bittaford PL21 .... 137 C8
  Yelverton PL20 .... 241 D8
Moorland Ct PL20 .... 126 F2
Moorland Dr PL7 .... 250 E6
Moorland Gate
  Bovey Tracey TQ12 .... 123 B2
  Roborough EX19 .... 43 B3
Moorland Gdns PL7 .... 250 F6
Moorland Rd PL7 .... 250 E5
Moorland Terr EX38 .... 159 B5
Moorland View
  Buckfastleigh TQ11 .... 236 A5
  Lapford EX17 .... 60 D3
  Newton Abbot TQ12 .... 208 A2
  Plymouth, Derriford PL6 .... 245 A5
  Plymouth, Plymstock PL9 ...256 B7
  Princetown PL20 .... 128 A8
  Saltash PL12 .... 242 F4
  South Molton EX36 .... 46 D8
Moorland Way
  Exeter EX4 .... 176 F8
  Exmouth PL18 .... 125 E5
Moorlands Tiverton EX16 ...161 E6
  West Hill EX11 .... 168 D5
Moorlands La PL12 .... 242 C4
Moorlands Rd EX9 .... 197 E1
Moorlands Trad Est
  PL12 .... 242 C4
Moormead EX9 .... 197 F1
Moorpark EX9 .... 202 C6
Moorpark Rd TQ12 .... 212 F6
Moorplot La EX18 .... 59 D3
Moors End TQ12 .... 207 D8
Moors Pk TQ14 .... 208 F7
Moorsend TQ12 .... 206 E4
Moorshead Cross
  Buckfastleigh TQ11 .... 135 B6
  Widecombe PL21 .... 136 D2
Moorside TQ7 .... 147 E7
Moorstone Leat TQ4 .... 226 C1
Moortown EX18 .... 59 F8
Moortown Cross
  Rackenford EX16 .... 47 B8
Mooreview
  Broadhempston TQ13 .... 131 B1
  Marldon TQ3 .... 218 D2
  North Tawton EX20 .... 77 C4
Moorview Cl EX4 .... 173 D1
Moorview Dr TQ10 .... 209 D8
Moorview End TQ10 .... 218 D2
Moory Mdw EX34 .... 2 F4
Moothill Cross TQ9 .... 216 A6
Morchard Bishop CE Prim
  Sch EX17 .... 61 B2
Morchard Road Sta EX17 ...78 F8
Morecombe Cross EX31 ...73 A4
Moreton Ave
  Bideford EX39 .... 156 E1
  Plymouth PL6 .... 244 F1
Moreton Dr EX39 .... 156 E2
Moreton Park Rd EX39 ...156 E1
Moreton Terr EX16 .... 161 C3
Moretonhampstead General
  Hospl TQ13 .... 111 F5
Moretonhampstead Prim Sch
  TQ13 .... 111 F5
Moretonhampstead Rd
☐ Morgan Ave TQ2 .... 220 A5
Morgan Ct EX14 .... 202 A6
Morganhayes Cross
  EX24 .... 102 D4
Morgans Quay TQ14 .... 210 B3

Morice Sq PL1 .... 247 E2
Morice St PL1 .... 247 E2
Morice Terr EX22 .... 54 A6
Morice Town Prim Sch
  PL2 .... 247 E4
Morin Rd TQ3 .... 226 C8
Morlaix Dr PL6 .... 245 B4
Morleigh Cross EX13 .... 139 A3
Morleigh Green Cross
  TQ9 .... 139 A3
Morley Cl TQ9 .... 139 C6
Morley Cl PL7 .... 250 A5
Morley Dr PL20 .... 126 D2
Morley Rd EX4 .... 177 E8
Morley View Rd PL7 .... 250 C6
Mornacott Cross EX36 ...31 A4
Mornacott Rd EX36 .... 31 A4
Morningside
  Dawlish EX7 .... 204 C4
  Torquay TQ2 .... 220 E5
Mornington Pk TA21 .... 160 E5
Morrell's Cross EX16 ......34 B4
Morrell's La EX16 .... 50 B6
Morris Cl EX20 .... 75 B7
Morris Pk PL9 .... 255 F6
Morshead Rd PL6 .... 244 F2
Mortain Rd PL12 .... 242 D4
Mortehoe Station Rd EX34 ...1 B1
Mortimer Ave TQ3 .... 226 B8
Mortimer Ct EX2 .... 178 A2
Mortimers Cross EX15 ...66 B4
Mortimore Ct PL12 .... 242 D2
Morton Cres EX8 .... 201 F6
Morton Crescent Mews
  EX8 .... 201 F6
Morton Rd EX8 .... 201 F6
Morton Way EX13 .... 167 D4
Morven Dr EX8 .... 196 A2
Morwell Gdns PL2 .... 248 A6
Morwellham Quay*
  PL19 .... 125 E4
Morwenna Park Rd
  EX39 .... 156 F7
Morwenna Ter ☐ EX39 ...156 F7
Moses Cl PL6 .... 244 E7
Moses Ct PL6 .... 244 E7
Mosshayne La EX1,EX5 ...175 B2
Mossop Cl EX11 .... 169 D3
Mostyn Ave PL4 .... 249 A4
Mote Pk PL12 .... 242 C3
Motehole Rd TQ12 .... 211 D2
Mothecombe PL8 .... 142 A6
Mothecombe Wlk PL6 ...245 E1
Mott's Cross EX15 .... 84 A7
Mott's La EX15 .... 84 B2
Moult Rd TQ8 .... 259 B2
Moulton Cl PL7 .... 251 B5
Mount Batten Waterside Pk*
  PL9 .... 254 F7
Mount Boone TQ6 .... 233 F4
Mount Boone Hill TQ6 .... 233 F4
Mount Boone La TQ6 .... 233 F4
Mount Boone Way TQ6 ...233 F4
Mount Cl EX14 .... 166 B5
Mount Edgcumbe Country
  Pk* PL10 .... 253 E6
Mount Gould Ave PL4 ...249 B2
Mount Gould Cres PL4 ...249 B3
Mount Gould Hospl PL4 ...249 B3
Mount Gould Rd PL4 .... 249 B3
Mount Gould Way PL4 ...249 B3
Mount Hermon Rd TQ2 ...220 B6
Mount House Sch PL19 ...171 E7
Mount Pleasant
  Bideford, East-the-Water
  EX39 .... 157 C3
  Bideford, Littleham EX39 ...25 D2
☐ Bishop's Tawton EX32 ...16 E1
☐ Chudleigh TQ13 .... 123 F6
☐ Crediton EX17 .... 165 C5
  Millbrook PL10 .... 252 E5
  Moretonhampstead TQ13 ...111 F4
  Plymouth PL5 .... 244 B2
Mount Pleasant Ave
  EX8 .... 196 B3
Mount Pleasant Cl
  Kingsbridge TQ7 .... 258 D6
  Kingskerswell TQ12 .... 213 A3
Mount Pleasant La ☐
  TQ14 .... 210 A3
Mount Pleasant Mews
  TQ5 .... 230 C4
Mount Pleasant Rd
  Brixham TQ5 .... 230 C4
  Dawlish Warren EX7 .... 201 B1
  Exeter EX4 .... 177 E8
  Kingskerswell TQ12 .... 213 A3
  Newton Abbot TQ12 .... 207 C2
☐ Torquay TQ2 .... 220 B6
Mount Radford Cres
  EX2 .... 261 C2
Mount Raleigh Ave
  EX39 .... 156 F4
Mount Raleigh Dr EX39 ...156 F4
Mount Rd TQ5 .... 230 D5
Mount Ridley Rd TQ6 ...234 C3
Mount Rise EX4 .... 177 E8
Mount St
  Plymouth, Mount Wise PL1 ...247 E1
  Plymouth, Mutley PL4 .... 263 A4
  Plymouth PL1 .... 254 A8
Mount Stone Rd PL1 .... 254 A8

Mount Street Prim Sch
PL4 ....263 A4
Mount Tamar Cl PL5 ....243 E2
Mount Tamar St PL5 ....243 E2
Mount Tavy Rd PL19 ....171 E6
Mount The
  52 Appledore EX39 ....15 A1
  Brixham TQ5 ....230 C6
  Teignmouth TQ14 ....210 B6
  Torquay TQ2 ....213 F4
  Totnes TQ9 ....223 C4
Mount View
  18 Colyton EX24 ....103 A4
  Feniton EX14 ....84 E2
Mount View Cotts EX32 ...155 F2
Mount View Terr 2
  TQ9 ....223 C5
Mount Wear Sq EX2 ....182 C8
Mount Wise Cl PL1 ....243 E1
Mount Wise Prim Sch
  PL1 ....247 E1
Mountain Cl EX8 ....202 F8
Mountain Hill EX8 ....197 A1
Mountbatten Cl
  Exmouth EX8 ....196 D2
  Plymouth PL9 ....255 D6
Mountbatten Rd PL4 ....161 C5
Mountbatten Way PL9 ......255 E6
Mounter's Hill TA20 ....69 E2
Mounthill Cotts TQ12 ......122 F1
Mounthill La EX13 ....103 E5
Mounticombe Cross
  EX18 ....45 C1
Mounticombe La EX18 ......45 C1
Mourne Villas PL9 ....255 F8
Mouse Hole La EX14 ....84 C4
Mouseberry Cross EX17 ...46 A4
Mouseberry La TQ13 ......124 B4
Mousehole Cross EX14 ....84 D5
Mowbars Hayes EX13 ......87 A3
Mowbray Ave EX4 ....261 B4
Mowbray Ct EX2 ....178 A5
Mowhay Mdw PL11 ....252 B8
Mowhay Rd
  Plymouth PL5 ....243 F1
  Plymouth PL5 ....244 A2
Mowlish La EX6 ....200 B7
Mowstead Pk EX33 ....152 B7
Mowstead Rd EX33 ....152 B7
Moxeys Cl EX17 ....62 E1
Moyses La EX20 ....170 B4
Moyses Mdw EX20 ....170 B4
Mrs Ethelston's Prim Sch
  DT7 ....260 A5
Mucky La EX19 ....57 D6
Mudbank La EX8 ....202 A8
Muddy La
  East Buckland EX32 ....18 E2
  Ottery St Mary EX11 ....101 B7
Mudford Gate EX16 ....62 E7
Mudgate Cross EX36 ....20 D3
Mudge La TQ12 ....217 E6
Mudge Way PL7 ....250 E5
Mudges Terr PL18 ....125 D6
Mudstone Cross EX19 ....58 B7
Mudstone La TQ5 ....230 E3
Mulberry Cl Exeter EX1 ...178 C7
  Paignton TQ3 ....225 E6
  Plymouth PL6 ....245 E7
  Willand EX15 ....162 D4
Mulberry Gr PL19 ....171 C2
Mulberry Rd PL12 ....242 E3
Mulberry St 3 TQ14 ....210 B4
Mulberry Way EX11 ....154 B2
Mulgrave St PL1 ....262 C2
Mullacott Cross EX34 ....1 E1
Mullet Ave PL3 ....249 C4
Mullet Cl PL3 ....249 C4
Mullet Rd PL3 ....249 C4
Mullion Cl PL11 ....246 F4
Munro Ave PL3 ....141 B8
Murchington Cross
  TQ13 ....110 E7
Murdock Rd PL11 ....246 F3
Murley Cl EX17 ....165 A6
Murley Cres TQ14 ....208 E8
Murley Grange TQ14 ....208 E8
Musbury Prim Sch
  EX13 ....103 D5
Musbury Rd EX13 ....167 C4
Museum Ct TQ2 ....258 C6
Museum Rd TQ1 ....220 C4
Musgrave Row EX4 ....261 B3
Musgraves TA22 ....33 E6
Musket Rd TQ12 ....180 F2
Mutley Cl PL4 ....263 A4
Mutley Plain PL4 ....248 E4
Mutley Plain La PL4 ....248 E4
Mutley Rd PL3 ....248 A3
Muttersmoor Rd EX10 .....187 E5
Mutton La TQ7 ....181 C8
Muxworthy La EX32 ....19 A8
Mylor Cl PL2 ....248 D8
Myra Cl 27 EX39 ....15 A1
Myrtle Cl Exeter EX2 ....177 B1
  Yelverton PL20 ....127 B3
Myrtle Cottage Rd EX39 .157 B8
Myrtle Farm View EX13 .....7 E2
Myrtle Gdns EX39 ....157 A2
Myrtle Gr EX39 ....157 A2
Myrtle Rd TQ1 ....210 C5
Myrtle La TA21 ....51 E7
Myrtle Rd EX4 ....176 E4
Myrtle Row Exmouth EX8 .202 A6
  4 Torquay TQ1 ....220 B5

Myrtle St 17 EX39 ....15 A1
Myrtles Ct PL12 ....242 D4
Myrtleville PL2 ....248 A6

N

Nadder Bottom EX4 ....176 B8
Nadder La
  Nadderwater EX4 ....176 B8
  South Molton EX36 ....158 B4
Nadder Park Rd EX4 ....176 D5
Nadrid Cross EX36 ....30 A8
Nadrid East Cross EX36 ...30 A8
Naish's La EX13 ....87 B3
Nancarrows PL12 ....242 C2
Nap La EX18 ....44 C1
Nap View EX14 ....85 B4
Napier St PL1 ....247 F3
Napier Terr Exeter EX4 ...261 A3
  Plymouth PL4 ....248 E4
Naps La EX10 ....186 C5
Narfords La TA20 ....69 F1
Narracott La
  Hollocombe EX18 ....58 E7
  South Molton EX36 ....158 A2
Narratons Rd EX20 ....93 E6
Narrow La
  Copplestone EX17 ....79 C4
  Saltash PL12 ....242 C7
Tiverton EX16 ....161 C2
Narrowmoor Cross TQ7 ..144 D4
Naseby Dr TQ12 ....180 F2
Nash Cl PL7 ....251 A5
Nash Gdns EX7 ....204 D4
Nash La DT6 ....88 H2
Nasmith Cl EX8 ....196 E1
Natcott La EX39 ....22 F2
National Marine Aquarium*
  PL4 ....263 A2
National Shire Horse Ctr
  The* PL8 ....136 B2
Nats La Cornwood PL21 ...133 D1
Sparkwell PL21 ....136 C8
Natson Mill La EX17 ....178 B4
Nattadon Rd TQ13 ....111 A6
Natty Cross EX38 ....43 A5
Neadon La EX6 ....112 F5
Neal Cl PL7 ....251 B4
Neath Rd PL4 ....263 C4
Needlewood Cl EX15 ....168 C3
Neet Way EX22 ....164 C6
Neilgate Cnr TQ13 ....131 A3
Nelson Ave PL1 ....247 F3
Nelson Cl Staverton TQ9 ..216 A5
  Teignmouth TQ14 ....210 A6
Nelson Cross TQ9 ....182 E5
  Torquay TQ1 ....220 D2
Nelson Dr Exmouth EX8 ...202 E8
  Westward Ho! EX39 ....156 C7
Nelson Gdns 5 PL1 ....247 F3
Nelson Pl TQ12 ....207 B5
Nelson Rd Brixham TQ5 ...230 C5
  Dartmouth TQ6 ....233 C3
  Exeter EX4 ....177 A5
  Westward Ho! EX39 ....156 C7
Nelson Terr
  Plymouth PL6 ....245 E6
  Westward Ho! EX39 ....156 C7
Neopardy Cross
  Yeoford, Neopardy EX17 ...79 D2
  Yeoford, Winstode EX17 ...79 D1
Nepean St 1 PL2 ....247 F5
Neptune Ct 3 EX1 ....261 A2
Ness Dr PL21 ....210 B2
Ness View Rd TQ14 ....210 C8
Neswick St PL1 ....262 B3
Nether Mdw TQ3 ....218 D3
Nethercott Cross
  Ashwater EX21 ....90 C7
  Oakford EX16 ....48 C8
Nethercott Hill EX14 ....48 B3
Nethercott Rd EX33 ....8 C2
Netherham Cross EX33 ....8 A2
Netherham Hill EX33 ....8 A2
Netherleigh Rd TQ1 ....220 B7
Netherton Cross EX34 ......3 A4
Netherton East PL20 ......126 D3
Netherton La EX34 ....3 A4
Netherton Rd TQ12 ....207 B8
Netacott Cross EX5 ....81 B2
Nettleford Hill EX6 ....46 F5
Nettlehayes PL9 ....256 D7
Netton Cl PL9 ....256 B6
Netton Cross PL3 ....249 D6
Neville Rd
  Newton Abbot TQ12 ....207 A4
  Okehampton EX20 ....170 C5
New Barn Hill PL7 ....250 F3
New Barns Rd EX4 ....8 A1
New Bldgs Bampton EX16 ..34 C1
  8 Barnstaple EX32 ....155 A6
  Broadclyst EX5 ....175 C7
  Chittlehampton EX37 ......28 F3
  Doddiscombsleigh EX6 ...113 D8
  3 Exeter EX4 ....177 D8
  Fremington EX31 ....153 E5
  Thurlestone TQ7 ....143 C1
New Bridge Cross EX31 ...27 E2
New Bridge St EX4 ....261 A2
New Cotts Exmouth EX8 ...202 F7
  Gunnislake PL18 ....125 D6

New Cross
  Avonwick TQ10 ....135 C2
  Kingsteignton TQ12 ....123 E1
New Cut Beer EX12 ....191 D5
  Crediton EX17 ....165 B5
New England Hill PL7 ......136 B5
New England Rd PL7 ....136 B5
New Esplanade Ct TQ4 ...226 C6
New Est EX5 ....81 A2
New Exeter Rd TQ13 ....123 F7
New Exeter St TQ13 ....123 E6
New George St PL1 ....262 C3
New Inn Cross 6 EX5 ....99 E8
New Inn Ct
  Cullompton EX15 ....163 C3
  6 Holsworthy EX22 ....96 D3
New La Bampton EX16 ....33 F2
  Broadhempston TQ9 ....131 E1
  Ottery St Mary EX11 ....169 E4
  Staverton TQ9 ....215 F5
  Tatworth TA20 ....88 C8
New Park (Cvn Site)
  TQ13 ....180 C4
New Park Cross TQ5 ....230 D4
New Park Cres TQ12 ....207 D8
New Park Rd
  Kingsteignton TQ12 ....207 D8
  Lee Mill PL7,PL21 ....136 B6
  Paignton TQ3 ....225 F7
  Plymouth PL7 ....251 A4
New Passage Hill PL1 .....247 E3
New Path EX17 ....97 C7
New Pk Bridford EX6 ....112 F5
  Horrabridge PL20 ....126 F4
New Quay La TQ5 ....230 D5
New Quay St
  Appledore EX39 ....15 A1
  Teignmouth TQ14 ....210 B4
  Paignton TQ3 ....225 F7
New Rd Barnstaple EX32 ...155 A4
  Bere Alston PL20 ....125 E2
  Bickleigh PL6,PL7 ....132 A5
  Bideford EX39 ....157 A1
  Bishop's Tawton EX32 ....16 E1
  Brendon EX35 ....6 D4
  Brixham TQ5 ....230 B4
  Buckfastleigh TQ11 ....236 B5
  Cawsand PL10 ....253 A1
  Cawsand, Kingsand PL10 .253 A2
  Chard Junction TA20 ....88 F8
  Clyst St Lawrence EX5 ......83 B3
  Great Torrington EX38 .....159 D5
  Instow EX39 ....15 C1
  Lifton PL16 ....105 F4
  Loddiswell TQ7 ....143 F7
  Lutton PL21 ....133 B2
  Merton EX20 ....57 A6
  Modbury PL21 ....137 B2
  Morchard Bishop EX17 .....61 B2
  Okehampton EX20 ....170 B6
  Roborough PL6 ....241 D2
  Saltash PL12 ....242 E3
  South Molton EX36 ....158 D4
  Starcross EX6 ....201 A8
  Stoke Fleming TQ6 ....146 B7
  Stoke Gabriel TQ9 ....227 F7
  Teignmouth TQ14 ....210 C7
  Totnes TQ9 ....223 D6
  Uppottery EX14 ....68 B1
  Watertow TA21 ....35 F4
  West Hill EX5 ....168 B5
  Wilmington EX14 ....86 D2
  Yealmpton PL8 ....136 A2
New Road Cl EX10 ....253 A2
New Road Cross
  Okehampton EX20 ....93 F5
  South Molton EX36 ....46 D6
  Wilmington EX14 ....86 D1
New Road Est EX20 ....93 F8
New Row 8 EX17 ....79 C4
New Sch The EX6 ....182 A5
New Sidmouth Rd EX20 ...102 F4
New St 6 Appledore EX39 ...15 A1
  Barnstaple EX32 ....157 A2
  Chagford TQ13 ....111 A6
  Chulmleigh EX18 ....44 E1
  Cullompton EX15 ....163 B3
  Exmouth EX8 ....202 A7
  Great Torrington EX38 .....159 C5
  Milton Damerel EX22 ....54 D3
  Okehampton EX20 ....93 F5
  Paignton TQ3 ....226 B6
  Plymouth PL1 ....263 A2
  Sidmouth EX10 ....188 B3
  Torrington EX38 ....159 C5
New Valley Rd EX4 ....176 F7
New Village Cross EX17 .....59 F2
New Way EX35 ....184 C6
New Way Est EX14 ....67 B2
New Wlk TQ9 ....223 D5
New Wood Cl PL6 ....245 E8
New Zealand Ho PL3 ......248 B4
Newacott Cross EX22 ....70 E5
Newberry Cl EX34 ....2 E4
Newberry Cotts EX33 ....8 A2
Newberry Hill EX34 ....2 F4
Newberry Rd
  Bideford EX39 ....157 A3

Newberry Rd
  Combe Martin EX34 ....2 F4
  Georgeham EX33 ....8 A2
Newberry's Patch TA3 .....68 D7
Newbery Cl
  Axminster EX13 ....167 E6
  Colyton EX24 ....103 A4
Newbery Comm Ctr EX5 ...99 A4
Newbridge Cross
  Bishop's Tawton EX32 ....27 F7
  Cowley EX5 ....172 D6
Newbridge Cswy EX31,
  EX32 ....27 E7
Newbridge Hill
  Cowley EX5 ....172 E6
  Gunnislake PL18 ....125 D6
  Holne TQ13 ....130 A6
  Witheridge EX16 ....46 D6
Newbuilding's Hill EX17 ...63 A3
Newbuildings Cross
  EX17 ....79 D6
Newbury Ct PL5 ....244 B4
Newbury Rd PL5 ....244 B4
Newcastle Gdns PL5 ....244 B5
Newcombe Cl EX20 ....170 D6
Newcombe St EX1 ....178 A6
Newcombe Street Gdns
  EX1 ....178 A6
Newcombe Terr EX1 ....177 F6
Newcombes 6 EX17 ....165 C5
Newcomen Rd TQ6 ....233 F3
Newcot Cross EX15 ....67 D5
Newcourt Rd
  Silverton EX5 ....82 B5
  Topsham EX3 ....182 E7
Newcross Pk 10 TQ12 ....123 E1
Newfoundland Cl EX4 .....173 E2
Newfoundland Way 1
  TQ12 ....207 B3
Newgate Cross TA22 ....33 D7
Newhay Cl EX7 ....204 C6
Newhay Cross TQ12 ....211 C1
Newhayes Cl EX2 ....177 A2
Newhayes TQ12 ....211 C1
Newhouse Hill EX14 ....46 E2
Newhouse La
  Chipstable TA4 ....35 E6
  Hittisleigh EX6 ....96 D5
Newland Cotts EX32 ....17 C1
Newland Cross
  King's Nympton TQ12 ....44 C8
  North Tawton EX20 ....77 B3
  Rackenford EX16 ....47 B2
Newlands Dawlish EX7 ....204 E7
  Honiton EX14 ....166 C6
Newlands Ave EX8 ....202 D8
Newlands Cl Exeter EX2 ...177 A2
  Landkey EX32 ....17 C2
  Sidmouth EX10 ....188 B8
Newlands Cross PL21 ......237 D3
Newlands Pk EX12 ....192 A6
Newlands Rd EX10 ....188 B8
Newlane End TQ9 ....215 F5
Newman Cres TQ2 ....213 B2
Newman Ct EX4 ....176 E5
Newman Rd Exeter EX4 ...176 E5
  Plymouth PL5 ....243 E2
  Saltash PL12 ....242 F3
Newnhall Ind Est PL7 ......250 F6
Newnham Cross EX37 ......44 C8
Newnham Ind Est PL7 .....250 F6
Newnham La EX18,EX37 ...44 C8
Newnham Way PL7 ....250 F6
Newport Comm Sch Sch EX32 ...155 B3
Newport Rd
  Barnstaple EX32 ....155 A3
  Exeter EX2 ....182 C7
Newport St
  Dartmouth TQ6 ....233 F3
  Millbrook PL10 ....252 E5
  Plymouth PL1 ....248 A1
  Tiverton EX16 ....161 D4
Newton Cross
  Blackawton TQ9 ....145 B7
  Denbury TQ12 ....211 B6
  Hartland EX39 ....22 C2
  Zeal Monachorum EX17 ....77 F7
Newton Ferrers CE Prim Sch
  PL8 ....140 F7
Newton Ferrers St PL2 ....248 C6
Newton Gdns PL5 ....243 F2
Newton Hall TQ12 ....207 C2
Newton Hill
  Darcombe TQ12 ....213 F6
  Newton Ferrers PL8 ....140 F7
Newton Ho PL5 ....80 F1
Newton Poppleford Prim Sch
  EX10 ....186 F8
Newton Rd
  Bideford EX39 ....157 A3

Newton Rd continued
  Bishopsteignton TQ14 .....208 D7
  Bovey Tracey TQ13 ....180 C6
  Bovey Tracey, Heathfield
    TQ13 ....180 E3
  Kingskerswell TQ12 ....213 A5
  Kingsteignton TQ12 ....207 D5
  Salcombe TQ8 ....259 D4
  Torquay TQ2 ....213 D1
Newton St EX38 ....55 C7
Newton Sq 6 EX16 ....34 B1
Newton St Cyres Prim Sch
  EX5 ....172 A8
Newton St Cyres Sta EX5 ..81 A1
Newton St Petrock Cross
  EX38 ....40 B1
Newtons Orch EX13 ....87 C1
Newtown Cornwood PL21 .133 C2
  Sidmouth EX10 ....188 B4
Newtown Cross EX36 ....31 A4
Newtown La EX36 ....31 A3
Nibbys Cross EX15 ....66 B5
Nicholas Cl EX2 ....33 E4
Nicholas Mdw EX17 ....125 B4
Nicholas Rd EX1 ....178 A6
Nichols Nymett Cross
  EX20 ....77 F4
Nichols Nymett La EX20 ...77 F5
Nichols Nymett Moors Cross
  EX20 ....77 F4
Nicholson Rd
  Plymouth PL5 ....244 F7
  Torquay TQ2 ....213 D1
Nick Reed's La EX15 ....52 D1
Nightingale Cl
  Plymouth PL5 ....256 C8
  Torquay TQ2 ....213 E2
Nightingale Lawns
  EX15 ....163 A2
Nilch Pk PL12 ....242 C2
Nilgala Cl EX39 ....156 E4
Nine Ash Cross EX16 ....49 D6
Nine Milestone Cross
  PL21 ....137 D2
Nine Oaks Aylesbeare EX5 ..99 C1
Dousland PL20 ....127 C3
Nirvana Cl PL21 ....237 C5
No Hill Pl TQ9 ....131 E1
No Man's Land EX33 ....3 B1
No Nans Chaple EX5 ....81 D3
No Place Hill TQ9 ....131 E1
Noelle Dr TQ12 ....207 A4
Noland Pk TQ10 ....135 A2
Nomandsland Cross
  EX16 ....62 B8
Nomansland EX17 ....80 D5
Nook The PL19 ....171 D6
Norcombe Ct EX12 ....192 B4
Norden La TQ7 ....143 B5
Nordon Cross TQ12 ....131 F3
Norfolk Cl PL3 ....249 C5
Norfolk Rd PL3 ....249 C4
Norfolk Terr 22 EX32 ......155 A4
Norleigh Cross EX20 ....75 C3
Norley Rd EX33 ....8 B1
Norman Cl Exmouth EX8 ..196 D2
  Newton Abbot TQ12 ....206 E5
Norman Dr EX15 ....163 C5
Norman Lockyer Obsy*
  EX10 ....188 D5
Norman Rd TQ3 ....226 C7
Norman Terr EX39 ....157 A7
Normandy y Way EX36 ....158 B4
Normandy Cl EX8 ....196 E1
Normandy Hill PL5 ....243 B2
Normandy Rd EX1 ....177 F6
Normandy Way
  Plymouth PL5 ....243 C2
  Salcombe TQ8 ....259 E5
Normans Cleave EX35 .....151 B5
Norns La TQ6 ....145 F6
Norsworthy's Grave EX17 ..97 E8
North Ave Bideford EX39 ...157 D1
  Exeter EX1 ....177 E6
  Lyme Regis DT7 ....260 D4
North Boundary Rd TQ5 ..230 B5
North Buckland Hill EX33 ...8 C3
North Combe Cross EX16 ..48 A3
North Combe Rd EX16 ......34 B4
North Country La EX16 .....47 A3
North Devon Coll EX31 ...154 E3
North Devon Cottage Rd
  EX16 ....161 B5
North Devon District Hospl
  EX31 ....155 A8
North Devon Maritime Mus*
  EX39 ....15 A1
North Devon Mus*
  EX32 ....154 F4
North Dimson PL18 ....125 D6
North Down Cres PL2 ......247 F6
North Down Cross EX37 ....79 B1
North Down Gdns PL2 .....247 F6
North Down Rd
  Braunton EX33 ....152 E6
  Plymouth PL2 ....248 B6
North East St EX17 ....47 A7
North Emb TQ6 ....233 F4
North End Cl TQ12 ....211 C2
North Ford Rd TQ6 ....233 F3
North Furzeham Rd
  TQ5 ....230 C6
North Gate Cl EX4 ....261 A3
North Gn 2 EX32 ....155 B4
North Grange EX2 ....178 D3
North Hele Cross EX16 .....31 A4
North Heasley Cross
  EX36 ....19 C4

North Hill PL4 .... 263 A4
North Hill Cl TQ5 .... 230 B5
North Hill La
  Morchard Bishop EX17 .... 61 B3
  Stockland EX14 .... 86 F8
North Huish Cross TQ10 138 B8
North La Ashford EX31 .... 16 A6
  Barnstaple, Bickington EX31 .... 154 A4
  Barnstaple, Middle Marwood EX31 .... 9 B3
  Barnstaple, Whiddon EX31 .. 9 D2
  Bratton Fleming EX31 .... 11 F4
North Lawn Ct EX1 .... 177 F6
North Lodge Cl EX7 .... 204 C5
North Molton Cross EX2 .... 261 C2
North Molton Prim Sch EX36 .... 30 D8
North Moor Cross EX36 38 C3
North Morte Rd EX34 .... 7 F8
North Park Almshouses EX2 .... 261 C2
North Park Rd
  Exeter EX4 .... 173 B1
  Tedburn St Mary EX6 .... 97 F4
North Park Villas PL12 .. 242 C4
North Prospect Prim Sch PL2 .... 248 A7
North Prospect Rd PL2 .. 248 A6
North Rd
  Barnstaple EX31 .... 155 A7
  Bideford EX39 .... 157 A2
  Bradworthy EX22 .... 38 E1
  Hartland EX39 .... 22 D3
  High Bickington EX37 .... 43 B7
  Holsworthy EX22 .... 164 D5
  Lee Mill PL21 .... 136 F4
  Okehampton EX20 .... 170 C7
  Saltash PL12 .... 242 F3
  South Molton EX36 .... 158 C5
  Torpoint PL11 .... 247 B3
  Yelverton PL20 .... 126 F3
North Rd E PL4 .... 262 C4
North Rd W PL1 .... 262 B4
North Road Ind Est EX20 .... 170 C6
North Rocks Rd TQ4 .... 229 C7
North St Ashburton TQ13 ..130 F5
  Axminster EX13 .... 167 D6
  Braunton EX33 .... 152 D6
  Chagford TQ13 .... 111 A6
  Crediton EX17 .... 165 C5
  Denbury TQ12 .... 211 A7
  Dolton EX19 .... 57 F7
  Exeter EX4 .... 261 A3
  Exeter, Heavitree EX1 .. 177 F6
  Ilfracombe EX34 .... 202 A7
  Hartland EX39 .... 22 D3
  Ipplepen TQ12 .... 211 D2
  North Tawton EX20 .... 77 C4
  Okehampton EX20 .... 170 B5
  Ottery St Mary EX11 ..169 E4
  Plymouth PL4 .... 263 A3
  Sheepwash EX21 .... 56 C1
  South Molton EX36 .... 158 C5
  Tavistock PL19 .... 171 C5
  Topsham EX3 .... 182 F4
  Wellington TA21 .... 160 D6
  Witheridge EX16 .... 46 E1
North Street 2 TQ9 .... 223 C6
North Tawton Prim Sch EX20 .... 77 C4
North Terr EX31 .... 154 A4
North View EX39 .... 156 F3
North View Hill EX39 .. 156 F3
North View Rd TQ5 .... 230 D5
North Walk Hill EX35 ..151 C6
North Weald Gdns PL5 .. 243 E5
North Wlk
  Barnstaple EX31 .... 154 F5
  Lynton EX35 .... 151 B6
Northam Burrows Ctry Pk* EX39 .... 14 E1
Northam Rd EX39 .... 156 F3
Northampton Cl PL5 .... 244 B5
Northams Mdw EX20 .. 170 A4
Northay Cross EX13 .... 88 H3
Northay La
  Axminster EX13 .... 88 G3
  Combe St Nicholas TA20 ..69 E6
Northbeer Cross EX17 .. 64 E2
Northbeer La EX17 .... 95 F8
Northclose Rd EX18 .... 59 D2
Northcombe La TA22 .... 33 E7
Northcote EX14 .... 166 C6
Northcote Cross EX37 .. 43 E4
Northcote Hill EX14 .. 166 F7
Northcote La
  Honiton EX14 .... 166 B6
  Witheridge EX16 .... 62 F8
Northcote Rd EX14 .. 166 E7
Northcott Gdns EX39 .. 157 A7
Northcott Terr 6 EX22 ..164 C4
Northdene EX14 .... 166 B6
Northdown Dr EX39 .. 156 F3
Northdown La EX36 .... 45 F6
Northdown Rd
  Bideford EX39 .... 156 F2
  Thorverton EX5 .... 81 F7
Northern La
  Branscombe EX12 .... 190 B5
  Sidmouth EX10 .... 189 E8
Northernhay 16 TQ12 ..207 C3

Northernhay Pl EX4 .... 261 B3
Northernhay Sq EX4 .... 261 A3
Northernhay St EX4 .... 261 A3
Northesk St PL2 .... 248 A4
Northfield EX13 .... 103 D5
Northfield La EX31 .... 154 F7
Northfield Pk EX31 .... 154 F7
Northfield Rd
  Bideford EX39 .... 157 C1
  Georgeham EX33 .... 8 B2
  Ilfracombe EX34 .... 150 B6
  Okehampton EX20 .... 170 B5
Northfield Terr 8 EX31 .. 154 F7
Northfields EX13 .... 103 D5
Northfields Ind Est TQ5 230 B5
Northfields La TQ5 .... 230 B5
Northgate EX39 .... 22 D3
Northgate La EX14 .... 86 A3
Northground La EX10 ..101 D1
Northland Cnr EX11 .... 11 D2
Northland Cross EX36 .. 19 A1
Northleat Ave TQ3 .... 225 E5
Northleigh Cross
  Barnstaple EX32 .... 17 C6
  Northleigh EX24 .... 102 B7
Northleigh Hill Rd
  Honiton EX14 .... 166 E3
  Offwell EX14 .... 84 A1
Northleigh Rd EX24 .. 102 D6
Northlew & Ashbury CE Prim Sch EX20 .... 74 E2
Northlew Rd EX20 .... 93 D6
Northleigh Hill Rd EX14 ..102 B8
Northmoor Rd TA22 .... 33 D7
Northmostworm Ct EX10 187 A7
Northolt Ave PL5 .... 243 D4
Northridge Cross EX5 .. 98 E7
Northridge La PL5 .... 98 E7
Northside TA21 .... 160 B5
Northumberland Pl TQ14 .... 210 B4
Northumberland St PL5 247 E8
Northumberland Terr PL1 .... 262 B1
Northview Rd EX9 .... 203 F8
Northville Pk TQ7 .... 258 C6
Northville Rd TQ7 .... 258 C6
Northways La PL21 .... 137 D7
Northwood Cross EX17 ..61 B3
Northwood La
  Buckfast TQ11 .... 236 C8
  Buckland Brewer EX39 .. 40 C7
  Morchard Bishop EX17 .. 61 B3
Northwoods TQ13 .... 180 C4
Norton Cross EX2 .... 263 C4
Norton Cl TA20 .... 233 A3
Norton View TQ6 .... 233 C3
Nortons Cross EX5 .... 81 A2
Norwich Ave PL5 .... 244 B5
Norwich Cl EX48 .... 166 C1
Norwich Rd EX44 .... 176 F6
Norwood Ave EX2 .... 261 C1
Norwood Ho EX4 .... 261 B4
Norwood Rd EX16 .... 161 D6
Notre Dame Cl PL6 .. 244 F5
Notre Dame RC Sch PL6 .... 244 F5
Notte St PL1 .... 262 C2
Nottiston Cross EX31 .. 16 A1
Novorossisk Rd PL6 .. 245 E2
Nower Rd EX13 .... 87 C3
Nowers La TA21 .... 160 C3
Nurseries Cl Exton EX3 ..183 C1
  Topsham EX3 .... 182 E6
Nursery Cl Exmouth EX8 202 C8
  Paignton TQ3 .... 226 A5
Nursery End EX13 .... 154 F7
Nursery Mews EX8 .. 202 C8
Nursery Rd TQ12 .... 207 E7
Nursery Cl CF16 .... 49 B2
Nut Bush La TQ2 .... 219 B7
Nut Bush La TQ2 .... 219 C6
Nut Tree Ct TQ5 .... 230 B2
Nut Tree Dr TQ5 .... 230 B2
Nutaberry Hill EX39 .. 157 B1
Nutbrook EX8 .... 196 B1
Nutcombe Hill EX34 .... 3 C2
Nuttaberry Bglws EX39 .. 25 F4
Nutwell Rd EX8 .... 196 E7
Nynet Ave EX17 .... 78 C4
Nynet Bridge Cross EX17 .... 60 B4
Nymet Villas EX17 .... 44 E6
Nymetwood Cross EX6 .. 96 D8
Nymphayes La EX17 .. 78 C8
Nynehead Rd TA21 .. 160 F8

O

Oak End Ct TQ3 .... 218 D2
Oak Gdns PL21 .... 237 E5
Oak Hill
  Budleigh Salterton EX9 ..198 C6
  Dawlish EX7 .... 204 C5
  East Budleigh EX9 .. 198 B6
Oak Hill Cross Rd
  Dawlish EX7 .... 204 C4
  Teignmouth TQ14 .... 210 D8
Oak La East Anstey TA22 ..32 E6
  Thorverton EX17 .... 81 A4
  Whitstone EX22 .... 70 E1
Oak Park Ave TQ4 .... 226 A4
Oak Park Cl TQ4 .... 226 A4
Oak Park Cl TQ2 .... 219 D8
Oak Park Rd Dawlish EX7 204 C4
  Newton Abbot TQ12 .. 206 F4
Oak Pl TQ12 .... 207 D3
Oak Ridge Ct EX4 .... 176 F4
  Okehampton EX20 .. 170 C6
  Tavistock PL19 .... 171 C2
  West Hill EX11 .... 168 C2
Oak Ridge PL16 .... 105 E4
Oak Tree Cl PL6 .... 244 F1
Oak Tree Dr
  Barnstaple EX32 .... 155 C4
  Newton Abbot TQ12 .. 212 F8
Oak Tree Gdns EX34 .. 150 D6
Oak Tree Gr 8 TQ14 .. 210 A3
  Tiverton EX16 .... 161 C3
Oak Tree Pk
  Plymouth PL6 .... 245 D6
  Sticklepath EX20 .... 95 A5
Oak Tree Pl EX2 .... 181 C8
Oak Units EX17 .... 165 F5
Oak View EX14 .... 166 A3
Oakapple Cl PL7 .... 250 B7
Oakbank TQ13 .... 180 C4
Oakcroft Rd PL2 .... 248 B6
Oakdale Ave EX2 .... 177 C2
Oakdene Rise PL9 .... 255 F6
Oaken Ground TA21 .. 160 B5
Oaken Hill
  Great Torrington EX31 ..42 E8
  Yarnscombe EX31 .... 27 D1
Oakery Cres PL20 .... 128 B8
Oakery Orch PL7 .... 250 E7
Oakfield Cl PL7 .... 251 C6
Oakfield La PL7 .... 160 E4
Oakfield Pl PL4 .... 249 B1
Oakfield Rd Exeter EX4 .. 177 A5
  Hatherleigh EX20 .... 75 C7
  Plymouth PL7 .... 250 C6
Oakfield St EX1 .... 177 F5
Oakfield Terr EX39 .. 157 A7
Oakfield Terrace Rd PL4 .... 249 B1
Oakford Cl EX36 .... 30 D8
Oakford Cross
  Kingsteignton TQ12 .. 207 D7
  North Molton EX36 .... 30 C8
Oakford Villas EX36 .. 30 C8
Oakham Rd PL5 .... 244 B5
Oakhayes Rd EX5 .. 184 B3
Oakhays EX36 .. 158 D4
Oakhill Rd TQ1 .... 219 F6
Oakhill Rise 3 EX31 .. 154 C3
Oakland Ave EX7 .... 204 D5
Oakland Dr EX7 .... 204 D5
Oakland Park Sch EX7 204 C5
Oakland Pk EX7 .... 204 C5
Oakland Rd TQ12 .... 207 F2
Oakland Wlk EX7 .. 204 D5
Oaklands Bideford EX39 ..25 D4
  Okehampton EX20 .... 56 F4
  Tavistock PL19 .... 171 D2
Oaklands Cl
  Buckfastleigh TQ11 .. 236 A5
  Plymouth PL6 .... 245 B5
  Seaton EX12 .... 192 A8
Oaklands Cvn Pk EX20 ..170 A6
Oaklands Dr
  Okehampton EX20 .. 170 B6
  Saltash PL12 .... 242 C3
Oaklands Gn TQ12 .. 242 D3
Oaklands Pk
  Buckfastleigh TQ11 .. 236 A5
  Okehampton EX20 .. 170 A6
Oaklawn Terr TQ1 .... 219 F7
Oaklea EX17 .... 165 B5
Oaklea TQ7 .... 258 C4
Oaklea Cres EX13 .... 153 D5
Oaklea Pk TQ12 .... 123 A1
Oakleigh Cl EX21 .... 73 E2
Oakleigh Rd
  Bovey Tracey TQ13 .. 180 E7
  4 Hemyock EX15 .... 67 B8
  Mary Tavy PL19 .... 117 E6
  Newton Abbot TQ12 .. 212 F8
  Yeoford EX17 .... 79 C1
Oakmere Ct
  Broadclyst EX5 .... 175 D6
  Exmouth EX8 .... 196 B3
  Ivybridge PL21 .... 237 A5
  Upottery EX14 .... 68 C2
Oakwell Cl EX38 .... 159 C5

Oakwood Cl
  Barnstaple EX31 .... 154 C2
  Dartmouth TQ6 .... 233 C3
Oakwood Pk PL20 .... 245 D7
Oakwood Cl EX36 .... 158 D4
Oakwood Dr PL21 .... 137 B3
Oakwood Pk TQ7 .... 143 E7
Oakwood Rise EX8 .... 196 E3
Oakymead Pk TQ12 .. 207 D6
Oates Rd PL2 .... 248 B5
Oatlands Ave EX32 .. 155 A1
Oatlands Dr TQ4 .... 226 A4
Oberon Rd PL7 .... 250 E5
Occombe Cross TQ3 .. 218 F3
Occombe Valley Rd TQ3 .... 219 A2
Ocean Ct PL1 .... 253 F8
Ocean Pk EX39 .... 156 B7
Ocean St TQ4 .... 247 E6
Ocean View Cres TQ5 .. 230 A1
Ochil Cl EX39 .... 26 A1
Octagon The PL1 .... 262 B2
Octon Gr TQ1 .... 219 E7
Odam Cross EX36 .... 45 E7
Odam Moor Cross EX36 ..45 E5
Oddicombe Beach Hill TQ1 .... 220 D8
Oddicombe Cliff Rly* TQ1 .... 220 D8
Odle Hill TQ12 .... 212 A6
Odle Hill Cross TQ12 .. 212 A6
Odun Rd 8 EX31 .... 154 F7
Offwell CE Prim Sch EX14 .... 86 B2
Offwell Turn EX24 .... 102 B8
Ogwell Cross TQ12 .. 206 E2
Ogwell End Dr TQ12 .. 206 F2
Ogwell Mill Rd TQ12 .. 206 E3
Ogwell Rd TQ12 .... 206 F1
Oilmill Cross EX5 .... 179 C2
Oilmill La
  Clyst St George EX5 .. 183 D8
  Clyst St Mary EX5 .... 179 C1
Oke Tor Cl TQ3 .... 219 A2
Okefield Ave EX17 .. 165 C6
Okefield Rd EX17 .. 165 C6
Okefield Ridge EX17 .. 165 C6
Okehampton & District Hospl EX20 .... 170 C5
Okehampton Castle* EX20 .... 170 A3
Okehampton Cl PL7 .. 251 B4
Okehampton Coll EX20 170 B4
Okehampton Mus of Dartmoor Life* EX20 .. 170 B5
Okehampton Prim Sch EX20 .... 170 B5
Okehampton Rd EX4 .. 177 A5
Okehampton St EX4 .. 177 A5
Okehampton Sta EX20 170 C6
Okehampton Way PL21 237 D4
Okement Cl EX20 .... 170 D6
Okewill Cross EX31 .. 10 A2
Okewood Ct EX8 .... 202 B5
Olands Rd TQ1 .... 220 A7
Olchard La TQ12,TQ13 ..124 A4
Old Bakery Cl EX4 .. 177 E2
Old Bakery Ct EX4 .. 176 F7
Old Bakery Cotts PL8 .. 257 F7
Old Bakery The EX8 .. 202 B7
Old Barn Cl EX5 .... 173 F8
Old Barnstaple Rd
  Bideford EX39 .... 157 D2
  Braunton EX31 .... 15 F7
  Ilfracombe EX34 .. 150 C6
Old Beer Rd EX12 .. 191 E6
Old Bell Hill EX16 .... 47 D5
Old Berrynarbor Rd EX34 .... 150 C5
Old Bideford Rd
  Barnstaple EX31 .... 154 B2
  Barnstaple EX31 .... 154 B2
Old Blundell's Sch EX16 161 D3
Old Bridge Rd EX15 .... 83 F6
Old Bridwell EX15 .... 65 F7
Old Butterleigh Rd EX5 ..82 B6
Old Bystock Dr EX8 .. 196 B2
Old Canal Cl EX23 .... 70 A6
Old Chapel Gdns EX19 ..58 F3
Old Chapel Way PL10 .. 252 F6
Old Chard Rd EX14 .. 86 C6
Old Cider Works La TQ12 .... 212 A7
Old Coach Rd EX5 .. 175 C6
Old Coast Rd EX34 .... 2 A2
Old Coastguard PL2 .. 140 E7
Old Coastguard Sta EX12 .... 192 D5
Old Corn Mill (Hele Mill) The* EX34 .... 150 E5
Old Dairy The PL3 .. 249 B6
Old Dawlish Rd EX6 .. 181 C2
Old Ebford La EX3 .. 183 C4
Old Exeter Rd
  Bishop's Tawton EX32 .. 16 E1
  Chudleigh TQ13 .. 123 F8
  Chudleigh TQ13,EX16 114 A2
  Newton Abbot TQ12 .. 207 A3
  Tavistock PL19 .... 171 D4
Old Exeter St TQ13 .. 123 E6
Old Farm Rd PL5 .... 247 C8
Old Farm Way EX7 .. 204 D5
Old Ferry Rd EX5 .... 243 A3

Old Fore St EX10 .... 188 B3
Old Foundry The PL19 .. 171 C6
Old Gatehouse Rd EX7 204 E7
Old George St PL1 .... 262 C2
Old Greystone Hill PL15, PL19 .... 115 D6
Old Hill Bickington TQ12 ..131 D7
  Cullompton EX15 .... 163 D2
Old Ide La EX2 .... 176 E2
Old Laira Rd PL3 .... 249 C4
Old Launceston Rd PL19 .... 171 B6
Old Laundry The PL3 .. 262 A3
Old Lyme Hill DT6 .... 104 F4
Old Lyme Rd DT6 .... 104 F4
Old Manor Cl TQ13 .. 130 E5
Old Manor Ct 20 EX7 .. 204 D6
Old Manor Gdns EX14 203 B3
Old Market Cl EX2 .... 177 B3
Old Market Dr EX39 .... 38 F8
Old Market Field EX16 ..46 E1
Old Matford La EX6,EX2 181 B6
Old Mill Cl EX2 .... 261 C1
Old Mill Ct PL7 .... 250 E5
Old Mill End Est EX5 .. 173 E7
Old Mill La TQ6 .... 233 C4
Old Mill Rd TQ2 .... 219 E7
Old Mill The EX15 .... 66 E8
Old Mine La PL18 .... 125 B6
Old Newton Rd
  Bovey Tracey TQ12 .. 180 E4
  Kingskerswell TQ12 .. 212 E5
Old Nursery Dr EX4 .. 178 B8
Old Orchard Cl EX23 ..70 A6
Old Orchard The EX20 ..74 E2
Old Paignton La TQ2 .. 219 D2
Old Pargiton Rd TQ2 .. 219 D3
Old Park Rd Exeter EX4 ..176 F8
  Plymouth PL3 .... 248 D6
Old Pavilion Cl EX2 .. 178 C2
Old Pinn La EX1 .... 174 E1
Old Plymouth Rd PL3 .. 249 E5
Old Priory PL7 .... 250 D5
Old Priory Jun Sch PL7 250 D5
Old Quarry Rd PL20 .. 126 D3
Old Quay La 8 EX39 .... 15 B1
Old Quay St TQ14 .... 210 B4
Old Rectory Cl EX15 .. 66 E8
Old Rectory Cross TQ13 .. 110 C2
Old Rectory Gdns
  Morchard Bishop EX17 ..61 B2
  Thurlestone TQ7 .... 143 A2
Old Rectory La
  Ashwater EX21 .... 90 E1
  Bratton Fleming EX31 ..18 A8
Old Rydon Cl EX2 .... 178 E3
Old Rydon La EX2 .... 178 D1
Old Rydon Ley EX2 .. 178 D2
Old Sawmill The EX10 ..186 C4
Old School Cl EX16 .. 161 B4
Old School Ct
  6 Hemyock EX15 .... 67 B8
  5 Honiton EX14 .... 166 C6
Old School La EX31 .. 153 E5
Old School Rd
  Barnstaple EX32 .. 247 C8
  Plymouth PL5 .... 247 C8
Old Sidmouth Rd EX24 ..103 A4
Old Smithy Cotts EX39 ..37 B4
Old Station Rd
  Barnstaple EX32 .... 155 B4
  Horrabridge PL20 .. 126 E4
Old Station The PL20 .. 126 E4
Old Sticklepath Hill EX31 .... 154 E3
Old Stone Cl EX39 .. 156 B6
Old Tannery Bsns Pk The 4 PL4 .... 263 A4
Old Teignmouth Rd EX7 .... 204 D4
Old Tithay PL6 .... 105 F4
Old Tiverton Rd
  Bampton EX16 .... 34 C1
  Crediton EX17 .... 165 E6
  Exeter EX4 .... 177 C7
Old Torquay Rd TQ3 .. 226 C8
Old Torrington Rd EX31 154 D2
Old Torwood Rd TQ1 .. 220 C4
Old Totnes Rd
  Ashburton TQ13 .... 130 F4
  Buckfastleigh TQ11 .. 236 C5
  Newton Abbot TQ12 .. 207 A1
Old Town Hill TQ12, TQ13 .... 122 C2
Old Town St
  Dawlish EX7 .... 204 D6
  Plymouth PL1 .... 263 A2
Old Vicarage Cl PL3 .. 176 D1
Old Vicarage Gdn DT7 .. 260 D3
Old Vicarage Rd EX2 .. 177 A2
Old Walls Mill TQ13 .. 124 D1
Old Way Chipstable TA4 ..35 D6
Old Wharf The PL9 .. 255 C2
Old Widdicombe La TQ3 .... 225 D6

Old Widdicombe Rd TQ3 225 C7
Old Widdicome La TQ3 225 B8
Old Woodlands Rd PL5 244 D3
Old Woods Hill TQ2 219 E7
Old Woods Trad Est TQ2 219 E8
Old's View EX4 177 A7
Oldaway La EX5 172 C7
Oldaway Tongue TQ7 143 E1
Oldbarn Cross TQ12 212 A7
Oldbarn La EX16 33 E1
Oldberry La TA22 33 D6
Oldborough Cross EX17 61 B1
Oldborough La EX17 61 B1
Olde Ct EX22 164 C3
Oldenburg Pk TQ3 226 C7
Oldfields EX8 202 C6
Oldhouse La TQ7 142 F7
Oldlands Cl PL6 245 B6
Oldridge Rd EX4 98 B6
Oldridge View EX6 97 F5
Oldshute La TA22 33 C7
Oldstone Cross TQ9 139 F2
Oldway Mansion* TQ3 226 B8
Oldway Pk TA21 160 F4
Oldway Prim Sch TQ3 226 B7
Oldway Rd
East Anstey TA22 32 F5
Paignton TQ3 226 B8
Wellington TA21 160 E4
Olga Terr EX8 195 F5
Olive Gdns EX7 201 B2
Olive Gr EX7 201 B2
Oliver Rd EX32 155 B5
Olivia Ct PL4 263 B4
Omega Ctr The EX2 178 E5
Once Upon A Time Childrens Theme Pk* EX34 8 C6
One End St 4 EX39 15 A1
Onslow Rd Plymouth PL2 248 C7
Salcombe TQ8 259 D5
Ora Cl EX33 7 E2
Ora La EX33 7 E2
Ora Stone Pk EX33 7 E1
Orange Gr TQ2 214 A2
Orange Moor Cross EX18 44 F3
Orbec Ave TQ12 207 F7
Orchard Ave PL6 249 B7
Orchard Cl
Ashprington TQ9 139 F7
Barnstaple EX31 154 C3
Beesands TQ7 149 D7
Braunton EX33 152 C6
8 Brixham TQ5 230 C3
7 Chudleigh TQ13 123 F6
Colyford EX24 103 B3
7 Combe Martin EX34 3 A3
Dawlish EX7 204 D6
Denbury TQ12 211 A6
East Budleigh EX9 198 B6
East Ogwell TQ12 206 D1
Exeter EX1 174 F1
Exmouth EX8 196 B1
Exmouth, Littleham EX8 203 A6
Frogmore TQ7 144 E1
Galmpton TQ5 229 C5
Kingsteignton TQ12 207 F7
Kingsteignton, Sandygate TQ12 123 E2
Lympstone EX8 195 E5
Newton Poppleford EX10 186 D8
Okehampton EX20 170 B4
Ottery St Mary EX11 169 E3
3 Plymouth PL7 251 C5
Rockwell Green TA21 160 A5
Sandford EX17 80 A5
Shaldon TQ14 209 D5
Sidmouth EX10 187 F3
St Giles on the Heath PL15 90 C1
Talaton EX5 84 A2
Tavistock PL19 126 A8
Uffculme EX15 66 A7
Upton Pyne EX5 173 A7
Whitford EX13 103 B6
Wilmington EX14 86 C2
Woodbury EX5 184 C3
Yealmpton PL8 257 F3
Orchard Cotts
Holbeton PL8 136 D1
Lamerton PL19 116 F3
Newton Tracey EX31 27 A6
Orchard Cres PL9 255 C7
Orchard Cross EX17 60 D3
Orchard Ct
1 Crediton EX17 165 C5
Exeter EX1 178 E6
Ivybridge PL21 237 B5
Lamerton PL19 116 E3
Wellington TA21 160 E6
3 Whimple EX5 99 E8
Orchard Dr
Ipplepen TQ12 211 D2
2 Kingskerswell TQ12 212 F4
Otterton EX9 198 E7
Orchard Gate EX19 57 F7
Orchard Gdns
Bideford EX39 157 A4
Broadclyst EX5 175 D6
14 Dawlish EX7 204 D6
Exeter EX4 176 F4
10 Teignmouth TQ14 210 C4
West Buckland TA21 52 F7
Orchard Gr Brixham TQ5 230 C3
Croyde EX33 7 E1
Orchard Hill
Bideford EX39 157 A4
Exeter EX2 176 F3
Yealmpton PL8 136 B3
Orchard Ho
8 Chudleigh TQ13 123 E6
1 Teignmouth TQ14 210 C4
Orchard Ind Est's TQ7 258 C5
Orchard La Silverton EX5 82 B6
Starcross EX6 201 A4
Orchard Leigh EX16 161 C3
Orchard Mdw TQ13 111 A6
Orchard Pk
Dartington TQ9 222 F8
Dittisham TQ6 228 C3
Orchard Pl 3 TQ1 220 A7
Orchard Rd
Ashburton TQ13 130 F4
Barnstaple EX32 155 B3
1 Ilfracombe EX34 150 C5
Knowle EX33 8 D1
Plymouth PL2 248 B7
4 Torquay, Ellacombe TQ1 220 B6
Torquay, Hele TQ2 213 F1
Wrafton EX33 152 E3
Orchard Rise EX39 157 A4
Orchard Terr
Abbotskerswell TQ12 212 B7
Barnstaple EX32 155 B2
3 Bovey Tracey TQ13 180 D8
Buckfastleigh TQ11 236 B5
Chagford TQ13 111 A6
Crediton EX17 165 B5
Kingskerswell TQ12 212 F5
Totnes TQ9 223 C5
Tuckenhay TQ9 139 F6
Orchard The
Abbotskerswell TQ12 212 B6
Avonwick TQ10 135 B1
Barnstaple EX31 154 A3
Bishopsteignton TQ14 208 F8
Gunnislake PL18 125 D6
Holcombe EX7 210 E8
Holywell Lake TA21 51 E7
Honiton EX14 166 B5
Kilmington EX13 87 D1
Seaton EX12 192 A5
Tipton St John EX10 100 D2
Totnes TQ9 223 C5
Yealmpton PL8 257 F3
Orchard Vale Com Sch EX32 155 E4
Orchard View
Frogmore TQ7 144 E1
Halberton EX16 65 B7
Orchard Way
1 Bovey Tracey TQ13 180 D8
Chillington TQ7 145 A1
Cullompton EX15 163 B2
Honiton EX14 166 D6
Kenton EX6 194 D3
Lapford EX17 60 D3
Stoke Gabriel TQ9 227 F8
Tiverton EX16 161 B3
Topsham EX3 182 E5
Uffculme EX15 66 A7
Willand EX15 162 D4
Orchard Waye TQ9 223 B5
Orchardon La EX33 8 B1
Orchards The
Galmpton TQ5 229 B5
Landkey EX32 17 B2
Swimbridge EX32 28 E8
Orchardside EX10 188 B7
Orchardton Terr PL9 255 F5
Orchid Ave
Ivybridge PL21 237 A6
Kingsteignton TQ12 207 E7
Orchid Cl 7 EX16 161 F6
Orchid Vale 14 TQ12 123 F1
Orcombe Ct EX8 202 D8
Ordnance St PL1 247 E2
Ordulf Rd PL19 171 A5
Oregon Way PL3 249 D6
Oreston Prim Sch PL9 255 C7
Oreston Rd PL9 255 C8
Orestone Cross TQ2 213 D3
Orestone Dr TQ1 214 C6
Orestone La TQ2,TQ12 213 E3
Orient Rd TQ3 226 D8
Oriole Dr EX4 173 D1
Orkney Cl TQ2 213 E2
Orkney Mews EX16 161 D6
Orleigh Ave TQ12 207 B5
Orleigh Cl EX39 40 C7
Orleigh Ct EX39 25 C1
Orleigh Pk TQ12 207 B5
Orley Rd TQ12 211 B2
Orplington Ct EX16 65 B7
Orstone Cross EX32 18 E3
Orway Ash Cross EX15 66 B2
Orway Cross EX15 66 C1
Orwell Garth EX4 178 C8
Osbern Rd TQ3 219 A2
Osborn Cl TQ12 211 D2
Osborne Cl EX39 156 D2
Osborne La EX39 156 D2
Osborne Rd
Ilfracombe EX34 150 A5
Plymouth PL3 248 A3
Osborne St TQ12 207 D3
Osborne Villas 2 PL3 248 A3
Osmond Lodge TQ4 226 C5
Osmond's La 11 TQ14 210 B4
Osney Ave TQ4 226 B4
Osney Cres TQ4 226 B4
Osney Gdns TQ4 226 B4
Osprey Dr TQ2 213 D3
Osprey Gdns PL9 256 C7
Osprey Rd EX2 178 F6
Oswald Browning Way 4 EX31 155 A7
Otter Cl
Okehampton EX20 170 D6
Tipton St John EX10 100 D3
West Hill EX11 168 D4
Otter Ct Bickington TQ12 131 F8
Budleigh Salterton EX9 198 C1
Exeter EX2 181 C8
Otter Estuary Nature Reserve* EX9 198 D1
Otter Rd TQ2 219 C7
Otter Reach EX10 186 F8
Otter Vale Cl EX14 68 C1
Otter Way EX32 155 D4
Otterbourne Ct EX9 198 B1
Otters The EX16 49 B2
Otterton CE Prim Sch EX9 198 E7
Otterton Mill* EX9 198 D7
Ottervale Rd EX9 198 C1
Ottery Cotts PL19 116 E2
Ottery La EX10 101 A1
Ottery Moor Ind Est EX14 166 B6
Ottery Moor La EX14 166 A6
Ottery Park Ind Est PL19 116 E2
Ottery St EX9 198 F8
Ottery St Mary Hospl EX11 169 C3
Ottery St Mary Prim Sch EX11 169 E3
Our Lady & St Patrick's RC Prim Sch TQ14 210 A6
Our Lady's RC Prim Sch EX32 155 B5
Oussaborough La EX34 8 C6
Outer Ting Tong EX9 197 B3
Outland Rd PL2 248 C7
Oval Gn EX2 178 C3
Overbeck's Mus & Gdn* TQ8 259 B1
Overbrook EX7 204 D6
Overcliff Ct EX7 204 E7
Overclose TQ3 225 F8
Overcott La EX36 46 D8
Overdale Cl TQ2 213 F4
Overdale Rd PL2 248 A7
Overgang TQ5 230 D5
Overgang Rd TQ5 230 C6
Overland Ct EX4 174 E2
Overlangs TQ7 142 C6
Overseas Est TQ6 146 B6
Overton Cl DT7 260 E5
Overton Gdns PL3 248 F5
Owen St TA21 160 C6
Owlaborough La EX36 32 B2
Owlacombe Cross TQ12 131 A7
Ox Hill La EX24 102 F4
Oxenham Cross EX20 95 C5
Oxenham Gn TQ2 219 D6
Oxenpark Gate EX6 112 F5
Oxenpark La
Berrynarbor EX34 2 C3
Ilfracombe EX34 2 C2
Morchard Bishop EX17 61 C1
Stockleigh Pomeroy EX17 80 F7
Oxford Ave PL3 248 E5
Oxford Cl EX8 196 E4
Oxford Cross EX33 8 A3
Oxford Ct TQ2 213 F1
Oxford Gdns PL3 248 E5
Oxford Gr EX34 150 B6
Oxford La TQ5 230 A4
Oxford Pk EX34 150 B5
Oxford Pl PL1 262 C3
Oxford Rd EX4 261 C4
Oxford St Dartmouth TQ6 233 F3
Exeter EX2 177 A4
Plymouth PL1 262 B3
Oxford Terr
Crediton EX17 165 D5
4 Plymouth PL1 262 B3
Sandford EX17 80 A5
Oxham Cross EX36 45 D8
Oxlea Cl TQ1 220 E4
Oxlea Rd TQ1 220 E4
Oxman's Cotts EX39 157 E6
Oxmon's La EX39 157 A7
Oyster Bend TQ4 226 C2
Oyster Cl TQ4 226 C2
Ozone Terr DT7 260 D2

P

Paccombe Pool La EX10 189 C7
Pacehayne La
Dalwood EX13 87 A1
Shute EX13 103 A8
Packhall La TQ5 230 A2
Packhorse Cl EX10 188 D8
Packington St PL2 248 A4
Packs Cl TQ9 139 C7
Padacre Rd TQ2 214 A4
Paddock Cl Plymouth PL9 255 E5
Saltash PL12 242 D4
Seaton EX12 191 F7
Paddock Dr PL21 237 D4
Paddock The
Brixham TQ5 230 B4
Dawlish EX7 204 E7
Dolton EX19 57 F7
Paddock The *continued*
Dulverton TA22 33 D6
Torquay TQ1 214 B1
Paddocks The
Abbotskerswell TQ12 212 B7
Honiton EX14 166 A2
Membury EX13 87 D6
Totnes TQ9 223 D6
Wellington TA21 160 E5
Paddons Coombe 9 TQ12 123 F1
Paddons La TQ14 210 A7
Pafford Ave TQ2 214 B2
Pafford Cl TQ2 214 A2
Page's Cross EX16 62 F7
Paige Adams Rd TQ9 223 B6
Paiges Farm PL9 255 C1
Paiges La 8 EX31 154 F5
Paignton & Dartmouth Rly* TQ4 226 C2
Paignton & Dartmouth Steam Rly* TQ5 229 C5
Paignton & District Hospl TQ3 226 B6
Paignton (Queen's Park) Sta TQ4 226 B6
Paignton Com Coll
Paignton TQ3 225 E5
Paignton TQ4 225 D4
Paignton Rd TQ9 228 A
Paignton Sta TQ4 226 B6
Paignton Zoological & Botanical Gdns* TQ4 225 F4
Pail Pk EX33 8 D1
Painsford Cross TQ9 139 D7
Painter's Cross EX13 102 F7
Painters Ct EX2 261 A1
Painton Water EX39 37 D8
Paizen La EX12 191 B6
Palace Ave TQ3 226 B6
Palace Gate EX1 261 B2
Palace Mdw TQ13 123 E6
Palace Pl TQ3 226 B6
Palace St PL1 263 A2
Palatine Cl TQ1 220 B5
Pale Gate Cl EX14 166 D7
Palegate Cross TQ7 258 A8
Palermo 10 TQ1 220 D4
Palermo Rd TQ1 220 C7
Palfrey's La EX16 49 C5
Palk Cl TQ14 209 D5
Palk St TQ2 220 B4
Palm Cl EX8 196 D3
Palm Cross PL21 137 B2
Palm Ct EX7 201 A2
Palm Rd TQ2 220 A5
Palmer Ct EX9 198 A1
Palmer's La EX5 99 E5
Palmers Cl EX33 152 D5
Palmers Ct EX38 159 E5
Palmerston Dr EX4 176 E7
Palmerston Pk EX16 161 B2
Palmerston St PL1 262 A4
Palms The 2 TQ1 220 D4
Pamela Rd EX1 177 F7
Pankhurst Cl EX8 202 E7
Panney The EX4 178 A7
Pannier Mkt
Great Torrington EX38 159 D5
Tavistock PL19 171 C5
Panorama TQ2 219 E2
Panson Cross PL15 90 B3
Papermakers La PL21 237 E6
Parade Chudleigh TQ13 123 E6
Exmouth EX8 202 A7
Plymouth PL1 263 A2
Parade Bsns Pk 4 PL19 171 B4
Parade Ope PL1 263 A2
Parade Rd PL5 244 A3
Parade The
Chardstock EX13 88 A7
Millbrook PL10 252 E5
Milton Abbot PL19 116 A6
Paradise Glen TQ14 210 B6
Paradise Lawn EX36 158 D4
Paradise Pk EX22 70 E1
Paradise Pl 1 TQ5 230 D5
Paradise Rd
Plymouth PL1 248 A2
Teignmouth TQ14 210 C6
Paradise Wlk TQ4 226 C4
Paramore Way EX36 158 C4
Parehayne La EX24 102 E7
Parely Hill TQ13 110 F6
Paris Rd TQ3 226 C8
Paris St EX1 261 B3
Park Ave
Barnstaple EX31 154 C4
Bideford EX39 157 A3
Brixham TQ5 230 B3
Plymouth, Devonport PL1 247 E3
Plymouth, Plymstock PL9 255 D7
Westward Ho! EX39 156 C7
Park Bglws EX16 51 B3
Park Cl Clyst Hydon EX15 83 D4
Fremington EX31 153 E5
Holsworthy EX22 164 C6
Ivybridge PL21 237 C5
Plymouth PL7 250 B7
Silverton EX5 82 C5
Tiverton EX16 161 D5
Woodbury EX5 184 C2
Park Com Sch The EX32 155 A3
Park Cotts PL21 137 D6
Park Cres
Combe Martin EX34 3 A3
Plymouth PL9 255 C7
Park Cross EX17 62 C3
Park Ct Brixham TQ5 230 E5
Chillaton PL16 106 D1
Ilfracombe EX34 150 B4
Park Field Terr EX12 190 D4
Park Five Bsns Ctr EX2 178 E4
Park Gate EX37 28 D2
Park Gdns EX35 151 B5
Park Hall TQ1 220 B3
Park Hill
Teignmouth TQ14 210 B5
Tiverton EX16 161 C5
Park Hill Rd EX34 150 B5
Park La Barnstaple EX32 155 A3
8 Bere Alston PL20 125 E1
Bideford EX39 157 A3
Blackawton TQ9 139 E1
Budleigh Salterton EX9 197 F1
Chittlehampton EX37 43 F8
Combe Martin EX34 3 A3
Combe St Nicholas TA20 69 F6
Dunkeswell EX14 67 C4
Exeter EX4 174 E2
Exmouth EX8 202 A8
Filleigh EX32 29 D7
Otterton EX9 198 E6
Plymouth PL9 255 C7
Sparkwell PL7 132 C1
Torquay TQ1 220 B3
Wellington TA21 160 C1
Wellington, Chelston TA21 52 E7
Whitford EX13 103 B6
Witheridge EX16 62 D6
Park Lane Cotts EX32 29 D7
Park Manor EX39 38 F8
Park Meadow Cl EX17 60 D3
Park Mews TQ5 230 E5
Park Mill Cross EX17 59 F3
Park Mill La EX18 59 F8
Park Pl
Exeter, Heavitree EX1 177 F6
Exeter, Mount Radford EX2 261 C2
Winkleigh EX19 58 F2
Park Place La 9 PL3 248 A4
Park Rd Beer EX12 191 C5
Crediton EX17 165 D4
Dartington TQ9 216 B2
Dawlish EX7 204 D6
Exeter EX1 177 E7
Exmouth EX8 202 A8
Hatherleigh EX20 75 C7
Kingskerswell TQ12 212 F5
Lapford EX17 60 D3
Lifton PL16 105 E3
Plymouth PL3 249 A6
Silverton EX5 82 C5
St Dominick PL12 125 A2
Tiverton EX16 161 D5
Torpoint PL11 247 B3
Torquay TQ1 214 B1
Park Rise Dawlish EX7 204 D4
Salcombe TQ8 259 C4
Park Row EX20 170 B5
Park Sch TQ9 216 C3
Park St Crediton EX17 165 D5
Ivybridge PL21 237 C4
Lynton EX35 151 B5
Plymouth PL3 248 A4
Tiverton EX16 161 D5
Willand EX15 162 C5
Park Street Mews PL21 237 C4
Park Street Ope PL3 248 A4
Park Terr
21 Barnstaple EX32 155 A4
Ivybridge PL21 237 C4
Park View Axminster EX13 88 A3
Beaford EX19 42 D1
Holsworthy EX22 71 D5
Kenton EX6 194 F3
Newton Abbot TQ12 212 F8
Plymouth PL4 263 C3
Park View Cl 18 EX34 3 A3
Park View Cotts
Great Torrington EX38 42 B6
Kingston TQ7 142 C6
Park View Rd EX32 155 A6
Park View Terr
Okehampton EX20 170 C3
Westward Ho! EX39 156 C7
Park Way Exmouth EX8 202 C8
Woodbury EX5 184 C2
Park Wood Rise PL16 105 E4
Parkelands TQ13 180 C7
Parker Cl Plymouth PL7 250 B5
Wellington TA21 160 E6
Parker Rd
Bigbury-on-Sea TQ7 142 E3
Plymouth PL2 248 B6
Parker's Gn PL18 125 C6
Parker's Rd EX6 201 A8
Parkers Cl TQ9 223 D4
Parkers Cross La EX1 174 F2
Parkers Farm Holiday Pk TQ13 131 C6
Parkers Hollow EX31 154 B3
Parkers Way TQ9 223 D4
Parkes Rd EX38 159 F5
Parkesway PL12 242 D2
Parkfield TQ7 143 A2
Parkfield Cl
Marldon TQ3 218 D3
Totnes TQ9 223 F5
Parkfield Cross TQ13 131 A3
Parkfield Dr PL6 245 F1
Parkfield Rd
Topsham EX3 182 F5
Torquay TQ1 219 F7

Parkfield Wlk TQ7 ...... 143 A2
Parkham Cross EX39 ...... 24 F1
Parkham Glade TQ5 ...... 230 C4
Parkham La TQ5 ...... 230 C4
Parkham Prim Sch EX39 ...... 39 E8
Parkham Rd TQ5 ...... 230 C4
Parkham Twrs 6 TQ5 ...... 230 C4
Parkhayes EX5 ...... 184 C7
Parkhill Cotts PL21 ...... 136 F4
Parkhill Ho TQ12 ...... 211 F3
Parkhill Rd TQ1 ...... 220 C3
Parkhouse Rd EX2 ...... 176 F3
Parkhurst Rd TQ1 ...... 219 F7
Parkland Dr EX2 ...... 178 C3
Parklands
  Barnstaple EX31 ...... 154 C3
  12 Hemyock EX15 ...... 67 B8
  Okehampton EX20 ...... 170 B3
  South Molton EX36 ...... 158 B3
  Totnes TQ9 ...... 223 C6
Parklands Ct EX36 ...... 158 B3
Parklands Rd TA21 ...... 160 D7
Parklands Way TQ13 ...... 180 C4
Parks Villas EX33 ...... 152 D5
Parkside Ivybridge PL21 ...... 237 E5
  Plymouth PL2 ...... 247 F5
  Salcombe TQ8 ...... 259 D5
Parkside Com Tech Coll
  PL10 ...... 247 E3
Parkside Cres EX1 ...... 174 F3
Parkside Ct EX2 ...... 261 B2
Parkside Dr EX8 ...... 196 E3
Parkside Rd Exeter EX1 ...... 174 F3
  Paignton TQ4 ...... 226 C6
Parkside Villas TQ1 ...... 220 C7
Parkstone La PL7 ...... 250 F6
Parkway Exeter EX2 ...... 176 F3
  Ilfracombe EX34 ...... 150 B3
Parkway CI PL6 ...... 249 E7
Parkway Ind Est The
  PL6 ...... 249 E7
Parkway Rd TQ13 ...... 123 E6
Parkway The PL3,PL5,
  PL6 ...... 244 B1
Parkwood CI PL6 ...... 241 B2
Parkwood Ct PL19 ...... 171 D6
Parkwood Rd
  Tavistock PL19 ...... 171 D6
  Tavistock PL19 ...... 171 E7
Parkyns Cross EX19 ...... 43 B4
Parliament Ct 7 EX34 ...... 150 C6
Parliament St EX17 ...... 165 C5
Parnell CI PL6 ...... 249 A8
Parr CI EX1 ...... 261 C4
Parr La PL4 ...... 263 B2
Parr St Exeter EX1 ...... 261 C4
  Plymouth PL4 ...... 263 B2
Parr's La TQ13 ...... 213 E6
Parracombe CE Prim Sch
  EX31 ...... 4 C1
Parracombe La EX31 ...... 4 D2
Parracombe Lane Head
  EX31 ...... 4 D2
Parricks La EX13 ...... 88 D3
Parrocks La TA20 ...... 88 C8
Parson CI EX8 ...... 196 C2
Parson St TQ14 ...... 210 B5
Parson's Ct EX15 ...... 66 A3
Parsonage Cross
  Chulmleigh EX18 ...... 44 F2
  Dartington TQ9 ...... 215 F2
  Germansweek EX21 ...... 91 D5
  Staverton TQ9 ...... 216 E3
  West Putford EX22 ...... 39 B2
  Woodbury EX5 ...... 184 C3
Parsonage Ct PL16 ...... 105 E4
Parsonage Hill EX36 ...... 31 A3
Parsonage La
  Awliscombe EX14 ...... 85 C1
  Combe Martin EX31 ...... 10 E5
  George Nympton EX36 ...... 29 F2
  Hittisleigh EX6 ...... 96 C6
  Honiton EX14 ...... 166 D5
  Morleigh TQ9 ...... 139 A3
  Silverton EX5 ...... 82 B6
  South Molton EX36 ...... 158 C5
  Staverton TQ9 ...... 216 E4
  Ugborough PL21 ...... 137 D6
Parsonage Lane Cross
  EX32 ...... 18 B2
Parsonage Lane End
  PL21 ...... 137 D6
Parsonage Rd PL8 ...... 141 A7
Parsonage St EX5 ...... 83 A7
Parsonage Way EX5 ...... 184 C4
Parsons CI
  Newton Poppleford EX10 ...... 186 D8
  Plymouth PL9 ...... 256 A4
Parsons La EX5 ...... 99 B5
Parthia Pl EX8 ...... 196 E1
Partridge Cross EX16 ...... 63 A8
Partridge Hill EX36 ...... 45 D7
Partridge La EX8 ...... 163 A8
Partridge Rd EX8 ...... 196 C2
Partwayes PL19 ...... 116 E3
Pasley St PL2 ...... 247 E4
Pasley St E PL2 ...... 247 F4
Passage Rd PL8 ...... 140 F6
Passmore Rd EX5 ...... 82 F6
Pasture Cross TQ9 ...... 144 F8
Pastures The EX20 ...... 92 A2
Patchacott Cross
  Bratton Clovelly EX21 ...... 92 A8
  Northlew EX21 ...... 74 B1
Patchel Cross EX20 ...... 56 F3
Patches Rd EX31 ...... 161 B4
Paternoster La TQ12 ...... 211 C2

Paternoster Row
  9 Barnstaple EX31 ...... 154 F5
  Ottery St Mary EX11 ...... 169 D4
Path Field CI EX32 ...... 18 B2
Path The 22 EX39 ...... 15 A1
Pathdown La EX33 ...... 7 F2
Pathfield EX38 ...... 159 F5
Pathfield CI EX31 ...... 154 A3
Pathfield Lawn EX31 ...... 154 E6
Pathfield Sch EX31 ...... 154 E6
Pathfields Croyde EX33 ...... 7 E2
  Totnes TQ9 ...... 223 D5
  Uffculme EX15 ...... 66 A7
Pathfields CI TQ9 ...... 223 D5
Pathfields Ind Est EX36 ...... 158 D6
Pathowlands EX10 ...... 188 A6
Patna Pl PL1 ...... 262 B4
Patricia CI EX4 ...... 173 C2
Pattard Cross EX39 ...... 22 D4
Patterdale CI PL6 ...... 245 D3
Patterdale Wlk PL6 ...... 245 D3
Patterson's Cross
  EX11 ...... 169 D8
Pattison CI EX11 ...... 100 F8
Pattison Dr EX11 ...... 169 F4
Pattison CI PL6 ...... 245 E2
Pattison Dr PL6 ...... 245 F2
Paul St EX4 ...... 261 A3
Paullet EX16 ...... 50 C1
Pauntley Gdn EX10 ...... 187 F3
Paviland Grange 6 PL1 ...... 248 A3
Pavilion Pl EX2 ...... 261 B2
Pavington Cross EX37 ...... 43 E3
Pavor Rd TQ2 ...... 214 B2
Paws Rd EX37 ...... 43 F2
Paya Ct EX4 ...... 178 B8
Payne's Cotts EX14 ...... 85 C3
Paynsford Mews 2
  TQ12 ...... 207 B4
Paynsford Rd 1 TQ12 ...... 207 B4
Paynter Wlk 5 PL7 ...... 251 B5
Payton Rd
  Holywell Lake TA21 ...... 51 F7
  Rockwell Green TA21 ...... 160 A5
Peacegate Cross EX20 ...... 76 E4
Peacehay La TA21 ...... 51 E4
Peacock Ave PL11 ...... 247 A3
Peacock CI PL7 ...... 250 F7
Peacock Pl EX6 ...... 201 A8
Peacocks CI TA21 ...... 52 F7
Peadhill La EX16 ...... 49 D2
Peak Cnr EX16 ...... 62 E7
Peak Cross TQ9 ...... 222 F3
Peak Hill Rd EX10 ...... 187 E3
Peak Tor Ave TQ1 ...... 220 C2
Peakfield Cross Ways
  EX5 ...... 82 E6
Pear Dr EX15 ...... 162 D4
Pear Tree Cotts PL8 ...... 257 A5
Pear Tree Way 5 EX32 ...... 17 B2
Peard Rd EX16 ...... 64 D6
Peards Down CI EX32 ...... 155 D4
Pearmain CI EX15 ...... 162 D4
Pearn Cotts 2 PL3 ...... 248 F6
Pearn Gdns PL3 ...... 249 A7
Pearn Rd PL3 ...... 249 A7
Pearn Ridge PL3 ...... 249 A7
Pearse CI EX20 ...... 75 B7
Pearson Ave 3 PL4 ...... 248 F4
Pearson CI EX22 ...... 164 C5
Pearson Dr PL4 ...... 248 F4
Peartree CI EX6 ...... 194 E3
Peartree Cross
  Ashburton TQ13 ...... 130 E4
  Denbury TQ12 ...... 211 A7
Peasedith TQ5 ...... 230 D3
Peasland Rd TQ2 ...... 214 A4
Peaslands Rd EX10 ...... 188 A5
Peaspark Cross TQ7 ...... 144 D3
Peazen Flats EX12 ...... 191 C6
Pebble Ct TQ4 ...... 226 B4
Pebbleridge Rd EX33 ...... 14 F1
Pecorama Pleasure Gdns*
  EX12 ...... 191 B5
Pedlerspool La EX17 ...... 165 E7
Peek La PL21 ...... 137 C8
Peek Mead D17 ...... 193 F7
Peek Moor Cross EX22 ...... 90 B4
Peeks Ave PL9 ...... 255 F7
Peel Row 3 EX4 ...... 178 C8
Peel St PL1 ...... 248 A1
Peep La 8 EX17 ...... 165 D5
Pegasus Ct Exeter EX1 ...... 177 F6
  Paignton TQ4 ...... 226 B8
Pegwell La TQ14 ...... 209 B3
Pellew Arc 5 TQ14 ...... 210 B4
Pellew Ho 9 TQ14 ...... 210 B4
Pellew Pl 4 PL2 ...... 247 F4
Pellew Way TQ14 ...... 210 A7
Pellinore Rd EX4 ...... 174 A1
Pembrey Wlk PL5 ...... 243 E4
Pembroke La PL1 ...... 247 E1
Pembroke Lodge 13
  EX34 ...... 150 B5
Pembroke Pk TQ3 ...... 218 E3
Pembroke Rd
  Paignton TQ3 ...... 225 E7
  Plymouth TQ2 ...... 220 B5
Pembroke St
  Plymouth PL1 ...... 247 E1
  Plymouth PL1 ...... 247 F1
Pembroke Pl PL5 ...... 243 C1
Pen-y-dre EX15 ...... 163 C4
Pencair Ave PL11 ...... 246 E2
Pencepool Cotts EX15 ...... 83 F6
Pencepool Orch EX15 ...... 83 F6
Pencombe Rocks EX31 ...... 4 C3

Pencorse Rd TQ2 ...... 219 F8
Pencreber Rd 3 PL20 ...... 126 F4
Pencross View 1 EX15 ...... 67 B8
Pendarves TQ9 ...... 222 D2
Pendean CI PL6 ...... 244 F6
Pendeen Cres PL6 ...... 245 A6
Pendeen Pk TQ7 ...... 145 A1
Pendennis CI
  Plymouth PL3 ...... 248 F8
  Plymouth PL7 ...... 246 F3
Pendennis Rd TQ2 ...... 219 F8
Pendilly Ave PL11 ...... 246 F2
Pendragon Rd EX4 ...... 174 A2
Penfield Gdns 11 EX7 ...... 206 D6
Pengelly CI PL11 ...... 246 F5
Pengelly Hill PL11 ...... 247 A5
Pengelly Pk PL11 ...... 246 F5
Pengilly Way EX39 ...... 22 E3
Penhale Dr EX22 ...... 164 B5
Penhayes Rd EX6 ...... 194 E3
Penhill Chalets TQ6 ...... 146 B7
Penhill Cross EX6 ...... 113 E3
Penhill La TQ5 ...... 234 E8
Peninsular Pk PL12 ...... 242 C4
Penlee EX9 ...... 199 G2
Penlee Cotts PL10 ...... 140 J2
Penlee Gdns PL3 ...... 248 A4
Penlee Pk PL4 ...... 248 F4
Penlee Rd PL3 ...... 248 A4
Penlee Way PL3 ...... 248 B4
Penleonard CI EX2 ...... 177 E5
Penn Cross PL16 ...... 260 F7
Penn Ho TQ12 ...... 207 E2
Penn Inn CI TQ12 ...... 207 D2
Penn La TQ5 ...... 230 D3
Penn Mdws TQ5 ...... 230 D3
Pennant Ho EX8 ...... 201 D6
Pennant Way PL21 ...... 136 D6
Pennball Cross TQ9 ...... 217 B3
Pennine Dr TQ4 ...... 225 D4
Pennington CI EX17 ...... 79 A5
Pennsland La TQ13 ...... 130 F7
Pennsylvania CI EX4 ...... 177 D8
Pennsylvania Cres EX4 ...... 177 C8
Pennsylvania Pk EX4 ...... 173 D1
Pennsylvania Rd
  Exeter EX4 ...... 173 C3
  Torquay TQ1 ...... 220 B5
Penny CI Exminster EX6 ...... 182 A4
  Wellington TA21 ...... 160 D7
Penny Plot D17 ...... 260 C4
Penny Thorn Cross EX14 ...... 85 E7
Penny's Hill TQ1 ...... 219 F7
Penny's La PL9 ...... 256 D6
Penny's Terr EX13 ...... 167 D5
Pennyacre Rd TQ14 ...... 210 C6
Pennycomequick Hill
  PL1,PL3 ...... 262 B4
Pennycross CI PL2 ...... 248 B8
Pennycross Park Rd
  PL2 ...... 248 C7
Pennycross Prim Sch
  PL2 ...... 248 B8
Pennywell Farm & Wildlife
  Ctr* TQ11 ...... 135 E6
Penpethy CI TQ5 ...... 230 B4
Penpethy Rd TQ5 ...... 230 B5
Penrith CI PL6 ...... 245 D3
Penrith Gdns PL6 ...... 245 D3
Penrith Wlk PL6 ...... 245 D3
Penrose Almshouses 4
  EX32 ...... 155 A4
Penrose St PL1 ...... 262 B3
Penrose Terr 7 EX1 ...... 261 A2
Penrose Villas 5 PL4 ...... 248 F4
Penroses Terr EX22 ...... 164 C4
Penryn Pl 4 TQ14 ...... 210 A3
Pens La EX15 ...... 67 B8
Penscombe Cross PL15 ...... 115 A6
Penshurst Rd TQ12 ...... 207 B1
Pensilva Pk TQ5 ...... 230 C2
Penson Cross EX20 ...... 59 B1
Penstone La Bondleigh EX20 ...... 77 B8
  North Tawton EX20 ...... 59 B1
Penswell Cross TQ10 ...... 135 E4
Pentamar St PL2 ...... 247 E4
Pentgrove Ct EX8 ...... 202 D7
Pentice La EX34 ...... 3 A3
Pentillie Rd
  Bere Alston PL20 ...... 125 E1
  Plymouth PL4 ...... 248 E4
Pentillie Cres PL4 ...... 248 D4
Pentire Rd PL11 ...... 246 F3
Pentland CI PL6 ...... 244 F7
Penton CI EX17 ...... 165 D6
Penton La EX17 ...... 165 D5
Penton Rise EX17 ...... 165 D6
Pentridge Ave TQ2 ...... 219 C2
Pentyre CI PL4 ...... 263 C4
Pentyre Terr PL4 ...... 263 C4
Penwill Way TQ4 ...... 226 A4
Peoples Park Rd EX17 ...... 165 C6
Pepper La
  Kingswear TQ6 ...... 234 E4
  Plymouth PL9 ...... 256 D2
Pepper's CI PL9 ...... 171 C6
Pepper's Cnr EX9 ...... 198 F7
Pepperdon Hall La
  TQ13 ...... 112 B3
Peppery La TQ14 ...... 209 D5
Pepys Pl PL5 ...... 244 B1
Perceval Rd EX4 ...... 174 A2
Perches CI PL8 ...... 141 B7
Percy Cross EX14 ...... 67 B2
Percy Rd EX2 ...... 177 B3
Percy St PL5 ...... 243 D1

Percy Terr PL4 ...... 249 A4
Peregrine CI TQ2 ...... 213 D3
Perinville CI TQ1 ...... 220 E6
Perinville Rd TQ1 ...... 220 D7
Periwinkle Dr
  Barnstaple EX31 ...... 154 B3
  Plymouth PL7 ...... 251 C5
Perkins Cross PL9 ...... 99 C1
Perranporth CI PL5 ...... 243 E4
Perriam's Pl EX9 ...... 199 G2
Perridge CI EX2 ...... 176 E3
Perridge Cross EX6 ...... 98 E1
Perriman's Row EX8 ...... 202 A7
Perriton Cross EX5 ...... 99 E8
Perriton CI TQ14 ...... 209 D8
Perry Cross TQ12 ...... 206 D7
Perry Hill EX17 ...... 80 E8
Perry La
  Doddiscombsleigh EX6 ...... 113 D5
  Newton Abbot TQ12 ...... 206 D6
Perry New Rd TA22 ...... 33 E4
Perry Rd EX4 ...... 177 B8
Perry St TA20 ...... 88 D8
Perryman CI PL7 ...... 250 E7
Perryman's Hill EX17 ...... 79 F7
Perrys Gdns EX11 ...... 168 D4
Perseverance Cotts 1
  PL7 ...... 250 E7
Perth CI EX4 ...... 173 E2
Peryam Cres EX2 ...... 178 A4
Peryn Rd PL19 ...... 171 A5
Peter Hopper's Hill PL5 ...... 240 C2
Peter St EX5 ...... 82 F7
Peter's CI PL9 ...... 256 C7
Peter's La EX17 ...... 61 A1
Peter's Park La PL5 ...... 243 E1
Peterborough Rd EX4 ...... 176 E7
Peterclose Rd EX16 ...... 161 F3
Peters Cres TQ13 ...... 218 D3
Peters Park CI PL5 ...... 243 E1
Petersfield CI PL3 ...... 249 B6
Petertavy Cross PL19 ...... 117 E3
Pethertons EX16 ...... 65 A7
Pethick CI PL6 ...... 244 D6
Pethill CI PL6 ...... 245 F2
Pethybridge TQ13 ...... 122 B8
Petit Well La TQ1 ...... 214 B1
Petitor Mews TQ1 ...... 214 C1
Petitor Rd TQ1 ...... 214 C1
Petrel CI TQ2 ...... 213 C3
Petticoat La EX13 ...... 167 A6
Petton Cross EX16 ...... 35 A3
Peverell Park Rd PL3 ...... 248 D6
Peverell Terr PL3 ...... 248 D5
Pew Tor CI
  Tavistock PL19 ...... 171 E5
  8 Yelverton PL20 ...... 126 F3
Phear Ave EX8 ...... 202 B7
Philham Cross EX39 ...... 22 D1
Philham La EX39 ...... 22 D1
Philham Water EX39 ...... 22 D1
Philip Ave EX31 ...... 154 D2
Philip CI PL9 ...... 256 A6
Philip Gdns PL9 ...... 255 F6
Philip Ho EX1 ...... 178 E6
Philip Rd EX4 ...... 177 E8
Phillimore St 3 PL2 ...... 247 F4
Phillipps Ave EX8 ...... 196 B1
Phillips Sq EX14 ...... 166 B6
Phoenix St 9 PL20 ...... 126 F4
Phoenix La EX13 ...... 161 D3
Phoenix PI TQ7 ...... 258 C5
Phoenix St PL1 ...... 262 A2
Piazza Terr EX2 ...... 261 B1
Pick Pie Dr PL6 ...... 245 E8
Picket Head Hill TQ14 ...... 210 A2
Pidgeley Rd EX7 ...... 204 F8
Pidgeon's La EX13 ...... 104 B7
Pidland La EX16 ...... 47 F1
Pidsley Hill EX17 ...... 79 F7
Pidsley La EX17 ...... 79 F8
Piece Hill EX6 ...... 97 E4
Piend La EX17 ...... 62 B1
Pier Head EX8 ...... 201 E6
Pier Quay TQ6 ...... 233 F3
Pier La PL10 ...... 253 A1
Pierremont Rd EX7 ...... 204 E6
Pig La EX13 ...... 167 D6
Piggy La EX39 ...... 37 E7
Pigs Leg Cross EX20 ...... 108 A8
Pigspark Cross TQ13 ...... 131 A5
Pike CI PL6 ...... 245 D5
Pike's Mead EX20 ...... 170 B4
Pikes Hill EX6 ...... 97 E3
Pilemoor La EX16 ...... 48 E3
Pilemore Cross EX16 ...... 48 E4
Piley La TA21 ...... 51 D8
Pilgrim CI PL2 ...... 248 B6
Pilgrim Prim Sch PL1 ...... 262 B3
Pilgrim Dr PL20 ...... 125 D6
Pill Gdns EX33 ...... 152 D5
Pill La Barnstaple EX32 ...... 162 A5
  Barnstaple, Chestwood
  EX32 ...... 155 A1
  Saltash PL12 ...... 242 E4
Pill Lawn EX32 ...... 155 A2
Pill Rd EX39 ...... 157 A2
Pilland Way EX31 ...... 154 C3
Pillar Ave TQ5 ...... 230 B5
Pillar CI TQ5 ...... 230 B5
Pillar Cres TQ5 ...... 230 B5
Pillar CI TQ5 ...... 230 B5
Pillar Flats TQ5 ...... 230 B5
Pillar Wlk PL6 ...... 244 E7
Pillavins La EX36 ...... 158 F6
Pilliven Cross EX16 ...... 46 F2

Pilliven La EX16 ...... 47 A2
Pillmere Dr PL12 ...... 242 F4
Pillory Hill PL8 ...... 140 F6
Pilmuir Ave TQ12 ...... 219 E5
Pilton Cswy EX32 ...... 154 F6
Pilton Inf Sch EX31 ...... 154 F6
Pilton La EX1 ...... 178 D8
Pilton Lawn EX31 ...... 154 F6
Pilton Quay EX31 ...... 154 F6
Pilton Sch & Com Coll
  EX31 ...... 154 E7
Pilton St EX31 ...... 154 F6
Pimlico TQ1 ...... 220 B5
Pimms Rd TQ3 ...... 225 E7
Pin La PL1 ...... 263 A2
Pinaster CI EX14 ...... 166 E5
Pinbrook Mews EX4 ...... 174 C2
Pinbrook Rd EX4 ...... 174 D1
Pinbrook Units EX4 ...... 174 D1
Pinces Gdns EX2 ...... 177 A3
Pinces Rd EX2 ...... 177 A3
Pinch Hill EX23 ...... 70 A7
Pinder Ct PL19 ...... 171 B5
Pine Ave EX4 ...... 176 F7
Pine CI Brixham TQ5 ...... 230 B2
  Ilfracombe EX34 ...... 150 E4
  Teignmouth TQ14 ...... 210 A6
  Tiverton EX16 ...... 161 B4
Pine Ct TQ1 ...... 220 D5
Pine Gdns EX14 ...... 166 D6
Pine Gr EX14 ...... 166 D6
Pine Park Rd EX14 ...... 166 D5
Pine Ridge D17 ...... 260 C5
Pine Tree CI EX7 ...... 201 B2
Pine View PL18 ...... 125 D6
Pine View Ave TQ1 ...... 220 C6
Pine View CI
  Exmouth EX8 ...... 196 F2
  Halwill Junction EX21 ...... 73 E3
Pine View Gdns TQ1 ...... 220 C6
Pine View Rd TQ1 ...... 220 C6
Pine Wlk D17 ...... 260 D2
Pinefields CI EX11 ...... 168 E3
Pinehurst Way PL6 ...... 237 A6
Pineridge CI EX14 ...... 176 F4
Pines CI EX39 ...... 22 E3
Pines Rd Exmouth EX8 ...... 196 D5
  Paignton TQ3 ...... 225 F8
Pines The Exeter EX4 ...... 176 F7
  Honiton EX14 ...... 166 D5
Pinewood CI
  Dawlish EX7 ...... 205 A8
  Plymouth PL6 ...... 250 F6
Pinewood Dr PL6 ...... 245 E7
Pinewood La EX4 ...... 174 B2
Pinewood Rd TQ12 ...... 207 E2
Pinhay Hollow D17 ...... 104 B2
Pinhey's Cross TQ9 ...... 144 F5
Pinhoe Bridge Halt Sta
  EX1 ...... 178 A7
Pinhoe CE Comb Sch
  EX4 ...... 174 E1
Pinhoe Rd EX4 ...... 174 E1
Pinhoe Sta EX1 ...... 174 E1
Pinhoe Trad Est EX4 ...... 174 D1
Pinksmoor La TA21 ...... 51 E7
Pinkworthy Cross EX16 ...... 48 C8
Pinkworthy Hill EX16 ...... 48 B7
Pinn Hill EX1 ...... 174 F2
Pinn La Exeter EX1 ...... 178 F8
  Otterton EX10 ...... 187 A3
Pinn Lane Cnr EX10 ...... 187 A1
Pinn Valley Rd EX1 ...... 174 F1
Pinnbridge Ct EX1 ...... 178 E8
Pinncourt La EX1 ...... 174 F2
Pinnex Moor Rd EX16 ...... 161 E6
Pins Pk EX22 ...... 164 C5
Pinslow Cross PL15 ...... 105 B8
Pinwood Meadow Dr
  EX4 ...... 174 B2
Pioneer Cotts EX12 ...... 191 D5
Pioneer Terr TQ11 ...... 236 A5
Piper CI EX16 ...... 64 C5
Pipers PI EX14 ...... 68 C2
Pippin CI EX1 ...... 178 C8
Pippins Field EX15 ...... 66 A7
Pippins The PL11 ...... 237 A5
Piscombe La EX9 ...... 198 F7
Pit Hill EX34 ...... 2 D4
Pitchingstone Cross
  TQ7 ...... 147 C7
Pitcombe La TA4 ...... 35 B1
Pitfield CI EX15 ...... 162 D3
Pitham La EX11 ...... 169 F7
Pitland Cnr PL19 ...... 117 B4
Pitland La TQ12 ...... 213 C6
Pitlands La EX15 ...... 163 A8
Pitley Cross TQ13 ...... 131 A5
Pitley Rd TQ13 ...... 131 B5
Pitman's La PL21 ...... 133 C2
Pits La PL10 ...... 140 H7
Pitsham La TA4 ...... 34 E6
Pitson La EX10 ...... 187 A5
Pitt Cres TQ4 ...... 224 B7
Pitt Cross EX39 ...... 22 C4
Pitt La EX39 ...... 23 D6
Pitt Hill Appledore EX39 ...... 157 B8
  Crediton EX17 ...... 79 F3
  Kenton EX6 ...... 194 D3
  Shebbear EX21 ...... 55 D4
Pitt Hill Rd TQ12 ...... 206 F4

Pitt Ho TQ13 . . . . .123 D5
Pitt La Bideford EX39 . . . .157 A2
Bow EX17 . . . . .78 B5
Butterleigh EX16 . . . . .64 C4
Cadbury EX5 . . . . .81 C8
Chevithorne EX16 . . . . .49 D2
Huish Champflower TA4 . . .35 E8
North Molton EX36 . . . . . . .30 F8
Thorverton EX5 . . . . .81 F7
Waterrow TA4 . . . . .35 F5
Pitton Cross EX6 . . . . .96 E5
Pitts Cnr EX16 . . . . .63 D3
Pitts Ct EX2 . . . . .261 C1
Pixey Plain EX36 . . . . .31 B3
Pixie Dell EX33 . . . . .152 B7
Pixie La EX33 . . . . .152 C6
Pixon La PL19 . . . . .171 A4
Pixon Trad Est 2 PL19 . .171 B4
Pixton Cross EX19 . . . . . .58 B2
Pixton Way TA22 . . . . . . .33 E6
Place Cross
Ashburton TQ13 . . . . .131 A6
Okehampton EX20 . . . . .93 E5
Place de Brest PL1 . . . . . .262 C3
Place La TQ13 . . . . .131 A5
Plainfield La EX16 . . . . . . .63 C7
Plainmoor Rd 2 TQ1 . . .220 B7
Plains The TQ9 . . . . .223 D5
Plaistow Cl PL5 . . . . .243 E2
Plaistow Cres PL5 . . . . . .243 E2
Plaistow Hill Inf Sch
PL5 . . . . .243 E2
Plant World Gdns★
TQ12 . . . . .213 C7
Plantagenet Dr EX15 . . . .163 C6
Plantation Cl TQ12 . . . . .207 F1
Plantation Terr EX7 . . . . .204 E6
Plantation Way
Torquay TQ2 . . . . .213 C2
Totnes TQ9 . . . . .222 F6
Plassey Cl EX4 . . . . .173 D2
Plaston Gn EX6 . . . . .112 D5
Platt The TQ6 . . . . .145 E5
Platt Ct TQ8 . . . . .259 B4
Platway La TQ14 . . . . . . .209 D5
Play Cross TQ13 . . . . .130 A4
Playmoor Dr EX1 . . . . . . .174 F1
Pleasant Terr 1 TQ3 . . .226 A6
Pleasure Hill Cl PL9 . . . .255 D8
Plintona View PL7 . . . . . .250 E7
Ploudal Rd EX15 . . . . .163 B2
Plougastel Dr PL12 . . . . .242 E3
Plough Gn PL12 . . . . .242 C3
Ploughman Way PL8 . . .136 A2
Plover Rise PL21 . . . . . . .237 B5
Plum Way EX15 . . . . .162 D4
Plume Of Feathers Cl
EX11 . . . . .169 C4
Plumer Rd PL6 . . . . .244 F2
Plumper's Cross EX38 . . .41 A7
Plumtree Dr EX2 . . . . .178 B4
Plumtree La EX5 . . . . .99 E7
Plym Cl TQ2 . . . . .219 B7
Plym Cres PL19 . . . . .171 D5
Plym St PL4 . . . . .263 A3
Plym Valley Rly★ PL7 . . .250 A7
Plym View Prim Sch
PL3 . . . . .249 D6
Plymbridge Gdns PL7 . . .250 C7
Plymbridge La PL6 . . . . . .245 B4
Plymbridge Rd
Plymouth, Estover PL6 . . . .245 E5
Plymouth, Plympton PL7 . .250 C7
Plymouth PL6 . . . . .245 A5
Plymouth City Airport
PL6 . . . . .245 C5
Plymouth Coll PL4 . . . . . .248 E4
Plymouth Coll of Art &
Design PL4 . . . . .263 A3
Plymouth Coll of Art &
Design (Sutton Annexe)
PL4 . . . . .263 A3
Plymouth Coll of F Ed
PL11 . . . . .248 A2
Plymouth Coll of F Ed
(Annexe) PL1 . . . . .262 C4
Plymouth Coll Prep Sch
PL3 . . . . .248 E6
Plymouth Dome Discovery
Ctr★ PL1 . . . . .262 A1
Plymouth High Sch for Girls
PL4 . . . . .263 A4
Plymouth Hill PL20 . . . . .128 A8
Plymouth International Bsns
Pk PL6 . . . . .245 A3
Plymouth Nuffield Hospl The
PL6 . . . . .245 A4
Plymouth Pavilions PL1 .262 B2
Plymouth Rd
Buckfastleigh TQ11 . . . . . .236 A3
Buckfastleigh TQ11 . . . . . .236 B4
Kingsbridge TQ7 . . . . .258 C6
Plymouth PL7 . . . . .250 B6
South Brent TQ10 . . . . .134 F2
Tavistock PL19 . . . . .171 B4
Totnes TQ9 . . . . .223 B5
Plymouth Road Ind Est
PL19 . . . . .171 C3
Plymouth Sta PL1,PL4 . . .262 C4
Plympton Cross TQ7 . . . .144 D5
Plympton Rd PL7 . . . . . . .250 F3
Plympton Hospl PL7 . . . .250 D5
Plympton St Mary CE Inf Sch
PL7 . . . . .250 D5

Plympton St Maurice Prim
Sch PL7 . . . . .250 F3
Plymstock Rd PL9 . . . . . . .255 D7
Plymstock Sch PL9 . . . . . .255 F8
Plymtree CE Prim Sch
EX15 . . . . .83 F5
Plymtree Dr PL7 . . . . .250 C7
Poadmarsh Cross EX6 . . .31 D1
Poadmarsh Hill
Bishops Nympton EX36 . . . .30 F1
Bishops Nympton, Rose Hill
EX36 . . . . .31 D1
Pocklington Rise PL7 . . .250 E5
Pocombe Hill EX2 . . . . . . .176 D3
Pod La EX13 . . . . .87 F4
Pode Dr PL7 . . . . .251 B4
Point In View Cotts EX8 .196 B3
Point Terr EX8 . . . . .201 E6
Pole Rue La TA20 . . . . .69 F6
Polehouse La EX2 . . . . . . .176 E1
Poles Hill EX31 . . . . .154 E7
Poleshill La EX31 . . . . . . .154 D7
Polhearne La TQ5 . . . . . .230 B3
Polhearne Way TQ5 . . . . .230 B3
Pollard Cl Plymouth PL9 .255 B5
Saltash PL12 . . . . .242 B2
Pollard's La TA21 . . . . .52 F7
Pollards The EX32 . . . . . .155 C3
Pollards Way PL12 . . . . . .242 E3
Pollyblank Rd 2 TQ12 . .207 B3
Pollybrook EX5 . . . . .184 C2
Polmer Mews EX9 . . . . . .199 G2
Polruan Terr PL1 . . . . .262 A3
Polsham Pk TQ3 . . . . .226 B7
Polsloe Rd EX1 . . . . .177 E6
Polson Hill EX17 . . . . .61 A2
Poltimore Cl EX36 . . . . . .158 D4
Poltimore Cross EX4 . . . .174 E6
Poltimore Ct EX4 . . . . . . .174 F7
Poltimore Lawn EX32 . . .155 B6
Poltimore Rd
Farway EX24 . . . . .101 F7
Offwell EX14 . . . . .102 A8
South Molton EX36 . . . . . . .158 D4
Poltimore Sq EX4 . . . . . . .261 B4
Polwhele Rd 14 EX16 . . .64 D7
Polywell EX39 . . . . .14 F1
Polzeath Gdns PL2 . . . . . .248 D8
Pomeroy Ave TQ5 . . . . . . .230 A5
Pomeroy Pl 8 TQ12 . . . .122 F1
Pomeroy Rd
Newton Abbot TQ12 . . . . . .207 B3
Tiverton EX16 . . . . .64 E8
Pomphlett Cl PL9 . . . . . . .255 D8
Pomphlett Farm Ind Est
PL9 . . . . .249 E1
Pomphlett Gdns PL9 . . . .255 D8
Pomphlett Prim Sch
PL9 . . . . .255 E8
Pomphlett Rd PL9 . . . . . .255 E8
Pond Hill EX16 . . . . .65 A7
Pond La TA21 . . . . .51 D3
Pondfield Rd PL12 . . . . . .242 B3
Ponsford Cross EX15 . . . .65 A4
Ponsford La EX15 . . . . .65 A4
Ponsonby Rd PL3 . . . . . . .248 B4
Poole La TQ13 . . . . .130 F5
Pool Anthony Dr EX16 . . .64 E8
Pool Cross EX20 . . . . .107 F8
Pool Hill Ashbrittle TA21 . .35 A5
Bridestowe EX20 . . . . .107 F8
Pool La Burrington EX37 . .44 A4
Chittlehampton EX37 . . . . . .29 A1
Woolacombe EX34 . . . . .1 A1
Pool Pk TQ10 . . . . .135 A3
Poole Cross TQ12 . . . . . .211 A1
Poole Hill TA22 . . . . .33 B5
Poole Park Rd PL5 . . . . . .247 C8
Poole's Ct EX17 . . . . .260 E3
Pooley Cross TQ7 . . . . . . .143 E4
Poolmill Cross TQ13 . . . .112 E1
Pools Weir TQ12 . . . . .214 B8
Pool La EX13,TA20 . . . . . . .88 B8
Pope's La Lapford EX17 . . .60 C3
Rockwell Green TA21 . . . . .160 B4
Popes Cl EX17 . . . . .165 C6
Popes La EX24 . . . . .103 A3
Popham Cross EX36 . . . . .19 A3
Popham Flats TA21 . . . . . .160 D6
Popham La EX36 . . . . .19 A3
Poplar Cl Brixham TQ5 . . .229 F2
Exeter EX2 . . . . .177 A3
Exmouth EX8 . . . . .196 D3
Newton Abbot TQ12 . . . . . .213 A8
Plymouth PL7 . . . . .251 B5
Poplar Dr TQ7 . . . . .258 C5
Poplar Mount EX13 . . . . .167 D6
Poplar Row EX9 . . . . .199 H2
Poplar Terr EX37 . . . . .43 C7
Poplar Tree Cnr EX12 . . .192 A8
Poplar Tree Dr EX12 . . . .192 A7
Poplars Dr TQ3 . . . . .218 D2
Poplars The
1 Chudleigh Knighton
TQ13 . . . . .123 C4
Exeter EX4 . . . . .174 E2
Poppy Cl EX4 . . . . .176 D8
Porch EX13 . . . . .88 A3
Pork Hill PL19 . . . . .117 F1
Porlock Way TQ4 . . . . .225 F2
Porsham Cl PL6 . . . . .241 B1
Porsham La PL5 . . . . .244 E8
Porspoder Pl PL10 . . . . . .253 A2
Port Cross
Bishops Nympton EX36 . . . .31 B4
Bratton Fleming EX31 . . . . .10 F5
Port Hill EX31 . . . . .10 F5

Port La
Bishops Nympton EX36 . . . .31 C4
Chillington TQ7 . . . . .145 A1
Dulverton TA22 . . . . .34 A5
Wotter PL7 . . . . .132 C4
Port Lane Cl TQ7 . . . . . . .144 F1
Port Mer Cl EX8 . . . . .196 E3
Port Rd EX6 . . . . .200 D4
Portal Pl PL21 . . . . .237 B5
Portbridge Cross TQ9 . . .215 F8
Portchester Hts EX4 . . . . .173 C2
Porteous Cl PL1 . . . . .247 F3
Porter Way PL12 . . . . .242 C3
Porter's La EX8 . . . . .195 E8
Portford Cross EX31 . . . . .27 E3
Portford La TQ10 . . . . . . .135 A2
Portgate Cross EX36 . . . . .30 B8
Portland Ave
Exmouth EX8 . . . . .202 B6
Teignmouth TQ14 . . . . .210 C7
Portland Bldgs 6 EX32 .155 A4
Portland Ct
19 Barnstaple EX32 . . . . .155 A4
Lyme Regis DT7 . . . . .260 C3
Plymouth PL1 . . . . .247 F3
Portland La
Kilmington EX13 . . . . .103 C8
Meavy PL20 . . . . .127 D2
Portland Pk EX34 . . . . .150 C6
Portland Pl PL4 . . . . .263 A4
Portland Rd
Plymouth PL1 . . . . .247 F3
Torquay TQ1 . . . . .220 D7
Portland Sq
Plymouth PL4 . . . . .262 C4
Plymouth PL4 . . . . .263 A4
Portland Square La N
PL4 . . . . .263 A4
Portland St
Barnstaple EX32 . . . . .155 B3
Exeter EX1 . . . . .177 E6
Ilfracombe EX34 . . . . .150 C6
Portland Villas EX4 . . . . .262 C4
Portledge Pl EX39 . . . . . . .25 A3
Portlemore Cl TQ7 . . . . . .147 E6
Portlemore Gdns TQ7 . . .147 E6
Portmarsh La EX32 . . . . . .155 A4
Portsmouth Arms Cross
EX18 . . . . .45 A8
Portsmouth Arms Sta
EX37 . . . . .43 F6
Portway EX15 . . . . .66 C7
Portway Cl PL9 . . . . .256 D7
Possession Cross EX37 . .28 E7
Post Box Cross
Bridgerule EX22 . . . . .70 F6
Cheriton Fitzpaine EX17 . . .63 A7
Post Cl TA21 . . . . .160 E4
Post Cross Bishops Nympton
EX18 . . . . .45 C8
Post Cross Bsns Pk EX15 .65 F2
Post Hill EX16 . . . . .64 C8
Post La Brendon EX35 . . . .6 C4
Upton TA4 . . . . .34 E7
Post Office La
Cheriton Fitzpaine EX17 . . .62 F1
Tatworth TA20 . . . . .88 C8
Post Office St EX1 . . . . . .261 B3
Potacre St EX38 . . . . .159 D5
Potem's Cross
Atherington EX37 . . . . .28 A1
Yarnscombe EX37 . . . . .27 F2
Potshop Cross EX37 . . . . .79 D2
Potter's Cross TA4 . . . . . . .35 C7
Potters Cl EX11 . . . . .168 D5
Potters Hill TQ1 . . . . .220 B5
Potters Stile EX14 . . . . . . .67 B1
Potters Way PL7 . . . . .250 D6
Potterswell EX11 . . . . .154 B3
Pottery Cl
Bovey Tracey TQ13 . . . . . . .180 C5
Honiton EX14 . . . . .166 D6
Pottery Ct TQ6 . . . . .233 D4
Pottery Est PL10 . . . . .252 E6
Pottery La EX14 . . . . .153 A4
Pottery Mews TQ3 . . . . . .218 D2
Pottery Rd
Bovey Tracey TQ13 . . . . . . .180 C5
Kingsteignton TQ12 . . . . . .207 D6
Plymouth PL1 . . . . .247 D3
Pottery Units TQ12 . . . . .207 D4
Pottington Bsns Pk
EX31 . . . . .154 C6
Pottington Dr EX31 . . . . .154 D6
Pottington Ind Est EX31 .154 D5
Pottington La TQ6 . . . . . . .146 A6
Potties Cl EX6 . . . . .182 B3
Poultney Cl PL7 . . . . .251 A5
Pouncers Cross EX14 . . . .86 F6
Pound Cl Burrington EX37 . .43 F3
Sidbury EX10 . . . . .101 B2
Topsham EX3 . . . . .182 E6
Pound Cnr
Clyst Honiton EX5 . . . . .179 E7
Whitestone EX4 . . . . .98 C5
Pound Cross EX4 . . . . .99 B5
Pound Down Cnr EX4 . . . .98 D5
Pound Field TQ9 . . . . .227 F8
Pound Gate EX16 . . . . .112 F5
Pound Hill Axmouth EX12 .192 D7
Holcombe Rogus TA21 . . . . .51 A5
Pound La Bridford EX6 . . .113 A5
Buckland Monachorum
PL20 . . . . .126 C3
Colaton Raleigh EX10 . . . . .186 C5
18 Combe Martin EX34 . . . .3 A3
High Bickington EX37 . . . . .43 C8

Pound La continued
Kingskerswell TQ12 . . . . . .212 F4
Nadderwater EX4 . . . . .98 F4
Raymond's Hill DT6 . . . . . .104 D8
Shaldon TQ14 . . . . .209 C5
Stoke Climsland PL17 . . . . .115 C1
5 Teignmouth TQ14 . . . . .210 C4
Topsham EX3 . . . . .182 E6
Uplyme DT7 . . . . .260 B5
Upottery EX14 . . . . .68 C1
Woodbury EX5 . . . . .184 C3
Yarcombe EX14 . . . . .69 B2
Pound Lane End EX37 . . . .43 B8
Pound Lane Trad Est
EX8 . . . . .196 C1
Pound Mdw
Great Torrington EX38 . . . . .42 B7
Hatherleigh EX20 . . . . .75 C7
Parkham EX39 . . . . .39 E8
Pound Pk EX20 . . . . .170 D6
Pound Pl TQ13 . . . . .180 D8
Pound Rd Axminster EX13 . .88 F2
Crapstone PL20 . . . . .126 E3
Lyme Regis DT7 . . . . .260 D3
Pound Sq EX15 . . . . .163 C2
Pound St Exmouth EX8 . . .202 A6
Lyme Regis DT7 . . . . .260 D3
Moretonhampstead TQ13 . .111 F4
Plymouth PL1 . . . . .254 A8
Pound Terr 1 TA21 . . . . .160 D5
Pound's Cross PL6 . . . . . .240 E5
Poundfield Cl EX31 . . . . . .153 F5
Poundhouse Cross TQ6 . .146 B8
Pounds Hill EX17 . . . . .165 D6
Pounds Park Rd
1 Bere Alston PL20 . . . . .125 E1
Plymouth PL3 . . . . .248 D7
Pounds Pk PL12 . . . . .242 F3
Poundsclose TA22 . . . . . . .33 E4
Poundsgate Cl TQ5 . . . . .230 E4
Poundshill Cross EX17 . . .165 D6
Poundsland EX5 . . . . .175 C6
Poundstone Ct TQ8 . . . . .259 C4
Poundwell St PL21 . . . . . .137 B2
Poundwell St PL21 . . . . . .137 C3
EX6 . . . . .194 F4
Powderham Castle★
. . . . .194 F4
Powderham Cl
Newton Abbot TQ12 . . . . . .207 B2
Topsham EX3 . . . . .182 E6
Powderham Cres EX4 . . .177 D8
Powderham Rd
Exeter EX2 . . . . .177 A4
Newton Abbot TQ12 . . . . . .207 B2
Plymouth PL3 . . . . .248 F7
Torquay TQ2 . . . . .213 F1
Powderham Terr
Newton Abbot TQ12 . . . . . .207 B2
Teignmouth TQ14 . . . . .210 C4
Powderham Wlk EX6 . . . .181 F5
Powell's Cl EX6 . . . . .96 E2
Powells Way EX14 . . . . . . .67 C1
Powis Gdns PL5 . . . . .244 B2
Powisland Dr PL6 . . . . . . .245 A5
Powlesland La EX17 . . . . . .95 E6
Poylen Rd TQ10 . . . . .188 A4
Poyers EX33 . . . . .152 E4
Pratt's La TQ7 . . . . .143 B7
Premier Pl EX2 . . . . .261 C2
Prescot Rd EX4 . . . . .176 C5
Prescott Rd EX15 . . . . .52 F8
Prestbury Pk 2 TQ2 . . . .219 F5
Preston Barns TQ9 . . . . . .222 D1
Preston Cross
West Alvington TQ7 . . . . . .148 C8
Preston Down Ave TA4 . . . .219 B2
Preston Down Rd TQ3 . . .219 B2
Preston Fork TQ9 . . . . . . .138 C2
Preston Gate EX31 . . . . . . .10 E6
Preston La EX17 . . . . .80 D7
Preston Prim Sch TQ2 . . .219 B2
Preston St EX1 . . . . .261 A2
Prestonbury Cl PL6 . . . . . .245 B7
Prestor EX13 . . . . .167 E5
Pretoria Rd EX1 . . . . .177 F7
Pretoria Terr EX34 . . . . . .150 A3
Pretty Top
Great Torrington EX20 . . . . .41 F1
Petrockstow EX20 . . . . .56 F8
Priddis Cl EX8 . . . . .196 C3
Priddles La TA20 . . . . .69 F8
Prideaux Cl PL12 . . . . .242 C5
Prideaux Cres EX16 . . . . .161 D6
Prideaux La TQ6 . . . . .145 F6
Prideaux Rd PL21 . . . . . . .237 D4
Prideax Mdw EX38 . . . . . .159 F5
Pridham La PL2 . . . . .248 D7
Pridhams Way EX6 . . . . . .182 A4
Priest Hill EX15 . . . . .66 A3
Priesthood Terr PL10 . . . .252 E5
Priestley Ave Exeter EX4 .173 A2
Plymouth PL5 . . . . .243 E2
Prigg Mdw TQ13 . . . . .130 F4
Primley Cross TQ3 . . . . . .225 F5
Primley Ct TQ3 . . . . .225 E5
Primley Gdns EX10 . . . . . .188 C7
Primley Mead EX10 . . . . .188 C7
Primley Paddock EX10 . .188 B7
Primley Pk TQ3 . . . . .225 E5
Primley Pk E TQ3 . . . . . . .226 A5
Primley Pk W TQ3 . . . . . .226 A5
Primrose Ave EX32 . . . . . .155 E4
Primrose Cl
Chillington TQ7 . . . . .144 F1
Ivybridge PL21 . . . . .237 D5

Primrose Cl continued
Kingsteignton TQ12 . . . . . .207 E7
6 Tiverton EX16 . . . . .161 F6
Torpoint PL11 . . . . .246 E4
Primrose Cres PL19 . . . . .171 E4
Primrose La EX39 . . . . . . .157 B8
Primrose Lawn EX4 . . . . .176 D8
Primrose Mdw PL21 . . . .237 A6
Primrose Way
Exeter EX12 . . . . .165 E6
Kingskerswell TQ12 . . . . . .212 F6
Launceston PL15 . . . . .105 A2
Seaton EX12 . . . . .192 B7
Primrose Wlk PL12 . . . . . .242 D4
Prince Charles Cl EX8 . . .196 C1
Prince Charles Ct TQ2 . . .214 A3
Prince Charles Rd EX4 . . .177 F8
Prince Charles Way
EX12 . . . . .192 A8
Prince Maurice Ct PL4 . .263 B3
Prince Maurice Rd PL4 . .248 F4
Prince Of Wales Dr
Dartmouth TQ6 . . . . .233 F4
Exmouth EX8 . . . . .196 E1
Prince Of Wales Rd
Crediton EX17 . . . . .58 A3
Exeter EX4 . . . . .177 B8
Kingsbridge TQ7 . . . . .258 C5
Prince Rock Prim Sch
PL4 . . . . .249 B2
Prince Rupert Way
TQ12 . . . . .123 B2
Prince St TQ12 . . . . .207 C3
Prince William Ct 1
TQ5 . . . . .230 C4
Prince William Quay
Plymouth PL3 . . . . .248 D7
TQ5 . . . . .230 D5
Prince's Sq EX2 . . . . .177 A3
Prince's St E EX2 . . . . . . .177 A3
Prince's St N EX2 . . . . . . .177 A4
Prince's St S EX2 . . . . . . .177 A3
Prince's St W EX2 . . . . . . .177 A4
Princes Point TQ1 . . . . . . .220 C3
Princes Rd Plymouth PL6 .245 E6
Torquay TQ1 . . . . .220 B5
Princes Rd E TQ1 . . . . . . .220 C5
Princes Rd W TQ1 . . . . . .220 B5
Princess St
15 Dawlish EX7 . . . . .204 D6
Exmouth EX8 . . . . .202 A6
Paignton TQ3 . . . . .226 B6
Plymouth PL1 . . . . .247 E2
Torquay TQ1 . . . . .220 D7
Princess Ave
Ilfracombe EX34 . . . . .150 C5
Plymouth, Mutley Plain PL5 .255 E6
Plymouth, West Park PL5 . .244 A3
Princess Cotts TQ12 . . . . .213 C6
Princess Cres PL9 . . . . . . .255 C6
Princess Elizabeth Terr
EX20 . . . . .107 F8
Princess Rd
Kingskerswell TQ12 . . . . . .213 A4
Kingsteignton TQ12 . . . . . .207 D8
Princess St
Barnstaple EX32 . . . . .155 A6
Plymouth PL1 . . . . .262 C2
Princess Street Ope
PL1 . . . . .262 C2
Princess Way PL1 . . . . . . .262 C2
Princesshay EX1 . . . . .261 B3
Princetown Prim Sch
PL20 . . . . .128 A8
Priorton Hill EX17 . . . . . . .80 B7
Priorton La EX17 . . . . .80 B7
Priory Bovey Tracey TQ13 .180 C8
Wellington TA21 . . . . .160 E6
Priory Ave
Kingskerswell TQ12 . . . . . .213 A5
Totnes TQ9 . . . . .223 C6
Priory Cl Barnstaple EX31 .154 F7
East Budleigh EX9 . . . . . . .198 B7
Ivybridge PL21 . . . . .237 B5
Tavistock PL19 . . . . .171 D3
Priory Ct 3 Totnes TQ9 . .223 C6
Wellington TA21 . . . . .160 E7
Priory Dr Plymouth PL7 . .250 D5
Totnes TQ9 . . . . .223 C6
Priory Gdns
Barnstaple EX31 . . . . .154 F7
1 Dawlish EX7 . . . . .204 E6
Exeter EX4 . . . . .261 A2
Tavistock PL19 . . . . .171 D3
Wellington TA21 . . . . .160 E6
Priory Gn EX4 . . . . .178 A7
Priory High Sch EX2 . . . .177 E2
Priory Hill
1 Dawlish EX7 . . . . .204 E6
Totnes TQ9 . . . . .223 C6
Priory La EX4 . . . . .113 B4
Priory Lawn Terr PL3 . . . .249 A6
Priory Mill PL7 . . . . .250 D5
Priory Park Rd EX4 . . . . . .204 D6
Priory RC Prim Sch
TQ1 . . . . .220 B8
Priory Rd
Abbotskerswell TQ12 . . . . .212 C7
Barnstaple EX31 . . . . .154 F7
Exeter EX4 . . . . .261 A2
Dawlish EX7 . . . . .204 E6
Exeter EX4 . . . . .177 E8
Plymouth PL3 . . . . .249 A6
Tiverton EX16 . . . . .161 F6
Totnes TQ9 . . . . .220 B8
Priory Ridge PL7 . . . . .250 D5
Priory St TQ9 . . . . .223 C6
Priory The
Abbotskerswell TQ12 . . . . .212 C7

Priory The continued
Modbury PL21 ....137 B2
Priory View TQ9 ....227 B4
Priory Wall Cross EX15 ..66 B2
Prisam La EX20 ....75 C2
Prisam Lane Cross EX20 ..75 F2
Priscott Way TQ12 ......207 E6
Prispen Dr EX5 ....82 B6
Prispen Ho EX5 ....82 B6
Prispen View EX5 ....82 B6
Prixford EX31 ....16 C7
Promenade
Ilfracombe EX34 ....150 B6
Kingsbridge TQ7 ....258 D5
Paignton TQ3 ....226 D8
Paignton, Goodrington
 TQ4 ....226 C4
Promenade The PL1 ....262 C1
Prospect EX7 ....204 E6
Prospect Cnr EX31 ......27 A7
Prospect Cres EX15 .....66 A7
Prospect Gdns EX4 .....177 E7
Prospect Hill
Okehampton EX20 ....170 B4
Stapton TQ7 ....145 C4
Prospect La PL12 ....242 C3
Prospect Pk EX4 ....177 D8
Prospect Pl
Barnstaple EX32 ....155 B3
Exeter EX4 ....177 A4
Ottery St Mary EX11 ....169 D3
Plymouth PL1 ....262 B2
 5 Tiverton EX16 ....161 B4
Prospect Rd 8 TQ5 .....230 C5
Prospect Row PL1 ....247 E1
Prospect St PL4 ....263 A3
Prospect Terr
Gunnislake PL18 ....125 D6
Gunnislake, St Ann's Chapel
 PL18 ....125 B5
Newton Abbot TQ12 .....207 C3
Prospect Way EX17 ......60 D3
Prospect Wlk PL12 ......242 C3
Prouse Cres PL2 ....248 C8
Prouse Rise PL2 ....242 E2
Providence Pl
Calstock PL18 ....125 D3
Plymouth PL1 ....248 A3
Providence Row 16
 EX39 ....157 A2
Providence St PL4 ......263 A4
Prowse La
Cheriton Fitzpaine EX17 ..80 C8
Lapford EX17 ....60 D3
Prowse's La EX16 ....63 E1
Prowses EX15 ....67 B8
Prynne Cl PL1 ....262 B3
Puckridge Rd EX4 ....174 D2
Puddavens Terr TQ9 .....223 A8
Pudleylake Rd
Axminster EX13 ....167 B1
Musbury EX13 ....103 E6
Puffin Way EX2 ....176 D3
Pugsley Rd 9 EX16 .....64 D7
Pulborough Farm Cvn Pk
 EX20 ....107 F4
Pulchrass St 11 EX32 ..155 A4
Pullen's Row EX16 ......46 E1
Pulleys Cl TQ7 ....143 C6
Pulling Rd EX4 ....174 D2
Pullins Terr 10 TQ13 ...123 E6
Pump La EX19 ....156 A2
Pump St 8 Brixham TQ5 .230 D5
 Newton St Cyres EX5 ....172 A8
Punchards Down TQ9 ....222 F6
Purbeck Ave TQ2 ....219 D2
Purcell Cl EX7 ....204 C3
Purcombe Cross TQ13 ...131 D3
Purdridge Cross EX24 ...102 D6
Purzebrook Cl EX13 .....167 D5
Pusehill Rd EX39 ....156 B5
Pusborough St EX13 ....8 A2
Pusborough Rd EX33 .....7 F3
Pushole La EX38 ....40 E1
Putson Cross EX16 ......64 E8
Putts Cnr EX10 ....101 C7
Pye Cnr
 Branshd Speke EX5 ......81 D1
 Cullompton EX15 ....163 C3
 Kennford EX6 ....181 B2
Pye La TA20 ....88 E8
Pykes Down PL21 ....237 F4
Pyles Thorne TA21 ......160 E5
Pyles Thorne Cl TA21 ...160 E5
Pyles Thorne Rd TA21 ...160 E4
Pym St Plymouth PL1 ....247 F3
 Tavistock PL19 ....171 C6
Pyne Gdns EX5 ....173 A7
Pyne Meadow Cross
 EX18 ....44 D3
Pynes Cl
 Cheriton Fitzpaine EX17 ..62 E1
 East Budleigh EX9 ......198 B6
Pynes Hill EX2 ....178 C2
Pynes Hill Bsns Pk EX2 .178 C3
Pynes Inf Sch EX39 .....156 F1
Pynes La EX39 ....156 E1
Pynes Rd EX16 ....64 D6
Pynsent Ct 4 TQ13 .....123 E6
Pytte Gdns EX3 ....183 C7
Pyworthy CE Prim Sch
 EX22 ....71 D5

Quadrangle The EX4 ....177 C8
Quadrant The EX2 ......261 C2

Quagmire La EX22 ......164 C7
Quant Pk PL19 ....171 C6
Quantock Rd TA21 ......160 D7
Quantocks EX33 ....158 B6
Quantocks Rd TQ2 ......219 C3
Quarries La EX37 ....43 C7
Quarries The EX4 ....176 D4
Quarry Cl Bideford EX39 .156 E2
 Totnes TQ9 ....222 C6
Quarry Cotts Beer EX12 .191 B5
 Plymouth PL1 ....262 A3
Quarry Foot Cross EX17 .79 C4
Quarry Gdns TQ3 ....226 A7
Quarry La Beer EX12 ....191 B5
 Down St Mary EX17 .....78 F6
 Exeter EX2 ....178 C4
 Gunnislake PL18 ....125 C6
 Silverton EX5 ....82 B5
 Thorverton EX5 ....81 D4
Quarry Park Ave PL9 ....255 D7
Quarry Park Rd
 Exeter EX2 ....178 C4
 Plymouth, Peverell PL3 .248 D5
 Plymouth, Plymstock PL9 .255 D7
Quarry Rd EX37 ....43 B7
Quarry St PL11 ....247 C3
Quarryfields EX20 ......170 C6
Quarter Mile La EX5 ....99 D3
Quarterdeck The PL1 ....254 A8
Quartley Hill EX16 ......34 E4
Quay Hill EX1,EX2 ......261 A2
Quay La Instow EX39 ....15 B1
 Lympstone EX8 ....195 D4
Quay Rd
 Newton Abbot TQ12 .....207 D3
 Plymouth PL1 ....263 A2
 Teignmouth TQ14 ....210 B4
Quay Terr TQ12 ....207 D3
Quay The Appledore EX39 .15 A1
 Ashprington TQ9 ....139 F7
 Bideford EX39 ....157 A2
 Brixham TQ5 ....230 D5
 Dartmouth TQ6 ....233 F3
 Dittisham TQ6 ....228 D2
 Exeter EX2 ....261 B2
 Ilfracombe EX34 ....150 C6
 Quayside **6** PL19 .....171 B5
Quayfield Rd EX34 ......150 C6
Quayside 6 PL19 ....171 B5
Quaywest Waterpark*
 TQ4 ....226 C3
Queen Anne's Ct
 EX31 ....154 F5
Queen Annes 14 EX39 ...157 A2
Queen Annes Copse
 TQ12 ....206 F1
Queen Dart Cross EX16 ..47 B4
Queen Dart Hill EX16 ....47 B3
Queen Elizabeth Ave
 TQ6 ....233 E4
Queen Elizabeth Ct
 EX39 ....156 C6
Queen Elizabeth Dr
 Crediton EX17 ....165 A6
 Torquay TQ3 ....225 E6
Queen Elizabeth's Com Coll
 EX17 ....165 B6
Queen Elizabeth's Lower Sch
 EX17 ....165 B5
Queen La 7 EX16 ....204 D6
Queen Sq EX15 ....163 C3
Queen St
 Barnstaple EX32 ....155 A5
 Bideford EX39 ....157 A2
 Budleigh Salterton EX9 .199 G2
 8 Colyton EX24 ......103 A4
 Dawlish EX7 ....204 D6
 Exeter EX4 ....261 A3
 11 Exmouth EX8 ......202 A6
 Honiton EX14 ....156 A6
 Lynton EX35 ....151 C5
 Newton Abbot TQ12 .....207 D3
 Northlew EX20 ....74 E2
 Plymouth PL1 ....247 D2
 Seaton EX12 ....192 A5
 South Molton EX36 .....158 C4
 12 Teignmouth TQ14 ..210 B4
 Tiverton EX16 ....161 C3
 Torquay TQ1 ....220 B5
 Winkleigh EX19 ....58 F3
Queen's Ave EX34 ......150 C5
Queen's Cres
 Brixham TQ5 ....230 D3
 Exeter EX4 ....261 B4
Queen's Ct 12 EX8 ......202 A6
Queen's Dr EX8 ....202 C5
Queen's Dr The EX4 .....177 B8
Queen's Gate
 Plymouth, Lipson PL4 ...263 B4
 Plymouth, Stoke PL3 ....262 A4
Queen's Gate Mews PL4 .263 B4
Queen's Gate Villas
 PL4 ....263 B4
Queen's Gate Villas Rd
 PL4 ....263 B4
Queen's Ho 4 EX31 .....154 F5
Queen's Park Rd TQ4 ...226 C6
Queen's Pk EX22 ....55 C1
Queen's Rd Brixham TQ5 .230 C6
 Budleigh Salterton EX9 .197 F2
 Moretonhampstead TQ13 ..121 E6
 Paignton TQ4 ....226 B6
Queen's Sq 8 EX24 .....103 A4
Queen's Terr EX4 ....261 A4

Queen's Terr
 Great Torrington EX38 ..159 B5
 4 Totnes TQ9 ....223 C6
Queens Cl
 Kingsteignton TQ12 ....207 F8
 Plymouth PL6 ....245 E6
Queens Pk EX17 ....80 D4
Queens Rd Exeter EX2 ..261 A1
 Plymouth PL5 ....243 F3
 Tavistock PL19 ....171 A5
 Torquay TQ1 ....220 B3
Queens Wlk DT7 ....260 E4
Queenshaye EX20 ....95 A5
Queensland Dr EX44 ....173 E2
Queensway
 Newton Abbot TQ12 ....207 E2
 Tiverton EX16 ....161 F5
 Torquay TQ2 ....219 D6
Queensway Cl TQ2 ......219 E7
Queensway Cres TQ2 ....219 E7
Queensway Ho TQ2 .....207 E2
Queensway Rc Sch TQ2 ..219 D7
Quentin Ave TQ5 ....230 B2
Questant La EX10 ......188 C6
Quicks Wlk EX38 ....159 F5
Quillets The TQ7 ....147 E6
Quince Cross
 South Molton EX36 .....46 B8
 Spreyton EX17 ....96 C7
Quince Hill EX36 ....31 A1
Quince Honey Farm*
 EX36 ....158 C5
Quinnel Ho 12 TQ14 ....210 B5
Quinta Cl TQ1 ....220 C6
Quinta Ct TQ1 ....220 C7
Quinta Rd TQ1 ....220 C6
Quintet Cl EX1 ....178 C5
Quirk Hill EX16 ....63 D7
Quoditch Cross EX21 ....73 B1
Quoitgate Cross EX22 ...38 D3

Rack Park Cl EX38 ......159 C5
Rack Park Rd EX38 .....258 D5
Rack St EX1 ....261 A2
Rackclose La EX4 ....261 A2
Rackenford CE Prim Sch
 EX16 ....47 D5
Rackenford Cross EX16 ..47 D5
Rackenford Rd
 Tiverton EX16 ....161 A6
 Witheridge EX16 ....46 E1
Rackfield TA21 ....160 A5
Rackfield Ct EX32 ......154 F6
Rackleigh La EX17 ......66 A2
Rackmead EX37 ....28 F4
Radcliffe Cl PL9 ....244 E6
Radcliffe Ct TQ3 ....226 C7
Raddenstile Ct EX8 .....202 B6
Raddick La PL20 ....127 F5
Raddicombe Cl TQ5 .....234 F8
Raddicombe Dr TQ5 .....234 F8
Raddicombe Farm TQ5 ..234 F8
Raddon Cross EX17 .....81 A5
Raddon Down Cross
 EX17 ....79 D4
Raddon Hill EX17 ....81 A6
Raddon Top EX17 ....81 A6
Radford Ave PL4 ....249 A1
Radford Ho EX2 ....226 B6
Radford La PL10 ....252 D4
Radford Park Dr PL9 ....255 D6
Radford Park Rd PL9 ....255 D6
Radford Rd Exeter EX2 ..261 C2
 Plymouth PL1 ....262 C2
Radford Way PL9 ....255 D6
Radfords Orch TQ9 .....131 E1
Radish La EX17 ....102 A2
Radnidge La EX36 ......30 D8
Radnor Hall PL4 ....263 A3
Radnor Pl Exeter EX2 ...261 C2
 Plymouth PL4 ....263 A3
Radway EX10 ....188 B4
Radway Ct TQ14 ....209 A8
Radway Gdns TQ14 .....209 A8
Radway Hill TQ14 ......209 A8
Radway La EX36 ....187 B1
Radway St TQ14 ....209 A8
Raeburn Rd PL5 ....244 B6
Rag La Aylesbeare EX5 ..99 D4
 Copplestone EX17 ......79 C7
 Yarcombe EX14 ....69 A2
Rage La EX9 ....199 G2
Ragged La EX18 ....44 B1
Raglan Cl PL1 ....247 F2
Raglan Gdns PL1 ....247 F2
Raglan Rd PL1 ....247 F2
Railway Cotts
 Holsworthy EX22 ....164 C3
 6 Plymouth, Ford PL2 .247 F5
 Plymouth, Plymstock PL9 .255 D7
 Tavistock PL19 ....171 B6
Railway Terr
 3 Bideford EX39 .....157 B1
 Broadclyst EX5 ....175 E3
Rainbow Ct TQ2 ....219 F2
Rainbow La TA3 ....67 F8
Raisey La TA20 ....69 F7
Rake Cnr TQ7 ....143 F6
Rakeham Hill EX38 .....41 B6
Rakelane Cross TQ7 ....143 F6

Raleigh Ave TQ2 ....219 D6
Raleigh Cl
 Dartmouth TQ6 ....233 C3
 Sidmouth EX10 ....188 B7
 South Molton EX36 .....158 C4
Raleigh Cotts 3 EX31 ...155 A7
Raleigh Ct
 Budleigh Salterton EX9 .198 B2
 Plymouth PL7 ....251 B6
 Torquay TQ2 ....219 D6
Raleigh Dr TQ4 ....226 B2
Raleigh Hill
 Bideford, Raleigh Hill EX39 .156 E4
 Bideford, Silford EX39 ..156 D5
Raleigh Hts EX31 ....154 F7
Raleigh Lawn EX31 .....154 F7
Raleigh Mdw EX31 ......155 A7
Raleigh Pk EX36 ....158 C4
Raleigh Rd
 Barnstaple EX32 ....154 F6
 Budleigh Salterton EX9 .198 B2
 Dartmouth TQ6 ....233 E4
 Exeter EX1 ....261 C2
 Exmouth EX8 ....202 A6
 Newton Abbot TQ12 ....207 F3
 Ottery St Mary EX11 ...169 E4
 Salcombe TQ8 ....259 D4
 Teignmouth TQ14 ......210 A8
Raleigh St PL1 ....262 B3
Raleigh View EX39 ......157 A3
Ralph Cl EX33 ....152 B6
Ralph Rd EX33 ....152 B6
Ralph's Ct PL19 ....171 B5
Ramage Cl PL6 ....245 F3
Rame Cotts PL10 ....140 H2
Rame La Cawsand PL10 ..252 F1
 Rame PL10 ....140 H1
Ramehead Cotts PL10 ...140 H1
Ramehead La PL10 ......140 H2
Ramillies Ave PL5 ......244 A4
Ramsey La
 Runnington TA21 ....51 F8
 Sampford Courtenay EX20 ..76 F3
Ramshill Cross TQ3 ....225 C8
Ramshill Rd TQ3 ....225 C8
Rance Dr EX8 ....196 E3
Randolph Ct TQ12 ......207 A4
Randwick Park Rd PL9 ..255 D7
Ranelagh Rd EX20 ......170 A5
Rangers Cl TQ11 ....236 B4
Ranscombe Cl TQ5 .....230 E5
Ranscombe Ct 9 TQ5 ...230 D5
Ranscombe Rd TQ5 .....230 D5
Ransum Way PL19 ......171 B4
Ranscombe Rd PL9 .....256 D6
Raphael Dr PL9 ....256 A6
Rapscott Cross EX36 ....18 F1
Rapscott Hill EX36 .....18 F1
Rashleigh Ave
 Plymouth PL7 ....250 F7
 Saltash PL12 ....242 D1
Rashleigh La EX18 ......59 D7
Ratcliffe Sch EX7 ......204 C4
Rathmore Rd TQ2 ......219 F4
Ratshole Gate EX24 ....102 F5
Rattan Cross EX44 .....174 D8
Rattenbury Cotts EX19 .191 C6
Rattenbury Cross EX19 ..76 A8
Rattle St TQ13 ....113 D1
Ravelin Gdns 4 EX32 ...155 B5
Ravelin Manor Rd EX32 .155 B5
Raven Cl EX4 ....173 C1
Ravensbourne La TQ6 ..146 B7
Ravensbury Dr TQ6 .....234 A2
Rawlin Cl PL6 ....249 C8
Rawlin La EX17 ....60 F4
Rawnsley La EX34 ......7 F6
Rayer Rd 18 EX16 ......64 D7
Raymond Way PL7 ......250 D6
Rayners EX6 ....181 A2
Raynham Rd PL3 ....248 B4
Rea Barn Cl TQ5 ....230 D4
Rea Barn Rd TQ5 ....230 D5
Read Cl EX8 ....196 C1
Reading Wlk PL5 ....243 E5
Recreation Rd PL2 .....248 C7
Recreation Way PL7 ....132 F4
Rectory Cl Filleigh EX32 ..29 B6
 3 Whimple EX5 ......99 E8
 Witheridge EX16 ....46 E1
 Wrafton EX33 ....152 F4
Rectory Close Cross
 EX33 ....152 F3
Rectory Cross TQ10 ....138 A7
Rectory Dr EX2 ....181 B8
Rectory Hill
 Berrynarbor EX34 ......2 D3
 Cheriton Fitzpaine EX17 ..62 E1
Rectory La Parkham EX39 ..39 E8
 Silverton EX5 ....82 C6
Rectory Pk EX39 ....156 F2
Rectory Rd Ashbrittle TA21 .50 F8
 Bridestowe EX20 ......107 F8
 Combe Martin EX34 ....3 A3
 Dolton EX19 ....57 F7
 East Ogwell TQ12 ......211 E8
 Morchard Bishop EX17 ..61 A2
 Plymouth PL1 ....248 A2
Rectory Rise EX20 ......56 F4
Red Brook Cl TQ4 ......226 D1
Red Cross Colyton EX24 ..102 F6
 Raymond's Hill EX13 ...104 C7
 Silverton EX5 ....82 C5
Red Cross Hill EX12 ....165 E6
Red Devon Ct PL21 ....137 B2

Red Gate
 Kings Nympton EX37 ....44 E8
 Winkleigh EX19 ....58 D2
Red House Ct 9 TQ13 ..123 C4
Red La Churchinford TA3 ..68 C7
 Plymouth PL9 ....75 C7
 Hemyock EX15 ....52 E3
 Raymond's Hill EX13 ...104 C6
Red Lion Hill PL8 ......257 B5
Red Lion La EX1,EX4 ...261 C4
Red Lion Pl 21 EX7 ....204 D6
Red Lion Yd EX20 ......170 B5
Red Post Cross
 Burrington EX37 ....43 F4
 Totnes TQ9 ....217 C4
Red Rock EX5 ....81 E2
Red Rock Rd EX5 ......81 D1
Redavon Rise TQ2 ......219 B8
Redburn Cl TQ3 ....226 A7
Redburn Rd TQ3 ....226 A7
Redcliff Ct EX9 ....199 G2
Redcliffe Rd TQ1 ....214 C1
Reddacleane Kiln Cross
 TQ11 ....135 A6
Reddaway Dr EX6 ......182 A4
Reddenhill Rd TQ1 .....220 C7
Reddicliff Cl PL9 ....255 D5
Reddicliff Rd PL9 ......255 D5
Reddington Rd PL3 .....249 B7
Redford Cross TQ7 .....258 A8
Redford Mdw TQ7 ......258 C5
Redford Way TQ7 ......258 C5
Redgate Cl TQ1 ....220 D6
Redhill Cl PL5 ....243 E4
Redhill Cotts EX11 .....169 F6
Redhills
 Budleigh Salterton EX9 ..199 G2
 Exeter EX4 ....176 E6
Redhills Cl EX4 ....176 E6
Redhills Comb Com Sch The
 EX4 ....176 F5
Redlake TQ9 ....222 F8
Redlake Cross TQ9 .....222 F8
Redland Cross EX18 ....58 F7
Redland Rd EX31 ....153 F5
Redlands EX16 ....161 F4
Redlands Cl EX4 ....178 A8
Redlands Ct TQ13 ......225 F7
Redlands The EX10 .....188 A3
Redlane Cross DT7 .....104 C6
Redlap Cross EX16 .....56 C8
Redlap Rd TQ6 ....146 C8
Redmoor Cl PL19 ......171 A7
Redolph Hill TQ6 ....234 B3
Redpost Cross
 North Tawton EX20 .....76 F5
 Sampford Courtenay EX20 ..76 F5
Redruth Cl PL5 ....244 A5
Redside Terr EX5 ....172 E5
Redstart Cl TQ12 ......206 F1
Redvers Gr PL7 ....250 E4
Redvers Rd EX4 ....177 A5
Redwalls Mdw TQ6 .....233 F3
Redwell La TQ3 ....225 F8
Redwell Rd TQ3 ....225 F8
Redwing Dr PL5 ....245 D8
Redwood Cl
 Bovey Tracey TQ13 .....180 C4
 Exeter EX18 ....196 D3
 10 Hemyock EX15 ....67 B8
 4 Honiton EX14 .....85 C2
Redwood Dr PL7 ....251 B5
Redwood Rd EX10 ......188 C5
Redyeates Cross EX17 ..63 A2
Reed Mdw EX20 ....75 C7
Reed Vale TQ14 ....210 A5
Reed's Cross
 Brushford EX16 ....9 E4
 Uffculme EX15 ....66 C6
Reeds Pl EX15 ....163 C3
Reedsdown Cross TQ7 ..79 F6
Reedy Hill EX6 ....112 F8
Reeves Cl PL6 ....245 D5
Reeves Cl TQ7 ....223 D5
Reeves Rd The TQ2 ....219 D5
Refarm St 3 EX31 ......154 F6
Regal Ct PL12 ....242 F2
Regency Cres EX8 .....202 C6
Regent Cl
 Barnstaple EX31 ....154 C2
 Fremington EX31 ......153 F5
 Torquay EX39 ....219 E8
Regent Gate EX4 ......177 E5
Regent St Dawlish EX7 ..204 D6
 Exeter EX2 ....177 A3
 Plymouth PL4 ....263 A3
 10 Teignmouth TQ14 ..210 C4
Regents Gate EX4 ......202 B6
Regents Gdns 6 TQ14 ..210 C4
Reigate Rd PL9 ....255 E8
Rema Dr EX4 ....202 C6
Rena Hobson Ct EX16 ..161 F3
Rendells Mdw TQ13 ....180 E7
Rendle St PL1 ....262 B3
Rendlesham Gdns PL6 ..245 E3
Rennes Dr EX4 ....173 C1
Rennes Rd EX16 ....178 B7
Renney Rd
 Down Thomas PL9 .....255 C1
 Heybrook Bay PL9 .....140 B8
Rennie Ave PL5 ....243 C1
Rennie Rd 2 EX16 .....64 D7

Renoir Cl PL9 ....256 A6
Renown St EX2 ....247 E6
Rensey La EX17 ....60 C4
Renton La TQ7 ....142 E7
Research Way PL6 ....245 C4
Reservoir Cres PL9 ....256 B7
Reservoir Cross PL16 ....91 A4
Reservoir La [1] PL3 ....248 F6
Reservoir Rd
  Plymouth, Hartley PL3 ....248 F6
  Plymouth, Plymstock PL9 ....256 B7
Reservoir Way PL7 ....256 E7
Resolution Ho PL4 ....263 B3
Rest Hill TQ12 ....131 D7
Restland La EX20 ....94 F7
Restormel Rd PL4 ....262 C4
Restormel Terr PL4 ....262 C4
Retail Park Cl EX22 ....177 B3
Retreat Cl TQ7 ....258 C5
Retreat Dr The EX3 ....182 D6
Retreat Rd EX3 ....182 E6
Retreat The PL3 ....249 B7
Revel Rd PL3 ....249 A6
Revell Park Rd PL7 ....250 D6
Revelstoke Rd PL8 ....140 F6
Revill Ind Units EX5 ....99 A4
Rew Cross
  Ashburton TQ13 ....130 F5
  Newton St Cyres EX5 ....81 A2
Rew Rd TQ13 ....130 F5
Rew's Cl EX34 ....2 F4
Rewdown Cross TQ13 ....130 F6
Rewe Barton EX5 ....82 A2
Rewe Cross EX5 ....82 A3
Rewe Ct EX5 ....82 B3
Rewe La EX5 ....99 D6
Rewes Cross EX5 ....82 F2
Rewes La EX5 ....82 F2
Rewles Cotts TQ13 ....130 F5
Rews Cross EX36 ....19 C2
Rews Mdw EX1 ....174 F1
Rews Park Dr EX1 ....174 F1
Rexon Cross PL16 ....106 B7
Rexona Cl EX2 ....177 A2
Reynell Ave TQ12 ....207 F3
Reynell Rd TQ12 ....211 F8
Reynolds Cl EX4 ....174 D1
Reynolds Gr PL5 ....247 C8
Reynolds Rd PL7 ....250 C6
Rheola Gdns PL6 ....245 D3
Rhodanthe Rd TQ1 ....219 B1
Rhode La DT7 ....260 C6
Rhodes Cl PL7 ....250 E7
Rhododendron Ave
  Barnstaple EX31 ....154 D3
  Dunkeswell EX14 ....67 B1
Rhude Cross EX22 ....53 D2
Rhydda Bank Cross EX31 ....4 A5
Rhyll Gate Cross TQ12 ....32 E7
Ribble Gdns PL3 ....249 D7
Ribston Ave EX1 ....178 C6
Rices Mews EX2 ....177 A4
Richard Cl EX39 ....25 E4
Richards Cl Dawlish EX7 ....204 D5
  Exmouth EX8 ....196 D2
  Wellington TA21 ....160 C8
Richards Row PL3 ....248 F7
Richards Terr PL10 ....252 E5
Richardson Dr PL8 ....141 B8
Richmond Ave EX34 ....150 A5
Richmond Cl
  Sampford Peverell EX16 ....50 D1
  Torquay TQ1 ....221 A4
Richmond Ct
  [4] Ilfracombe PL4 ....204 E6
  Paignton TQ3 ....226 B7
Richmond Gn EX39 ....14 F1
Richmond Hill TQ12 ....213 A5
Richmond Pk EX39 ....156 F7
Richmond Pl [3] EX7 ....204 E6
Richmond Rd
  Appledore EX39 ....15 A1
  Exeter EX4 ....261 A3
  Exmouth EX8 ....202 D7
  Ilfracombe EX34 ....150 A4
  Plymouth PL6 ....245 A2
Richmond St EX32 ....155 A5
Richmond Terr
  [9] Appledore EX39 ....15 A1
  Buckland Monachorum PL20 ....126 C3
  Kingsbridge TQ7 ....258 D6
Richmond Wlk
  [10] Barnstaple EX32 ....155 A6
  Plymouth PL1 ....262 A1
Rickards Gn EX39 ....156 B2
Rickham Cross TQ8 ....148 D4
Riddell Ave EX32 ....154 F6
Riddistone Cross EX20 ....77 A8
Riddistone La EX20 ....77 A8
Ride The PL7,PL9 ....249 D2
Ridge Cross
  Chillington TQ7 ....149 B8
  Plymouth PL9 ....266 A3
  Wilmington EX14 ....86 E4
Ridge Hill Berrynarbor EX34 ....2 E3
  Combe Martin EX34 ....3 A2
  Dartmouth TQ6 ....233 F4
Ridge Ho PL4 ....249 A4
Ridge La Chudleigh TQ13 ....124 D7
  Cornworthy TQ9 ....139 F4
  Paignton TQ3 ....218 F8
  Tiverton EX16 ....63 F8
  Wilmington EX14 ....86 C3
Ridge Lane Cross TQ9 ....139 E4

Ridge Park Ave PL4 ....248 D4
Ridge Park Rd PL7 ....250 F5
Ridge Pk PL7 ....250 E5
Ridge Rd
  Combeinteignhead TQ12 ....208 D2
  Maidencombe TQ1,TQ12 ....214 B7
  Modbury PL21 ....137 B4
  Plymouth PL7 ....250 E3
  Stokeinteignhead TQ12 ....209 A1
  Ugborough PL21 ....137 D7
  West Anstey TA22 ....32 D7
Ridge Way EX6 ....194 E2
Ridgeleish Ct [10] EX14 ....166 C6
Ridgemark Cl TQ5 ....230 E5
Ridges The TQ6 ....233 D1
Ridgeway Exeter EX4 ....173 A3
  Honiton EX14 ....166 B4
  Ottery St Mary EX11 ....169 E4
  Plymouth PL7 ....250 D5
  Saltash PL12 ....242 D1
  Sidbury EX10 ....101 B2
Ridgeway Ave EX39 ....156 E7
Ridgeway Cl
  Newton Abbot TQ12 ....207 F1
  Sidbury EX10 ....101 B2
  Westward Ho! EX39 ....156 D7
Ridgeway Ct EX39 ....156 D7
Ridgeway Dr EX39 ....156 D7
Ridgeway Gdns EX11 ....169 E4
Ridgeway Gn EX37 ....43 B7
Ridgeway Hill TQ12 ....218 D6
Ridgeway Hts [15] TQ1 ....220 D4
Ridgeway La
  Awliscombe EX14 ....85 A5
  Coffinswell TQ12 ....213 D6
  Shillingford EX16 ....34 D2
Ridgeway Mead EX10 ....187 F7
Ridgeway Rd
  Newton Abbot TQ12 ....207 F1
  Torquay TQ1 ....220 D4
  Torquay TQ1 ....220 E4
Ridgeway's Cross EX17 ....79 E6
Ridgewood Cross EX15 ....67 D8
Ridgewood La EX15 ....67 D8
Ridgway Cross TQ13 ....130 B4
Ridgway Cross EX36 ....20 E1
Ridgway Ct EX13 ....167 D5
Ridgway La EX14 ....102 F4
Riding Cross EX37 ....29 E6
Ridings The EX3 ....183 C4
Ridley Hill TQ6 ....234 A3
Rifford Rd EX2 ....178 B4
Rifton La EX16 ....48 B4
Riga Terr PL3 ....249 C4
Rigdale Cl PL6 ....249 A7
Riggles Cross EX14 ....68 A3
Rill Cnr EX5 ....99 D3
Rill La EX9 ....199 H2
Rillage La TQ2 ....219 F6
Ring Hill EX20 ....95 C5
Ringdown La EX15 ....52 F2
Ringhill Cross EX20 ....95 D5
Ringmore Cl TQ14 ....209 D5
Ringmore Dr TQ7 ....142 E3
Ringmore Rd
  Shaldon TQ14 ....209 D5
  Teignmouth TQ14 ....210 A3
Ringmore Way PL5 ....244 B3
Ringrona TQ8 ....259 B2
Ringslade Cl TQ12 ....206 F1
Ringslade Rd TQ12 ....206 F5
Ringswell Ave EX1 ....178 C6
Ringswell Cross TQ9 ....216 E6
Riphay Cross TA22 ....33 E3
Ripon Cl EX4 ....176 E6
Rippon Cl Brixham TQ5 ....229 F2
  [1] Tiverton EX16 ....64 D7
Riscombe Hill EX5 ....98 F8
Risdon Ave PL4 ....249 B1
Rising Sun EX13 ....87 A3
Ritson La TQ9 ....139 D3
Rivenford La EX5,EX17 ....81 C3
River Cl EX5 ....173 F8
River Ct Saltash PL12 ....242 D5
  Tavistock PL19 ....171 D6
River Dart Country Pk*
  TQ13 ....130 D5
River Dr EX15 ....163 D3
River Exe Ctry Pk* EX2 ....181 F8
River Front EX3 ....183 C2
River Mdws EX2 ....177 D3
River Pk TQ13 ....137 A4
River Tamar Way EX22 ....164 C6
River Valley Rd [13] TQ13 ....123 C4
River View
  Barnstaple EX32 ....155 C2
  Brushford TA22 ....33 F3
  Gunnislake PL18 ....125 B5
  Plymouth PL3 ....249 B1
  Saltash PL12 ....242 F3
River View Cl
  [2] Chudleigh Knighton
  TQ13 ....123 C4
  [20] Colyton EX24 ....103 A4
River View Commercial Ctr
River View Dr [4] EX34 ....150 A6
River View La PL4 ....249 B1
River View Terr EX6 ....182 B3
Riverbank Cotts EX39 ....157 B4
Riverdale
  Harbertonford TQ9 ....139 C7
  Seaton EX12 ....192 B7
Riverdale Cl EX12 ....192 B7
Riverford Cl PL6 ....245 D7
Rivermead EX15 ....163 C2

Rivermead Ave EX8 ....196 A3
Rivermead Rd EX2 ....177 D3
Rivers Cl PL21 ....237 E5
Rivers The PL12 ....242 E1
Rivers Wlk EX2 ....182 C7
Riversdale Ave EX34 ....150 A6
Riverside
  Kingsbridge TQ7 ....258 D4
  Teignmouth TQ14 ....210 A3
  Totnes TQ9 ....223 B7
  Wellington TA21 ....160 B7
Riverside Apartments
  EX36 ....158 E4
Riverside Bsns Pk PL1 ....247 E3
Riverside Cl
  Bideford EX39 ....157 B4
  Honiton EX14 ....166 B6
Riverside Cotts EX17 ....62 A3
Riverside Cott PL12 ....242 C1
Riverside Ct
  Bideford EX39 ....157 B4
  Dartmouth TQ6 ....233 F3
  Exeter EX2 ....261 B2
  Newton Abbot TQ12 ....207 D4
Riverside Mews PL12 ....243 A3
Riverside Pl PL1 ....247 D2
Riverside Rd
  Barnstaple EX31 ....154 C6
  Dittisham TQ6 ....228 C3
  Lynmouth EX35 ....151 C6
  Sidmouth EX10 ....188 B3
Riverside Rd E PL8 ....140 F6
Riverside Rd W PL8 ....140 F6
Riverside Terr TQ9 ....223 D5
Riverside Units EX31 ....154 C6
Riverside View EX11 ....169 D3
Riverside Way EX12 ....192 C5
Riverside Wlk
  Plymouth PL6 ....244 B6
  Yealmpton PL8 ....136 A2
Riverside Workshops
  EX12 ....192 C5
Riversmeet EX39 ....15 A1
Riverside Cl TQ13 ....110 F6
Riverview Dr EX4 ....176 F8
Riverview Pl TQ7 ....258 C5
Riviera Terr Dawlish EX7 ....204 F7
  Exminster EX6 ....182 B3
Riviera The Paignton TQ2 ....226 B5
  Paignton TQ3 ....226 B5
Riviera Way TQ2 ....213 D1
Rixafer Rd TQ13 ....124 B4
Rixdale Rd TQ13 ....124 C4
Rixey La EX17 ....61 B2
Rixeypark Cnr TQ13 ....123 D3
Roach Hill EX36 ....31 F7
Roach La EX5 ....82 C6
Roachill Cross EX36 ....32 C1
Road Down Cross EX6 ....96 F7
Road End Cross EX14 ....67 A3
Road Pk TQ13 ....123 B7
Roadway Cnr EX34 ....8 A5
Robartes Ct EX2 ....261 C2
Robclave Cl PL7 ....251 C6
Robert Adams Cl PL7 ....250 B5
Robert Way EX10 ....186 F8
Roberts Ave PL11 ....247 B3
Roberts Cl
  Cullompton EX15 ....163 B2
  Torquay TQ2 ....214 B2
Roberts Rd Exeter EX2 ....261 B2
  Plymouth PL5 ....247 D8
Roberts Way TQ12 ....206 F4
Robin Cl EX15 ....163 B2
Robin Dr PL15 ....105 A2
Robins Field TQ7 ....144 F1
Robins Hill EX39 ....156 E4
Robins Way PL9 ....255 E8
Robinson's Row TQ8 ....259 E4
Roborough Ave PL6 ....245 B5
Roborough Down La PL6 ....241 F5
Roborough La
  Ashburton TQ13 ....130 F5
  Plymouth PL5 ....244 D8
Roborough Rd EX31 ....155 A8
Roborough Terr TQ13 ....130 F5
Robyns Cl PL7 ....251 B5
Roche Gdn EX2 ....182 A8
Rochester Rd [4] PL4 ....248 E4
Rochford Cres PL5 ....243 F5
Rock Ave
  Barnstaple EX32 ....155 A3
  Lynton EX35 ....151 B5
Rock Cl TQ4 ....229 C7
Rock End Ave TQ1 ....220 C2
Rock Gdns
  Barnstaple EX32 ....155 A3
  Plymouth PL9 ....249 D1
Rock Head EX17 ....28 C2
Rock Hill
  Aveton Gifford TQ7 ....143 C6
  Berrynarbor EX34 ....2 D2
  Braunton EX33 ....152 D6
  Chulmleigh EX18 ....59 E8
  Georgeham EX33 ....8 A2
  Lynton EX35 ....151 B5
  Umberleigh EX37 ....28 C2
Rock House La TQ1 ....214 C5
Rock La
  Cheriton Bishop EX17 ....97 B7

Rock La continued
  Chudleigh TQ13 ....123 F8
  [14] Combe Martin EX34 ....3 A3
  Offwell EX14 ....86 C1
Rock Lodge Pk EX35 ....151 B5
Rock Park Terr [22] EX32 ....155 A4
Rock Pk
  [4] Ashburton TQ13 ....131 A5
  Dartmouth TQ6 ....233 D4
Rock Rd Chudleigh TQ13 ....123 E5
  Torquay TQ2 ....220 B4
Rock Terr PL7 ....250 D4
Rock The EX31 ....154 F7
Rock View EX16 ....65 B7
Rockbeare CE Prim Sch
  EX5 ....99 B5
Rockbeare Hill EX5 ....168 A5
Rockdale Rd PL8 ....136 A2
Rockerhayne Cross
  EX24 ....102 D7
Rockey La Bideford EX39 ....157 A2
Rockfield [5] EX16 ....161 C3
Rockfield Ave PL6 ....244 F6
Rockfield Cl TQ14 ....210 D7
Rockfield Cotts
  Exeter EX4 ....176 F8
  Holywell Lake TA21 ....51 F7
Rockfield Rd EX14 ....7 F7
Rockhill PL5 ....244 C7
Rockingham Rd PL3 ....249 A5
Rocklands TQ13 ....123 E5
Rockley La EX32 ....11 F1
Rockmount Terr [6]
  EX39 ....157 A2
Rockpark Cross TQ13 ....131 A5
Rockridge Cross EX36 ....156 B6
Rockshead Hill EX32 ....18 F3
Rockville Pk PL9 ....255 E8
Rockwell Green Prim Sch
  TA21 ....160 B5
Rockwood Rd PL6 ....245 E8
Rocky Hill PL19 ....171 B5
Rocky La
  Abbotsham EX39 ....156 A3
  Buckfastleigh TQ11 ....236 A3
  Combe Martin EX34 ....3 A4
Rosebarn Ave EX4 ....173 E1
Rosebarn La EX4 ....173 E1
Rosebery Ave PL4 ....263 C4
Rosebery La PL4 ....263 C4
Rosebery Rd Exeter EX4 ....177 E8
Rocky Park Ave PL9 ....255 E8
Rocky Park Rd PL9 ....255 E8
Rocombe Cl TQ2 ....213 F4
Rocombe Cross
  Daccombe TQ12 ....213 F6
  Raymond's Hill EX13 ....104 C6
Rocombe Hill TQ12 ....213 F7
Rodda Cl PL18 ....125 D7
Roddick Way [8] PL7 ....251 C5
Rodgemonts Cross EX18 ....59 E8
Rodgemont's La EX18 ....59 F8
Rodgemonts Cross EX18 ....59 E8
Rodgers Ind Est TQ4 ....225 D3
Rodney Cl
  Exmouth EX8 ....203 A7
Rodney St PL5 ....247 D8
Rods La PL19 ....117 E6
Rodway Cross EX14 ....87 A6
Roeselare Ave PL11 ....247 A3
Roeselare Cl PL11 ....247 A3
Rogada Ct TQ5 ....230 D3
Rogate Dr PL6 ....245 D4
Rogate Wlk PL6 ....245 D4
Roland Bailey Gdns
  PL19 ....171 A6
Rolle Barton EX9 ....198 D7
Rolle Cotts EX9 ....197 E2
Rolle Ct EX38 ....159 C5
Rolle Rd
  Budleigh Salterton EX9 ....199 G2
  Exmouth EX8 ....202 A6
  Great Torrington EX38 ....159 A5
Rolle St Barnstaple EX31 ....154 F6
  Exmouth EX8 ....202 A6
Rolle The EX9 ....199 G2
Rolle Villas EX8 ....202 A6
Rolle's Quay EX31 ....154 F5
Rolles Terr EX30 ....42 D7
Rollestone Cres EX4 ....173 E2
Rollis Park Cl PL9 ....255 C8
Rollis Park Rd PL9 ....255 C8
Rolston Cl PL6 ....244 D6
Romalyn Gdns TQ4 ....226 B4
Roman Rd Fenton EX5 ....84 C2
  Kilmington EX13 ....87 C1
  Lyme Regis DT7 ....260 D4
  Plymouth PL5 ....243 E2
Roman Way
  Honiton EX14 ....166 E7
  Plymouth PL5 ....243 E2
  Seaton EX12 ....192 A6
Romansleigh Cross EX36 ....45 C7
Romansleigh Ridge EX18 ....45 C5
Romilly Gdns PL7 ....250 B5
Romney Cl PL5 ....244 B1
Romsey Dr EX2 ....177 E5
Ronald Terr PL2 ....247 F5
Roncombe Cnr EX24 ....101 E6
Roncombe Gate EX24 ....101 E5
Rondle Cl EX16 ....64 D7
Ronsdale Cl PL9 ....255 D8
Rook La PL7 ....133 C3
Rook Lane End PL21 ....133 C3
Rookbear La EX33 ....9 D2
Rookery Ct EX6 ....194 E2
Rookery Hill EX16 ....48 C8
Rookery La DT7 ....260 D8
Rookery Terr TA21 ....160 C5

Rooklands Ave TQ2 ....219 E6
Rooks Cl EX31 ....154 B3
Rooks Cross EX31 ....27 D3
Rooks Farm Rd EX31 ....153 A4
Rooks Nest EX31 ....153 E5
Rooks Way EX16 ....161 E6
Rookswood La EX5 ....99 C5
Rookwood Cl EX14 ....166 B5
Rookwood Ho EX14 ....166 B6
Room Hill Rd TA24 ....21 D7
Roope Cl PL5 ....247 C7
Rooty Cross EX31 ....27 A7
Rope Wlk
  [2] Teignmouth TQ14 ....210 B5
  Wellington TA21 ....160 C4
Roper Ave PL9 ....255 D8
Roper's La EX9 ....198 E7
Roperidge Cross PL21 ....137 F6
Ropers Ct EX9 ....198 E7
Ropery Rd EX34 ....150 C6
Ropewalk Bideford EX39 ....157 A2
  Kingsbridge TQ7 ....258 C4
Ropewalk Hill TQ5 ....230 C5
Ropewalk Ho EX8 ....201 E6
Rorkes Cl PL5 ....243 E2
Roscoff Ct EX38 ....159 E5
Rose & Crown Hill EX17 ....80 A5
Rose Acre Terr TQ5 ....230 D4
Rose Cl EX14 ....161 F6
Rose Cotts Beer EX12 ....191 D5
  [8] Bishop's Tawton EX32 ....28 B1
  Plymouth PL6 ....249 B8
Rose Dene TQ2 ....213 F2
Rose Duryard EX4 ....173 A1
Rose Gdns PL6 ....245 E6
Rose Hill
  Kingskerswell TQ12 ....212 F4
  Wembury PL9 ....140 D7
Rose Hill Cl [3] TQ12 ....212 F4
Rose Hill Terr PL17 ....125 D3
Rose La EX33 ....152 B7
Rose Mary Ho [9] EX15 ....67 B8
Rose Moor Rd EX38 ....159 E5
Rose Terr PL18 ....125 B5
Rosea Bridge La EX34 ....3 A4
Rosebank Cres EX4 ....173 E1
Rosebarn Ave EX4 ....173 E1
Rosebarn La EX4 ....173 E1
Rosebery Ave PL4 ....263 C4
Rosebery La PL4 ....263 C4
Rosebery Rd Exeter EX4 ....177 E8
  Plymouth PL4 ....263 C4
Rosedale Ave PL2 ....248 D7
Rosedown Ave PL2 ....248 A7
Rosehill Cl TQ1 ....220 C5
Rosehill Rd TQ1 ....220 C5
Rosehip Cl PL6 ....245 E7
Roseland Ave EX1 ....178 A6
Roseland Cres EX1 ....178 A6
Roseland Cross EX22 ....54 C8
Roseland Dr EX1 ....178 A6
Roseland Sq TQ12 ....207 E7
Roselands PL10 ....188 A4
Roselands Dr TQ4 ....225 F2
Roselands Prim Sch
  TQ4 ....225 F2
Roselands Rd TQ4 ....226 B2
Rosemary Ave TQ12 ....206 F4
Rosemary Cl TQ3 ....226 C8
Rosemary Gdns TQ3 ....225 F8
Rosemary La
  Colyton EX24 ....103 A5
  Dulverton TA22 ....33 D6
  Holne TQ13 ....130 A3
  Musbury EX13 ....103 D5
Rosemary St EX14 ....176 F5
Rosemarrow Cross
  EX15 ....52 D1
Rosemont [8] PL4 ....263 A2
Rosemont Ct EX2 ....177 B1
Rosemoor Gdn* EX38 ....159 D2
Rosemoor Rd EX38 ....159 E5
Rosemount TQ4 ....226 C5
Rosemount Cl EX14 ....166 B5
Rosemount Ct TQ8 ....259 D5
Rosemount La EX14 ....166 B5
Rosery Rd TQ2 ....219 E5
Rosevean Ct [8] PL3 ....248 F6
Rosevean Gdns PL3 ....248 F6
Rosevean Ho [7] PL3 ....248 F6
Roseveare Cl PL9 ....256 A8
Roseville St TQ6 ....233 F3
Rosewarne Ave TQ2 ....207 F2
Roseway EX3 ....202 F8
Rosewell Cl EX14 ....166 D7
Rosewood Cl PL9 ....255 F5
Rosewood Cres EX39 ....156 B2
Rosewood Ct EX31 ....154 C3
Rosewood Terr [5] EX4 ....177 D8
Rospeath Cres PL2 ....248 D8
Ross Cl EX1 ....174 F1
Ross St PL2 ....247 F4
Rossall Dr TQ3 ....226 A5
Rosse Rd EX16 ....161 D6
Rosshayne La EX14 ....68 F2
Rosslyn Park Rd PL3 ....248 D5
Rosyl Ave EX7 ....204 C6
Rothbury Cl PL6 ....245 E4
Rothbury Gdns PL6 ....245 D4
Rotherfold TQ9 ....223 B5
Rothesay Gdns PL5 ....244 B3
Rothin TQ1 ....220 B8
Rougemont EX13 ....167 D5
Rougemont Ave TQ2 ....213 D1
Rougemont Cl PL3 ....249 B6
Rougemont Ct EX6 ....181 F4

Round Berry Dr TQ8 .... 259 C4
Round Cross TQ11 .... 236 B6
Roundball Cl EX4 .... 166 C4
Roundball La EX14 .... 166 B2
Roundham Ave TQ4 .... 226 D5
Roundham Cres TQ4 .... 226 D5
Roundham Gdns TQ4 .... 226 D4
Roundham Ho TQ4 .... 226 C5
Roundhead Rd TQ12 .... 180 F3
Roundhill EX16 .... 161 B3
Roundhill Cl EX4 .... 173 A3
Roundhill Rd TQ2 .... 219 D2
Roundhouse La EX8 .... 196 B2
Roundings The TQ5 .... 229 B5
Roundmoors Cl TQ12 .... 213 A3
Roundsleys La PL19 .... 117 E6
Roundtable Meet EX4 .... 174 B1
Roundway The TQ12 .... 212 F6
Rousdown Rd TQ2 .... 219 E4
Row La PL5 .... 243 E2
Row The EX36 .... 30 A2
Row Tor Cl EX20 .... 170 C5
Rowan Cl
East Ogwell TQ12 .... 206 F1
[2] Honiton EX14 .... 85 C2
Plymouth PL7 .... 251 B5
Tavistock PL19 .... 171 C3
Tiverton EX16 .... 161 F5
Rowan Cl PL12 .... 242 C2
Rowan Dr EX12 .... 192 A8
Rowan Pk [2] EX31 .... 154 C2
Rowan Way Brixham TQ5 .... 230 A2
Exeter EX4 .... 176 F7
Plymouth PL6 .... 245 E7
Rowans EX17 .... 78 B7
Rowans The PL16 .... 105 E4
Rowantree Rd TQ12 .... 207 E1
Rowbrook Cl TQ4 .... 225 E3
Rowcliffe Cotts TA21 .... 50 F8
Rowcroft Ct EX4 .... 166 B5
Rowcroft Rd TQ3 .... 226 C8
Rowden Cross
Salcombe TQ7 .... 148 A8
Teignmouth TQ14 .... 124 C1
Widecombe in the Moor
TQ13 .... 121 A3
Rowden Ct PL8 .... 141 A6
Rowden St PL3 .... 248 E5
Rowdens Ho The TQ14 .... 210 D6
Rowdens Rd TQ2 .... 219 F5
Rowdens The TQ14 .... 210 C6
Rowdon Brook EX6 .... 112 F5
Rowdown Cl PL7 .... 251 D4
Rowe Cl TA21 .... 160 A4
Rowe St
Plymouth PL1,PL4 .... 262 C3
Torpoint PL11 .... 247 B3
Rowells Mead [4] TQ12 .... 122 F1
Rowes Orch EX15 .... 162 C3
Rowhorne Rd EX4 .... 176 C8
Rowland Cl PL9 .... 255 E5
Rowley Cross EX31 .... 4 D1
Rowley Rd TQ1 .... 214 C1
Rowlstone Cl EX8 .... 196 C3
Rows La Bampton EX16 .... 34 A1
[16] Combe Martin EX34 .... 3 A3
Rowse Gdns PL18 .... 125 D3
Rowsell's La TQ9 .... 223 D5
Rowtry Cross EX7 .... 196 A1
Royal Albert Meml Mus*
EX4 .... 261 A3
Royal Ave The EX8 .... 201 F7
Royal Charter Pk EX18 .... 44 E1
Royal Cl EX2 .... 181 B7
Royal Ct Princetown PL20 .... 128 A8
Torquay TQ1 .... 220 D7
Royal Devon & Exeter Hospl
(Heavitree) EX1 .... 177 E6
Royal Devon & Exeter Hospl
(Wonford) EX2 .... 177 F4
Royal Eye Intmy PL4 .... 248 E4
Royal Navy Ave PL2 .... 247 F6
Royal Oak Cross EX14 .... 86 E6
Royal Par PL1 .... 262 C2
Royal Pines TQ1 .... 220 E3
Royal Way EX6 .... 200 A8
Royal West of England Sch
for the Deaf EX2 .... 261 C1
Royal William Rd PL1 .... 254 A8
Royston Cl [4] EX1 .... 178 C8
Royston Rd
Bideford EX39 .... 156 F1
Churchinford IA3 .... 68 D7
Rozel TQ1 .... 220 D3
Rubby Cross EX6 .... 97 E5
Ruckamore Rd TQ2 .... 219 E5
Ruckham La EX16 .... 62 F6
Rudda Bldgs [4] EX16 .... 161 B4
Rudolf Steiner Sch TQ9 .... 215 C3
Rudyard Way EX39 .... 156 B6
Rudyerd Wlk PL3 .... 249 D6
Rue de Courseulles sur Mer
TQ6 .... 233 F4
Rue St Pierre PL21 .... 237 E5
Rufford Cl PL2 .... 248 A7
Rugby Rd EX4 .... 177 A4
Ruggadon La TQ12 .... 123 D8
Ruggaton La EX34 .... 2 D2
Rule Cross EX23 .... 37 B2
Rull Cross EX16 .... 48 C5
Rull Hill Oakford EX16 .... 48 C5
West Worlington EX17 .... 61 B8
Rull La EX15 .... 163 B6
Rumbelow Rd EX16 .... 161 E6
Rumsam Gdns EX32 .... 155 C2
Rumsam Rd EX32 .... 155 B2
Rumsams Cl EX32 .... 155 B2

Runaway La PL21 .... 137 A2
Rundle Rd TQ12 .... 207 C4
Runnacleave Rd EX34 .... 150 B6
Runnymede Ct PL6 .... 245 E2
Rupert Price Way TQ12 .... 123 B2
Rupertswood EX34 .... 150 C6
Rupertswood Terr [2]
EX34 .... 150 C6
Rus Cotts EX17 .... 165 A5
Rush Park Terr PL18 .... 125 C7
Rush Way TQ9 .... 223 F5
Rushcott Cl EX31 .... 153 A4
Rushcott Cross EX31 .... 27 B7
Rushforth PI EX4 .... 176 E8
Rushiade Cl TQ4 .... 225 F2
Ruskin Cres PL5 .... 244 D2
Rusper Cl EX15 .... 83 F6
Russel Cl EX32 .... 17 C1
Russel La EX15 .... 65 A1
Russell Ave PL3 .... 248 F7
Russell Cl
East Budleigh EX9 .... 198 B6
Gunnislake PL18 .... 125 D7
Plymouth PL9 .... 256 B7
Saltash PL12 .... 242 C2
Russell Court Gdns
PL19 .... 171 B6
Russell Ct Plymouth PL1 .... 262 C2
Saltash PL12 .... 242 C3
Tavistock PL19 .... 171 B6
Russell Dr EX9 .... 198 B6
Russell PI PL1 .... 262 B4
Russell St Exeter EX1 .... 261 C3
Sidmouth EX10 .... 188 B3
Tavistock PL19 .... 171 C5
Russell Terr EX4 .... 261 A4
Russell Way EX7 .... 178 D2
Russet Ave EX1 .... 178 C6
Russet Cl EX15 .... 66 A7
Russet Wood PL5 .... 243 F4
Russets La TQ11 .... 236 C5
Ruston Hill EX17 .... 61 A6
Rutger PI PL1 .... 262 A4
Rutherford St EX2 .... 178 A4
Ruthven Cl PL6 .... 248 F8
Rutland Rd PL4 .... 248 F4
Rutt's Cross EX14 .... 84 E2
Ruxhill La EX31 .... 10 D5
Ryall's Cnr Beaford EX20 .... 42 A1
Merton EX20 .... 57 A8
Ryalls Ct EX12 .... 192 A5
Rydal Cl PL6 .... 245 D2
Rydal Mews EX14 .... 176 F5
Ryde Cl TQ2 .... 214 A2
Ryde Ct [16] EX16 .... 64 D7
Ryder Rd PL2 .... 247 F4
Rydon Acres
Kingsteignton TQ12 .... 207 E8
Stoke Gabriel TQ9 .... 227 E8
Rydon Ave TQ12 .... 207 E8
Rydon Cross
Denbury TQ12 .... 211 D6
Stoke Gabriel TQ9 .... 227 F8
Rydon Est TQ12 .... 207 E8
Rydon Ind Est TQ12 .... 207 D6
Rydon La
Abbotskerswell TQ12 .... 212 C6
Exeter EX2 .... 178 C3
Exton EX3,EX5 .... 183 E2
Holsworthy EX22 .... 71 E7
Payhembury EX14 .... 84 B4
Rydon Park Sch TQ12 .... 207 E8
Rydon Rd
Holsworthy EX22 .... 164 B5
Kingsteignton TQ12 .... 207 E8
Rydonball Cross TQ12 .... 211 F7
Rydons TQ5 .... 230 A4
Rye Hill PL12 .... 242 C2
Rye La TQ7 .... 144 B5
Rye Park Cl EX19 .... 42 D1
Rye Pk Beaford EX19 .... 42 D1
Monkton EX14 .... 86 C5
Ryeland Cl PL9 .... 140 D8
Ryll Cl EX8 .... 202 B7
Ryll Court Dr EX8 .... 202 B7
Ryll Gr EX8 .... 202 B7

S

Sabre Cl TQ [1] EX32 .... 180 E3
Sabre Wlk [1] EX32 .... 155 B5
Sackery TQ12 .... 208 D4
Sacred Heart RC Prim Sch
EX4 .... 261 A3
Saddle The TQ4 .... 226 C2
Saddlers Cl EX6 .... 96 B3
Saddlers Way EX20 .... 170 D6
Sadler Cl EX8 .... 202 E8
Safewater La TQ12 .... 213 D6
Saffron Cl EX4 .... 176 D3
Saffron Pk TQ7 .... 258 D5
Sage Cl EX13 .... 167 F7
Sage Gr EX13 .... 167 F7
Sage Park Rd EX33 .... 152 E7
Sages Lea EX14 .... 184 C6
Sailmakers Ct EX8 .... 201 E6
Saint Luke's Campus
EX1 .... 177 E6
Saint Luke's Coll EX1 .... 177 E6
St Agnes La TQ2 .... 214 A2
St Albans Cl EX4 .... 176 E6
St Albans Pk PL20 .... 127 A2
St Albans Rd TQ1 .... 220 C8
St Andrew St
Millbrook PL10 .... 252 E5
Plymouth PL1 .... 262 B2
Tiverton EX16 .... 161 C3
St Andrew's CE Prim Sch
PL20 .... 126 C3

St Andrew's CE Prim Sch
PL1 .... 262 B2
St Andrew's Cl
Calstock PL18 .... 125 D3
Feniton EX14 .... 84 D2
Kennford EX6 .... 114 E4
Yarnscombe EX31 .... 27 E2
St Andrew's Cross [1]
PL1 .... 263 A2
St Andrew's Est EX15 .... 163 B4
St Andrew's PI PL10 .... 253 A1
St Andrew's Rd
Cowley EX4 .... 172 F2
Exmouth EX8 .... 201 F6
St Andrews Sch EX13 .... 88 A7
St Andrew's Sq EX24 .... 103 A5
St Andrew's St PL10 .... 253 A1
St Andrews Cl
Ashburton TQ13 .... 130 F4
[8] Bere Alston PL20 .... 125 E1
Cullompton EX15 .... 163 C3
Saltash PL12 .... 242 C2
Sutcombe EX22 .... 54 A6
St Andrews Ct TQ2 .... 219 C8
St Andrews Dr EX13 .... 167 F7
St Andrews Ho EX8 .... 201 F6
St Andrews Mdw DT7 .... 260 D4
St Andrews Orch EX24 .... 103 A5
St Andrews Prim Sch
EX15 .... 163 B3
St Andrews Rd
Cullompton EX15 .... 163 C3
Fremington EX31 .... 153 D6
Paignton TQ4 .... 226 C5
St Andrews Way EX15 .... 163 C3
St Anne's Chapel Mus*
EX31 .... 154 F5
St Anne's Rd Exeter EX1 .... 177 E7
Plymouth PL6 .... 245 D6
Saltash PL12 .... 242 E3
Torquay TQ2 .... 220 D7
St Annes EX6 .... 194 D3
St Annes Ct EX22 .... 70 E1
St Annes Ct TQ12 .... 207 B3
St Annes Well Brewery
EX4 .... 261 A3
St Annes Well Mews
EX4 .... 261 A3
St Anthony's Cl EX11 .... 169 E4
St Aubyn Ave PL2 .... 247 F5
St Aubyn Rd PL1 .... 247 E3
St Aubyn St PL1 .... 247 E2
St Aubyn Terr PL1 .... 132 F4
St Aubyn's Villas EX16 .... 161 F3
St Augustines Cl TQ2 .... 214 A3
St Austin Cl PL21 .... 237 B5
St Austin's Priory Private Sch
PL21 .... 136 D7
St Barnabas Hospl PL12 .... 242 F2
St Barnabas Terr PL1 .... 262 A4
St Bartholomew Way
TQ12 .... 206 D1
St Bernard's Cl
Buckfast TQ11 .... 236 B7
Exeter EX2 .... 261 C1
St Bernards Sch TQ12 .... 207 C2
St Boniface Cl PL2 .... 248 C7
St Boniface Dr PL2 .... 248 C7
St Boniface Prim Sch
PL1 .... 262 B3
St Boniface Rd EX17 .... 165 A5
St Boniface's RC Coll
PL5 .... 244 E1
St Brannock's Hill EX33 .... 152 D7
St Brannock's Park Rd
EX34 .... 150 B4
St Brannock's Rd EX34 .... 150 B4
St Brannock's Well Cl
EX33 .... 152 D7
St Briac Way EX4 .... 190 E3
St Bridget Ave PL6 .... 244 F1
St Budeaux Cl EX11 .... 169 E3
St Budeaux Ferry Rd Sta
PL5 .... 247 D8
St Budeaux Foundation Jun
Sch PL5 .... 243 F2
St Catherine's Rd TQ1 .... 220 B8
St Catherines Pk PL8 .... 141 A7
St Clement's Terr TQ9 .... 222 D2
St Clements Ct TQ6 .... 233 D4
St Columba Cl TQ12 .... 207 E8
St Cyres Rd EX4 .... 166 B6
St David's CE Fst Sch
EX4 .... 261 A3
St David's Dr EX12 .... 192 A6
St David's Hill EX4 .... 177 A7
St David's Rd PL19 .... 171 E5
St David's Sta EX4 .... 177 A7
St David's Terr EX4 .... 261 A3
St Davids [12] EX39 .... 157 A1
St Davids Cl EX13 .... 167 F7
St Davids Rd TQ9 .... 223 B6
St Dominic's Cl TQ1 .... 220 B8
St Dominick CE Sch
PL12 .... 125 A2
St Dunstan's Abbey Sch
PL1 .... 262 A3
St Dunstan's Rd TQ8 .... 259 C4
St Dunstan's Terr PL4 .... 263 C3
St Edmund's Rd TQ7 .... 258 C6
St Edmund's Rd TQ7 .... 258 C6
St Edmunds wlk TQ7 .... 258 C6
St Edward Gdns PL6 .... 245 B1
St Edward's CE Prim Sch
PL6 .... 245 C1
St Efride's Rd TQ2 .... 219 F5
St Elizabeth Cl PL7 .... 250 F4
St Elmo Ct TQ9 .... 259 C3

St Erth Rd PL2 .... 248 D7
St Eval PI PL5 .... 243 E4
St Francis Ct PL5 .... 244 B3
St Gabriel's Ave PL3 .... 248 D5
St George's Ave EX2 .... 261 C4
St George's CE Inf Sch
EX39 .... 156 F8
St George's CE Prim Sch
PL1 .... 262 A1
St George's Rd
Barnstaple EX32 .... 155 A6
Saltash PL12 .... 242 E3
Torquay TQ1 .... 220 C7
St George's Terr [1]
EX32 .... 155 A6
St George's Terr
Plymouth PL1 .... 247 F4
Shillingford St George EX2 .... 114 C6
St George's View EX15 .... 163 B4
St George's Way EX16 .... 161 C3
St George's Well EX15 .... 163 C4
St George's Well Ave
EX15 .... 163 B4
St Georges Ave EX13 .... 167 F7
St Georges Cl PL21 .... 137 B2
St Georges Cres TQ1 .... 220 C7
St Georges Ct [1] PL2 .... 247 F4
St Georges Hill DT7 .... 260 C4
St Georges Rd PL12 .... 242 D3
St German's Rd EX4 .... 177 C8
St Giles on the Heath Prim
Sch PL15 .... 90 C1
St Gregorys Cl EX2 .... 192 A6
St Helen's CE Prim Sch
EX19 .... 156 A1
St Helen's Cl EX33 .... 7 E2
St Helens EX39 .... 156 A2
St Helens Wlk PL5 .... 244 C5
St Hilary Terr EX4 .... 263 C3
St Hill Cl EX2 .... 177 A2
St Ida's Cl EX2 .... 176 D1
St Ives Cl [3] TQ2 .... 220 A6
St Jame's Prec [15]
TQ1 .... 210 B5
St James Cl Exeter EX4 .... 261 C4
Landkey EX32 .... 17 C1
Parkham EX39 .... 39 E1
St James Ct
Plymouth PL1 .... 262 B2
Torpoint PL11 .... 247 B3
St James High Sch EX4 .... 174 B1
St James PI PL1 .... 262 B2
St James Rd
Torpoint PL11 .... 247 B2
Torquay TQ1 .... 220 A7
St James St EX20 .... 170 B5
St James Terr EX4 .... 261 C4
St James' Ho [16] TQ4 .... 210 B5
St James' Park (Exeter City
AFC) EX4 .... 261 C4
St James' Park Halt
EX4 .... 261 C4
St James' PI E PL1 .... 262 B2
St James' PI W PL1 .... 262 B2
St James's Cl EX34 .... 150 C6
St John the Baptist RC Prim
Sch TQ6 .... 233 C2
St John's Bridge Rd
PL4 .... 263 B2
St John's CE Prim Sch
TQ9 .... 223 E5
St John's CE Prim Sch
TA21 .... 160 E6
St John's Cl
Bishopsteignton TQ14 .... 208 F7
Bovey Tracey TQ13 .... 180 C6
Honiton EX14 .... 166 C3
Ivybridge PL21 .... 237 B5
Millbrook PL10 .... 252 E5
St John's Cotts SX10 .... 187 F5
St John's Ct PL4 .... 263 B2
St John's Dr
Bradworthy EX22 .... 53 E8
Plymouth PL9 .... 255 B6
St John's La
Barnstaple EX32 .... 155 C3
Bovey Tracey TQ13 .... 180 C7
St John's Rd Exeter EX1 .... 177 F7
Exmouth EX8 .... 196 C2
Horrabridge PL20 .... 126 F4
Ivybridge PL21 .... 237 B5
Millbrook PL10 .... 252 E5
Plymouth,Turnchapel PL9 .... 255 A6
St John's Sch EX10 .... 187 F5
St John's St PL4 .... 263 B2
St John's Terr TQ2 .... 214 B1
St John's Villas EX2 .... 177 E6
St Johns TQ1 .... 171 C5
St Johns PI [16] Colyton EX24 .... 103 A4
Wellington TA21 .... 160 E6
St Johns Ave PL19 .... 171 C5
St Johns Cl EX22 .... 53 E8
St Johns Ct EX13 .... 167 F7
St Johns Farm Mews
EX8 .... 196 C2
St Johns La PL11 .... 252 B8
St Johns RC Prim Sch
EX16 .... 161 C6
St Johns St TQ14 .... 210 C5
St Johns St PL4 .... 207 D4
St Joseph's Cl PL6 .... 244 F1

St Joseph's RC Prim Sch
Exmouth EX8 .... 202 B7
Plymouth PL1 .... 247 E2
St Jude's Rd EX4 .... 263 B2
St Julian's Cotts PL10 .... 253 E7
St Katharine's Rd TQ2 .... 219 E6
St Katherine's Cl EX13 .... 153 A5
St Katherine's Way TQ9 .... 223 C5
St Katherines Rd EX4 .... 178 A8
St Katherine's Mews [5]
TQ9 .... 223 C5
St Keverne PI PL2 .... 248 D8
St Keyes Cl [10] EX32 .... 17 B2
St Kitts Cl TQ2 .... 213 F2
St Lawrence Cl [12] EX16 .... 64 D7
St Lawrence Cres EX11 .... 178 D6
St Lawrence Ct EX17 .... 165 B5
St Lawrence La TQ13 .... 130 F4
St Lawrence Mews EX4 .... 263 A4
St Lawrence Rd EX4 .... 263 A4
St Lawrence's Gn EX17 .... 165 B5
St Leo PI PL2 .... 248 D7
St Leonard's Ave EX2 .... 261 B1
St Leonard's Cl [10] TQ12 .... 207 B3
St Leonard's PI EX2 .... 261 C2
St Leonard's Rd
Exeter EX2 .... 261 C2
Newton Abbot TQ12 .... 207 B3
Plymouth PL4 .... 263 C2
St Leonards Cl EX14 .... 166 A5
St Levan Rd PL2 .... 247 F5
St Loye's Cl EX2 .... 178 A4
St Loye's Coll EX2 .... 177 F2
St Loye's Terr EX2 .... 178 A4
St Loyes Rd EX2 .... 178 A4
St Luke's CE High Sch
EX1 .... 178 C6
St Luke's Cl TQ12 .... 207 F1
St Luke's Pk TQ2 .... 220 A4
St Luke's Rd
Kingskerswell TQ12 .... 212 E8
Torquay TQ2 .... 220 B4
St Luke's Rd N TQ2 .... 220 A4
St Luke's Rd S TQ2 .... 220 A4
St Malo Cl EX8 .... 196 E1
St Marco Gdns TQ7 .... 258 D6
St Margaret Clitherow RC
Prim Sch TQ5 .... 230 B3
St Margaret's Ave
EX39 .... 156 E7
St Margaret's Cl TQ1 .... 220 B8
St Margaret's Ct [7]
EX39 .... 156 E7
St Margaret's Prim Sch
TQ1 .... 220 B8
St Margaret's Rd
Exeter EX4 .... 178 A8
St Margaret's Sch TQ2 .... 220 B7
St Margaret's Terr EX33 .... 177 E5
St Margaret's View EX8 .... 203 A7
St Margarets Cl EX13 .... 67 B8
St Margarets Ct EX33 .... 182 E5
St Margarets Gdn [1]
EX1 .... 154 F6
St Margarets La TQ12 .... 88 C8
St Margarets Rd PL2 .... 258 B7
St Margarets Terr EX3 .... 182 F5
St Mark's Prim Sch
EX23 .... 37 B2
St Mark's Rd
Honiton EX14 .... 166 A4
Torquay TQ1 .... 220 D3
St Marks [8] EX7 .... 204 E6
St Marks Ave EX1 .... 177 F7
St Marks Rd EX1 .... 177 F7
St Martin's Ave PL6 .... 245 D5
St Martin's Cl EX17 .... 248 D7
St Martin's La EX17 .... 165 B6
St Martin's Mews TQ12 .... 165 B6
St Martins Cl TQ1 .... 220 B8
St Martins Ct TQ2 .... 213 F1
St Martins Rd EX23 .... 70 A8
St Marwenne Cl EX23 .... 70 A6
St Mary St PL1 .... 262 A2
St Mary Steps Terr [6]
EX1 .... 261 A2
St Mary's
Bideford EX39 .... 157 A4
Brixton PL8 .... 257 A4
St Mary's C
Axminster EX13 .... 167 F5
Brixham TQ5 .... 230 B2
Great Torrington EX38 .... 159 B4
St Mary's Cotts EX7 .... 200 F4
St Mary's Ct
Newton Abbot TQ12 .... 214 B1
[4] Newton Abbot TQ12 .... 207 B3
Paignton TQ3 .... 219 C5
St Mary's Flats [7]
EX39 .... 157 A1
St Mary's La EX17 .... 104 B6
St Mary's Pk TQ2 .... 225 C8
St Mary's RC Prim Sch
EX13 .... 167 C5
St Mary's Rd TQ11 .... 236 C2
St Mary's Rd
Barnstaple EX32 .... 155 A6
Brixham TQ5 .... 230 D2
Croyde EX33 .... 7 E2
Newton Abbot TQ12 .... 207 A2
Plymouth PL7 .... 250 C6
Teignmouth TQ14 .... 210 C6
St Marychurch CE Prim Sch
TQ1 .... 214 B1

St Marychurch Rd
Newton Abbot TQ12 . . . .**207** F1
Torquay, Plainmoor TQ1 . .**220** B6
Torquay, St Marychurch
TQ1 . . . .**214** C1
St Maryhaye PL19 . . . .**171** A5
St Marys Cl
Abbotskerswell TQ12 . . . . .**212** A6
12 Chudleigh TQ13 . . . . . .**123** E6
Plymouth PL7 . . . .**250** D5
St Marys Ct
Plymouth PL7 . . . .**250** D5
Teignmouth TQ14 . . . .**210** C5
St Marys Pk EX11 . . . .**169** F3
St Marys View
Silverton EX5 . . . .**82** B5
West Hill EX11 . . . .**168** E5
St Matthew's Rd TQ2 . . . .**219** D4
St Matthews Cl EX1 . . . . . .**177** E6
St Matthews Wlk EX1 . . . .**261** C3
St Matthias Church Rd
TQ1 . . . .**220** E5
St Maurice Mews PL7 . .**250** E4
St Maurice Rd PL7 . . . . . .**250** F3
St Maurice View PL7 . . .**251** B4
St Mawes Dr TQ4 . . . .**229** B8
St Mawes Terr 3 PL2 . . . .**247** F5
St Mawgan Rd PL2 . . . . . .**247** F5
St Michael's TQ2 . . . .**219** E6
St Michael's Bsns Ctr
DT7 . . . .**260** E3
St Michael's CE Mid Sch
EX1 . . . .**177** F6
St Michael's CE Prim Sch
TQ12 . . . .**207** E7
St Michael's Cl
Clyst Honiton EX5 . . . .**179** D8
Exeter EX2 . . . .**177** E1
Plymouth PL1 . . . .**247** E1
Torquay TQ1 . . . .**219** E6
St Michael's Ct
Paignton TQ4 . . . .**226** A4
7 Plymouth PL1 . . . .**247** F3
St Michael's Hill EX5 . . .**179** D8
St Michael's Prim Sch
DT7 . . . .**260** E4
St Michael's Rd
Newton Abbot TQ12 . . . . .**207** D1
Paignton TQ4 . . . .**226** B5
Torquay TQ1 . . . .**219** E7
St Michael's Terr
Plymouth PL4 . . . .**262** C4
8 Plymouth, Devonport
PL1 . . . .**247** F3
St Michaels Terr 3
TQ1 . . . .**220** B5
St Michaels Cl
Launceston PL15 . . . .**105** B1
Otterton EX9 . . . .**198** E7
St Michaels Rd
Kingsteignton TQ12 . . . . .**207** D6
Teignmouth TQ14 . . . .**210** C7
St Michaels Sch EX31 . . . . .**27** D8
St Michaels Terr 3
TQ10 . . . .**134** F2
St Michaels View EX21 . . .**55** E4
St Modwen Rd PL6 . . . . . .**249** F7
St Nazaire App PL1 . . . . .**247** F2
St Nazaire Cl PL1 . . . .**247** E2
St Nicholas CE Jun Sch
EX10 . . . .**188** A7
St Nicholas RC Comb Sch
EX2 . . . .**261** C1
St Olave's Cl EX4 . . . .**261** A3
St Pancras Ave PL2 . . . . .**248** D8
St Paul St Plymouth PL1 . .**248** A4
Tiverton EX16 . . . .**161** C4
St Paul's Cres TQ1 . . . . . .**220** B7
St Paul's RC Prim Sch
PL5 . . . .**243** D1
St Paul's Rd
Honiton EX14 . . . .**166** C5
12 Newton Abbot TQ12 . .**207** C3
Paignton TQ3 . . . .**219** D1
Torquay TQ1 . . . .**220** B7
St Paul's Sq EX16 . . . .**161** C3
St Pauls Cl
Bovey Tracey TQ13 . . . . . .**180** D7
Plymouth PL3 . . . .**249** C5
St Peter Cl PL7 . . . .**250** F4
St Peter St EX16 . . . .**161** C4
St Peter's Cath EX1 . . . .**261** B3
St Peter's CE High Sch
EX2 . . . .**178** C5
St Peter's CE Jun Sch
PL19 . . . .**171** D5
St Peter's Cl TQ13 . . . . . .**180** E8
St Peter's Hill 5 TQ5 . . .**230** D5
St Peter's Prim Sch
TQ3 . . . .
St Peter's Quay TQ9 . . . .**223** D4
St Peter's RC Prim Sch
PL5 . . . .**244** B5
St Peter's Terr EX14 . . . .**166** A6
St Peter's Sch EX8 . . . .**196** A6
St Peters CE Prim Sch
PL1 . . . .**262** A3
St Peters West Buckland EX32 . .**18** B2
St Peters Cl Torquay TQ2 .**219** D6
West Buckland EX32 . . . .**18** B2
St Peters Mount EX4 . . . .**262** A3
St Peters Rd
Fremington EX31 . . . .**153** D5

St Peters Rd continued
Holsworthy EX22 . . . .**164** B5
Plymouth PL5 . . . .**244** C2
St Peters Terr 2 EX34 . .**150** C5
St Peters Way
Ivybridge PL21 . . . .**237** E3
Ivybridge PL21 . . . .**237** E5
St Peters Well La EX22 . . .**53** E8
St Petrock's Cl EX2 . . . . . .**261** C2
St Phillips Ct EX4 . . . .**176** F4
St Rumon's CE Inf Sch
PL19 . . . .**171** C6
St Saviour's Way EX17 . .**165** D5
St Saviours Rd EX11 . . . . .**169** D3
St Scholastica's Abbey
EX4 . . . .**210** D7
St Sevan Way EX8 . . . .**196** E3
St Sidwell's Ave EX4 . . . .**261** B4
St Sidwell's CE Comb Sch
EX4 . . . .**261** C4
St Sidwell's Ct EX4 . . . . . .**261** B4
St Simon's La PL4 . . . .**249** B3
St Stephen Rd PL2 . . . . . .**250** F3
St Stephen St PL1 . . . .**247** F1
St Stephen's Hill PL12 . .**242** C1
St Stephen's Pl PL7 . . . . .**250** D5
St Stephen's Rd PL12 . . .**242** E2
St Stephens Com Prim Sch
PL12 . . . .**242** E2
St Swithin's Gdns EX17 . . .**80** A5
St Teresa Ho PL4 . . . .**263** A3
St Teresa's Cl EX39 . . . . .**156** F7
St Teresa's Ct 6 EX39 . .**156** F7
St Therese's Rd PL1 . . . . .**247** F2
St Thomas Cl
Bovey Tracey TQ13 . . . . . .**180** E7
Plymouth PL7 . . . .**250** F3
St Thomas Ct EX4 . . . .**177** A4
St Thomas Fst Sch EX4 . . .**177** A4
St Thomas Sh Ctr EX4 . . . .**177** A4
St Vincent Cl TQ1 . . . .**220** C3
St Vincent St PL2 . . . .**247** E4
St Vincent's Rd TQ1 . . . . .**219** F7
St Vincents Cl TQ1 . . . . . .**219** F6
St Werburgh Cl PL9 . . . . .**140** D7
St Wilfrid's Sch EX4 . . . . .**261** A3
Salamanca St PL11 . . . . . .**247** B3
Salcombe CE Prim Sch
TQ8 . . . .**259** C5
Salcombe Ct EX10 . . . .**188** B4
Salcombe Hill Cl EX10 . . .**188** B4
Salcombe Hill Rd EX10 . .**188** B4
Salcombe Lawn EX10 . . . .**188** B4
Salcombe Rd
Malborough TQ7, TQ8 . . . .**147** F6
Sidmouth EX10 . . . .**188** B4
Salcombe The TQ8 . . . . . .**259** C5
Salem Almshouses **7**
EX32 . . . .**155** A4
Salem Pl 12 TQ12 . . . . . .**207** B3
Salem St 8 EX32 . . . .**155** A4
Salisbury Ave
Feniton EX14 . . . .**84** D2
Torquay TQ1 . . . .**213** F1
Salisbury Cl EX14 . . . .**84** D2
Salisbury Ope PL3 . . . . . .**248** B5
Salisbury Rd Exeter EX4 . .**177** E8
Exmouth EX8 . . . .**202** A7
Newton Abbot TQ12 . . . . .**207** D4
Plymouth PL4 . . . .**263** C4
Salisbury Road Jun Sch
PL4 . . . .**263** C4
Salisbury Terr
Paignton EX13 . . . .**87** C1
3 Teignmouth TQ14 . . . .**210** D5
Sallicombe Rd EX24 . . . . .**101** F6
Salmonhutch Cotts
EX17 . . . .**165** B3
Salmonpool La EX2 . . . . .**177** E3
Salston Barton EX11 . . . .**169** C2
Salston Ride EX11 . . . .**169** C2
Salt Mill PL12 . . . .**242** F4
Salt Wood La EX34 . . . .**7** F3
Saltash Bsns Pk PL12 . . . .**242** C4
Saltash Coll PL12 . . . .**242** C6
Saltash Com Sch PL12 . . . .**242** E1
Saltash Ctr (Coll of F Ed)
PL12 . . . .**242** D2
Saltash Ind Est PL12 . . . . .**242** D4
Saltash Parkway Ind Est
PL12 . . . .**242** B4
Saltash Rd Plymouth PL3 .**262** C4
Plymouth, Keyham PL2 . . .**247** E7
Saltash Sta PL12 . . . .**243** A2
Saltburn Rd PL5 . . . .**243** C1
Salter's Cross EX10 . . . . .**187** D6
Salter's La EX24 . . . .**103** A4
Salter's Rd EX2 . . . .**178** B4
Salterns Rd TQ4 . . . .**226** C1
Salterns Terr EX39 . . . . . .**157** B2
Salters Ct EX2 . . . .**178** A4
Salters Mdw EX10 . . . .**188** B5
Salterton Rd
Budleigh Salterton EX8,
EX9 . . . .**197** B1
Exmouth EX8 . . . .**202** C7
Salterton Workshops **1**
EX9 . . . .**198** A1
Salting Hill EX9 . . . .**199** J2
Saltings The
Seaton EX12 . . . .**192** B7
Shaldon TQ14 . . . .**209** D5
Saltmer Cl EX34 . . . .**150** A2
Saltram Ho * PL7 . . . .**250** A4
Saltram Terr
Lee Moor PL7 . . . .**132** F4
Plymouth PL7 . . . .**250** E5
Saltways La EX10 . . . .**100** F1

Salty La TQ14 . . . .**209** D5
Salway Cl EX15 . . . .**163** B3
Salway Gdns EX13 . . . . . .**167** F5
Samara Bsns Pk TQ12 . . .**180** F3
Sampford Arundel Com Prim
Sch TA21 . . . .**52** B3
Sampford Cross EX20 . . . . .**76** F3
Sampford Gdns PL20 . . . .**127** A5
Sch EX16 . . . .**50** C1
Sampford Terr 7 PL20 . .**126** F5
Sampson Cl PL18 . . . .**125** A6
Sampson Cross EX37 . . . . .**44** D8
Sampson's Hill EX2 . . . . .**114** C6
Sampsons La EX1 . . . .**177** E7
San Remo Terr EX7 . . . . .**204** E7
Sanctuary Cl EX32 . . . .**16** E1
Sanctuary La
Hatherleigh EX20 . . . .**75** C7
Woodbury Salterton EX5 . .**185** B7
Sanctuary Rd EX22 . . . . .**164** C4
Sand Down La EX5 . . . . . .**172** A8
Sand Hill PL18 . . . .**125** B3
Sand La Calstock PL18 . . .**125** D3
Totnes TQ9 . . . .**224** A8
Sand Pit Hill La EX24 . . . .**102** F4
Sandaway La EX34 . . . .**2** A3
Sandclose La EX34 . . . .**31** D7
Sanders Cl EX5 . . . .**175** D6
Sanders Cross EX22 . . . . . .**54** C8
Sanders La 2 EX32 . . . . . .**16** E1
Sanders Rd Bow EX17 . . . . .**78** C4
Brixham TQ5 . . . .**230** A5
Exeter EX4 . . . .**174** E1
Sanders' La EX22 . . . .**164** C5
Sandersfield EX15 . . . .**83** F6
Sanderspool Cross
TQ10 . . . .**135** C2
Sandford Ash La EX17 . . . .**79** A7
Sandford Cl EX13 . . . .**165** C4
Sandford Cross EX20 . . . . .**77** C4
Sandford La EX20 . . . .**77** F3
Sandford Orleigh TQ12 . .**207** B5
Sandford Rd PL9 . . . .**255** F8
Sandford Sch EX17 . . . .**80** A5
Sandford Wlk EX1 . . . . . .**261** C3
Sandford Wlk EX1 . . . . . .**261** C3
Sandfords EX6 . . . .**181** B1
Sandfords Gdns EX38 . . .**159** B4
Sandgate La EX11 . . . .**100** D4
Sandheap Cross TQ7 . . . .**143** C2
Sandhill Cross TQ13 . . . .**111** E5
Sandhill St EX11 . . . .**169** E4
Sandhills TQ8 . . . .**259** C3
Sandhills Rd TQ8 . . . .**259** C3
Sandhole Cross EX39 . . . . .**37** A8
Sandick Cross EX22 . . . .**57** A2
Sandon Wlk PL6 . . . .**245** A1
Sandown Rd TQ4 . . . .**225** F2
Sandpark La EX31 . . . .**10** D5
Sandpark Rd EX18 . . . .**59** D2
Sandpath Rd TQ12 . . . . . .**207** B6
Sandpiper Ct EX4 . . . .**174** D1
Sandpiper Dr EX3 . . . .**183** C2
Sandpiper Gn EX2 . . . . . .**176** D3
Sandpit Hill EX24 . . . .**101** E6
Sandridge Cl PL9 . . . .**255** E8
Sandringham Dr TQ3 . . . .**219** B2
Sandringham Gdns TQ3 .**219** D1
Sandringham Rd TQ12 . .**207** A5
Sands EX15 . . . .**65** D7
Sands Gate Cross TQ13 . . .**95** F1
Sands Rd Paignton TQ4 . .**226** C5
Slapton TQ7 . . . .**145** D3
Sanduck Cross TQ13 . . . .**112** A2
Sandy Cross EX9 . . . .**198** A8
Sandy La
Brampford Speke EX5 . . . . .**81** E1
Braunton EX33 . . . .**152** B6
Broadclyst EX5 . . . .**175** D5
Chittlehampton EX37 . . . . .**29** A5
Croyde EX33 . . . .**7** F2
Ivybridge PL21 . . . .**237** D5
Kingsbridge TQ7, TQ9 . . . .**144** B5
Staverton TQ9 . . . .**216** A6
Woolacombe EX34 . . . .**1** A1
Sandy Mdw EX33 . . . .**7** C1
Sandy's La EX11 . . . .**68** C2
Sandygate Bsns Pk
TQ12 . . . .**123** E1
Sandygate Mill TQ12 . . . .**123** E1
Sandygate La EX38 . . . . . .**41** A2
Sandymere Rd EX39 . . . . .**156** F7
Sandymoor Cross EX22 . . .**72** E1
Sandypark La EX17 . . . .**82** B6
Sandyway Cross EX36 . . . .**20** F4
Sanford Ct EX9 . . . .**197** J7
Sanford Rd TQ2 . . . .**219** E5
Sango Ct PL10 . . . .**252** F6
Sango Rd PL11 . . . .**252** F6
Sannerville Way EX6 . . . .**182** B5
Sanson Cl EX5 . . . .**173** B8
Sarah Ct PL20 . . . .**125** E1
Sargent Cl EX1 . . . .**178** C6
Sargents Mdw EX23 . . . .**4** A1
Sarlsdown Rd EX8 . . . . . .**202** D7
Sarum Cl PL3 . . . .**248** F7
Satterleigh Cross EX37 . . .**43** A3
Saturday's La TQ12 . . . . .**212** F1
Saunders Way
Cullompton EX15 . . . .**163** E4
West Charleton TQ7 . . . . . .**144** C1
Saunton Beach Villas
EX33 . . . .**14** E8

Saunton Cl EX33 . . . .**152** C6
Saunton Rd EX33 . . . .**152** B6
Savage Rd PL5 . . . .**247** D7
Savery Cl PL21 . . . .**237** E6
Savile Rd EX4 . . . .**176** F5
Savoy Hill EX4 . . . .**174** A2
Sawmill La EX9 . . . .**197** F7
Sawmills Way 3 EX14 . .**166** C5
Sawpit La TQ9 . . . .**222** F7
Sawrey St PL1 . . . .**262** A2
Sawyer Dr TQ14 . . . .**124** E1
Sawyer St TQ14 . . . .**124** E1
Sawyers Mill EX16 . . . .**34** E2
Saxon Ave EX4 . . . .**174** F2
Saxon Hts 2 TQ5 . . . .**230** C4
Saxon Mdw TQ3 . . . .**225** C5
Saxon Rd EX1 . . . .**177** F6
Saxon Way EX15 . . . .**163** C6
Saxons Croft EX32 . . . . . .**155** C3
Scabbacombe La TQ6 . . .**235** A6
Scadsbury La EX20 . . . .**75** A4
Scalders La PL21 . . . .**237** C6
Scalwell La EX12 . . . .**192** A7
Scalwell Mead EX12 . . . . .**192** A7
Scalwell Pk EX12 . . . .**192** A7
Scarborough Pl TQ2 . . . . .**219** F5
Scarborough Rd TQ2 . . . .**219** F5
Scarhill Cross EX20 . . . . . .**95** D4
Scarsdale EX8 . . . .**202** C5
Scattor View EX6 . . . .**112** F5
School Cl Bampton EX16 . . .**34** B1
Fremington EX31 . . . .**153** E5
Plymouth PL7 . . . .**250** D7
Shobrooke EX17 . . . .**80** E4
Tavistock PL19 . . . .**171** D5
School Cnr EX39 . . . .**22** E3
School Cotts TQ12 . . . . . .**207** A8
School Cl TQ6 . . . .**233** D3
School Dr PL6 . . . .**245** D7
School Hill
Cockwood EX6 . . . .**201** B6
6 Dawlish EX7 . . . .**204** D6
Lympstone EX8 . . . .**195** D3
Stoke Gabriel TQ9 . . . .**227** F7
School La
6 Bishop's Tawton EX32 . .**16** E1
Blackawton TQ9 . . . .**139** E1
Broadclyst EX5 . . . .**175** C7
Chulsworthy EX22 . . . .**53** E1
6 Colyton EX24 . . . .**103** A4
Exeter EX2 . . . .**178** A1
Exmouth EX8 . . . .**196** C1
Great Torrington EX38 . . . .**159** D5
Hartland EX39 . . . .**22** E3
Honiton EX14 . . . .**166** C6
Newton Poppleford EX10 . .**186** E8
Plymouth PL7 . . . .**250** E4
Rousdon DT7 . . . .**193** F7
Tatworth TA20 . . . .**88** C8
Tedburn St Mary EX6 . . . . .**97** F4
3 Teignmouth TQ14 . . . .**210** A3
Thorverton EX5 . . . .**81** E4
West Hill EX11 . . . .**168** E5
School Rd
Ermington PL21 . . . .**136** F4
Exeter EX2 . . . .**177** A4
Kingskerswell TQ12 . . . . . .**212** F4
Lydford EX20 . . . .**107** F4
Newton Abbot TQ12 . . . . .**207** D1
Silverton EX5 . . . .**82** B5
Stoke Fleming TQ6 . . . . . .**146** A7
Teigngrace TQ12 . . . .**206** F8
Whitchurch PL19 . . . .**171** D2
School St 5 EX10 . . . .**101** B1
School Way EX20 . . . .**170** B5
Schooners Ct EX8 . . . .**201** E6
Scobhill Rd EX35 . . . .**5** E3
Sconner Rd PL11 . . . .**247** B2
Score Farm Cvn Pk
EX33 . . . .**152** C5
Score View EX34 . . . .**150** C3
Scoresby Cl TQ2 . . . .**214** B3
Scotchmead EX5 . . . .**99** D3
Scott Ave
18 Appledore EX39 . . . . . .**15** A1
Exeter EX2 . . . .**177** F3
Plymouth PL5 . . . .**247** C8
Scott Dr EX8 . . . .**196** B2
Scott Hospl PL2 . . . .**248** A6
Scott Rd PL2 . . . .**248** B6
Scott's Cl TQ7 . . . .**143** E4
Scott's Hill TA4 . . . .**35** E8
Scott's La
Raymond's Hill EX13 . . . . .**104** C7
Wellington TA21 . . . .**160** E6
Scottleigh TQ2 . . . .**219** F3
Scouse Cross EX13 . . . .**88** E2
Scouse La EX13 . . . .**88** E2
Scrapton La TA20 . . . .**69** F5
Scratch Face La EX12 . . .**192** A7
Scratchface La
Bideford EX39 . . . .**25** D4
Bideford, Littleham EX39 . . .**25** D6
Buckland Brewer EX39 . . . . .**40** B6
Thorverton EX17 . . . .**81** B6
Screechers Hill TQ13 . . . .**130** F5
Scurfield Cl EX33 . . . .**152** D7
Sea Hill Beer EX12 . . . . . .**191** E5
Seaton EX12 . . . .**192** A4
Sea Lawn Terr EX7 . . . . . .**204** F7
Sea Trout Mews TQ9 . . . .**216** A5
Sea View PL18 . . . .**125** B5
Sea View Ave PL4 . . . .**263** A4
Sea View Dr 7 PL9 . . . . . .**140** D8
Sea View Gdns TQ7 . . . . .**258** F6
Sea View Terr
Beer EX12 . . . .**191** D5
Brixham TQ5 . . . .**230** C6

Sea View Terr continued
Plymouth PL4 . . . .**263** B4
Sidmouth EX10 . . . .**188** A5
Thurlestone TQ7 . . . .**143** A2
Seabourne Ct TQ4 . . . . . .**226** C4
Seabrook Ave EX2 . . . . . .**182** C7
Seacroft Rd PL5 . . . .**243** C2
Seafield Ave EX8 . . . .**196** A2
Seafield La EX10 . . . .**188** A3
Seafield Rd Seaton EX12 .**192** A5
Sidmouth EX10 . . . .**188** A4
Seaforth Lodge EX12 . . .**191** F6
Sealands EX34 . . . .**8** C6
Seale Cl TQ6 . . . .**233** D4
Seale-Hayne (Univ of
Plymouth) TQ12 . . . .**206** B7
Seapoint 11 TQ14 . . . . . .**210** B4
Searle Cl EX17 . . . .**165** C5
Searle Terr EX39 . . . .**157** A7
Seashore Ctr * TQ4 . . . . . .**226** C4
Seaside EX34 . . . .**2** B5
Seaton EX12 . . . .**192** B5
Seaton & District Electric
Tramway * EX12 . . . .**192** C3
Seaton & District Hospl
EX12 . . . .**192** A5
Seaton Ave PL4 . . . .**248** E4
Seaton Bsns Pk PL6 . . . . .**245** B3
Seaton Cl TQ1 . . . .**220** D7
Seaton Down Cl EX12 . . .**191** F8
Seaton Down Hill EX12 . .**191** F8
Seaton Down Rd EX12 . . .**192** A5
Seaton La PL4 . . . .**248** E4
Seaton Orch PL7 . . . .**136** A8
Seaton Pl PL2 . . . .**247** F5
Seaton Prim Sch EX12 . . .**192** A6
Seaton Rd
Branscombe EX12,EX24 . .**102** A2
Colyford EX24 . . . .**103** A3
Farway EX24 . . . .**101** E5
Musbury EX13 . . . .**103** D6
Seaton EX12 . . . .**192** B8
Seaton Way PL20 . . . .**126** D2
Seaview TQ7 . . . .**149** A3
Seaview Cres TQ3 . . . . . .**219** C3
Seaview Rd
Thurlestone TQ7 . . . .**143** A2
Uplyme DT7 . . . .**104** B4
Seaward Cl EX12 . . . .**190** E4
Seaway Cl TQ2 . . . .**219** E3
Seaway Cres TQ3 . . . .**226** D8
Seaway Ct TQ5 . . . .**230** B4
Seaway Gdns TQ3 . . . . . .**226** D8
Seaway La
Tipton St John EX10 . . . . .**100** D2
Torquay TQ2 . . . .**219** E3
Seaway Rd TQ3 . . . .**226** D8
Seckerleigh Cross EX16 . . .**48** E4
Seckington Cross EX19 . . .**58** E4
Secmaton La EX7 . . . .**200** E3
Secmaton Rise EX7 . . . . .**200** E3
Second Ave
Axminster EX13 . . . .**167** F7
Dawlish EX7 . . . .**204** C5
Exeter, Countess Wear
EX2 . . . .**182** D7
Exeter, Heavitree EX1 . . . .**177** F7
Plymouth, Billacombe PL9 .**250** A3
Plymouth, Devonport PL1 .**248** A2
Plymouth, Weston Mill PL2 .**247** E7
Teignmouth TQ14 . . . .**210** A3
Torquay TQ1 . . . .**220** A8
Second Dr
Teignmouth TQ14 . . . .**210** B5
Torquay TQ1 . . . .**220** A8
Second Field La EX33 . . .**152** C6
Sector Hill EX13 . . . .**88** B3
Sector La EX13 . . . .**167** F5
Sedemuda Cl EX10 . . . . . .**188** A6
Sedemuda Rd EX10 . . . . .**187** F6
Sedge Cl PL21 . . . .**237** D4
Sedgeclaire Cl EX1 . . . . .**174** F1
Sedgewell Cross EX21 . . . .**55** F4
Sedley Way PL5 . . . .**244** D3
Sefton Ave PL4 . . . .**249** B3
Sefton Cl PL4 . . . .**263** C4
Sefton Ct 8 EX7 . . . .**204** E6
Segrave Rd PL2 . . . .**248** A5
Selcombe Cross TQ9 . . . .**144** E4
Seldons Cl PL21 . . . .**137** D6
Selkirk Pl PL5 . . . .**244** E2
Sellbed Cross TA24 . . . .**21** A8
Seller's Grave EX24 . . . . .**103** A4
Seller's Wood Hill EX12 .**190** E6
Sellick Ave TQ5 . . . .**230** D3
Selsden Cl PL9 . . . .**256** C6
Senate Ct EX8 . . . .**196** E1
Senate Way EX8 . . . .**196** E1
Sendall's Way PL6 . . . . . .**244** E4
Sennen Cl PL11 . . . .**246** F4
Sennen Pl PL2 . . . .**247** E5
Sentry Cnr EX39 . . . .**157** C1
Sentry Cross EX31 . . . .**18** A8
Sentry La
Bishop's Tawton EX32 . . . . .**16** E1
Huntsham EX16 . . . .**49** E6
Sentrys Orch EX6 . . . .**182** B3
Sercombes Gdns EX6 . . .**201** B8
Serge Ct EX2 . . . .**261** A2
Serpell Cl PL6 . . . .**244** E6
Serstone Cross EX17 . . . . .**78** C5
Sessland La
North Tawton EX17 . . . .**77** E1
Zeal Monachorum EX17 . . .**95** D8
Sett Cl TQ13 . . . .**180** D7
Seven Acre Cross EX36 . . .**31** E6
Seven Acre La
Braunton EX33 . . . .**152** E5

Seven Acre La continued
Bridford EX6 ....112 F5
Seven Acres Pk EX33 ....152 E5
Seven Ash Cross EX34 ......3 C1
Seven Brethren Ind Est
  EX31 ....154 F3
Seven Crosses 63 F6
Seven Crosses Rd EX16 ..161 A3
Seven Hills Ho TQ2 ....220 A5
Seven Stars La PL5 ....244 C6
Seven Stars Cross
  TQ7 ....142 E8
Seven Thorns EX35 ....5 D5
Seven Trees Ct PL4 ....263 B4
Seventh St ◢ EX32 ....154 F6
Severn Pl PL3 ....249 C5
Severn Rd TQ2 ....219 B7
Sewell Ct PL3 ....248 E5
Sexton's Cross EX6 ....113 E6
Seymour Ave PL4 ....263 B4
Seymour Bglws EX34 ....1 A1
Seymour Dr Exmouth EX8 ..196 B2
  9 Totnes TQ9 ....223 D5
Seymour Dr
  Plymouth PL3 ....233 C3
  Plymouth PL3 ....248 F5
  Torquay TQ2 ....214 B4
Seymour Mews PL4 ....263 C4
Seymour Pk PL3 ....249 A5
Seymour Pl TQ9 ....223 D5
Seymour Rd
  Exmouth EX8 ....196 B2
  Newton Abbot TQ12 .....207 C4
  Plymouth, Mannamead
  PL3 ....248 F5
  Plymouth, Plympton PL7 ..250 C6
Seymour St
  Plymouth PL4 ....263 A3
  Wellington TA21 ....160 C6
Seymour Terr EX16 ....161 C4
Seymour Villas EX34 ....1 A1
Shackel Cross TA3 ....67 E8
Shackhayes EX34 ....3 A4
Shackleton Cl EX8 ....196 B2
Shadycombe Ct TQ8 ....259 D5
Shadycombe Rd TQ8 ......259 D5
Shaftesbury Cl 22 EX17 ..204 E6
Shaftesbury Cotts PL4 ...263 A4
Shaftesbury Ct 8 PL4 ....263 A4
Shaftesbury Rd
  Exeter EX2 ....177 A4
  4 Ilfracombe EX34 ...150 C5
Shaftsborough La EX34 ....1 C1
Shaftsbury Pl 8 TQ9 .....223 C5
Shakespeare Cl
  Tiverton EX16 ....161 D6
  Torquay TQ2 ....219 D6
Shakespeare Rd
  Exeter EX2 ....177 F3
  Plymouth PL5 ....244 C2
Shakespeare Way EX4 ....196 C4
Shaldon Cres PL5 ....244 B3
Shaldon Prim Sch TQ14 ..210 A3
Shaldon Rd
  Combeinteignhead TQ12 ..208 F5
  Newton Abbot TQ12 .....207 F2
Shallowford Cl PL6 ....249 C8
Shallowford Rd PL6 ....249 C8
Shamble Way EX35 ....151 E2
Shameface La TQ13 ....123 B7
Shamel's End EX16 ....64 E7
Shand Pk EX13 ....167 C5
Shapcott La EX36 ....32 C2
Shapcott Wood Hill EX36 ..31 F2
Shapland Pl EX16 ....161 C2
Shapley Tor Cl TQ5 ......230 A2
Shapley Way TQ12 ....180 C1
Shapleys Gdns PL9 ....256 A5
Shapters Ct PL4 ....263 C2
Shapters Way PL4 ....255 B8
Shaptor Cross TQ13 ......122 F8
Shaptor View TQ13 ....180 B5
Sharland La EX17 ....78 F8
Sharland La TA33 ....152 C6
Sharlands Rd EX22 ....70 A6
Sharon Way PL4 ....245 A5
Sharp Rock EX34 ....7 F7
Sharper La TQ14 ....209 C3
Sharpham Dr TQ9 ....223 D4
Sharphay Cl TQ13 ....218 F1
Sharpitor Row PL20 ......127 B4
Sharpland La EX33 ....7 E3
Sharps Cl TQ12 ....123 B2
Sharps Crest TQ12 ....123 B2
Sharps Ct EX8 ....201 F6
Sharrose Rd PL9 ....255 B5
Shaugh Prior Prim Sch
  PL7 ....132 C6
Shaw Way PL9 ....255 A7
Sheafhayne Cross EX14 ...69 B4
Shearford La EX31 ....154 F8
Shearman Ct 10 EX2 .....261 A2
Shearwater Dr TQ2 ......213 D3
Shearwood Cl PL7 ....250 C6
Shebbear Coll EX21 ....55 E4
Shebbear Cross EX38 .....41 A2
Shebbear Sch EX21 ....55 E4
Shedden Hill Rd TQ2 .....220 A4
Sheepstor Rd PL6 ....245 D1
Sheepwash Cross EX36 ...31 C6
Sheepwash Hill EX34 ......31 C6
Sheilds The EX34 ....150 C4
Sheldon Cross EX14 ....66 F2
Sheldon's La TA22 ....33 A7
Shell Cl PL6 ....245 E1

Shell La EX16 ....47 F1
Shell's La TA20 ....69 D3
Shelley Ave
  Tavistock PL19 ....171 D5
  10 TQ1 ....220 B8
Shelley Cl EX2 ....177 A2
Shelley Ct EX8 ....201 E6
Shelley Way PL5 ....243 D1
Shells La EX24 ....103 A3
Shelly Ct EX20 ....95 B4
Shelly Rd Exmouth EX8 ...201 E6
  South Zeal EX20 ....95 B4
Shelly Reach EX8 ....201 F6
Shelston Tor Dr TQ4 .....223 F3
Shepherd Cl TQ13 ....225 E5
Shepherd's La
  Hemyock EX15 ....52 F1
  Plymouth PL4 ....263 B2
Shepherds La
  Colaton Raleigh EX10 ...186 E4
  Teignmouth TQ14 ....124 E1
Shepherds Mdw
  Abbotsham EX39 ....156 A8
  Beaford EX19 ....42 D1
Sheplegh Ct TQ9 ....145 B8
Sheppard's Knap EX13 ...87 A2
Sheppards Row EX8 ......202 A7
Sheppards Rd EX4 ....173 D2
Sheppaton La EX18,EX19,
  EX17 ....43 B2
Sherborne Cl PL9 ....256 C6
Sherborne Rd TQ12 ......207 B3
Sherbourne La DT7 ......260 E3
Sherbrook Cl EX9 ....203 F8
Sherbrook Hill EX9 ....203 F8
Shercroft Cl EX5 ....175 E2
Sherford Cres
  Plymouth, Elburton PL9 ..256 C7
  Plymouth, West Park PL5 ..244 A3
Sherford Down Cross
  TQ7 ....144 D3
Sherford Down Rd TQ7 ..144 E3
Sherford Rd PL9 ....256 D7
Sherford Wlk PL9 ....256 D7
Sheridan Rd Exeter EX4 ..178 C8
  Plymouth PL5 ....244 C1
Sherman Ho EX11 ....169 E3
Sherracombe Cross
  EX36 ....19 C6
Sherratt's Oak EX31 .....155 B7
Sherrell Pk PL20 ....125 E1
Sherril Ct PL4 ....255 F4
Sherwell Cl
  Dawlish Warren EX7 .....201 A2
  Staverton TQ9 ....216 A5
Sherwell Ct TQ1 ....236 B5
Sherwell Hill TQ2 ....219 E5
Sherwell La
  Plymouth PL4 ....263 A4
  Torquay TQ2 ....219 E5
Sherwell Park Rd TQ2 ....219 E5
Sherwell Rise S TQ2 .....219 D5
Sherwell Valley Prim Sch
  TQ2 ....219 C2
Sherwill Valley Rd TQ2 ..219 D6
Sherwill Cl EX21 ....37 A6
Sherwill La TQ9 ....216 A5
Sherwood Cl EX2 ....177 F5
Sherwood Cross EX14 ....84 D2
Sherwood Dr EX8 ....196 B3
Sherwood Gn EX38 ....42 E7
Shetland Cl TQ2 ....213 E2
Shewte Cross TQ13 ......122 D5
Shields The EX34 ....150 C4
Shieling Rd EX13 ....103 A7
Shiers Orch EX7 ....197 F8
Shillands EX16 ....161 B5
Shillingate Cl EX7 ....204 A6
Shillingford Fst Sch
  EX16 ....34 F3
Shillingford Rd EX4 ......181 A3
Shillingford Rd EX12 ....181 A7
Shilston Gate PL21 ......137 D4
Shilstone Cross EX32 .....28 C5
Shilstone La TQ13 ....113 C1
Shindle Pk TQ7 ....144 E6
Shinners Cotts TQ6 ......228 C2
Ship La EX15 ....179 D8
Shiphay Ave TQ2 ....219 C8
Shiphay Com Prim Sch
  TQ2 ....219 C8
Shiphay La TQ2 ....219 D7
Shiphay Manor Dr TQ2 ..219 D7
Shiphay Park Rd TQ2 ....219 D7
Shipley Rd EX14 ....166 E6
Shipley Wlk PL6 ....245 A1
Shipney La TQ13 ....124 A7
Shirburn Rd
  Plymouth PL4 ....249 B8
  Torquay TQ1 ....220 A7
Shire Ct Honiton EX14 ...166 A5
  Paignton TQ4 ....229 B8
Shire Horse Ctr The*
  EX34 ....150 A1
Shire La DT7 ....260 B3
Shirley Cl EX8 ....196 D4
Shirley Cnr EX17 ....79 B5
Shirley Gdns PL5 ....244 C1
Shirley Twrs TQ1 ....220 C3
Shirwell Cross
  Barnstaple EX31 ....16 E6
  Shirwell EX31 ....17 B8
Shirwell Prim Sch EX31 ..17 B8
Shirwell Rd EX31 ....17 A7
Shoalgate Cross EX20 ....94 F8
Shobbrook Hill TQ13 ....206 E4

Shobrook La EX17 ....78 F7
Shobrooke Cross EX17 ...80 D4
Shoot's La EX14 ....67 A3
Shooting La EX15 ....60 B7
Shooting Marsh Stile
  EX2 ....261 A1
Shoots Barn Cross EX14 ..84 D3
Shop Cotts PL7 ....132 F4
Shore Head EX14 ....86 F5
Shoreland Cross EX18 ....44 F5
Shorelands Rd EX31 .....154 D3
Shorelands Way
  Barnstaple EX31 ....154 D3
  Northam EX39 ....156 E7
Shoreline The EX12 ......192 C4
Shoresgate Cross EX19 ..76 F8
Shorland Cl EX7 ....204 F8
Shorneywell TQ7 ....145 A1
Short Cl EX39 ....156 D2
Short Cotts PL11 ....247 A3
Short Cross TQ9 ....139 B3
Short La Halwell TQ9 ....139 B3
  Shaldon TQ14 ....209 C8
Short Park Rd PL3 ....248 D5
Shorta Cross TQ7 ....143 C7
Shortacombe Cnr EX31 ..10 A5
Shortacombe Dr EX33 ...152 B7
Shorter Cross TQ9 ......135 D2
Shortlands
  Budleigh Salterton EX9 ..197 F8
  Holsworthy EX22 ....71 D5
Shortlands La EX15 ......163 B3
Shortlands Rd EX15 ......163 B3
Shortmoor Cross EX14 ...86 E6
Shortwood Cl EX32 ......155 C3
Shortwood La EX15 ....86 D1
Shotridge Cl
  Honiton EX14 ....166 C4
  Witheridge EX16 ....46 E1
Shotridge Mead 11
  EX16 ....161 B4
Shorts Way TQ9 ....222 E6
Shortwood Cl PL9 ....197 F2
Shortwood Cres PL9 ....256 A7
Shovelpiece La EX32 ....11 D1
Shrewsbury Ave TQ2 ....214 A1
Shrewsbury Rd PL5 .....244 C4
Shrinkhill La EX16 ....161 D3
Shrubbery Cl EX32 ......155 C3
Shrubbery La EX14 ....86 E6
Shrubbery The EX20 .....76 C5
Shubbery The EX13 ......167 D5
Shute TQ7 ....147 E6
Shute La EX16 ....46 F7
Shute Cross
  Newton St Cyres EX17 ...81 B2
  South Brent TQ10 ......134 E1
Shute Ct TQ14 ....209 A8
Shute Hill
  Bishopsteignton TQ14 ..209 A8
  Malborough TQ7 ....147 E6
  Teignmouth TQ14 ....210 C5
Shute Hill Cres TQ10 ...210 C5
Shute La Combe Martin EX34 ..3 A4
  Denbury TQ12 ....211 A6
  Huish Champflower TA4 ..35 C8
  Monkton Wyld DT6 ......199 C1
  Morehampstead TQ13 ..111 F5
  Winkleigh EX19 ....58 F2
Shute Meadow St 2
  EX8 ....202 A7
Shute Park Rd PL9 ......256 A7
Shute Pk TQ7 ....147 E6
Shute Prim Sch EX13 ...103 B8
Shute Rd Kilmington EX13 ..87 C1
  Totnes TQ9 ....223 A7
Shute Row TQ11 ....160 E5
Shute Wood EX38 ....58 F6
Shuteleigh TA21 ....160 E5
Shutes Mead EX11 ....169 E4
Shutscombe Hill EX32 ...18 E5
Shutter Water Rd
  Westwood EX15 ....83 C1
  Whimple EX5 ....99 C8
Shuttern Cl EX5 ....172 A8
Shutterton La End EX7 ..200 F1
Shutterton La EX7 ....201 A3
Sicklemans Ct TQ7 ......144 C1
Sid La EX10 ....188 C5
Sid Park Rd EX10 ....188 B5
Sid Vale Cl EX10 ....101 B1
Sidborough Hill EX17 ....61 B1
Sidbury CE Prim Sch
  EX10 ....101 C2
Sidcliffe EX10 ....188 C6
Siddalls Gdns EX16 ......161 E5
Siddals Gdns EX14 ......166 B4
Side Wood La EX36 ....32 A1
Sideling Cl EX2 ....114 A6
Sideling Fields EX16 ....161 E5
Sidford Cross EX10 ......188 E7
Sidford Rd EX10 ....188 B7
Sidgard Rd EX10 ....188 C6
Sidholme Cotts EX10 ....188 B5
Siding Cross TQ10 ....137 E8
Sidings The
  Braunton EX33 ....152 D6
  Kingsbridge TQ7 ....258 C5
Sidleigh EX10 ....188 C5
Sidmont Gdns EX10 ......188 C5
Sidmouth Coll EX10 .....188 C7
Sidmouth Hosp EX10 ....188 B4
Sidmouth Int Sch EX10 ..188 B3
Sidmouth Junc Cross
  EX14 ....84 D2
Sidmouth Rd
  Bradninch EX5 ....83 B5

Sidmouth Rd continued
  Clyst St Mary EX2,EX5 ...179 A3
  Colyton EX24 ....103 A4
  Exeter EX2 ....178 D5
  Exeter EX2 ....178 E4
  Honiton EX14 ....166 A3
  Lyme Regis DT7 ....260 C3
  Ottery St Mary EX11 ...169 E2
Sidney Cl 3 EX7 ....200 D6
Sidvale Ct 2 EX10 ......101 B1
Sidwell St EX4 ....261 C4
Sidwell St EX4 ....261 C4
Sigford Cross TQ13 ......122 B2
Sign of the Owl Cross
  TQ10 ....137 E8
Signal Terr EX31 ....154 F6
Signal Terr EX31 ....154 F4
Signals The EX14 ....84 D2
Signpost La EX17 ....80 A7
Silbury Terr EX17 ....165 C5
Silver Head Hill TQ9 ....216 F1
Silver La Exeter EX4 ....261 C4
  Rockbeare EX5 ....99 C5
Silver Lea EX13 ....87 C1
Silver St
  Appledore EX39 ....155 A1
  Axminster EX13 ....167 D5
  11 Barnstaple EX16 ..34 B1
  Barnstaple EX32 ....155 A5
  Bere Ferrers PL20 ......240 A3
  Berrynarbor EX34 ....2 E3
  Bideford EX39 ....157 A1
  Braunton EX33 ....152 D7
  Buckfastleigh TQ11 ....236 B5
  Colyton EX24 ....103 A5
  Culmstock EX15 ....66 D8
  Honiton EX14 ....166 C6
  Ipplepen TQ12 ....211 C1
  Kentisbeare EX15 ....66 A3
  Kilmington EX13 ....87 C1
  Lydford EX20 ....107 F3
  Lyme Regis DT7 ....260 D3
  Ottery St Mary EX11 ...169 D4
  Saltash PL12 ....243 A2
  Thorverton EX5 ....81 E4
  Tiverton EX16 ....161 D4
  West Buckland TA21 .....52 F7
  Willand EX15 ....162 D4
Silver Stream Way PL8 ...257 B5
Silver Terr Exeter EX4 ...261 C4
  Plymouth PL4 ....263 A3
Silverdale Exmouth EX8 ..196 E3
Silverdale Cres EX5 ......82 B6
Silverdale Cl TA12 ....33 E4
Silverhills Rd TQ12 .....212 D8
Silvers The EX3 ....178 F2
Silverton CE Prim Sch
  EX5 ....82 B5
Silverton Rd EX2 ....181 D8
Silverway EX17 ....80 E4
Silverwell Pk PL21 ......137 C2
Silverwood Ave TQ12 ....207 E1
Silworthy Cross EX22 ...38 F2
Simcoe Pl EX15 ....67 B8
Simcoe Way EX14 ....67 B1
Simey Cl EX4 ....176 F7
Simmonds Pl EX15 ......163 E4
Simmons Cl EX20 ....170 C5
Simmons Way EX20 ......170 C4
Simms Hill TQ12,TQ13 ..122 C2
Simon Cl PL7 ....255 E6
Simonsburn Cross EX13 ..87 E4
Sinai Hill EX35 ....151 B5
Sing's La EX33 ....152 D5
Singer Cl TQ3 ....219 D3
Singmore Rd TQ3 ....218 E2
Sir Alex Wlk EX3 ....182 E5
Sir John Hunt Com Coll
  PL5 ....244 D4
Sir Robert's Path EX31 ...4 D5
Siskin Chase EX2 ....163 A2
Sitwell Mews EX2 ....177 F5
Sivell Pl EX2 ....177 F5
Six Acre Cross EX35 ......5 A4
Six Acre La EX35 ....5 A5
Six Mile Hill
  Doddiscombsleigh EX6 ...113 A8
  Tedburn St Mary EX6 ...98 A5
Skardale Gdns PL6 ......249 D8
Skardon Pl PL4 ....263 A4
Skern Cl EX39 ....156 F8
Skern Way EX39 ....156 F8
Skerries Rd PL6 ....244 F7
Skinnard La PL18 ....125 C5
Skinner Cl EX16 ....161 B4
Skirhead La EX14 ....84 A4
Skye Cl TQ2 ....213 E2
Skylark Rise PL6 ....245 E8
Skylark Spinney 3
  EX31 ....154 A2
Skyways Bsns Pk EX5 ...99 A4
Slade EX39 ....156 E2
Slade Cl
  Ottery St Mary EX11 ...169 F4
  Plymouth PL9 ....256 A5
Slade Cross
  Kingsbridge TQ7 ....144 B6

Slade Cross continued
  Lustleigh TQ13 ....122 D8
  North Tawton EX20 ......77 D5
Slade La
  Abbotskerswell TQ12 ...212 B6
  Combe Martin EX31 ......3 B4
  Galmpton TQ5 ....229 B5
  Hawkridge TA22 ....21 D1
  Sidmouth EX10 ....189 C7
  West Anstey EX36 ....32 B6
Slade Lane Cross EX34 ...3 E1
Slade Rd
  Ilfracombe EX34 ....150 F3
  Ottery St Mary EX11 ...169 F3
Slade Valley Rd EX34 ...150 A3
Sladnor Park Rd TQ1 ...214 C5
Sladnor Pk TQ1 ....214 C5
Slannes Mdw TQ12 ......207 D6
Slappers Hill TQ4,TQ5 ..234 E7
Slatelands Cl PL7 ....251 B3
Slattenslade La EX31 .....4 D5
Sleap Hill EX9 ....198 C7
Sleepy La TQ3 ....219 A1
Sletchcott Cross EX37 ...44 E8
Slew Hill EX34 ....2 C2
Slewhill Cross EX20 .....95 B5
Slewton Cres EX5 ....99 E8
Slipper Stone Dr PL21 ...237 A6
Slipperstone TQ9 ....139 A7
Slipperstone Cross TQ9 ..216 C7
Slipperstone La TQ9 .....216 C7
Slittercombe La EX6 ....194 E3
Sloe La 4 EX32 ....17 B2
Slough La
  Bishops Nympton EX36 ...30 F3
  Upottery EX14 ....68 C5
Small La Broadclyst EX5 ..175 D7
  Burlescombe EX16 ....62 E5
Small Pt TQ7 ....135 D3
Rattery TQ10 ....135 D3
Smallack Cl PL6 ....244 F2
Smallack Dr PL6 ....244 F2
Smallacombe Dross
  TQ10 ....135 D6
Smallacombe Hill EX16,
  EX36 ....32 D4
Smallacombe La EX36 ....31 F8
Smallacombe Rd EX16 ..161 B4
Smallacott Hill EX16 .....27 D7
Smallcombe Cross TQ3 ..225 E8
Smallcombe Rd TQ3 ....225 E8
Smalldon La TQ2 ....214 B3
Smallridge Cl PL9 ....255 F5
Smallridge Rd EX13 ......87 F4
Smallwell La
  Ashprington TQ9 ....139 E7
  Marldon TQ3 ....218 C3
Smardon Ave TQ5 ....230 A5
Smeardon La EX20 ......170 A5
Smeathy La EX15 ....52 F3
Smeaton Sq PL3 ....249 D6
Smiter's Pit La EX13 ....167 A1
Smith Field Rd EX2 .....181 A8
Smith Hill TQ14 ....208 F8
Smith Rd TQ6 ....233 F3
Smith's La
  Calverleigh EX16 ....48 E3
  Hollocombe EX18 ....58 E6
Smithay Mdws EX6 .....113 A8
Smithfield Dr PL12 ......242 B3
Smithfields TQ9 ....223 A6
Smiths Ct EX2 ....261 A1
Smiths Way PL12 ....242 B3
Smockpark La PL9 ....140 B8
Smokey Cross TQ13 ....122 B3
Smugglers' La EX7 ......210 F8
Smythen Cross EX34 .....9 E6
Smythen St EX1,EX4 ...261 A2
Smythen St EX1,EX4 ...261 A2
Snell Dr PL12 ....242 B3
Snobrook Cross EX10 ...101 C1
Snowberry Cl TQ1 ....219 F7
Snowdonia Cl TQ4 ......225 D4
Snowdrop Cl 2 EX14 ...84 D2
Snowdrop La PL6 ....245 D8
Snowdrop Mews EX4 ...176 D8
Snows EX17 ....80 B5
Snydles La EX37 ....44 B6
Sog's La EX10 ....100 C2
Solar Cres EX4 ....176 F4
Soldon Cross EX22 ....53 E5
Solland Cross EX20 ....76 D4
Solland La EX20 ....177 A1
Soloman Dr EX39 ....157 A1
Solsbro Rd TQ2 ....219 E4
Solways DT7 ....260 C5
Somerfields DT7 ....260 C3
Somerlea EX21 ....73 E2
Somers Rd DT7 ....260 D3
Somerset Ave EX4 ......176 E4
Somerset Cotts 7 PL3 ..248 A4
Somerset Ct
  10 Brixham TQ5 .....230 C5
  17 Totnes TQ9 ......223 D5
Somerset Pl
  8 Barnstaple EX32 ..154 F5
  Plymouth PL3 ....248 A4
  10 Teignmouth TQ14 ..210 B4
  Totnes TQ9 ....223 D5
Somerset Place La 8
  PL3 ....248 A4
Somerslea EX21 ....73 E2
Something La EX33 ....7 E1
Somerville Cl
  Exmouth EX8 ....196 D1

Somerville Cl continued
Willand EX15 ....162 C5
Somerville Pk EX15 ......162 C4
Somerville Rd EX15 ......162 C5
Sommers' Cres EX34 ....150 C6
Soper Rd TQ14 ....210 A7
Soper's Wlk TQ14 ....210 A7
Soper's Hill PL5 ....240 E1
Sophia Way TQ12 ....207 A2
Sorley Green Cross TQ7 .143 F5
Sorley La TQ7 ....143 F5
Sorley Tunnel Adventure
  Farm* TQ7 ....143 F5
Sorrell Cl TQ12 ....207 D7
Sorrento TQ2 ....220 C5
South Ave Bideford EX39 .157 D1
  Exeter EX1 ....177 E6
  Lyme Regis DT7 ....260 D4
South Bank Dr EX39 ......156 F2
South Brent Prim Sch
  TQ10 ....135 A3
South Brent Rd TQ7 .....143 E7
South Burrow Rd [10]
  EX34 ....150 B5
South Church La EX20 .170 A4
South Common La EX13 ..88 A5
South Dartmoor Com Coll
  TQ13 ....131 A5
South Dartmoor Com Coll
  Sixth Form Ctr TQ13 ..131 A6
South Dean Cnr EX31 ......4 A5
South Dean La EX31 ....4 A5
South Devon Coll TQ1 ..219 F6
South Devon Rly*
  Buckfastleigh TQ11 ......236 E4
  * Staverton TQ9 ....215 D4
South Down Cross EX19 ..76 C7
South Down Farm TQ7 .147 E5
South Down La EX36 ......31 E6
South Down Rd
  Beer EX12 ....191 D5
  Plymouth PL2 ....248 B6
South Downs Rd EX7 ....204 D4
South Dr EX38 ....159 B5
South Emb TQ6 ....233 F3
South End Cl [6] EX13 ...152 D5
South Farm Rd EX9 ....198 C3
South Ford Rd TQ6 ....233 F3
South Furzeham Rd
  TQ5 ....230 C5
South Gate EX2 ....261 B2
South Gn [4] EX32 ....155 B4
South Grange EX2 ....178 D3
South Hams Bsns Pk
  TQ7 ....143 E4
South Hams Hospl TQ7 .258 C6
South Hayes Copse EX32 .17 B2
South Hayne Cross EX36 .31 B4
South Hele Cross EX16 ..35 C1
South Hill
  Plymouth, Hooe PL9 ....255 C5
  Plymouth, Stoke PL1 ....248 A3
South Hill Rd TQ1 ....220 C4
South La
  Braunton Fleming EX31 .11 F3
  Braunton EX33 ....15 E8
  Hartland EX39 ....22 E2
  Lynton EX35 ....5 F5
South Lawn Exeter EX2 .261 C2
  Sidmouth EX10 ....188 C8
South Lawn Terr EX1 ....177 F6
South Lea EX33 ....152 E5
South Lea Cl EX33 ....152 E5
South Lee Cross EX34 ..107 E6
South Ley Cross EX31 ....3 D1
South Milton St PL4 .....263 C2
South La
  EX36 ....158 C3
South Molton Com Hospl
  EX36 ....158 C4
South Molton Inf Sch
  EX36 ....158 C4
South Molton Mus*
  EX36 ....158 C4
South Molton Rd EX14 ..34 B1
South Molton St EX18 ...44 E1
South Molton United CE Jun
  Sch EX36 ....158 C5
South Moor La EX17 ......59 E1
South Par EX9 ....199 H2
South Parks Rd TQ2 .....213 F2
South Pk
  Barnstaple EX32 ....155 B3
  Braunton EX33 ....152 F5
  Woolfardisworthy EX39 ..38 F7
South Rd
  [10] Appledore EX39 ....15 A1
  Newton Abbot TQ12 ....207 B2
South Sands TQ4 ....226 C2
South Sq [10] EX24 ......103 A4
South St Axminster EX13 .167 D5
  Barnstaple EX32 ....155 B2
  Barnstaple EX32 ....155 B3
  Braunton EX33 ....152 D5
  Colyton EX24 ....103 A4
  Denbury TQ12 ....211 A6
  Dolton EX19 ....57 F7
  Exeter EX1 ....261 B2
  Exmouth EX8 ....202 A6
  Great Torrington EX38 ..159 C5
  Hatherleigh EX20 ....75 C7
  Holcombe Rogus TA21 ..50 F5
  Sheepwash EX21 ....56 C1
  South Molton EX36 ....158 C4
  Torquay TQ2 ....219 F6

South St continued
Totnes TQ9 ....223 C5
Wellington TA21 ....160 E5
Winkleigh EX19 ....58 F3
Woodacombe EX34 ....7 F6
South Tawton Prim Sch
  EX20 ....95 B4
South Trelawny Prim Sch
  PL2 ....248 A8
South View
  Abbotskerswell TQ12 ....212 B6
  Ashford EX31 ....16 C7
  Barnstaple EX31 ....154 D7
  Bideford EX39 ....156 F2
  Bovey Tracey TQ13 ......180 D7
  Braunton EX33 ....152 D4
  [5] Hempock EX15 ....67 B8
  [10] Horrabridge PL20 ..126 F4
  Ilfracombe EX34 ....1 E3
  Lydford EX20 ....171 B8
  Mary Tavy PL19 ....117 E6
  Plymouth, Crownhill PL5 ..244 E2
  Plymouth, Elburton PL9 ..256 B6
  Westleigh EX16 ....51 A3
South View Cl
  Braunton EX33 ....152 D4
  Plymouth PL7 ....250 D7
  Willand EX15 ....162 D5
South View Est EX15 ....162 D5
South View Pk PL7 ....250 D7
South View Rd EX15 ....162 D5
South View Terr
  Exeter EX4 ....177 D8
  Exminster EX6 ....182 B4
  Plymouth PL4 ....263 C3
  Sidmouth EX10 ....188 A5
South Yeo Cross
  Cheriton Fitzpaine EX17 ..62 E3
  Northlew EX20 ....74 F2
  Bovey Tracey TQ13 ......180 E8
  Otterton EX10 ....187 B1
  Rockbeare EX5 ....99 C7
Southbrook Rd
  Bovey Tracey TQ13 ......180 C8
  Exeter EX4 ....178 A2
Southcott CE EX2 ....178 A2
Southcombe Cross
  Hittisleigh EX6 ....96 F4
  Widecombe in the Moor
  TQ13 ....121 B3
Southcombe Hill EX6 .....96 F4
Southcombe St TQ13 ....111 A6
Southcoombe Terr
  EX12 ....192 E7
Sparrow La TA24 ....21 C7
Sparrow Pk TQ7 ....147 F6
Sparrow Rd TQ9 ....223 B5
Speakers Rd PL21 ....237 E5
Speares The PL22 ....242 B2
Spearfield Cl EX36 ....158 D4
Spears La TA21 ....155 F3
Speedwell Cl
  Barnstaple EX32 ....155 B3
  Brixham TQ5 ....230 C3
  Millbrook PL10 ....252 F5
  Speedwell Units TQ6 ...233 C3
Speedwell Wlk PL6 ....249 B7
Spekes Cross EX18 ......59 C4
Spence Combe Cross
  EX17 ....79 C4
Spence Cross EX14 ....84 D4
Spence La DT6 ....104 F7
Spencer Cl EX8 ....196 E2
Spencer Ct EX11 ....169 D3
Spencer Dr EX16 ....161 F3
Spencer Gdns PL12 .....242 F1
Spencer Rd
  Newton Abbot TQ12 ....207 C2
  Paignton TQ3 ....225 E7
  Plymouth PL9 ....255 E8
  Spenser Ave EX2 ....94 C3
  Speranza Gr [7] TQ14 ..210 B5
  Spestos La EX17 ....78 C1
  Spicer Cl EX15 ....163 B2
  Spicer Rd EX1 ....261 C3
  Spicers Rd TQ13,EX6 ..114 A1
  Spider's La EX8 ....196 C3
  Spidery Mdw TQ6 ....233 B3
  Spinaker Quay PL9 ......255 B5
  Spindlebury EX15 ....163 A2
  Spindlewood Cl EX14 ...166 C2
  Spinney Cl EX2 ....178 C4
  Spinney The
  Ivybridge PL21 ....237 A5
  Plymouth PL7 ....251 A4
  Uffculme EX15 ....66 A8
Spinning Bath Gdns
  EX17 ....165 C4
Spinning La EX13 ....104 B8
Spire Ct PL3 ....249 B5
Spire Hill Pk PL12 ....242 C2
Spire Lake Cl EX36 ......79 C4
Spire's Cross EX20 ....77 A3
Spirelake Cross EX17 ....79 C8
Spirelake Hill EX17 ....79 C8
Spitfire Wlk EX32 ....155 C2
Spithead TQ6 ....233 F3
Spittis Pk TQ6 ....234 B3
Spittle Cross EX18 ....44 D4
Spittles La DT7 ....260 E4
Spitup La EX10 ....187 E7

Southford La TQ9 ....216 A4
Southgate Ave PL9 ....255 E4
Southgate Cl PL9 ....255 E4
Southgate Ct [7] EX2 ....261 B2
Southland Park Cres [8]
  PL9 ....140 D8
Southland Park Rd PL9 .140 D8
Southlands EX33 ....152 E4
Southleigh EX39 ....156 D6
Southleigh Hill Cross
  EX24 ....102 B3
Southleigh Rd EX24 .....102 E5
Southley Rd EX36 ....158 C4
Southmead Prim Sch
  EX33 ....152 E4
Southport Ave EX4 ....176 E5
Southside Ope [4] PL1 ..263 A2
Southside St PL1 ....263 A2
Soutown
  Dartmouth TQ6 ....233 F2
  Kenton EX6 ....194 F3
Southview PL10 ....253 A6
Southview Rd TQ3 ....226 A7
Southville Gdns TQ4 ...258 D3
Southway Sidmouth EX10 .188 C4
  Tedburn St Mary EX6 ....97 F4
Southway Ave TQ2 ....213 F1
Southway Com Coll PL6 .244 F6
Southway Dr PL6 ....244 E6
Southway La TA20 ....69 C4
Southway La
  Plymouth, Southway PL6 .245 B6
  Plymouth, Tamerton Foliot
  PL6 ....244 C6
  Southway Prim Sch PL6 .244 E6
Southwell Rd PL6 ....244 E6
Southwood Cross EX5 ....99 C4
Southwood Ct TQ1 ....220 C5
Southwood Dr EX39 .....157 A3
Southwood Rd PL18 .....125 D6
Sovereign Cl EX8 ....196 E1
Sovereign Ct PL7 ....250 C5
Sovereign Mews TQ2 ...214 B2
Sowden La
  Barnstaple EX32 ....155 B5
  Lympstone EX8 ....195 E4
Sowden Pk EX32 ....155 C4
Sowton Ind Est EX2 .....178 E5
Sowton La EX5 ....179 B6
Spa Ct TQ1 ....220 C4
Space Pl EX2 ....177 C1
Spanish Lane End TQ9 .139 A5
Spanishlake Cross EX6 .113 C6
Sparhanger Cross EX35 ..5 B3
Sparhanger La EX35 ......5 B3
Sparkatown La PL20 .....127 B3
Sparke Cl PL7 ....251 B4
Sparks Barn Rd TQ4 ....226 C3
Sparkwell CE Prim Sch
  PL7 ....251 F8

Splatford Dr EX15 ....163 C5
Splatts Cross EX19 ....76 C7
Splitwell Cross EX17 ......82 B2
Spreacombe Gdns EX33 ...8 C4
Spreyton Cross EX17 .....96 A7
Spreyton Prim Sch EX17 ..96 A7
Spring Cl
  Newton Abbot TQ12 ....206 E4
  Northam EX39 ....156 E6
Spring Field EX39 ....22 D3
Spring Gdns EX11 ....169 E3
Spring Head Rd DT7 ....260 B6
Spring Hill PL19 ....171 B5
Spring Pk PL6 ....245 E7
Spring Rd PL9 ....140 B8
Springdale Cl TQ5 ....230 C2
Springfield
  Dunkeswell EX14 ....67 C2
  Membury EX13 ....87 D6
Springfield Ave
  Barnstaple EX32 ....155 B3
  Plymouth PL9 ....256 B6
Springfield Cl PL9 ....256 B7
Springfield Cres
  Fremington EX31 ....153 F6
  Northam EX39 ....156 F7
Springfield Dr
  Kingsbridge TQ7 ....258 C5
  Plymouth PL3 ....248 A4
  Tiverton EX16 ....161 B4
Springfield Gdns EX7 ...200 F1
Springfield La PL9 ....256 B7
Springfield Pk EX20 .....107 F8
Springfield Rd
  Barnstaple EX31 ....154 B3
  Exeter EX4 ....177 D8
  Exmouth EX8 ....196 B1
  Honiton EX14 ....166 F5
  Ilfracombe EX34 ....150 B6
  Offwell EX14 ....86 A3
  Plymouth PL9 ....256 B6
  South Brent TQ10 ....134 F3
  Torquay TQ1 ....220 B7
  Wellington TA21 ....160 C7
  Woolacombe EX34 ....8 A6
Springfield Rise PL9 ....256 B7
Springfield Terr
  [1] Bideford EX39 ....157 B1
  [11] Combe Martin EX34 ..3 A3
  Dawlish EX7 ....204 E6
  Westward Ho! EX39 .....156 C7
Springfields EX24 ....103 A3
Springhead Cross EX13 .193 A6
Springhead La EX13 ......87 C1
Springhill PL2 ....248 C8
Springhill Down Hill
  EX16 ....47 A2
Springhill Gdns DT7 ....260 D4
Springhill Gn PL2 ....248 C8
Springhill Rd TQ9 ....223 E5
Springwood Cl
  Ivybridge PL21 ....237 E5
  Plymouth PL7 ....251 A3
Spruce Cl Exeter EX4 ...176 E2
  Exmouth EX8 ....196 D3
Spruce Gdns PL7 ....251 B5
Spruce Pk EX17 ....165 C4
Spruce Way TQ3 ....225 E8
Spry La PL16 ....106 A4
Sprys Shop Cross EX21 .72 D2
Sprytown Cross PL16 ...106 B4
Spryfield Cross EX21 ....56 A1
Spur Cross EX39 ....22 C7
Spurway Gdns EX34 ......3 B3
Spurway Hill EX16 ....48 A7
Spurway Hill Cross EX16 .48 A8
Spurway Rd EX16 ....161 F3
Square [6] EX22 ....38 D1
Square The
  Barnstaple EX32 ....154 F4
  Beer EX12 ....191 D5
  [10] Beere Alston PL20 .125 E1
  [3] Bishop's Tawton EX32 ..16 E1
  Bridestowe EX20 ....107 F8
  Cawsand PL10 ....253 A1
  Chagford TQ13 ....111 A6
  Chittlehampton EX37 ....28 E4
  Chulmleigh EX18 ....44 E1
  Ermington PL21 ....136 F4
  Exeter EX4 ....176 F8
  Galmpton TQ7 ....147 B6
  Hatherleigh EX20 ....75 C7
  [5] Ilfracombe EX34 .....150 B6
  Kingswear TQ6 ....234 A3
  Lutton PL21 ....133 B2
  Moretonhampstead TQ13 .111 F5
  North Molton EX36 ......30 D8
  [6] Northam EX39 ....156 F7
  Petrockstow EX20 ....56 D6
  Plymouth, Hooe PL9 ....256 A4
  Plymouth, Stonehouse PL1 .248 A2
  Saltash PL12 ....242 C3
  Sandford EX17 ....80 A5
  [7] Seaton EX12 ....192 A5
  Sidbury EX10 ....101 B2
  Sidmouth EX10 ....188 D7
  South Molton EX36 ......158 C4
  Ugborough PL21 ....137 D6
  Wellington TA21 ....160 F9
  Witheridge EX16 ....46 E1
Square's Quay TQ7 ......258 C4
Squire's La EX12 ....192 C5
Squires Cl EX32 ....155 B2

Squires Cotts PL20 ......128 B8
Squires' La Shebbear EX21 .55 D6
  Shebbear EX21 ....55 D7
Squirrel Ct TA21 ....160 D5
Stabb Cl TQ4 ....226 A1
Stabb Dr TQ4 ....226 A1
Stabdon La EX20 ....59 C1
Stable La TQ1 ....214 B1
Stables The TQ9 ....223 D6
Stadbury Cross EX14 .....86 B7
Stadbury La EX14 ....86 C5
Staddens Lea La TQ2 ...219 C6
Staddiscombe Rd PL9 ..255 F4
Staddon Cl
  Braunton EX33 ....152 C6
  Exeter EX4 ....178 B7
Staddon Court Cotts
  PL9 ....140 B8
Staddon Cres PL9 ....255 E6
Staddon Cres EX22 ....72 C6
Staddon Gate EX20 ....77 D5
Staddon Gdns TQ2 .....214 B2
Staddon Gn PL9 ....255 D6
Staddon La PL9 ....255 B4
Staddon Moor Cross
  EX20 ....77 D5
Staddon Park Rd PL9 ..255 E6
Staddon Rd
  Appledore EX39 ....15 A3
  Holsworthy EX22 ....164 F3
  Tedburn St Mary EX6 ....97 E2
Staddon Terrace La
  PL1 ....262 B4
Staddonhill Rd TA24 .....21 F6
Staddons View TQ13 ...180 C8
Stadium Dr TQ12 ....213 A2
Stafflick Cl EX6 ....194 E3
Stafford Cross EX24 .....102 D2
Stafford Ct [1] TQ9 ......223 E5
Stafford Hill EX14 ....84 F8
Stafford La EX24 ....103 A3
Stafford Rd Dolton EX19 .57 F7
  Exeter EX4 ....176 F5
  Paignton TQ4 ....226 C5
Stafford Way EX19 ....57 F7
Stag La
  Plymouth, Elburton PL9 .256 B8
  Plymouth, Plympton PL7 .250 B3
Stag Mill Cross EX16 ....50 B3
Staggers La EX33 ....152 E3
Stags Wood Dr EX21 .....73 E2
Stakes Hill TQ7 ....143 A5
Stallards Braunton EX33 .152 C7
  Wellington TA21 ....160 C3
Stamford Cl PL9 ....255 B6
Stamford Fort Cotts
  PL9 ....255 A6
Stamford La PL9 ....255 A6
Stammery Hill EX13 ....88 C1
Stamps Hill PL8 ....257 A6
Stamps The PL17 ....125 A5
Stanborough Cross PL9 .256 B7
Stanborough Rd PL9 ...256 B7
Stanbridge Pk EX39 ....156 D2
Stanbury Ave PL6 ....244 F1
Stanbury Cl PL15 ....90 C1
Stanbury Copse EX34 ..150 A4
Stanbury Cross
  Holsworthy EX22 ....164 D6
  Morwenstow EX23 ....36 F3
Stanbury Cross EX7 .....54 A6
Stanbury Rd Knowle EX33 .8 D1
  Torquay TQ2 ....219 C7
Stanbury's Orch EX6 ....96 F8
Stancombe Cross TQ7 .144 E4
Standard Ct PL19 ....117 E6
Standard Rd PL2 ....248 B8
Standarhay Cl PL9 ....256 C7
Standarhay Villas PL9 ..256 C7
Stanfield TQ2 ....213 D3
Stanford Rd EX2 ....178 C5
Stang La EX34 ....8 F5
Stangray Ave PL4 ....248 F4
Stanhope Cl EX22 ....164 C5
Stanhope Dr EX22 ....164 C4
Stanhope Rd PL5 ....243 D7
Stanhope Sq [7] EX22 ..164 C4
Stanhope Terr EX39 .....157 A3
Stani Forth Dr PL21 ....237 D4
Stanley Gdns TQ3 ....226 A7
Stanley Mews EX9 ......198 A1
Stanley Pl PL4 ....249 B2
Stanley Rd TQ1 ....220 C8
Stanley Sq EX33 ....8 B3
Stanley St [1] PL4 ....249 A2
Stanley Wlk EX38 ....196 D4
Stanmere Rise EX7 .....204 E7
Stanmore Tor TQ3 ....226 A5
Stannary Bridge Rd
  PL19 ....171 D6
Stannary Cl PL21 ....237 E5
Stannary Pl TQ13 ....111 A6
Stansfeld Ave TQ3 ....226 A6
Stant Way TA20 ....69 F6
Stantaway Hill TQ1 .....219 F7
Stantaway Pk TQ1 ....219 F7
Stanton Ct TQ7 ....143 A3
Stantor La TQ3 ....218 F7
Stantway Cross EX39 ..156 B8
Stantyway Ct EX9 ....198 F5
Stantyway Rd EX9 ....198 F5
Stanwell Dr EX39 ....156 C6
Stanwell Hill EX39 ....156 C6
Stanwey EX1 ....178 A5
Staplake La EX6 ....201 A7
Staplake Rd EX6 ....195 B1
Staplake Rise EX6 ....195 A1
Staple Back La EX19 ....57 B8

Staple Cl Pl.6 ....241 C1
Staple Cross EX19 ....57 F5
Staple Orch TQ9 ....222 F8
Stapleback Cross EX19 .....57 E5
Stapledon La TQ13 ....130 F5
Stapleford Gdns PL5 ......243 F5
Staplegate EX16 ....50 A3
Staplehill Rd
  Liverton TQ12 ....122 F1
  Newton Abbot TQ12 ......206 B8
Staples Mdw TA20 ....88 D8
Staples Mews 4 EX8 ......202 A7
Staples Terr DT7 ....260 E4
Stapleton Cl TQ4 ....225 E3
Star Barton La EX5 ....172 D4
Star Cross EX13 ....87 E6
Star Pk PL18 ....125 D6
Starcombe La EX10 ....101 D4
Starcross Prim Sch EX6 ....201 A8
Starcross Sta EX6 ....201 B8
Starkey Cl TQ12 ....64 D7
Starlings Roost EX15 ......163 A2
Starpitts Gr TQ2 ....214 B3
Starpitten La W TQ2 ......214 A2
Starre Cl EX22 ....192 A7
Start Ave Chillington TQ7 .145 E3
  Teignmouth TQ14 ....210 C7
Start Bay Pk TQ6 ....145 F6
Start Cross TQ12 ....211 A7
Starved Oak Cross EX5 .....81 D1
Station App TQ10 ....134 F3
Station Bsns Pk TQ14 ......210 C5
Station Cl EX33 ....152 D5
Station Cotts
  Bittaford TQ10 ....137 E8
  Brandis Corner EX22 .....73 A5
Station Cross
  Bittaford TQ10 ....137 E8
  Crediton EX17 ....165 E4
Station Ct TQ13 ....180 C7
Station Fields EX21 ....73 E2
Station Hill
  Bideford EX39 ....157 B1
  Bratton Fleming EX31 .....11 A1
  Brixham TQ5 ....230 C5
  Great Torrington EX38 ...159 A6
  Lynton EX35 ....151 B4
  Swimbridge EX32 ....17 E1
Station La Calstock PL18 ..125 D3
  Paignton TQ4 ....226 B5
Station Rd Bampton EX16 ..34 B1
  Barnstaple EX31 ....154 F4
  Bere Alston PL20 ....125 E1
  Bere Ferrers PL20 ....239 E3
  Bovey Tracey TQ13 ......180 C7
  Bow EX17 ....78 B3
  Bratton Fleming EX31 .....18 A8
  Braunton EX33 ....152 D5
  Bridestowe EX20 ....107 F7
  Broadclyst EX5 ....175 E3
  Bucklastleigh TQ11 ......236 C5
  Budleigh Salterton EX9 ..198 A1
  Burlescombe EX16 ....51 B3
  Chard Junction TA20 .....88 D8
  Chudleigh EX18 ....44 C3
  Colyton EX24 ....103 A5
  Cullompton EX15 ....163 C4
17 Dawlish EX7 ....204 E6
  Exeter, Pinhoe EX1 ......174 E6
  Exeter, St David's EX4 ...177 A8
  Exminster EX6 ....182 D3
  Exton EX3 ....183 C1
  Feniton EX14 ....84 D2
  Gunnislake PL18 ....125 C6
  Halwill Junction EX21 ....73 E2
  Hele EX5 ....82 F5
  Hemyock EX15 ....67 B8
  Holsworthy EX22 ....164 C4
  Horrabridge PL20 ....126 F4
  Ide EX2 ....176 D1
  Ilfracombe EX34 ....150 A4
  Ivybridge PL21 ....237 D6
  Lifton PL16 ....105 F4
  Lydford EX20 ....108 A6
  Mary Tavy PL19 ....117 E6
  Moreton TQ13 ....57 C2
  Moretonhampstead TQ13 ..111 F4
  Newton Abbot TQ12 ......207 D3
  Newton Poppleford EX10 ..186 F8
  Newton St Cyres EX5 ......81 A1
  North Brentor PL19 ......117 C8
  Northlew EX20 ....74 E1
  Okehampton EX20 ....170 B4
  Plymouth, Elburton PL9 ..256 C7
  Plymouth, Keyham PL2 ...247 E5
  Plymouth, Plympton PL7 .250 E5
  Plymouth, Tamerton Foliot
    PL5 ....244 A6
  Princetown PL20 ....128 A8
  Saltash PL12 ....243 A2
  Sidmouth EX10 ....188 A4
7 South Brent TQ10 ......134 F3
  South Molton EX36 ....158 D5
3 Teignmouth TQ14 ......210 C4
  Tiverton EX16 ....161 D4
  Topsham EX3 ....182 F5
  Totnes TQ9 ....223 C6
  Wellington TA21 ....160 C7
  Willand EX15 ....162 C5
  Woolacombe EX34 ....8 A6
  Yelverton PL20 ....127 A2
  Yeoford EX17 ....79 C1
Station Road Ind Est
  EX15 ....67 B8
Station View PL19 ....117 C8
Station Yard Ind Est
  TQ7 ....258 C5
Staverton Cotts TQ13 .....130 F4

Staverton Sta* TQ9 ....215 E4
Stawley Prim Sch TA21 ....51 B8
Ste Honorine Du Fay Cl
  EX32 ....28 E8
Steamer Quay Rd TQ9 ....223 D4
Steamer Quay Wharf 11
  TQ9 ....223 D5
Stearfield Rd TQ13 ....226 C7
Steddaford Ct EX20 ....95 A5
Steed Cl TQ4 ....229 A8
Steel Cl EX14 ....166 D6
Steep Head EX36 ....19 B1
Steep Hill TQ1 ....214 D6
Steephill La Landkey EX32 .17 D2
  Upton TA22 ....34 C8
Steepleton Cl EX20 ......170 D5
Steeple Cl PL9 ....255 F5
Steeple Dr EX2 ....181 B8
Steer Park Rd PL7 ....251 C5
Steer Point Cotts PL8 ....256 F2
Steer Point Rd PL8 ......257 A4
Stefan Cl PL9 ....255 B5
Stella Maris Ct EX39 .....157 A2
Stella Rd TQ3 ....219 A1
Stenlake Pl PL4 ....249 B2
Stenlake Terr PL4 ....249 B2
Stentaway Cl PL9 ....255 F8
Stentaway Dr PL9 ....255 F8
Stentaway La EX33 ....7 E2
Stentaway Rd PL9 ....255 F8
Stentiford Hill TQ7 ......258 D7
Stentiford Hill Rd TQ1 ...220 B5
Stentiford La TQ13 ......122 D4
Stepcote Hill EX1 ....261 A2
Steppes Mdw TQ12 ......207 A2
Steppingstone Cross EX33 .8 D1
Stepps Cross La EX12,DT7 .193 A5
Stepps Cl La EX17 ....174 F1
Steps Cross TQ2 ....214 B3
Steps Cross Specl Sch
  TQ2 ....214 B3
Steps La TQ2 ....214 B3
Stepstone La EX33 ....220 C1
Stern's Cross EX10 ....188 D8
Stevens Cross Cl EX10 ...188 E8
Stevens La EX10 ....188 A7
Stevenstone Ct EX38 .....42 A6
Stevenstone Rd EX4 ......196 C1
Stewart Cl EX8 ....196 E1
Stibb La PL21 ....136 D7
Stickle Path EX16 ....35 C1
Sticklepath Cl EX31 ......154 E3
Sticklepath Hill EX31 ....154 E4
Sticklepath Prim Sch
  Barnstaple EX31 ....154 C3
  Okehampton EX20 ....94 F5
Sticklepath Terr EX31 ....154 F4
Stidson Cross TQ10 ......135 B3
Stile La EX35 ....135 A3
Stile La DT7 ....260 D3
Stile Orch TQ7 ....143 F7
Stillman Ct 8 PL4 ....263 A2
Stillman St PL4 ....263 A2
Stiniel Cross TQ13 ......111 A4
Stintway La EX10 ....187 E5
Stirling Ct PL5 ....243 C1
Stirling Rd PL5 ....243 C1
Stitchill Rd TQ1 ....220 C4
Sitworthy Cross EX39 ....23 C1
Stoat Pk EX32 ....7 E3
Stoats Cl EX36 ....158 C2
Stoats Mews EX20 ....77 C4
Stock Hill EX35 ....151 A1
Stock La EX12 ....192 A5
Stock Rd EX35 ....5 B3
Stockadon La EX17 ....63 A1
Stocker Rd EX4 ....173 B1
Stockeydown La EX17 ....79 E2
Stockham Hill TA22 ......33 E8
Stockland CE Prim Sch
  EX14 ....87 A7
Stockland Head Cross
  EX15 ....84 B7
Stockland Hill EX14 ......86 E6
Stockleigh Cross
  Cheriton Fitzpaine EX17 ..62 C1
  Stockleigh Pomeroy EX17 .80 F6
Stockman La TA20 ....88 C7
Stockmeadow Gdns
  TQ14 ....209 A7
Stockstyle La EX17 ....88 A8
Stockton Ave EX7 ....204 E6
Stockton Hill EX7 ....204 D6
Stockton La EX7 ....204 D6
Stockton Rd EX7 ....204 D6
Stockwell Cross EX5 .....82 D5
Stoford La TA21 ....52 F7
Stoggy La PL7 ....251 A6
Stoke Canon CE Prim Sch
  EX5 ....173 F8
Stoke Climsland Prim Sch
  PL17 ....115 B3
Stoke Cross PL8 ....141 B5
Stoke Damerel Bsns Ctr 5
  PL3 ....248 A4
Stoke Damerel Coll
  PL3 ....248 A4
Stoke Damerel Prim Sch
  PL1 ....248 A3
Stoke Fleming Prim Sch
  TQ6 ....146 A2
Stoke Gabriel Prim Sch
  TQ9 ....227 F7
Stoke Gabriel Rd
  Galmpton TQ5 ....229 A5
  Paignton TQ5 ....228 E6

Stoke Hill Exeter EX4 ....173 E2
Stoke Canon EX5 ....173 F6
Stoke Gabriel TQ9 ....227 F7
Stoke Hill Cres EX4 ......173 E2
Stoke Hill Fst Sch EX4 ...173 E1
Stoke Hill La PL20 ....126 E2
Stoke Hill Mid Sch EX4 ..173 E1
Stoke House Gdns TQ6 ..146 B7
Stoke Lyne EX8 ....196 C1
Stoke Meadow Cl EX4 ....173 E2
Stoke Rd
  Higher Gabwell TQ1,TQ12 .214 C7
  Noss Mayo PL8 ....141 A6
  Paignton, Higher Yalberton
    TQ4 ....225 C3
  Paignton, Waddeton TQ5 .228 F6
  Plymouth PL1 ....262 A3
  Stoke Canon EX4,EX5 ....173 D5
Stoke Valley Rd EX4 .....173 D2
Stoke Woods Forest Wlks*
  EX4,EX5 ....173 B4
Stokeinteignhead Prim Sch
Stokelake TQ13 ....123 D5
Stokenham Area Prim Sch
  TQ7 ....145 B1
Stokenham Cross TQ7 ....145 B1
Stokes La EX15 ....263 A2
Stokes Mead EX5 ....184 D3
Stokingway Cl PL9 ....255 E5
Stone Barton Cl EX17 ....61 C3
Stone Barton La PL7 .....250 C6
Stone Barton Rd PL7 ....250 C6
Stone Cl EX14 ....166 B4
Stone Cross
  Chagford TQ13 ....96 A1
  Lifton PL16 ....105 E5
  Meeth EX20 ....57 C4
  Molland EX36 ....31 F7
  North Tawton EX20 ......77 E4
  West Buckland EX32 .....18 A4
  Widecombe in the Moor
    TQ13 ....121 B1
Stone La Lympstone EX8 ..195 E5
  Thorverton EX5 ....81 F7
Stone Lane Ret Pk Ex2 ...177 B3
Stone Moor Cross EX18 ..45 C1
Stone Pk TQ4 ....229 D6
Stone's Hill EX17 ....80 A7
Stoneacre Cl TQ5 ....230 C3
Stonebarrow La EX13 ....88 F2
Stoneborough Cnr EX9 ..198 B1
Stoneborough La EX9 ...198 B1
Stonebridge Hill EX9 ....198 B1
Stonecombe Hill EX31 ..10 C6
Stonehall Flats PL1 ......248 A1
Stonehanger Ct TQ8 ....259 D4
Stonehedge Cl PL21 .....237 D4
Stonehouse Bridge PL1 ..248 A1
Stonehouse St PL1 ......262 A2
Stoneland Cross EX16 ...47 F4
Stoneland La EX16 ......47 F5
Stonelands EX6 ....96 F3
Stonelands EX7 ....204 C6
Stonelands Mews EX7 ...204 C6
Stonelands Pk EX7 ......204 C6
Stonelands Terr EX7 ....204 C6
Stoneleigh
  Sidmouth EX10 ....189 C7
  Wellington TA21 ....160 B8
Stoneleigh Cl TQ12 ......168 A4
Stoneleigh Dr TQ2 ......219 D3
Stoneman's Hill TQ12 ...212 D7
Stonemans La EX38 ......159 C5
Stonemoor Cross EX38 ..56 B7
Stonemoor La EX36 ......31 F7
Stonepark TQ13 ....130 F4
Stonepark Cres TQ13 ...130 F4
Stoneridge La TA4 ....35 F5
Stones Cl
  6 Kingsteignton TQ12 ..123 F1
  Modbury PL21 ....137 C2
Stonewall Cross EX17 ...80 A7
Stonewall La EX17 ....165 C6
Stoney La Bradninch EX5 .82 F7
  Honiton EX14 ....166 D2
Stoney Lane Cross EX14 .50 B3
Stoney Lane Hill EX16 ...48 C2
Stoney Park La EX20 ....170 A4
Stoneyford Pk EX9 ......198 B1
Stoneyhill TQ12 ....212 B3
Stoneyhouse La EX14 ...86 D1
Stoneylands EX15 ....99 C5
Stoneywell Hill EX16 ....48 B3
Stoneywell 3 EX39 .....15 B1
Stoning Cross EX20 ......75 C7
Stony Close La EX12 ....192 E5
Stony Cnr EX34 ....3 D3
Stony Hill Cross EX36 ...31 A3
Stonylands La EX33 .....167 E6
Stony La Axminster EX13 .167 E6
  Gunnislake PL18 ....125 D6
  Hawkridge TA22 ....21 C3
  Landkey EX32 ....17 E1
  Lympstone EX8 ....195 F8
  Parracombe EX31 ....4 D1
  Swimbridge EX32 ....28 B8
  Woodbury Salterton EX5 .184 C6
Stony La End EX32 ......17 B1
Stonybridge Cross EX30 .30 B8
Stonybridge Hill EX36 ...30 B8
Stonypark La EX17 ......165 B5
Stoodleigh Cross
  Calverleigh EX16 ....48 B4
  West Buckland EX32 .....18 B2
Stoodleigh Moor Cross
  EX16 ....48 D6
Stoodley Knowle Convent
  Sch TQ1 ....220 F5

Stooke Bridge Rd EX15 ..83 C1
Stooks Cl EX5 ....81 E1
Stoop Cross TQ9 ....131 C1
Stooper's Hill TA20 ......69 F6
Stopford Pl PL1 ....247 F3
Stopgate Cross
  East Monachorum EX17 ..78 C8
  Zeal Monachorum EX17 ..78 C8
Stormsdown Cotts
  TQ12 ....131 B7
Storridge La EX13 ....188 B6
Storrs Cl TQ13 ....180 C8
Stott Cl PL3 ....249 D5
Stour Cl PL3 ....249 D6
Stourscombe Wood
  PL15 ....105 A2
Stout Cross EX14 ....68 F5
Stover Long La EX12 ....191 D6
Stover Country Pk*
  TQ12 ....123 B2
Stover Sch EX14 ....261 C4
Stover Sch TQ12 ....123 B1
Stowell La EX20 ....76 C4
Stowell La TA20 ....88 D8
Stowford Bsns Pk PL21 ..237 D6
Stowford Cl PL20 ....127 B3
Stowford Cross
  Bradworthy EX22 ....53 C8
  Bratton Fleming EX31 ...11 C3
  Chittlehampton EX37 ....29 A5
  Cobbaton EX37 ....28 E5
  Halwill EX21 ....91 D8
  South Molton EX36 .....19 B2
  West Putford EX22 ......39 C2
Stowford Gate EX17 ....61 A7
Stowford Hill EX17 ......61 A7
Stowford Mts EX17 ......61 F8
Stowford Prim Sch
  PL21 ....237 C5
Stowford Rise EX10 .....187 F8
Straightway Head EX5 ..100 A7
Strand Teignmouth TQ14 .210 A3
  Topsham TQ3 ....182 F4
  Torquay TQ1 ....220 B4
Strand Ct
  1 Barnstaple EX31 .....157 A2
  Topsham EX3 ....182 F4
Strand Hill EX7 ....204 C6
Strand La EX31 ....16 B6
Strand Ringmore TQ14 ..209 C5
Strand St PL1 ....254 A8
Strand The
  Barnstaple EX32 ....154 F5
  Bideford EX39 ....157 A2
3 Brixham TQ5 ....230 D5
  Culmstock EX15 ....66 E8
  Dawlish EX7 ....204 E6
  Exmouth EX8 ....202 A6
  Ilfracombe EX34 ....150 C6
  Lympstone EX8 ....195 D5
  Starcross EX6 ....201 B8
Strand View EX3 ....182 F4
Strashleigh View PL21 ...136 D6
Stratford Ave EX4 ....178 C8
Strathculm Rd EX5 .....82 F7
Stratton Wlk PL2 ....248 D8
Strawberry Ave EX2 .....181 C8
Strawberry Hill EX8 .....195 F5
Strawberry La EX7 ......204 C3
Strawberry Terr TQ12 ...207 E8
Stray Pk PL9 ....257 F4
Straypark Cnr EX35 ......5 E4
Stream Cl EX2 ....261 A1
Streamcombe La TA22 ..33 B5
Streamers Mdws EX14 ..166 D5
Streams La EX31 ....9 B2
Streatham Dr EX4 ....177 B8
Streatham Rise EX4 .....177 A8
Street Ash La TA20 ......69 F8
Street The
  Kilmington EX13 ....87 C1
  Musbury EX13 ....103 D5
  Stoke Raleigh EX5 .....168 A8
Strode Rd
  Bucklastleigh TQ11 .....236 B4
  Plymouth PL7 ....250 F6
Stroma Cl PL6 ....244 F7
Strongs Hill Cross EX21 ..73 F1
Stroud Park Rd PL2 .....248 C7
Stroxworthy Cross EX39 ..38 F6
Stuart Cres EX15 ....163 C6
Stuart Ct EX7 ....204 D4
Stuart Rd Exeter EX1 ...177 F6
  Plymouth PL3 ....262 A4
Stuart Road Prim Sch
  PL1 ....262 A4
Stubbing Cross EX14 ....102 C5
Stubbins Cross TQ12 ...211 D7
Stubborn Cross EX16 ...47 C1
Stuckeridge Cross EX16 .48 D8
Stucley Rd EX39 ....156 E1
Studd Cr EX32 ....7 C3
Studhayes Cross EX13 ..87 C1
Studhayes Rd EX13 .....87 B2
Studley Ho 8 EX14 .....166 C5
Studley Rd TQ1 ....220 A4
Stumpy Cross
  Shobrooke EX17 ....80 A8
  Silverton EX5 ....82 B8
Sturnpypost Cross TQ7 ..144 B6
Sturcombe Ave TQ4 .....225 F3
Sturdee Rd PL2 ....248 A5
Sturges Rd EX8 ....202 D8
Sturt Cotts EX17 ....78 E7
Sturtlebury La TQ7 ......143 F5
Style Cl EX32 ....155 B2

Suddon's Cross EX24 ....102 B6
Suddon's La EX24 ....102 B6
Sugar Mill Bsns Pk PL9 .249 C1
Sullivan Rd PL2 ....178 C5
Summer Ct Exeter EX4 ..178 B8
  Exmouth EX8 ....202 E8
15 Hemyock EX15 ....67 B8
Summer La
  Bovey Tracey TQ13 .....123 C2
  Brixham TQ5 ....230 B2
  Exeter EX4 ....174 B1
  Exmouth EX8 ....196 B4
  Northlew EX20 ....74 F2
  Ottery St Mary EX11 ...100 F8
Summer Well La EX34 ....9 A5
Summercourt Way TQ5 .230 A2
Summerfield
  Sidmouth EX10 ....188 B8
  Woodbury EX5 ....184 C4
Summerfield Ave TA21 ..52 D8
Summerfield Ct
  Ivybridge PL21 ....237 A5
  Paignton TQ4 ....226 C5
Summerfield Rd TQ2 ....219 E8
Summerfield Way TQ1 ..52 D8
Summerhaye Rd PL21 ...242 D1
Summerhayes EX7 ......204 D4
Summerhill Cl TQ12 .....122 F1
Summerhill Cres 16
  TQ12 ....122 F1
Summerhill Rd TQ13 ...130 E4
Summerhill Rd
  15 Newton Abbot TQ12 .122 F1
  Lyme Regis DT7 ....260 E4
Summerland EX14 ......166 C5
Summerland Ave EX7 ...204 D7
Summerland Cl EX7 .....204 D7
Summerland Cotts
  10 Newton Abbot TQ12 .207 C3
  Ottery St Mary EX11 ...100 F8
Summerland Ct 11
  TQ1 ....207 C3
Summerland St
  Barnstaple EX32 ....155 A5
  Exeter EX1,EX4 ....261 C4
Summerland Terr 1 EX34 .3 A3
  Plymouth TQ12 ....123 A1
Summerlands Cl
  Brixham TQ5 ....230 A2
  Plymouth PL7 ....251 C5
Summerlands Gdns PL7 .251 C5
Summermoor La EX37 ...28 E6
Summers Cl PL9 ....249 B7
Summers Moor Cross
  EX19 ....58 F1
Summersby Cl EX12 ....192 A6
Summerville Cross EX39 .37 F6
Summerway EX4 ....178 C8
Summerway Mid Sch
  EX4 ....178 C8
Summerwell La EX16 ...162 D4
Sumner Rd PL21 ....137 C7
Sun Cl TQ12 ....207 B3
Sun Valley Cl TQ5 ......230 C5
Sunbury Hill TQ1 ....220 A6
Sunbury Rd TQ1 ....226 B5
Sunbury Terr 2 TQ1 ....220 A6
Sunday Cl TQ2 ....213 F3
Sunderland Cl PL3 ......255 A6
Sunflower Rd EX32 .....155 A5
Sunhill Ave EX3 ....182 F6
Sunhill La EX3 ....182 F6
Sunningbrook Rd EX16 .161 E5
Sunningdale EX39 ......157 A3
Sunningdale Rd PL12 ...242 C2
Sunny Bank EX32 ......155 B4
Sunny Cl TQ4 ....207 F3
Sunny Ct EX16 ....161 D4
Sunny Dene PL5 ....243 D1
Sunny Gdns TQ1 ....220 A6
Sunny Hollow TQ12 ....211 D8
Sunny View EX19 ....58 F3
Sunnybank EX6 ....194 E3
Sunnyfield EX5 ....175 C7
Sunnylands Cross EX13 .87 A2
Sunnylands Way EX7 ...210 F8
Sunnymead EX17 ....79 B5
Sunnymead Terr 3
  TQ9 ....223 C5
Sunnymoor Cl EX1 .....174 F2
Sunnyside
  Awliscombe EX14 ....85 C4
9 Bideford EX39 ....157 B1
2 Braunton EX33 ......152 D5
  Burlescombe EX16 ......51 C2
  Combe Martin EX34 .....3 A3
  Sandford EX38 ....42 B5
  Woolfardisworthy EX39 .38 F8
Sunnyside Cotts 10 EX34 .3 B8
Sunnyside Rd
  Kingskerswell TQ12 ....213 A4
  Plymouth PL4 ....249 B2
Sunset No 1 EX12 ......192 A4
Sunset Hts EX7 ....155 A5
Sunway Cl PL19 ....171 A6
Sunwell La PL11 ....252 A8
Surname Pl EX8 ....208 C6
Surbiton Cres EX4 .....176 F4

Surf Bay Cvn Pk EX39 ....156 D8
Surridge La TQ2 ....220 A5
Sussex Cl Exeter EX4 ......176 E4
  Torquay TQ2 ....214 A3
Sussex Pl PL1 ....262 C2
Sussex Rd PL2 ....247 F5
Sussex St PL1 ....262 C2
Sussex Terr ⑤ PL2 ....247 F5
Sutcliffe Cl TQ9 ....222 F7
Sutcombe Com Prim Sch
  EX22 ....54 A6
Sutherland Cl TQ12 ....212 F8
Sutherland Dr TQ2 ....214 B2
Sutherland Rd
  Plymouth PL4 ....263 A4
  Torquay TQ1 ....220 C5
Sutton Cl Dawlish EX7 ....204 D7
  Torquay TQ2 ....213 F4
Sutton Cross
  Moretonhampstead TQ13 .111 E5
  Thurlestone TQ7 ....143 D1
Sutton Ct PL1 ....247 F1
Sutton Mews ② PL4 ....263 A2
Sutton Rd PL4 ....263 B2
Suttons Cross EX14 ....86 D1
Swaddicott Cross EX21 ....56 C2
Swaindale Rd ⑤ PL3 .....248 E6
Swains TA21 ....160 D4
Swains Ct EX3 ....182 E5
Swains La TA21 ....160 D4
Swains Rd EX9 ....198 B1
Swale Cl Plymouth PL3 ....249 B6
  Torquay TQ2 ....214 A3
Swallerton Gate TQ13 .....121 D6
Swallow Cl EX32 ....155 E4
Swallow Dr EX2 ....176 D3
Swallow Field EX31 ....154 A2
Swallow Units EX2 ....177 D1
Swallow Way EX15 ....163 B2
Swallowfield Rd EX2 ......178 B2
Swallowfield Rise TQ2 ....213 C2
Swallowfields TQ9 ....223 B7
Swallows Acre EX7 ....204 E7
Swallows End PL9 ....255 E8
Swallowtree Cross EX6 ....96 C7
Swan Cl PL10 ....253 A6
Swan Ct Dartmouth TQ6 ..233 E3
  Exeter EX1 ....261 B1
Swan Gdns PL7 ....250 F5
Swan Hill Rd EX24 ....103 A3
Swan Rd EX4 ....201 A8
Swan Units EX2 ....178 E5
Swan Yd Exeter EX4 ....177 A5
Swanaford Rd EX6 ....112 F7
Swanborough Rd TQ12 ...208 A2
Swannaton La
  Crediton EX17 ....79 E8
  Morchard Bishop EX17 ....61 E1
Swannaton Rd TQ6 ....233 E1
Swannywell Hill EX17 ......78 F8
Swanswood Gdns EX39 ..156 D7
Swedwell La TQ2 ....214 A4
Swedwell Rd TQ2 ....214 A4
Sweetbriar Cl EX7 ....204 C3
Sweetbriar La EX7 ....204 C3
Sweetbriar La EX11 ....168 B3
Sweidacombe La EX36 ....32 C7
Swift Gdns PL5 ....244 C2
Swift Ind Est TQ12 ....207 D6
Swimbridge CE Prim Sch
  EX32 ....17 D1
Swinburne Gdns PL5 .....244 C1
Swincombe Dr TQ3 ....225 F6
Swincombe La EX31 ....11 C4
Swing Gate EX6 ....194 A4
Swing Gate Cross EX37 ...29 A2
Swingate Cross EX22 ....90 B8
Swiss Cl EX8 ....196 B3
Sycamore Ave
  Dawlish Warren EX7 .....201 A2
  Plymouth PL4 ....263 C2
  Tavistock PL19 ....171 C2
Sycamore Cl
  Broadclyst EX5 ....175 D6
  Exeter EX1 ....178 B5
  Exmouth EX8 ....196 E2
  Exmouth EX8 ....196 F2
  Honiton EX14 ....166 A4
  Paignton TQ4 ....229 D2
  Willand EX15 ....162 C4
Sycamore Dr
  Plymouth PL6 ....245 C7
  Torpoint PL11 ....247 A3
Sycamore Rd
  Saltash PL12 ....242 B3
  Tiverton EX16 ....161 E5
Sycamore Way
  Plymouth PL6 ....245 A4
  Plymouth PL6 ....245 B8
Sydenham Cross PL19 ....116 A2
Sydenham La EX16 ....47 A6
Sydney Cl PL7 ....250 E4
Sydney Rd Exeter EX2 ....177 A4
  Torpoint PL11 ....247 A3
Sydney St PL1 ....262 B4
Sylvan Ave EX4 ....173 D1
Sylvan Cl EX8 ....196 A2
Sylvan Ct EX8 ....196 A2
Sylvan Rd Exeter EX4 .....173 E1
  Wellington TA21 ....160 E5
Sylvania Dr EX4 ....173 E2
Symons Rd PL12 ....242 F2
Synagogue Pl EX4 ....261 A3
Syncock's Cross EX39 ....157 F3

T

Tabernacle Ct ⑤ EX1 ....261 A2
Tackbear Rd EX22,EX23 ...70 C4
Tacket Ct TQ7 ....258 C4
Taddiford Est EX4 ....177 A8
Taddiford Rd EX4 ....177 A8
Tadworthy Rd EX39 ......156 E7
Tail Cnr EX17 ....79 D7
Tailyour Rd PL6 ....244 F2
Talbot Gdns PL5 ....247 D7
Talbot Rd DT7 ....260 D5
Tale Common Head Cross
  EX14 ....84 B4
Taleford Cl EX11 ....169 C7
Taleford Villas EX11 ......169 C7
Talewater Cross EX5 ....84 C2
Tallow Wood Cl TQ3 ......225 E6
Tamar Ave Plymouth PL2 .247 E5
  Tavistock PL19 ....171 D5
  Torquay TQ2 ....219 B7
Tamar Bridge PL5 ....243 A2
Tamar Cl ⑦ PL20 ....125 E3
Tamar Cotts PL19 ....116 A1
Tamar Rd PL1 ....15 E5
Tamar St Plymouth PL1 ...247 E3
  Saltash PL12 ....243 A2
  Torpoint PL11 ....247 C3
Tamar Terr
  Calstock PL17 ....125 D3
  Saltash PL12 ....243 A2
Tamar Valley Donkey Pk*
  PL18 ....125 A5
Tamar View
  Milton Abbot PL19 ....116 A6
  St Dominick PL12 ....125 A2
Tamar View Ind Est
  PL12 ....242 D5
Tamar Villas PL19 ....242 D5
Tamar Way PL18 ....125 D6
Tamar Wharf PL1 ....247 E3
Tamar's Dr EX15 ....162 C4
Tamarind EX15 ....162 C4
Tamarisk EX14 ....174 B2
Tamarside Com Coll
  PL5 ....243 E1
Tamerton Ave PL5 ....243 D1
Tamerton Cl PL5 ....244 A6
Tamerton Foliot Rd
  PL6 ....244 C6
Tamerton Rd PL6 ....241 B2
Tamerton Vale Prim Sch
  PL6 ....244 C6
Tan La EX2 ....177 B3
Tangmere Ave PL5 ....243 D7
Tanner's Hill TA4 ....35 E7
Tanners Ct EX15 ....163 D1
Tanners Rd Landkey EX32 ..17 C2
  Paignton TQ4 ....226 C4
Tannery Flats ④ EX16 ...161 C5
Tanpits Cross TQ7 ....145 A1
Tanpits Mdw TQ7 ....145 A1
Tanworth Ho TQ7 ....143 A1
Tanyard La TQ12 ....217 F6
Tanyards Ct ⑥ EX12 .....192 A5
Tape La EX14 ....85 B3
Tapfield Cross TQ7 ....142 F4
Tapley Gdns TQ14 ....209 A8
Tapp's La PL8 ....257 B5
Tappers Ct EX3 ....182 E7
Tappers Knapp DT7 ......260 B5
Taps Cl EX6 ....182 B4
Tapson Dr PL9 ....255 A6
Tarbet Ave EX1 ....177 F7
Tarka Cl EX20 ....170 D6
Tarr Stps* TA22 ....21 D3
Tarr's Ave TQ12 ....207 E2
Tarraway Rd TQ3 ....219 D1
Tarrs End TQ12 ....207 E2
Tarrs La TQ12 ....207 E2
Tatworth Prim Sch TA20 ..88 C8
Tatworth St TA20 ....88 C8
Taunton Ave PL5 ....244 B5
Taunton Cl EX13 ....177 A3
Taunton Cross EX13 ....87 A1
Taunton Ct ⑧ TQ9 ....223 D5
Taunton Pl PL5 ....244 B5
Taunton Rd TA21 ....160 E7
Tavern Gdns EX39 ....26 B1
Tavis Rd TQ3 ....225 F8
Tavistock Coll PL19 ....171 A3
Tavistock Cross PL20 .....116 E5
Tavistock General PL19 ...171 B5
Tavistock Mus* PL19 ....171 C6
Tavistock Pl
  Paignton TQ4 ....229 B8
  Plymouth PL4 ....263 A3
Tavistock Prim Sch
  PL19 ....171 B4
Tavistock Rd Exeter EX4 ..177 A7
  Launceston PL15 ....105 A2
  Okehampton EX20 ....193 D4
  Plymouth PL6 ....245 B5
  Plymouth, Manadon PL5 ..248 F8
  Princetown PL20 ....128 A8
  Yelverton PL20 ....126 F3
Tavy Ave TQ2 ....219 B8
Tavy Pl PL4 ....248 F4
Tavy Rd Saltash PL12 .....242 C3
  Tavistock PL19 ....171 D5
Taw Bridge Cross EX20 ...77 B4
Taw Cl PL3 ....249 D6
Taw Cres EX31 ....155 E6
Taw Ct ⑨ EX32 ....155 A5
Taw Green Cross EX20 ....95 B7
Taw Meadow Cres EX31 ..153 F6
Taw Mills La EX18 ....59 C1

Taw Rd EX31 ....15 E5
Taw Vale EX32 ....154 F4
Taw Vale Ave EX20 ....77 B4
Taw Vale Cl EX20 ....77 B4
Taw View
  ❶ Bishop's Tawton EX32 ...16 E1
  Fremington EX31 ....153 F6
Tawgreen La EX18 ....59 C1
Tawgreen Rd EX20 ....95 C7
Tawmoor Cross EX20 .....95 C7
Tawny Cl TQ3 ....226 C8
Tawton La EX20 ....95 B4
Tay Gdns PL3 ....249 D6
Taylor Cl Dawlish EX7 ....204 D5
  Ottery St Mary EX11 .....169 B4
  Saltash PL12 ....242 C3
Taylor Rd PL12 ....242 C4
Taylor Sq PL19 ....171 B6
Taylor's Cross EX17 ....62 E3
Taylor's Hill EX16,EX17 ..62 E4
Taylor's La EX17 ....43 D6
Taylors Ct EX16 ....161 E7
Taylors Field EX20 ....77 B4
Taylors Newtake ②
  TQ12 ....122 F1
TDC Units EX22 ....164 C6
Teal Cl TQ2 ....213 C2
Teats Hill Flats PL4 ....263 B1
Teats Hill Rd PL4 ....263 B1
Teazle Ct EX2 ....176 A2
Tedburn Rd EX4 ....176 B5
Tedburn St Mary Prim Sch
  EX6 ....97 F5
Tedburrow La EX15 ....67 A8
Tedders Cl ⑧ EX15 ....67 B8
Tedstone La EX8 ....196 A7
Tees Cl PL3 ....249 C7
Teign Cl TQ14 ....208 E8
Teign Ct
  Bishopsteignton TQ12 ...209 A8
  Stokeinteignhead TQ12 ..209 B1
Teign La Chudleigh TQ13 .123 D7
  Trusham TQ13 ....113 D1
Teign Rd
  Newton Abbot TQ12 ......207 D4
  Plymouth PL3 ....249 B6
Teign Sch TQ12 ....207 D8
Teign St TQ14 ....210 B4
Teign View TQ13 ....123 C4
Teign View Pl ❺ TQ14 ..210 B4
Teign Village TQ13 ....113 A3
Teignbridge Bsns Ctr
  TQ12 ....180 F3
Teignbridge Crossing LC
  TQ12 ....207 A7
Teignbridge Gate TQ12 ..207 A7
Teigncombe Ct EX6 ......113 A4
Teignharvey Rd TQ12 ....209 A3
Teignholt Cross EX6 ......96 F3
Teignmouth Com Coll
  TQ14 ....210 B5
Teignmouth Hill EX7 .....204 E5
Teignmouth Hospl
  TQ14 ....210 B5
Teignmouth Invertegin Inf
  Sch TQ14 ....209 D8
Teignmouth Mus*
  TQ14 ....210 C4
Teignmouth Rd
  Bishopsteignton TQ12 ...208 F8
  Holcombe EX7 ....210 E7
  Kingsteignton TQ12,TQ14 .208 A4
  Shaldon TQ1,TQ14 ....210 A1
  Torquay TQ1 ....220 A8
Tekoa Bldgs EX2 ....177 C1
Telegraph Cross PL11 ....136 D4
Telegraph Hill EX6 ....114 D2
Telegraph La EX5,EX11 ...168 B6
Telegraph View TQ12 .....180 B1
Telegraph Wharf PL1 .....254 A8
Telford Cres PL5 ....243 F2
Telford Rd EX4 ....177 A2
Temeraire Rd PL5 ....244 D2
Temperance Pl ❻ TQ5 ..230 D5
Temperance St TQ2 ......220 A5
Templar Way
  Newton Abbot TQ12 ......206 F8
Temple Cres EX16 ....161 F4
Temple Gdns EX16 ....188 B5
Temple St EX16 ....188 B5
Templer Rd TQ3 ....219 A3
Templer's Way ❶ TQ12 ..123 E1
Templers Rd TQ12 ....219 A3
Templeton Cross EX16 ....48 A1
Templeton La EX16 ....47 F1
Ten Acre Gate EX33 ....87 E7
Tenby Rd PL5 ....243 C1
Tencery Orch EX14 ....86 A3
Tenerife TQ1 ....220 C5
Tennacott Hts EX39 ......26 A4
Tennacott La EX39 ....26 B4
Tennyson Ave EX2 ....177 F3
Tennyson Dr TQ1 ....220 B8
Tennyson Gdns PL5 ......244 B1
Tennyson Way EX8 ....196 C4
Tern Gdns PL7 ....250 F5
Terra Nova Gn PL2 ....248 A6
Terrace The
  Braunton EX33 ....152 D6
  Harrowbarrow PL17 .....125 B4
  Torquay TQ1 ....220 B4

Terris Cross EX20 ....76 A6
Tewkesbury Cl PL2 ....248 A8
Tews La
  Barnstaple, Bickington
  EX31 ....154 A3
  Barnstaple, Roundswell
  EX31 ....154 A2
Tewsley Cl EX11 ....169 B4
Thackeray Gdns PL5 .....244 B1
Thackeray Rd EX4 ....178 C8
Thames Gdns PL3 ....249 D5
Thanckes Cl PL11 ....247 A3
Thanckes Dr PL11 ....247 A4
Thatcher Ave TQ1 ....221 A4
Thatcher Dr TQ1 ....210 C8
Thatcher Hts TQ1 ....220 F3
Thatcher's La EX5 ....81 E6
Thatcher's Lane End EX5 .81 E5
Theatre La ❸ EX31 ......154 F5
Theatre Ope PL1 ....247 F1
Theatre Royal PL1 ....262 C2
Thelbridge Cross EX17 ...61 D6
Thelbridge Hill EX17 ......61 C7
Therlow Rd PL3 ....249 B6
Thetford Gdns PL6 ....248 D8
Third Ave Dawlish EX7 ...204 D5
  Exeter, Countess Wear
  EX2 ....182 C7
  Exeter, Heavitree EX1 ....177 F6
  Plymouth, Beacon Pk PL2 .248 A4
  Plymouth, Camels Head
  PL2 ....247 E7
Thirlmere Gdns PL6 ......244 F4
Thistle Cl PL4 ....245 E7
Thomas Bassett Rd
  EX24 ....103 A3
Thomas Cl EX8 ....196 C4
Thomas Newcomen Ct
  TQ6 ....233 C3
Thomas's Cross EX16 ....112 F8
Thompson Rd EX1 ....178 A7
Thorn Cl Exeter EX1 ......178 B6
  Newton Abbot TQ12 ......206 E4
Thorn Cnr EX18 ....77 E8
Thorn Cross
  Bovey Tracey TQ13 ....180 C5
  Chagford TQ13 ....110 E5
  Slapton TQ7 ....145 C6
Thorn Cross Way TA21 ...50 D8
Thorn Hill EX16 ....63 B6
Thorn La Membury EX13 ..87 D7
  Saltash PL12 ....242 B2
Thorn Moor Cross PL15 .105 C7
Thorn Orch TQ12 ....211 E2
Thorn Pk PL3 ....248 F5
Thorn Villas TQ12 ....208 A6
Thornberry Ave EX1 ......178 B6
Thornbury Cross
  Sampford Courtenay EX20 .76 D2
  Shebbear EX22 ....55 A3
Thornbury Mill EX22 .....55 A4
Thornbury Park Ave
  PL3 ....248 D6
Thornbury Prim Sch
  PL6 ....245 D4
Thornbury Rd PL6 ....245 E4
Thorncliff Cl TQ2 ....208 E1
Thorndale Cres EX4 .....176 D8
Thorndon Cross EX22 ....71 E5
Thorne Cotts EX11 ....169 B3
Thorne Cross EX6 ....96 C4
Thorne Farm Way EX14 .169 C3
Thorne La Bow EX17 .....236 C3
Thorne Moor Cross EX6 ..96 E4
Thorne Pk Rd TQ2 ....219 D5
Thorne Rd EX34 ....9 A5
Thornemoor La EX17 .....77 C8
Thornes Cross EX16 ......64 E5
Thornes Mdw EX12 ......114 A6
Thornes Terr EX36 ....158 C4
Thorney Cross EX21 ....90 E7
Thornfield Cl
  Exmouth EX8 ....196 A2
  Seaton EX12 ....192 A7
Thornham Chapel Cross
  EX17 ....46 B1
Thornham La EX17 ....46 B5
Thornhedges Cross EX17 .80 B5
Thornhedges La EX17 ....80 B5
Thornhill Rd PL3 ....248 E6
Thornhill Way PL3 ....248 E6
Thornhole St TQ8 ....259 E5
Thornlea Ave EX31 ....153 D5
Thornley Rd TQ14 ....210 A5
Thornmoor La TQ12 ......210 A5
Thornpark Cross EX1 ....178 B7
Thornpark Rise EX1 ......178 B6
Thorns Cross TQ13 ......111 B7
Thorns Cross PL20 ....126 B4
Thornton Hill EX4 ....261 C4
Thorntree Bsns Units
  EX8 ....196 F1
Thornville Terr PL9 ....255 C8
Thornyville Cl PL9 ....255 C8
Thornyville Dr PL9 ....255 D8
Thornyville Villas PL9 ....255 C8
Thorpe Ave EX8 ....196 B3
Thorverton CE Prim Sch
  EX5 ....81 E4
Three Ash Cross EX14 ....87 B5
Three Close La EX13 ......88 E2
Three Corner Cross EX36 .31 C5
Three Corner Pl EX2 ......181 C8

Three Corners Cross
  EX14 ....85 A6
Three Cross Ways EX19 ...58 D2
Three Crossways
  Chulmleigh EX18 ....44 E1
  Zeal Monachorum EX17 ..78 A4
Three Elms Cross EX15 ...83 D1
Three Firs EX15 ....83 D4
Three Gate Cross
  Cheriton Bishop EX17 .....97 B6
  Yeoford EX17 ....79 D2
Three Gates Cross
  Dulverton TA22 ....33 C6
  Huntsham EX16 ....49 E6
  Yarnscombe EX31 ....27 D3
Three Gates Hill EX16 ....49 D7
Three Hammers Cross
  EX17 ....61 A6
Three Lane End EX7 ....38 E7
Three Limbed Oak EX5 ...81 D3
Three Mariners Cross
  EX14 ....86 C6
Three Sycamores Cross
  EX24 ....102 F4
Three Tree La TQ4 ....124 C2
Three Ways EX11 ....18 A1
Threefoot Stool EX6 ....98 A1
Threshers EX17 ....165 A5
Threwstones Cl EX16 ....161 E5
Thriverton Cross EX22 ....90 F4
Throgmorton Ho ❶
  TQ9 ....223 D5
Throwcombe Cross EX16 .48 A6
Throwcombe La EX16 .....48 A6
Thrushel Cl TQ5 ....230 A2
Thuborough Cross EX22 ..54 A4
Thurlescombe Cross
  EX16 ....64 E6
Thurlestone Gdns TQ6 ...233 E1
Thurlestone Rd ❼ TQ12 .207 B4
Thurlestone Rock TQ7 ...147 B8
Thurlestone Wlk PL6 ....249 D7
Thurlow Cl EX17 ....165 A5
Thurlow Hill TQ1 ....220 A4
Thurlow Pk TQ1 ....220 A4
Thurlow Rd Exeter EX4 ..177 A7
  Torquay TQ1 ....220 A4
Tichfield Gdns TQ3 ....225 F...
Tick La EX6 ....113 E5
Ticklemore St TQ9 ....225 C5
Tidcombe Cl ❶ EX16 ....64 D7
Tidcombe La EX16 ....64 D7
Tidderson Cross EX16 ....47 E3
Tidderson La EX16 ....47 E3
Tiddy Cl PL19 ....171 B3
Tideford Cross TQ9 ......227 A3
Tidlake La EX36 ....30 C6
Tidwell Cl EX9 ....198 A2
Tidwell La EX9 ....198 B5
Tidwell Rd EX9 ....198 A2
Tidwell Tops TQ9 ....135 F3
Tilery EX14 ....169 A2
Tillard Cl PL7 ....251 C5
Tilly Cl PL9 ....255 F4
Timber Hill DT7 ....260 E5
Timber Terr TQ12 ....212 F4
Timber Vale Cvn Pk
  DT7 ....260 E5
Timbers Cl EX11 ....236 A3
Timbers La EX11 ....236 A3
Timewell Hill EX16 ....34 C4
Timridge La EX6 ....113 E6
Tin La PL4 ....263 A2
Tincombe TQ12 ....242 C2
Tinhay Cross PL16 ....105 F4
Tinhay Mill Ind Est PL16 .105 F4
Tinker's Cross EX18 ......59 A5
Tinkers Wood Ct ❹
  TQ5 ....230 C4
Tinkley La TQ13 ....123 C6
Tinpit Hill EX5 ....98 F7
Tintagel Cl Exeter EX4 ...174 A2
  Torquay TQ2 ....219 F8
Tintagel Cres TQ2 ....248 C8
Tintern Ave PL4 ....263 C2
Tip Hill EX11 ....169 D3
Tipleyhill Cross TQ12 ....122 D8
Tipleyhill La TQ12,TQ13 .122 D8
Tipnacott La EX35 ....6 A4
Tipple Cross PL15 ....105 B6
Tipton Cross EX11 ....168 B2
Tipton Rd EX11 ....168 B2
Tipton St John CE Prim Sch
  EX10 ....168 B2
Tipton Vale EX11 ....100 C3
Titchen's La
  Calverleigh EX16 ....48 B1
  Tiverton EX16 ....63 B8
Titching Park La EX34 ....9 B5
Titham Hill EX16 ....47 C6
Tithe Barn Cross EX15 ...51 D2
Tithe Rd PL7 ....250 B7
Tithebarn Copse EX1 ....178 F8
Tithebarn La EX1 ....178 A8
Titterton Cross EX20 .....77 C7
Tiverton Castle* EX16 ...161 C4
Tiverton Cl PL6 ....245 B8
Tiverton Craft Ctr*
  EX16 ....161 C4
Tiverton High Sch EX16 .161 B5
Tiverton Parkway Sta
  EX16 ....65 E8
Tiverton Rd Bampton EX16 .49 E8
  Cullompton EX15 ....163 B3
Silverton EX5 ....82 B6
Silverton Way EX16 ......161 F5
Tiverton Mus* EX16 .....161 C4
Toadpit La EX11 ....168 E6

Tobruk Rd PL12 ....242 E3
Toby Cross PL21 ....137 D6
Toby La EX5 ....184 E5
Tod Moor Cross PL21 ....237 A1
Tolchers TQ9 ....222 F8
Tolcis Cross EX13 ....87 D3
Toll Bar Cross EX18 ....44 E3
Tollards Rd EX12 ....178 B2
Tollbar Cl PL21 ....237 F5
Tollbar Cross EX31 ....17 B8
Tolleys EX17 ....165 E5
Tollit Gdn 12 TQ9 ....223 D5
Tollox Pl PL3 ....249 B4
Tolman Cross EX12 ....192 B6
Tom Maddock Gdns
  PL21 ....237 E4
Tom Sanders Cl EX34 ....3 A3
Tom's La EX39 ....25 A3
Tombstone La EX16 ....63 D8
Tomhead Cross EX4 ....98 B6
Tomouth Cres 14 EX39 ....15 A1
Tomouth Rd EX39 ....15 A1
Tomouth Sq 15 EX39 ....15 A1
Tomouth Terr 16 EX39 ....15 A1
Tomsclose La EX18 ....59 C2
Tone Hill TA21 ....160 B8
Tonedale Bsns Pk TA21 ....160 B7
Tongue End Cross EX20 ....94 E5
Tongue Gate EX36 ....45 E7
Tongue Gate Hill EX36 ....45 E7
Tongue Lake La EX37 ....44 E5
Tonyfield Wood Cross
  EX17 ....60 B4
Top Cliff TQ14 ....209 D5
Top O The Town Clyd
  PL12 ....242 F2
Topcliff Rd TQ14 ....209 D5
Topsham Mus* EX3 ....182 F4
Topsham Rd The EX3 ....178 A1
Topsham Sch The EX3 ....182 F5
Topsham Sta EX3 ....182 F5
Tor Church Rd TQ2 ....220 A5
Tor Cross Exeter EX4 ....174 A1
  Paignton TQ4 ....229 B7
  Plymouth, Hartley PL3 ....248 E7
  Plymouth, Marsh Mills PL3 ....249 F5
Tor Dale 1 TQ1 ....220 A6
Tor Down EX20 ....94 D5
Tor Gdns TQ12 ....206 D1
Tor Haven TQ2 ....220 B4
Tor Hill Rd TQ2 ....220 A5
Tor La PL12 ....242 B1
Tor Lane End TQ9 ....144 C7
Tor Mare Ct TQ2 ....219 F4
Tor Park Rd
  Paignton TQ4 ....225 D3
  Torquay TQ2 ....219 F6
Tor Rd PL3 ....249 A4
Tor Vale TQ1 ....219 F6
Tor View
  Buckfastleigh TQ11 ....236 A4
  8 Horrabridge PL20 ....126 F4
Tor View Ave TQ12 ....207 F2
Tor View Gdns TQ3 ....226 A6
Torbay Ct TQ5 ....230 E5
Torbay Hospl TQ2 ....219 D8
Torbay Hospl Annexe
  TQ2 ....213 D1
Torbay Rd Paignton TQ4 ....226 C6
  Torquay TQ2 ....219 F3
Torbay Trad Est TQ5 ....230 C4
Torbridge Cl PL12 ....242 D2
Torbridge Rd
  7 Horrabridge PL20 ....126 F4
  Plymouth PL7 ....250 E6
Torbryan Cl PL6 ....249 E8
Torbryan Hill TQ12 ....211 A3
Torches Cnr EX19 ....42 D1
Tordown Gn EX32 ....17 F2
Torland Rd PL3 ....248 E7
Toronto Ho EX4 ....177 E8
Toronto Rd EX4 ....261 C4
Torpeek Cross PL21 ....137 C7
Torpoint Com Sch PL11 ....247 A4
Torpoint Inf Sch PL11 ....247 B3
Torquay Boy's Gram Sch
  TQ2 ....219 D7
Torquay Com Coll TQ2 ....219 F8
Torquay Gram Sch for Girls
  TQ2 ....219 D7
Torquay Mus* TQ1 ....220 C4
Torquay Rd
  Kingskerswell TQ12 ....213 A3
  Newton Abbot TQ12 ....207 C3
  Newton Abbot, Milber
  TQ12 ....212 E8
  Paignton TQ3 ....226 C8
  Teignmouth TQ14 ....210 A3
Torquay Sta TQ2 ....219 F4
Torr Bridge Pk PL8 ....136 A2
Torr Cres PL3 ....248 F7
Torr Hill PL8 ....257 F4
Torr La East Allington TQ9 ....144 B7
  Plymouth PL3 ....248 E7
  Yealmpton PL8 ....136 A2
Torr Rd PL3 ....248 D7
Torr View Ave PL3 ....248 D7
Torre Cl PL21 ....237 F5
Torre City Prim Sch TQ1 ....219 E7
Torre Sta TQ2 ....219 E6
Torrfge Ave TQ2 ....219 D7
Torridge Cl
  12 Bideford EX39 ....157 B1
  Plymouth PL7 ....251 A6
Torridge Hill EX39 ....157 B1
Torridge Mount EX39 ....157 B1
Torridge Pl 13 EX39 ....157 B1

Torridge Rd
  Appledore EX39 ....15 A1
  Braunton EX33 ....15 A1
  Plymouth PL7 ....250 F6
Torridge St EX39 ....157 B1
Torridge View EX38 ....159 B5
Torridge View Bglws
  EX38 ....159 B5
Torridge Way
  Holsworthy EX22 ....164 C6
  Plymouth PL3 ....249 C5
Torrington 1646*
  EX38 ....159 C4
Torrington Cottage Hospl
  EX38 ....159 D5
Torrington Cross EX37 ....29 C4
Torrington La EX19 ....58 E4
Torrington Pl EX19 ....194 D3
Torrington Rd EX19 ....58 E3
Torrington St 10 EX39 ....157 B1
Torrs Pk EX34 ....150 A5
Torrs Walk Ave EX34 ....150 A6
Tors Pk EX35 ....151 D5
Tors Rd Lynmouth EX35 ....151 D5
  Okehampton EX20 ....170 B3
Tors The TQ12 ....212 F4
Tors View EX39 ....156 B6
Torver Cl PL6 ....245 D7
Torview Flats 6 TQ13 ....180 D8
Torwood Cl TQ1 ....220 D3
Torwood Ct 4 TQ1 ....220 D4
Torwood Gardens Rd
  TQ1 ....220 D4
Torwood Ho 4 TQ1 ....220 D4
Torwood Mount 6 TQ1 ....220 D4
Torwood St TQ1 ....220 D4
Tory Brook Ave PL7 ....250 E6
Tory Brook Ct PL7 ....250 D6
Tory Way PL7 ....250 D6
Tosberry Cross EX39 ....37 E8
Tothill Ave PL4 ....263 B3
Tothill Cl 2 TQ14 ....210 A3
Tothill Rd PL4 ....263 B3
Totnes Castle* TQ9 ....223 B6
Totnes Cl PL21 ....251 B4
Totnes Com Hospl TQ9 ....223 C6
Totnes Cross TQ9 ....139 C3
Totnes Down Hill TQ9 ....223 D3
Totnes Mus* TQ9 ....223 C5
Totnes Rd
  Buckfastleigh TQ11 ....236 D5
  Ipplepen TQ12 ....211 F5
  Marldon TQ3 ....218 C1
  Paignton TQ3,TQ4 ....225 F5
  6 South Brent TQ10 ....134 F3
  Strete TQ6 ....145 E5
  Totnes TQ9 ....223 C7
Totnes Riverside Sta*
  TQ9 ....223 C7
Totnes Sta TQ9 ....223 C6
Tottons Ct EX2 ....281 A8
Touts Ct EX36 ....158 D2
Towell La EX19 ....42 D2
Tower Ct
  Duncheideck EX6 ....114 A5
  Saltash PL12 ....242 C2
Tower Gdns EX17 ....165 C6
Tower Hill
  Cheriton Fitzpaine EX17 ....62 E1
  Holcombe Rogus TA21 ....50 D5
Tower Hill Cross EX17 ....62 E1
Tower Ho Pl 247 E1
Tower House Sch TQ4 ....226 B5
Tower La PL21 ....137 C8
Tower Moor EX37 ....28 F6
Tower Pk EX36 ....158 C3
Tower Rd Honiton EX14 ....166 F4
  Offwell EX14 ....86 A3
  Paignton TQ3 ....226 B6
Tower St
  5 Bideford EX39 ....157 A1
  12 Exmouth EX8 ....202 A6
  Northam EX39 ....156 F7
Tower View
  Broadclyst EX5 ....175 C5
  Saltash PL12 ....242 D1
Tower Way EX14 ....67 B1
Tower Wlk EX2 ....181 C8
Towerfield EX3 ....182 E7
Towerfield Dr PL6 ....245 C8
Towerhill La TA24 ....124 B4
Towers Cl PL6 ....245 F2
Town Cl TQ6 ....233 E3
Town Ct EX13 ....87 A3
Town End EX5 ....175 D7
Town End Cross EX20 ....76 C5
Town Farm Cl
  4 Honiton EX14 ....166 B6
  6 Horrabridge PL20 ....126 F4
Town Farm Cotts TQ9 ....139 E1
Town Farm Ct EX33 ....152 C6
Town Farm La TQ13 ....124 B4
Town Hall Pl 4 TQ13 ....180 D8
Town Hill Broadclyst EX5 ....175 C7
  Culmstock EX15 ....66 E8
  Ermington EX21 ....136 F3
  Staverton TQ9 ....216 A5
  West Anstey EX36 ....32 C6
Town La
  Bratton Fleming EX31 ....11 E3
  Rackenford EX16 ....47 D4
  Woodbury EX5 ....184 C3
Town Living Cross EX20 ....76 B5
Town Mdw
  Great Torrington EX38 ....41 D3

Town Mdw continued
  Ilsington TQ13 ....122 C3
Town Mdws EX39 ....38 E8
Town Mill Gdns PL19 ....171 C6
Town Moor Cross EX17 ....46 B1
Town Moor Hill EX17 ....46 B1
Town Pk M Crediton EX17 ....165 B5
  6 Great Torrington EX38 ....159 C5
  Southleigh TQ7 ....143 E7
  West Alvington TQ7 ....258 A4
Town Quay TQ6 ....233 F3
Tree Hill Hill 16 EX7 ....204 D6
Town View EX17 ....165 C5
Town Wlk EX32 ....155 B4
Town's End Cross TQ7 ....145 C3
Town's La TQ7 ....143 E7
Townfield EX6 ....182 A4
Townlands Bradninch EX5 ....82 F6
  Willand EX15 ....162 D3
Townliving Cross EX36 ....30 E1
Townsend EX12 ....191 C6
Townsend Ave EX12 ....192 A4
Townsend Ci TQ7 ....258 A4
Townsend Cross
  Malborough TQ7 ....147 F6
  Winkleigh EX19 ....58 E2
Townsend Hill TQ12 ....211 C3
Townsend Rd
  Seaton EX12 ....192 A5
  West Alvington TQ7 ....258 A4
Townshend Ave PL2 ....247 E5
Townstal Cres TQ6 ....233 D4
Townstal Hill TQ6 ....233 D3
Townstal Pathfields
  TQ6 ....233 D3
Townstal Rd TQ6 ....233 D4
Tracey Almshouses 7
  ....180 D8
Tracey Ct PL1 ....262 B3
Tracey Vale TQ13 ....180 C6
Tracey View 2 EX14 ....166 B6
Traceys Ave EX7 ....191 F8
Trackfordmoor Cross
  ....33 B3
Trafalgar Cl
  Newton Abbot TQ12 ....207 B5
  Plymouth PL3 ....249 B6
Trafalgar Ct EX3 ....182 E5
Trafalgar Gdns EX32 ....155 A3
Trafalgar Lawn EX32 ....155 A3
Trafalgar Pl
  8 Bideford EX39 ....156 F1
  4 Plymouth PL1 ....247 F3
Trafalgar Place La PL1 ....247 F3
Trafalgar Rd EX8 ....195 E6
Trafalgar St PL4 ....263 A3
Trafalgar Terr TQ5 ....230 D6
Trafford Mews EX4 ....178 C3
Trago Mills L Pk*
  TQ12 ....123 A1
Tragos Brake PL9 ....256 C1
Traine Rd PL9 ....140 D8
Traine Terr PL21 ....137 C2
Traine Villas PL21 ....137 C3
Tramway Rd PL4 ....245 E7
Transit Way PL5 ....244 C2
Travershes Cl EX8 ....196 B1
Traylane EX37 ....28 B1
Treable La EX6 ....96 B3
Treago Gdns PL6 ....245 C8
Treasbeare La EX5 ....99 A5
Trebblepark Rd TQ7 ....258 C5
Treburley Cl PL15 ....115 A4
Treburley Ind Est PL15 ....115 A4
Treby Rd PL7 ....250 F4
Trecott Cross EX20 ....76 F3
Tree Cl EX32 ....17 F4
Treefield EX31 ....18 A8
Treefield Wlk EX32 ....155 C4
Treefields EX33 ....225 F6
Treesdale Ct TQ1 ....220 B6
Trefusis Gdns PL3 ....249 A4
Trefusis Pl EX8 ....202 A5
Trefusis Terr
  Exmouth EX8 ....202 A5
  Millbrook PL10 ....252 A6
Trefusis Way EX9 ....198 B6
Tregenna Ct PL4 ....263 C3
Tregoning Rd PL11 ....246 F2
Trehill La PL10 ....140 H2
Trehill Rd PL21 ....237 E5
Trehanner Prim Sch
  PL15 ....115 A5
Trelawney Ave PL5 ....243 D1
Trelawney Cl PL15 ....115 A4
Trelawney Pl PL21 ....243 D1
Trelawney Rd
  Plymouth PL3 ....248 D5
  Saltash PL12 ....242 E2
Trelawney Rise PL11 ....246 E3
Trelawney Way PL11 ....246 E3
Trelew Rd
  Plymouth PL7 ....251 C6
  Tavistock PL19 ....171 C6
Trelissick Cl TQ3 ....225 D7
Trelissick Rd TQ3 ....225 D7
Treloggan Cl PL8 ....257 D8
Tremaine Ct EX14 ....166 D6
Trematon Ave TQ1 ....220 B6
Trematon Cl PL11 ....237 E4
Trematon Dr PL21 ....237 E5
Trematon Terr PL4 ....248 E4
Tremayne Rise PL19 ....171 B5
Tremere Ct 20 EX32 ....155 A4

Tremlett Gr TQ12 ....211 D2
Tremletts Cl EX6 ....97 F5
Trencher La PL10 ....252 D2
Trenchfirs Cnr TQ9 ....139 E2
Trendlewood Rd PL6 ....245 D7
Trengrouse Ave PL11 ....246 F3
Trennaway Cross EX6 ....96 C1
Trenode Ave EX34 ....2 F4
Trent Bideford EX39 ....26 A4
  Plymouth PL3 ....249 B6
Trentbridge Sq EX2 ....178 C4
Trentham Cl
  Paignton TQ3 ....225 E8
  Plymouth PL6 ....245 B6
Trentishoe Hill EX31 ....4 A5
Trentishoe La EX31 ....4 A5
Trentworthy Cross EX22 ....38 B2
Trescote Way EX20 ....92 F1
Tresilian Cotts EX3 ....182 F3
Tresilian Gdns EX3 ....182 F4
Tresilian Rd EX4 ....177 E8
Tresillian St PL4 ....263 C2
Tresluggan Rd PL5 ....243 D1
Treston Cl EX7 ....204 E7
Trethewey Gdns PL7 ....132 D4
Tretower Cl PL6 ....244 F1
Trevanna Rd TQ7 ....258 C4
Trevanno La PL6 ....249 A8
Trevandon PL17 ....115 B1
Trevennage Gdns PL2 ....248 D8
Treven Dr TQ12 ....213 A3
Trevoor Gdns PL21 ....137 C3
Treverbyn Cl PL7 ....250 D6
Treverbyn Rd PL7 ....250 D6
Tfevessa Cl PL2 ....248 D8
Trevethan Pk PL20 ....239 F4
Trevithick Ave PL11 ....246 F4
Trevithick Rd PL5 ....243 E2
Trevol Bsns Pk PL11 ....246 D3
Trevol Pl PL11 ....246 E3
Trevol Rd PL11 ....246 D3
Trevone Gdns PL2 ....248 D8
Trevorder Cl PL11 ....246 F2
Trevorder Rd PL11 ....246 F2
Trevose Way PL3 ....249 C6
Trevythan Dr PL6 ....244 F1
Trewns Weir Reach EX2 ....261 C1
Trewin Ave PL6 ....244 E7
Trewin Rd EX22 ....164 B5
Triangle Pl 18 TQ14 ....210 C4
Triangle The 10 TQ14 ....210 C4
Trickey Cl EX16 ....161 F5
Tridley Foot Cross EX17 ....61 F4
Tridley Foot Hill EX17 ....61 F4
Trigger's Hill EX19 ....42 D3
Trill Cross EX13 ....103 E6
Trill La Axminster EX13 ....167 C2
  Musbury EX13 ....103 E6
Trimstone Cnr EX34 ....8 F5
Trimstone Cross EX34 ....8 E6
Trimstone La
  Ilfracombe EX34 ....8 E5
  Woolacombe EX34 ....8 D6
Trinfield Ave EX8 ....196 A1
Trinity Cl
  Bere Alston PL20 ....125 E1
  11 Teignmouth TQ14 ....210 B6
  Wellington TA21 ....160 C5
Trinity Cross
  Westward Ho! EX39 ....156 B6
  Sidmouth EX10 ....188 B3
Trinity Gdns EX34 ....150 A5
Trinity Hill TQ1 ....220 C3
Trinity Hill Rd
  Axminster EX13 ....167 F1
  Raymond's Hill EX13 ....104 B7
  Uplyme EX13 ....104 A5
Trinity Pl 18 EX32 ....155 A4
Trinity Row TA21 ....160 C5
Trinity Sch TQ14 ....210 B7
Trinity St PL1 ....267 D6
Trinity St EX32 ....155 A4
Trinity Way PL19 ....171 A4
Trinnaman Cl PL21 ....237 D4
Trinnicks Orch PL21 ....137 D6
Tristan Cl EX4 ....174 A2
Tristford Ho TQ9 ....223 A4
Tristford Rd TQ9 ....222 D2
Trittencott Cross EX36 ....46 A8
Troarn Way 21 TQ13 ....123 E6
Trobridge Cross EX17 ....165 D2
Trojan Ind Pk TQ4 ....225 E3
Trood La EX2 ....181 D7
Trough La TQ13 ....123 A6
Trouville 12 EX32 ....155 A4
Trove Hill EX10 ....188 D8
Trow Hill EX10 ....188 D8
Trowell La TA4 ....35 E4
Truckham La EX14 ....86 F8
Trumlands Rd TQ1 ....214 B6
Trumpers Cl PL21 ....237 A6
Trumps Cross EX15 ....65 C6
Trumps Orch EX15 ....163 A4
Truro Ave TQ2 ....214 A1
Truro Dr Exeter EX4 ....176 F7
  Plymouth PL5 ....244 D8
Trusham Cross TQ13 ....113 D1
Trusham Rd EX2 ....177 C2
Tub Cnr EX5 ....99 C7
Tucker Cl PL5 ....247 F8
Tucker Ct EX14 ....166 C6
Tucker's Hill PL21 ....133 C1

Tucker's Hill Head PL21 ....133 C2
Tucker's Moor Cross
  EX16 ....32 F3
Tuckers EX17 ....32 A5
Tuckers Maltings*
  TQ12 ....207 C3
Tuckers Mdw EX17 ....165 A5
Tuckers Pk
  Bradworthy EX22 ....38 E1
  Buckland Brewer EX39 ....40 B7
Tuckfield Cl EX7 ....178 A4
Tucking Mill La EX36 ....158 E3
Tuckmill Cross EX14 ....84 C4
Tudor Cl Northam EX39 ....156 F7
  Paignton TQ4 ....226 A2
  Plymouth PL6 ....255 E5
Tudor Ct Exeter EX4 ....261 A2
  Saltash PL12 ....243 A2
Tudor Dr EX31 ....154 D2
Tudor Gr EX15 ....163 C5
Tudor Rd TQ12 ....207 B3
Tudor St PL4 ....261 A2
Tudor St EX4 ....261 A2
Tuffery Ct EX4 ....177 F8
Tugela Terr EX5 ....179 A3
Tully Gdns EX10 ....188 B7
Tuly St EX31 ....154 F5
Tumbles The EX20 ....76 C5
Tumbling Field La EX16 ....161 D3
Tumbling Fields EX16 ....161 D3
Tumbly Hill TQ7 ....258 D4
Tunnaford Cross TQ13 ....110 E4
Tunnel La EX14 ....166 F8
Tunnel La EX5 ....82 B5
Tunworth Ct 1 EX1 ....261 A2
Tuphill EX8 ....203 B7
Turbill Gdns 4 PL7 ....251 B5
Turbury Cross EX14 ....85 A8
Turk's Head La EX14 ....166 A6
Turkey La EX5 ....99 E5
Turlake Ho EX5 ....172 F5
Turlake Mews EX5 ....172 F5
Turner Ave EX8 ....202 B7
Turner Cl EX10 ....186 F7
Turner's La EX39 ....88 H2
Turners Cres EX39 ....22 E3
Turnpike Halberton EX16 ....65 C8
  Honiton EX14 ....166 D6
  Sampford Peverell EX16 ....50 C1
Turnpike Cl Clovelly EX39 ....23 D3
  Whiddon Down EX20 ....95 F3
Turnpike Cross EX34 ....8 C6
Turnpike Rd EX20 ....95 F3
Turnquay PL9 ....255 C2
Turret Gr PL4 ....248 F4
Tute's La EX34 ....3 B4
Tuxton Cl PL7 ....251 C4
Tuxton Cl EX14 ....166 C4
Tweed Cl EX14 ....166 C4
Tween Moor Cross EX17 ....60 F6
Tweenaways Ct TQ4 ....225 E4
Tweenaways TQ11 ....236 A4
Tweenaways Cross TQ4 ....225 E4
Tweenways TQ12 ....207 D7
Twelve Acre Post TA22 ....33 A4
Twelve Milestone Hill
  EX17 ....79 D7
Twelve Oaks Cross EX18 ....58 E6
Twickenham Rd TQ12 ....208 A1
Twinaway La EX7 ....114 B8
Twindle Beer TQ13 ....123 C6
Twiscombe Cnr EX4 ....98 D5
Twistgates La EX14 ....68 D4
Twitchen Ball Cnr EX36 ....20 C3
Twitchen Cross
  Great Torrington EX38 ....26 F2
  Ilfracombe EX34 ....8 E6
Twitchen Gate EX31 ....11 F4
Twitchen La
  Bratton Fleming EX31 ....10 F4
  Burrington EX37 ....43 F3
Two Acre Ct TQ1 ....225 E6
Two Bridges Rd
  Princetown PL20 ....128 B8
  Sidford EX10 ....101 B1
Two Crosses
  Dodiscombsleigh EX6 ....113 A8
  Ugborough PL21 ....136 A1
Two Gate Cross EX17 ....44 A4
Two Gates Cross EX15 ....47 E5
Two Hills Pk PL12 ....242 C3
Two Mile Oak Cross
  TQ12 ....211 F5
Two Moors Prim Sch
  EX16 ....161 E5
Two Post Cross
  Spreyton EX17 ....95 D7
  Thornford EX17 ....95 D7
Two Rivers Ind Est
  EX31 ....154 E6
Two Stone La EX4 ....114 C5
Two Trees Rd EX31 ....153 D5
Twoacre Ct EX2 ....181 A8
Twyford Pl 11 Tiverton EX16 ....161 D4
  Wellington TA21 ....160 D5
Tyes Orch EX15 ....83 F5
Tylney Cl PL6 ....245 B6
Tyndale Cl PL5 ....244 B1
Tyrrell Hospl (Private)
  EX34 ....150 B5
Tyrrell Mead EX10 ....188 B7
Tyrrell Rd EX16 ....161 B4
Tytheing Cl EX15 ....172 A8
Tything Wlk 4 PL3 ....248 E6

U

Uffculme Ct EX15 ....66 A7
Uffculme Prim Sch EX15 ..66 A7
Uffculme Rd
Culmstock EX15 ....66 D8
Uffculme EX15 ....66 A7
Willand EX15 ....162 E6
Uffculme Sch EX15 ....66 A7
Ugborough Prim Sch
PL21 ....137 D6
Ugborough Rd PL21 ....137 C7
Ugbrooke Ho* TQ13 ....123 F5
Uggaton Cross EX14 ....84 D5
Uilcombe La EX14 ....68 C4
Uilswater Cres PL6 ....244 E4
Uilswater Ct EX4 ....176 F5
Umber Cl EX34 ....2 F4
Umberleigh Prim Sch
EX37 ....28 D2
Umberleigh Sta EX37 ....28 C2
Umberside 17 EX34 ....3 A3
Under La
Bovey Tracey TQ13 ....180 A5
Holsworthy EX22 ....164 C3
Sidbury EX10 ....101 C1
Under Minnow Rd EX31 ...154 E7
Under Rd Bridgerule EX22 ..70 F5
Gunnislake PL18 ....125 D6
Under Way TQ12 ....213 A6
Undercliff TQ6 ....233 F4
Undercliff Rd PL9 ....255 B7
Underdown EX6 ....114 A4
Underdown Cotts EX39 .....23 D3
Underdown La EX20 ....76 D4
Underfleet The EX12 ....192 B5
Underground Passages
Mus* EX4 ....261 B3
Underhay PL8 ....257 E4
Underheath 4 TQ1 ....220 D5
Underhill EX8 ....195 E5
Underhill Cl EX8 ....195 E4
Underhill Cres EX8 ....195 E4
Underhill Rd
Plymouth PL3 ....248 A4
Torquay TQ2 ....219 E3
Underhill Terr EX3 ....182 F5
Underhill Villas 1 PL3 .....248 A3
Underidge Cl TQ3 ....225 E6
Underidge Dr TQ3 ....225 E6
Underidge Rd TQ3 ....225 E6
Underlane Boyton PL15 .....99 D3
Marhamchurch EX23 ....70 A6
Plymouth, Plympton PL7 ...250 C5
Plymouth, Plymstock PL9 ...255 E6
Underleat Cl 3 TQ13 ......123 F6
Underleys EX12 ....191 C5
Undertown PL21 ....137 D6
Underways PL20 ....125 E1
Underwood Cl EX7 ....204 D4
Underwood Rd PL7 ....250 B6
Unicorn Cl PL7 ....250 B6
Union Cl EX39 ....156 F1
Union Hill EX17 ....78 E7
Union La 9 TQ5 ....230 C5
Union Pl EX1 ....262 A2
Union Rd Crediton EX17 ..165 C5
Exeter EX4 ....177 D8
Union Sq TQ1 ....220 B5
Union St Dartmouth TQ6 ..233 F3
Dulverton TA22 ....33 D6
Exeter EX2 ....177 B4
8 Exmouth EX8 ....202 A6
Newton Abbot TQ12 ....207 C3
Plymouth PL1 ....262 A2
Salcombe TQ8 ....259 E5
Torquay TQ2 ....220 A5
Union Terr
Barnstaple EX32 ....155 A4
Barnstaple, Bickington
EX31 ....154 A4
Crediton EX17 ....165 C5
Unity Cl PL6 ....245 D5
Univ of Exeter EX4 ....177 B8
Univ of Plymouth
Exeter EX2 ....177 E2
Plymouth PL1,PL4 ....262 C3
Univ of Plymouth
(Cookworthy Bldg)
PL4 ....263 A3
Univ of Plymouth Bsns Sch
PL4 ....262 C4
Univ of Plymouth Faculty of
Art & Education
Exeter EX2 ....177 E2
Exeter EX4 ....261 A3
Univ of Plymouth Faculty of
Arts & Education EX8 .....202 B6
Univ of Plymouth The Hoe
Ctr PL1 ....262 C2
Upcott Ave EX31 ....154 C6
Upcott Cross
Cobbaton EX32 ....28 C5
Halwill EX21 ....91 D8
Holsworthy EX22 ....72 D7
Iddesleigh EX19 ....57 F4
St Giles on the Heath PL16 ..90 E1
Welcombe EX39 ....37 C5
West Buckland EX32 ....18 C3
Upcott Gate EX18 ....59 B3
Upcott Hill
Barnstaple EX31 ....154 D8
Bideford EX39 ....25 F4

Upcott Hill continued
Okehampton EX20 ....170 A6
Upcott La Thorverton EX5 ..81 E6
West Buckland EX32 ....18 C3
Upcott Mead Rd EX16 .....161 B4
Upcott Valley EX20 ....170 A6
Upexe La EX5 ....82 B5
Upham Cross EX17 ....63 A3
Upham La EX5 ....99 C1
Uphay La EX13 ....167 B8
Uphill Cl PL21 ....237 E5
Upland Chase EX14 ....166 B3
Upland Dr PL6 ....245 A5
Upland Gdns PL9 ....140 D8
Uplands Saltash PL12 .....242 E1
Tavistock PL19 ....171 A4
Uplands Dr EX4 ....174 A1
Uplands Rd TQ3 ....219 A2
Uplands Terr EX22 ....164 C3
Uplowman CE Prim Sch
EX16 ....50 B2
Uplowman Rd
Chevithorne EX16 ....49 F1
Tiverton EX16 ....64 E8
Uplyme Rd DT7 ....260 C4
Uplyme Road Ind Est
DT7 ....260 A6
Upottery Prim Sch EX14 ...68 C2
Uppacott Cnr EX31 ....50 E7
Uppacott Cross
Moretonhampstead TQ13 ..111 D7
South Molton EX36 ....45 F8
Uppaton La PL21 ....133 D1
Upper Braddons Hill Rd
TQ1 ....220 C4
Upper Church St 9 ....202 A6
Upper Churston Rise
EX12 ....191 E8
Upper Claypark EX34 ....2 F7
Upper Cockington La
TQ2 ....219 C7
Upper Headland Park Rd
TQ3 ....219 C1
Upper Hermosa Rd 8
TQ14 ....210 B5
Upper Highfield EX10 .....188 A5
Upper Knollys Terrace La
PL3 ....248 C4
Upper Longlands EX7 ....248 D7
Upper Manor Rd TQ3 .....226 B8
Upper Morin Rd TQ3 ....226 C7
Upper Paul St EX4 ....261 A3
Upper Penns Rd TQ3 ......219 C1
Upper Ridings PL7 ....251 B7
Upper Stoneborough La
EX9 ....198 A1
Upper Torrs EX34 ....2 E4
Upper West Terr EX9 ......198 A1
Upper Westhill Rd DT7 ....260 C3
Upper Wood La TQ6 ....234 B3
Upperton La PL6 ....241 F3
Upperton Rd EX6 ....97 D1
Uppincott Hill EX5 ....63 C1
Uppincott La EX5 ....81 C8
Upright Villas 3 EX33 ....152 D5
Upton Cl PL3 ....249 B7
Upton Cross
Payhembury EX14 ....84 D5
Thurlestone TQ7 ....143 D2
Upton Hill TQ1 ....220 D6
Upton Hill Rd TQ5 ....230 C2
Upton Manor Ct TQ5 ......230 C2
Upton Manor Pk TQ5 .....230 C2
Upton Manor Rd TQ5 .....230 C2
Upton Pyne Cross EX5 .....172 F6
Upton Pyne Hill EX5 ....172 F6
Upton Rd
11 Bideford EX39 ....157 B1
Torquay TQ2 ....219 F6
Upton St James CE Prim Sch
TQ1 ....220 A7
Usticke La EX34 ....3 B3
Uton Steep Cross EX17 ...165 B1
Uxbridge Dr PL5 ....243 E4

V

Vaagso Cl PL1 ....247 E2
Vachell Cres EX2 ....178 C3
Vale Cl Barnstaple EX32 ..155 A6
Galmpton TQ5 ....229 B5
Vale La EX13 ....167 D6
Vale Rd Exmouth EX8 .....202 D7
Kingskerswell TQ12 ....213 A5
Newton Abbot TQ12 ....207 D1
Valentines TA22 ....33 E6
Vales Rd EX9 ....198 B1
Valiant Ave PL5 ....244 A4
Valletort Flats PL1 ....248 A2
Valletort Ho PL1 ....262 C3
Valletort La PL1 ....248 A3
Valletort La PL1 ....248 A3
Valletort Pl PL1 ....248 A2
Valletort Rd PL1 ....248 A2
Valley Cl Barnstaple EX32 ..155 B5
Valley Dr PL9 ....140 D8
Valley La 6 EX34 ....3 A3
Valley of Rocks The*
EX35 ....3 A2
Valley Park Cl EX4 ....173 D2
Valley Path TQ12 ....206 E4
Valley Rd
Clyst St Mary EX5 ....179 E3
Exeter EX4 ....176 F7
Plymouth PL7 ....250 B5

Valley Rd continued
Saltash PL12 ....242 E2
Valley View
Axminster EX13 ....167 E5
Bampton EX16 ....34 B3
Bideford EX39 ....156 D2
Chagford TQ13 ....111 A6
Farway EX24 ....101 F6
Landkey EX32 ....17 C1
Millmoor EX15 ....51 E1
Plymouth PL6 ....245 D7
Seaton EX12 ....192 A6
Shebbear EX21 ....55 E4
Valley View Cl
Plymouth PL3 ....249 B6
Seaton EX12 ....192 B6
Torquay TQ1 ....219 F7
Valley View Rd PL3 ....249 B7
Valley Way EX8 ....196 E3
Valley Wlk PL6 ....245 E6
Valleyside TQ7 ....143 A2
Van Buren Pl EX2 ....178 D3
Van Post EX14 ....49 D6
Vanehill Rd TQ1 ....220 C3
Vanguard Cl PL5 ....244 E6
Vanpost Hill EX16 ....49 D5
Vansittart Dr EX8 ....196 C3
Vansittart Rd TQ2 ....219 F6
Vapron Rd PL3 ....248 F6
Varco Sq EX2 ....178 C4
Varian Cl 4 TQ9 ....223 E5
Varley Ct EX16 ....161 E6
Vauban Pl PL2 ....247 F4
Vaughan Cl PL2 ....248 C7
Vaughan Par TQ2 ....220 B4
Vaughan Rd Exeter EX1 ..178 B6
Torquay TQ2 ....220 B3
Vaughan Rise EX1 ....178 B6
Vauxhall Ct 11 PL4 ....263 A2
Vauxhall St PL4 ....263 A2
Vauxhall Street Flats 10
PL4 ....263 A2
Vavasours Slip TQ6 ....233 F4
Veale Cl EX20 ....75 B6
Vealenia Terr TQ13 ....130 D4
Veales Rd TQ7 ....258 C4
Veaspark PL9 ....140 D8
Veille La TQ7 ....219 C8
Veitch Gdns EX2 ....181 B8
Velator Cl EX33 ....152 D4
Velator Cr EX33 ....152 D4
Velator Lane Ave EX33 ...152 D5
Velator Rd EX33 ....152 D4
Vellacott La EX34 ....3 C3
Vellaford Cross EX16 ....87 A7
Velland Ave TQ2 ....213 F4
Velator Way EX33 ....152 D4
Velwell Rd EX4 ....261 A4
Venbrough Cl EX12 ....191 F8
Venbridge Hill EX6 ....97 B4
Venford Cl TQ2 ....229 B8
Venford Hill
East Anstey TA22 ....32 E8
Hawkridge TA22 ....21 D1
Venford Villas EX36 ....30 D4
Venhay Cross EX36 ....46 D6
Venlake DT7 ....260 A5
Venlake Cl DT7 ....260 A5
Venlake End DT7 ....260 A5
Venlake Mdw DT7 ....260 A5
Venn Cl Barnstaple EX32 ..155 D1
Venmore Orch EX5 ....184 B2
Venn Cl Instow EX39 ....15 C2
6 Plymouth PL3 ....248 E6
Stoke Fleming TQ6 ....146 B7
Venn Cotts EX39 ....15 C2
Venn Cres PL3 ....248 E6
Venn Cross
Barnstaple EX32 ....155 D1
Broadhempston TQ12 .....131 D4
Clayhanger TQ9 ....144 E5
Stoke Fleming TQ6 ....146 B7
Ugborough PL21 ....137 E7
Waterrow TA4 ....35 D3
West Putford EX22 ....39 D3
Venn Ct Brixton PL8 ....257 A4
Plymouth PL3 ....248 E6
Venn Dr PL8 ....257 A4
Venn Gdns PL3 ....248 E7
Venn Gr PL3 ....248 E6
Venn Hill
Copplestone EX17 ....79 B8
Milton Abbot PL19 ....116 A6
Venn La
Cheriton Fitzpaine EX17 ....63 A1
Dartmouth TQ6 ....233 B1
Plymouth PL2,PL3 ....248 C6
Stoke Fleming TQ6 ....146 A8
Venn La End EX32 ....17 B7
Venn Ottery Rd EX10 ......186 E8
Venn Pk TQ6 ....146 B8
Venn Way Plymouth PL3 ..248 E7
Stoke Fleming TQ6 ....146 B7
Venny Bridge EX4 ....174 D1
Ventiford Cotts TQ12 ......123 C2
Vention La EX33 ....7 E3
Venton Cross
Highampton EX21 ....74 E6
Totnes TQ9 ....139 B5
Venton Dr EX39 ....156 C6
Venton La Plymouth PL7 ..207 A3
Verbena Terr TQ14 ....209 D5
Vermont Gdns PL2 ....247 F7
Verna Pl PL5 ....243 D2
Verna Rd PL5 ....243 E2
Verney St EX1 ....261 C4

Vernhill Cross PL7 ....132 E3
Vernon Cl TQ1 ....220 C2
Vernon Rd EX8 ....196 D2
Vernons La 12 EX9 ....15 A1
Verona Ct 8 EX32 ....155 A6
Verwill La EX34 ....3 D3
Vestry Dr EX2 ....181 B8
Viaduct View EX22 ....164 C4
Vial's Cnr EX16 ....48 D5
Vicarage Ball TQ9 ....222 C2
Vicarage Cl Brixham TQ5 ..230 C5
Hartland EX39 ....22 D3
Stoke Gabriel TQ9 ....227 F7
Vicarage Gdns
Dawlish EX7 ....204 C6
Milton Abbot PL19 ....116 A6
Plymouth PL5 ....243 B1
Vicarage Gr TQ9 ....227 F8
Vicarage Hill
Cornwood PL21 ....133 D3
Dartmouth TQ6 ....233 E3
Dulverton TA22 ....33 D6
Holbeton PL8 ....136 D1
Kingsteignton TQ12 ....207 F7
Marldon TQ3 ....218 E3
Torquay TQ2 ....219 D4
Vicarage La
15 Chudleigh TQ13 ....123 E6
Exeter EX4 ....174 E2
Longdown EX6 ....98 E1
South Tawton EX20 ....95 B5
Strete TQ6 ....145 F6
Vicarage Lawn EX32 .....155 A5
Vicarage Rd
Abbotskerswell TQ12 ......212 B6
Blackawton TQ9 ....139 E1
Brixham TQ5 ....230 C2
Cockwood EX6 ....201 B6
East Budleigh EX9 ....198 B6
Kenton EX6 ....148 B2
Marldon TQ3 ....218 E3
Village St 8 EX12 ....192 A5
Marldon TQ3 ....218 E3
Okehampton EX20 ....170 A5
Plymouth PL7 ....250 C6
Sidmouth EX10 ....188 B4
South Brent TQ10 ....134 F3
Stoke Gabriel TQ9 ....227 F8
Torpoint PL11 ....247 B2
Torquay TQ2 ....219 D4
Vicarage St
Barnstaple EX32 ....155 A5
Colyton EX24 ....103 A5
Vicary Cl TQ12 ....207 A3
Vickers Ground EX39 .....156 F8
Vickery Cl EX15 ....163 B3
Vicrage Hill TQ5 ....230 C5
Victor La TQ9 ....139 E1
Victor St EX1 ....178 A5
Victoria Ave PL1 ....262 A4
Victoria Cl
5 Barnstaple EX32 ....155 B4
Kenton EX6 ....148 C4
Willand EX15 ....162 D4
Victoria Cottage Hospl
EX10 ....188 B4
Victoria Cotts
2 Holsworthy EX22 ......164 C4
Lee Mill PL21 ....136 D6
North Tawton EX20 ....77 C4
Plymouth PL6 ....249 B8
Victoria Cres EX17 ....165 D6
Victoria Ct
Dartmouth TQ6 ....233 D3
4 Totnes TQ9 ....223 C5
Victoria Gdns 1 EX39 ....157 A1
Kingsbridge TQ7 ....159 A1
Victoria Hill TQ6 ....164 C5
Victoria Hts TQ6 ....233 D3
Victoria La PL12 ....242 F2
Victoria Lawn EX32 ....155 B4
Victoria Par TQ1 ....220 B3
Victoria Park Rd
Exeter EX2 ....177 E5
Torquay TQ1 ....220 B7
Victoria Pl
Axminster EX13 ....167 D6
Brixham TQ5 ....230 C6
Budleigh Salterton EX9 ...199 G2
Chardstock EX13 ....88 A2
Dartmouth TQ6 ....233 F3
6 Exmouth EX8 ....202 A6
Newton Abbot TQ12 ....207 C3
Plymouth PL2 ....262 A2
Plymouth, Devonport PL2 ..247 F4
Victoria Rd
Barnstaple EX32 ....155 A4
Barnstaple EX32 ....155 A6
Black Torrington EX21 ......74 A8
Dartmouth TQ6 ....233 F6
Exeter EX4 ....177 D8
Plymouth PL5 ....243 D1
1 Exeter EX4 ....177 D8
Exmouth EX8 ....201 F6
Plymouth PL5 ....243 D2
Saltash PL12 ....242 F2
Sidmouth EX10 ....188 B3
Topsham EX3 ....182 F5
Totnes TQ9 ....223 C5
Victoria Road Prim Sch
PL5 ....243 D1
Victoria Sh Ctr TQ4 ....226 C6
Victoria Sq
Paignton TQ4 ....226 C6
Victoria St
Combe Martin EX34 ....3 B3
Exeter EX4 ....177 D8

Victoria St continued
Holsworthy EX22 ....164 C4
Okehampton EX20 ....170 C5
Paignton TQ4 ....226 B6
Torpoint PL11 ....247 B3
Totnes TQ9 ....223 C5
Wellington TA21 ....160 D6
Victoria Terr
Barnstaple EX32 ....155 A4
2 Bovey Tracey TQ13 ....180 D8
3 Brixham TQ5 ....230 C4
Honiton EX14 ....166 B6
Kingsteignton TQ12 ....207 F7
Ottery St Mary EX11 ....169 C3
Plymouth PL6 ....249 B8
Tiverton EX16 ....161 B4
Victoria Way EX8 ....201 F6
Victory Rd
Dartmouth TQ6 ....233 D3
North Tamerton EX22 ....89 D8
Victory St PL2 ....247 E6
Vieux Cl EX9 ....198 E7
View Rd DT7 ....260 D3
Vigo Mews PL19 ....171 C6
Vigoridge Rd PL19 ....171 C6
Vila Cl EX32 ....155 B2
Villa Rd EX38 ....159 C5
Village Cl EX8 ....202 F7
Village Cross
Coldridge EX17 ....59 F2
Loddiswell TQ7 ....143 E7
Morchard Bishop EX17 .....61 B2
Village Cross Rd TQ7 ....143 E7
Village Dr PL6 ....241 C1
Village Farm Cl EX23 .....70 A6
Village La EX14 ....86 B1
Village Rd Christow EX6 ..113 B3
Marldon TQ3 ....218 D3
Woodbury Salterton EX5 ..184 C6
Village St 8 EX12 ....192 B6
Village The PL20 ....126 C3
Village Way PL19 ....117 F4
Villiers Ave TQ12 ....207 F2
Villiers Cl PL9 ....255 D7
Vincent Way PL12 ....242 F2
Vincents Rd TQ12 ....258 B6
Vine Cl EX22 ....261 C2
Vine Cres PL7 ....248 B6
Vine Gdns PL2 ....248 B6
Vine Pas EX14 ....166 C6
Vine Rd TQ2 ....219 F6
Vine St EX19 ....58 F2
Vinery La PL7,PL9 ....250 E1
Vinery The TQ1 ....220 B4
Viney Cross EX14 ....86 B6
Viney Ct TQ5 ....230 B6
Ipottery EX14 ....68 C2
Viney Lane Cross EX14 ...86 B5
Vineyard TQ9 ....223 A8
Vineyard Hill TQ9 ....223 A8
Vineyard La EX13 ....167 C7
Vineyard Terr TQ9 ....144 D7
Vineyards The EX22 ....164 C5
Vinicock Cl EX10 ....188 F7
Vinicroft La EX10 ....188 F7
Vinivers Cross TQ8 ....148 F4
Vinnicombes Rd PL5 .....173 F8
Vinstone Way PL5 ....243 E3
Violet Dr PL6 ....245 E8
Violet La PL19 ....171 E6
Virginia Cl EX39 ....157 A1
Virginia Cotts EX4 ....155 D6
Virginia Lodge 17 TQ1 ..220 D4
Vision Hill Rd EX9 ....198 B2
Visitors Hill EX16 ....63 D4
Vittery Cl TQ5 ....230 B5
Vix Ct TQ5 ....230 B5
Vixen Tor Cl
Okehampton EX20 ....170 E5
Yelverton PL20 ....126 E3
Vognacott Cross EX22 .....53 F3
Voscombe Cross EX31 .....26 F7
Voulsdon Cross EX20 ......92 A4
Voysey Hill EX17 ....220 B7
Vuefield Hill EX2 ....177 A1
Vulscombe Cross EX16 .....63 A6
Vulscombe La EX16 ....63 A6
Vyvyan Ct EX1 ....178 A5

W

Wadbrook Cross EX13 ......88 C4
Waddens Cross EX24 .....102 D4
Wadderly Hill EX17 ....79 F7
Waddeton Cl TQ4 ....225 F1
Waddeton Ind Est TQ4 ...225 F1
Waddeton Rd
Paignton TQ4 ....225 F1
Stoke Gabriel TQ5 ....228 D6
Waddington Cross EX36 ...31 A3
Waddington La EX16 ....45 A5
Waddles Down Cross
EX4 ....98 E5
Waddon Cl PL7 ....250 E7
Waddons Cross TQ9 ....216 C6
Wade Cl EX18 ....202 E8
Wadham Cross
Dunsford TQ9 ....32 A2
West Anstey SS6 ....32 A4
Wadham Hill EX36 ....32 A2
Wadham Ho EX4 ....173 A1
Wadham Terr 6 PL2 ....248 A5
Waggoners Way EX17 ......86 A3
Waggons Way EX4 ....177 A8
Waggs Plot EX13 ....88 B4
Waie Cotts EX17 ....78 C6
Waie Cross EX17 ....78 B6
Wain La TQ12 ....122 F1

Wain Pk PL7 . . . . .250 F4
Wake St PL4 . . . . .262 B4
Wakefield Ave PL5 . . . . . . .243 E1
Wakehams CI PL21 . . . . . .137 C2
Walborough CE Prim Sch
TQ12 . . . . .207 C3
Walcot CI PL6 . . . . .245 E3
Walcott Way EX14 . . . . .67 C1
Walden Rd EX14 . . . . .67 C1
Waldon CI PL7 . . . . .251 B6
Waldon Ct TQ2 . . . . .220 B4
Waldon Ho TQ2 . . . . .220 B4
Waldon Point TQ2 . . . . . . .220 B4
Waldon Way EX22 . . . . . . .164 C6
Waldons Cross EX19 . . . . . .57 F1
Waldron's Cross TA21 . . . . .35 E1
Walk La EX36 . . . . .30 F6
Walker Terr PL1 . . . . .262 B1
Walkers Gate TA21 . . . . . .160 D5
Walkham Bsns Pk PL5 . . . .244 B1
Walkham CI PL19 . . . . .171 D5
Wall Park CI TQ5 . . . . .230 E5
Wall Park Rd TQ5 . . . . .230 E5
Wall Pk TQ9 . . . . .222 F6
Wallace Ave Dawlish EX7 204 E7
Exeter EX4 . . . . .178 B8
Torquay TQ2 . . . . .219 C8
Wallace La
Kingsbridge TQ7 . . . . .258 B3
Lynton EX35 . . . . .5 A3
Wallace Rd PL7 . . . . .251 A4
Wallaford Rd TQ11 . . . . . . .135 C8
Walland Cross EX32 . . . . . .18 E3
Wallaton Cross TQ9 . . . . . .145 A7
Wallfield Rd TQ13 . . . . . . .180 B5
Wallingford Rd TQ7 . . . . .258 D6
Wallis Gr PL3 . . . . .209 A8
Wallon Cross TQ13 . . . . . .110 F7
Wallpark CI PL7 . . . . .250 F7
Walls CI EX8 . . . . .196 D2
Walls Hill Rd TQ1 . . . . .220 D7
Walnut CI Exminster EX6 182 A4
Plymouth PL7 . . . . .251 B5
Totnes TQ9 . . . . .223 B6
Walnut Ct Brixham TQ5 . . .230 D4
Torquay TQ2 . . . . .219 E4
Walnut Dr Crediton EX17 165 D6
Plymouth PL7 . . . . .251 C5
Tiverton EX16 . . . . .161 F5
Walnut Gdns PL7 . . . . .251 C5
Walnut Gr EX8 . . . . .202 C7
Walnut Gr TQ12 . . . . .219 E4
Walnut Rd Exeter EX2 . . . .177 F2
Honiton EX14 . . . . .166 A4
Torquay TQ2 . . . . .219 E4
Walnut Way EX32 . . . . . . .155 D4
Walpole CI EX4 . . . . .174 C1
Walreddon CI PL19 . . . . . .171 B4
Walshams EX14 . . . . .87 A7
Walsingham Ct PL7 . . . . . .251 B6
Walson Cross EX17 . . . . . . .78 D3
Walson La EX19 . . . . .76 E7
Walson Rd EX17 . . . . .78 D3
Waltacre PL8 . . . . .257 F3
Walter Daw Fst Sch
EX2 . . . . .178 B4
Walters Rd PL5 . . . . .243 C2
Waltham PI PL2 . . . . .248 A8
Waltham Rd TQ12 . . . . . . .207 A3
Waltham Way PL21 . . . . . .237 E4
Walton Cres PL5 . . . . .244 C1
Walton Rd EX2 . . . . .178 C5
Walton Way EX32 . . . . . . .155 C5
Wandle PI PL3 . . . . .249 D5
Wanstead Gr PL5 . . . . . . .244 A2
Wantage Gdns PL5 . . . . . .262 A3
Warberry CE Prim Sch
TQ1 . . . . .220 C5
Warberry Rd W TQ1 . . . . .220 B5
Warberry Vale ❸ TQ1 . . . .220 B6
Warboro Terr EX4 . . . . . . .201 B8
Warborough Hill EX6 . . . .194 E3
Warborough Rd TQ5 . . . . .229 C6
Warbrightsleigh Hill
EX16 . . . . .48 B7
Warbro CI ❶ TQ1 . . . . . . .220 B7
Warbro Rd TQ1 . . . . .220 C7
Warburton Gdns PL5 . . . .243 C1
Warcombe La EX34 . . . . . . .1 B2
Ward La EX19 . . . . .59 A2
Ward PI PL3 . . . . .249 B5
Wardens CI EX17 . . . . .63 C7
Wardleworth Way TA21 . .160 C7
Wardlow CI PL6 . . . . .248 F8
Wardlow Gdns PL6 . . . . . .248 F8
Wardrew Rd EX4 . . . . .176 F5
Wards Cross EX5 . . . . .99 C8
Ware CI TQ12 . . . . .207 F7
Ware Cliff Chalets DT7 . .260 D2
Ware Cross
Kingsteignton TQ12 . . . . . .207 F7
Ugborough PL21 . . . . .137 D6
Ware La DT7 . . . . .260 B2
Wareborough Rd EX22 . . . .72 A5
Warecross Gdns TQ12 . . . .207 F7
Warefield Rd TQ3 . . . . . . .226 C7
Wareham Cross EX13 . . . . .88 E1
Wareham Rd EX13 . . . . .88 E2
Warestoot Dr EX17 . . . . . .165 B6
Warfelton Cres PL12 . . . . .242 E2
Warfelton Gdns PL12 . . . .242 E2
Warfelton Terr PL12 . . . . .242 E2
Warfield Villas EX34 . . . . .150 C5

Warfleet Creek Rd TQ6 . .234 A1
Warfleet Rd TQ6 . . . . .234 A2
Waring Bowen Ct EX2 . . . .177 F1
Waring Rd PL6 . . . . .244 D7
Warkleigh Ave PL2 . . . . . .248 A5
Warkleigh Cross EX37 . . . .29 B1
Warland TQ9 . . . . .223 C5
Warleigh Ave PL2 . . . . . . .247 E5
Warleigh Cres PL6 . . . . . . .244 F5
Warleigh La PL2 . . . . .247 E5
Warleigh Rd ❶ PL4 . . . . . .248 E4
Warn Hill TQ13 . . . . .123 B7
Warmwell Rd PL5 . . . . . . .243 E4
Warne La PL19 . . . . .117 E6
Warneford Gdns EX8 . . . . .196 E2
Warnicombe La EX16 . . . . .64 D6
Warne La PL19 . . . . .171 C3
Warraton Cl PL12 . . . . .242 D3
Warraton Gn PL12 . . . . . . .242 D3
Warraton La PL12 . . . . .242 D3
Warraton Rd PL12 . . . . . . .242 D3
Warren Cl
Great Torrington EX38 . . . .159 C5
Wembury PL9 . . . . .140 D7
West Hill EX11 . . . . .168 D4
Warren Cotts PL9 . . . . . . .140 E6
Warren Cross EX16 . . . . . .161 B7
Warren Dr EX9 . . . . .198 B2
Warren Hill TQ2 . . . . .220 B4
Warren La
Dartington TQ9 . . . . .216 B3
Exeter EX4 . . . . .261 B4
Farway EX24 . . . . .102 A7
Great Torrington EX38 . . . .159 C5
Lee Mill PL21 . . . . .136 D6
Plymouth PL5 . . . . .244 A8
Wembury PL9 . . . . .140 E7
Warren Pk Plymouth PL6 245 D7
West Hill EX11 . . . . .168 D4
Warren Rd
Bigbury-on-Sea TQ7 . . . . .142 E3
Dawlish EX7 . . . . .205 A8
Kingsbridge TQ7 . . . . .258 E3
Mary Tavy PL19 . . . . .117 E6
Thurlestone TQ7 . . . . .143 A1
Torquay TQ2 . . . . .220 B4
Warren St Plymouth PL2 247 E4
Rockwell Green TA21 . . . . .160 A4
Warren The TQ12 . . . . .206 F3
Warren View EX39 . . . . . . .156 E2
Warrens Mead EX10 . . . . .188 D8
Warsprite Gdns PL5 . . . . .244 A2
Warton CI PL5 . . . . .244 D3
Warwick Ave Exeter EX1 .178 C5
Plymouth PL5 . . . . .244 D3
Warwick CI Feniton EX14 . .84 E2
Torquay TQ2 . . . . .220 E7
Warwick Orchard CI
PL5 . . . . .244 B3
Warwick Rd EX1 . . . . .178 C6
Warwick Terr ❼ EX32 . . . .154 F6
Wasdale CI PL6 . . . . .245 D2
Wasdale Gdns PL6 . . . . . .245 D2
Wash Cross TQ11 . . . . .215 B8
Washabrook La TQ7 . . . . .258 E6
Washabrook Way TQ7 . . .258 E5
Washbourne Cl
Brixham TQ5 . . . . .230 E5
Plymouth PL1 . . . . .247 E3
Washbourne Cross TQ9 . .139 D6
Washbrook View EX11 . . .169 E4
Washfield La
Calverleigh EX16 . . . . .48 E2
Tiverton EX16 . . . . .161 B7
Washford Pyne Cross
EX17 . . . . .61 E4
Washington Cl TQ13 . . . . .219 B1
Wastor Cross PL21 . . . . . . .142 D7
Wastor Pk PL21 . . . . .142 D7
Watch The TQ7 . . . . .143 A2
Watching Place Cross
TQ13 . . . . .111 B3
Watcombe Heights Rd
TQ1 . . . . .214 C4
Watcombe Prim Sch
TQ2 . . . . .214 B3
Water Bridge Cross EX17 .78 F6
Water Cotts TQ13 . . . . . . .121 F7
Water Gate EX21 . . . . .261 B2
Water La
Barnstaple EX32 . . . . .155 B3
Bow EX17 . . . . .78 C4
Combe Martin EX34 . . . . . . .3 A3
Cornworthy TQ9 . . . . .227 A3
Exeter EX2 . . . . .177 C3
Kingskerswell TQ12 . . . . . .213 A4
Sidmouth EX10 . . . . .188 B5
Tiverton EX16 . . . . .162 B6
Torquay TQ2 . . . . .219 C8
Water Lane CI ❷ EX32 . . .155 B3
Water Lane End TQ9 . . . . .215 B3
Water Mdw EX15 . . . . .163 C2
Water Park Rd EX39 . . . . .156 D2
Water Terr ❺ EX34 . . . . .3 A3
Water Turn TQ13 . . . . .130 E5
Waterbeer St EX4 . . . . . . .261 A3
Waterdale Farm TQ12 . . .213 A4
Waterford Cross TQ9 . . . .131 B3
Waterford La EX13 . . . . . . .103 C5
Watergate Cotts PL9 . . . .140 D8
Watergate Cross EX20 . . .107 E6
Waterhaynes La TQ10 . . . .68 F8
Waterhead CI TQ5 . . . . . .234 B4
Waterhead Terr TQ6 . . . . .234 B4
Waterhouse Cross EX17 . .62 E1
Waterhouse Hill EX20 . . . .74 F1

Waterhouse La EX13,
EX14 . . . . .87 C6
Watering Ct EX9 . . . . .198 E7
Waterlake La EX31 . . . . . . .16 A7
Waterlands Rd TA20 . . . . .88 C8
Waterlears Cross TQ7 . . .147 D8
Waterleat Ave
Honiton EX14 . . . . .166 D5
Paignton TQ3 . . . . .225 E6
Waterleat CI TQ3 . . . . .225 E5
Waterleat Ct TQ3 . . . . .225 F5
Waterleat Rd TQ3 . . . . . . .225 E5
Waterloo CI PL1 . . . . .248 A2
Waterloo Cross EX15 . . . . .65 F8
Waterloo Ct PL1 . . . . .248 A2
Waterloo Hill EX16 . . . . . . .47 B6
Waterloo Rd Exeter EX2 . .177 A3
Holsworthy EX22 . . . . .164 D5
Kingsbridge TQ7 . . . . .258 D6
Torquay TQ1 . . . . .220 B6
Wellington TA21 . . . . .160 C6
Waterloo St
Plymouth PL4 . . . . .263 A4
Plymouth, Stoke PL1 . . . . .248 A3
❶₄ Teignmouth TQ14 . . . .210 C4
Waterloo Terr ❻ EX39 . . .156 F1
Waterloo Yard Flats
PL1 . . . . .248 A2
Watermead TA20 . . . . .88 D8
Watermill Ct ❺ TQ5 . . . . .230 C4
Watermore Ct EX4 . . . . . .177 E7
Watermouth Castle*
EX34 . . . . .2 D3
Watermouth Rd EX34 . . . .150 E6
Waterpool Rd TQ6 . . . . . .233 E2
Waterside Exeter EX2 . . . .261 A1
Kingsbridge TQ7 . . . . .258 D4
Waterside Ho
Ivybridge PL21 . . . . .237 C4
❽ Totnes TQ9 . . . . .223 D5
Waterside Rd TQ4 . . . . . . .226 C1
Watersloade Dr PL21 . . . .237 F4
Waterslade La EX5 . . . . . .179 E8
Watersmeet* EX35 . . . . . . .5 E5
Watersmeet Ho* EX35 . . . .5 E5
Watersmeet Rd EX35 . . . .151 E4
Waterstream Sq ❺
TQ13 . . . . .123 F6
Waterwell La TQ12 . . . . . .213 C8
Waterworks La TQ14 . . . .209 D4
Watery La Axminster EX13 .88 A3
Barnstaple, Bear EX32 . . . . .9 A1
Barnstaple, Whiddon EX31 . .9 C1
Braunton EX33 . . . . .152 F5
Budlake EX5 . . . . .82 E3
Colyton EX13,EX24 . . . . . .103 A6
Combe Martin EX34 . . . . . . .3 A3
Croyde EX33 . . . . .7 E2
Great Torrington EX38 . . . .159 E5
Great Torrington, Taddiport
EX38 . . . . .159 B4
Milton Combe PL6 . . . . . . .240 D6
Thorverton EX5 . . . . .83 F3
Tiverton EX16 . . . . .161 E5
Woodbury EX5 . . . . .184 B4
Watkins Way TQ3 . . . . . . .225 D7
Watson CI PL4 . . . . .263 B4
Watson PI PL4 . . . . .263 B2
Watts Park Rd PL2 . . . . . .248 C7
Watts Rd PL19 . . . . .171 B5
Watts' Rd PL4 . . . . .263 C3
Waveney Gdns PL5 . . . . . .244 C3
Waverley Ave EX4 . . . . . . .261 B4
Waverley Rd
Exmouth EX8 . . . . .202 A8
Kingsbridge TQ7 . . . . .258 C4
Newton Abbot TQ12 . . . . .207 B4
Plymouth PL5 . . . . .243 D2
Wawish Pk PL11 . . . . .246 E3
Way CI EX16 . . . . .63 A5
Way Cross TQ9 . . . . .131 D2
Way Down Cross TQ13 . . .110 F8
Way La EX6 . . . . .98 B5
Way's La EX15 . . . . .163 C2
Waybrook Cotts EX2 . . . . .181 B7
Waybrook Cres EX2 . . . . .181 C8
Waybrook La EX2 . . . . .181 B6
Waycott Wlk PL6 . . . . .244 D6
Waye Cross TQ13 . . . . . . .110 E5
Wayfaring EX32 . . . . .155 D3
Wayland Ave EX2 . . . . . . .261 C1
Wayside Brixham TQ5 . . . .230 A4
Ivybridge PL21 . . . . .237 C4
Wayside CI TQ5 . . . . .230 A4
Wayside Cres EX1 . . . . . . .178 B7
Waytown Cross TQ9 . . . . .131 D2
Wear Barton Rd EX2 . . . . .182 B7
Wear Cl EX2 . . . . .182 C7
Wear House Dr EX2 . . . . . .182 C6
Weardown Dr PL21 . . . . . .237 F5
Weatherill Rd EX14 . . . . . .166 C4
Weaver Cross EX15 . . . . . . .83 E6
Weaver Ct TQ2 . . . . .219 B8
Weaver La EX15 . . . . .83 E6
Weavers Cl EX2 . . . . .261 A2
Weavers Ct EX2 . . . . .261 A2
Weavers Way TQ12 . . . . . .213 A4
Weavers Wlk EX15 . . . . . .163 B2
Webber CI TQ12 . . . . .211 F8
Webbers CE Prim Sch
TA21 . . . . .160 D5
Webbers CI
Wellington TA21 . . . . .160 E4
Whimple EX5 . . . . .99 E8
Webbers Way
Dartington TQ9 . . . . .222 F8
Willand EX15 . . . . .162 D4
Webbers Yard Est TQ9 . . .222 E8
Webberton Cross EX2 . . .113 F6

Webbery Cross EX39 . . . . . .26 D4
Webbery Moor Cross
EX36 . . . . .31 A3
Webble Green Cross
EX13 . . . . .87 C8
Webland La TQ10 . . . . . . .135 C3
Webley Rd EX2 . . . . .176 F3
Weddicott Cross TQ13 . . .111 A4
Wedding Well La EX33 . . . .8 F1
Weech Cl EX7 . . . . .204 C6
Weech Rd EX7 . . . . .204 C6
Week Cross
Bishop's Tawton EX31 . . . . .27 F6
Burrington EX37 . . . . .43 C5
Chulmleigh EX18 . . . . .45 D3
Moretonhampstead TQ13 .111 C4
South Zeal EX20 . . . . .95 B3
Witheridge EX16 . . . . .62 D6
Zeal Monachorum EX17 . . .78 C7
Week La
Dawlish Warren EX7 . . . . .201 A1
Huntsham EX16 . . . . .43 D5
Week Lane End EX31 . . . . .27 F5
Week Park Cross EX37 . . . .43 C5
Weekaborough Dr TQ3 . .218 D2
Weekaborough Oak Cross
TQ12 . . . . .217 E4
Weeke Cross PL21 . . . . . . .137 D4
Weeke Hill TQ6 . . . . .146 C8
Weekes Mdw TA21 . . . . . . .51 E6
Weeksland Rd TQ2 . . . . . .219 C6
Weekstone Cross EX22 . . .71 B8
Weir CI PL6 . . . . .245 F2
Weir Gdns PL6 . . . . .245 F2
Weir Head Cotts TA22 . . . .33 D7
Weir Rd PL6 . . . . .245 F2
Weirfield Ho EX2 . . . . .261 B1
Weirfield Rd EX2 . . . . .261 B1
Weirfields TQ9 . . . . .223 C6
Weirford La EX20 . . . . .76 F4
Weirside Rd EX32 . . . . .18 B1
Weirside Way EX32 . . . . . .155 B6
Welbeck Ave PL4 . . . . .262 C4
Welch's La EX31 . . . . .15 C2
Welcombe Cross EX39 . . . .37 E4
Welcome St EX2 . . . . .261 A2
Well Park Ave ❶ EX34 . . .150 D5
Well Cross PL21 . . . . .137 E6
Well Gdns PL1 . . . . .262 B3
Well Hill TQ7 . . . . .147 E6
Well Hill CI TQ7 . . . . .147 E6
Well La EX39 . . . . .37 B5
Well Mead EX13 . . . . .87 C1
Well Oak Pk EX2 . . . . .177 F3
Well Park Flats EX38 . . . . .159 D5
Well Rd
Great Torrington EX38 . . . .159 D5
Torpoint PL11 . . . . .247 B3
Well Spring CI EX39 . . . . . .22 E3
Well St Exeter EX4 . . . . . . .261 C4
Great Torrington EX38 . . . .159 D5
Paignton TQ3 . . . . .226 B6
Starcross EX6 . . . . .201 B8
Well The TA21 . . . . .160 B5
Welland Gdns PL3 . . . . . . .249 C5
Wellands Cl EX15 . . . . .66 B7
Wellands Cross EX13 . . . . .87 D4
Wellbrook Gn EX16 . . . . . .161 B4
Wellbrook St EX16 . . . . . .161 B4
Wellbrook Terr
❽ Tiverton EX16 . . . . .161 B4
❸ Bideford EX39 . . . . . . .163 A4
Welle House Gdns TQ7 . .258 D6
Wellesley Park Prim Sch
TA21 . . . . .160 C4
Wellesley Rd TA21 . . . . . .160 C4
Wellesley Way TA21 . . . . . .68 D7
Wellfield CI PL7 . . . . .251 C5
Wellfield Hill EX13,DT6 . . .88 H2
Wellhay CI PL9 . . . . .256 C6
Welling Ct TA20 . . . . .88 C8
Wellings CI TA20 . . . . .88 C8
Wellington Cottage Hospl
TA21 . . . . .160 C5
Wellington Hill TA21 . . . . .160 F2
Wellington Jun Sch
TA21 . . . . .160 D5
Wellington Mus TA21 . . . .160 D6
Wellington PI ❶ TQ1 . . . .220 B6
Wellington Rd
Exeter EX2 . . . . .177 A3
Torquay TQ2 . . . . .220 B6
Wellington Sch TA21 . . . .160 E5
Wellington Sq ❶₄ TQ10 .134 F3
Wellington St
Plymouth PL4 . . . . .263 A4
Plymouth, Stoke PL1 . . . . .248 A3
❶₀ Teignmouth TQ14 . . . .210 C4
Torpoint PL11 . . . . .247 B3
Wellpark CI EX4 . . . . .176 F6
Wellpark Rd PL18 . . . . . . .125 C5
Wells Ave PL11 . . . . .246 E4
Wells CI EX16 . . . . .196 E4
Wells Ct PL10 . . . . .252 E6
Wells St EX32 . . . . .154 F5
Wellsbourne Pk PL3 . . . . .249 A6
Wellsprings EX16 . . . . . . .161 C6
Wellstones CI PL21 . . . . . .237 E4
Wellswood Ave TQ1 . . . . .220 E5
Wellswood Gdns
Exeter EX4 . . . . .176 E5
Torquay TQ1 . . . . .220 D5
Wellswood Manor ❷
TQ1 . . . . .220 D5
Wellswood Path TQ1 . . . .220 D5
Wellswood Pk TQ1 . . . . . .220 D5

Welman Rd PL10 . . . . .252 F6
Welsbere La EX17 . . . . .62 C3
Welsford Ave PL2 . . . . . . .247 F5
Welstor Cross TQ13 . . . . .130 D7
Wembury Dr TQ2 . . . . . . .214 B2
Wembury Marine Ctr*
PL9 . . . . .140 C7
Wembury Mdw ❶ PL9 . . .140 D8
Wembury Park Rd PL3 . . .248 D6
Wembury Prim Sch PL9 .140 D8
Wembury Rd
Plymouth PL9 . . . . .256 A4
Wembury PL9 . . . . .140 E8
Wemworthy Down La
EX18 . . . . .59 C4
Wendover Way EX2 . . . . . .178 B2
Wenlock Gdns PL2 . . . . . .248 B8
Wensum CI PL7 . . . . .251 A4
Wentwood Gdns PL6 . . . .245 E3
Wentwood PI PL6 . . . . . . .245 E3
Wentworth Gdns EX4 . . . .176 E4
Wentworth PI PL4 . . . . . . .249 B2
Wentworth Rd TQ12 . . . . .180 F3
Wentworth Way PL12 . . . .242 C2
Wesley Ave PL3 . . . . .248 E5
Wesley CI
❸ Tiverton EX16 . . . . .64 D7
Torquay TQ2 . . . . .214 A3
Wesley Ct PL11 . . . . .247 C3
Wesley La PL12 . . . . .242 F2
Wesley Mews TQ2 . . . . . .214 A2
Wesley PI
Plymouth, Mutley PL3 . . . .248 E5
❶ Plymouth, Stoke PL2 . .248 A4
Wesley Rd PL12 . . . . .242 F2
Wesley Terr TQ12 . . . . . . .211 D2
Wesley View TQ12 . . . . . .211 D2
Wesley Way EX32 . . . . . . .155 B4
Wessex Est EX4 . . . . .182 D6
Wessex Ct EX4 . . . . .177 A7
Wessiters EX12 . . . . .192 A5
West & East Putford Prim
Sch EX22 . . . . .39 C2
West Acres EX32 . . . . .191 F7
West Alvington Butts
TQ7 . . . . .143 E2
West Alvington CE Prim Sch
TQ7 . . . . .258 A4
West Alvington Hill
TQ7 . . . . .258 C5
West Anstey School Cross
EX36 . . . . .32 C5
West Ave
Barnstaple EX31 . . . . .154 D3
Exeter EX4 . . . . .177 C8
❹ Tavistock PL19 . . . . . . .171 B5
West Ball Hill EX39 . . . . . . .22 D3
West Barton La EX20 . . . . .76 E4
West Beckon Cl EX23 . . . . .70 A4
West Brushford La EX18 . .59 C2
West Buckeridge TQ14 . . .210 B6
West Buckland Com Prim
Sch TA21 . . . . .52 F7
West Buckland Cross
EX37 . . . . .18 B2
West Buckland Rd TA21 . .52 D7
West Buckland Sch EX32 . .18 C2
West Burridge Cross
EX18 . . . . .60 E7
West Challacombe La
EX34 . . . . .3 A4
West Charleton Ct TQ7 . .144 C1
West Cl EX13 . . . . .167 C5
West Cliff EX7 . . . . .204 D5
West Cliff Ct EX7 . . . . .204 D5
West Cliff Park Dr EX7 . . .204 D5
West Cliff Rd EX7 . . . . . . .204 D6
West Cliff Terr ❷ EX12 . . .192 A4
West Coombe La TA4 . . . . .35 D8
West Cotts TA24 . . . . .13 A2
West Country Amb Trust HQ
EX2 . . . . .178 F5
West Croft Jun Sch
EX39 . . . . .156 F1
West Croft Rd EX22 . . . . .164 B4
West Cross EX13 . . . . .152 D6
West Devon Bsns Pk
PL19 . . . . .171 B3
West Down EX16 . . . . .65 A6
West Down Hill EX33,EX34 .8 F4
West Down La EX34 . . . . . . .8 E5
West Down Prim Sch
EX34 . . . . .8 F5
West Down Rd PL2 . . . . . .248 B6
West Down View EX38 . . .159 C5
West Efford La EX17 . . . . . .81 A4
West Emlett La EX17 . . . . .61 E3
West End EX16 . . . . .48 D5
West End Cross EX16 . . . . .48 D5
West End Rd
Bradninch EX5 . . . . .82 F6
Buckfastleigh TQ11 . . . . . .236 B4
West End Terr
Ashburton TQ13 . . . . .130 F4
Denbury TQ12 . . . . .211 A6
South Molton EX36 . . . . . .158 C4
West Exe N EX16 . . . . .161 C4
West Exe S EX16 . . . . .161 C3
West Exe Tech Coll EX12 .192 A5
West Field Rd EX6 . . . . . . .182 B3
West Ford Cross TQ12 . . .211 C2
West Garth Ct EX4 . . . . . .172 F2
West Garth Rd EX4 . . . . . .172 F2
West Grove Rd EX2 . . . . . .261 C2

West Hill
Budleigh Salterton EX9 . . . . **203** F8
Heybrook Bay PL9 . . . . **140** A7
Heybrook Bay PL9 . . . . **140** B7
West Hill Ct EX9 . . . . **203** F8
West Hill La
Braunton EX33 . . . . **152** C6
Budleigh Salterton EX9 . . . **197** F1
Parracombe EX31 . . . . **4** B2
West Hill Prim Sch
EX11 . . . . **168** D4
West Hill Rd
Lyme Regis DT7 . . . . **260** D3
Plymouth PL4 . . . . **248** F4
West Hill EX11 . . . . **168** D4
West Hoe Rd PL1 . . . . . . **262** B1
West La
Bratton Fleming EX31 . . . . . **11** D4
Dolton EX19 . . . . **57** E6
Knowle EX33 . . . . **8** C2
Lapford EX17 . . . . **60** C3
Paignton TQ3 . . . . **225** A6
West Leigh Cross TQ9 . . **135** F1
West Lyn Rd EX35 . . . . . . **151** C2
West Malling Ave PL5 . . **243** E5
West Manley La EX16 . . . . **64** E7
West Meadow Cl EX33 . . **152** B7
West Meadow Rd EX33 . . **152** A7
West Mill Cross TQ11 . . **236** B4
West Molland La EX30 . . . **32** F6
West Moor Cl EX39 . . . . . **156** F8
West Moor Way EX39 . . **156** F8
West Mount TQ12 . . . . . . **207** D1
West of England Sch for
Children with Little or no
Sight EX2 . . . . **178** B1
West Ogwell Cross
TQ12 . . . . **211** C8
West Pafford Ave TQ2 . . **214** B3
West Park Dr PL7 . . . . . . **251** C5
West Park Hill PL7 . . . . . **251** B7
West Park Prim Sch
PL5 . . . . **244** A2
West Park Rd EX10 . . . . . **188** A5
West Pk Braunton EX33 . . **152** C6
Galmpton TQ7 . . . . **147** B7
South Molton EX36 . . . . . . **158** B4
Stoke Fleming TQ6 . . . . . . **146** B8
West Point (County
Showground) EX5 . . . . . **179** C3
West Pugsley Cross
EX37 . . . . **29** A2
West Rd Roborough PL19 . . **42** F4
Sheepwash EX21 . . . . **56** C1
Westward Ho! EX39 . . . . **7** F6
West Spurway La EX16 . . . **48** A8
West St Ashburton TQ13 . . **130** F4
Axminster EX13 . . . . **167** D5
Bampton EX16 . . . . **34** B1
Bishops Nympton EX36 . . . . **30** F2
Bishopsteignton TQ14 . . . . **208** F8
Denbury TQ12 . . . . **211** A6
Exeter EX1,EX4 . . . . **261** A2
Hartland EX39 . . . . **22** D3
Millbrook PL10 . . . . **252** E5
Okehampton EX20 . . . . **170** B5
South Molton EX36 . . . . . . **158** C4
Tavistock PL19 . . . . **171** B5
Witheridge EX16 . . . . **46** C1
West Terr
Budleigh Salterton EX9 . . . **198** A1
Churston Ferrers TQ5 . . . . **229** E4
Exeter EX1 . . . . **177** F6
West Town Cross EX39 . . . **38** E8
West Town Mdw TQ14 . . **208** E8
West Town Rd EX5 . . . . . . **98** F8
West Ugworthy Cross
EX22 . . . . **53** E3
West Underleys EX12 . . . **191** C5
West View Beer EX12 . . . **191** D5
Holsworthy EX22 . . . . **164** C5
Tavistock PL19 . . . . **171** E2
West View Ave EX39 . . . **157** B2
West View Cl TQ12 . . . . . **206** F1
West View Rd
图 Bere Alston PL20 . . . . **125** E1
Marldon TQ3 . . . . **218** D2
Okehampton EX20 . . . . **170** C5
West View Terr
Exeter EX4 . . . . **261** A2
图 Honiton EX14 . . . . . . **166** B6
Lympstone EX8 . . . . **195** F5
West Waters La EX31 . . . . . **4** D5
West Yelland EX31 . . . . . . **15** C2
West Yeo Cross EX16 . . . . **46** C3
West Yeo Moor Hill EX16 . . **46** C3
Westabrook Ave TQ13 . . **130** F5
Westabrook Cl TQ13 . . . . **130** F5
Westabrook Dr TQ13 . . . . **130** F5
Westacombe EX31 . . . . **27** B8
Westacott Cross
Inwardleigh EX20 . . . . **75** C3
North Tawton EX20 . . . . **77** E5
South Molton EX36 . . . . **45** E8
Westacott La
Coldridge EX17 . . . . **59** E2
East Buckland EX32 . . . . **18** D2
North Tawton EX20 . . . . **77** E5
Westacott Mdw EX32 . . . **155** E4
Westacott Rd EX32 . . . . . **155** E4
Westaway EX31 . . . . **153** E5
Westaway Cl EX31 . . . . . . **155** A7
Westaway Plain EX31 . . . **155** A8
Westaway Rd 图 EX24 . . . **103** A4
Westbourne Gr EX34 . . . **150** A5

Westbourne Rd
Plymouth PL3 . . . . **248** D5
Torquay TQ1 . . . . **220** A7
Westbourne Terr
Budleigh Salterton EX9 . . . **203** F8
Saltash PL12 . . . . **242** F3
Westward Ho! EX39 . . . . . . **156** C7
Westbridge Cl EX20 . . . . **170** B5
Westbridge Cotts PL19 . . **171** B4
Westbridge Ind Est 图
PL19 . . . . **171** B4
Westbrook Ave TQ14 . . . **210** A5
Westbrook Cl EX14 . . . . . **178** B8
Westbury Cl PL5 . . . . **244** B4
Westcliff Rd DT6 . . . . **104** F4
Westcliff Sch EX7 . . . . . . **204** C5
Westclyst EX1 . . . . **175** A3
Westcombe EX2 . . . . **188** D4
Westcombe Cres PL9 . . . **255** D5
Westcombe La EX39 . . . . **156** F2
Westcotts Dr EX19 . . . . . . **58** F2
Westcott Cl PL6 . . . . **249** A8
Westcott Cross EX14 . . . . **66** F2
Westcott La
Aylesbeare EX5 . . . . **99** D4
Aylesbeare EX5 . . . . **9** A1
Witheridge EX16 . . . . **61** E7
Westcott Rd 图 EX16 . . . . **64** D7
Westcott Way EX14 . . . . . **166** D6
Westcountry Cl PL2 . . . . . **247** F7
Westcroft Ct 图 EX19 . . . . **58** F1
Westcroft Rd PL5 . . . . **243** D1
Westcroyde PL15 . . . . **7** D1
Westella Rd PL20 . . . . **127** A2
Westentown TQ7 . . . . **142** C6
Wester-Moor Cl 图
EX31 . . . . **154** A2
Wester-Moor Dr EX31 . . . **154** A2
Wester-Moor Way
EX31 . . . . **154** A2
Western Terr PL2 . . . . **248** C7
Westerland Cotts
TQ3 . . . . **234** B3
Westerland Gn TQ3 . . . . . **218** D2
Westerland La TQ3 . . . . . **218** D2
Western App PL1 . . . . **262** B2
Western Ave
Appledore EX39 . . . . **15** A1
Exeter EX2 . . . . **182** D7
Western Bsns Pk TQ4 . . . . **225** F2
Western By-Pass TQ9 . . . **223** B5
Western By-Pass TQ9 . . . **223** B6
Western College Rd
PL4 . . . . **248** F5
Western Cotts EX20 . . . . **107** E1
Western Dr
Newton Abbot TQ12 . . . . . **206** F4
Plymouth PL3 . . . . **249** B4
Starcross EX6 . . . . **201** B8
Western Gardens Rd EX34 . . **3** A3
Western Ho EX7 . . . . **204** E7
Western Pl EX24 . . . . **103** A4
Western Rd
Ashburton TQ13 . . . . **130** F4
Crediton EX17 . . . . **165** A6
Exeter EX4 . . . . **177** A5
Holsworthy EX22 . . . . **164** C4
Ivybridge PL21 . . . . **237** C4
Newton Abbot TQ12 . . . . . **207** C3
Torquay TQ1 . . . . **214** B1
Western Rise EX34 . . . . **8** A6
Western Terr
Barnstaple EX31 . . . . **154** E5
Ilfracombe EX34 . . . . **150** A4
Totnes TQ9 . . . . **223** B6
Western Units TQ13 . . . . . **180** D5
Western Villas EX17 . . . . **165** B5
Western Way Exeter EX1 . . **261** A2
Exeter EX1 . . . . **261** C3
Western Way Ind Est
EX15 . . . . **163** C4
Western Wood Way
PL7 . . . . **251** D5
Westerweck Cl EX31 . . . . **154** D4
Westfield Bradninch EX5 . . **82** F6
Plymouth PL7 . . . . **251** A6
Westfield Ave
Barnstaple EX31 . . . . **154** D4
Plymouth PL7 . . . . **255** C6
Westfield Cl
Brixham TQ5 . . . . **230** B3
Budleigh Salterton EX9 . . . **198** A1
Westfield Rd
Budleigh Salterton EX9 . . . **198** A1
Tiverton EX16 . . . . **161** C3
Westfield Terr 图 EX16 . . **161** C3
Westford Cl TA21 . . . . **160** A5
Westgate Ct EX7 . . . . **60** D3
Westhampnett Pl PL5 . . . **243** F4
Westhay Cross EX13 . . . . . **88** B6
Westhayes Cvn Pk DT7 . . **193** D8
Westhays Cl PL9 . . . . **255** F4
Westhead Rd PL10 . . . . . . **140** H2
Westhill Ave TQ1 . . . . **220** B7
Westhill Avenue Cl TQ1 . . **220** B7
Westhill Cres TQ3 . . . . . . **220** B7
Westhill Rd
Paignton TQ3 . . . . **226** A7
Torquay TQ1 . . . . **220** B8
Torwood Terr TQ12 . . . . . . **213** A4
Westholme TQ1 . . . . **220** B7
Westlake Cl PL9 . . . . **140** A8
Westlake Rd PL9 . . . . **140** A8
Westlake Rise PL9 . . . . . . **140** A8
Westland La EX16 . . . . **62** C6
Westlands Exmouth EX8 . . **202** D6
Wrafton EX33 . . . . **152** B4
Westlands La TQ1 . . . . . . **220** B7

Westlands Lwr Sch TQ1 . . **220** B8
Westlands Upper Sch
TQ1 . . . . **220** C7
Westleat Ave TQ3 . . . . . . **225** F6
Westleigh La EX34 . . . . **3** C2
Westmead Cl EX33 . . . . . **152** C6
Westminster Cl
Exmouth EX8 . . . . **196** D3
Feniton EX14 . . . . **84** D2
Westminster Rd EX4 . . . . **176** E6
Westminster Villas
EX34 . . . . **150** D5
Westmoor Cl PL7 . . . . **251** C6
Westmoor Pk PL19 . . . . . **171** C4
Weston Cl Brixham TQ5 . . **230** C3
Broadhembury EX14 . . . . . . **84** D7
Weston Cross
Awliscombe EX14 . . . . **85** C3
Sidmouth EX10 . . . . **189** D8
Weston La
Awliscombe EX14 . . . . **85** B3
Honiton TQ9 . . . . **223** E4
Weston Mill Com Prim Sch
PL2 . . . . **247** E7
Weston Mill Hill PL5 . . . . **243** F1
Weston Mill La PL5 . . . . . **244** A1
Weston Mill Rd PL5 . . . . . **243** E1
Weston Park Rd PL3 . . . . **248** D6
Weston Rd TQ9 . . . . **223** D5
Westonfields TQ9 . . . . . . **223** E5
Westover Cl
Brixham TQ5 . . . . **230** D4
Ivybridge PL21 . . . . **237** B5
Westover Hill DT6 . . . . . . **104** F5
Westover Ind Est PL21 . . . **237** C4
Westover La PL21 . . . . . . **237** A4
Westover Rd EX1 . . . . **178** B4
Westridge Cross EX16 . . . . **63** C4
Westview Cl EX5 . . . . **99** E8
Westward Cl TQ9 . . . . **223** C5
Westward Dr EX8 . . . . **202** B7
Westward View TQ12 . . . **208** A2
Westwater Hill EX6 . . . . . . **97** E5
Westway Cross EX16 . . . . . **61** F8
Westways PL9 . . . . **255** B5
Westwood Cl TQ9 . . . . . . **245** C6
Westwood Cotts EX6 . . . . **98** E2
Westwood Hill EX6 . . . . . **201** A5
Westwood La EX6 . . . . . . **176** B4
Westwood Rd
Crediton EX17 . . . . **165** A5
East Ogwell TQ12 . . . . **212** A8
Westwood Units EX2 . . . . **177** D1
Westwood Way EX12 . . . . **192** B7
Westworthy Cross EX20 . . **77** E6
Westyard La EX18 . . . . **59** B8
Wet La Christow EX6 . . . . **113** B4
图 Combe Martin EX34 . . . . **3** A3
Wethered Cl EX14 . . . . . . **161** C3
Weycroft Ave EX13 . . . . . **167** F7
Weycroft Cl EX1 . . . . **178** D6
Weymouth Pk TQ7 . . . . . . **147** B7
Whalley La DT7 . . . . **260** B4
Wharf Cotts TA21 . . . . . . **160** B8
Wharf Rd TQ12 . . . . **207** D4
Whatley La TA20 . . . . **69** A7
Wheadon Cross EX16 . . . . **46** D4
Wheal Betsy * PL19 . . . . . **117 F8
Wheal Maria Cotts PL16 . . **116** B1
Wheal Rd PL19 . . . . **117** E6
Wheat Pk TQ9 . . . . **138** D8
Wheatclose Cross EX36 . . **20** D2
Wheatcombe Cl TQ2 . . . . **214** B3
Wheatfield Cl EX15 . . . . . **163** B2
Wheatland Cross EX16 . . . **48** C6
Wheatland La EX16 . . . . . . **48** C6
Wheatlands Rd TQ4 . . . . . **226** B4
Wheatley Cl EX4 . . . . **176** E5
Wheatley Ct 图 EX1 . . . . . **261** A2
Wheatly La EX31 . . . . **4** B2
Wheatridge PL7 . . . . **250** B7
Wheathury Cl TQ12 . . . . . **219** E2
Wheatsheaf Way EX17 . . **177** A1
Wheel Cross EX34 . . . . **2** F1
Wheel La EX34 . . . . **2** E1
Wheelbarrow La EX15 . . . . **67** C8
Wheelers Cross EX22 . . . . **39** B1
Wheelwright Ct PL20 . . . **127** B4
Whelmstone Cross EX17 . . **78** E4
Whetcombe Cross PL21 . . **137** F6
Whey Cross EX37 . . . . **28** D3
Whidborne Ave TQ1 . . . . **221** A4
Whidborne Cl TQ1 . . . . . . **220** F3
Whiddon Cross TQ12 . . . **212** B4
Whiddon Dr EX32 . . . . . . **155** D3
Whiddon La
Barnstaple EX31 . . . . **9** D1
Ide EX2 . . . . **114** A8
Whiddon Rd TQ12 . . . . . . **212** B4
Whiddon Valley Ind Est
EX32 . . . . **155** D3
Whidley La EX14 . . . . **167** A8
Whilborough Rd PL12 . . . **212** E2
Whimble Hill EX22 . . . . . . **164** D3
Whimple Prim Sch EX5 . . . **99** E8
Whimple St PL1 . . . . **262** C2
Whimple Sta EX5 . . . . **99** E8
Whin Bank Rd PL5 . . . . . . **244** C3
Whippescott Hill EX36 . . . **46** B8
Whipple's Cross PL21 . . . **136** E4
Whipton Barton Ho EX1 . . **178** B7
Whipton Barton Mid Sch
EX1 . . . . **178** C7
Whipton Barton Rd EX1 . . **178** C7
Whipton First Sch EX1 . . **178** C7
Whipton La EX1 . . . . **178** C7

Whipton La EX1 . . . . **178** A6
Whipton Rd EX4 . . . . **178** A8
Whipton Village Rd EX4 . . **178** B8
Whistley Down PL20 . . . . **126** E2
Whistley Hill TQ13 . . . . . **131** A4
Whistley Hill Cross
TQ13 . . . . **131** A4
Whitby Cres PL6 . . . . **245** A1
Whitby Rd PL6 . . . . **245** A1
Whitchurch Ave EX2 . . . . **178** B4
Whitchurch Prim Sch
PL19 . . . . **171** D2
Whitchurch Rd
Horrabridge PL20 . . . . **126** F5
Tavistock PL19 . . . . **171** C3
Whitcott Hill EX36 . . . . . . **31** A8
White Ash La TA20 . . . . . . **69** D5
White Cl TQ3 . . . . **219** B2
White Cross
Aylesbeare EX5 . . . . **99** C1
Cheriton Fitzpaine EX17 . . . **62** F1
Malborough TQ7 . . . . **147** E6
Ottery St Mary EX11 . . . . . **100** F3
White Cross Ct PL4 . . . . . **263** A3
White Cross Hill EX17 . . . . **62** F1
White Cross Rd EX5 . . . . . **184** D6
White Ct EX7 . . . . **204** B8
White Down Cross EX16 . . **64** E5
White Farm La EX11 . . . . **168** D3
White Gate EX24 . . . . **102** E3
White Gates Cross TQ13 . . **110** F7
White Hart La TA21 . . . . . **160** D6
White Heather Terr
TQ13 . . . . **180** D8
White Hill Dro TA20 . . . . . **69** F5
White Hill La PL1 . . . . **263** A2
White Ladies TQ6 . . . . . . **146** B7
White Lodge EX9 . . . . **198** B1
White Pk TQ9 . . . . **139** A3
White Post EX36 . . . . **20** F2
White Rock Prim Sch
TQ4 . . . . **229** A8
White St EX3 . . . . **182** F4
White Tor Cl EX20 . . . . . . **170** E5
White Tor Rd EX20 . . . . . **170** E5
White's La EX38 . . . . **159** C5
Whiteaburcy Cross TQ13 . . **111** C7
Whitear Cl TQ14 . . . . **124** E1
Whitear's Way TQ12 . . . . **207** E7
Whitebeam Cl
Exeter EX4 . . . . **174** B2
Paignton TQ3 . . . . **225** E7
Whitebourgh La
Chudleigh TQ13 . . . . **123** D8
Trusham TQ13 . . . . **113** D1
Whitebridge EX14 . . . . . . **166** C5
Whitebridges EX14 . . . . . **166** B4
Whitebrook Terr TA21 . . . **160** F5
Whitechapel La EX16 . . . . **64** C7
Whitecleave Cross EX37 . . **43** F2
Whitedown Cross EX15 . . **67** E4
Whitefield EX14 . . . . **86** C3
Whitefield Cross EX36 . . . **32** D3
Whitefield Hill EX31 . . . . . **9** D2
Whitefield La EX32 . . . . . . **19** A6
Whitefield Terr PL4 . . . . . **263** B4
Whitefriars La PL4 . . . . . . **263** B3
Whitegates EX24 . . . . **103** A5
Whitehall Cl EX36 . . . . . . **158** C3
Whitehall Dr
B Bere Alston PL20 . . . . **125** E1
Plymouth PL9 . . . . **256** B7
Whitehall La EX3 . . . . **182** F8
Whitehall Manor TQ7 . . . **143** E4
Whiteheads Cross TQ11 . . **135** C7
Whitehill Cl TQ12 . . . . **206** F1
Whitehill Cotts TQ12 . . . **206** F5
Whitehill Cross PL15 . . . . **105** B6
Whitehill Gdns PL7 . . . . . **132** F4
Whitehill La TQ9,TQ9 . . . **228** B8
Whitehill Rd TQ12 . . . . . . **206** F1
Whitehouse Cl 图 EX39 . . . **15** B1
Whitehouse Cross EX16 . . **64** C5
Whitehouse Cross EX39 . . **156** B3
Whitehouse La EX18 . . . . . **58** D5
Whitehouse La EX18 . . . . . **58** B5
Whiteland Head EX20 . . . . **58** B8
Whiteleg Ave TQ9 . . . . . . **222** F6
Whiteley Cross PL21 . . . . **137** B5
Whitemoor Cross PL8 . . . **142** A8
Whitemoor Hill EX16 . . . . **61** E1
Whitemoor La EX5 . . . . . . **82** F4
Whiterocks Pk PL18 . . . . **125** A6
Whites Cotts EX20 . . . . . . **95** B4
Whites La EX31 . . . . **154** F7
Whiteside Cl EX4 . . . . **178** C4
Whitestaunton Cross
TA20 . . . . **69** E8
Whitestone Cross TQ7 . . . **145** C5
Whitestone La EX33 . . . . . . **8** D1
Whitethorn Cl
Honiton EX14 . . . . **166** C4
Sidmouth EX10 . . . . **187** B4
Whitethorn Pk EX4 . . . . . **173** C3
Whiteway Cl 图 EX5 . . . . . **99** E8
Whiteway Dr EX1 . . . . **178** B6
Whiteway La TQ12 . . . . . . **214** D8
Whiteway Rd TQ12 . . . . . **207** D7
Whitford Rd
Kilmington EX13 . . . . **103** D8
Musbury EX13 . . . . **103** D7
Whitham Pk PL19 . . . . **171** C4
Whitleigh Ave PL5 . . . . . . **244** D2
Whitleigh Cotts PL5 . . . . **244** C4
Whitleigh Ct PL5 . . . . **244** C4
Whitleigh Gn PL5 . . . . **244** C4

Whitleigh Prim Sch
PL5 . . . . **244** D4
Whitleigh Villas PL5 . . . . **244** E2
Whitleigh Way PL5 . . . . . **244** C4
Whitley Cross TQ7 . . . . . **143** C3
Whitley Rd Farway EX24 . . **101** F7
Paignton TQ4 . . . . **226** A4
Whitley Rocks EX36 . . . . . **31** C7
Whitlow Copse EX2 . . . . **178** C4
Whitman Cl EX8 . . . . **196** C4
Whitmore La PL21 . . . . . . **137** C4
Whitmore Way EX14 . . . . **166** A4
Whitnage La EX16 . . . . **50** C2
Whitnole Cross EX16 . . . . **48** A5
Whitnole La EX16 . . . . **48** A4
Whitsam Cross PL20 . . . . **125** D1
Whitsheaf Cross EX14 . . . **85** C8
Whitsley Cross EX19,EX38 . **42** C4
Whitson Cross PL5 . . . . . **244** C2
Whitsoncross La PL5 . . . . **244** C2
Whitstone Cty Prim Sch
EX22 . . . . **70** E1
Whitstone Head Sch
EX22 . . . . **70** E1
Whitstone La
Bovey Tracey TQ13 . . . . . . **180** C8
South Molton EX36 . . . . **46** B5
Whitstone Rd TQ4 . . . . . . **226** B5
Whittingham Rd
Ilfracombe EX34 . . . . **150** C5
Yealmpton PL8 . . . . **141** B8
Whittington St PL3 . . . . . **262** B4
Whitton Ct EX10 . . . . **187** F7
Whitwell La EX24 . . . . . . **103** A3
Whity Cross PL12 . . . . . . **242** A4
Whitycombe Way EX4 . . . **176** D8
White Stones EX8 . . . . . . **202** C6
Whympston Cross PL21 . . **137** D1
Wicaford Cross EX16 . . . . . **31** A2
Wicaford La EX36 . . . . **31** A2
Wick Cross EX14 . . . . **85** F7
Wicket The EX2 . . . . **178** C3
Wickington La EX20 . . . . . **95** E5
Widdicombe Cross TQ13 . **218** E5
Widdicombe Dr PL21 . . . **237** D4
Widecombe in the Moor Prim
Sch TQ13 . . . . **121** B3
Widecombe Way EX4 . . . **173** E1
Widegate Nursery PL9 . . **256** D8
Widend Camping Pk
TQ3 . . . . **225** A8
Widepost La EX13 . . . . . . **167** C5
Widewell La PL6 . . . . **244** F8
Widewell Prim Sch PL6 . . . **245** B7
Widewell Rd PL6 . . . . **245** B7
Widey Court Prim Sch
PL6 . . . . **244** F1
Widey Cross PL6 . . . . **244** F1
Widey Hill PL14 . . . . **141** A7
Widey La PL6 . . . . **244** F1
Widey View PL3 . . . . **248** F6
Widgery Dr EX36 . . . . **158** C4
Widgery Rd EX4 . . . . **178** A8
Widworthy Ct EX14 . . . . . . **86** C2
Wigford Cross TQ7 . . . . . **138** C1
Wigley Cross EX31 . . . . . . **16** C8
Wilbarn Rd TQ3 . . . . **226** C7
Wilburton Cross PL21 . . . **136** E5
Wilbury Way EX7 . . . . **204** F7
Wilcocks Rd EX4 . . . . **174** D1
Wilcombe Cross EX32 . . . . **18** E4
Wilcove La PL11 . . . . **246** E5
Wilder Pk EX34 . . . . **150** B5
Wilder Rd EX34 . . . . **150** B6
Wilderness La EX14 . . . . . **84** D6
Wilderness Rd PL3 . . . . . **248** E5
Wildmoor La EX15 . . . . **52** F6
Wildor Top EX35 . . . . **4** E4
Wildwoods Cres TQ12 . . . **207** F4
Wilford Rd EX2 . . . . **178** B5
Wilingcott Cross EX34 . . . **8** C5
Wilkey Cl EX32 . . . . **155** C4
Wilkinson Rd PL5 . . . . . . **247** D8
Willake Rd TQ12 . . . . **213** A5
Willand Moor Mews
EX15 . . . . **162** E5
Willand Moor Rd EX15 . . **162** E5
Willand Old Village
EX15 . . . . **162** C3
Willand Rd
Braunton EX33 . . . . **152** C6
Cullompton EX15 . . . . **163** C4
Willand EX15 . . . . **162** D4
Willas Rd PL16 . . . . **105** E4
Willcocks Cl 图 TA21 . . . **160** D5
Willet St 图 EX39 . . . . . . **157** A2
Willey's Ave EX2 . . . . **261** A1
Willeys Ct EX2 . . . . **261** A1
Willhay La EX13 . . . . **167** D7
Willhayes Cross EX16 . . . **113** E6
Willhayes Hill EX16 . . . . . **113** E6
Willhayes Pk EX13 . . . . . **167** D6
Willhays Cl 图 TQ12 . . . . **123** F1
William Evans Cl PL6 . . . **245** D7
William St EX16 . . . . **161** C4
Williams Ave Exeter EX2 . **261** A1
Plymouth PL4 . . . . **249** B1
Williams Cl Dawlish EX7 . . **204** C5
Wrafton EX33 . . . . **152** E5
Williams Ct EX31 . . . . . . **155** A3
Williamson Cl EX33 . . . . . . **8** A2
Williamson Way EX36 . . . **158** C4
Willing Cross TQ10 . . . . . **135** E5
Willingcott Cross EX34 . . . **8** C5
Willingcott Hill EX34 . . . . . **8** D4

Willis Ct **1** TQ1 ....220 A7
Willis's Cross TQ12 ....122 D2
Willmott Cl EX8 ....196 E1
Willoughby Cl EX8 ....196 A3
Willoughby Rd TQ1 ....220 C6
Willow Ave Exmouth EX8 .196 B3
  Torquay TQ2 ....214 A3
Willow Cl
  Ilfracombe EX34 ....150 E4
  Newton Abbot TQ12 .....213 A8
  Plymouth PL3 ....249 E5
  Seaton EX12 ....192 A8
  Stoke Canon EX5 ....173 F8
Willow Cotts PL7 ....250 D4
Willow Ct
  Buckfastleigh TQ11 .....236 B5
  Exeter EX2 ....178 A4
  Plymouth PL6 ....249 E7
Willow Gdns EX5 ....175 C6
Willow Gn PL12 ....242 D2
Willow Gr Bideford EX39 ..25 D5
  Stibb Cross EX38 ....40 D1
Willow La
  Cornworthy TQ9 ....227 B3
  ⁕ Hemyock EX15 ....52 F2
Willow Rd PL19 ....171 C3
Willow Sq **2** TQ14 ......210 B4
Willow Tree Cl EX2 ....170 C5
Willow Tree Rd EX32 .....155 B2
Willow Way EX7 ....201 A2
Willow Wlk
  Crediton EX17 ....165 E6
  3 Exeter EX4 ....177 D8
  Honiton EX14 ....166 B4
  Plymouth PL6 ....245 D5
Willoway Gr EX33 ....152 C6
Willoway La EX33 ....152 C7
Willoways Cl EX33 ....152 C6
Willowbank Prim Sch
  EX15 ....163 B3
Willowbrook Sch EX4 .....174 B1
Willowby Pk PL20 ....127 A2
Willowdale Cl **4** EX14 .166 B6
Willowfield EX33 ....152 C7
Willowpark La TQ12 ......213 C4
Willows Cl TQ7 ....144 E1
Willows The
  Chilsworthy EX22 ....53 E1
  Shillingford St George EX2 .114 C6
  Torquay TQ2 ....213 D2
Wills Ave TQ3 ....219 C1
Wills Cl PL6 ....244 E7
Wills Rd TQ9 ....223 D6
Willsdown Rd EX2 ....181 C8
Willshere Rd EX2 ....155 C4
Willsland Cl EX6 ....194 D3
Wilmington La EX13,EX14 .86 E2
Wilminstone Ind Est
  PL19 ....171 E7
Wilmot Gdns PL5 ....244 D3
Wilncote Lodge **4** TQ1 ..220 A6
Wilsham Cross EX35 ......6 A5
Wilshere La EX35 ....5 F5
Wilson Cres PL7 ....248 B5
Wilson La Rackenford EX16 .47 B4
  Witheridge EX17 ....46 B1
Wilton Cl TQ12 ....212 B6
Wilton Rd Paignton TQ3 ..219 B2
  Plymouth PL1 ....248 A3
Wilton St PL1 ....262 A4
Wilton Way
  Abbotskerswell TQ12 ....212 B6
  Exeter EX1 ....178 D6
Wiltown La EX15 ....52 F3
Wiltshier Cl EX5 ....175 C7
Wiltshire Cl Exeter EX4 ..176 E4
  Plymouth PL4 ....248 F4
Wimble Cross EX22 ....164 D3
Wimple La TQ12 ....33 C6
Winchester Ave
  Exeter EX4 ....176 F7
  Torquay TQ2 ....213 F1
Winchester Cl EX14 ......84 D2
Winchester Dr EX8 ....196 D4
Winchester Gdns PL5 .....244 A5
Wind Whistle Cross EX35 .66 C1
Windabout Cross EX39 ....39 B7
Winddard Terr EX20 ......93 B1
Windball Hill TQ12 ......33 B7
Windbow La EX15 ....48 D3
Windeatt Sq **4** TQ9 ....223 D5
Windermere Cl EX4 ....176 F6
Windermere Cres PL6 .....244 F4
Windermere Rd TQ1 ......220 C6
Windford Hill EX31 ......10 C4
Windjammer Ct EX8 ......201 E6
Windmill Ave TQ3 ....219 A1
Windmill Cl TQ5 ....230 D4
Windmill Cross EX31 .....27 A3
Windmill Ct **5** TQ5 ....230 C4
Windmill Gdns TQ3 ......219 A1
Windmill Hill
  Brixham TQ5 ....230 D4
  Saltash PL12 ....242 E2
Windmill La
  North Whilborough TQ12 .212 D1
  Northam EX39 ....157 B7
  Paignton TQ3 ....218 F1
  West Hill EX11 ....168 D5
Windmill Rd
  Brixham TQ5 ....230 D4
  Holsworthy EX22 ....164 D4
  Paignton TQ3 ....219 A1
Windout La EX6 ....97 E3
Windrush Rise EX11 .....169 D3
Windsor Ave TQ12 ......207 F3

Windsor Cl
  Cullompton EX15 ....163 C6
  Exeter EX4 ....177 A7
  Ivybridge PL21 ....237 E4
  Newton Abbot TQ12 ....207 C2
  Torquay TQ1 ....220 B6
Windsor Ct
  Ilfracombe EX34 ......150 B5
  Kingsbridge TQ7 ......258 D5
Windsor Dr EX7 ....200 E2
Windsor La PL12 ....242 E2
Windsor Mead EX10 .....101 A1
Windsor Pl PL1 ....262 C2
Windsor Rd
  Barnstaple EX31 ......154 E7
  Dartmouth TQ6 ....233 C3
  Kingsbridge TQ7 ......258 D5
  Northam EX39 ....156 F7
  Plymouth PL3 ....249 B7
  Torquay TQ1 ....220 C6
Windsor Sq EX8 ....202 A7
Windsor Terr DT7 ......260 D4
Windsor Villas PL1 ....262 C2
Windthorn Cross TQ12 ..218 A7
Windthorn La TQ3,TQ12 .218 B7
Windward La EX7 ....210 F8
Windward Rd TQ2 ......213 E3
Windway Hill TA4 ....34 D6
Windwhistle Cross EX5 ..81 C8
Windwhistle La EX16 ....49 B8
Windy Ash Cross EX32 ..16 F1
Windy Ash Hill EX32 ...155 C1
Windy Cnr TQ4 ....229 B6
Windy Cross Ashford EX31 .16 A6
  Chulmleigh EX18 ......44 E1
  Doddiscombsleigh EX6 ..113 E7
  Great Torrington EX38 .159 C5
  Holsworthy Beacon EX22 .54 F2
Windypost Cross EX35 ..151 C2
Wingfield TQ7 ....143 A1
Wingfield Cl **3** EX16 .161 C3
Wingfield Rd PL3 ......262 A4
Wingfield Way PL3 .....262 A4
Winham La EX15 ....83 B6
Winifred Baker Ct **5**
  PL4 ....263 A4
Winifred Cliff Ct **1** EX16 .34 B1
Winkleigh Cl EX2 ......177 A2
Winkleigh Moor Cross
  EX19 ....58 C7
Winkleigh Prim Sch
  EX19 ....58 F2
Winneford La EX14 .....85 C3
Winner Hill Rd TQ3 ....226 A6
Winner St TQ3 ....226 A6
Winnicott Cl PL6 ......244 E7
Winnings Way TQ12 ....220 D7
Winnow Cl PL9 ....255 F4
Winsbeer La
  Rockwell Green TA21 ..160 A6
  Runnington TA21 ......51 F8
Winsbury Ct PL6 ....245 A1
Winscott Cross
  Holsworthy EX21 ....72 A4
  Newton St Cyres EX5 ..81 B1
Winsford Rd TQ12 .....219 C3
Winsham Cross
  Knowle EX33 ....8 D1
  Knowle EX33 ....8 D1
Winsham Rd EX33 ....8 D1
Winslade Cl TQ7 ......144 E1
Winslade Park Ave EX5 .179 B2
Winslade Rd EX10 .....188 B6
Winsland Ave TQ9 .....97 F4
Winsland Mdw EX5 ....222 E6
Winson Cross EX37 ....29 A4
Winsor Cross PL8 .....136 C4
Winstanley Wlk PL3 ...249 D6
Winstitchen Cross TQ14 ..13 C6
Winstitchen La TA24 ...13 C2
Winston Ave PL4 ......262 C4
Winston Cl TQ12 ......207 E7
Winston Ct TQ14 .....210 C6
Winston Ho TQ36 .....158 C5
Winston Pk EX36 .....158 C5
Winston Rd EX8 ......196 E2
Winstone Ave TQ2 ....214 A1
Winstone La PL8 .....257 B4
Winsu Ave TQ2 ....226 A8
Winswood EX17 ....165 D4
Winsworthy EX39 ......23 D3
Winter Gdn TQ2 ......220 B4
Winter's La EX11 .....169 D3
Winterbourne Rd TQ14 .210 C5
Winterland La EX22 ...164 D2
Winters Cross TA4 ....35 C8
Wiriga Way EX16 ......46 E1
Wishings Rd TQ5 .....230 D3
Wiston Cross EX36 ....32 D2
Witch La EX14 ....86 F8
Witcombe La EX16 ....194 D3
Witham Gdns PL3 .....249 C5
Witheby EX10 ....187 F3
Withecombe Cross
  TQ13 ....110 F8
Withen Cross EX5 .....99 C1
Withen La EX5 ....99 D2
Witherdon Cross EX21 ..91 D5
Witheridge CE Prim Sch
  EX16 ....46 E1
Witheridge Mill Cross
  EX16 ....46 E2
Witheridge Moor Cross
  (East) EX16 ....47 E1
Witheridge Moor Cross
  (West) EX16 ....47 D1
Witheridge Pl EX14 ...150 E5
Withleigh Cross EX16 ..63 C8

Withleigh La EX16 .....63 D7
Withycombe La PL10 ...252 B8
Withy Bed La EX5 .....99 E3
Withy Cl EX16 ....161 F3
Withy Cross EX38 .....42 E6
Withy La EX15 ....52 B1
Withy The EX5 ....99 E8
Withycombe Park Dr
  EX8 ....196 A3
Withycombe Raleigh CE Prim
  Sch EX8 ....196 C1
Withycombe Rd EX8 ...202 B8
Withycombe Village Rd
  EX8 ....196 B1
Withygate La EX32 ....19 A5
Withypool Cross
  Hawkridge TA22 ......21 C2
  Twitchen EX36 ....20 E4
Withywell La EX33 ....7 E1
Withywine La TA22 ...34 C5
Wixon Cross EX18 .....45 B3
Wixon La EX18 ....45 B3
Woburn Cl TQ3 ....225 D7
Woburn Terr PL9 .....255 C2
Wolborough Cl TQ2 ...207 C2
Wolborough Gdns
  Brixham TQ5 ....230 E6
  Newton Abbot TQ2 ...207 C2
Wolborough Hill Sch
  TQ12 ....207 B2
Wolborough St TQ12 ..207 B3
Wolford Cross EX14 ..85 B8
Wollaton Cross PL8 ..257 A6
Wollaton Gr EX1 .....243 F3
Wolrige Ave PL7 .....251 B5
Wolrige Way PL7 .....251 A5
Wolsdon Pl PL1 ......262 A3
Wolsdon St PL1 ......262 B3
Wolseley Bsns Pk **2**
  PL1 ....248 A5
Wolseley Cl PL2 .....248 A5
Wolseley Rd
  Plymouth, Camels Head
  PL5 ....247 F6
  Plymouth, St Budeaux PL5 .243 C1
Wolseley Road Flats
  PL2 ....247 F6
Wolston Cl TQ5 ......230 B6
Wolverstone Dr EX13 .85 A8
Wolverstone Hill EX14 .85 A7
Wolverton Dr TQ12 ..207 D7
Wolverwood Cl PL7 ..251 C3
Wolverwood La PL7 ..251 B3
Wombwell Cres PL2 ..247 E7
Wonders Cnr EX38 ...42 E6
Wonford Rd EX2 .....178 A4
Wonford St EX2 .....178 A4
Wonnacott's Rd EX20 .170 C5
Wonton Cross TQ9 ...135 D2
Wood Acre PL12 .....242 B6
Wood Cl Christow EX6 .113 B4
  Saltash PL12 ....242 B3
Wood Cnr EX6 ....97 C2
Wood Cotts TQ12 ...180 C1
Wood Cross EX14 ...86 C6
Wood La
  Abbotskerswell TQ12 .212 A5
  Ashreigney EX18 .....43 D1
  Broadhembury EX14 ..84 E7
  Christow EX6 ....113 B4
  Combe Martin EX34 ..9 B2
  Exmouth EX8 ....196 D1
  Ilfracombe EX34 .....8 F4
  Kingswear TQ6 ......234 B3
  Monkton EX14 ....86 C6
  Morchard Bishop EX17 .61 A2
  Slapton TQ7 ....145 D4
  Thorverton EX17 .....81 B4
  West Alvington TQ7 ..258 A4
Wood Park La EX34 ..9 D3
Wood Pk Ivybridge PL21 .237 D6
  Plymouth PL6 ....132 A2
Wood Rock EX36 ......32 C5
Wood View TQ1 ......207 A3
Wood Way EX8 ....196 A4
Wood's Cross EX36 ..32 C5
Wooda Rd EX39 .....157 C8
Woodacott Cross EX22 .54 E2
Woodah Rd EX4 .....176 F5
Woodbine Cross PL7 ..250 E4
Woodbine Pl **4** EX12 .192 A5
Woodbine Terr EX4 ..261 A4
Woodbridge La
  Bondleigh EX18 .....77 D8
  Fareway EX24 ....102 B6
  North Tawton EX17 ..57 E1
Woodbrook Rd TQ9 ..223 E5
Woodburn Cl PL21 ...237 B5
Woodburn Cross EX16 .32 F2
Woodburn La EX16 ..32 F1
Woodbury Water Cross
  EX16 ....32 F1
Woodbury CE Prim Sch
  EX5 ....184 C3
Woodbury Ct EX8 ....202 C6
Woodbury Gdns PL5 ..244 A3
Woodbury La EX13 ...167 E3
Woodbury Pk EX13 ..167 C4
Woodbury Rd EX3,EX5 .183 E5
Woodbury Salterton CE Prim
  Sch EX5 ....184 C7
Woodbury View
  Exeter EX2 ....177 A2
  Broadclyst EX5 ......175 D6
Woodbury Way EX13 ..167 D4
Woodchurch PL20 ....126 D4
Woodcock Cl PL10 ...253 A6
Woodcock Way EX13 ..85 B7

Woodcote Ct EX5 ....184 C3
Woodcourt Rd TQ9 ...139 C7
Woodcroft Cross EX19 .76 D7
Woodcroft La EX19 ..76 D8
Woodcroft Mdws TA20 .69 F7
Woodend Rd
  Plymouth PL6 ....245 D7
  Torquay TQ2 ....220 D4
Wooder Wharf **8** EX34 .157 A1
Woodfield Cl EX4 ....196 E2
Woodfield Cres PL21 .237 E4
Woodfield Ct TQ1 ...220 D3
Woodfield Prim Sch
  PL5 ....244 C5
Woodfields EX12 ....192 A7
Woodford Ave PL7 ...250 A7
Woodford Cl PL7 ....250 A7
Woodford Cres PL7 ..250 A6
Woodford Gn PL7 ....250 A7
Woodford Inf Sch PL7 .250 B6
Woodford Jun Sch PL7 .250 B7
Woodford Rd PL6 ....245 D6
Woodhaye Cl TQ10 ..134 F2
Woodhaye Gdns **5** TQ1 .220 D4
Woodhaye Terr **1** TQ10 .134 F2
Woodhead Cross
  Branscombe EX12 ....190 E7
  Totnes TQ9 ....217 D4
Woodhead La
  Tiverton EX16 ....63 A7
  Totnes TQ9 ....217 E4
Woodhey Rd PL2 .....248 A7
Woodhill View EX14 ..166 B4
Woodhouse Cl TQ2 ..258 C4
Woodhouse Cross TQ13 .122 D3
Woodhouse Fields DT7 .104 B4
Woodhouse La
  Axminster EX13 ......88 D1
  Uplyme DT7 ....104 B4
Woodhouse Rd EX13 ..88 B1
Woodhuish La TQ5,TQ6 .235 B7
Woodland Ave
  Kingskerswell TQ12 ..212 F5
  Plymouth PL9 ....256 A8
  Teignmouth TQ14 ...210 D7
Woodland Barn Bsns Pk TQ12 .219 E8
Woodland Cl
  Barnstaple EX32 ....155 C4
  Denbury TQ12 ......131 F3
  Saltash PL12 ....237 B5
  Staverton TQ9 .....216 A4
  Torquay TQ2 ....237 E8
Woodland Cotts PL21 .237 A5
Woodland Cross EX31 ..27 B4
Woodland Dr
  8 Barnstaple EX32 .155 A4
  Ivybridge PL21 ....237 A5
  Paignton TQ3 ......226 B7
Woodland Dr PL7 ....250 B4
Woodland Hill EX17 ..97 B8
Woodland La TQ9 ...227 C4
Woodland Mews PL9 .175 D6
Woodland Pk
  Northam EX39 ......157 A5
  Paignton TQ3 ......226 B7
Woodland Rd
  Ashburton TQ13 ....130 F4
  Broadclyst EX5 ....175 C6
  Denbury TQ12 .....211 A6
  Exeter EX1 ....178 D7
  Harbertonford TQ9 ..139 C7
  Ivybridge PL21 ....237 B5
  Ivybridge, Lee Mill PL21 .136 D7
  Plymouth PL7 ......250 C6
  Torquay TQ2 ....219 E8
Woodland Terr
  Ivybridge PL21 ....237 B4
  Kingswear TQ6 ....234 A3
  Plymouth PL4 .....263 B4
Woodland Way
  Gunnislake PL18 ..125 D7
  Torpoint PL11 ....246 F3
Woodland Way Cl PL18 .125 C6
Woodlandhead Cross
  EX17 ....97 B7
Woodlands
  Budleigh Salterton EX9 .203 E8
  Churchstow TQ7 ....143 E4
  Combe Martin EX34 ..2 F4
  Dousland PL20 .....127 B3
  Halwill EX21 ......73 D3
  Kingsbridge TQ12 ..122 E2
  Newton St Cyres EX5 .98 F8
  Plymouth PL9 .....255 F6
  Sidmouth EX10 ....188 A4
  Wellington TA21 ..160 F3
  Whimple EX5 ......99 F8
Woodlands Bsns Pk
  EX16 ....51 C3
Woodlands Cl
  Churchstow TQ7 ...143 E4
  Offwell EX14 ......88 A8
  Teignmouth TQ14 ..210 C5
Woodlands Ct
  Exmouth EX8 ......196 B3
  Plymouth PL5 .....244 A3
  Totnes TQ9 ....223 B6
Woodlands End PL6 ..245 D5
Woodlands Gdns **5**
  TQ12 ....207 F2
Woodlands La PL6 ...245 F1
Woodlands Leisure Pk ⁕
  TQ9 ....139 F3
Woodlands Park Prim Sch
  PL21 ....237 C5
Woodlands Rd TQ12 ..207 F2
Woodlands Sch PL5 ..244 B4
Woodlands Way EX5 .179 C5

Woodlands Wlk TQ13 ..180 C4
Woodlark La **2** EX31 ..154 A2
Woodleigh Cl EX4 ....173 A3
Woodleigh Cross EX19 .42 B3
Woodleigh Pk TQ14 ..210 B2
Woodleigh Rd TQ12 ..206 F3
Woodley Cross EX5 ..98 F8
Woodley La EX5 .....98 E8
Woodleys Dr EX10 ..186 D8
Woodman's Cnr PL20 .127 A3
Woodmans Cres **2**
  EX14 ....166 C5
Woodmans Orch EX5 .84 A2
Woodmead Rd
  Axminster EX13 ....167 C5
  Lyme Regis DT7 ...260 D3
Woodmere Way TQ12 .207 E6
Woodmill Hospl EX15 .163 C1
Woodovis Holiday Pk
  PL19 ....116 D1
Woodpark Cross EX17 .61 A8
Woodpark La
  Midland EX36 ......31 E6
  Paignton TQ3 .....218 E8
Woodpecker Way EX6 .97 B4
Woodplace La EX16 ..162 E6
Woodridge Cross EX19 .57 E6
Woodroffe Sch The
  DT7 ....260 C4
Woods Cross EX36 ...31 D6
Woods The TQ1 .....220 E3
Woodside
  Crapstone PL20 ....126 E2
  Plymouth PL4 .....263 B4
Woodside Ave PL9 ..255 C6
Woodside Cl PL21 ..237 D4
Woodside Ct PL7 ...250 E4
Woodside Dr TQ1 ..220 D4
Woodside La PL4 ...263 B4
Woodside Wlk EX14 .166 D6
Woodstock Gdns PL5 .243 D1
Woodstock Rd EX2 ..178 A5
Woodview Pk TQ9 ..256 A6
Woodview Rd TQ4 ..225 E1
Woodville Ave PL20 .128 A8
Woodville Cl
  Barnstaple EX32 ..154 C4
  Plymouth PL2 .....247 F7
Woodville Cross EX23 .36 F1
Woodville Rd Exeter EX2 .177 B3
  Exmouth EX8 ......202 A8
  Morwenstow EX23 ..37 F6
  Plymouth PL2 .....247 F6
Woodward Rd EX16 ..161 B2
Woodwater La
  Exeter EX2 ....178 B4
  Exeter EX2 ....178 C3
Woodway Pl9 ......256 A7
Woodway Cl TQ14 ..210 C7
Woodway Dr TQ14 .210 C6
Woodway Rd TQ14 .210 C6
Woodway St TQ13 ..123 E6
Woolacombe Cross
  PL20 ....125 F1
Woolacombe Prim Sch
  EX34 ....8 A6
Woolacombe Rd PL20 .125 F1
Woolacombe Rise EX34 ..8 A6
Woolacombe Sands Cvn Pk
  EX34 ....8 A6
Woolacombe Station Rd
  EX34 ....8 A6
Woolaway Ave EX16 ..182 B4
Woolbarn Lawn EX32 .155 D4
Woolbrook Cl EX10 ..188 A6
Woolbrook Mead EX10 .187 F7
Woolbrook Pk EX10 ..188 A7
Woolbrook Rd EX10 ..188 A7
Woolbrook Rise EX10 .188 A7
Woolcombe La
  Ivybridge PL21 ....237 D4
  Sidmouth EX10 ....188 B5
Woolcott Way EX15 ..163 B2
Woolfardisworthy Cross
  Cheriton Fitzpaine EX17 ..62 A3
  Clovelly EX39 ....23 D2
Woolfardisworthy West Prim
  Sch EX39 ....38 F7
Woolhanger's La EX34 ..2 E3
Woollcombe Ave PL7 .250 F4
Woolms Mdw PL21 ..213 E2
Woolsage La TA24 ..21 B7
Woolsery Ave EX4 ..178 B8
Woolsery Cl EX4 ...178 B8
Woolsery Gr EX4 ...178 B8
Woolster Ct **8** PL4 .263 A2
Woolwell Cres PL6 ..245 C8
Woolwell Dr PL6 ...245 D7
Woolwell Rd PL6 ...245 C7
Wootton Cross EX13 .88 F1
Worcester Cres PL5 .162 D4
Worden Cross
  Milton Damerel EX22 .54 E6
  Sutcombe EX22 ....53 E6
Wordland Cross EX17 .80 F8
Wordsworth Ave EX31 .154 F7
Wordsworth Cl
  Exmouth EX8 ......196 C4
  Torquay TQ2 ......219 E6
Wordsworth Cres PL2 .247 F7
Wordsworth Rd PL2 .247 F7

Worham's La EX13 ....86 F2
Works The EX16 ....161 C4
World of Country Life*
  EX8 ....203 B6
Worlington Cross EX39 ...15 C1
Worlington Hill EX39 ....15 C1
Wormsworthy Hill EX16 ..48 D6
Worth La Hele EX5 ....82 E5
  Withypool TA22,TA24 ...21 C4
Worth Rd EX34 ....150 C5
Worthele CI PL21 ......237 A4
Worthele Cross PL21 ...237 B1
Worthy La EX16 ....47 C6
Wotton Cross TQ12 ....131 E4
Wotton La EX8 ....196 B5
Wotton Pound EX8 .....196 A5
Wotton Way TQ9 ....131 E1
Wrafton Rd EX33 ......152 E4
Wragcombe La TA21 ......52 A4
Wrangaton Rd PL21,
  TQ10 ....137 D8
Wrangcombe Rd TA21 ....52 A4
Wrangway Rd EX15 ......52 A3
Wrangworthy Cross EX39 ..39 E4
Wreford's CI EX4 ......173 A3
Wreford's Dr EX4 ......173 A3
Wreford's La Exeter EX4 .173 A3
  Exeter EX4 ....173 B3
Wreford's Link EX4 ....173 A3
Wren CI Honiton EX14 ..166 B4
  Northam EX39 ....157 A6
Wren Ct [10] TQ5 ......230 C4
Wren Gdns PL7 ....250 C6
Wren Hill TQ5 ....230 C4
Wren Pk TQ2 ....213 D2
Wrens Gate PL9 ....255 E8
Wrentham Bsns Ctr
  EX4 ....177 D8
Wrentham Est EX4 .....177 D8
Wrenwell Cross TQ12 ..131 F3
Wressing View EX15 .....66 A3
Wrey Ave EX31 ....154 D4
Wright CI PL1 ....247 E3
Wright Dr EX17 ....79 A5
Wright's La Exmouth EX8 .196 F6
  Torquay TQ1 ....220 A7
Wrights La PL8 ....140 F7
Wrigwell Cross TQ12 ...211 E1
Wrigwell La TQ12 .....217 F8
Wrinkleberry La EX39 ...23 D3
Wroxall Grange TQ1 ...220 C4
Wulphere CI EX14 ......67 B1
Wyatts La PL19 ....171 B6
Wych Ct EX13 ....88 E3
Wychall Orch EX12 ....192 A6

Wychall Pk EX12 ......192 A7
Wychwood CI EX7 ......204 E7
Wycliffe Rd PL3 ......249 B4
Wye Gdns PL3 ....249 D7
Wyke Cross EX17 ....80 F2
Wyke Hill EX17 ....80 F2
Wyke La EX13 ....167 D2
Wyke Moor Cross EX20 ...95 C8
Wyke Rd EX13 ....167 D3
Wykeham Dr PL2 ......248 A7
Wykes Rd EX1 ....177 F7
Wynards EX2 ....261 B2
Wynards CI EX9 ....198 B6
Wynards La [2] EX2 ...261 B2
Wynards Rd EX9 ......198 B6
Wyndham Ave EX1 ....177 F6
Wyndham La PL1 ......262 A3
Wyndham Rd EX5 ....82 B6
Wyndham Sq PL1 .....262 A3
Wyndham St E PL1 ....262 B3
Wyndham St W PL1 ...262 B3
Wynford Rd EX4 ......173 F1
Wyoming CI PL3 ......249 C6
Wyre Ct TQ4 ....226 A2
Wytch Gn EX13 ....88 E3
Wythburn Gdns PL6 ...245 D3

Y

Yalberton Ind Est TQ4 ..225 D3
Yalberton Ind Management
  Units TQ4 ....225 E3
Yalberton Rd TQ4 ....225 D3
Yalberton Tor Ind Est
  TQ4 ....225 D3
Yalland Cross TQ10 ...134 F5
Yallop Way EX14 .....166 B4
Yanhey Hill EX16 ......32 E4
Yannon Dr TQ14 .....210 B5
Yannon La TQ12 ......212 E5
Yannon Terr TQ14 ....210 B6
Yannons The TQ14 ...210 B6
Yapham Cross EX39 ....23 A4
Yard Cross EX14 ....86 B7
Yard Down Cross EX36 ..19 C6
Yard Downs La EX5 ....82 D6
Yard Hill TQ13 ....111 D2
Yard La EX36 ....46 B8
Yarda Wlk PL8 ....257 A4
Yardbury Hill Rd EX24 ..102 E7
Yarde CI EX10 ....188 B7
Yarde Cotts EX38 ......41 D1
Yarde Cross EX32 ......18 A4
Yarde Gate Cross EX36 ..19 B6
Yarde Hill Orch EX10 ..188 B7
Yarde Mead EX10 ....188 B7

Yarde Medieval Farmhouse*
  TQ7 ....147 F7
Yarde's Grave Cross
  TQ9 ....222 F7
Yardelands EX10 .....188 B7
Yardelands CI EX10 ..188 B7
Yardewells Cross EX36 ...19 B5
Yardleigh Cross EX13 ...88 D4
Yardley Gdns PL6 ....245 E3
Yards La TQ5 ....230 C2
Yarnleigh La EX17 .....79 E7
Yarnacott Cnr EX32 ....17 E1
Yarnapitts Cross TQ13 ..110 E7
Yarrow Mead PL9 ....256 D7
Yawl Cres DT7 ....104 B5
Yawl Cross DT7 ......104 B6
Yawl Hill DT7 ....104 C6
Yawl La DT7 ....104 B5
Yealm Gr TQ2 ....219 C7
Yealm Pk PL8 ....257 E4
Yealm Rd PL8 ....140 F6
Yealm View Rd PL8 ...141 A6
Yealmbury Hill PL8 ...257 F4
Yealmpstone CI PL7 ..251 B4
Yealmpstone Dr PL7 ..251 B3
Yealmpstone Farm Prim Sch
  PL7 ....251 B3
Yealmpton Prim Sch
  PL8 ....257 E4
Yearlstone Vineyard*
  EX16 ....63 F3
Yearnor Mill La TA24 ....6 F5
Yeats CI PL5 ....244 C2
Yeatt Cross TQ12 ....131 F3
Yellaford Way [1] EX31 .154 B3
Yelland Bglws TQ10 ...135 E5
Yelland Cross
  Bratton Fleming EX31 ..11 D4
  Rattery TQ10 ....135 E5
  Yelland EX31 ....153 A5
Yelland Rd EX31 .....153 C5
Yellands Pk TQ7 .....142 C6
Yellaton La EX34 ......3 B1
Yellow Moor La EX19 ...58 F1
Yellow Tor CI PL12 ...242 C2
Yellow Tor La PL12 ...242 C2
Yellowtor Rd PL12 ...242 B2
Yelverton Bsns Pk PL20 .126 E2
Yelverton CI PL5 ....243 E4
Yelverton Paperweight Mus*
  PL20 ....126 F2
Yelverton Terr
  Tavistock PL19 ....171 D6
  Yelverton PL20 ....127 A2
Yendacott La EX17 .....81 B3
Yeo CI PL3 ....249 B5
Yeo Dr [20] EX39 ......15 A1
Yeo Gate EX36 ....31 C4

Yeo La Molland EX36 ....31 C5
  North Tawton EX20 .....77 B5
Yeo Mill Cross EX36 ...32 C5
Yeo Pk PL8 ....136 A3
Yeo Rd Braunton EX31 ..15 E5
  Zeal Monachorum EX17 ..78 D7
Yeo Vale Cross EX17 ....60 C2
Yeo Vale Cross Ind Est
  EX17 ....60 C2
Yeo Vale Ho [4] EX32 ..154 F6
Yeo Vale Rd EX32 ....154 F6
Yeo Valley Prim Sch
  EX32 ....155 A6
Yeoford Com Prim Sch
  EX17 ....79 C1
Yeoford Mdws EX17 ....79 C1
Yeoford Sta EX17 ......79 C1
Yeoford Way EX2 .....181 D8
Yeoland La
  Swimbridge EX32 ......17 F1
  Yelverton PL20 ....126 F1
Yeolands The TQ9 ....227 F8
Yeolland La PL21 ....237 D5
Yeolland Pk PL21 ....237 E5
Yeomadon Cross EX22 ...71 D4
Yeomans Way PL7 ....251 A4
Yeotown Cross EX37 ...44 C8
Yerris Rd EX15 ....65 F2
Yetsonais Cross TQ9 ..144 D8
Yettington Rd EX9 ...198 A7
Yew CI Brixham TQ5 ..229 F2
  Honiton EX14 ....166 A4
Yew Tree CI Exeter EX4 .173 E1
  Exmouth EX8 ....196 C3
Yew Tree Dr TQ12 ....207 E6
Yew Wood Cross EX15 ..66 A4
Yewdale Gdns PL6 ...245 D2
Yolhey La TQ12 ......212 C5
Yon St TQ12 ....212 F4
Yonder CI EX11 ......169 E3
Yonder Cnr EX11 ....169 E3
Yonder Mdw TQ9 ....227 F8
Yonder Mount EX13 ..103 D5
Yonder St
  Ottery St Mary EX11 ..169 E3
  Plymouth PL9 ....255 B6
York CI Axminster EX13 .167 C6
  Exmouth EX8 ....196 C2
  Feniton EX14 ....84 D2
York Cres Feniton EX14 ..84 D2
  Torquay TQ1 ....220 C8
York Gdns TQ4 ......226 B4
York PI Bideford EX39 ..157 A3
  Cullompton EX15 .....163 C5
  Plymouth PL2 ....247 F4
York Rd Exeter EX4 ...261 C4
  Paignton TQ4 ....226 B4
  Plymouth PL5 ....247 E8

Seaton EX12 ....192 A5
Torpoint PL11 ....247 B3
Torquay TQ1 ....220 C8
York St Plymouth PL1 .247 E2
York St continued
  Sidmouth EX10 ......188 B3
York Terr
  [7] Plymouth PL2 ...247 F4
  Sidmouth EX10 ......188 B3
York Villas TQ1 .....220 C8
Yorke Rd TQ6 ....233 D7
Youngs Dr EX31 .....155 A2
Youlden La EX20 ......95 C2
Youldon Moor Cross
  EX22 ....53 E4
Youldon Way PL20 ...126 F4
Youldons CI TQ9 ....139 C2
Youlston CI EX31 ......17 A2
Youltree Cross EX39 ...22 E4
Young's Park Rd TQ4 .226 C4
Youngaton Rd EX39 ..156 C2

Z

Zeal Cross EX6 ......112 F8
Zeal Rd Dunsford EX6 ..112 F8
  Tedburn St Mary EX6 ...97 F8
Zealley Est TQ12 ....207 E6
Zempson Cross TQ10 ..135 B5
Zephyr Cres EX32 ....155 B5
Zeth Hill La PL21 ....136 D6
Zion PI Dartmouth TQ6 ..233 F4
  Ivybridge PL21 ....237 C5
Zion Rd [3] TQ2 .....219 F5
Zion St PL1 ....262 C2

NG NH NJ NK
NM NN NO NP
NR NS NT NU
NX NY NZ
SC SD SE TA
SH SJ SK TF TG
SM SN SO SP TL TM
SR SS ST SU TQ TR
SW SX SY SZ TV

Any feature in this atlas can be given a unique reference to help you find the same feature on other Ordnance Survey maps of the area, or to help someone else locate you if they do not have a Street Atlas.

The grid squares in this atlas match the Ordnance Survey National Grid and are at 500 metre intervals. The small figures at the bottom and sides of every other grid line are the National Grid kilometre values (**00** to **99** km) and are repeated across the country every 100 km (see left).

To give a unique National Grid reference you need to locate where in the country you are. The country is divided into 100 km squares with each square given a unique two-letter reference. Use the administrative map to determine in which 100 km square a particular page of this atlas falls.

The bold letters and numbers between each grid line (**A** to **F**, **1** to **8**) are for use within a specific Street Atlas only, and when used with the page number, are a convenient way of referencing these grid squares.

Example   The railway bridge over DARLEY GREEN RD in grid square B1

Step 1: Identify the two-letter reference, in this example the page is in **SP**

Step 2: Identify the 1 km square in which the railway bridge falls. Use the figures in the southwest corner of this square: Eastings **17**, Northings **74**. This gives a unique reference: **SP 17 74**, accurate to 1 km.

Step 3: To give a more precise reference accurate to 100 m you need to estimate how many tenths along and how many tenths up this 1 km square the feature is (to help with this the 1 km square is divided into four 500 m squares). This makes the bridge about **8** tenths along and about **1** tenth up from the southwest corner.

This gives a unique reference: **SP 178 741**, accurate to 100 m.

Eastings (read from left to right along the bottom) come before Northings (read from bottom to top). If you have trouble remembering say to yourself "Along the hall, THEN up the stairs"!

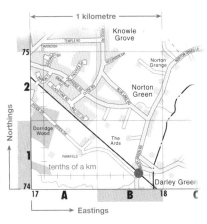

Addresses

Name and Address	Telephone	Page	Grid reference

Name and Address	Telephone	Page

Street Atlases from Philip's

Philip's publish an extensive range of regional and local street atlases which are ideal for motoring, business and leisure use. They are widely used by the emergency services and local authorities throughout Britain.

Key features include:

◆ Superb county-wide mapping at an extra-large scale of 3½ inches to 1 mile, or 2½ inches to 1 mile in pocket edition

◆ Complete urban and rural coverage, detailing every named street in town and country

◆ Each atlas available in two handy sizes – standard spiral and pocket paperback

'The mapping is very clear... great in scope and value'
★★★★ BEST BUY   AUTO EXPRESS

<table>
<tr><td>1 Bedfordshire</td><td>3 Birmingham and West Midlands</td><td>15 North Essex</td></tr>
<tr><td>2 Berkshire</td><td>4 Bristol and Bath</td><td>16 South Essex</td></tr>
<tr><td></td><td>5 Buckinghamshire</td><td>17 Glasgow and W Central Scotland</td></tr>
<tr><td></td><td>6 Cambridgeshire</td><td>18 Gloucestershire</td></tr>
<tr><td></td><td>7 Cardiff, Swansea and The Valleys</td><td>19 North Hampshi</td></tr>
<tr><td></td><td>8 Cheshire</td><td>20 South Hampshire</td></tr>
<tr><td></td><td>9 Cornwall</td><td>21 Herefordshire an Monmouthshire</td></tr>
<tr><td></td><td>10 Derbyshire</td><td>22 Hertfordshire</td></tr>
<tr><td></td><td>11 Devon</td><td>23 East Kent</td></tr>
<tr><td></td><td>12 Dorset</td><td>24 West Kent</td></tr>
<tr><td></td><td>13 County Durham and Teesside</td><td>25 Lancashire</td></tr>
<tr><td></td><td>14 Edinburgh and East Central Scotland</td><td>26 Leicestershire and Rutland</td></tr>
<tr><td></td><td></td><td>27 Lincolnshire</td></tr>
<tr><td></td><td></td><td>28 London</td></tr>
<tr><td></td><td></td><td>29 Greater Manche</td></tr>
<tr><td></td><td></td><td>30 Merseyside</td></tr>
<tr><td></td><td></td><td>31 Norfolk</td></tr>
<tr><td></td><td></td><td>32 Northamptonshir</td></tr>
<tr><td></td><td></td><td>33 Nottinghamshire</td></tr>
<tr><td></td><td></td><td>34 Oxfordshire</td></tr>
<tr><td></td><td></td><td>35 Shropshire</td></tr>
<tr><td></td><td></td><td>36 Somerset</td></tr>
<tr><td></td><td></td><td>37 Staffordshire</td></tr>
<tr><td></td><td></td><td>38 Suffolk</td></tr>
<tr><td></td><td></td><td>39 Surrey</td></tr>
<tr><td></td><td></td><td>40 East Sussex</td></tr>
<tr><td></td><td></td><td>41 West Sussex</td></tr>
<tr><td></td><td></td><td>42 Tyne and Wear Northumberland</td></tr>
<tr><td></td><td></td><td>43 Warwickshire</td></tr>
<tr><td></td><td></td><td>44 Worcestershire</td></tr>
<tr><td></td><td></td><td>45 Wiltshire and Sw</td></tr>
<tr><td></td><td></td><td>46 East Yorkshire an Northern Lincoln</td></tr>
<tr><td></td><td></td><td>47 North Yorkshire</td></tr>
<tr><td></td><td></td><td>48 South Yorkshire</td></tr>
<tr><td></td><td></td><td>49 West Yorkshire</td></tr>
</table>

How to order

The Philip's range of street atlases is available from good retailers or directly from the publisher by phoning 01903 828503